GLEIM®

2018 EDITION

CPA Review

Regulation

by

Irvin N. Gleim, Ph.D., CPA, CIA, CMA, CFM

Gleim Publications, Inc.
PO Box 12848
University Station
Gainesville, Florida 32604
(800) 87-GLEIM or (800) 874-5346
(352) 375-0772
Website: www.gleim.com
Email: admin@gleim.com

For updates to this 2018 edition of
CPA Review: Regulation

Go To: www.gleim.com/CPAupdate

Or: Email update@gleim.com with **CPA REG 2018-1** in the subject line. You will receive our current update as a reply.

Updates are available until the next edition is published.

ISSN: 1547-8092

ISBN: 978-1-61854-079-9 *CPA Review: Auditing and Attestation*
ISBN: 978-1-61854-148-2 *CPA Review: Business Environment and Concepts*
ISBN: 978-1-61854-149-9 *CPA Review: Financial Accounting and Reporting*
ISBN: 978-1-61854-150-5 *CPA Review: Regulation*
ISBN: 978-1-61854-151-2 *CPA Exam Guide: A System for Success*

First Printing: November 2017

ACKNOWLEDGMENTS

Material from *Uniform CPA Examination, Selected Questions and Unofficial Answers*, Copyright © 1974-2017 by the American Institute of Certified Public Accountants, Inc., is reprinted and/or adapted with permission. Visit the AICPA's website at www.aicpa.org for more information.

The author is indebted to the Institute of Certified Management Accountants for permission to use problem materials from past CMA examinations. Questions and unofficial answers from the Certified Management Accountant Examinations, copyright by the Institute of Certified Management Accountants, are reprinted and/or adapted with permission.

Environmental Statement -- This book is printed on recyclable, environmentally friendly groundwood paper, sourced from certified sustainable forests and produced either TCF (totally chlorine-free) or ECF (elementally chlorine-free).

ABOUT THE AUTHOR

Irvin N. Gleim is Professor Emeritus in the Fisher School of Accounting at the University of Florida and is a member of the American Accounting Association, Academy of Legal Studies in Business, American Institute of Certified Public Accountants, Association of Government Accountants, Florida Institute of Certified Public Accountants, The Institute of Internal Auditors, and the Institute of Management Accountants. He has had articles published in the *Journal of Accountancy*, *The Accounting Review*, and *The American Business Law Journal* and is author/coauthor of numerous accounting books, aviation books, and CPE courses.

REVIEWERS AND CONTRIBUTORS

Alexis L. Davis, Esq., is a graduate of Nova Southeastern University Shepard Broad College of Law and received both her Bachelor of Arts and Bachelor of Science degrees from the University of Florida. Ms. Davis provided substantial editorial assistance throughout the project.

Garrett W. Gleim, B.S., CGMA, received a Bachelor of Science degree from the University of Pennsylvania, The Wharton School. He also holds a CPA certificate issued by the State of Delaware. Mr. Gleim coordinated the production staff, reviewed the manuscript, and provided production assistance throughout the project.

Lorie M. Gleim, B.S., B.A., J.D., graduated from The Wharton School and the College of Arts and Sciences at the University of Pennsylvania. She went on to receive a Juris Doctor with honors from the University of Florida College of Law. Ms. Gleim practiced complex commercial business litigation for over 22 years at Greenberg Traurig. She is a member of the executive management team at Gleim Publications and provided significant editorial assistance for the law content in Regulation.

Solomon E. Gonite, J.D., CPA, is a graduate of the Florida State University College of Law and the Fisher School of Accounting at the University of Florida. He has practiced as an auditor (in both the private and government sectors) and as a tax practitioner. Mr. Gonite provided substantial editorial assistance throughout the project.

Grady M. Irwin, J.D., is a graduate of the University of Florida College of Law, and he has taught in the University of Florida College of Business. Mr. Irwin provided substantial editorial assistance throughout the project.

D. Scott Lawton, B.S., is a graduate of Brigham Young University-Idaho and Utah Valley University. He has worked as an auditor for the Utah State Tax Commission. Mr. Lawton provided substantial editorial assistance throughout the project.

Mark S. Modas, M.S.T., CPA, received a Bachelor of Arts in Accounting from Florida Atlantic University and a Master of Science in Taxation from Nova Southeastern University. He was the Sarbanes-Oxley project manager and internal audit department manager at Perry Ellis International, and the former Acting Director of Accounting and Financial Reporting for the School Board of Broward County, Florida. Mr. Modas provided substantial editorial assistance throughout the project.

A PERSONAL THANKS

This manual would not have been possible without the extraordinary effort and dedication of Jacob Bennett, Julie Cutlip, Ethan Good, Doug Green, Blaine Hatton, Fernanda Martinez, Kelsey Olson, Bree Rodriguez, Teresa Soard, Justin Stephenson, Joanne Strong, Elmer Tucker, and Candace Van Doren, who typed the entire manuscript and all revisions and drafted and laid out the diagrams, illustrations, and cover for this book.

The authors also appreciate the production and editorial assistance of Levi Bradford, Steven Critelli, Jim Harvin, Jessica Hatker, Kristen Hennen, Belea Keeney, Katie Larson, Diana León, Bernadyn Nettles, Jake Pettifor, Shane Rapp, Drew Sheppard, and Alyssa Thomas.

The authors also appreciate the critical reading assistance of Felix Chen, Corey Connell, Nathan Giron, Justin Hamilton, Nichole Hyde, Andrew Johnson, Dean Kingston, Melissa Leonard, Monica Metz, Timothy Murphy, Cristian Prieto, Crystal Quach, Martin Salazar, and Lily Zhao.

Finally, we appreciate the encouragement, support, and tolerance of our families throughout this project.

TABLE OF CONTENTS

DETAILED TABLE OF CONTENTS

PREFACE FOR CPA CANDIDATES

This is the 2018 Edition of CPA Review. It reflects relevant business law, ethical, and federal tax laws through December 2017.

The purpose of this Gleim CPA Review study book is to help you prepare to pass the 2018 Regulation (also referred to throughout the rest of this text as REG) section of the CPA examination. Our overriding consideration is to provide a comprehensive, effective, and easy-to-use study program. This book

1. Explains how to optimize your grade by focusing on the Regulation section of the CPA exam.
2. Defines the subject matter tested on the Regulation section of the CPA exam.
3. Outlines all of the subject matter tested on the Regulation section in 20 easy-to-use-and-complete study units.
4. Presents multiple-choice questions from recent CPA examinations to prepare you for questions in future CPA exams. Our answer explanations are presented to the immediate right of each question for your convenience. Use a piece of paper to cover our answer explanations as you study the questions.

The outline format, the spacing, and the question and answer formats in this book are designed to facilitate readability, learning, understanding, and success on the CPA exam. Our most successful candidates use the Gleim Premium CPA Review System,* which includes Gleim Instruct videos; our Access Until You Pass Guarantee; SmartAdapt technology; expertly authored books; the largest test bank of multiple-choice questions, Task-Based Simulations, and Written Communications; audio lectures; and the support of our team of accounting experts. This review book and all Gleim CPA Review materials are compatible with other CPA review materials and courses that follow the AICPA Blueprints.

To maximize the efficiency and effectiveness of your CPA review program, augment your studying with *CPA Exam Guide: A System for Success*, which has been carefully written and organized to provide important information to assist you in passing the CPA examination.

Thank you for your interest in the Gleim CPA Review materials. We deeply appreciate the thousands of letters and suggestions received from CPA, CIA, CMA, and EA candidates during the past 5 decades.

If you use the Gleim materials, we want YOUR feedback immediately after the exam and as soon as you have received your grades. The CPA exam is NONDISCLOSED, and you will sign an attestation including, "I hereby agree that I will maintain the confidentiality of the Uniform CPA Examination. In addition, I agree that I will not divulge the nature or content of any Uniform CPA Examination question or answer under any circumstance . . ." We ask only for information about our materials, i.e., the topics that need to be added, expanded, etc. Our approach has AICPA approval.

Please go to www.gleim.com/feedbackREG to share your suggestions on how we can improve this edition.

Good Luck on the Exam,

Irvin N. Gleim

November 2017

* Visit www.gleimcpa.com or call (800) 874-5346 to order.

OPTIMIZING YOUR REGULATION SCORE

UNIFORM CPA EXAMINATION

CPA Exam Section	Auditing & Attestation	Business Environment & Concepts	Financial Accounting & Reporting	**Regulation**
Acronym	AUD	BEC	FAR	**REG**
Exam Length	4 hours	4 hours	4 hours	**4 hours**
Testlet 1: Multiple-Choice	36 questions	31 questions	33 questions	**38 questions**
Testlet 2: Multiple-Choice	36 questions	31 questions	33 questions	**38 questions**
Testlet 3: Task-Based Simulations	2 tasks	2 tasks	2 tasks	**2 tasks**
Standardized Break	Clock stops for 15 minutes			
Testlet 4: Task-Based Simulations	3 tasks	2 tasks	3 tasks	**3 tasks**
Testlet 5: Task-Based Simulations or Written Communications	3 tasks	3 written communications	3 tasks	**3 tasks**

2018 CPA Exam User Interface Changes

At time of print, updates to the CPA exam user interface are slated for mid-2018. These changes affect the layout, functionality, and general appearance of all testlets. Additionally, the basic spreadsheet tool currently available in the exam will be replaced by Microsoft Excel. Learn about the new user interface by visiting www.gleim.com/CPAchanges.

Passing the CPA exam is a serious undertaking. Begin by becoming an expert in the content, formatting, and functionality of the REG exam before you take it. The objective is no surprises on exam day. Also, you will save time and money, decrease frustration, and increase your probability of success by learning all you can about how to prepare for and take REG.

Review *CPA Exam Guide: A System for Success* at www.gleim.com/PassCPA for a complete explanation of how to prepare for and take each section of the CPA exam. This free guide includes over 40 pages of test-taking techniques, time management strategies, and more.

More exam tactics and information, as well as breaking news and updates from the AICPA and NASBA, are available on our blog at www.gleim.com/CPAblog. Follow us on all your favorite social media networks for blog updates and other critical information.

CPA Exam Pass Rates

	Percentage of Candidates		
	2015	2016	2017
AUD	47	46	49
BEC	57	57	52
FAR	47	46	45
REG	49	49	48

The implication of these pass rates for you as a CPA candidate is that you have to be, on average, in the top 45% of all candidates to pass. The major difference between CPA candidates who pass and those who do not is their preparation program. You have access to the best CPA review material; it is up to you to use it. Even if you are enrolled in a review course that uses other materials, you will benefit with the Gleim Premium CPA Review System.

GLEIM CPA REVIEW WITH SmartAdapt

Gleim CPA Review features the most comprehensive coverage of exam content and employs the most efficient learning techniques to help you study smarter and faster. The Gleim CPA Review System is powered by SmartAdapt technology, an innovative platform that continually zeros in on your knowledge gaps when you move through the following steps for optimized CPA review:

Step 1:

Complete a Diagnostic Quiz. Based on your quiz results, our SmartAdapt technology will create a custom learning track.

Step 2:

Solidify your knowledge by studying the suggested Knowledge Transfer Outline(s) or watching the suggested Gleim Instruct video(s).

Step 3:

Focus on weak areas and perfect your question-answering techniques by taking the adaptive quizzes and simulations that SmartAdapt directs you to.

Final Review:

After completing all study units, take the Exam Rehearsal. Then, SmartAdapt will walk you through a Final Review based on your results.

To facilitate your studies, the Gleim Premium CPA Review System uses the largest test bank of CPA exam questions on the market. Our system's content and presentation precisely mimic the whole AICPA exam environment so you feel comfortable on test day.

Learning from Your Mistakes

One of the main building blocks of the Gleim studying system is that learning from questions you answer incorrectly is very important. Each question you answer incorrectly is an **opportunity** to avoid missing actual test questions on your CPA exam. Thus, you should carefully study the answer explanations provided so you understand why the original answer you chose is wrong as well as why the correct answer indicated is correct. This learning technique is the difference between passing and failing for many CPA candidates.

The Gleim Premium CPA Review System has built-in functionality for this step. After each quiz and simulation you complete, the Gleim system directs you to study why you answered questions incorrectly so you can learn how to avoid making the same errors in the future. Reasons for answering questions incorrectly include

1. Misreading the requirement (stem)
2. Not understanding what is required
3. Making a math error
4. Applying the wrong rule or concept
5. Being distracted by one or more of the answers
6. Incorrectly eliminating answers from consideration
7. Not having any knowledge of the topic tested
8. Using a poor educated guessing strategy

SUBJECT MATTER FOR REGULATION

Below, we have provided the AICPA's major content areas from the Blueprint for Regulation. The averaged percentage of coverage for each topic is indicated.

  I. (15%) Ethics, Professional Responsibilities, and Federal Tax Procedures
 II. (15%) Business Law
III. (17%) Federal Taxation of Property Transactions
IV. (20%) Federal Taxation of Individuals
 V. (33%) Federal Taxation of Entities

Appendix A contains the Blueprint for REG with cross-references to the subunits in our materials where topics are covered. Remember that we have studied and restudied the Blueprint and explain the subject matter thoroughly in our CPA Review. Accordingly, you do not need to spend time with Appendix A. Rather, it should give you confidence that Gleim CPA Review is the best review available to help you PASS the CPA exam.

Candidates are expected to demonstrate knowledge and skills related to

- Federal taxation,
- Ethics and professional responsibilities related to tax practice, and
- Business law.

The following general topics will be tested:

- Ethics and responsibilities in tax practice
- Licensing and disciplinary systems
- Federal tax procedures
  - Income taxation
    - ☐ Property transactions
    - ☐ Estate and gift taxation
    - ☐ Tax preparation and planning for individuals
    - ☐ Tax preparation and planning for entities, including sole proprietorships, partnerships, limited liability companies, C corporations, S corporations, joint ventures, trusts, estates, and tax-exempt organizations

- Legal duties and responsibilities
- Business law
  - Legal implications of business transactions
  - Agency, contracts, debtor-creditor relationships, government regulation of business, and business structure
  - Federal and widely adopted uniform state laws

WHICH PRONOUNCEMENTS ARE TESTED?

The following is the section of the AICPA's pronouncement policy that is relevant to the REG section:

Changes in the federal taxation area, the Internal Revenue Code, and federal taxation regulations may be included in the testing window beginning six (6) months after the change's effective date or enactment date, whichever is later.

For all other subjects covered in the Regulation (REG) and Business Environment and Concepts (BEC) sections, materials eligible to be tested include federal laws in the window beginning six (6) months after their effective date, and uniform acts in the window beginning one (1) year after their adoption by a simple majority of the jurisdictions.

AICPA's NONDISCLOSURE AGREEMENT

As part of the AICPA's nondisclosure policy and to prove each candidate's willingness to adhere to this policy, a confidentiality and break policy statement must be accepted by each candidate during the introductory screens at the beginning of each exam. Nonacceptance of this policy means the exam will be terminated and the test fees will be forfeited. This statement is reproduced here to remind all CPA candidates about the AICPA's strict policy of nondisclosure, which Gleim consistently supports and upholds.

"Policy Statement and Agreement Regarding Exam Confidentiality and the Taking of Breaks

I hereby agree that I will maintain the confidentiality of the Uniform CPA Examination. In addition, I agree that I will not:

- Divulge the nature or content of any Uniform CPA Examination question or answer under any circumstance
- Engage in any unauthorized communication during testing
- Refer to unauthorized materials or use unauthorized equipment during testing; or
- Remove or attempt to remove any Uniform CPA Examination materials, notes, or any other items from the examination room

I understand and agree that liability for test administration activities, including but not limited to the adequacy or accuracy of test materials and equipment, and the accuracy of scoring and score reporting, will be limited to score correction or test retake at no additional fee. I waive any and all right to all other claims.

I further agree to report to the AICPA any examination question disclosures, or solicitations for disclosure of which I become aware.

I affirm that I have had the opportunity to read the Candidate Bulletin and I agree to all of its terms and conditions.

I understand that breaks are only allowed between testlets. I understand that I will be asked to complete any open testlet before leaving the testing room for a break.

In addition, I understand that failure to comply with this Policy statement and Agreement may result in the invalidation of my grades, disqualification from future examinations, expulsion from the testing facility and possible civil or criminal penalties."

GLEIM CPA REVIEW ESSENTIALS

Gleim CPA Review has the following features to make studying easier:

1.   **Backgrounds:** In certain instances, we have provided historical background or supplemental information. This information is intended to illuminate the topic under discussion and is set off in bordered boxes with shaded headings. This material does not need to be memorized for the exam.

> ### Background
>
> Accelerated depreciation is a tax relief measure highly desired by businesses. Quickly expensing the cost of investment in plant and equipment for tax purposes allows businesses to significantly reduce their tax liability. In 1971, Congress regularized the haphazard use of accelerated depreciation by introducing the Asset Depreciation Range (ADR) system. Assets of a similar nature or use could be classed together, thereby simplifying the calculation of depreciation expense.

2.   **Examples:** Illustrative examples, both hypothetical and those drawn from actual events, are set off in shaded, bordered boxes.

> ### EXAMPLE
>
> John submitted reimbursement requests to his employer for $10,500 in airfare. John was later refunded for $500 of the airfare. If John does not remit the funds to his employer, John must include the $500 in gross income.

3.   **Gleim Success Tips:** These tips supplement the core exam material by suggesting how certain topics might be presented on the exam or how you should prepare for an issue.

> The accounting rules for income and deduction items under both the cash and accrual methods have often been tested. The AICPA has used questions that have focused on the timing of the inclusions of various income and expense items under each method.

4.   **Memory Aids:** The mnemonic devices are designed to assist you in memorizing important concepts.

     For example, "Harry Uses Tax Information" helps candidates remember the itemized deductions subject to the 2%-of-AGI exclusion: Hobby expenses, Unreimbursed employee expenses, Tax preparation fees, and Investment expenses.

5.   **Detailed Table of Contents:** This information at the beginning of the book is a complete listing of all study units and subunits in the Gleim CPA Regulation Review program. Use this list as a study aid to mark off your progress and to provide jumping-off points for review.

6.   **Blueprint with Gleim Cross-References:** Appendix A contains a reprint of the AICPA Blueprint for REG along with cross-references to the corresponding Gleim study units.

7.   **Optimizing Your Score on the Task-Based Simulations (TBSs):** Appendix B explains how to approach and allocate your time for the TBS testlets. It also presents several example TBSs for your review.

8.   **Core Concepts:** We have also provided additional study materials to supplement the Knowledge Transfer Outlines in the digital Gleim CPA Review Course. The Core Concepts, for example, are consolidated documents providing an overview of the key points of each subunit that serve as the foundation for learning. As part of your review, you should make sure that you understand each of them.

TIME BUDGETING AND QUESTION-ANSWERING TECHNIQUES FOR REGULATION

To begin the exam, you will enter your Launch Code on the Welcome screen. If you do not enter the correct code within 5 minutes of the screen appearing, the exam session will end.

Next, you will have an additional 5 minutes to view a brief exam introduction containing two screens: the nondisclosure policy and a section information screen. Accept the policy and then review the information screen, but be sure to click the Begin Exam button on the bottom right of the screen within the allotted 5 minutes. If you fail to do so, the exam will be terminated and you will not have the option to restart your exam.

These 10 minutes, along with the 5 minutes you may spend on a post-exam survey, are not included in the 240 minutes of exam time.

Once you complete the introductory screens and begin your exam, expect two testlets of 38 multiple-choice questions (MCQs) each and three testlets of Task-Based Simulations (TBSs) (one with 2 TBSs and two with 3 TBSs each). You will have 240 minutes to complete the five testlets.

1. **Budget your time so you can finish before time expires.**

    a.   Here is our suggested time allocation for Regulation:

	Minutes	Start Time	
Testlet 1 (MCQ)	47*	4 hours	00 minutes
Testlet 2 (MCQ)	47*	3 hours	13 minutes
Testlet 3 (TBS)	36	2 hours	26 minutes
Break	15	Clock stops	
Testlet 4 (TBS)	54	1 hour	50 minutes
Testlet 5 (TBS)	54	0 hours	56 minutes
**Extra time	2	0 hours	02 minutes
*Rounded down			

    b.   Before beginning your first MCQ testlet, prepare a Gleim Time Management plan as recommended in *CPA Exam Guide: A System for Success.*

    c.   As you work through the individual questions, monitor your time. In Regulation, we suggest 47 minutes (1.25 minutes per question) for each testlet of 38 MCQs. If you answer five items in 6 minutes, you are fine, but if you spend 8 minutes on five items, you need to speed up. In the TBS testlets, spend no more than 18 minutes on each TBS. For more information on TBS time budgets, refer to Appendix B, "Optimizing Your Score on the Task-Based Simulations."

    **Remember to allocate your budgeted extra time, as needed, to each testlet. Your goal is to answer all of the items and achieve the maximum score possible. As you practice answering TBSs in the Gleim Premium CPA Review System, you will be practicing your time management.

2. **Answer the questions in consecutive order.**

    a.   Do not agonize over any one question. **Stay within your time budget.**

    b.   Never leave an MCQ unanswered. Your score is based on the number of correct responses. You will not be penalized for answering incorrectly. If you are unsure about a question,

        1)   Make an educated guess.

        2)   Flag it for review by clicking on the flag icon at the bottom of the screen.

        3)   Return to it before you submit the testlet as time allows. Remember, once you have selected the Submit Testlet option, you will no longer be able to review or change any answers in the completed testlet.

3. **Read the question carefully to discover exactly what is being asked.**

   a.   Ignore the answer choices so they do not affect your precise reading of the question.

   b.   Focusing on what is required allows you to

        1)   Reject extraneous information
        2)   Concentrate on relevant facts
        3)   Proceed directly to determining the best answer

   c.   **Careful!** The requirement may be an exception that features negative words.

   d.   Decide the correct answer before looking at the answer choices.

4. **Read the answer choices, paying attention to small details.**

   a.   Even if an answer choice appears to be correct, do not skip the remaining choices. Each choice requires consideration because you are looking for the best answer provided.

   b.   **Only one answer option is the best.** In the MCQs, four answer choices are presented, and you know one of them is correct. The remaining choices are distractors and are meant to appear correct at first glance. Eliminate them as quickly as you can.

   c.   Treat each answer choice like a true/false question as you analyze it.

   d.   In computational MCQs, the distractor answers are carefully calculated to be the result of common mistakes. Be careful, and double-check your computations if time permits.

        1)   There will be a mix of conceptual and calculation questions. When you take the exam, it may appear that more of the questions are calculation-type because they take longer and are more difficult.

5. **Click on the best answer.**

   a.   You have a 25% chance of answering correctly by guessing blindly, but you can improve your odds with an educated guess.

   b.   For many MCQs, you can **eliminate two answer choices with minimal effort** and increase your educated guess to a 50/50 proposition.

        1)   Rule out answers that you think are incorrect.
        2)   Speculate what the AICPA is looking for and/or why the question is being asked.
        3)   Select the best answer or guess between equally appealing answers. Your first guess is usually the most intuitive.

6. **Do not click the Submit Testlet button until you have consulted the question status list at the bottom of each MCQ screen.**

   a.   Return to flagged questions to finalize your answer choices if you have time.

   b.   Verify that you have answered every question.

   c.   Stay on schedule because time management is critical to exam success.

Doing well on the **task-based simulations** requires you to be an expert on how to approach them both from a question answering and a time allocation perspective. Refer to Appendix B, "Optimizing Your Score on the Task-Based Simulations," for a complete explanation of task-based simulations and how to optimize your score on each one.

HOW TO BE IN CONTROL

Remember, you must be in control to be successful during exam preparation and execution. Perhaps more importantly, control can also contribute greatly to your personal and other professional goals. Control is the process whereby you

1. Develop expectations, standards, budgets, and plans
2. Undertake activity, production, study, and learning
3. Measure the activity, production, output, and knowledge
4. Compare actual activity with expected and budgeted activity
5. Modify the activity, behavior, or study to better achieve the expected or desired outcome
6. Revise expectations and standards in light of actual experience
7. Continue the process or restart the process in the future

Exercising control will ultimately develop the confidence you need to outperform most other CPA candidates and PASS the CPA exam!

QUESTIONS ABOUT GLEIM MATERIALS

Gleim has an efficient and effective way for candidates who have purchased the Gleim Premium CPA Review System to submit an inquiry and receive a response regarding Gleim materials **directly through their course**. This system also allows you to view your Q&A session online in your Gleim Personal Classroom.

Questions regarding the information in this **introduction and/or the Gleim *CPA Exam Guide*** (study suggestions, study plans, exam specifics) may be emailed to personalcounselor@gleim.com.

Questions concerning **orders, prices, shipments, or payments** should be sent via email to customerservice@gleim.com and will be promptly handled by our competent and courteous customer service staff.

For **technical support**, you may use our automated technical support service at www.gleim.com/support, email us at support@gleim.com, or call us at (800) 874-5346.

FEEDBACK

Please fill out our online feedback form (www.gleim.com/feedbackREG) IMMEDIATELY after you take the CPA Regulation section so we can adapt our material based on where candidates say we need to increase or decrease coverage. Our approach has been approved by the AICPA.

STUDY UNIT ONE
ETHICS AND PROFESSIONAL RESPONSIBILITIES

(11 pages of outline)

When a dispute or disagreement over tax issues arises, a taxpayer may have to appear before the IRS. CPAs, enrolled agents (EAs), attorneys, and other individuals authorized to practice before the IRS may represent taxpayers. This study unit discusses the various individuals who may practice before the IRS, their standards of conduct, and their licensing disciplinary systems.

1.1 PRACTITIONERS

Rules for practice before the IRS are in Treasury Department Circular 230.

1. **Practice before the IRS**

   a. Practice before the **Internal Revenue Service (IRS)** is the presentation to the IRS or any of its officers or employees of any matter relating to a client's rights, privileges, or liabilities under laws or regulations administered by the IRS.

   b. Practicing before the IRS includes

      1) Representing a taxpayer at conferences, hearings, or meetings with the IRS
      2) Preparing necessary documents and filing them with the IRS for a taxpayer
      3) Rendering written advice with respect to any entity, transaction, plan, or arrangement having a potential for tax avoidance or evasion

   c. The following do **not** constitute practicing before the IRS:

      1) Preparing less than substantially all of a tax return, an amended return, or a claim for refund
      2) Furnishing information upon request to the IRS
      3) Appearing as a witness for a person

   d. A practitioner who for compensation prepares or assists with the preparation of **all or substantially all** of a tax return, an amended return, or claim for refund must comply with the following:

      1) Have a preparer tax identification number.
      2) Be subject to the duties and restrictions relating to practice before the IRS.
      3) Be subject to the sanctions for violation of the regulations of Circular 230.

2.   **Persons Authorized to Practice**

    a.   The following persons may practice before the IRS:

        1)   Attorneys

            a)   An attorney who is a member in good standing of the bar of the highest court of any state, possession, territory, commonwealth, or the District of Columbia

            b)   An attorney who is not under suspension or disbarment from practice before the IRS

        2)   CPAs

            a)   A CPA is an individual qualified to practice as a CPA in any state, territory, or possession of the U.S.

            b)   A CPA who is not suspended from practice by the IRS Office of Professional Responsibility.

        3)   Enrolled agents (EAs)

            a)   An EA is an individual, other than an attorney or a CPA, who is eligible, qualified, and certified as authorized to represent a taxpayer before the IRS.

            b)   The EA designation is issued by the IRS to individuals passing the EA exam.

        4)   Enrolled actuaries, enrolled retirement plan agents, and annual filing season program (AFSP) participants

    b.   To practice before the IRS, an attorney or a CPA must

        1)   Not be suspended or disbarred

        2)   File a **written declaration** for each party (s)he represents that (s)he

            a)   Is currently qualified

            b)   Has been authorized to represent the party

	Type of Practitioners*	Attorney, CPA, EA	AFSP Participants
Type of Practice Before the IRS	Allowed Practice before the IRS	Unlimited	Limited
	Preparation of return or claim for refund	Sign returns and refunds when completed "all or substantially all" of a return or refund	Sign returns and refunds when completed "all or substantially all" of a return or refund
	Representation	1) Before anyone at the IRS 2) Examination and appeals 3) Any return or refund	1) Before IRS revenue agents, customer service representatives, and employees 2) During examination only 3) Return that tax return preparer signed him or herself for the period under examination
	Tax Advice	Unlimited including tax planning	Limited to return or refund preparation

*For brevity, the chart excludes enrolled actuaries and enrolled retirement plan agents because the extent of their practice rights is not likely to be tested on the CPA exam.

3.   **Rules of Conduct before the IRS**

   a.   **Conflict of Interest**

   1)   A conflict of interest exists if

   a)   The practitioner's representation of a client will be **directly adverse** to another client or

   b)   There is a significant risk that the representation of one or more clients will be **materially limited** by the practitioner's responsibilities to another or former client, a third person, or by the practitioner's personal interest(s).

   2)   A practitioner may represent conflicting interests before the IRS only if

   a)   All directly affected parties provide informed, written consent once the existence of the conflict is known by the practitioner (written consent must be within 30 days of informed consent);

   b)   The representation is not prohibited by law; and

   c)   The practitioner reasonably believes that (s)he can provide competent and diligent representation to each client.

   3)   A practitioner is not required to disclose the conflict of interest to the IRS.

   b.   **Diligence** must be exercised in preparing and in assisting in preparing, approving, and filing returns, documents, and other papers relating to IRS matters.

   1)   Diligence is presumed if the practitioner (a) relies upon the work product of another person and (b) uses reasonable care in engaging, supervising, training, and evaluating the person.

   2)   A practitioner may not unreasonably delay the prompt disposition of any matter before the IRS.

   c.   **Information or records** properly and lawfully requested by a duly authorized officer or employee of the IRS must be promptly submitted.

   1)   However, if reasonable basis exists for a good-faith belief that (a) the information is privileged or (b) the request is not proper and lawful, the practitioner is excused from submitting the requested information.

   2)   A practitioner also is required to provide information about the identity of persons that (s)he reasonably believes may have possession or control of the requested information if the practitioner does not.

   d.   A practitioner who **knows** that a client (1) has **not complied** with the revenue laws of the U.S. or (2) has made an error or omission is required promptly to advise the client of noncompliance and the consequences of such noncompliance, error, or omission under the Code and regulations.

   1)   Circular 230 does not require the practitioner to notify the IRS.

   e.   A practitioner must not negotiate, including by endorsement, any **income tax refund check** issued to a client.

   f.   A practitioner may not charge an **unconscionable fee** in connection with any matter before the IRS.

g.   A practitioner may not charge a **contingent fee** in relation to any matter before the IRS except in relation to an IRS examination of (1) an original return, (2) an amended return, or (3) a claim for refund or credit.

h.   A practitioner must **return client records** on request, regardless of any fee dispute. Records deemed returnable for purposes of this requirement are those records necessary for a client to comply with his or her federal tax obligations.

    1)   However, documents **prepared by the practitioner** that (s)he is withholding pending payment of a fee, with respect to such documents, are not included (provided state law permits retention of records in a fee dispute).

i.   Circular 230 allows **advertising** and **solicitation** with the following conditions:

    1)   False, fraudulent, misleading, deceptive, or unfair statements or claims are not allowed. Claims must be subject to factual verification.

    2)   Specialized expertise may not be claimed except as authorized by federal or state agencies having jurisdiction over the practitioner.

    3)   Each of the following fees may be advertised:

        a)   Fixed fees for specific routine services
        b)   A range of fees for particular services
        c)   The fee for an initial consultation
        d)   Hourly rates
        e)   Availability of a written fee schedule

    4)   Fee information may be communicated in professional lists, telephone directories, print media, mailings, electronic mail, facsimile, hand delivered flyers, radio, television, and any other method.

    5)   A practitioner may not assist or accept assistance from any person or entity that the practitioner knows has obtained clients in violation of Circular 230's advertising and solicitation rules.

4.   **Best Practices for Tax Advisors**

a.   Tax advisors should provide clients with the highest quality representation regarding federal tax issues. They should adhere to best practices in providing advice and in preparing or assisting in the preparation of a submission to the IRS.

b.   Best practices include

    1)   (a) Establishing the facts, (b) determining which facts are relevant, (c) evaluating the reasonableness of any assumptions or representations, (d) relating applicable law to the relevant facts, and (e) arriving at a conclusion supported by the law and the facts

    2)   Communicating clearly with the client about the terms of the engagement

    3)   Advising the client regarding the importance of the conclusions reached, including, for example, whether a taxpayer may avoid accuracy-related penalties under the Internal Revenue Code (IRC) if a taxpayer acts in reliance on the advice

    4)   Acting fairly and with integrity in practice before the IRS

c.   Tax advisors with responsibility for overseeing a firm's provision of advice about federal tax issues should take reasonable steps to ensure that the firm's procedures for all members, associates, and employees are consistent with the best practices.

5. **Written Tax Advice**

   a. When providing written advice about any federal tax matter, a practitioner must

      1) Base the advice on reasonable assumptions,
      2) Reasonably consider all relevant facts that are known or should be known, and
      3) Use reasonable efforts to identify and determine the relevant facts.

   b. The advice cannot rely upon representations, statements, findings, or agreements that are unreasonable, i.e., are known to be incorrect, inconsistent, or incomplete.

   c. The advice must not consider the possibility that (1) a tax return will not be audited or (2) a matter will not be raised during the audit in evaluating a federal tax matter.

   d. When providing written advice, a practitioner may rely in good faith on the advice of another practitioner only if that advice is reasonable given all the facts and circumstances.

   e. The practitioner cannot rely on the advice of a person who (1) the practitioner knows or should know is not competent to provide the advice or (2) has an unresolved conflict of interest.

6. **Sanctions for Violations**

   a. Practitioner may be censured (public reprimand), suspended, or disbarred from practice before the IRS for willful violations of any of the regulations contained in Circular 230.

   b. The Secretary of the Treasury may censure, suspend, or disbar from practice before the IRS any practitioner who

      1) Is shown to be incompetent or disreputable
      2) Refuses to comply with the rules and regulations relating to practice before the IRS
      3) Willfully and knowingly, with intent to defraud, deceives, misleads, or threatens any client

   c. The following is a brief list of conduct that may result in suspension or disbarment:

      1) Being convicted of an offense involving dishonesty or breach of trust
      2) Providing false or misleading information to the Treasury Department, including the IRS
      3) Negotiating a client's refund check or not promptly remitting a refund check
      4) Circulating or publishing matter related to practice before the IRS that is deemed libelous or malicious
      5) Using abusive language
      6) Suspension from practice as a CPA by any state licensing authority, any Federal court of record, or any Federal agency, body, or board
      7) Conviction of any felony involving conduct that renders the practitioner unfit to practice before the IRS
      8) Attempting to influence the official action of any IRS employee by bestowing a gift, favor, or anything of value

   d. A notice of disbarment or suspension of a CPA from practice before the IRS is issued to (1) IRS employees, (2) interested departments and agencies of the federal government, and (3) state licensing authorities.

Stop and review! You have completed the outline for this subunit. Study multiple-choice questions 1 through 6 beginning on page 20.

1.2 TAX RETURN PREPARERS

1. **Tax Return Preparers**

   a. A tax return preparer is **any person** who prepares **for compensation**, or employs one or more persons to prepare for compensation, **all or a substantial portion** of any return of tax or claim for refund under the Internal Revenue Code (IRC).

      1) A portion of any return or claim for refund is deemed substantial unless a condition for unsubstantiality is satisfied.

      2) An **unsubstantial portion** is either

         a) Less than $10,000 or

         b) Less than $400,000 **and** also less than 20% of the gross income on the return or claim.

      3) If **more than one** schedule, entry, or other portion is involved, all schedules, entries, or other portions **shall be combined** in determining whether a tax return preparer has prepared a substantial portion of any return or claim for refund.

   b. Preparation with respect to the following is within the scope of the rules governing tax return preparers:

Individual income tax	Corporate income tax
Individual returns	Corporate returns
Partnership returns	DISC returns
S corporation returns	Estate taxes
Employment tax	Excise taxes
Gift tax	

   c. Persons who are tax return preparers (provided they are compensated) include the following:

      1) A person who provides to a taxpayer or other preparer sufficient information and advice so that completion of the return is simply a mechanical matter.

      2) A **nonsigning** tax return preparer who prepares all or a substantial portion of a return or claim for refund. Examples include preparers who provide advice that constitutes a substantial portion of the return.

   d. Persons who are not tax return preparers include the following:

      1) An employee who prepares a return for the employer by whom (s)he is regularly and continuously employed

      2) A fiduciary who prepares a return or refund claim for any person (the trust)

      3) A person who prepares a refund claim in response to a notice of deficiency issued to another

      4) A person who provides typing, reproducing, or other mechanical assistance, i.e., clerical

      5) A person who merely gives an opinion about events that have not happened, i.e., planning

2. **Due Diligence**

   a. Significant aspects of return preparation require

      1) Making factual inquiries to ensure clients' accuracy and truthfulness and

      2) Taking a position relative to tax law. In other words, assessing the scenario and appropriately applying tax law to the facts.

    b.   A tax return preparer may rely, if in good faith, on information provided by the taxpayer without having to obtain third-party verification.

        1)   However, the preparer may not ignore the implications of the information.

        2)   The preparer must make **reasonable inquiries** if the information appears inaccurate or incomplete.

        3)   The preparer should make appropriate inquiries of the taxpayer about the existence of documentation for deductions.

    c.   When a tax return preparer discovers that a taxpayer has made an error in or omission from any document filed with the IRS, (s)he must notify the taxpayer of the error or omission immediately.

        1)   The tax return preparer also must advise the taxpayer of the consequences of the error or omission.

3.   **Procedural Requirements**

    a.   A return preparer is required to sign the return or claim for refund after it has been completed and before it is presented to the taxpayer.

        1)   If more than one tax return preparer is involved, the preparer who has primary responsibility for overall substantive accuracy is required to sign the return or claim for refund.

    b.   A return or refund claim prepared by a return preparer and filed with the IRS must include the return preparer's identifying number.

    c.   A return preparer is required to provide a completed copy of the return or refund claim to the taxpayer no later than the time it is presented for the taxpayer's signature.

    d.   A person who employs one or more return preparers is required to retain a record of (1) the name, (2) identifying number, and (3) principal place of work of each employed tax return preparer.

    e.   A return preparer is required to retain a completed copy of each return or claim prepared for 3 years after the close of the return period.

        1)   An alternative is to keep a list that includes, for the returns and claims prepared, the following information:

            a)   The taxpayers' names
            b)   Taxpayer identification numbers
            c)   Their tax years
            d)   Types of returns or claims prepared

        2)   The return period is the 12-month period beginning on July 1 each year.

4.   **Penalties**

    a.   Tax return preparers are subject to severe penalties for violations. The degree of severity varies among the penalties. Individuals with overall supervisory responsibility for advice given by a firm are also subject to penalties.

    b.   **Unreasonable positions.** Taking an **undisclosed** position **without a reasonable belief** that substantial authority exists that it will be sustained on its merits results in a penalty of an amount equal to the greater of $1,000 or 50% of the income to be derived.

        1)   If the position is **disclosed**, its tax treatment must have a **reasonable basis**.

        2)   The penalty does not apply if the preparer proves that

            a)   (S)he acted in good faith and
            b)   Reasonable cause exists for the understatement.

        3)   The return preparer can charge a reasonable fee for time and expense incurred to copy such records.

c. **Negligence.** Negligence includes any failure to make a reasonable attempt to (1) comply with the provisions of the internal revenue laws or (2) exercise ordinary and reasonable care in the preparation of a return.

d. **Willful or reckless conduct.** If the understatement was caused by the preparer's willful or reckless conduct, the penalty is the greater of $5,000 or 75% of the income to be derived.

e. **Frivolous submission.** Filing a frivolous return is penalized. A frivolous return (1) omits information necessary to determine the taxpayer's tax liability, (2) shows a substantially incorrect tax or willful understatement of tax liability, (3) is based on a frivolous position (e.g., that wages are not income), or (4) is based on the taxpayer's desire to impede the collection of tax.

f. The tax code provides that any tax return preparer who endorses or otherwise **negotiates** any check issued to a taxpayer with respect to taxes imposed by the IRC is subject to a penalty. Furthermore, any tax return preparer who operates a check cashing agency that cashes, endorses, or negotiates tax refund checks for returns prepared also is subject to a penalty.

g. **Aiding or abetting** in preparation of any document is subject to a penalty if using the document would result in an **understatement** of tax liability.

   1) Any act that constitutes a **willful** attempt to evade federal tax liability, even that of another person, is subject to criminal penalties, including imprisonment. Furthermore, any person who willfully aids or assists in preparation or presentation of a materially false or fraudulent return is guilty of a felony.

   2) Violations of these rules may result in disciplinary action by the director of the IRS, and an injunction may be issued prohibiting the violator from acting as a tax preparer.

h. **Fraud.** Fraudulent transactions ordinarily involve a willful or deliberate action with the intent to obtain an unauthorized benefit.

5. **Disclosure of Taxpayer Information**

   a. **Penalty**

      1) A penalty is imposed on any tax return preparer who discloses or uses any tax return information without the consent of the taxpayer. But the penalty is **not** imposed if the disclosure was specifically for (a) preparing, (b) assisting in preparing, or (c) providing services in connection with the preparation of any tax return of the taxpayer.

      2) The penalty is $250 per disclosure, with a maximum of $10,000 per year.

      3) If convicted of knowingly or recklessly disclosing the information, a preparer is guilty of a misdemeanor and subject to up to $1,000 in fines and up to a year in prison.

   b. **Exceptions**

      1) The penalty for disclosure is not imposed if the disclosure was made in the following circumstances:

         a) In accordance with the Internal Revenue Code

         b) To a related taxpayer, provided the taxpayer did not expressly prohibit the disclosure

         c) Under a court order

         d) To tax return preparers within the same firm

         e) For the purpose of a quality or peer review to the extent necessary to accomplish the review

   c. **Consent**

      1) The taxpayer's consent must be a written, formal consent authorizing the disclosure for a specific purpose.

      2) The taxpayer must authorize a preparer to

         a) Use the taxpayer's information to solicit additional current business from the taxpayer in matters not related to the IRS

         b) Disclose the information to additional third parties

         c) Disclose the information in connection with another person's return

   d. **Confidentiality**

      1) The confidentiality privilege is extended to certain nonattorneys.

         a) The privilege may **not** be asserted to prevent the disclosure of information to any regulatory body other than the IRS.

      2) In noncriminal tax proceedings before the IRS, a taxpayer is entitled to common-law protections of confidentiality with respect to the tax advice given by any **federally authorized tax practitioner**. They are the same protections a taxpayer would have if the advising individual were an attorney.

         a) A federally authorized tax practitioner includes any nonattorney who is authorized to practice before the IRS, such as a CPA.

         b) **Tax advice** is advice given by an individual with respect to matters that are within the scope of the individual's authority to practice before the IRS.

      3) The privilege also applies in any noncriminal tax proceeding in federal court brought by or against the United States.

Stop and review! You have completed the outline for this subunit. Study multiple-choice questions 7 through 18 beginning on page 22.

1.3 LICENSING AND DISCIPLINARY SYSTEMS

1. **State Boards of Accountancy**

   a. State boards of accountancy are governmental agencies that license accountants to use the designation **Certified Public Accountant**.

      1) **Requirements for licensure** vary from state to state. In addition to passing the CPA examination and paying the applicable license fee, a candidate may need to satisfy a state's educational, experience, and residency criteria.

      2) Continuing professional education (CPE), peer review, and ethics standards also may vary by state. Meeting these standards is necessary to remain licensed.

      3) State boards can suspend or revoke licensure through administrative process, for example, in board hearings.

      4) **State CPA societies** are voluntary, private entities that can admonish, suspend, or expel members.

      5) CPA examination questions do not test specific state disciplinary systems.

2. **AICPA Disciplinary Mechanisms**

   a. **Professional Ethics Division**

      1) The Professional Ethics Division investigates ethics violations by AICPA members.

      2) It imposes sanctions in less serious cases. For example, it may require a member to take additional CPE courses as a remedial measure.

b. **Joint Trial Board**

1) More serious infractions come before a joint trial board, which can acquit, admonish (censure), suspend, or expel a member. It may also take such other disciplinary, remedial, or corrective action as it deems to be appropriate.

2) The *CPA Letter* publishes information about suspensions and expulsions.

3) A decision of a trial board panel may be appealed to the **full trial board**. The determination of this body is conclusive.

4) Upon the member's exhaustion of legal appeals, **automatic expulsion** without a hearing results when a member has been convicted of, or has received an adverse judgment for,

   a) Committing a felony
   b) Willfully failing to file a tax return
   c) Filing a fraudulent tax return on the member's or a client's behalf
   d) Aiding in preparing a fraudulent tax return for a client

5) **Automatic expulsion** also occurs when a member's **CPA certificate is revoked** by action of any governmental agency, e.g., a state board of accountancy.

6) Expulsion from the AICPA or a state society does not bar the individual from the **practice of public accounting**.

7) **Joint Ethics Enforcement Program (JEEP)**

   a) The AICPA and most state societies have agreements that permit referral of an ethics complaint either to the AICPA or to a state society.

   b) The AICPA handles matters of national concern, those involving two or more states, and those in litigation.

      i) JEEP also promotes formal cooperation between the ethics committees of the AICPA and of the state societies.

3. **Other Disciplinary Bodies**

   a. The **SEC**

   1) The SEC may seek an **injunction** from a court to prohibit future violations of the securities laws. Moreover, it may conduct **administrative proceedings** that are quasi-judicial.

      a) Such proceedings may result in **suspension** or permanent **revocation** of the right to practice before the SEC, including the right to sign any document filed by an SEC registrant. Sanctions are imposed if the accountant

         i) Does not have the qualifications to represent others
         ii) Lacks character or integrity
         iii) Has engaged in unethical or unprofessional conduct
         iv) Has willfully violated, or willfully aided and abetted the violation of, the federal securities laws or their rules and regulations

   2) Suspension by the SEC also may result from

      a) Conviction of a felony or a misdemeanor involving moral turpitude
      b) Revocation or suspension of a license to practice
      c) Being permanently enjoined from violation of the federal securities acts

   3) Some proceedings have prohibited not only individuals but also **accounting firms** from accepting SEC clients. Furthermore, the SEC can initiate administrative proceedings against accounting firms.

      a) The SEC may, for example, prohibit a firm from appearing before the SEC if it engages in unethical or improper professional conduct. Such misconduct may include negligence.

4) The SEC may impose civil penalties in administrative proceedings.

    a) Furthermore, the SEC may order a violator to account for and surrender any profits from wrongdoing and may issue cease-and-desist orders for violations.

b. The **IRS**

1) The IRS may prohibit a CPA from practicing before the IRS if the person is incompetent or disreputable or does not comply with tax rules and regulations.

2) The IRS also may impose fines.

c. The **Public Company Accounting Oversight Board (PCAOB)**

1) The PCAOB was established by the Sarbanes-Oxley Act of 2002 to oversee auditors of issuers.

2) The SEC has oversight authority over the PCAOB, including approval of rules, standards, and budgets.

3) Public accounting firms are required to register with the PCAOB to prepare, issue, or participate in audit reports of issuers.

4) The PCAOB has **rule-making authority** regarding quality control, ethics, and auditing standards.

    a) These rules, especially those governing quality control, have great relevance to enforcement actions.

5) The PCAOB **inspects** registered CPA firms that regularly provide audit reports for more than 100 issuers. It inspects firms that regularly provide audit reports for 100 or fewer issuers every 3 years. Violations are reported to the SEC and state licensing authorities.

    a) All **attestation engagements** may be reviewed.

    b) The inspection also involves a **quality control assessment**.

    c) Furthermore, the inspection report must include the **firm's response**. The firm then has 12 months to correct the reported weaknesses.

6) The PCAOB has substantially the same **investigatory scope** with respect to accountants as the SEC.

    a) The PCAOB may request that the SEC issue subpoenas to third parties, and it may **deregister** any uncooperative firm.

7) The PCAOB has no power to issue injunctions, but it may initiate **administrative proceedings**.

    a) It may suspend or revoke a firm's registration or seek (1) disassociation of a person from a registered firm, (2) suspension (temporary or permanent) of the firm's registration, or (3) a penalty of up to $15 million.

8) Each registered public accounting firm must **report annually** to the PCAOB.

    a) A firm also may be required to submit **special (event-based) reports**.

        i) Annual reports must provide information about such matters as audit reports issued during the year and disciplinary history of new members of the firm.

        ii) Special reports must be filed within 30 days after reportable events, including the initiation of certain actions against the firm or certain classes of individuals.

Stop and review! You have completed the outline for this subunit. Study multiple-choice questions 19 and 20 on page 25.

QUESTIONS

1.1 Practitioners

1. Frank Maple, CPA, represents his brother Joe Maple and Joe's business partner Bill Smith. Joe Maple and Bill Smith are equal shareholders in the Joe & Bill Corporation. The Internal Revenue Service examined the corporation and determined that one of the shareholders committed fraud, but could not determine which shareholder it was. Frank has made an appointment with the Internal Revenue Service to determine which partner was guilty. Which of the following statements reflects what Frank should do in accordance with Circular 230?

A. Frank should meet with the Internal Revenue Service and try to convince the examiner that each shareholder is equally guilty.

B. Advise Joe & Bill that they should dissolve the corporation, thereby making it difficult for the Internal Revenue Service to pursue the issue.

C. Advise Joe & Bill that he cannot represent them because there is a conflict of interest.

D. Advise Joe & Bill on creating documents that will convince the Internal Revenue Service that neither shareholder is guilty of fraud.

Answer (C) is correct.
REQUIRED: The appropriate action in accordance with Circular 230.
DISCUSSION: An agent may represent conflicting interests before the IRS only if all directly interested parties expressly consent in writing after full disclosure. According to Sec. 10.29(a) of Circular 230, a conflict of interest exists if

1. The representation of one client will be directly adverse to another client or

2. There is a significant risk that the representation of one or more clients will be materially limited by the practitioner's responsibilities to another client, a former client or a third person, or by a personal interest of the practitioner.

Frank Maple should determine whether a conflict of interest exists and get all appropriate consents to the representation. Because acquiring the consent of the parties is required to continue representation of both parties and since that is not given as an option, Frank should advise Joe and Bill that he cannot represent them.

2. Mike is a CPA. Widget, Inc., is an accrual-basis taxpayer. In Year 3, while preparing Widget's Year 2 return, Mike discovered that Widget failed to include income on its Year 1 return that Widget received in Year 2 but that should have been included in income in Year 1 under the accrual method of accounting. What must Mike do?

A. Advise Widget of the error and the consequences of the error.

B. Include the income on the Year 2 return.

C. Refuse to prepare Widget's Year 2 return until Widget agrees to amend its Year 1 return to include the amount of income.

D. Change Widget to the cash method of accounting.

Answer (A) is correct.
REQUIRED: The action required by a CPA who knows that a client has not complied with the revenue laws.
DISCUSSION: An agent who knows that a client has not complied with the revenue laws of the U.S. is required to promptly advise the client of noncompliance as well as the consequences of noncompliance under the Code and Regulations. Under Circular 230, the agent is not required to notify the IRS.
Answer (B) is incorrect. An amended return would need to be filed, and the agent would file an amended return at the request of the taxpayer. Answer (C) is incorrect. It is the client's responsibility to request for the amended return to be filed for Year 1. Answer (D) is incorrect. Widget, Inc., may be required to maintain an accrual method of accounting due to the Code and Regulations. Also, amending the Year 1 return would be the only way to properly correct the understatement of income.

3. Identify the appropriate action that a practitioner should take when (s)he becomes aware of an error or omission on a client's return.

A. Amend the return and provide it to the client.

B. Inform the IRS of the noncompliance, error, or omission.

C. Do nothing.

D. Promptly advise the client of such noncompliance, error, or omission and the consequences thereof.

Answer (D) is correct.
REQUIRED: The appropriate action when a practitioner is aware of an error or omission.
DISCUSSION: Section 10.21 of Treasury Department Circular 230 requires an attorney, a certified public accountant, or an enrolled agent who knows that a client has not complied with the revenue laws of the United States to promptly advise the client of the noncompliance, error, or omission and the consequences of the noncompliance, error, or omission as provided in the IRC and regulations.
Answer (A) is incorrect. A practitioner may not amend the return without first informing a client. Answer (B) is incorrect. A practitioner is not required to inform the IRS. Answer (C) is incorrect. A practitioner must promptly advise the client of the noncompliance, error, or omission.

4. Which of the following statements is true with respect to a client's request for records of the client that are necessary for the client to comply with his or her Federal tax obligations?

A. The practitioner may never return records of the client to the client even if the client requests prompt return of the records.

B. The existence of a dispute over fees always relieves the practitioner of his or her responsibility to return records of the client to the client.

C. The practitioner must, at the request of the client, promptly return the records of the client to the client unless applicable state law provides otherwise.

D. The practitioner must, at the request of the client, return the records of the client to the client within 3 months of receiving the request.

Answer (C) is correct.

REQUIRED: The true statement about a client's request for records of the client.

DISCUSSION: A practitioner must return a client's records on request, regardless of any fee dispute. Records deemed returnable for purposes of this requirement are those records necessary for a client to comply with his or her federal tax obligations. Returns or other documents prepared by the practitioner that the practitioner is withholding pending payment of a fee are not includible unless applicable state law provides otherwise.

Answer (A) is incorrect. The client's records are required to be returned if the taxpayer makes such a request to comply with federal tax laws. Answer (B) is incorrect. A fee dispute does not relieve the practitioner of his responsibility to return documents that the taxpayer needs to comply with federal tax laws. Answer (D) is incorrect. The practitioner must return the documents to the taxpayer as quickly as is reasonable.

5. Which of the following is **not** an example of disreputable conduct (as described in Sec. 10.51 of Circular 230) for which a CPA may be suspended or disbarred from practice before the IRS?

A. Knowingly giving false or misleading information to the Treasury Department.

B. Willful failure to make a federal tax return in violation of federal revenue laws.

C. Failure to respond to a request by the Director of the Office of Professional Responsibility to provide information.

D. Misappropriation of funds received from a client for the purpose of payment of federal tax.

Answer (C) is correct.

REQUIRED: The action for which a CPA may not be disbarred or suspended from practice.

DISCUSSION: Section 10.51 of Circular 230 lists several examples of disreputable conduct for which a CPA may be disbarred or suspended from practice before the Internal Revenue Service. Failure to respond to a request by the Director of the Office of Professional Responsibility to provide information is not disreputable conduct under Sec. 10.51 of Circular 230.

Answer (A) is incorrect. Knowingly giving false or misleading information to the Treasury Department is prohibited by Circular 230. Answer (B) is incorrect. Willful failure to make a federal tax return in violation of federal revenue laws is prohibited by Circular 230. Answer (D) is incorrect. Misappropriation of funds received from a client for the purpose of payment of federal tax is prohibited by Circular 230.

6. All of the following are examples of disreputable conduct for which a CPA may be disbarred or suspended from practice before the Internal Revenue Service **except**

A. Soliciting by mailings, the contents of which are designed for the general public.

B. Suggesting that (s)he is improperly able to obtain special consideration from an Internal Revenue Service employee.

C. Maintaining a partnership for the practice of tax law and accounting with a person who is under disbarment from practice before the Internal Revenue Service.

D. Failing to properly and promptly remit funds received from a client for the purpose of payment of taxes.

Answer (A) is correct.

REQUIRED: The action for which a CPA may not be disbarred or suspended from practice.

DISCUSSION: Section 10.51 of Circular 230 lists several examples of disreputable conduct for which a CPA may be disbarred or suspended from practice before the Internal Revenue Service. Solicitation by mailings, the contents of which are designed for the general public, is not prohibited under Sec. 10.30(a)(2) and is not disreputable conduct under Sec. 10.51 of Circular 230.

1.2 Tax Return Preparers

7. A CPA must sign the preparer's declaration on a federal income tax return

- A. Only when the CPA prepares a tax return for compensation.
- B. Only when the CPA can declare that a tax is based on information of which the CPA has personal knowledge.
- C. Whenever the CPA prepares a tax return for others.
- D. Only when the return is for an individual or corporation.

Answer (A) is correct.
REQUIRED: The condition for signing the preparer's declaration on a federal income tax return.
DISCUSSION: Treasury Regulations require preparers to sign all the returns they prepare and to include their identification numbers. However, a preparer is defined as a person who prepares (or employs persons to prepare) for compensation any tax return, amended return, or claim for refund of tax imposed by Subtitle A of the Internal Revenue Code (which covers income taxes on all entities).
Answer (B) is incorrect. The CPA may prepare a return based on information provided by the taxpayer. Personal knowledge of the information is not required. Answer (C) is incorrect. The CPA must sign only when (s)he receives compensation. Answer (D) is incorrect. The signature requirement applies to returns and claims for refund by all income tax-paying entities.

8. Which of the following statements is **false** regarding tax return preparers?

- A. Only a person who signs a return as the preparer may be considered the preparer of the return.
- B. Unpaid preparers, such as volunteers who assist low-income individuals, are not considered to be preparers for purposes of preparer penalties.
- C. An employee who prepares the return of his or her employer does not meet the definition of a tax preparer.
- D. The preparation of a substantial portion of a return for compensation is treated as the preparation of that return.

Answer (A) is correct.
REQUIRED: The false statement about tax return preparers.
DISCUSSION: Under Sec. 7701(a)(36), a tax return preparer is any person who prepares for compensation, or employs others to prepare for compensation, any tax return or claim for refund under Title 26. A person who prepares a substantial portion of a return is considered a preparer even though someone else may be required to sign the return.

9. Mike is a CPA. For the past 5 years, the information that Anne provided Mike to prepare her return included a Schedule K-1 from a partnership showing significant income. However, Mike did not see a Schedule K-1 from the partnership among the information Anne provided to him this year. What does due diligence require Mike to do?

- A. Without talking to Anne, Mike should estimate the amount that would be reported as income on the Schedule K-1 based on last year's Schedule K-1 and include that amount on Anne's return.
- B. Call Anne's financial advisor and ask him about Anne's investments.
- C. Nothing, because Mike is required to rely only on the information provided by his client, even if he has a reason to know the information is not accurate.
- D. Ask Anne about the fact that she did not provide him with a Schedule K-1.

Answer (D) is correct.
REQUIRED: The actions required to perform due diligence.
DISCUSSION: A tax return preparer may rely, if in good faith, upon information furnished by the taxpayer without having to obtain third-party verification. However, the preparer may not ignore the implications of the information furnished. The preparer must make reasonable inquiries if the information appears inaccurate or incomplete.
Answer (A) is incorrect. The tax return preparer is not supposed to make up numbers. The tax return preparer is required to use the actual amounts in preparing a tax return. Answer (B) is incorrect. The tax return preparer cannot contact Anne's financial advisor without Anne's consent. Answer (C) is incorrect. A tax return preparer is required to make reasonable inquiries if information provided by the taxpayer appears inaccurate or incomplete.

10. Arnie is a Certified Public Accountant who prepares income tax returns for his clients. One of his clients submitted a list of expenses to be claimed on Schedule C of the tax return. Arnie qualifies as a return preparer and, as such, is required to comply with which one of the following conditions?

   A. Arnie is required to independently verify the client's information.

   B. Arnie can ignore implications of information known by him.

   C. Inquiry is not required if the information appears to be incorrect or incomplete.

   D. Appropriate inquiries are required to determine whether the client has substantiation for travel and entertainment expenses.

Answer (D) is correct.
   REQUIRED: The conditions with which a return preparer must comply.
   DISCUSSION: A practitioner (i.e., a CPA) may rely on information provided by a client without further inquiry or verification. However, if the information so provided appears incorrect, incomplete, or inconsistent, the practitioner must make reasonable inquiries about the information. This requirement includes inquiry about unsubstantiated travel and entertainment expenses (Circular 230).
   Answer (A) is incorrect. Arnie may rely in good faith on the client's information. Answer (B) is incorrect. Arnie may not ignore implications of information known by him. Answer (C) is incorrect. Arnie is required to make reasonable inquiries about information that appears to be incorrect or incomplete.

11. All of the following are tax return preparers **except**

   A. A person who prepares a substantial portion of the return for a fee.

   B. A person who prepares a claim for a refund for a fee.

   C. A person who gives an opinion about theoretical events that have not occurred.

   D. A person who prepares a United States return for a fee outside the United States.

Answer (C) is correct.
   REQUIRED: The person who is not a tax return preparer.
   DISCUSSION: A tax return preparer is any person who prepares for compensation, or employs others to prepare for compensation, any tax return or claim for refund under Title 26. A person who gives an opinion about events that have not happened is not a tax return preparer.
   Answer (A) is incorrect. A person who prepares a substantial portion of the return for a fee represents tax return preparers under the regulations. Answer (B) is incorrect. A person who prepares a claim for a refund for a fee represents tax return preparers under the regulations. Answer (D) is incorrect. A person who prepares a United States return for a fee outside the United States represents tax return preparers under the regulations.

12. Jane is a Certified Public Accountant who specializes in preparing federal tax returns. Which of the following returns would **not** qualify Jane as a tax return preparer?

   A. Estate or gift tax returns.

   B. Excise tax returns.

   C. Withholding tax returns.

   D. None of the answers are correct.

Answer (D) is correct.
   REQUIRED: The types of returns that qualify an individual as a tax return preparer.
   DISCUSSION: A tax return preparer is any person who prepares for compensation any return of tax or claim for refund under the IRC. Estate returns, gift tax returns, excise tax returns, and withholding returns are covered by the IRC.
   Answer (A) is incorrect. Preparation of gift tax returns does qualify Jane as a tax preparer. Answer (B) is incorrect. Preparation of excise tax returns does qualify Jane as a tax preparer. Answer (C) is incorrect. Preparation of employment tax returns, including withholding tax returns, does qualify Jane as a tax preparer.

13. When must a tax return preparer provide a copy of a tax return to a taxpayer?

   A. Within 45 days after the return is filed, including extensions.

   B. Within 48 hours after the taxpayer requests a copy of the tax return.

   C. Not later than the time the original return is presented to the taxpayer for signature.

   D. None of the answers are correct.

Answer (C) is correct.
   REQUIRED: The time when a preparer must provide a copy of the return to the taxpayer.
   DISCUSSION: Section 6107(a) requires all tax return preparers to furnish a completed copy of the return to the taxpayer not later than the time such return or claim for refund is presented for the taxpayer's signature.
   Answer (A) is incorrect. The taxpayer must receive a copy no later than the time the original return is presented for a signature. Answer (B) is incorrect. The taxpayer must receive a copy no later than the time the original return is presented for a signature. Answer (D) is incorrect. A correct answer choice is provided.

14. Jack, a return preparer, did not retain copies of all returns that he prepared but did keep a list that reflected the taxpayer's name, identification number, tax year, and type of return for each of his clients. Which of the following statements best describes this situation?

A. Jack is in compliance with the provisions of the tax code if he retains the list for a period of 1 year after the close of the return period in which the return was signed.

B. Jack is in compliance with the provisions of the tax code, provided he retains the list for a 3-year period after the close of the return period in which the return was signed.

C. Jack is not in compliance with the tax code since he must retain copies of all returns filed.

D. Jack is not in compliance with the tax code since he has not kept all the information required by the Code.

Answer (B) is correct.

REQUIRED: The statement that best describes record retention requirements for tax return preparers.

DISCUSSION: The person who is an income tax return preparer of any return or claim for refund shall "retain a completed copy of the return or claim for refund; or retain a record by list, card file, or otherwise of the name, taxpayer identification number, and taxable year of the taxpayer for whom the return or claim for refund was prepared and the type of return or claim for refund prepared." The material shall be retained and kept available for inspection for the 3-year period following the close of the return period during which the return or claim for refund was presented for signature to the taxpayer.

Answer (A) is incorrect. The list must be retained for a 3-year period. Answer (C) is incorrect. Jack is in compliance with the tax code. Answer (D) is incorrect. Jack is in compliance with the tax code.

15. Which of the following persons would be subject to the penalty for improperly negotiating a taxpayer's refund check?

A. A tax return preparer who operates a check cashing agency that cashes, endorses, or negotiates tax refund checks for returns he prepared.

B. A tax return preparer who operates a check cashing business and cashes checks for her clients as part of a second business.

C. The firm that prepared the tax return and is authorized by the taxpayer to receive a tax refund but not to endorse or negotiate the check.

D. A business manager who prepares tax returns for clients who maintain special checking accounts against which the business manager is authorized to sign certain checks on their behalf. The clients' federal tax refunds are mailed to the business manager, who has the clients endorse the checks and then deposits them in the special accounts.

Answer (A) is correct.

REQUIRED: A tax return preparer's obligations and penalty for improperly negotiating a refund check.

DISCUSSION: Section 6695(f) provides that any tax return preparer who endorses or otherwise negotiates any check issued to a taxpayer with respect to taxes imposed by the IRC will be subject to a penalty of $500 for each such check. A tax return preparer who operates a check cashing agency that cashes, endorses, or negotiates tax refund checks for returns that (s)he prepared is subject to the penalty.

Answer (B) is incorrect. The preparer's second business meets the definition of a bank. Answer (C) is incorrect. A preparer may receive checks provided (s)he does not cash it. Answer (D) is incorrect. The clients endorsed the checks.

16. A CPA who prepares clients' federal income tax returns for a fee must

A. File certain required notices and powers of attorney with the IRS before preparing any returns.

B. Keep a completed copy of each return for a specified period of time or keep a summarized list of specified return information.

C. Receive client documentation supporting all travel and entertainment expenses deducted on the return.

D. Indicate the CPA's federal identification number on a tax return only if the return reflects tax due from the taxpayer.

Answer (B) is correct.

REQUIRED: The duty of a CPA when preparing federal income tax returns.

DISCUSSION: A CPA who prepares clients' federal income tax returns for a fee meets the definition in the federal tax code of an income tax return preparer. An income tax return preparer is subject to penalties for certain types of failures. For example, for each failure to retain a copy of a prepared return, the penalty is $50. The copy must be retained for 3 years.

Answer (A) is incorrect. The IRC does not require such filing. Answer (C) is incorrect. The preparer is not required to examine documents to verify independently information provided by the taxpayer. But (s)he must make reasonable inquiry, if the information appears to be incorrect or incomplete, or determine the existence of required facts and circumstances incident to a deduction. Answer (D) is incorrect. The preparer is required to indicate his or her federal identification number on each return filed.

17. Which of the following acts by a CPA will **not** result in a CPA's incurring an IRS penalty?

- A. Failing, without reasonable cause, to provide the client with a copy of an income tax return.

- B. Failing, without reasonable cause, to sign a client's tax return as preparer.

- C. Understating a client's tax liability as a result of an error in calculation.

- D. Negotiating a client's tax refund check when the CPA prepared the tax return.

Answer (C) is correct.
REQUIRED: The act that will not result in a CPA's incurring an IRS penalty.
DISCUSSION: Understating a client's tax liability as a result of an error in calculation will not result in imposition of an IRS penalty unless it is the result of gross negligence or a willful attempt to avoid tax liability.
Answer (A) is incorrect. A CPA is required to provide his or her client with a copy of the tax return. Answer (B) is incorrect. A tax preparer is required to sign the return. Answer (D) is incorrect. Any tax return preparer who endorses or otherwise negotiates a refund check issued to a taxpayer is liable for a $500 penalty.

18. Which of the following acts, if any, constitute grounds for a tax preparer penalty?

I. Without the taxpayer's consent, the tax preparer disclosed taxpayer income tax return information under an order from a state court.

II. At the taxpayer's suggestion, the tax preparer deducted the expenses of the taxpayer's personal domestic help as a business expense on the taxpayer's individual tax return.

- A. I only.

- B. II only.

- C. Both I and II.

- D. Neither I nor II.

Answer (B) is correct.
REQUIRED: The acts, if any, that constitute grounds for a tax preparer penalty.
DISCUSSION: A penalty equal to the greater of $5,000 or 75% of the income derived is imposed on a tax return preparer if any part of an understatement of tax liability resulted from a willful attempt to understate the liability or from an intentional disregard of rules or regulations. A penalty will not be imposed if client information is disclosed under a court order.

1.3 Licensing and Disciplinary Systems

19. Which of the following professional bodies has the authority to revoke a CPA's license to practice public accounting?

- A. National Association of State Boards of Accountancy.

- B. State board of accountancy.

- C. State CPA Society Ethics Committee.

- D. Professional Ethics Division of AICPA.

Answer (B) is correct.
REQUIRED: The body with the authority to revoke a CPA's license.
DISCUSSION: A valid license is a prerequisite to the practice of public accounting. State boards of accountancy are the governmental agencies that license CPAs. Revocation or suspension of a CPA's license may be made only by the issuing board.
Answer (A) is incorrect. Only individual boards have the power to revoke licenses. Answer (C) is incorrect. State CPA societies and their ethics committees are not authorized to suspend or revoke a CPA's license. Expulsion by a state society does not prohibit the practice of public accounting. Answer (D) is incorrect. The AICPA and its committees are not authorized to suspend or revoke a CPA's license. Expulsion by the AICPA does not prohibit the practice of public accounting.

20. The SEC can suspend or revoke the right of an accountant to sign any document filed by an SEC registrant if the accountant

	Lacks Integrity	Engages in Unethical Conduct
A.	No	No
B.	No	Yes
C.	Yes	No
D.	Yes	Yes

Answer (D) is correct.
REQUIRED: The basis for discipline of an accountant by the SEC.
DISCUSSION: The SEC may conduct quasi-judicial proceedings. Pursuant to such proceedings, it may suspend or permanently revoke the right to practice before the SEC, including the right to sign any document filed by an SEC registrant, if the accountant does not have the qualifications to represent others, lacks character or integrity, has engaged in unethical or unprofessional conduct, or has willfully violated the federal securities laws or their rules and regulations.

STUDY UNIT TWO
SECURITIES LAW AND LIABILITY OF CPAs

(21 pages of outline)

This study unit covers CPAs' responsibilities to clients and third parties under state and federal laws. CPAs may be liable to clients and third parties upon breach of contract, negligence, fraud, or violations of securities laws.

The three main federal laws on which the AICPA tests candidates' knowledge are the Securities Act of 1933, the Securities Exchange Act of 1934, and the Sarbanes-Oxley Act of 2002.

States also have enacted laws governing securities for which CPAs must comply. State securities laws are collectively known and referred to as "blue-sky laws."

The impetus of federal securities laws and blue-sky laws was the Stock Market Crash of 1929, when the state and federal governments began to regulate securities and hold those who market and trade in them accountable, including CPAs and their clients.

The AICPA tests candidates' knowledge on the responsibilities of CPAs under these laws and to whom CPAs are liable if these laws are not followed.

As you review the relevant laws covered in this study unit, it is important to always understand what CPAs must do to fulfill their responsibilities (and thus protect themselves against liability), as well as to understand to what type of party (client, third-party user of financial statements, etc.) CPAs could be liable for errors and omissions, whether committed intentionally or unintentionally.

2.1 SECURITIES ACT OF 1933

1. **Overview**

    a. The 1933 act regulates the initial offering of securities by requiring the filing of a registration statement with the **Securities and Exchange Commission (SEC)** prior to sale or an offer to sell. State securities laws also apply. The functions of the SEC are explained in Subunit 2.2, which covers the Securities Exchange Act of 1934 in detail.

    b. Each **state** has adopted its own securities laws, often called **blue-sky laws**.

    1) Generally, both federal and state securities laws must be complied with. However, federal securities laws typically preempt blue-sky laws.

2. **Objectives**

    a. The objectives of the 1933 act are to

    1) Disclose to potential investors all material information that may impact their decisions regarding the securities and
    2) Prevent fraud, deceit, and misrepresentation in initial offerings.

    b. The goal is to provide investors with adequate information so they can make informed investment decisions.

    c. The SEC does **not** judge the merits of an investment, guarantee the accuracy of the information contained in the registration statement, or disclose the associated risks.

    1) Registration does not insure investors against loss.

3. **Definition and Parties**

   a. The 1933 act defines the term "security" to include almost any offering that constitutes an investment. A few examples are stocks, stock subscriptions, bonds, debentures, stock options and warrants, and limited partnership interests.

   b. **Every person involved** in the initial offering and sale of securities is subject to the securities laws.

      1) An **issuer** initially offers a security for sale to the public (generally, to raise money).

         a) Issuers include governments, trusts, corporations, or any person who owns more than 10% of a company's stock. In other words, the SEC views a person or entity that owns more than 10% of a company as an issuer in parallel to the corporation.

      2) An **underwriter** participates in the original offering of securities from the issuer with the intention of distributing the proceeds to the issuer.

      3) A **dealer** offers, sells, buys, deals, or otherwise trades in securities issued by another.

         a) A **broker** is an agent who executes securities transactions for clients.

4. **Categories of Issuers**

   a. Under the SEC's integrated disclosure system, four categories of issuers are recognized:

      1) A **nonreporting issuer** does not file under the 1934 act and must file a detailed initial registration statement under the Securities Act of 1933.

      2) An **unseasoned issuer** has reported for at least 3 consecutive years under the 1934 act.

      3) A **seasoned issuer** has filed for at least 1 year under the 1934 act and has a market capitalization of at least $75 million.

      4) A **well-known seasoned issuer** has filed for at least 1 year under the 1934 act and (a) has a worldwide market capitalization of at least $700 million or (b) has issued securities for cash in a registered offering of at least $1 billion of debt or preferred stock in the past 3 years.

5. **Registration under the 1933 Act**

   a. **Any offer to sell or sale of securities to the public** requires registration unless a specific exemption applies to the securities or the transaction.

   b. To comply with the 1933 act, an issuer must prepare and publicly file

      1) A registration statement
      2) A prospectus

   c. A **registration statement** is a public disclosure to the SEC of all material financial and other information regarding an issue of specific securities. It includes the prospectus given to each potential investor and any other information about the securities not required in the prospectus.

      1) The purpose of registration is to help investors evaluate the merits of securities. A registration statement includes

         a) A description of

            i) The registrant's business, property, and competition
            ii) The significant provisions of the security to be offered for sale
            iii) Management, compensation of directors and officers, material transactions with them, and their holdings of the registrant's securities

           iv)   Material legal proceedings

           v)   The principal purposes for which the proceeds will be used

    b)   The most recent audited financial statements and management's discussion and analysis (MD&A)

    c)   The signatures of the issuer, CEO, CFO, chief accounting officer, and a majority of the directors

   d.   A **prospectus** is an offer of securities for sale that includes key information from the registration statement. Certain communications are prohibited.

      1)   A preliminary prospectus is known as the "red-herring" prospectus.

      2)   In specified circumstances, a well-known seasoned issuer may make oral and written communications at any time. These may include a **free-writing prospectus**, a written offer (including one by electronic means) that is **not** a statutory prospectus.

      3)   Subject to certain limitations, **any issuer** may communicate a free-writing prospectus after the registration statement is filed. The intent is to ensure the public equal access to information about the business.

   e.   The registration statement is **effective on the 20th day** after filing unless the SEC accelerates the effective date or requires an amendment. A new 20-day period begins after an amendment. Sales or offers to sell may occur after the effective date if the buyer has received a final prospectus.

6.   **Shelf Registration under the 1933 Act**

   a.   Shelf registration benefits large corporations that frequently offer securities to the public.

   b.   Corporations that are **seasoned** or **well-known seasoned issuers** can file registration statements covering an unlimited amount of securities that may be issued within 3 years of the effective date of the registration. The securities then are issued **without**

      1)   Filing a new registration statement,

      2)   Observing a 20-day waiting period, or

      3)   Preparing a new prospectus.

   c.   The issuer must (1) update the information so that it is accurate and current or (2) refer investors to quarterly and annual statements filed with the SEC.

7.   **Exempt Securities under the 1933 Act: Issuers Who Are Not Subject to the 1933 Act**

   a.   Securities issued by the following are exempt from registration:

      1)   Domestic governments **if** used for a governmental purpose

      2)   Not-for-profit organizations

      3)   Domestic banks and savings and loan associations

      4)   Issuers that are federally regulated common carriers (e.g., railroads or public utilities)

      5)   A receiver or trustee in bankruptcy with prior court approval

      6)   Insurance policies and annuity contracts of state-regulated insurers

      7)   A corporation in reorganization if approved by a court or other governmental body

      8)   An issuer that exchanges securities with its current security holders if no commission or other consideration is paid

         a)   Thus, stock dividends and stock splits generally are exempt.

   b.   **Commercial Paper (Negotiable Instruments)**

      1)   Any note, draft, or banker's acceptance issued to acquire working capital is exempt if it has a maturity of not more than 9 months when issued.

8. **Exempt Transactions by Issuers under the 1933 Act: Types of Security Offerings Not Subject to the 1933 Act**

   a. **Rule 147** provides a safe harbor for an **intrastate offering**. But noncompliance with Rule 147 does not necessarily prevent use of the exemption. The following are the requirements of the safe harbor:

      1) The issuer is organized or incorporated in the state in which the issue is made;
      2) 80% of the proceeds are to be used in that state;
      3) 80% of its assets are located there, and the issuer does at least 80% of its business (gross revenues) within that state;
      4) **All** purchasers and offerees are residents of the state;
      5) No resales to nonresidents occur for at least 9 months after the initial sale by the issuer is completed; and
      6) Steps (e.g., a legend on the securities) are taken to prevent interstate distribution.

   b. **Regulation A** (also referred to as Regulation A+) permits certain issuers to offer up to $50 million of securities in any 12-month period without filing a formal registration statement and prospectus. General solicitation and advertising are allowed, and resale is **not** restricted.

      1) Offers and sales still may be made by general solicitation and advertising, and the securities continue to be unrestricted. But all issuers must file financial statements for the last 2 complete fiscal years.

         a) Persons (**bad actors**) who are convicted of (or subject to sanctions for) securities fraud or other offenses involving transactions in securities or SEC filings cannot use the exemption.

      2) An **offering statement** with certain disclosures must be filed and approved by the SEC. Also, each offeree and purchaser must receive an **offering circular** with concise narrative disclosures.

      3) The issuer may **test the waters** by using broadcast or written advertisements. But no oral communications with buyers are allowed until the SEC receives the advertisements. **No** sales are allowed until the offering statement is approved by the SEC.

      4) The criteria for Tier 1 (maximum of $20 million) and Tier 2 (maximum of $50 million) offerings are as follows:

         a) Under **Tier 1**, the number and nature of investors are not limited and no ongoing reporting requirements apply.

         b) Under **Tier 2**, a **nonaccredited** investor in unlisted securities cannot purchase an amount exceeding 10% of the greater of the investor's net worth or annual income. Furthermore, Tier 2 requires the following:

            i) Annual, semiannual, and current events filings must be made;
            ii) Audited statements must be included in the offering statement; and
            iii) Issuers are exempt from registration and qualification under state securities (**blue-sky**) laws.

   c. **Regulation D** of the Securities Act of 1933 provides certain exemptions for small issuances of securities and small issuers. There are two types of Regulation D exemptions that have been tested in detail on past CPA exams: Rule 504 and Rule 506. These rules are discussed in detail below and on the following pages.

      1) Certain procedural requirements must be followed to qualify for a Regulation D exemption.

         a) The issuer must exercise reasonable care to ensure that the purchasers of the securities are not underwriters and that such investors are purchasing strictly for their own investment purposes (only Rule 506).

        b)   The SEC must be notified within 15 days of the first offering.

        c)   The exemption is only for transactions in which the securities are offered or sold by the issuer (only Rule 506). In other words, the resale of securities is restricted.

2)   Regulation D affects two types of investors:

        a)   **Accredited investors** are individuals that meet income or net worth thresholds (excluding the value of a person's primary residence). Most institutional investors (hedge funds, mutual funds, etc.) are considered accredited investors. Accredited investors are not as regulated as nonaccredited investors because they are assumed by the SEC to be more knowledgeable and, therefore, they do not need to be supplied as much detailed information.

        b)   **Nonaccredited investors** are all investors who are not accredited investors. Nonaccredited investors must be given material information about the issuer, its business, and the securities being offered prior to the sale.

3)   **Rule 504** permits qualified issuers to sell up to **$5 million** of securities during a 12-month period to any number or type of purchasers. Registration is not required, and the issuer need not provide specific financial information. But the issuer must notify the SEC of Rule 504 sales.

        a)   Nonaccredited and accredited investors may purchase the securities.

              i)   **Accredited investors** include most institutional investors and individuals that meet income or net worth thresholds (excluding the value of a person's primary residence). All other investors are **nonaccredited**. If the offer is to nonaccredited investors, they must be given material information about the issuer, its business, and the securities being offered prior to the sale. Specified information is not required to be given to accredited investors.

        b)   General solicitation is allowed, and the securities issued are **not** restricted and can be freely traded, if the offering is

              i)   Registered in a state that requires a publicly filed registration statement, and disclosure documents are delivered to investors, or

              ii)   Sold exclusively according to state law exemptions that permit general solicitation and advertising, if sale is only to accredited investors.

4)   **Rule 506** implements the **private placement** exemption from registration for "transactions by an issuer not involving any public offering." Rule 506, unlike Rule 504, has **no** maximum amount.

        a)   The offering may be purchased by an unlimited number of accredited investors.

        b)   General solicitation and advertising are permitted if (1) sales are to accredited investors only, (2) the issuer takes reasonable steps to confirm that all purchasers are accredited, and (3) the issuer notifies the SEC and takes precautions against unregistered and nonexempt resale.

        c)   No more than 35 of the purchasers are nonaccredited investors. All nonaccredited investors must be **sophisticated**–they must have knowledge and experience sufficient to evaluate the risks and merits of the investment.

        d)   Generally, the issuer requires the purchaser to sign an investment letter stating that (s)he is purchasing for investment only and not for resale. For this reason, the shares are called lettered stock.

d.   **Section 4(6)** exempts up to $5 million of offers and sales if made only to **accredited investors**. The number of such investors may be unlimited, and no information is required to be given to them, but general advertising and solicitation are not permitted. Moreover, this exemption has the following requirements:

1)   The SEC must be informed of sales under the exemption,
2)   Resale is restricted, and
3)   Precautions must be taken to prevent nonexempt or unregistered resales.

Exempt Transactions by Issuers

Exemption	Aggregate Maximum Amount	Investors	Offer and Filings	Resale
Rule 147 (intrastate offerings)	No maximum	Purchasers and offerees must be state residents	General solicitation and advertising, but interstate distribution not permitted	No resales to nonresidents for at least 9 months
Regulation A -- *Tier 1* (excludes issuers reporting under the 1934 act, investment companies, and bad actors)	$20 million in 12-month period	Unlimited number of accredited and nonaccredited investors	Testing the waters, offering circular, approval of filed offering statements, general solicitation and advertising, 2 years of financial statements	Not restricted
-- *Tier 2* (excludes issuers filing under the 1934 act, investment companies, and bad actors)	$50 million in 12-month period	Nonaccredited investors limited to 10% of the greater of annual income or net worth if securities unlisted + unlimited number of accredited investors	Same as Tier 1 plus audited statements in offering statement; annual, semiannual, current events filings; exemption from blue-sky laws	Not restricted
Regulation D -- *Rule 504* (excludes most issuers that report under 1934 act)	$1 million in 12-month period	Unlimited number of accredited and nonaccredited investors	General solicitation allowed if compliant with state law	Not restricted if compliant with state law
-- *Rule 505*	$5 million in 12-month period	Unlimited number of accredited investors and no more than 35 nonaccredited purchasers (who are sophisticated or not sophisticated)	No general solicitation or advertising	Restricted
-- *Rule 506*	No maximum	Unlimited number of accredited investors and no more than 35 nonaccredited purchasers who must be considered sophisticated	No general solicitation and advertising unless all sales are confirmed to be to accredited investors and resale precautions are taken	Restricted
Rule 4(6)	$5 million	Only accredited but number unlimited	No general solicitation or advertising	Restricted

Stop and review! You have completed the outline for this subunit. Study multiple-choice questions 1 through 5 beginning on page 48.

2.2 SECURITIES EXCHANGE ACT OF 1934

1. **Overview**

   a. In contrast to the 1933 act, which regulates the **initial** offerings of securities, the 1934 act regulates the **secondary** distribution (resale) of securities. The following are the main elements of the 1934 act:

      1) This act establishes the following SEC powers:

         a) The SEC is an administrative agency created by the 1934 act to enforce the federal securities laws. It has the power to (1) issue rules, (2) investigate violations, (3) conduct hearings to decide whether violations have occurred (adjudication), (4) subpoena witnesses and records, and (5) impose civil penalties.

         b) The SEC may deny, suspend, or revoke registration, or it may order a suspension of trading of the securities. These sanctions are in addition to civil and criminal liability imposed by the federal securities laws.

         c) The SEC may prohibit an individual who has committed **securities fraud** from serving as an officer or director of a public company.

         d) The SEC oversees the Public Company Accounting Oversight Board (PCAOB).

         e) The SEC has recognized the FASB as the standards-setter for U.S. GAAP.

         f) As an administrative agency, the SEC cannot prosecute criminal cases. But it may refer cases to the Justice Department, e.g., willful falsehoods in a registration statement.

         g) The SEC supervises and disciplines accountants, attorneys, brokers, dealers, stock exchanges, investment advisors, etc.

      2) Periodic reporting, which requires providing up-to-date statements about all business operations and matters potentially affecting the value of securities

      3) Proxy solicitation and tender offers

      4) Insiders

      5) Antifraud provisions

2. **Registration under the 1934 Act**

   a. All regulated, publicly held companies must make a one-time **registration with the SEC**.

      1) Registration is required for

         a) All securities listed on a national exchange and

         b) Equity securities of companies that have total gross assets exceeding $10 million and a class of equity securities with (1) at least 2,000 shareholders or (2) 500 who are nonaccredited investors.

      2) National securities exchanges and registrants under the 1933 act also must register.

      3) Issuers that have registered securities under the 1934 act must file periodic reports and comply with the sections on insider trading and proxy solicitation and tender offers (Subunit 2.3).

   b. Registration and reporting requirements under the 1934 act are in addition to, not a substitute for, those under the 1933 act.

c.   In addition to disclosing financial statements for the 3 preceding years audited by a firm registered with the PCAOB, registration requires disclosure of the following:

1)   Nature of the business, corporate organization, and financial structure

2)   A description of the terms, rights, and positions of all outstanding securities

3)   Names of officers, directors, underwriters, and holders of more than 10% of a nonexempt equity security

4)   A description of bonus and profit-sharing arrangements.

3.   **Periodic Reporting Subsequent to Registration**

a.   **Annual reports** certified by the CEO and CFO are filed on **Form 10-K**. The elements of the annual report to shareholders may be incorporated by reference.

1)   The 10-K report contains information about the registrant's

a)   Business activities

b)   Securities (including common equity and the market for it)

c)   Stock prices (but not all price changes)

d)   Management-related persons (including all compensation for the CEO, CFO, next three highest paid officers, and directors)

e)   Disagreements about accounting and disclosures

f)   Audited balance sheets for the past 2 years and statements of income, cash flows, and equity for the past 3 years

g)   Management's discussion and analysis (MD&A) of the business

h)   Selected 5-year financial data

i)   Other matters included in the basic information package common to most SEC filings

b.   **Quarterly reports** certified by the CEO and CFO are filed on **Form 10-Q**. They need not contain audited financial statements. But the quarterly financial information must be reviewed by an independent auditor. Form 10-Q must be filed within 40 days of the last day of the first 3 fiscal quarters by large accelerated filers and within 45 days by nonaccelerated filers.

c.   **Current reports** must be filed on **Form 8-K** within 4 business days after certain material events. They include (1) changes in control of the registrant, (2) the acquisition or disposition of a significant amount of assets other than in the ordinary course of business, (3) bankruptcy or receivership, (4) resignation of a director, and (5) a change in the registrant's certifying accountant.

d.   The following table breaks down periodic issuer reporting to the SEC under the 1934 act.

Periodic Issuer Reporting to the SEC under the 1934 Act

Report	Form	Content	Timing
Annual (certified by CEO and CFO)	10-K	Audited financial statements and many other matters	60, 75, or 90 days after fiscal year end
Quarterly (certified by CEO and CFO)	10-Q	Reviewed quarterly financial information and changes during quarter	40 or 45 days after end of first 3 quarters
Current	8-K	Material events	Within 4 business days of event

e.   Any person or group of persons who acquires beneficial ownership of more than 5% of a class of registered equity securities of certain issuers must file a beneficial ownership report with the SEC within 10 days after the acquisition.

4. **Proxy Solicitation under the 1934 Act**

   a. A **proxy** is a power of attorney given by a shareholder to a third party authorizing the party to exercise the voting rights of the shares.

   b. Solicitation includes any request for a proxy or any request to revoke a proxy.

   c. The 1934 act makes it unlawful for any person to solicit any proxy with respect to any registered security in violation of SEC rules and regulations.

   d. The issuing company must file copies of the proxy statement and proxy form with the SEC 10 days prior to mailing to shareholders.

5. **Tender Offers under the 1934 Act**

   a. A tender offer is a general invitation by an individual or a corporation to all shareholders of the target corporation to purchase their shares for a specified price.

      1) The following must file a disclosure statement with the SEC, the issuer, and the securities exchanges:

         a) Any person or group that acquires beneficial ownership of more than 5% of a class of registered securities

         b) A person or group that makes a tender offer for more than 5% of such securities

         c) An issuer offering to repurchase its registered securities

6. **Insiders under the 1934 Act**

   a. Insiders required to report to the SEC are (1) directors, (2) officers, and (3) any person beneficially owning more than 10% of the stock of a corporation listed on a national stock exchange or registered with the SEC. Insiders must make an initial filing, report status changes, and file annually.

7. **Antifraud Provisions**

   a. **Insider trading** under Rule 10b-5 is the purchase or sale of **any security** by an individual who (1) has access to **material, nonpublic information**; (2) has not disclosed it before trading; and (3) has a fiduciary obligation to the issuer, the shareholders, or any other source of information. Thus, the definition of an insider in this context is much broader than previously discussed.

      1) Insiders for Rule 10b-5 purposes include (a) officers, directors, employees, and agents of the issuer; (b) persons entrusted with the issuer's information, such as auditors, attorneys, underwriters, and government employees; and (c) tippees (recipients of information from insiders).

      2) The SEC may bring a civil action for insider trading. Also, a private suit for damages may be brought by a purchaser or seller of shares.

Stop and review! You have completed the outline for this subunit. Study multiple-choice questions 6 through 8 on page 50.

2.3 FEDERAL STATUTORY LIABILITY OF CPAs AND OTHERS

1. **Overview**

    a. This subunit explains the liability provisions of the securities laws introduced in the previous subunits. They apply not only to accountants but also to other parties subject to the securities laws.

    b. A statute of limitations determines the maximum amount of time after an act or event occurs during which civil or criminal legal action can be taken.

2. **Claims and Defenses under Section 11 of the 1933 Act**

    a. Any person who acquires a security issued under a registration statement or prospectus that contains a **misstatement or omission of a material fact** may sue the issuer, directors, underwriters, signers, and expert preparers (e.g., auditors and attorneys).

    b. To recover under Section 11, a plaintiff must prove

    1) The plaintiff acquired a security subject to registration,
    2) The plaintiff incurred a loss (damages), and
    3) The registration statement contained a material misstatement or omission.

        a) But the accountant is liable only for a material misstatement or omission in a part of the statement for which (s)he was responsible.

            i) A misstatement or omission is **material** if a reasonable investor would be substantially likely to consider it important when deciding whether to buy the registered security.

    c. Plaintiffs need not prove **intent, negligence, causation by the defendant, or reliance by the plaintiff on the misstatement or omission**. The existence of a material misstatement or omission is enough to state a claim.

    d. A defendant's (e.g., an auditor's) liability for material misstatements or omissions contained in the registration statement or the prospectus extends to acquirers of a security (e.g., third party investors).

    1) The acquirer need not have given value to obtain the security.
    2) Privity of contract (the doctrine that the defendant must be a party to the contract with plaintiff) is not required between the acquirer and the defendant.
    3) The acquirer need not prove reliance, negligence, or fraud.

EXAMPLE

Public Corp. engages Accountant to review events subsequent to the date of a certified balance sheet. The objective is to determine whether any material change has occurred that should be disclosed to prevent the balance sheet from being misleading with regard to the registration statement required for a bond issue. Accountant does not discover a material uninsured loss. Astute purchases some of the bonds. Public files for protection from creditors under the Bankruptcy Act. It defaults on payment of interest on the bonds. No contract exists between Astute and Accountant. Nevertheless, Accountant is liable to Astute for damages incurred because the registration statement did not include the material loss.

e. The best defense to a Section 11 claim is **due diligence**. Any defendant except the issuer may assert this defense. Accordingly, this defense is what a CPA would most likely assert.

1) Due diligence means the accountant reasonably believed, at the time the registration statement became effective, that the financial statements did not contain an omission or misstatement of a material fact.

a) The belief must be based on a reasonable investigation, for example, adherence to GAAP and PCAOB standards, including extending procedures to the effective date (or as close as practicable to the effective date) of the filing.

2) Other defenses are that (a) the buyer knew of the misstatement or omission, (b) the misstatement or omission was immaterial, (c) the registration statement contained no misstatement or omission, or (d) the plaintiff's loss was not caused by the misstatement or omission.

f. A successful plaintiff is entitled only to monetary damages under Section 11. They are generally measured by the plaintiff's loss, but resale is not required to prove loss.

1) The loss equals the difference between the price paid for the security and either the market value of the security or the sale of the security as follows:

Action	Before Suit	After Suit
Security sold	Purchase price – Sales price	Purchase price – Greater of market value or sales price
Security not sold	Purchase price – Market value	Purchase price – Market value

2) The purpose of this measure of damages is to prevent unjust enrichment of the plaintiff. The plaintiff should be compensated for actual loss but not receive a windfall.

EXAMPLE

Reni successfully sued CPA under Section 11. Reni paid $50 per share for the stock that was the basis for the suit. The suit was brought on June 1. The market value of the stock on June 1 was $45. Reni sold the stock for $47 on June 5 before the jury reached a verdict. Reni's damages are $3 per share ($50 – $47). If Reni had not sold the stock, damages would be $5 per share ($50 – $45). If Reni had sold the stock on June 5 for $40, damages also would be $5 per share ($50 – $45).

---

g. Under the 1933 act, the period of the statute of limitations on an action by a purchaser of securities is 1 year after discovery of the misstatement or omission. But the maximum period after the first offer to the public is 3 years.

3. **Failure to Register under the 1933 Act**

a. Section 12(a)(1) imposes strict civil liability (liability that has no requirement to prove fault, negligence, or intention) if

1) The required registration was not made;

2) A registered security was sold, but a prospectus was not delivered or was not current; or

3) An offer to sell was made before a required registration.

b. The purchaser may sue only his or her seller (privity is required).

4. **Antifraud Provisions under the 1933 Act**

    a. These apply to all securities, both **registered and exempt**.

    b. Section 12(a)(2) imposes liability on any person to the immediate purchaser for material misstatements or omissions in any communication made with respect to the offer or sale of any security. The SEC or the defrauded purchaser may sue.

        1) The purchaser may sue only his or her seller.
        2) The seller's defenses include proving that

            a) (S)he did not know, and should not have known, about the misstatement or omission, or
            b) The decline in value was not caused by the seller's misstatements.

    c. Under Section 17(a), liability is imposed for fraud, material misrepresentations, and omissions in any securities sale. However, this broad provision does **not allow** the purchaser to sue. Only the SEC may sue.

    d. A safe harbor is provided for forward-looking statements (about revenues, income, EPS, etc.) made by issuers required to register under the 1934 act. Civil liability is avoided if the predictions are (1) not material, (2) made without actual knowledge that they are false or misleading, or (3) accompanied by meaningful cautionary statements that identify risk factors that could cause actual results to differ materially from those in the statement.

        1) The safe harbor does not apply to, for example, statements about IPOs, tender offers, and ongoing private transactions.

    e. The following table summarizes civil remedies under the 1933 act.

Civil Remedies under the 1933 Act

Section	Prohibition	Plaintiffs	Defendants	Liability
11	Misstatement or omission in registration statement or prospectus	Acquirers of the covered securities	Issuer Signers Directors Experts Underwriters	Strict for issuer Negligence for others
12(a)(1)	No registration No delivery of current prospectus Sale before registration	Purchaser	Seller	Strict
12(a)(2)	Material misstatement or omission in any communication about offer or sale of any security	Purchaser or SEC	Seller	Negligence
17(a)	Fraud, material misrepresentation, omission in any securities sale	SEC enforcement (no implied private remedy)	Offerors and sellers	Civil or criminal

5. **Criminal Liability under the 1933 Act**

    a. Liability is based on **willful** violations of the act in the sale of securities.

        1) Willful violations are essentially fraud.

6. **Claims for False or Misleading Statements under the 1934 Act**

   a. The 1934 act imposes civil liability for making or causing a **false or misleading statement (or omission) of a material fact** in any **filing** with the SEC under the act.

   b. A plaintiff must prove the following:

      1) A false statement about, or omission of, a material fact
      2) Reliance on the misstatement in buying or selling the security

         a) Proof that the price of the security was affected by the misstatement **(fraud-on-the-market theory)** may substitute for proof of reliance.

      3) Damages (loss)

   c. A **defense** to a suit is to prove that the defendant acted in good faith and had **no knowledge** that the statement was false or misleading.

      1) **Good faith** is an absence of an intent to deceive.

   d. For false or misleading statements, the 1934 act requires a plaintiff to file suit before the earlier of (1) 2 years after discovery of the false or misleading statement or (2) 5 years after the cause of action arose.

7. **Antifraud Provisions under the 1934 Act: Section 10(b)**

   a. Section 10(b) is the antifraud provision of the 1934 act.

      1) The SEC's **Rule 10b-5** states that it is illegal for any person, directly or indirectly, to use the mail, interstate commerce, or a national securities exchange to defraud anyone in connection with the purchase or sale of any security, whether or not exempt from registration.

         a) Rule 10b-5 most often is applied to **insider trading** and corporate misstatements.

         b) A person may violate Rule 10b-5 without actually participating in the purchase or sale of the security.

            i) All that is required is that the party's activity be connected with the purchase or sale.

         c) Rule 10b-5 has no exemption.

   b. Liability is only to actual purchasers or sellers. They need **not** be in privity with the defendant.

   c. The SEC or a private party may sue under Rule 10b-5.

   d. A **plaintiff must prove** each of the following:

      1) An oral or written misstatement or omission of a material fact or other fraud

         a) A misstatement or omission is **material** if a reasonable investor would be substantially likely to consider it important when deciding whether to buy or sell the security.

      2) Its connection with any purchase or sale of securities
      3) The defendant's intent to deceive, manipulate, or defraud **(scienter)**
      4) Reliance on the misstatement

         a) If the plaintiff is the SEC, reliance is not required.

         b) A private plaintiff ordinarily need not prove reliance in omission cases. Indirect reliance is presumed (fraud-on-the-market theory).

      5) Loss caused by the reliance

    e.   Remedies include

        1)   Damages (the recovery is at least the amount caused by the fraud, and no resale is necessary)

        2)   Rescission of a securities contract

        3)   Injunctions

    f.   An accountant may be liable for misrepresentations contained in unaudited financial statements if (s)he knew or should have known of them.

        1)   The accountant has a duty to perform a minimal investigation and not to ignore suspicious circumstances.

    g.   An accountant is liable for **aiding and abetting** violations of the 1934 act when (s)he

        1)   Is generally aware of his or her participation in an activity that, as a whole, is improper and

        2)   Knowingly aids the activity. Silence may constitute aiding, not abetting.

The CPA exam tests on the similarities and differences between Section 11 of the 1933 act and Section 10(b) of the 1934 act.

A plaintiff needs to prove scienter, reliance, and causation under Section 10(b), whereas he or she does not under Section 11. Under both provisions, the plaintiff needs to prove loss (damages) and misstatement or omission of a material fact.

A Section 10(b) plaintiff must prove either the purchase or sale of securities, while a Section 11 plaintiff must prove purchase of securities.

Remedies for Section 11 plaintiffs include only monetary damages, while remedies for Section 10(b) plaintiffs include damages, rescission of a securities contract, and injunctions.

---

8.   **Proxy Statements under the 1934 Act**

    a.   If a **proxy statement** contains a false or misleading statement or omission of material fact, a shareholder who reasonably relies on it may sue the proxy solicitor.

9.   **Tender Offers under the 1934 Act**

    a.   In a **tender offer**, it is illegal for any person to

        1)   Make a misstatement of a material fact or omission of such a fact or

        2)   Engage in any fraudulent or deceptive practice.

    b.   The following table summarizes civil remedies under the 1934 act.

Civil Remedies under the 1934 Act

Subject	Conduct	Plaintiffs	Defendants
Misleading Statements	Material false or misleading statement or omission in any SEC filing	Purchasers or sellers who rely and incur damages	Filers (defense is good faith or no knowledge)
Proxy Statements	Material false or misleading proxy statement	Government, Shareholders	Parties making the solicitation
Tender Offers	Material misstatement or omission of fact or fraud with respect to a tender offer	Government, Possible private suit by target or its shareholders	Tender offeror
Rule 10b-5	Fraud with regard to purchase or sale of any security	Government, Purchaser or seller	Any person who commits fraud (but scienter must be proven)
Anti-Fraud Provision	Insider trading	Government, Purchasers or sellers	Any purchaser or seller having material, nonpublic information

10. **Criminal Liability under the 1934 Act**

    a. The 1934 act imposes **criminal penalties** for **willfully** making a materially false or misleading statement.

        1) **Reckless disregard** for the truth of a statement sometimes is considered the equivalent of a willful violation.

11. **Private Securities Litigation Reform Act of 1995 (PSLRA)**

    a. This act was primarily enacted to curb abusive securities lawsuits under the Securities Act of 1933 and the Securities Exchange Act of 1934.

    b. Under PSLRA, more evidence is required for the plaintiff to file the case with the courts.

    c. Furthermore, auditors are required to include procedures designed to provide reasonable assurance of detecting illegal acts.

12. **Sarbanes-Oxley Act of 2002 (SOX)**

    a. This act was a response to numerous accounting scandals. It applies to issuers of publicly traded securities subject to federal securities laws.

    b. Among other things, the act established the **Public Company Accounting Oversight Board (PCAOB)** to regulate, inspect, and investigate public accounting firms. To prepare an audit report for an SEC registrant, a CPA firm must register with the PCAOB.

        1) Violations of the PCAOB's rules are violations of the Securities Exchange Act of 1934 and are subject to the same penalties.

    c. The **audit committee** must be directly responsible for appointing, compensating, and overseeing the work of the public accounting firm employed by the issuer. In addition, the accounting firm must report directly to the audit committee, not to management.

        1) The act requires that each member of the audit committee, including at least one who is a financial expert, be an independent member of the issuer's board.

13. **Section 404 of SOX**

    a. Under Section 404 of the act, **management of an issuer** must establish and document internal control procedures and include in the annual report **a report on the company's internal control over financial reporting**.

        1) Because of Section 404, **two audit opinions** are expressed: one on internal control and one on the financial statements.

            a) However, a corporate issuer with a market capitalization of less than $75 million is exempt from the required audit of assertions about control and procedures for financial reporting.

        2) The auditor must evaluate whether the control structure and procedures

            a) Include records accurately and fairly reflecting the firm's transactions and

            b) Provide reasonable assurance that transactions are recorded so as to permit statements to be prepared in accordance with GAAP.

        3) The auditor's report also must **describe any material weaknesses** in the controls.

b. **Auditors of issuers** must **not** perform the following nonaudit services without an exemption created by the PCAOB on a case-by-case basis or audit committee preapproval:

1) Appraisal and other valuation services, designing and implementing financial information systems, actuarial functions, and bookkeeping if the results are subject to audit

2) Management and human resource services

3) Legal and other expert services not pertaining to the audit

4) Investment banking, advisory, and broker-dealer services

5) Internal audit outsourcing that involves financial accounting

6) Certain tax services

c. Still another provision of the act prohibits the conflict of interest that arises when the CEO, CFO, controller, chief accounting officer, or the equivalent was employed by the company's public accounting firm within 1 year preceding the audit.

d. Auditors must retain their audit **working papers** for at least 7 years.

1) It is a **crime** for auditors to fail to maintain all audit or review working papers for at least 5 years.

a) If retention is for more than 5 years but fewer than 7 years, sanctions that are not criminal penalties may be imposed by the PCAOB.

e. Second-partner review and approval of audit reports is required.

1) Furthermore, the lead audit partner and the reviewing partner must rotate off the audit every 5 years.

f. Public accounting firms must register with the PCAOB and be subject to **inspection every 3 years (1 year for large firms)**.

g. The act created a **felony** for defrauding shareholders of issuers. It prohibits the knowing or attempted execution of any fraud upon persons in connection with securities of issuers or the purchase or sale of such securities.

Stop and review! You have completed the outline for this subunit. Study multiple-choice questions 9 through 13 beginning on page 50.

2.4 STATE LAW LIABILITY TO CLIENTS AND THIRD PARTIES

1. **Contractual Liability to Client (also called Privity of Contract)**

a. The contract between an accountant and a client is a personal service contract, so it can be litigated like any other type of contract. The usual remedy for **breach** of the contract is compensatory **monetary damages**.

b. Legal issues arising from contract disputes include (1) whether the elements of a contract are present, (2) the duties of the parties, (3) who may enforce the contract, (4) who is liable for breach of contract, (5) what remedies are available for breach, and (6) whether the accountant may delegate responsibility for an engagement.

1) These and other matters are covered in the contract law outline in Study Unit 18.

2. **Contractual Liability to Third Parties**

a. An accountant potentially may be liable to third-party beneficiaries of the contract.

3. **Accountant's Duties**

    a. The accountant is implicitly bound by the contract to perform the engagement with **due care** (nonnegligently) and in compliance with **professional standards**.

        1) Moreover, an accountant must comply with the law and is responsible for exercising independent professional judgment.

EXAMPLE

An accountant and a client entity contract for the accountant to perform an audit for $2,500. The audit is contracted to be done within 3 months. The audit actually takes 6 months. A breach of contract has occurred.

---

    b. An understanding should be established regarding what services the accountant is to perform for the client. An **engagement letter** puts this contract in writing.

        1) The engagement letter should describe (a) the services agreed upon by the client and accountant (whether or not required by professional standards), (b) fees to be paid, and (c) other pertinent details.

EXAMPLE

The engagement letter may provide for positive confirmation of all accounts receivable. Professional standards may, in the circumstances of the specific engagement, permit negative confirmation of a sample of accounts receivable.

---

4. **Contractual Defenses**

    a. Typical defenses include the absence of one or more elements of a contract, substantial performance, or the failure of the other party to perform. For example, suspension or termination of performance may be justified because of the other party's prior breach.

5. **Tort Liability to Client for Negligence**

    a. An accountant may be liable in tort for losses caused by the accountant's negligence.

        1) A **tort** is a private wrong resulting from the breach of a legal duty imposed by society.

            a) The duty is not created by contract or other private relationship.

    b. Types of Negligence.

        1) **Ordinary negligence** may result from an accountant's act or failure to act given a duty to act, for example, failing to observe inventory or confirm receivables.

        2) **Negligent misrepresentation** is a false representation of a material fact not known to be false but intended to induce reliance as opposed to intentional misrepresentation (fraud).

            a) The plaintiff must have reasonably relied on the misrepresentation and incurred damages.

        3) **Gross negligence** is failure to use even slight care.

            a) In extreme circumstances, an accountant may be liable for **punitive damages** if (s)he is grossly (not ordinarily) negligent.

    c.   An accountant has a duty to exercise **reasonable care and diligence**.

        1)   The accountant should have the degree of skill commonly possessed by other accountants in the same or similar circumstances, but an accountant is not a guarantor of the work.

        2)   **Compliance with professional standards** demonstrates that the accountant exercised reasonable care and diligence and is therefore a defense against negligence claims.

        3)   Accountants may be liable for failure to communicate to the client findings or circumstances that indicate misstatements in the accounting records or fraud.

            a)   They also must communicate all significant deficiencies and material weaknesses in internal control.

    d.   A client must prove all of the elements of negligence.

        1)   The accountant owed the plaintiff a **duty**.

        2)   The accountant **breached** this duty.

        3)   The accountant's breach **actually and proximately caused** harm to the plaintiff.

            a)   Proximate cause is a chain of causation that is not interrupted by a new, independent cause. Moreover, the harm would not have occurred without the proximate cause. However, actual causation is insufficient. The harm also must have been reasonably foreseeable. Thus, proximate cause is a limit on liability and a possible defense.

        4)   The plaintiff incurred **damages**.

6.   **Tort Liability to Third Parties for Negligence**

    a.   The majority rule is that the accountant is liable to **foreseen** (not necessarily identified in the contract) **third parties** (foreseen users and users within a foreseen class of users).

        1)   Foreseen third parties are those to whom the accountant intends to supply the information or knows the client intends to supply the information.

            a)   They also include persons who use the information in a way the accountant knows it will be used.

EXAMPLE

Smith, CPA, was engaged by Client, Inc., to audit its annual financial statements. Client's president told Smith that the financial statements would be distributed to South Bank in connection with a loan application. Smith was negligent in performing the audit. Subsequently, the financial statements were given to West Bank as well. West Bank lent Client $50,000 in reliance on the financial statements. West Bank suffered a loss on the loan. Smith is liable to West Bank because it is within a foreseen class of users, and the loan is a transaction similar to that for which the financial statements were audited.

---

    b.   In some states, the accountant is liable to all **reasonably foreseeable third parties**. They are all members of the class of persons whose reliance on the financial statements the accountant may reasonably anticipate.

EXAMPLE

Smith, CPA, is engaged to audit the annual financial statements of Client. Smith is not informed of the intended use of the statements. However, Smith knows that they are routinely distributed to lessors, suppliers, trade creditors, and lending institutions. Client uses the statements, which were negligently prepared, to obtain a lease from XYZ, Inc., a reasonably foreseeable party. Smith will be liable to XYZ because it is a member of a class of reasonably foreseeable third parties.

---

    c.   The traditional view was that an accountant was liable for **negligence** only to a plaintiff (1) in **privity of contract** with the accountant or (2) a primary (intended third-party) beneficiary of the engagement. A third party is a primary beneficiary if

        1)   The accountant is retained principally to benefit the third party,

        2)   The third party is identified, and

        3)   The benefit pertains to a specific transaction. Thus, the accountant knows the particular purpose for which the third party will use and rely upon the work.

EXAMPLE

Smith, CPA, was engaged by Client, Inc., to audit Client's annual financial statements. Client told Smith that the audited financial statements were required by Bank in connection with a loan application. Bank is a primary beneficiary and may recover damages caused by the CPA's negligence.

---

7. **Strict Liability in Tort**

    a.   Strict liability without fault is not a basis for recovery from an accountant.

8. **Liability for Fraud**

    a.   Fraud is an intentional misrepresentation. It is a willful and deceitful act. An accountant is liable for losses that result from his or her commission of fraud. Punitive and compensatory damages are both permitted.

EXAMPLE

An accountant is engaged to audit financial statements. To increase profits from the engagement, the accountant planned to and did omit necessary audit procedures. The accountant committed fraud.

---

    b.   A finding of fraud requires proof of the following elements:

        1)   The accountant made a **misrepresentation**.

        2)   The misrepresentation was made with **scienter**, that is, with actual knowledge of fraud.

        3)   The misrepresentation was of a **material fact**.

        4)   The misrepresentation induced **reliance**.

        5)   Another person **justifiably relied** on the misstatement to his or her detriment.

    c.   **Constructive fraud** is a fraud claim with the scienter requirement of actual knowledge satisfied by gross negligence.

        1)   **Gross negligence** is such a reckless disregard for the truth that fraud is implied.

    d.   Auditor-accountants have **no general duty to discover fraud**.

        1)   Nevertheless, an auditor is held liable for failure to discover fraud when the auditor's negligence prevented discovery.

        2)   An auditor who fails to follow professional standards and therefore does not discover fraud will probably be liable if compliance with professional standards would have detected the fraud.

EXAMPLE

U.S. GAAS and PCAOB standards require an auditor to plan and perform the audit to provide **reasonable assurance** about whether the financial statements are free of material misstatement, whether caused by error or fraud. An auditor must (1) identify risks of material misstatement due to fraud; (2) assess the identified risks; and (3) respond by changing the nature, timing, and extent of audit procedures.

---

9. **Liability to Third Parties for Fraud**

    a. Liability is to all **reasonably foreseeable users** of the work product. A foreseeable user is any person that the accountant should have reasonably foreseen would be injured by justifiable reliance on the misrepresentation.

        1) Privity is not required. The accountant can be sued by others who rely on the work product. The plaintiff does not have to be the person or entity that entered into the contract with the accountant.

        2) A foreseeable user has the right to sue.

10. **Defenses to Fraud**

    a. A plaintiff must prove each element of fraud with particularity. Credible evidence that disproves one of the elements tends to negate liability.

Stop and review! You have completed the outline for this subunit. Study multiple-choice questions 14 through 18 beginning on page 52.

2.5 PRIVILEGED COMMUNICATION AND CONFIDENTIALITY

1. **Accountant-Client Privilege – Federal Law**

    a. Federal law does not recognize a broad privilege of confidentiality for accountant-client communications.

        1) However, a confidentiality privilege covers most **tax advice** provided to a current or prospective client by any individual (CPA, attorney, enrolled agent, or enrolled actuary) qualified under federal law to practice before the IRS.

            a) The privilege is available only in matters brought before the IRS or in proceedings in federal court in which the U.S. is a party.

            b) The privilege applies only to advice on legal issues.

            c) The privilege does **not** apply to criminal tax matters, private civil matters, disclosures to other federal regulatory bodies, or state and local tax matters.

2. **Accountant-Client Privilege – State Law**

    a. State law does not recognize a privilege for accountant-client communications **except** in a minority of states.

EXAMPLE

State law provides for an accountant-client privilege. The IRS, in conducting a proper investigation, requests Accounting Firm to provide it with records on Client. The federal privilege does not apply. Firm complies, and Client sues Firm in state court. Firm asserts that federal law does not recognize the privilege and preempts state law. State court determines that, because the disclosure was without notice to Client and was made in the absence of service of legal process compelling disclosure, Firm is liable to Client for the voluntary disclosure.

---

        1) If the privilege exists, it belongs to the client.

        2) If any part of the privileged communication is disclosed by either the client or the accountant, the privilege is lost completely.

EXAMPLE

In the previous example, disclosure by Firm to a third party (the IRS) negates the privilege with respect to the information. The information is no longer recognized as a protected confidential communication under the law of the state. However, Firm may still be liable to Client. Given the existence of a state privilege, Firm is still liable if, in the specific case, federal law does not preempt state law. Firm has a professional duty under the AICPA *Code of Professional Conduct*. It must not disclose confidential client information without consent except, for example, to comply with an enforceable summons or subpoena.

---

3. Client communications with accountants retained by attorneys to aid in litigation are protected by the **attorney-client** privilege. This privilege is recognized in federal and state courts.

4. **Working Papers**

    a. Working papers are confidential records of an accountant's performance of an engagement. They document the procedures performed, evidence obtained, and conclusions reached.

    b. Working papers are the **property of the accountant**.

        1) Because they are prepared by the accountant, they provide the best evidence of the accountant's performance.

        2) However, working papers may be subpoenaed by a third party for use in litigation in the many states that do not recognize a privilege for accountant-client communications.

        3) Without a court order or client consent, third parties have no right of **access** to working papers.

        4) Working papers may be disclosed to another CPA partner of the accounting firm without the client's consent because such information has not been communicated to outsiders.

    c. **Confidential Client Information Rule**

        1) A member of the AICPA in public practice must not disclose confidential client information without the client's consent. However, this Rule does **not** affect the following:

            a) Professional obligations under the Compliance with Standards Rule and the Accounting Principles Rule

            b) The duty to comply with a valid subpoena or summons or with applicable laws and regulations

            c) An official review of the member's professional practice

                i) But a member's practice may be reviewed as part of a purchase, sale, or merger of the practice. However, appropriate precautions (e.g., a written agreement) should prevent disclosures by a prospective buyer.

            d) The member's right to initiate a complaint with or respond to any inquiry made by an appropriate investigative or disciplinary body, e.g., the professional ethics division or a trial board of the AICPA or a state CPA society peer review body

    d. At a minimum, an accountant who does **not** audit public companies should **retain** working papers until the state statute of limitations on legal action has lapsed. The limitations period varies by state and according to the type of claim.

    e. Auditors of public companies must retain working papers for at least 7 years.

Stop and review! You have completed the outline for this subunit. Study multiple-choice questions 19 and 20 on page 54.

QUESTIONS

2.1 Securities Act of 1933

1. Under the Securities Act of 1933, which of the following statements, if any, are correct regarding the purpose of registration?

I.   The purpose of registration is to allow for the detection of management fraud and prevent a public offering of securities when management fraud is suspected.

II. The purpose of registration is to adequately and accurately disclose financial and other information upon which investors may determine the merits of securities.

    A. I only.

    B. II only.

    C. Both I and II.

    D. Neither I nor II.

Answer (B) is correct.
    REQUIRED: The true statements, if any, about the purpose of registration under the Securities Act of 1933.
    DISCUSSION: One purpose of the Securities Act of 1933 is disclosure. The act was designed to provide complete and fair disclosure to potential investors. It applies only to the initial issuance of securities. Disclosure is accomplished through the requirement that a registration statement be filed with the SEC. Once potential investors have complete disclosure, the assumption is that they can make reasonable decisions. The second purpose is prevention, not detection, of fraud through enforcement of its antifraud provisions. Thus, although the 1933 act does not provide for evaluation of the merits of securities or examination by government auditors, its civil remedies, criminal penalties, and disclosure requirements (including financial statements audited by CPAs) help prevent fraud.

2. Dee is the owner of 12% of the shares of common stock of D&M Corporation that she acquired in Year 1. She is the treasurer and a director of D&M. The corporation registered its securities in Year 2 and made a public offering pursuant to the Securities Act of 1933. If Dee decides to sell part of her holdings in Year 9, the shares

    A. Would be exempt from registration because the corporation previously registered them within 3 years.

    B. Must be registered regardless of the amount sold or manner in which they are sold.

    C. Would be exempt from registration because she is not an issuer.

    D. Must be registered if Dee sells 50% of her shares through her broker to the public.

Answer (D) is correct.
    REQUIRED: The true statement as to whether a controlling person's stock sale must be registered.
    DISCUSSION: In general, any offer to sell securities in interstate commerce is subject to registration unless the securities or the transaction is exempt. Most transactions are exempt because they involve sales by persons other than issuers, underwriters, or dealers, e.g., transactions by ordinary investors selling on their own account. Dee, however, is considered an issuer because she is a controlling person, that is, one who owns more than 10% of the company's stock and who has the direct or indirect ability to control the company. A sale of 6% (12% × 50%) of D&M's common stock to the public in the ordinary course of business (e.g., through a broker) is not a basis for an exemption under the Securities Act of 1933. Thus, it is subject to SEC registration.
    Answer (A) is incorrect. The previous registration is irrelevant. Answer (B) is incorrect. Under Rule 144, an insider who has held restricted securities for at least 1 year may resell without registration in any 3-month period the greater of 1% of the total shares of that class outstanding or the average weekly volume traded. Notice must be given to the SEC, adequate information about the issuer must be publicly available, and sales must be through brokers' transactions or in transactions with a market maker. Also, the sale might be exempt if no public offer is made or if certain other requirements are met. Answer (C) is incorrect. A controlling person is an issuer.

3. An offering made under the provisions of Regulation A Tier 1 requires that the issuer

A. File an offering statement with the SEC.

B. Sell only to accredited investors.

C. Provide investors with the prior 4 years' audited financial statements.

D. Provide investors with a proxy registration statement.

Answer (A) is correct.

REQUIRED: The requirement for a stock offering made under Regulation A Tier 1.

DISCUSSION: Under Tier 1, a public issue of securities up to $20,000,000 is exempt from full registration with the SEC if certain requirements are met. The issuer must file an offering statement with the SEC on EDGAR that contains specified disclosures. Moreover, each offeree and purchaser must receive an offering circular containing concise narrative disclosures, and the issuer must file 2 years of financial statements. Advantages of a Tier 1 offering are that (1) ongoing reporting requirements do not apply and (2) the number and nature of investors are unlimited.

Answer (B) is incorrect. The rules for Tier 1 do not restrict resale, have an investor sophistication requirement, or limit the number of buyers. Answer (C) is incorrect. Regulation A requires the issuer to file financial statements for the last 2 complete fiscal years. Answer (D) is incorrect. Filing proxy statements is required under the 1934 act. Regulation A provides an exemption from filing certain requirements of the 1933 act.

4. Frey, Inc., intends to make a $2 million common stock offering under Rule 505 of Regulation D of the Securities Act of 1933. Frey

A. May sell the stock to an unlimited number of nonaccredited investors.

B. May make the offering through a general advertising.

C. Must notify the SEC within 15 days after the first sale of the offering.

D. Must provide all investors with a prospectus.

Answer (C) is correct.

REQUIRED: The true statement about a securities offering under Rule 505.

DISCUSSION: Rule 505 provides exemption from the requirements of the 1933 act to all issuers other than investment companies for sales of securities up to $5 million in any 12-month period. Under Rule 505, securities may be sold to no more than 35 nonaccredited investors and to an unlimited number of accredited investors. Rule 505 also provides that the issuer must notify the SEC within 15 days after the first offering.

Answer (A) is incorrect. Rule 505 prohibits sale to more than 35 nonaccredited investors. Answer (B) is incorrect. Exemption under Rules 505 and 506 of Regulation D is conditioned on no general solicitation. Answer (D) is incorrect. A prospectus need not be provided. However, if some investors are nonaccredited, they must be furnished with material information about the issuer, its business, and the securities being offered.

5. Which of the following most likely is a violation of federal securities law regarding communications before and during registered securities offerings?

A. A well-known seasoned issuer makes an oral offer 10 days after filing a registration statement with the SEC.

B. An unseasoned issuer publishes its regularly released forward-looking information 15 days before filing a registration statement with the SEC.

C. A seasoned issuer files hard-copy documents with the SEC that include its registration statement and prospectus.

D. An issuer files a free-writing prospectus a day after filing a registration statement.

Answer (C) is correct.

REQUIRED: The likely violation of federal securities law regarding communications before and during registered securities offerings.

DISCUSSION: An issuer must file its registration statement, prospectus, periodic reports, etc., on EDGAR, the SEC's Electronic Data Gathering, Analysis, and Retrieval computer system. The filings are available on the SEC's website within 24 hours.

Answer (A) is incorrect. A well-known seasoned issuer may make oral and written communications at any time. Answer (B) is incorrect. In general, fact-based information that is routinely published may continue to be communicated. For example, a reporting issuer may continue to issue its fact-based business information and forward-looking information. Answer (D) is incorrect. Subject to certain limitations, any issuer may communicate a free-writing prospectus after the registration statement is filed.

2.2 Securities Exchange Act of 1934

6. Integral Corp., with assets in excess of $4 million, has issued common and preferred stock and has 350 shareholders. Its stock is sold on the New York Stock Exchange. Under the Securities Exchange Act of 1934, Integral must be registered with the SEC because

- A. It issues both common and preferred stock.
- B. Its shares are listed on a national stock exchange.
- C. It has more than 300 shareholders.
- D. Its shares are traded in interstate commerce.

Answer (B) is correct.
REQUIRED: The basis for required registration under the 1934 act.
DISCUSSION: The 1934 act requires all regulated, publicly held corporations to register with the SEC. Covered corporations either (1) list shares on a national securities exchange or (2) have at least 500 shareholders of equity securities and total gross assets exceeding $10 million.
Answer (A) is incorrect. Issuing preferred stock is not a sufficient condition for registering or reporting under the 1934 act. Answer (C) is incorrect. The threshold is 500 shareholders and total gross assets of $10 million or more. Answer (D) is incorrect. Shares trading in interstate commerce are insufficient to trigger registration requirements under the 1934 act.

7. Under Section 12 of the Securities Exchange Act of 1934, in addition to companies whose securities are traded on a national exchange, what class of companies is subject to the SEC's registration requirements?

- A. Companies with annual revenues in excess of $5 million and 300 or more shareholders.
- B. Companies with annual revenues in excess of $10 million and 500 or more shareholders.
- C. Companies with assets in excess of $5 million and 300 or more shareholders.
- D. Companies with assets in excess of $10 million and 500 or more shareholders.

Answer (D) is correct.
REQUIRED: The companies subject to registration requirements under Section 12 of the 1934 act.
DISCUSSION: All regulated, publicly held companies must register with the SEC. Registration is required of all companies that have at least 500 shareholders of equity securities and total gross assets exceeding $10 million.
Answer (A) is incorrect. A minimum amount of assets, not annual revenues, and more than 300 shareholders are required for registration requirements. Answer (B) is incorrect. A minimum amount of assets, not annual revenues, is required for registration requirements. Answer (C) is incorrect. The minimum amount of assets and shareholders required for registration requirements is higher than $5 million in assets and 300 or more shareholders.

8. Which of the following events must be reported to the SEC under the reporting provisions of the 1934 act?

	Tender Offers	Insider Trading	Solicitation Proxies
A.	Yes	Yes	Yes
B.	Yes	Yes	No
C.	Yes	No	Yes
D.	No	Yes	Yes

Answer (A) is correct.
REQUIRED: The events that must be reported to the SEC under the 1934 act.
DISCUSSION: The 1934 act governs dealings in securities subsequent to their initial issuance. The act requires all regulated, publicly held companies to register with the SEC. The act requires disclosure of matters concerning tender offers, insider trading, and the solicitation of proxies.

2.3 Federal Statutory Liability of CPAs and Others

9. One of the elements necessary to recover damages if there has been a material misstatement in a registration statement filed under the Securities Act of 1933 is that the

- A. Issuer and plaintiff were in privity of contract with each other.
- B. Issuer failed to exercise due care in connection with the sale of the securities.
- C. Plaintiff gave value for the security.
- D. Plaintiff suffered a loss.

Answer (D) is correct.
REQUIRED: The element necessary to recover damages under the 1933 act.
DISCUSSION: Under Section 11, the plaintiff must prove that (s)he was an acquirer of a security covered by a registration statement, (s)he suffered a loss, and the statement misstated or omitted a material fact.
Answer (A) is incorrect. Plaintiff may have obtained the security from a party other than defendant. Answer (B) is incorrect. Neither negligence nor fraud need be proven by the plaintiff. However, any defendant except an issuer may employ the due diligence defense by proving that (s)he was not negligent and that (s)he reasonably investigated the statement and reasonably believed it to be free of material falsehoods or omissions. Answer (C) is incorrect. That the plaintiff gave value for the security need not be shown.

10. Burt, CPA, issued an unmodified opinion on the financial statements of Midwest Corp. These financial statements were included in Midwest's annual report, and Form 10-K was filed with the SEC. As a result of Burt's reckless disregard for GAAS, material misstatements in the financial statements were not detected. Subsequently, Davis purchased stock in Midwest in the secondary market without ever seeing Midwest's annual report or Form 10-K. Shortly thereafter, Midwest became insolvent, and the price of the stock declined drastically. Davis sued Burt for damages based on Section 10(b) and Rule 10b-5 of the Securities Exchange Act of 1934. Burt's best defense is that

A. There has been no subsequent sale for which a loss can be computed.

B. Davis did not purchase the stock as part of an initial offering.

C. Davis did not rely on the financial statements or Form 10-K.

D. Davis was not in privity with Burt.

Answer (C) is correct.
   REQUIRED: The best defense of a grossly negligent accountant sued under Rule 10b-5.
   DISCUSSION: The plaintiff must have relied on the misstatement or omission of a material fact with regard to the purchase or sale of a security if (s)he is to recover under Rule 10b-5. In the case of an omission, reliance is implied by materiality. Davis did not see the relevant annual report or Form 10-K and will therefore have difficulty in proving reliance.
   Answer (A) is incorrect. Damages may be proven without a subsequent sale. Answer (B) is incorrect. Rule 10b-5 applies to a misstatement or an omission of a material fact in connection with any purchase or sale of a security if the wrongful act involved interstate commerce, the U.S. mail, or a national securities exchange. Answer (D) is incorrect. Privity is not required.

11. Under the Securities and Exchange Act of 1934, which of the following penalties could be assessed against a CPA who intentionally violated the provisions of Section 10(b), Rule 10b-5 of the act?

	Civil Liability for Monetary Damages	Criminal Liability for a Fine
A.	Yes	Yes
B.	Yes	No
C.	No	Yes
D.	No	No

Answer (A) is correct.
   REQUIRED: The penalty(ies), if any, for an intentional violation of Section 10(b), Rule 10b-5 of the Securities Exchange Act of 1934.
   DISCUSSION: Section 10(b) of the 1934 act and SEC Rule 10b-5 are antifraud provisions. They make it unlawful for any person to employ, in connection with the purchase or sale of any security, any manipulative or deceptive device or any contrivance in contravention of SEC rules and regulations. Any buyer or seller of any security who suffers a monetary loss may bring a private civil suit to rescind the transaction or to receive monetary damages. Punitive damages are not recoverable. The 1934 act also provides for criminal sanctions for willful violations. Liability is imposed for false material statements in applications, reports, documents, registration statements, and press releases. For an individual, the penalty is a fine not to exceed $5 million, 20 years in prison, or both. An individual who proves (s)he had no knowledge of the rule or regulation will not be imprisoned. If the person is not a natural person (e.g., a corporation), the maximum fine is $25 million.

12. The antifraud provisions of Rule 10b-5 of the Securities Exchange Act of 1934

A. Apply only if the securities involved were registered under the Securities Act of 1933 or the Securities Exchange Act of 1934.

B. Require that the plaintiff show negligence on the part of the defendant in misstating facts.

C. Require that the wrongful act be accomplished through the mail, any other use of interstate commerce, or through a national securities exchange.

D. Apply only if the defendant acted with intent to defraud.

Answer (C) is correct.
   REQUIRED: The element of a violation of the antifraud provisions of Rule 10b-5.
   DISCUSSION: The scope of Rule 10b-5 is broad but not absolute. Rule 10b-5 applies to certain wrongful acts done in connection with the purchase or sale of any security by use of (1) any means or instrumentality of interstate commerce, (2) the mails, or (3) any facility of any national securities exchange.
   Answer (A) is incorrect. Rule 10b-5 also applies to unregistered securities. Answer (B) is incorrect. Intent to deceive must be proved. Answer (D) is incorrect. An intent to deceive or manipulate suffices.

13. The Sarbanes-Oxley Act of 2002 (SOX) has strengthened auditor independence by requiring a public company to

A. Engage auditors to report in accordance with the Foreign Corrupt Practices Act (FCPA).

B. Report the nature of disagreements with former auditors.

C. Select auditors through audit committees.

D. Hire a different CPA firm from the one that performs the audit to perform the company's tax work.

Answer (C) is correct.
REQUIRED: The Sarbanes-Oxley requirement that strengthened auditor independence.
DISCUSSION: The audit committee must hire and pay the external auditors. Such affiliation inhibits management from changing auditors to gain acceptance of a questionable accounting method. Also, a successor auditor must inquire of the predecessor before accepting an engagement.
Answer (A) is incorrect. No report under the FCPA is required. Answer (B) is incorrect. Reporting the nature of disagreements with auditors is a long-time SEC requirement. Answer (D) is incorrect. The SOX does not restrict who may perform tax work. Other engagements, such as outsourcing internal auditing or certain consulting services, are limited.

2.4 State Law Liability to Clients and Third Parties

14. A client suing a CPA for negligent preparation of a tax return in a state court must prove each of the following factors **except**

A. Breach of duty of care.

B. Proximate cause.

C. Reliance.

D. Injury.

Answer (C) is correct.
REQUIRED: The factor not required to be proven in a negligence lawsuit.
DISCUSSION: A client suing an accountant for the unintentional tort of negligence must establish the following elements: (1) The accountant owed the client a duty, (2) the accountant breached this duty, (3) the accountant's breach actually and proximately caused the client's injury, and (4) the client suffered damages. Reasonable reliance on a misrepresentation is an element of fraud or of negligent misrepresentation.
Answer (A) is incorrect. Breach of a duty to conform to a specific standard of conduct for the protection of the plaintiff from unreasonable risk of injury is an element of the tort of negligence. Answer (B) is incorrect. Proximate cause is an element of the tort of negligence. Thus, liability is imposed not for all consequences of a negligent act but for those with a relatively close connection. Answer (D) is incorrect. The plaintiff must prove that damage to the defendant's person or property resulted from the negligent act.

15. Which of the following penalties is usually imposed against an accountant who, in the course of preparing a tax return, breaches common law contract duties owed to a client?

A. Specific performance.

B. Punitive damages.

C. Money damages.

D. Rescission.

Answer (C) is correct.
REQUIRED: The penalty usually imposed on an accountant for breach of contract.
DISCUSSION: The accountant-client contract is a personal service contract. Recovery for breach of contract ordinarily is limited to compensatory damages, and punitive damages are rarely allowed. Thus, an accountant is usually liable for money damages.
Answer (A) is incorrect. Specific performance for a personal service contract is not granted. Answer (B) is incorrect. Punitive damages for breach of contract are rarely allowed. Answer (D) is incorrect. Rescission returns the parties to the positions they would have occupied if the contract had not been made. It would only be applicable if the breach were material, such as an unjustifiable failure to perform.

16. Under state law, which of the following statements most accurately reflects the liability of a CPA who fraudulently prepares a client's tax return?

    A. The CPA is liable only to third parties in privity of contract with the CPA.

    B. The CPA is liable only to known users of the financial statements.

    C. The CPA probably is liable to any person who suffered a loss as a result of the fraud.

    D. The CPA probably is liable to the client even if the client was aware of the fraud and did not rely on the opinion.

Answer (C) is correct.
    REQUIRED: The liability of a CPA for fraud.
    DISCUSSION: The distinctive feature of fraud is scienter, that is, intentional misrepresentation or reckless disregard for the truth (sometimes found in gross negligence). Because fraud involves intentional wrongdoing, the courts permit all foreseeable users of an accountant's work product to sue for damages proximately caused by the fraud.
    Answer (A) is incorrect. Accountant liability can extend to all persons who incur loss resulting from the accountant's fraud regardless of privity. Answer (B) is incorrect. Accountant liability can extend to all persons who incur loss resulting from the accountant's fraud, not only those known to the accountant. Answer (D) is incorrect. An element of a fraud action is that the plaintiff relied justifiably on the material misstatement.

17. Which of the following facts must be proven for a lender to prevail in a state-law negligent misrepresentation action against a CPA who prepared a borrower's tax return that was disclosed to the lender?

    A. The defendant made the misrepresentations with a reckless disregard for the truth.

    B. The plaintiff justifiably relied on the misrepresentations.

    C. The misrepresentations were in writing.

    D. The misrepresentations concerned opinions.

Answer (B) is correct.
    REQUIRED: The fact that must be proven to establish negligent misrepresentation.
    DISCUSSION: Negligent misrepresentation occurs when the accountant makes a false representation of a material fact not known to be false but intended to induce reliance. The plaintiff must reasonably have relied on the accountant's misrepresentation and incurred damages.
    Answer (A) is incorrect. Reckless disregard for the truth is an element in proving that a misrepresentation was grossly negligent. Answer (C) is incorrect. Under the negligence theory, the misrepresentation relied upon may be oral or written. A written misstatement is not necessary to prove negligent misrepresentation. Answer (D) is incorrect. Facts, not opinions, form the bases of a negligent misrepresentation case.

18. Which of the following elements, if present, would support a finding of common law constructive fraud on the part of a CPA who prepared a tax return?

    A. Gross negligence.

    B. Ordinary negligence.

    C. Identified third-party users.

    D. Scienter.

Answer (A) is correct.
    REQUIRED: The element supporting a finding of constructive fraud on the part of a CPA.
    DISCUSSION: Scienter is a prerequisite to liability for fraud. Scienter exists when the defendant makes a false representation with knowledge of its falsity or with reckless disregard as to its truth. For constructive fraud, the scienter requirement is met by proof of gross negligence (reckless disregard for the truth).
    Answer (B) is incorrect. A good faith failure to comply with applicable standards is evidence of negligence. To prove fraud, more is required. Answer (C) is incorrect. For fraud, a CPA may be liable to all foreseeable users of his or her work. Answer (D) is incorrect. Scienter is a necessary element of fraud. For constructive fraud, the scienter element is proven by evidence of gross negligence.

2.5 Privileged Communication and Confidentiality

19. Which of the following statements is true regarding a CPA's working papers related to tax practice? The working papers must be

- A. Transferred to another accountant purchasing the CPA's practice even if the client has not given permission.
- B. Transferred permanently to the client if demanded.
- C. Turned over to any government agency that requests them.
- D. Turned over pursuant to a valid federal court subpoena.

Answer (D) is correct.
    REQUIRED: The true statement about working papers.
    DISCUSSION: The AICPA's Confidential Client Information Rule does not affect a CPA's obligation to comply with a validly issued and enforceable subpoena. Because no federal accountant-client privilege exists, a federal court may subpoena working papers.
    Answer (A) is incorrect. A CPA is required to obtain the client's permission before transferring his or her working papers to another CPA. This is true even if the other accountant is purchasing the CPA's firm. Answer (B) is incorrect. Working papers are the property of the CPA and ordinarily need not be transferred to the client upon request. Answer (C) is incorrect. Unless a summons or subpoena is issued, a governmental request need not be honored. Moreover, some states have provided for an accountant-client privilege.

20. Which of the following statements about disclosure of confidential client data resulting from a CPA's tax practice is generally true?

- A. Disclosure may be made to any state agency without subpoena.
- B. Disclosure may be made to any party with the consent of the client.
- C. Disclosure may be made to comply with an IRS audit request.
- D. Disclosure may be made to comply with generally accepted accounting principles.

Answer (B) is correct.
    REQUIRED: The condition allowing disclosure of confidential client data.
    DISCUSSION: Under the Confidential Client Information Rule, an accountant may disclose any confidential client information with the specific consent of the client.
    Answer (A) is incorrect. Disclosure may be made to a state agency only pursuant to a subpoena or summons or with the client's consent. Answer (C) is incorrect. Without a client's consent, an accountant may disclose confidential information to the IRS only in response to a subpoena or summons. Answer (D) is incorrect. Compliance with GAAP is a responsibility of clients who issue financial statements, not the accountants who advise them on tax matters or prepare their tax returns.

Online is better! To best prepare for the CPA exam, access **thousands** of exam-emulating MCQs and TBSs through Gleim CPA Review online courses with SmartAdapt technology. Learn more at www.gleimcpa.com or contact our team at 800.874.5346 to upgrade.

STUDY UNIT THREE
FEDERAL TAX AUTHORITY, PROCEDURES, AND INDIVIDUAL TAXATION

(25 pages of outline)

This study unit provides an understanding of federal tax authority, tax procedures, and tax planning before beginning our coverage of individual taxation.

Federal tax authority consists of legislative, administrative, and judicial law. Understanding the hierarchy and intent of each authoritative source is critical for CPAs to conduct effective and efficient tax research.

Tax procedures cover the processes for (1) determining a need to file a tax return, (2) collecting tax through estimated payments, (3) claiming refunds of taxes paid, and (4) assessing or collecting a deficiency in payment.

Tax planning is a continuous process of analyzing options available for a business or individual that will minimize tax liabilities, but it is done in a way that maintains the overall objective of maximizing income. Planning options include timing of income, shifting of income, and conversion of income property. A critical aspect of tax planning is distinguishing between tax avoidance and tax evasion.

Filing status determines the amount of the standard deductions, personal exemptions, and applicable tax rates. Certain taxpayers may also be able to claim a dependency exemption. To qualify as a taxpayer's dependent, an individual must be either a qualifying child or a qualifying relative; the criteria for both are heavily tested on the CPA exam.

Related portions of IRS tax forms for reporting have been reproduced in the Knowledge Transfer Outline as a detailed practical reference to the related text. Some candidates find it helpful to have the entire tax form side-by-side with our Knowledge Transfer Outline when studying. The full versions of the most up-to-date forms are easily accessible at www.gleim.com/taxforms. These forms and the form excerpts used in our outline are periodically updated as the latest versions are released by the IRS.

3.1 TAX AUTHORITY

Background

The U.S. Constitution, in Article I, Section 8, grants Congress the power to lay and collect taxes. However, Section 9 states that a direct tax cannot be levied unless it is proportional to population. Since this depends on the outcome of a census, the early federal government would have found such a tax unwieldy and simply relied on tariffs (duties on imported goods) for most of its revenue.

The first tax imposed on the incomes of the citizens was levied from 1862 until 1872 to raise the huge amounts of money needed to carry on the Civil War. Some observers claimed that this directly violated the prohibition against direct taxes that are based on something other than proportional population.

In order to clear up the Constitutional issue once and for all, supporters of the income tax managed to get the Sixteenth Amendment ratified in 1913: "The Congress shall have power to lay and collect taxes on incomes, from whatever source derived, without apportionment among the several States, and without regard to any census or enumeration." Just over 7 months after ratification of this amendment, Congress enacted the Revenue Act of 1913.

The code received its most drastic overhaul in 1954 and its most recent in 1986. The current designation of the tax code is IRC 1986.

1.   **Authoritative Hierarchy**

   a.   Authoritative tax law consists of legislative law, administrative law, and judicial law.

Tax Authority Hierarchy

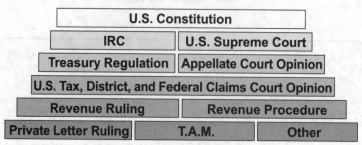

Figure 3-1

   b.   **Conflicting authority.** When there are conflicting sources of tax law within the same tier of the hierarchy, the most recent rule or law takes precedence.

2.   **Legislative Law**

   a.   Legislative law, which comes from Congress, is authorized by the Constitution and consists of the IRC and committee reports.

   b.   *The Internal Revenue Code* **of 1986** is the primary source of Federal tax law. It imposes income, estate, gift, employment, miscellaneous excise taxes, and provisions controlling the administration of Federal taxation. The Code is found at Title 26 of the United States Code (U.S.C.). The United States Code consists of 50 titles.

   c.   *Committee Reports* are useful tools in determining Congressional intent behind certain tax laws and helping examiners apply the law properly.

3.   **Administrative Law**

   a.   Administrative tax law is promulgated by the Treasury department, of which the IRS is a part, and includes regulations, rules, and procedures.

   b.   Section 7805(a) grants general authority to the Secretary of the Treasury to "prescribe all needful rules and regulations for the enforcement" of the Code. All regulations are written by the Office of the Chief Counsel, IRS, and approved by the Secretary of the Treasury.

   1)   Regulations are issued as **interpretations** of specific Code sections and are organized in a sequential system consistent with the Code.

      a)   Every regulation is prefixed by a number that designates the area of taxation referred to by the regulation.

   2)   **Treasury Regulations** are authorized by law. Nevertheless, courts are not bound to follow such administrative interpretations to the extent they conflict with the Code.

   3)   The Supreme Court has stated that "Treasury Regulations must be sustained unless unreasonable and plainly inconsistent with the revenue statutes."

   4)   Regulations can be proposed, temporary, or final.

      a)   **Proposed regulations** are issued to elicit comments from the public. Public hearings are held if written requests are made.

         i)   Proposed regulations might be used as somewhat of an authority for taking a tax position, but the regulations themselves do not state this and must be considered as a **weak authority** at best.

       b) **Temporary regulations** provide guidance to the IRS, tax practitioners, and the public until final regulations are issued. Temporary regulations have the same force and effect of law as final regulations until the final regulations are issued. Public hearings are not held on temporary regulations unless written requests are made. Temporary regulations

          i) Can be used as somewhat of an authority
          ii) May remain effective for a maximum of 3 years
          iii) Must be issued concurrently as proposed regulations

       c) **Final regulations** are adopted after public comment on the proposed versions has been evaluated by the Treasury.

          i) When a proposed regulation becomes final or an existing regulation is amended, the document that describes the finalization or amendment is referred to as a **Treasury Decision (TD)**.

    5) **The IRS is bound by the regulations. The courts are not.**

       a) If both temporary and proposed regulations have been issued on the same Code section and the text of both are similar, taxpayers' positions should be based on the temporary regulations because they can be cited as an authority for proposing an adjustment.

       b) When no temporary or final regulations have been issued, taxpayers may use a proposed regulation to support a position. The taxpayer should indicate that the proposed regulation is the best interpretation of the Code section available.

  c. A **revenue ruling** is an official interpretation of Internal Revenue law as applied to a given set of facts and is issued by the Internal Revenue Service.

    1) Revenue rulings are published in Internal Revenue Bulletins (and later the Cumulative Bulletin) to inform and advise taxpayers, the IRS, and others on substantive tax issues.

    2) Publication of revenue rulings is intended to promote uniform application of tax laws by IRS employees and to reduce the number of letter ruling requests.

    3) Revenue rulings may be cited as precedent and relied upon when resolving disputes, but they do not have the force and effect of regulations.

       a) A revenue ruling is not binding on a court.

  d. A **revenue procedure** is an official IRS statement that prescribes procedures that affect the rights or duties of either a particular group of taxpayers or all taxpayers.

    1) Revenue procedures primarily address administrative and procedural matters, e.g., in what format and to whom should a letter ruling request be submitted.

    2) Revenue procedures do not have the force and effect of law, but they may be cited as precedent.

  e. The **Internal Revenue Bulletin (IRB)** is the authoritative instrument of the Commissioner of Internal Revenue for announcing official IRS rulings and procedures and for publishing Treasury Decisions, Executive Orders, Tax Conventions, legislation, court decisions, and other items of general interest. It is published on a weekly basis by the Government Printing Office.

  f. Rulings do not have the force and effect of Treasury Department Regulations, but they may be used as precedent. In applying published rulings, the effects of subsequent legislation, regulations, court decisions, rulings, and procedures must be considered. Caution is urged against reaching the same conclusion in other cases, unless the facts and circumstances are substantially the same.

g. IRS **Publications** explain the law in plain language for taxpayers and their advisors. They typically highlight changes in the law, provide examples illustrating Service positions, and include worksheets. Publications are not binding on the Service and do not necessarily cover all positions for a given issue. While a good source of general information, publications should not be cited to sustain a position.

h. **Private Letter Rulings and Technical Advice Memoranda**

1) A *Private Letter Ruling* (PLR) represents the conclusion of the Service for an individual taxpayer. The application of a private letter ruling is confined to the specific case for which it was issued, unless the issue involved was specifically covered by statute, regulations, ruling, opinion, or decision published in the Internal Revenue Bulletin.

2) Technical Advice Memoranda (TAMs) are requested by IRS area offices after a return has been filed, often in conjunction with an ongoing examination. TAMs are binding on the Service in relation to the taxpayer who is the subject of the ruling.

3) A private letter ruling to a taxpayer or a technical advice memorandum to an area director, which relates to a particular case, should not be applied or relied upon as a precedent in the disposition of other cases. However, they provide insight with regard to the Service's position on the law and serve as a guide.

4) Existing private letter rulings and memoranda [including Confidential Unpublished Rulings (CUR), Advisory Memoranda (AM), and General Counsel Memoranda (GCM)] may not be used as precedents in the disposition of other cases but may be used as a guide with other research material in formulating an area office position on an issue.

5) Whenever an area office finds that a CUR, AM, or GCM represents the sole precedent or guide for determining the disposition of an issue and cannot to its own satisfaction find justification in the Code, regulations, or published rulings to support the indicated position, technical advice should be requested from the Headquarters Office.

6) **Technical Advice** should be requested where taxpayers or their representatives take the position that the basis for the proposed action is not supported by statute, regulations, or published positions of the Service. If it is believed that the position of the Service should be published, the request for technical advice will contain a statement to that effect. Instructions for requesting technical advice from the Headquarters Office are contained in the second revenue procedure issued each year. Questions regarding the procedures should be addressed to the functional contacts listed in the revenue procedure.

7) **General Counsel Memoranda (GCM)** are legal memoranda from the Office of Chief Counsel prepared in connection with the review of certain proposed rulings (Rev. Ruls., PLRs, TCMs). They contain legal analyses of substantive issues and can be helpful in understanding the reasoning behind a particular ruling and the Service's response to similar issues in the future.

8) **Technical Memoranda (TM)** function as transmittal documents for Treasury Decisions or Notices of Proposed Rule Making (NPRMs). They generally summarize or explain proposed or adopted regulations, provide background information, state the issues involved, and identify any controversial legal or policy questions. Additionally, they are helpful in tracing the history and rationale behind a regulation or regulation proposal.

4. **Judicial Law**

   a. Judicial law originates from the federal court system and is primarily comprised of court opinions.

   b. The court system is comprised as follows:

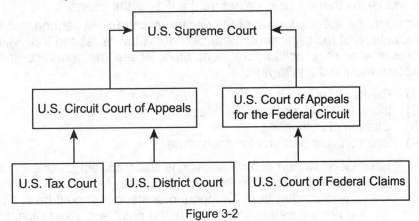

Figure 3-2

   c. **Tax Court**

   1) Decisions of the Tax Court are issued as either regular decisions or memorandum decisions.

      a) **Regular decisions** establish precedent either through a new tax matter or unique facts and circumstances for a tax matter that has been previously settled.

      b) A **Tax Court memorandum** decision is a report of a Tax Court decision thought to be of little value as a precedent because the issue has been decided one or more times before.

   d. Cases from the U.S. Tax Court and the U.S. District Courts are appealed to the appropriate U.S. Circuit Court of Appeals. Cases from the U.S. Court of Federal Claims are appealed to the U.S. Court of Appeals for the Federal Circuit.

   e. **U.S. Supreme Court**

   1) The U.S. Supreme Court can exercise its discretionary authority to review decisions of the courts of appeals and other federal courts.

   2) An appellant in an appropriate case may petition the Supreme Court to hear an appeal from the lower court's decision. A **writ of certiorari** is an order by the Supreme Court to send the case up for its consideration. The court's certiorari jurisdiction is purely discretionary. A denial of a petition for a writ of certiorari by the Supreme Court expresses no opinion on the merits of the case.

   3) If the Court determines that various lower courts are deciding a tax issue in an inconsistent manner, it may pronounce a decision and resolve the contradiction.

5. **Tax Research**

   a.   Tax research is the process of gathering situational facts, applying the most appropriate tax authorities, and clearly communicating the findings to the taxpayer/client or other interested parties. It involves analysis of information and drawing conclusions that will hold up before the IRS or the courts.

   b.   Although the specific format of the **communication** will depend upon the audience (e.g., level of technical comprehension of tax law or related topics), the medium of presentation (e.g., written, oral), and other issues, the general organized format should include the following:

      1)   Review of relevant facts
      2)   Individual listing of specific issues
      3)   Citation of authorities
      4)   Solutions/conclusions for each issue

         a)   Good written communication is clear, correct, concise, consistent, constructive, coherent, and complete. As with other business writing, less is often best. Compound sentences should be avoided. The communication should make the point and avoid repeating.

Stop and review! You have completed the outline for this subunit. Study multiple-choice questions 1 through 5 beginning on page 80.

3.2 TAX PROCEDURES

1. **Tax Prepayments and Penalties for Individuals**

   a.   The IRC is structured to obtain at least 90% of the final tax through **withholding** and **estimated tax** payments. Individuals who earn income not subject to withholding must pay estimated tax on that income in quarterly installments.

      1)   For a calendar-year taxpayer, the installments are due by April 15, June 15, and September 15 of the current year and January 15 of the following year. Dates are adjusted for weekends and holidays.

      2)   Each of the following is treated as prepayment of tax:

         a)   Overpayment of tax in a prior tax year, which has not been refunded

            i)   An individual may so elect on the prior year's tax return.
            ii)   It is applied to the first required installment due.

         b)   Amounts withheld (by an employer) from wages

            i)   The aggregate amount is treated as if equal parts were paid on each due date, unless the individual establishes the actual payment dates.

         c)   Direct payment by the individual (or another on his or her behalf)

            i)   It is applied to the first estimated tax payment due.

         d)   Excess FICA withheld when an employee has two or more employers during a tax year who withheld (in the aggregate) more than the ceiling on FICA taxes

      3)   Each installment must be at least 25% of the lowest of the following amounts:

         a)   100% [110% for taxpayers whose prior year's AGI exceeds $150,000 ($75,000 for married filing separately)] of the prior year's tax (if a return was filed)

         b)   90% of the current year's tax

         c)   90% of the annualized current year's tax (applies when income is uneven)

　　　4)　Tax refers to the sum of the regular tax, AMT, self-employment tax, and household employee tax.

From Form 1040-ES Instructions

[Year] Estimated Tax Worksheet

c	**Total [Year] estimated tax.** Subtract line 13b from line 13a. If zero or less, enter -0- . . . ▶	**13c**	

14a	Multiply line 13c by 90% (66⅔% for farmers and fishermen)	**14a**		
b	Required annual payment based on prior year's tax (see instructions) .	**14b**		
c	**Required annual payment to avoid a penalty.** Enter the **smaller** of line 14a or 14b . . . ▶	**14c**		

　　　Caution: Generally, if you do not prepay (through income tax withholding and estimated tax payments) at least the amount on line 14c, you may owe a penalty for not paying enough estimated tax. To avoid a penalty, make sure your estimate on line 13c is as accurate as possible. Even if you pay the required annual payment, you may still owe tax when you file your return. If you prefer, you can pay the amount shown on line 13c. For details, see chapter 2 of Pub. 505.

15	Income tax withheld and estimated to be withheld during [Year] (including income tax withholding on pensions, annuities, certain deferred income, etc.)	**15**	

16a	Subtract line 15 from line 14c	**16a**	

Is the result zero or less?
☐ **Yes.** Stop here. You are not required to make estimated tax payments.
☐ **No.** Go to line 16b.

b	Subtract line 15 from line 13c	**16b**	

Is the result less than $1,000?
☐ **Yes.** Stop here. You are not required to make estimated tax payments.
☐ **No.** Go to line 17 to figure your required payment.

17	If the first payment you are required to make is due [April 15], enter ¼ of line 16a (minus any [prior year] overpayment that you are applying to this installment) here, and on your estimated tax payment voucher(s) if you are paying by check or money order	**17**	

　　b.　A penalty is imposed if, by the quarterly payment date, the total of estimated tax payments and income tax withheld is less than 25% of the required minimum payment for the year.

　　　1)　The penalty is determined each quarter.
　　　2)　The penalty is the federal short-term rate plus 3% times the underpayment.
　　　3)　The penalty is not allowed as an interest deduction.

　　c.　The penalty will not be imposed if any of the following apply:

　　　1)　Actual tax liability shown on the return for the current tax year (after reduction for amounts withheld by employers) is less than $1,000.

EXAMPLE

Taxpayer has AGI of $170,000 and a tax liability of $11,000 for 2017. Taxpayer's employer withheld $7,000 for 2017. Taxpayer's 2016 liability was $7,000.

Even though only $700 [($7,000 prior year liability × 110%) – $7,000 current year withholding] is subject to the penalty, the $1,000 minimum exception does not apply due to the fact that the exception is based on the current year. The total tax liability shown on the tax return of $11,000 minus the amount paid through withholding of $7,000 is greater than $1,000. Hence, the taxpayer will be subject to an underpayment penalty.

---

　　　2)　No tax liability was incurred in the prior tax year.
　　　3)　The IRS waives it for reasonable cause shown.

d. Any tax liability must be paid by the original due date of the return. An automatic extension for filing the return does not extend time for payment. Interest will be charged from the original due date.

1) A penalty of 5% per month up to 25% of unpaid liability is assessed for **failure to file** a return. Additionally, the minimum penalty for filing a return over 60 days late is the lesser of $210 or 100% of tax due.

2) A penalty of 0.5% per month up to 25% of unpaid liability is assessed for **failure to pay** tax.

a) In general, a failure-to-pay penalty is imposed from the due date for taxes (other than the estimated taxes) shown on the return. A failure-to-pay penalty may offset a failure-to-file penalty. When an extension to file is timely requested, a failure-to-pay penalty may be avoided by paying at least 90% of the actual liability by the original due date of the return and paying the remaining balance when the return is filed. Exceptions and adjustments to these rules may apply in unique situations.

2. **Filing Requirements**

a. An individual must file a federal income tax return if gross income is above a threshold, net earnings from self-employment is $400 or more, or (s)he is a dependent with more gross income than the standard deduction or with unearned income over $1,050.

NOTE: In contrast to individuals, corporations (including S corps) must file an income tax return regardless of gross income.

1) The gross income threshold amount generally is the sum of the standard deduction, excluding any amount for being blind, and personal exemption amounts, excluding dependency exemptions.

Standard Deduction
+ Personal Exemption
= Filing Requirement Threshold

2) Net unearned income of a dependent child is taxed to the dependent at the parent's marginal rate. This is referred to as the **"Kiddie Tax."** Net unearned income is unearned income minus the sum of

a) $1,050 (first $1,050 clause) and

b) The greater of (1) $1,050 of the standard deduction or $1,050 of itemized deductions or (2) the amount of allowable deductions that are directly connected with the production of unearned income.

NOTE: A dependent is allowed at least $2,100 ($1,050 + $1,050) reduction in unearned income.

 Historically, exam questions have provided the applicable standard deduction amount for dependents with unearned income, eliminating the need to memorize the specific amount. However, you should have a general idea of the amount, and you need to be well practiced in calculating the amount taxable at the parent's rate.

b.   Another significant filing requirement is the reporting of foreign financial accounts and specified foreign assets. Generally, any U.S. citizen, resident, or person doing business in the United States who has an ownership interest in or signatory authority or other authority over any number of financial accounts in a foreign country with an aggregate value in excess of $10,000 at any time during the calendar year, must file a Form FinCEN Report 114, *Report of Foreign Bank and Financial Accounts* (commonly referred to as an FBAR), reporting certain information with respect to those accounts by April 15 of the subsequent year or the extension due date of October 15, if applicable. Failure to file an FBAR is subject to both civil and criminal penalties. A related form is Part III of Form 1040 Schedule B. This is presented below and assists taxpayers in making sure they comply with foreign account reporting rules.

From Form 1040 Schedule B

			Yes	No
	You must complete this part if you **(a)** had over $1,500 of taxable interest or ordinary dividends; **(b)** had a foreign account; or **(c)** received a distribution from, or were a grantor of, or a transferor to, a foreign trust.			
Part III Foreign Accounts and Trusts (See instructions on back.)	**7a**	At any time during [Year], did you have a financial interest in or signature authority over a financial account (such as a bank account, securities account, or brokerage account) located in a foreign country? See instructions		
		If "Yes," are you required to file FinCEN Form 114, Report of Foreign Bank and Financial Accounts (FBAR), to report that financial interest or signature authority? See FinCEN Form 114 and its instructions for filing requirements and exceptions to those requirements		
	b	If you are required to file FinCEN Form 114, enter the name of the foreign country where the financial account is located ▶ _____		
	8	During [Year], did you receive a distribution from, or were you the grantor of, or transferor to, a foreign trust? If "Yes," you may have to file Form 3520. See instructions on back		

For Paperwork Reduction Act Notice, see your tax return instructions.   Cat. No. 17146N   Schedule B (Form 1040A or 1040) [Year]

1)   Individuals must use Form 8938 to report specified foreign financial assets with an aggregate value that exceeds $50,000 on the last day of the year or exceeds $75,000 at any time during the tax year (this threshold is doubled for married individuals filing jointly). Form 8938 is required to be filed with an individual's annual income tax return. Individuals not required to file an annual income tax return are not required to file Form 8938.

2)   The purposes of Form 8938 and the FBAR are similar, and there is significant overlap. Yet, filing Form 8938 does not relieve an individual of the requirement to file an FBAR. Many individuals will be required to file both Form 8938 and an FBAR to report substantially the same information. Despite the similarities, there are some differences between Form 8938 and the FBAR. The FBAR is not filed with an individual's federal income tax return to the IRS, but is instead filed electronically through the Bank Secrecy Act (BSA) e-file system with the Treasury's Financial Crimes Enforcement Network (FinCEN).

3.   **Due Dates and Related Extensions**

a.   **Individual** tax returns must be filed (postmarked) no later than the 15th day of the **4th** month (or 3 months and 15 days) following the close of the tax year. This is April 15 for calendar-year taxpayers.

1)   An automatic **6-month** extension is available by filing Form 4868. This extends the deadline to October 15 for calendar-year taxpayers.

2)   The extension does not grant any additional time to pay taxes due.

b.   **C corporation** tax return due dates changed significantly beginning with the 2016 tax year. Eventually, all C corporations will have original due dates on the 15th day of the 4th month following the end of the tax year, and extended due dates 6 months later on the 15th day of the 10th month following the end of the tax year. The following table shows the due dates and extension dates beginning in 2016 through to 2026 when all are again unified. Changes/differences are in bold:

Tax Year Type	2016-2025	2026
June 30 Fiscal Year	Original: **3rd month** (Sept. 15) Extended: 10th month (April 15)	Original: **4th month** (Oct. 15) Extended: 10th month (April 15)
Calendar/Other Fiscal Year	Original: 4th month Extended: 10th month	

c.   **S corporation** tax returns must be filed (postmarked) no later than the 15th day of the **3rd** month following the close of the tax year. This is March 15 for calendar-year taxpayers.

   1)   An automatic **6-month** extension is available by filing Form 7004. This extends the deadline to September 15 for calendar-year taxpayers.

   2)   The extension does not grant any additional time to pay taxes due.

d.   **Partnership** tax returns must be filed (postmarked) no later than the 15th day of the **3rd** month following the close of the tax year. This is March 15 for calendar-year taxpayers.

   1)   An automatic **6-month** extension is available by filing Form 7004. This extends the deadline to September 15 for calendar-year taxpayers.

e.   **Exempt organizations** are generally required to file annual information returns by the 15th day of the **5th** month following the close of the taxable year.

   1)   Form 8868 can be filed to request an automatic **6-month** extension if needed.

f.   **Estate** and **trust** tax returns must be filed (postmarked) no later than the 15th day of the 4th month following the close of the tax year. This is April 15 for trusts and calendar-year estates.

   1)   An extension of up to 5 1/2 months may be granted by filing Form 7004.

g.   If the 15th day falls on a Saturday, Sunday, or legal holiday, the due date is extended until the next business day.

Summary of Due Dates for Calendar-Year Taxpayers Other than C Corporations

Return Type	Original Due Date	Extension Due Date
S Corporation	March 15th	September 15th
Partnership	March 15th	September 15th
Estate and Trust	April 15th	September 30th
Individual	April 15th	October 15th
Exempt Organization	May 15th	November 15th

4.   **Disclosure of Tax Positions**

a.   A taxpayer's accuracy-related penalty due to disregard of rules and regulations, or substantial understatement of income tax, may be avoided if the return position is adequately disclosed and has a reasonable basis. Generally, the penalty is equal to 20% of the underpayment. The penalty is not figured on any part of an underpayment on which the fraud penalty is charged.

1) Disregard of the rules and regulations includes any careless, reckless, or intentional disregard.

2) Substantial understatement of income tax occurs when the understatement is more than the larger of 10% of the correct tax or $5,000. In addition to adequate disclosure and a reasonable basis, the amount of the understatement may be reduced to the extent the understatement is due to substantial authority.

3) Whether there is substantial authority for the tax treatment of an item depends on the facts and circumstances. Some of the items that may be considered are court opinions, Treasury regulations, revenue rulings, revenue procedures, and notices and announcements issued by the IRS and published in the IRB that involve the same or similar circumstances as the taxpayer's.

4) To adequately disclose the relevant facts about the tax treatment of an item, use Form 8275, *Disclosure Statement*. There must also be a reasonable basis for the taxpayer's treatment of the item. Form 8275-R, *Regulation Disclosure Statement*, is used to disclose items or positions contrary to regulations.

5) Adequate disclosure has no effect on items attributable to tax shelters.

6) Showing a reasonable cause also includes showing actions were taken in good faith.

7) The reasonable basis is a significantly higher standard than the not frivolous standard applied to preparers for the same penalty.

5. **Recordkeeping**

   a. Books of account or records sufficient to establish the amount of gross income, deductions, credit, or other matters required to substantiate any tax or information return must be kept.

   1) Records must be maintained as long as the contents may be material in administration of any internal revenue law.

   2) Employers are required to keep records on employment taxes until at least 4 years after the due date of the return or payment of the tax, whichever is later.

6. **Claims for Refund**

   a. A claim for refund of federal income tax overpaid for the current tax year is made by filing a return (Form 1040). A refund claim for a prior year is made by filing an amended return (Form 1040X). Form 843 is used to claim a refund of any other tax.

   b. Application for a tentative carryback adjustment to get a quick refund for carryback of a net operating loss, corporate net capital loss, or general business credit is made on Form 1045 (individuals) or Form 1139 (corporations).

   c. A claim for refund must be made within the **statute of limitations** period for refunds. A claim must be filed by the later of 3 years from filing the return or 2 years after the tax was paid.

   1) An early return is treated as filed on the due date.

   2) If the claim relates to worthless securities or bad debts, the period of limitation is 7 years from the date prescribed for filing the return for the year with respect to which the claim is made.

   3) If a taxpayer does not file a return, a refund must be claimed within 2 years from the time the tax was paid. Tax deducted and withheld at the source during any calendar year is deemed paid by the recipient of the income on the 15th day of the 4th month following the close of his or her tax year.

7.   **Assessment of Deficiency**

a.   A deficiency is any excess of tax imposed over the sum of amounts shown on the return plus amounts previously assessed (reduced by rebates). Assessment of tax is made by recording the liability of the taxpayer in the office of the Secretary of the Treasury. The following flowchart is provided to illustrate the process.

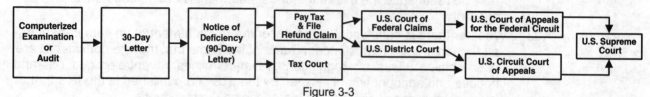

Figure 3-3

b.   Computerized examination or audit of a return may result in an IRS examiner proposing an addition to tax. A letter stating the proposal is sent to the taxpayer. It is referred to as a **30-day letter**.

c.   If consensus is not reached with the examiner in a conference with his or her supervisor or from an administrative appeal, a **notice of deficiency (ND)** is mailed to the taxpayer, but no sooner than 30 days after a 30-day letter.

1)   A notice of deficiency is referred to as a 90-day letter.

2)   A notice of deficiency is a prerequisite to assessment.

3)   However, immediate assessment, i.e., without a notice of deficiency, is allowed for the following:

a)   Tax shown on a return filed by a taxpayer

b)   Mathematical and clerical errors in a return

c)   Overstatement of credits

d)   Tax for which assessment is waived

d.   A taxpayer may institute a proceeding in the U.S. Tax Court within the 90 days following mailing of the ND (150 days if the taxpayer lives outside the U.S.). The ND is a prerequisite to a U.S. Tax Court proceeding.

1)   Payment of the deficiency is not required. Payment after the ND is mailed does not deprive the U.S. Tax Court of jurisdiction.

e.   If a petition is not filed with the U.S. Tax Court, taxes may be assessed 90 days after the ND is mailed.

1)   Filing the petition suspends the 90-day period.

f.   Partial or full payment of a deficiency prior to mailing of the ND deprives the Tax Court of jurisdiction. After full payment of any deficiency balance, the taxpayer may file a claim for refund and, if it is denied by the IRS, may institute a refund proceeding in a U.S. district court or the U.S. Court of Federal Claims.

1)   A jury is available only in a U.S. district court. One or more judges decide all issues in the U.S. Tax Court and the U.S. Court of Federal Claims.

g.   Authority to assess tax liability is limited by statute to specific periods.

1)   The general **statute of limitations** (S/L) for assessment of a deficiency is 3 years from the later of the date the return was due or the date it was filed.

a)   A return filed before the due date is treated as filed on the due date.

b)   The IRS generally has 10 years following the assessment to begin collection of tax by levy or a court proceeding.

2)   The S/L is 6 years if there is omission of items of more than 25% of gross income stated in the return. Specifically for goods or services from a trade or business, gross income includes gross receipts before deduction for cost of goods sold. Only items completely omitted are counted.

EXAMPLE

A sole proprietor had the following income transactions:

Gross receipts	$300,000
Less: COGS	(200,000)
Net business income	$100,000
Capital gains	40,000
Gross income	$140,000

For determining the 25% GI threshold, the sole proprietor's GI is as follows:

Gross receipts	$300,000
Capital gains	40,000
Gross income for 25% threshold	$340,000

Note that for the nonbusiness item, i.e., capital gains, only the gain and not the sale amount is included.

---

      3) **Failure to file.** The S/L period does not commence before a return is filed.

         a) When no return has been filed, the assessment period is unlimited.

      4) **Fraud.** Attempting to evade tax results in an unlimited assessment period. Fraud cannot be cured by filing a correct amended return.

      5) The S/L period begins to run when a return filed late is received by the IRS.

      6) Extension. The S/L period may be extended by an agreement between the taxpayer and the IRS entered into before the S/L expires.

         a) Each time an extension has been requested (or after expiration if there has been a levy), the IRS must notify the taxpayer that the taxpayer may refuse to extend the period of limitations or may limit the extension to particular issues or to a particular period of time.

   h. Mitigation of the statute of limitations. In certain circumstances, the statute of limitations may unjustly penalize the taxpayer or the government for a given return position.

EXAMPLE

The taxpayer reports an item of income in 2015. Later, the IRS asserts that this item should be reported in 2017. Since each year's assessment stands alone, the payment in 2015 does not impact the liabilities for 2017. Therefore, without the mitigation provisions outlined below, the taxpayer would have to pay twice for the same income item.

---

      1) The mitigation provisions are limited to **income tax**, not gift, etc., when the following circumstances are met:

         a) There is a "determination" for a tax year concerning the treatment of an item of income (i.e., Tax Court decision);

         b) On the date of determination, correction of the error must be barred (i.e., statute of limitations);

         c) There must be a condition necessary for adjustment, i.e., double income (deduction); and

         d) In the proceeding of determination, the successful party must have taken a position inconsistent with the position in the closed year.

The statute of limitations, both for a taxpayer claiming a refund and for the IRS assessing a deficiency, is a consistently tested topic on the exam.

8. **Closed Cases**

   a. Cases closed after examination will not be reopened to make adjustments unfavorable to the taxpayer except under certain circumstances. Qualifying circumstances include evidence of fraud, malfeasance, collusion, concealment, or misrepresentation of a material fact.

Stop and review! You have completed the outline for this subunit. Study multiple-choice questions 6 through 10 beginning on page 81.

3.3 TAX PLANNING

Background
Reduction of tax may always be important but should not be the deciding factor behind every financial action. The goal of maximizing "after-tax" wealth is not always the same as minimizing taxes. The role of tax planning is to assist individuals and businesses in reaching maximization of after-tax wealth in the most tax-efficient way possible.

1. Tax planning is the consideration of tax implications for individual or business decisions, usually with the intent of minimizing, or at least reducing, the tax liability. It includes, among other things, considering alternative treatments, projecting the tax consequences, and determining the role of taxes in decision making.

   a. The three most basic and common types of tax planning are (1) timing of income recognition, (2) shifting of income among taxpayers and jurisdictions, and (3) conversion of income among high- and low-rate activities.

2. **Timing**

   a. The timing technique accelerates or defers recognition of income and/or deductions. The advice most often heard is to defer income and accelerate deductions. This results in the lowest tax liability for the current year. However, in a year in which the taxpayer's rates are lower than the rates will be the following year, it is advisable to do just the opposite.

   b. The following items should be considered when evaluating the use of timing techniques:

      1) Time value of money (e.g., can the taxpayer make a higher return on income realized and reinvested this year than the taxpayer can save in taxes by deferring the income to a future date by not selling the capital asset until later?)
      2) Future (or likelihood of proposed) tax law (i.e., will it stay the same or change?)
      3) Individual circumstances of the taxpayer (i.e., a strategy good for one is not necessarily the best strategy for another)

EXAMPLE
An accrual basis corporation has low cash flow at the end of Year 1 but will have cash on hand to pay a considerably large charitable donation by March 15, Year 2. Because the corporation has projected a lower marginal tax rate in Year 2, the board should authorize the donation for Year 1 and elect to make the payment by March 15, Year 2. Claiming the deduction in Year 1 will create a higher tax savings than it will in Year 2.

   c. A taxpayer typically has more control over the recognition of some types of income (e.g., sale of capital gain property) than a taxpayer has over other types (e.g., salaries).

3. **Shifting**

   a. The basics of income shifting typically relate to moving income and therefore the accompanying tax liability from one family member to another who is subject to a lower marginal rate, or moving income between entities and their owner(s). However, tax planning also involves shifting income from one tax jurisdiction to another with different marginal tax rates.

   b. Three key terms when discussing shifting income are **"assignment of income doctrine," "related party transaction,"** and **"arm's-length transaction."** An arm's-length transaction occurs when the involved parties act independently, regardless of any relation between the parties. The purpose of these transactions is to guarantee that all parties act in their own self-interest and not for the common good of all the parties involved to the detriment of the IRS.

   c. Other rules that may limit or otherwise make income shifting difficult include the "Kiddie Tax" rules and gift/wealth transfer rules.

   d. Successful shifting of income among family members or entities depends on determining the following:

      1) Income/assets available for shifting
      2) Best strategy for realizing the shift
      3) Best recipient of income/asset within the family or entity

---

EXAMPLE

Parents with a 33% marginal rate want to invest some of their savings and minimize the overall tax liability on the family. One way these parents can accomplish this goal is to have their adult children, who have only a 15% marginal rate, purchase a rental home and borrow the money from the parents at the lowest allowable rate (i.e., applicable federal rate). This strategy will result in the rental income being taxed at only 15% instead of the higher 33% of the parents and at the lowest cost possible (due to the low rate). The parents have also shifted income to the adult children without being subject to gift tax limits, etc.

---

   e. In the case of shifting income among tax jurisdictions, the jurisdictions among which the income is moved could be city, county, or state jurisdictions within the U.S. In addition, shifting of income also could involve moving the income from U.S. jurisdiction to that of another nation.

   f. In the case of multiple nations claiming the right to tax an individual or business, credit (subject to specific laws and treaties) will usually be given by each country for tax paid to the other. This helps to avoid double taxation and encourages international business.

EXAMPLE

A player for the National Basketball Association is drawing near to the end of his original/rookie contract in Ohio. He has offers from franchises in Ohio, New York, Illinois, Florida, and California and wishes to minimize his overall tax liability in his next contract. All other issues being equal, the player should accept the offer from the franchise in Florida. By doing so, the player would be shifting his income from a state (Ohio) with a state income tax to the only state of those making offers with no state income tax. Though the federal income tax would go unchanged, the player's overall tax liability would be reduced.

---

4.   **Conversion**

   a.   Converting income from a less favorable category to a more favorable one can be achieved in various ways. Favorable conversions include converting ordinary income property into capital gain property. The opposite applies for losses.

EXAMPLE

A taxpayer wants to convert $10,000 FMV of inventory with a basis of $3,000 to capital gain property. The taxpayer will accomplish the goal by transferring the inventory to a controlled corporation for stock (the FMV would be $10,000). The taxpayer's basis in the stock is $3,000; therefore, selling the stock will result in a $7,000 capital gain for the taxpayer.

If the taxpayer simply sells the inventory (i.e., no conversion), the $7,000 gain will be ordinary.

---

   b.   Even better than converting property from a high tax rate to a low rate is converting it to nontaxable property. Examples of this include the following:

   1)   Employee benefits, e.g., employer-paid medical reimbursement
   2)   Investing in municipal bonds (i.e., nontaxable investment interest)
   3)   Convert nondeductible personal expense to a business expense

   c.   Some conversions involve a comparative analysis of minimization of current taxes to minimization of future taxes.

EXAMPLE

Contributions to an individual retirement account are deductible (subject to limitations) in the year made; however, tax applies to 100% of the withdrawals. So there is a current tax savings or deferral. On the other hand, contributions to a Roth IRA are currently taxed; however, the withdrawals are tax-exempt, including any increase in the investment over the years. This results in tax avoidance.

---

5.   **Avoidance vs. Evasion**

Background

In a 1947 case, Judge Learned Hand stated, "Over and over again courts have said that there is nothing sinister in so arranging one's affairs as to keep taxes as low as possible. Everybody does so, rich or poor; and all do right, for nobody owes any public duty to pay more than the law demands: taxes are enforced extractions, not voluntary contributions. To demand more in the name of morals is mere cant."

---

   a.   **Tax avoidance** is the minimization of tax liability through legal arrangements and transactions. The goal of a business is to maximize profits, and tax avoidance is a key element in obtaining this goal. Avoidance maneuvers take place prior to incurring a tax liability.

   b.   **Tax evasion** takes place once a tax liability has already been incurred (i.e., taxable actions have been completed). A key distinction between avoidance and evasion is taxpayer "intent." A taxpayer's intent is called into question when one of the "badges" of fraud is identified. These indicators include understatement of income, improper allocation of income, claiming of fictitious deductions, questionable conduct of the taxpayer, and accounting irregularities.

   c.   Concerning fraud, Sec. 7201 reads as follows: "Any person who willfully attempts in any manner to evade or defeat any tax imposed by this title or the payment thereof shall, in addition to other penalties provided by law, be guilty of a felony and, upon conviction thereof, shall be fined not more than $100,000 ($500,000 in the case of a corporation), or imprisoned not more than five years, or both, together with the costs of prosecution."

Stop and review! You have completed the outline for this subunit. Study multiple-choice questions 11 and 12 beginning on page 82.

3.4 FILING STATUS

From Form 1040

Filing Status Check only one box.	1 ☐ Single 2 ☐ Married filing jointly (even if only one had income) 3 ☐ Married filing separately. Enter spouse's SSN above and full name here. ▶	4 ☐ Head of household (with qualifying person). (See instructions.) If the qualifying person is a child but not your dependent, enter this child's name here. ▶ 5 ☐ Qualifying widow(er) with dependent child

1. **Overview**

    a. The amounts of the standard deductions, personal exemptions, and applicable tax rates vary with filing status.

    b. Filing status on the last day of the year determines the filing status for the entire year.

2. **Single -- Form 1040 Box 1**

    a. An individual must file as single if (s)he neither is married nor qualifies for widow(er) or head of household status.

3. **Married Filing a Joint Return -- Form 1040 Box 2**

    a. Married individuals who file a joint return account for their items of income, deduction, and credit in the aggregate.

    1) A joint return is allowed when spouses use different accounting methods.
    2) Spouses with different tax years may not file a joint return.

    b. Two individuals are treated as legally married for the entire tax year if, on the last day of the tax year, they are

    1) Legally married and cohabiting as spouses,
    2) Legally married and living apart but not separated pursuant to a valid divorce decree or separate maintenance agreement, or
    3) Separated under a valid divorce decree that is not yet final.

    c. If a spouse dies and the surviving spouse does not remarry before the end of the tax year, a joint return may be filed.

    d. Since 2013, same-sex couples have qualified for married filing status. The related Supreme Court rulings of 2015 have little effect on federal taxes, other than an expected increase in the volume of married same-sex taxpayers filing joint returns now that all states are required to license marriages between people of the same sex.

4. **Married Filing a Separate Return -- Form 1040 Box 3**

    a. Each spouse accounts separately for items of income, deduction, and credit. A spouse who uses his or her own funds to pay expenses of jointly owned property is entitled to any deduction attributable to the payments.

    b. If one spouse files separately, so must the other.

5. **Head of Household -- Form 1040 Box 4**

    a. An individual qualifies for head of household status if (s)he satisfies conditions with respect to filing status, marital status, and household maintenance.

    b. **Filing status.** The individual may not file as a qualifying widow(er).

    c. **Marital status.** A married person does not qualify for head of household status unless the conditions below are satisfied. A married individual who lives with a dependent apart from the spouse qualifies for head of household status if, for the tax year,

    1) (S)he files separately;
    2) (S)he pays more than 50% toward maintaining the household; and
    3) For the last 6 months,

        a) The spouse is not a member of the household,
        b) The household is the principal home of a child of the individual, and
        c) The individual can claim a dependency exemption for the child.

d.   **Household maintenance.** To qualify for head of household status, an individual must maintain a household that is the principal place of abode for a qualifying individual for at least half of the tax year.

1)   To maintain a household for federal filing status purposes, an individual must furnish more than 50% of the qualifying costs of maintaining the household during the tax year.

Qualifying Costs	Nonqualifying Costs
Property tax	Clothing
Mortgage interest	Education
Rent	Medical treatment
Utilities	Life insurance
Upkeep	Transportation
Repair	Vacations
Property insurance	Services by the taxpayer
Food consumed on premises	Services by the dependent

NOTE: Nonresident aliens cannot qualify for the head of household status.

2)   **Qualifying person and time.** The taxpayer must maintain a household that constitutes the principal place of abode for more than half of the taxable year for at least one qualified individual who is

   a)   An unmarried son or daughter, unmarried grandchild, or unmarried stepchild or

   b)   Any other person eligible to be claimed as a dependent, except for those eligible under a multiple-support agreement.

3)   There are two special rules concerning a qualifying person.

   a)   First, the taxpayer with a dependent parent qualifies even if the parent does not live with the taxpayer. Otherwise, the IRS maintains that the qualifying individual must occupy the same household (except for temporary absences).

   b)   Second, in the case of divorce, the custodial parent of a qualifying child qualifies for head of household status even if the noncustodial parent claims the dependency exemption for the child.

4)   On the following page is a summary of the qualifications for a person qualifying the taxpayer as head of household.

Who Is a Qualifying Person Qualifying the Taxpayer to File as Head of Household?

IF the person is the taxpayer's . . .	AND . . .	THEN that person is . . .
qualifying child (such as a son, daughter, or grandchild who lived with the taxpayer more than half the year and meets certain other tests)	he or she is single	a qualifying person, whether or not the taxpayer can claim an exemption for the person.
	he or she is marred **and** the taxpayer can claim an exemption for him or her	a qualifying person.
	he or she is married **and** the taxpayer can't claim an exemption for him or her other than just because they are married	not a qualifying person.
qualifying relative who is the taxpayer's father or mother	the taxpayer can claim an exemption for him or her	a qualifying person.[1]
	the taxpayer can't claim an exemption for him or her	not a qualifying person.
qualifying relative other than the taxpayer's father or mother.	he or she lived with the taxpayer more than half the year, **and** the taxpayer can claim an exemption for him or her, **and** is one of the following: son, daughter, stepchild, foster child, or a descendant of any of them; the taxpayer's brother, sister, half-brother, half-sister, or a son or daughter of any of them; an ancestor or sibling of the taxpayer's father or mother; or stepbrother, stepsister, stepfather, stepmother, son-in-law, daughter-in-law, father-in-law, mother-in-law, brother-in-law, or sister-in-law	a qualifying person.
	he or she didn't live with the taxpayer more than half the year	not a qualifying person.
	he or she isn't related to the taxpayer in one of the ways listed above **and** is the taxpayer's qualifying relative only because he or she lived with the taxpayer all year as a member of the taxpayer's household (for example, a companion or a friend)	not a qualifying person.
	the taxpayer can't claim an exemption for him or her	not a qualifying person.

[1]The taxpayer is eligible to file as head of household even if the taxpayer's parent, whom the taxpayer can claim as a dependent, doesn't live with the taxpayer. The taxpayer must pay more than half the cost of keeping up a home that was the main home for the entire year for the taxpayer's parent. This test is met if the taxpayer pays more than half the cost of keeping the taxpayer's parent in a rest home or home for the elderly.

6. **Qualifying Widow(er) or Surviving Spouse -- Form 1040 Box 5**

   a.   The qualifying widow(er) status is available for 2 years following the year of death of the husband or wife if the following conditions are satisfied:

   1)   The taxpayer did not remarry during the tax year.

   2)   The widow(er) qualified (with the deceased spouse) for married filing joint return status for the tax year of the death of the spouse.

   3)   A qualifying widow(er) maintains a household for the entire taxable year. Maintenance means the widow(er) furnishes more than 50% of the costs to maintain the household for the tax year.

      a)   The household must be the principal place of abode of a dependent of the widow(er). The widow(er) must be entitled to claim a dependency exemption amount for the dependent.

      b)   The dependent must be a son or daughter, a stepson or daughter, or an adopted child. This does not include a foster child.

   4)   A widow(er) can file a joint return in the tax year of the death of the spouse. (S)he is also entitled to the full personal exemption amount for the deceased spouse.

7. **Summary**

   a.   The decision chart on the next page in general summarizes the determination of filing status.

Determination of Filing Status

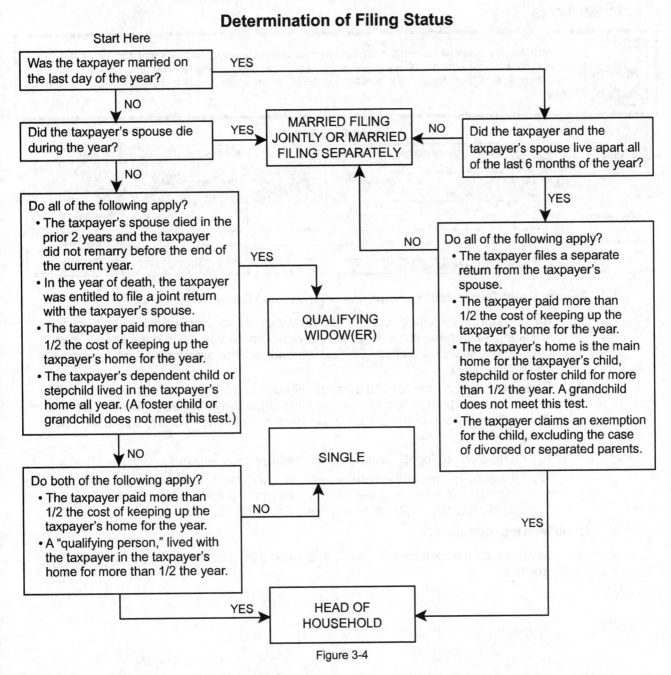

Figure 3-4

Stop and review! You have completed the outline for this subunit. Study multiple-choice questions 13 through 17 beginning on page 83.

3.5 EXEMPTIONS

 The AICPA has consistently tested the rules and regulations pertaining to the personal and dependent exemptions. Take the time necessary to understand this information, as the requirements for each can easily be confused. Work through the questions in the Gleim materials to reinforce your knowledge of these topics.

From Form 1040

Exemptions								Boxes checked on 6a and 6b	
	6a	☐ **Yourself.** If someone can claim you as a dependent, **do not** check box 6a							
	b	☐ **Spouse**						No. of children on 6c who:	
	c	**Dependents:**	**(2)** Dependent's social security number	**(3)** Dependent's relationship to you	**(4)** ✓ if child under age 17 qualifying for child tax credit (see instructions)			• **lived with you**	
		(1) First name Last name						• **did not live with you due to divorce or separation** (see instructions)	
If more than four dependents, see instructions and check here ▶ ☐		_____			☐				
		_____			☐			Dependents on 6c not entered above	
		_____			☐				
		_____			☐			Add numbers on lines above ▶	
	d	Total number of exemptions claimed							

1. **Personal and Dependent Exemptions -- Form 1040 Boxes 6a to 6d**

    a. An individual's (including resident aliens) deduction for exemptions is the sum of a personal exemption amount for the individual and a spouse, along with a dependent exemption amount for each qualified dependent. The amount for each individual is $4,050 for 2017.

    b. **Personal exemptions for the spouse.** Normally, a joint return must be filed. However, a taxpayer filing as married filing separately may deduct an exemption for the spouse if the spouse has no gross income and is not a dependent of another taxpayer.

        1) If divorced or legally separated, no exemption is allowed.

        2) If a spouse dies in the current year, an exemption is allowed as long as the spouse would have qualified for an exemption on the date of death and the qualifying widow(er) does not remarry during that year.

2. **Qualified Dependent**

    a. To qualify as a dependent, the individual must be a qualifying child or a qualifying relative.

Overview of the Rules for Claiming an Exemption for a Dependent

Caution: This table is only an overview of the rules. For details, see Publication 17.

- The taxpayer can't claim any dependents if the taxpayer, or the taxpayer's spouse if filing jointly, could be claimed as a dependent by another taxpayer.
- The taxpayer can't claim a married person who files a joint return as a dependent unless that joint return is only to claim a refund of income tax withheld or estimated tax paid.
- The taxpayer can't claim a person as a dependent unless (s)he is the taxpayer's **qualifying child** or **qualifying relative**.

Tests To Be a Qualifying Child	Tests To Be a Qualifying Relative
1. **Relationship.** The child must be the taxpayer's son, daughter, stepchild, foster child, brother, sister, half brother, half sister, stepbrother, stepsister, or a descendant of any of them. Adopted individuals qualify.	1. **Relationship.** The relationship requirement is satisfied if the person is related as indicated in **item 3., Qualifying Relative Relationship Criteria**, following this table, or meets the principal residence requirement.
2. **Principal Residence.** The child must have lived with the taxpayer for more than half of the year.	2. **Principal Residence.** The residence requirement is satisfied if the person lives with the taxpayer all year as a member of the taxpayer's household.
3. **Age.** The child must be: (a) under age 19 at the end of the year, (b) under age 24 at the end of the year and a full-time student,[1] or (c) any age if permanently and totally disabled.	3. **Gross Taxable Income.** The person's gross income for the year must be less than $4,050. Gross income means all income the person received in the form of money, goods, property, and services that isn't exempt from tax (e.g., taxable interest income and taxable scholarships). Don't include social security benefits for low-income taxpayers.
4. **Not Self-Supporting.** The child must not have provided more than half of his or her own support for the year.	4. **Support.** The taxpayer must provide more than half of the person's total (economic) support for the year. **Item 4., Qualifying Relative Support Criteria**, on page 78, has a detailed explanation.
5. If the child meets the rules to be a qualifying child of more than one person, the taxpayer must be the person entitled to claim the child as a qualifying child.	5. The person can't be the taxpayer's qualifying child or the qualifying child of any other taxpayer. A child isn't the qualifying child of any other taxpayer if the child's parent (or any other person for whom the child is defined as a qualifying child) isn't required to file an income tax return or files an income tax return only to get a refund of income tax withheld.
6. The child isn't filing a joint return for the year (unless that joint return is filed only to claim a refund of income tax withheld or estimated tax paid).	

[1]To qualify as a full-time student, the dependent must be enrolled at an educational organization for at least 5 months during the tax year.

3. **Qualifying Relative Relationship Criteria**

   a. The relationship requirement is satisfied by existence of an extended (by blood) or immediate (by blood, adoption, or marriage) relationship. The relationship need be present to only one of the two married persons who file a joint return. Any relationship established by marriage is not treated as ended by divorce or by death.

      1) Extended relationships: Grandparents and ancestors, grandchildren and descendants, uncles or aunts, nephews or nieces

      2) Immediate relationships

         a) Parent: Natural, adoptive, stepparent, father- or mother-in-law

         b) Child: Natural, adoptive, stepchild, son- or daughter-in-law, foster child (who lives with the claimant for the entire tax year)

         c) Sibling: Full or half brother or sister, adoptive brother or sister, stepbrother or sister, brother- or sister-in-law

      NOTE: Cousins do not meet the relationship test. However, if they lived with the taxpayer all year, they meet the residence test.

4. **Qualifying Relative Support Criteria**

   a. Support includes welfare benefits, Social Security benefits, and any support provided by the exemption claimant, the dependent, and any other person.

   ### EXAMPLE

   A dependent earns $2,000 and the exemption claimants provide $3,000 of support to the dependent. The total support equals $5,000 ($2,000 provided by dependent + $3,000 provided by exemption claimants).

   ---

   b. Only amounts provided during the calendar year qualify as support.

      1) Amounts paid in arrears (i.e., payment for child support for a previous year) are not considered support for the current year.

   c. Support includes money and items, or amounts spent on items, such as

      1) Food, clothing, shelter, utilities
      2) Medical and dental care and insurance
      3) Education
      4) Child care, vacations, etc.

   d. **Excluded.** Certain items (or amounts spent on them) have not been treated as support, e.g., scholarship received by a dependent, taxes, or life insurance premiums.

   e. A **divorced or separated** individual need not meet the support test if (s)he and the (ex-)spouse meet (or have met) the following conditions:

      1) Provided more than 50% of the support
      2) Had (between them) custody for more than 50% of the year
      3) Lived apart for the last half of the year
      4) Did not have a multiple support agreement in effect

      NOTE: The parent having custody for more than 50% of the year is entitled to the exemption, but the exemption amount may be allocated to the noncustodial parent if there is an agreement signed by both parents and attached to the noncustodial parent's return.

   f. **Multiple support agreement.** One person of a group that together provides more than 50% of the support of an individual may, pursuant to an agreement, be allowed the dependency exemption amount.

      1) The person must be otherwise eligible to claim the exemption and must provide more than 10% of the support.
      2) No other person may provide more than 50% of the support.
      3) Each other person in the group who provides more than 10% of the support must sign a written consent filed with the return of the taxpayer who claims the exemption.

5. **Dependent Rules**

   a. There are special rules that apply to an individual qualifying as a dependent.

      1) **Ineligible dependents.** If an individual meets the requirements to be classified as a dependent on another person's tax return, the individual (dependent) is not entitled to the deduction for personal exemptions for himself or herself.

      2) **Filing status** (occasionally referred to as the joint return test). An individual does not qualify as a dependent on another's return if the individual is married and files a joint return.

         a) However, such an individual can qualify as a dependent if (s)he files a joint return solely to claim a refund of withheld tax without regard to the citizenship test.

EXAMPLE

Mr. and Mrs. Kind provided more than half the support for their married daughter and son-in-law who lived with the Kinds all year. Neither the daughter nor the son-in-law is required to file a 2017 tax return. They do so only to get a refund of withheld taxes. The Kinds may claim the daughter and the son-in-law as dependents on their 2017 joint return.

---

    3) The individual must **not be a qualifying child** of any other taxpayer.

        a) A child being adopted is eligible to be claimed as a dependent by the adopting parents if the adoption taxpayer identification number (ATIN) is assigned.

        b) Both a dependent who dies before the end of the year and a child born during the year may be claimed as dependents.

    4) **Citizenship.** To qualify as a dependent, an individual must be, for any part of the year, a U.S. citizen, resident, or national, or a Canadian or Mexican resident.

EXAMPLE

Resident aliens living in the U.S. provide all the support for their four minor children even though they all live with various relatives in other countries. One is in Mexico, two others are in Canada, and the fourth is in Chile. All family members are citizens of Chile. The resident aliens may claim dependent exemptions for only the three children residing in Mexico and Canada.

---

    5) **Taxpayer identification number (TIN).** The taxpayer must provide the correct TIN of a dependent on the income tax return.

6. **Phaseout of Personal Exemptions**

    a. The amount of each exemption that an individual may claim is phased out if the individual's AGI exceeds a threshold amount. Each exemption amount ($4,050 in 2017) is reduced by 2% for each $2,500 ($1,250 MFS) by which the individual's AGI exceeds the applicable threshold amount.

    b. The deduction for personal exemptions is completely phased out when the taxpayer's AGI exceeds an applicable cap threshold.

EXAMPLE

Taxpayer A and B file a joint return for this year. They are entitled to five personal exemptions (three children). Their gross amount of personal exemptions is $20,250 ($4,050 × 5). Their AGI of $318,800 exceeds the applicable threshold amount of $313,800 by $5,000. They must reduce the gross exemption amount by $810 ($5,000 ÷ $2,500 = 2; 2 × 2% = 4%; $20,250 × .04 = $810). Their allowable deduction for personal exemptions is $19,440 ($20,250 – $810).

THE DEDUCTION FOR PERSONAL EXEMPTIONS -- 2017					
Filing Status	Amount per Exemption	Threshold AGI Amount	Step Size	Phaseout Rate	AGI Cap
Married Filing Jointly	$4,050	$313,800	$2,500	2%	$436,300
Surviving Spouse	4,050	313,800	2,500	2%	436,300
Head of Household	4,050	287,650	2,500	2%	410,150
Unmarried (other than above)	4,050	261,500	2,500	2%	384,000
Married Filing Separately	4,050	156,900	1,250	2%	218,150

Stop and review! You have completed the outline for this subunit. Study multiple-choice questions 18 through 20 beginning on page 84.

QUESTIONS

3.1 Tax Authority

1. Which of the following is the primary source of Federal Tax Law?

- A. The Internal Revenue Code of 1913.
- B. Treasury Regulations.
- C. The Internal Revenue Code of 1986.
- D. The Internal Revenue Bulletin.

Answer (C) is correct.
REQUIRED: The primary source of Federal Tax Law.
DISCUSSION: The Internal Revenue Code of 1986 is the primary source of Federal Tax Law. It imposes income, estate, gift, employment, and miscellaneous excise taxes and provisions controlling the administration of Federal taxation. The Code is found at Title 26 of the United States Code.
Answer (A) is incorrect. The Internal Revenue Code (IRC) of 1913 was the first IRC to implement a federal income tax and is superseded by the 1986 Code. Answer (B) is incorrect. Treasury Regulations are administrative pronouncements that interpret and illustrate the rules contained in the Internal Revenue Code. They are a secondary source of Federal Tax Law. Answer (D) is incorrect. The Internal Revenue Bulletin is an instrument used to publish treasury decisions, executive orders, tax conventions, legislation, court decisions, and other items of general interest.

2. When a revenue ruling conflicts with a revenue procedure, which of the two tax authorities has precedence?

- A. Revenue ruling.
- B. The one established first.
- C. Revenue procedure.
- D. The most recently established.

Answer (D) is correct.
REQUIRED: The tax authority with precedence when there is a conflict.
DISCUSSION: When there are conflicting sources of tax law within the same tier of the hierarchy (as is the case with revenue rulings and procedures), the most recent rule/law takes precedence.
Answer (A) is incorrect. Revenue rulings are in the same hierarchical tier as revenue procedures. Answer (B) is incorrect. More recent tax law within the same hierarchical tier has precedence. Answer (C) is incorrect. Revenue procedures are in the same hierarchical tier as revenue rulings.

3. In order to show that a tax preparer's application of tax law was in line with the intent of the tax law, the preparer should cite which of the following types of authoritative sources to make the most convincing case?

- A. IRS publication.
- B. Technical advice memorandum of another, similar case.
- C. Committee report.
- D. Delegation order.

Answer (C) is correct.
REQUIRED: The authoritative source for determining the intent behind certain tax law.
DISCUSSION: Committee reports are useful tools in determining Congressional intent behind certain tax laws and helping examiners apply the law properly. The committee reports are very high authority to which the courts are bound.
Answer (A) is incorrect. Publications do an excellent job of plainly explaining the law; however, they are not binding on the IRS or courts. Answer (B) is incorrect. TAMs are binding on the IRS only in relation to the taxpayer who is the subject of the ruling. Answer (D) is incorrect. Delegation orders are not authoritative sources for tax research. They simply delegate authority to perform tasks/make decisions to specified IRS employees.

4. Which of the following statements with respect to revenue rulings and revenue procedures is **false**?

- A. Revenue procedures are official statements of procedures that either affect the rights or duties of taxpayers or other members of the public or should be a matter of public knowledge.
- B. The purpose of revenue rulings is to promote uniform application of the tax laws.
- C. Taxpayers cannot appeal adverse return examination decisions based on revenue rulings and revenue procedures to the courts.
- D. IRS employees must follow revenue rulings and revenue procedures.

Answer (C) is correct.
REQUIRED: The false statement regarding revenue rulings and revenue procedures.
DISCUSSION: Revenue rulings and revenue procedures do not have the force and effect of regulations but are published to provide precedents to be used in the disposition of other cases. While taxpayers may rely on the rulings and procedures, they can also appeal adverse return examination decisions based on those rulings to the Tax Court or other federal courts.

5. To research whether the Internal Revenue Service has announced an opinion on a Tax Court decision, refer to which of the following references for the original announcement?

    A.   Circular 230.

    B.   Federal Register.

    C.   Internal Revenue Bulletin.

    D.   Tax Court Reports.

Answer (C) is correct.

    REQUIRED: The reference that contains the original announcement of an IRS opinion on a Tax Court decision.

    DISCUSSION: The Internal Revenue Bulletin is published weekly and includes Treasury decisions, statutes, committee reports, U.S. Supreme Court decisions affecting the IRS, lists of the acquiescences and nonacquiescences of the IRS to decisions of the courts, and administrative rulings.

    Answer (A) is incorrect. Circular 230 does not contain the original announcement of an IRS opinion on a Tax Court decision. Answer (B) is incorrect. The Federal Register does not contain the original announcement of an IRS opinion on a Tax Court decision. Answer (D) is incorrect. Tax Court Reports do not contain the original announcement of an IRS opinion on a Tax Court decision.

3.2 Tax Procedures

6. A taxpayer understated the tax liability by $10,000. The total tax liability was $50,000. No disclosure of the return position was made by the taxpayer; however, the basis for the position is reasonable. How much of an accuracy-related penalty will the taxpayer be assessed?

    A. $0

    B. $1,000

    C. $2,000

    D. $10,000

Answer (C) is correct.

    REQUIRED: The amount of an accuracy-related penalty.

    DISCUSSION: A taxpayer's accuracy-related penalty due to disregard of rules and regulations, or substantial understatement of income tax, may be avoided if the return position is adequately disclosed and has a reasonable basis. Generally, the penalty is equal to 20% of the underpayment. Substantial understatement of income tax occurs when the understatement is more than the larger of 10% of the correct tax ($5,000 is 10% of the correct tax) or $5,000. This taxpayer failed to adequately disclose the return position. The penalty is $2,000 ($10,000 understatement × 20%).

    Answer (A) is incorrect. Because the taxpayer substantially understated the liability and failed to adequately disclose the return position, an accuracy-related penalty is due. Answer (B) is incorrect. The penalty is greater than 10%. Answer (D) is incorrect. The penalty is less than 100% of the understatement.

7. Keen, a calendar-year taxpayer, reported gross income of $100,000 on his 2017 income tax return. Inadvertently omitted from gross income was a $20,000 commission that should have been included in 2017. Keen filed his 2017 return on March 17, 2018. To collect the tax on the $20,000 omission, the Internal Revenue Service must assert a notice of deficiency no later than

    A.   March 17, 2021.

    B.   April 15, 2021.

    C.   March 17, 2024.

    D.   April 15, 2024.

Answer (B) is correct.

    REQUIRED: The statute of limitations on assessment of a deficiency.

    DISCUSSION: The general statute of limitations for assessment of a deficiency is 3 years from the date the return was filed or due. An income tax return filed before the due date for the return is treated as if filed on the due date for statute of limitations purposes. Since Keen's return was due April 15, 2018, the statute of limitations will expire 3 years from that date.

    Answer (A) is incorrect. An income tax return filed before the due date for the return is treated as if filed on the due date. Answer (C) is incorrect. A 6-year statute applies only when income items that would increase stated gross income by more than 25% are omitted. Answer (D) is incorrect. A 6-year statute applies only when income items that would increase stated gross income by more than 25% are omitted.

8. A taxpayer filed his income tax return after the due date but neglected to file an extension form. The return indicated a tax liability of $50,000 and taxes withheld of $45,000. On what amount is the penalties for late filing and late payment computed?

    A. $0

    B. $5,000

    C. $45,000

    D. $50,000

Answer (B) is correct.

    REQUIRED: The amount used to assess late filing and late payment penalties.

    DISCUSSION: When an income tax return is filed later than its due date and no extension has been filed, the IRS may assess a penalty on the taxpayer. The penalty is assessed only on the outstanding taxes due. The taxpayer therefore receives credit for the $45,000 in withholding taxes and the penalty is only assessed on the difference, $5,000 [Sec. 6651(b)].

    Answer (A) is incorrect. The net tax due is used to assess the penalty. Answer (C) is incorrect. Only the net tax still due, not the tax already remitted, is used to assess the penalty. Answer (D) is incorrect. The taxpayer receives a credit for the taxes withheld.

9. A claim for refund of erroneously paid income taxes, filed by an individual before the statute of limitations expires, must be submitted on Form

    A.   1139.

    B.   1045.

    C.   1040X.

    D.   843.

Answer (C) is correct.

    REQUIRED: The required form for submitting a claim for refund of individual income taxes.

    DISCUSSION: A claim for refund of previously paid income taxes is made by filing an amended return on Form 1040X within the appropriate statute of limitations period.

    Answer (A) is incorrect. Application for a tentative carryback adjustment to get a quick refund for carryback of a net operating loss, corporate net capital loss, and general business credit may be made on Form 1139 for corporations. Answer (B) is incorrect. Form 1045 is used to apply for a quick refund on a carryback for individuals. Answer (D) is incorrect. Form 843 is used to file a claim for refund of taxes paid other than income taxes.

10. Krete, an unmarried taxpayer with income exclusively from wages, filed her initial income tax return for the 2017 calendar year. By December 31, 2017, Krete's employer had withheld $16,000 in federal income taxes, and Krete had made no estimated tax payments. On April 15, 2018, Krete timely filed an extension request to file her individual tax return and paid $300 of additional taxes. Krete's 2017 income tax liability was $16,500 when she timely filed her return on April 30, 2018, and paid the remaining income tax liability balance. What amount is subject to the penalty for the underpayment of estimated taxes?

    A. $0

    B. $200

    C. $500

    D. $16,500

Answer (A) is correct.

    REQUIRED: The amount subject to penalty for underpayment of estimated taxes.

    DISCUSSION: No amount is subject to the penalty for the underpayment of estimated taxes. The amount withheld from wages by Krete's employer, $16,000, is treated as if an equal part was paid on each due date. Each of these installments meets the 25% of 90% of the current year's tax threshold.

    Answer (B) is incorrect. This amount results from subtracting the $300 taxes paid from the additional $500 income tax liability computed on the return ($16,500 – $16,000). Answer (C) is incorrect. This amount is the additional $500 income tax liability computed on the filed return. Answer (D) is incorrect. This figure is the entire amount of income tax liability computed on the filed return.

3.3 Tax Planning

11. Company A, a U.S. company, deducted costs from research and development of a product in the U.S., then licensed rights to the product to a foreign subsidiary in a lower tax jurisdiction. The subsidiary then manufactured the product and sold each unit back to Company A (the parent company). This is an example of which tax planning technique?

    A.   Timing of income/deductions.

    B.   Shifting of income.

    C.   Conversion of income property.

    D.   Deferral of income.

Answer (B) is correct.

    REQUIRED: The tax planning technique exemplified in the question.

    DISCUSSION: In addition to moving income among related parties, shifting of income also involves moving income from one tax jurisdiction to another with a lower tax rate. By deducting all of the R&D expenses in the U.S. and licensing the rights to a foreign subsidiary, Company A minimized their U.S. taxable income and shifted profits to a foreign tax jurisdiction with a lower tax rate.

    Answer (A) is incorrect. Timing of income deals with the recognition period of income, not the jurisdiction. Answer (C) is incorrect. Conversion of income property relates to the change in the type of income property, resulting in a different tax liability, not the jurisdiction. Answer (D) is incorrect. Deferral of income is an element of timing of income/deductions and is not exemplified in the question.

12. Electing MACRS depreciation (accelerating the depreciation deduction) over straight-line depreciation is an example of which tax planning technique?

A. Conversion.

B. Shifting.

C. Timing.

D. Assignment.

Answer (C) is correct.

REQUIRED: The tax planning technique exemplified by electing a depreciation method.

DISCUSSION: The three most basic and common types of tax planning are

1. Timing of income recognition,
2. Shifting of income among taxpayers and jurisdictions, and
3. Conversion of income among high and low rate activities.

The timing technique accelerates or defers recognition of income and/or deductions. Because election of depreciation methods accelerate or defer the depreciation deduction, it is a timing strategy.

Answer (A) is incorrect. Conversion of income involves changing the type/class of income producing property. Electing a depreciation method does not change the income property but does change the period of income recognition. Answer (B) is incorrect. Shifting of income involves a change in ownership of the income or change in the tax jurisdiction of the income. Electing a depreciation method does not change the ownership or jurisdiction of income but does change the period of income recognition. Answer (D) is incorrect. Assignment of income is an element of income shifting and is not related to the effects of electing a depreciation method.

3.4 Filing Status

13. A husband and wife can file a joint return even if

A. The spouses have different tax years, provided that both spouses are alive at the end of the year.

B. The spouses have different accounting methods.

C. Either spouse was a nonresident alien at any time during the tax year, provided that at least one spouse makes the proper election.

D. They were divorced before the end of the tax year.

Answer (B) is correct.

REQUIRED: The condition under which a husband and wife may file a joint return.

DISCUSSION: There is no provision disallowing spouses from filing a joint return because they have different accounting methods.

Answer (A) is incorrect. The IRC disallows spouses with different tax years from filing a joint return. Answer (C) is incorrect. The IRC provides that neither spouse can be a nonresident alien during the tax year and still file a joint return, unless the nonresident alien spouse is married to a U.S. citizen or resident alien at year end and both spouses elect to have the nonresident alien treated as a resident alien. Answer (D) is incorrect. Spouses must be married on the last day of the tax year to be allowed to file a joint return.

14. Which of the following, if any, are among the requirements to enable a taxpayer to be classified as a "qualifying widow(er)"?

I. A dependent has lived with the taxpayer for 6 months.

II. The taxpayer has maintained the cost of the principal residence for 6 months.

A. I only.

B. II only.

C. Both I and II.

D. Neither I nor II.

Answer (D) is correct.

REQUIRED: The requirements, if any, to file as a qualifying widow(er).

DISCUSSION: Filing as a surviving spouse or qualifying widow(er) requires the individual's spouse to have died during one of the previous 2 tax years. In addition, the survivor must maintain a household that is the principal place of residence for a dependent child. "Maintain" means the spouse furnishes over 50% of the costs of the household for the entire year.

15. A taxpayer's spouse dies in August of the current year. Which of the following is the taxpayer's filing status for the current year?

A. Single.

B. Qualifying widow(er).

C. Head of household.

D. Married filing jointly.

Answer (D) is correct.

REQUIRED: The taxpayer's filing status for the current year.

DISCUSSION: The qualifying widow(er) status is available for 2 years following the year of death of the husband or wife; however, the surviving spouse can file a joint return in the tax year of the death of the deceased spouse. (S)he is also entitled to the full personal exemption amount for the deceased spouse.

Answer (A) is incorrect. A taxpayer cannot file as single in the year his or her spouse dies. Answer (B) is incorrect. A taxpayer cannot file as a qualifying widow(er) in the year his or her spouse dies. However, the qualifying widow(er) status is available for the 2 years following the year of death of the spouse under certain conditions. Answer (C) is incorrect. A taxpayer cannot file as head of household in the year his or her spouse dies because the taxpayer will not be considered unmarried.

16. A couple filed a joint return in prior tax years. During the current tax year, one spouse died. The couple has no dependent children. What is the filing status available to the surviving spouse for the first subsequent tax year?

A. Qualified widow(er).

B. Married filing separately.

C. Single.

D. Head of household.

Answer (C) is correct.

REQUIRED: The filing status of the surviving spouse for years subsequent to death.

DISCUSSION: For the year of death, the living spouse may choose MFJ status. Because the surviving spouse has no dependents (qualifying individuals), the only filing status available for subsequent years is single.

Answer (A) is incorrect. In order to elect to file as widow(er), the household must be the principal place of abode of a dependent of the surviving spouse. The spouse must be entitled to claim a dependency exemption amount for the dependent. Answer (B) is incorrect. Both filing statuses for married individuals require the taxpayer to be married. Married status is terminated for years subsequent to death. Answer (D) is incorrect. The surviving spouse does not have any qualifying (dependent) individuals as required for head of household status.

17. For head of household filing status, which of the following costs are considered in determining whether the taxpayer has contributed more than one-half the cost of maintaining the household?

	Food Consumed in the Home	Value of Services Rendered in the Home by the Taxpayer
A.	Yes	Yes
B.	No	No
C.	Yes	No
D.	No	Yes

Answer (C) is correct.

REQUIRED: The item(s) considered keeping up a home for head of household filing status.

DISCUSSION: The cost of maintaining a household for head of household status includes expenditures for the mutual benefit of the occupants, e.g., food consumed in the home, rent, or real estate taxes. Not included is the value of services rendered in the home by the taxpayer or the rental value of a home owned by the taxpayer.

3.5 Exemptions

18. Joe and Barb are married, but Barb refuses to sign a Year 1 joint return. On Joe's separate Year 1 return, an exemption may be claimed for Barb if

A. Barb was a full-time student for the entire Year 1 school year.

B. Barb attaches a written statement to Joe's income tax return, agreeing to be claimed as an exemption by Joe for Year 1.

C. Barb was under the age of 19.

D. Barb had no gross income and was not claimed as another person's dependent in Year 1.

Answer (D) is correct.

REQUIRED: The circumstance(s) under which a married person filing separately may claim a personal exemption for the spouse.

DISCUSSION: A taxpayer filing as married filing separately may claim an exemption for his or her spouse if that spouse has no gross income and is not a dependent of another taxpayer.

19. Al and Mary Lew are married and filed a joint 2017 income tax return in which they validly claimed the $4,050 personal exemption for their dependent 17-year-old daughter, Dora. Since Dora earned $8,650 in 2017 from a part-time job at the college she attended full-time, Dora was also required to file a 2017 income tax return. What amount was Dora entitled to claim as a personal exemption in her 2017 individual income tax return?

   A. $0

   B. $1,050

   C. $1,550

   D. $4,050

Answer (A) is correct.
   REQUIRED: The personal exemption deduction allowed a dependent.
   DISCUSSION: An exemption is allowed for each dependent whose gross income for the taxable year is less than the exemption amount ($4,050 in 2017) or who is a child of the taxpayer and has not attained the age of 19. No personal exemption may be taken on the return of an individual who can be claimed as a dependent on another taxpayer's return. Dora's parents are entitled to claim her as a dependent on their return. Therefore, Dora is not entitled to a personal exemption herself.

20. Jim and Kay Ross contributed to the support of their two children, Dale and Kim, and Jim's widowed parent, Grant. For 2017, Dale, a 19-year-old, full-time college student, earned $6,200 as a bookkeeper. Kim, a 23-year-old bank teller, earned $13,700. Grant received $7,875 in dividend income and $6,875 in nontaxable Social Security benefits. Grant, Dale, and Kim are U.S. citizens and were over one-half supported by Jim and Kay. How many exemptions can Jim and Kay claim on their 2017 joint income tax return?

   A. 2

   B. 3

   C. 4

   D. 5

Answer (B) is correct.
   REQUIRED: The number of exemptions that a married couple filing a joint return can claim.
   DISCUSSION: On a joint return, there are two taxpayers, and an exemption is allowed for each. An exemption is also allowed for each dependent. Kim does not qualify as a dependent because she had gross income in excess of the exemption amount ($4,050 in 2017). Although a parent can also qualify as a dependent, Grant has gross income in excess of the exemption and therefore cannot be claimed. The gross income test does not apply to a person such as Dale, who is a child of the claimant, under age 24, and a full-time student. Thus, Jim and Kay can claim themselves and Dale for a total of three exemptions on their return.

STUDY UNIT FOUR
ACCOUNTING METHODS AND GROSS INCOME

(27 pages of outline)

Explanation of the timing of inclusions, exclusions, and deductions is integrated into the discussion of accounting methods in the third subunit of this study unit.

This study unit also presents taxable and nontaxable income items, income items for which there are no exclusions, and income items for which the Internal Revenue Code provides partial or complete exclusion from gross income.

The following table provides an overview of the steps to compute federal income tax liability for individual taxpayers and each corresponding study unit. It will be a useful reference throughout this course's tax-related knowledge transfer outline.

Individual Income Tax	Information covered in
FORMULA	SU 4
GROSS INCOME	
– Adjustments (above the line)	
= **ADJUSTED GROSS INCOME**	SU 6
– Greater of Itemized Deductions or Standard Deduction	
– Personal Exemptions	SU 3
= **TAXABLE INCOME**	
× Tax Rate	SU 6
= **GROSS TAX** Liability	
– Credits	
= **NET TAX** Liability or Refund Receivable	SU 7

Some candidates find it helpful to have the entire tax form side-by-side with our Knowledge Transfer Outline when studying. The full versions of the most up-to-date forms are easily accessible at www.gleim.com/taxforms. These forms and the form excerpts used in our outline are periodically updated as the latest versions are released by the IRS.

4.1 ACCOUNTING METHODS

1. **Background**

   a. A person must use the method of accounting regularly used to compute income in keeping books and records. The method must clearly reflect income. The **cash method** and the **accrual method** are the most common. Specific provisions of the Internal Revenue Code (IRC) may override and require specific treatment of certain items.

   b. Generally, IRS consent is required for **changes in accounting method** which includes, but is not limited to, change in either the overall system of accounting for gross income or deductions or treatment of any material item used in the system. Form 3115, *Application for Change in Accounting Method*, must be completed and submitted to the IRS. IRS consent is not required for the following changes:

      1) Adopting LIFO inventory valuation
      2) Switching from declining-balance depreciation to straight-line
      3) Making an adjustment in useful life of certain assets
      4) Correcting an error in computing tax
      5) Changing from the accrual method to the installment method of reporting income

   c. Income is reported when it can be estimated with reasonable accuracy. Adjustments are made in a later year for any differences between the actual amount and the previously reported amounts.

2. **Tax Year**

   a. The accounting method determines the tax year, which is the annual accounting period used to keep the person's books and records, in which an item is includible or deductible in computing taxable income. Federal income tax is imposed on taxable income.

   b. The taxable period is adopted in a person's first tax year and includes the following:

      1) A **calendar year** is the 12-month period ending on December 31.
      2) A **fiscal year** is any 12-month period ending on the last day of a month.
      3) A **52- or 53-week tax year** is also allowed.
      4) A **short tax year** is allowed for a business not in existence for an entire year (365 or 366 days), e.g., the start-up year or the year at dissolution.

         a) In calculating the tax for a short tax year, the income must first be annualized. Then the tax on the annualized income is calculated, and the final step is to determine the short tax year portion of tax.

$$Annualized\ income = Short\ tax\ year\ income \times \frac{12\ months}{Short\ tax\ year\ months}$$

Calculate tax:

$$Short\ tax\ year\ tax = Annualized\ income\ tax \times \frac{Short\ tax\ year\ months}{12\ months}$$

      5) A change of tax year generally requires IRS consent, and a short tax year return is then required.

3. **Cash Method**

   a. A cash-method taxpayer accounts for income when one of the following occurs:

      1) Cash is actually received
      2) A cash equivalent is actually received
      3) Cash or its equivalent is constructively received

   b. At the time a person receives noncash forms of income, such as property or services, the fair market value is included in gross income. This applies even if the property or service can be currently converted into cash at an amount lower than face value.

1) A **cash equivalent** is property that is readily convertible into cash and typically has a maturity of 3 months or less. Cash equivalents are so near to maturity that the risk of loss due to a change in value is immaterial. Cash equivalents include

   a) Checks (valued at face)
   b) Promissory notes (valued at FMV)
   c) Property (e.g., land, transferable at current FMV)

2) If the value of property received cannot be determined, the value of what was given in exchange for it is treated as the amount of income received.

EXAMPLE

A CPA performs various services for a start-up company in exchange for stock options. If the value of the stock options cannot be determined, the value of the services performed is included in income.

---

3) If both the property received and the property given are impossible to value (e.g., an unsecured promise to pay from a person with unknown creditworthiness), the transaction is treated as open, and the consideration is not viewed as income until its value can be ascertained.

c. Under the doctrine of **constructive receipt**, an item is included in gross income when a person has an unqualified right to immediate possession.

   1) A person constructively receives income in the tax year during which it is credited to his or her account, set apart for him or her, or otherwise made available so that (s)he may draw upon it at any time.

      a) It is more than a billing, offer, or promise to pay.
      b) It includes ability to use on demand, as with escrowed funds subject to a person's order.
      c) Deferring deposit of a check does not defer income. However, dishonor (i.e., bounced or returned checks) retroactively negates the income.

   2) Constructive receipt **by an agent** is imputed to the principal.

   3) Income is not constructively received if the taxpayer's control of its receipt is subject to substantial restrictions or limitations (e.g., a valid deferred compensation agreement).

EXAMPLE

John is awarded a $10,000 bonus in 2017. If only half of the bonus is payable in 2017 with the other half paid at the end of 2018, contingent upon John completing another year of service for his employer, only $5,000 is taxable in 2017.

---

d. The **claim-of-right** doctrine indicates that a taxpayer receiving income under a claim of right and without restrictions on its use is taxed on that income in the year received even though the right to retain the income is not yet fixed or the taxpayer may later be required to return it.

e. The **economic or financial benefit** conferred on an employee as compensation has been determined by the courts to be included in the definition of gross income. This economic benefit theory is applied by the IRS in situations in which an employee or independent contractor receives a transfer of property that confers an economic benefit that is equivalent to cash.

   1) The economic benefit theory applies even when the taxpayer cannot choose to take the equivalent value of the income in cash.

EXAMPLE

The fair rental value of a car that a dealership provides for the personal use of its president is gross income.

f.   **Dividends** are constructively received when made subject to the unqualified demand of a shareholder.

1)   If a corporation declares a dividend in December and pays such that the shareholders receive it in January, the dividend is not treated as received in December.

g.   When a **bond** is sold between interest payment dates, the interest accrued up to the sale date is added to the selling price of the bond. The seller includes the accrued interest in gross income.

h.   **Prepaid rent** is gross income when received.

1)   Lease cancellations are included.

2)   Tenant improvements, in lieu of rent, are included.

3)   Security deposits are not considered income when the property owner is obligated to return it to the tenant.

4)   Advance rental payments must be deducted by the payee during the tax periods to which the payments apply.

i.   Tips are gross income when reported. An employee who receives $20 or more in tips a month working for any employer must report the tips to the employer by the 10th day of the following month.

j.   A cash-method taxpayer's **deductions** include expenditures when actually paid, except for prepaid expenses (e.g., rent or insurance). Rules regarding actual payment include the following:

1)   A promise to pay, without more, is not payment.

2)   A check represents payment when delivered or sent.

3)   A third-party (e.g., bank) credit card charge transaction represents current payment with loan proceeds. A second-party (e.g., store) credit card charge transaction is not paid until the charge is paid off.

4)   Adjusted basis in accounts receivable is deductible when the debt becomes worthless. Since a cash-method taxpayer usually has no basis in accounts receivable, (s)he may not deduct bad debts.

5)   Interest on a loan issued at discount, or unstated (imputed) interest, is deductible pro rata over the life of the loan.

6)   A person who uses the cash method to report gross income must use the cash method to report expenses.

4.   **Accrual Method**

a.   An accrual-method taxpayer accounts for income in the period it is actually earned. **Income** is included when all the events have occurred that fix the right to receive it and the amount can be determined with reasonable accuracy.

1)   A right is not fixed if it is contingent on a future event.

2)   The all-events test is satisfied when goods shipped on consignment are sold.

3)   Only in rare and unusual circumstances, in which neither the FMV received nor the FMV given can be ascertained, will the IRS respect holding a transaction open once the right to receive income is fixed. In those circumstances, income is accrued upon receipt.

a)   Proceeds from settlement of a lawsuit are determinable in amount with reasonable accuracy when received.

    b.   **Prepaid income** must generally be included in income when received.

        1)   Prepaid income for **services** may be accrued over the period for which the services are to be performed, but only if it does not extend beyond the end of the next tax year.

            a)   If the taxpayer does not complete the performance within that period, the prepaid income is included in the year following receipt.

        2)   Prepaid **rent** is includible in gross income in the year received (the same as for cash-method and accrual-method taxpayers).

        3)   Prepayments for **merchandise sales** must be included when reported for accounting purposes if reported earlier than when earned.

            a)   The right to income is fixed when it is earned (e.g., when goods are shipped).

    c.   **Expenses** are generally deductible in the period in which they accrue. A taxpayer who uses the accrual method to report gross income must use the accrual method to report expenses.

        1)   The accrual-method taxpayer may claim an allowable deduction when both of the following requirements are met:

            a)   All events have occurred that establish the fact of the liability, including that economic performance has occurred.

            b)   The amount can be determined with reasonable accuracy.

        2)   To the extent the amount of a liability is disputed, the test is not met. But any portion of a (still) contested amount that is paid is deductible.

        3)   **Economic performance** occurs as services are performed or as property is provided or used.

        4)   Under current case law, reserves for contingent liabilities (such as product warranties) are not determinable in amount with reasonable accuracy.

        5)   Accrued vacation pay is generally deductible when paid.

        6)   Deduction of an amount payable to a related party is allowed only when includible in gross income of the related party.

    d.   The accrual method is required of certain persons and for certain transactions.

        1)   If the accrual method is used to report expenses, it must be used to report income items.

        2)   A taxpayer that maintains inventory must use the accrual method with regard to purchases and sales. Exceptions to this inventory rule include

            a)   **Qualifying taxpayers** who satisfy the gross receipts test for each test year.

               i)   The average annual gross receipts (consisting of the test year and the preceding 2 years) for each test year must be $1 million or less.

            b)   **Qualifying small business taxpayers** who satisfy the gross receipts test for each test year (i.e., tax year ending on or after December 31, 2000). The requirements that must be satisfied are

               i)   Average annual gross receipts must be $10 million or less;

              ii)   Taxpayer must not be a corporation (other than an S corp) or a partnership with a corporate partner; and

              iii)   Principal business activity cannot be mining, manufacturing, wholesale trade, retail trade, or information industries.

3) Generally, C corporations, partnerships with a C corporation as a partner, and tax shelters must use the accrual method. **Tax shelters** include any arrangement for which the principal purpose is avoidance of tax, any syndicates, and any enterprise in which the interests must be registered as a security. Exceptions to the general rule allow the following taxpayers to use the cash method if the entity is not a tax shelter:

a) Qualified personal service corporations

b) Entities that meet the gross receipts test by having $5 million or less average gross receipts in the 3 preceding years

c) Farming or tree-raising businesses

4) The accrual method of accounting is generally required when there are inventories.

The accounting rules for income and deduction items under both the cash and accrual methods have often been tested. The AICPA has used questions that have focused on the timing of the inclusions of various income and expense items under each method.

---

5. **Inventory Method**

a. The inventory method used must clearly reflect income and conform to generally accepted accounting principles of the trade or business.

1) Gross income includes receipts reduced by cost of goods sold (COGS), whether purchased or manufactured.

2) Regulations require the particular treatment of certain items or an alternative acceptable treatment.

b. Inventory may be valued at cost or at the lower of cost or FMV.

c. **Purchased merchandise** is invoice price reduced by trade discounts and increased by handling charges, such as freight.

$$Cost = Purchase\ price - Trade\ discounts + Handling\ charges$$

1) Cash discounts may instead be treated as income.

2) Taxpayers with average annual gross receipts over $10 million for the 3 preceding tax years must allocate purchasing costs (e.g., administrative, warehousing) between COGS and inventory.

d. **Produced merchandise** cost must be calculated using the full absorption costing method.

1) **Direct costs** of material and labor are included in inventory.

2) **Overhead costs** for manufacturing are also included (e.g., costs for plant administration, plant maintenance such as rent, utilities, insurance, and support costs such as payroll and warehousing).

3) **Nonmanufacturing costs** (e.g., marketing) need not be included in inventory, but interest must be included in inventory on property that is real or requires more than 2 years of production (1 year if it costs more than $1 million).

e. Any of the following **standard methods** may be used to determine inventory costs: specific identification, average cost, FIFO, and LIFO.

1) **FIFO** assumes that the first items acquired are the first items sold. Ending inventory contains the most recently acquired items.

2) **LIFO** assumes that the latest items acquired are the first items sold. If LIFO is used, inventory must be valued at cost. In a period of rising prices, LIFO results in a higher cost of goods sold than FIFO. Because COGS is higher, net income (NI) is lower, resulting in lower current tax liability.

   a) LIFO may only be used for tax purposes if it is used for financial reporting.

   NOTE: Since 2008, taxpayers using a rolling-average method for financial accounting purposes are allowed to use the same method for tax purposes if the related safe harbor rules are satisfied.

6. **Long-Term Contracts**

   a. A long-term contract is a contract completed in a tax year subsequent to the one in which it was entered into for building, construction, installation, or manufacturing. Long-term manufacturing contracts are for items that normally require more than 12 months to complete or that are unique and not usually inventory items.

      1) A trade or business of a taxpayer must use the same method for each of its long-term contracts.

      2) Long-term contract rules apply to direct costs and allocable portions of labor, material, and overhead costs.

      3) Costs of the following do not need to be allocated to a specific contract:

         a) Unaccepted bids
         b) Marketing
         c) Research and development (if not restricted to the specific contract)

   b. The **completed-contract method** accounts for (reports) receipts and expenditures in the tax year in which the contract is completed. The method is allowed only for

      1) Home construction projects or
      2) Small businesses (average annual gross receipts not greater than $10 million for the 3 preceding tax years) whose construction contracts are expected to take not greater than 2 years to complete.

   c. The **percentage-of-completion method** reports as income that portion of the total contract price that represents the percentage of total work completed in the year. It may be measured by the ratio of costs for the tax year to total expected costs.

      Formula:

Contract price	$ XXX
Minus: Total estimated cost **of contract**[1]	(XXX)
Estimated total gross profit	$ XXX
Times: Percent completed[2]	XXX
Gross profit recognized to date	$ XXX
Minus: Gross profit recognized in prior periods	(XXX)
Gross profit recognized in current period	$ XXX

      [1]Cost incurred to date plus remaining estimated cost **to complete**

      [2] $\dfrac{\text{Total cost to date}}{\text{Total estimated cost \textbf{of contract}}}$

      1) When the contract is complete, the taxpayer must pay interest on any additional tax that would have been incurred if actual total costs had been used instead of expected costs.

      2) The taxpayer may elect not to apply the above rule if the cumulative taxable income or loss using estimated costs is within 10% of the cumulative taxable income or loss using actual costs.

7. **Installment Method**

   a. The installment method is required for installment sales by both cash-method and accrual-method taxpayers, unless an election is made not to apply the method.

      1) An installment sale is a disposition of property in which at least one payment is received after the year of sale.

      2) The method applies only to gains.

      3) A loss on an installment sale is fully recognized in the year realized (unless recognition would be deferred even if the sale was not an installment sale).

   b. The installment sales method is generally not applied to the following sales:

      1) Inventory personal property sales
      2) Revolving credit personal property sales
      3) Dealer dispositions
      4) Securities, generally, if publicly traded
      5) Sales by manufacturers of tangible personal property

   c. Installment sale income is determined as follows:

      1) Calculate gross profit:

         $$Contract\ price\ -\ Cost\ of\ goods\ sold$$

      2) Calculate gross profit percentage:

         $$\frac{Gross\ profit}{Contract\ price}$$

      3) Calculate current-year installment sale income:

         $$Current\text{-}year\ receipts\ \times\ Gross\ profit\ percentage$$

   d. The full amount of any depreciation recapture recharacterized as ordinary income must be recognized in the year of sale, regardless of the payments received. This does not apply to S-L depreciation recapture of Sec. 1250 property because it is not recharacterized as ordinary income.

8. **Hybrid Methods**

   a. Any combination of permissible accounting methods may be employed if the combination clearly reflects income and is consistently used.

   b. If inventory is used, the accrual method must be used for purchases and sales. The cash method may be used for other receipts and expenses if income is clearly reflected.

   c. A person may use different methods for separate businesses.

Stop and review! You have completed the outline for this subunit. Study multiple-choice questions 1 through 5 beginning on page 114.

4.2 GROSS INCOME

1. **Overview**

    a. The Internal Revenue Code (IRC) defines gross income as all income from whatever source derived except as otherwise provided.

    b. The IRC enumerates a non-exhaustive list of the types of income that constitute gross income as follows:

        1) Compensation for services, including fees, commissions, and fringe benefits
        2) Gross income derived from business
        3) Gains derived from dealings in property
        4) Interest
        5) Rents
        6) Royalties
        7) Dividends
        8) Alimony and separate maintenance payments
        9) Annuities
        10) Income from life insurance and endowment contracts
        11) Pensions
        12) Income from discharge of indebtedness
        13) Distributive share of partnership gross income
        14) Income in respect of a decedent (income earned but not received before death)
        15) Income from an interest in an estate or trust

    c. Some types of gross income not enumerated in Sec. 61 are specifically included by other IRC sections or case law.

        1) Other types of income also constitute gross income unless a statute specifically excludes them.

EXAMPLE

John receives a lump sum for signing a noncompete agreement. John should recognize the entire lump sum as ordinary income in the year received.

NOTE: To enable better understanding of the numerous gross income categories, we have provided a "snap-shot" of the applicable Form 1040 line number(s), forms, and schedules with which the gross income items are associated. The forms referenced on the following pages may be accessed at www.irs.gov/forms-pubs.

2.   Compensation for Services

From Form 1040

| 7 | Wages, salaries, tips, etc. Attach Form(s) W-2 . . . . | 7 | |

a.   **All compensation for personal services (including fees, commissions, and similar items) is gross income** regardless of form of payment.

   1)   If property or credit is given in lieu of cash or check, the FMV of the property or credit is included in gross income.

   2)   Gross income of an employee includes any amount paid by an employer for a liability (including taxes) or an expense of the employee.

EXAMPLE

Rick's employer pays his car payment in lieu of direct deposit into Rick's personal account, and the payment is reported as gross income.

b.   All wages (including tips) received by the taxpayer are listed on Form W-2, *Wage and Tax Statement*. A sample of Form W-2 appears below.

22222	Void ☐	a Employee's social security number	For Official Use Only ▶ OMB No. 1545-0008	

b Employer identification number (EIN)	**1** Wages, tips, other compensation	**2** Federal income tax withheld
c Employer's name, address, and ZIP code	**3** Social security wages	**4** Social security tax withheld
	5 Medicare wages and tips	**6** Medicare tax withheld
	7 Social security tips	**8** Allocated tips
d Control number	**9** Verification code	**10** Dependent care benefits
e Employee's first name and initial Last name Suff.	**11** Nonqualified plans	**12a** See instructions for box 12
	13 Statutory employee ☐ Retirement plan ☐ Third-party sick pay ☐	**12b**
	14 Other	**12c**
		12d
f Employee's address and ZIP code		

15 State Employer's state ID number	**16** State wages, tips, etc.	**17** State income tax	**18** Local wages, tips, etc.	**19** Local income tax	**20** Locality name

Form **W-2** Wage and Tax Statement

Copy A For Social Security Administration — Send this entire page with Form W-3 to the Social Security Administration; photocopies are **not** acceptable.

Department of the Treasury—Internal Revenue Service

For Privacy Act and Paperwork Reduction Act Notice, see the separate instructions.

Cat. No. 10134D

Do Not Cut, Fold, or Staple Forms on This Page

c.   The following types of income must also be included on Form W-2 and in the total on line 7 of Form 1040.

1)   All wages received as a household employee. An employer is not required to provide a Form W-2 to the taxpayer if the employer paid the taxpayer wages of less than $2,000 in 2017.

2)   Tip income the taxpayer did not report to the employer. This should include any allocated tips reported in box 8 on Form W-2. Also include the value of any noncash tips the taxpayer received, such as tickets, passes, or other items of value.

3)   Dependent care benefits that are reported in box 10 of Form W-2. Form W-2 instructions list income exclusion requirements.

4)   Employer-provided adoption benefits, which should be shown in box 12 of Form(s) W-2 with code T. Form W-2 instructions list income exclusion requirements.

5)   Scholarship and fellowship grants not reported on Form W-2.

6)   Excess salary deferrals. The amount deferred is reported in box 12 of Form W-2. Form W-2 instructions list income exclusion requirements.

d.   If an employer transfers property to an employee at less than its FMV **(bargain purchase)**, the difference may be income to the employee and treated as compensation for personal services.

e.   **Scholarships or fellowships** received for room, board, or incidental expenses are gross income.

f.   **Reimbursed employee expenses** plans include those that are

1)   Non-accountable. Under non-accountable plans, employee reimbursements (advances) are included in gross income, and all expenses may be deducted from AGI subject to the 2% floor.

2)   Accountable. Under accountable plans, employees must submit requests for reimbursement. Only reimbursements in excess of expenses must be included in gross income.

EXAMPLE

John submitted reimbursement requests to his employer for $10,500 in airfare. John was later refunded for $500 of the airfare. If John does not remit the funds to his employer, John must include the $500 in gross income.

---

g.   **Qualified reimbursements for moving expenses** are excluded from gross income. If the reimbursement is not for qualified moving expenses, it is included in gross income.

3. Interest and Dividends

From Form 1040

8a	**Taxable** interest. Attach Schedule B if required	**8a**	
b	**Tax-exempt** interest. **Do not** include on line 8a **8b**		
9a	Ordinary dividends. Attach Schedule B if required	**9a**	
b	Qualified dividends **9b**		

a. **Interest income** is gross income for tax purposes unless an exclusion applies. Examples of interest income include

1) Merchandise premium (e.g., a toaster given to a depositor for opening an interest-bearing account).
2) Imputed interest on below-market term loans.
3) Interest on state, local, and federal tax refunds.

b. Generally, payers of interest income send the taxpayer Form 1099-INT listing the interest income amount.

1) **Taxable interest** is reported on Form 1040 with Schedule B (sample provided on next page) attached if the total is over $1,500.

c. **Original Issue Discount (OID)** is the excess, if any, of the stated redemption price at maturity over the issue price and is included in income based on the effective interest rate method of amortization.

EXAMPLE

Cathy purchases a 20-year, 7% bond at original issue for $10,000. The stated redemption price is $12,400, and interest is paid annually. The ratable monthly portion of OID is $10. Assume that the effective rate of interest is 10%. During the first year held, interest income is $1,000 ($10,000 × 10%) and interest received is $868 ($12,400 × 7%). The difference of $132 ($1,000 – $868) is included in income under the effective interest rate method. This amount increases the investor's book value from $10,000 to $10,132. The second year's interest is $1,013.20, and the discount amortization is $145.20.

---

d. Generally, payers of dividends send the taxpayer Form 1099-DIV listing ordinary and qualified dividends amounts.

1) **Ordinary dividends** are reported on Form 1040 with Schedule B attached if the total is over $1,500 or the taxpayer received, as a nominee, ordinary dividends that actually belong to someone else.
2) **Qualified dividends** are reported on Form 1040 and are also included in the ordinary dividend total.

e. **Dividend reinvestment plans (DRP)** allow a taxpayer to use his or her dividends to buy more shares of stock in the corporation instead of receiving the dividends in cash. The dividends are included in gross income.

1) The basis of stock received as a result of a DRP is the FMV of the stock (determined on the dividend payment date).
2) If the DRP allows a member to use the dividends to buy stock at a price less than FMV, the discount (FMV – Discounted price) is gross income to the member.
   a) If the DRP allows a member to use cash to purchase stock at a discounted price, the discount is included in gross income.
3) Any service charge subtracted from the cash dividends before the dividends are used to buy additional stock is considered dividend income.

EXAMPLE

David is a member of a DRP. He received $500 in dividends. On that date, he purchased five shares for $100 per share (FMV = $150 per share). David must report the $500 dividend as gross income and the $250 discount as gross income.

SCHEDULE B **(Form 1040A or 1040)** Department of the Treasury Internal Revenue Service (99)	**Interest and Ordinary Dividends** ▶ Attach to Form 1040A or 1040. ▶ Go to *www.irs.gov/ScheduleB* for instructions and the latest information.	OMB No. 1545-0074 **[Year]** Attachment Sequence No. **08**

Name(s) shown on return | Your social security number

Part I

Interest

(See instructions and the instructions for Form 1040A, or Form 1040, line 8a.)

Note: If you received a Form 1099-INT, Form 1099-OID, or substitute statement from a brokerage firm, list the firm's name as the payer and enter the total interest shown on that form.

		Amount
1	List name of payer. If any interest is from a seller-financed mortgage and the buyer used the property as a personal residence, see the instructions and list this interest first. Also, show that buyer's social security number and address ▶	**1**
2	Add the amounts on line 1	**2**
3	Excludable interest on series EE and I U.S. savings bonds issued after 1989. Attach Form 8815	**3**
4	Subtract line 3 from line 2. Enter the result here and on Form 1040A, or Form 1040, line 8a . . . . ▶	**4**

Note: If line 4 is over $1,500, you must complete Part III.

Part II

Ordinary Dividends

(See instructions and the instructions for Form 1040A, or Form 1040, line 9a.)

Note: If you received a Form 1099-DIV or substitute statement from a brokerage firm, list the firm's name as the payer and enter the ordinary dividends shown on that form.

		Amount
5	List name of payer ▶	**5**
6	Add the amounts on line 5. Enter the total here and on Form 1040A, or Form 1040, line 9a . . . . ▶	**6**

Note: If line 6 is over $1,500, you must complete Part III.

Part III

Foreign Accounts and Trusts

(See instructions.)

You must complete this part if you **(a)** had over $1,500 of taxable interest or ordinary dividends; **(b)** had a foreign account; or **(c)** received a distribution from, or were a grantor of, or a transferor to, a foreign trust.

		Yes	No
7a	At any time during [Year], did you have a financial interest in or signature authority over a financial account (such as a bank account, securities account, or brokerage account) located in a foreign country? See instructions		
	If "Yes," are you required to file FinCEN Form 114, Report of Foreign Bank and Financial Accounts (FBAR), to report that financial interest or signature authority? See FinCEN Form 114 and its instructions for filing requirements and exceptions to those requirements		
b	If you are required to file FinCEN Form 114, enter the name of the foreign country where the financial account is located ▶		
8	During [Year], did you receive a distribution from, or were you the grantor of, or transferor to, a foreign trust? If "Yes," you may have to file Form 3520. See instructions		

For Paperwork Reduction Act Notice, see your tax return instructions. | Cat. No. 17146N | Schedule B (Form 1040A or 1040) [Year]

4. Taxable State and Local Refunds or Credits

From Form 1040

| 10 | Taxable refunds, credits, or offsets of state and local income taxes . . . . . . | 10 | |

a. Payers of state or local income tax refunds, credits, or offsets send the taxpayer Form 1099-G listing the amount to be reported.

b. None of the refund is taxable if, in the year the taxpayer paid the tax, the taxpayer either

1) Did not itemize deductions or
2) Did not elect to deduct state and local income taxes.

EXAMPLE

In 2017, a taxpayer who files single elected to itemize deductions, claiming $7,000 of state income tax paid. In 2018, the state refunded $2,000. The taxpayer must include the refund in gross income for 2018 to the extent the 2017 deduction exceeded the 2017 standard deduction, which is $650 ($7,000 itemized deduction – $6,350 standard deduction for 2017).

---

5. **Alimony and separate maintenance payments** are included in the gross income of the recipient (payee) and are deducted from the gross income of the payor.

From Form 1040

| 11 | Alimony received . . . . | 11 | |

a. A payment is considered to be alimony (even if paid to a third party) when it is

1) Paid in cash
2) Paid pursuant to a written divorce or separation instrument
3) Terminated at death of recipient
4) Not designated as other than alimony (e.g., child support)
5) Not paid to a member of the same household
6) Not paid to a spouse with whom the taxpayer is filing a joint return

b. **Payments to a third party** for the benefit of the payor's ex-spouse are considered qualified alimony payments if all other requirements are met.

c. **Property settlements** are not treated as alimony.

1) Property transferred to a spouse or former spouse incident to a divorce is treated as a transfer by gift, which is specifically excluded from gross income.

a) **"Incident to a divorce"** means a transfer of property within 1 year after the date the marriage ceases or a transfer of property related to the cessation of the marriage.

b) This exclusion does not apply if the spouse or former spouse is a nonresident alien.

d. **Child support** payments are an exclusion from the gross income of the recipient and are not deductible by the payor. These payments are not alimony.

1) If the divorce or separation instrument specifies payments of both alimony and child support and only **partial payments** are made, the payments are considered to be child support until this obligation is fully paid, and any excess is then treated as alimony.

2) If the payment amount is to be reduced based on a contingency relating to a child (e.g., attaining a certain age, marrying), the amount of the **payment reduction** will be treated as child support.

6. Business, Supplemental, and Farm Income

From Form 1040

12	Business income or (loss). Attach Schedule C or C-EZ	**12**		
17	Rental real estate, royalties, partnerships, S corporations, trusts, etc. Attach Schedule E	**17**		
18	Farm income or (loss). Attach Schedule F	**18**		

a. **Business income** includes service and non-service income.

   1) Gross income is calculated in a manner similar to individuals.

   2) Supplemental income is reported on Schedule E and includes rental real estate, royalties, partnerships and LLCs (from Schedule K-1), S corporations (K-1), estates (K-1), and trusts (K-1).

b. Net earnings reported on Schedule C (Form 1040), *Profit or Loss From Business*; Schedule F (1040), *Profit or Loss From Farming*; or other schedules used for reporting self-employment income are included in gross income.

   1) The director of a corporation is considered self-employed, and all director and consulting fees received are included in gross income.

   2) Generally, prepaid income is taxable in the year received whether the taxpayer uses the cash or the accrual method of accounting. However, service and certain non-service advanced payments are allowed a limited 1-year deferral (Rev. Proc. 2004-34).

   3) Prepayments for merchandise inventory are not income until the merchandise is shipped.

EXAMPLE

Beth is a piano instructor. She is a calendar-year taxpayer using the accrual method of accounting. On November 2 of Year 1, she received $4,800 for a contract for 96 1-hour lessons beginning on that date. The contract provided Beth give 8 lessons in Year 1 and 48 lessons in Year 2, with the remaining lessons to be given in Year 3. Beth should report $400 on her Year 1 return and the remaining prepayment of $4,400 on her Year 2 return.

---

c. **Rent** is income from an investment, not from the operation of a business. Lessor gross income includes

   1) A bonus received for granting a lease. However, a lessee's refundable deposit is not income to the lessor.

   2) Value received to cancel or modify a lease. Amounts received by a lessee to cancel a lease, however, are treated as amounts realized on disposition of an asset/property (a capital gain).

   3) An amount paid by a lessee to maintain the property in lieu of rent, e.g., property tax payments. The lessor may be entitled to a deduction for all or part of the amount, e.g., property tax deduction.

   4) The FMV of lessee improvements made to the property in lieu of rent. The **cost of maintenance** can be deducted by the lessee as a rental expense. The **cost of capital expenditures** can be capitalized and depreciated by the lessee. The FMV of lessee improvements not made in lieu of rent are excluded.

NOTE: Study Unit 8, Subunit 1, has more detailed coverage of when to expense and when to capitalize costs.

   5) Prepaid rent, with no restriction as to its use, which is income when received regardless of the method of accounting

   6) Rental income from a residence unless the residence is rented out for less than 15 days a year.

     a) If rental income is excluded, the corresponding rental deductions are also disallowed.

d. **Bartered services or goods** are included in gross income at the fair market value of the item(s) received in exchange for the services.

1) Bartered exchanges are required to file Form 1099-B, and the transaction is recorded on Form 1040 Schedule C.

e. **Royalties** are payments to an owner by people who use some right belonging to that owner; thus, royalties constitute gross income.

f. A partner's share of **partnership income** is included in the partner's gross income, whether distributed or not. An owner's pro rata share of **S corporation income** is also included, whether distributed or not.

g. **Income in respect of a decedent** (income earned but not received before death) and **income from an interest in an estate or trust** is included in gross income.

NOTE: Gross Income from Self-Employment (Schedule C) and Farming Income (Schedule F) are discussed in detail in Study Unit 5.

7. **Investment income (including gains derived from dealings in property).** An investor in property seeks a return of the investment (capital) and gross income from the investment, which may be in the form of gains, interest, rents, royalties, or dividends.

From Form 1040

13	Capital gain or (loss). Attach Schedule D if required. If not required, check here ▶ ☐	13		
14	Other gains or (losses). Attach Form 4797	14		

a. A gain on disposition of investment property is generally the net increase (appreciation) in the value of the property.

1) **Realization** of investment income occurs upon a taxable event such as a disposition of the property by a sale or an exchange. **Realized gain** is calculated as follows:

Total money received and to be received
+ FMV[1] of property received and to be received
+ Amount of liabilities transferred with the property
− Any selling expenses
= **Amount realized**
− Adjusted basis
= **Gain (or loss) realized**

[1]FMV = Fair market value at time of disposition

b. All gain realized is **recognized gain** unless a statutory provision provides for its nonrecognition by way of exclusion or deferral. Recognition means the income is to be included in gross income.

c. **Adjusted basis (AB)** indicates the amount of capital invested in the property and not yet recovered by tax benefit (i.e., depreciation). Adjusted basis generally is computed as follows:

Basis on acquisition (e.g., cost)
+ Debt on property
± Adjustments to basis (e.g., depreciation, improvements)
= AB

d. If the taxpayer **sold a capital asset** (e.g., stock), the taxpayer must attach Form 8949, *Sales and Other Dispositions of Capital Assets,* and Schedule D, *Capital Gains and Losses.*

e. If the taxpayer **sold or exchanged assets used in a trade or business** (e.g., delivery trucks), the taxpayer must complete and attach Form 4797, *Sales of Business Property,* and report the results as other gains or losses on Form 1040.

8. Retirement Income

From Form 1040

15a	IRA distributions .	**15a**			**b** Taxable amount . . .	**15b**	
16a	Pensions and annuities	**16a**			**b** Taxable amount . . .	**16b**	

a. An **individual retirement account (IRA)** is a personal savings plan that gives the taxpayer tax advantages for setting aside money for retirement. Advantages of an IRA include

   1) Contributions the taxpayer makes to an IRA may be fully or partially deductible, depending on which type of IRA the taxpayer has and the taxpayer's circumstances.

   2) Generally, amounts in the taxpayer's IRA (including earnings and gains) are not taxed until distributed. In some cases, amounts are not taxed at all (or partially taxed) if distributed according to the rules.

b. Payers of IRA distributions send the taxpayer Form 1099-R listing the gross distribution and the taxable amount (if known) before income tax or other deductions were withheld.

c. A **pension** is generally a series of definitely determinable payments (most often paid in the form of an annuity) made to a taxpayer after the taxpayer retires from work.

   1) Pension payments are made regularly and are based on such factors as years of service and prior compensation. Therefore, the rules for pensions are similar to the rules for annuities.

      a) The investment in the pension is the amount contributed by the employee in after-tax dollars.

      b) Amounts withdrawn early are treated as a recovery of the employee's contributions (excluded from gross income) and of the employer's contributions (included in gross income). After all contributions are withdrawn, additional withdrawals are fully included in gross income.

         i) However, a noncontributory plan results in all withdrawals being included in gross income.

d. **Annuity** payments are included in gross income unless a statute provides for their exclusion.

   1) Retirees are able to recover their contributions to their pensions (cost of annuity) tax-free.

   2) Any proceeds in excess of the cost of the annuity or contributions are included in gross income.

e. Generally, the taxpayer will receive Form 1099-R listing the total amount of the taxpayer's pension and annuity payments before income tax or other deductions were withheld.

From Form 1040

19	Unemployment compensation	**19**	

9. **Unemployment benefits** received under a federal or state program are gross income.

a. The payer of unemployment compensation sends the taxpayer Form 1099-G listing the amount to be reported.

b. **Supplemental unemployment benefits** from a noncontributory fund that is company financed are taxable as wages (not unemployment).

   1) Supplemental unemployment benefits to be reported are listed on Form W-2.

From Form 1040

20a	Social security benefits	20a			b	Taxable amount . . .	20b		

10. **Social Security Benefits (SSB)** are generally not taxable unless additional income is received. The gross income inclusion is dependent upon the relation of provisional income (PI) to the base amount (BA) and the adjusted base amount (ABA).

    a. Treating SSB as other annuity benefits are treated is not practical because SS amounts are very difficult to predict. Taxpayers' earnings change drastically over a lifetime, and Congress occasionally readjusts benefit formulas.

    b. Congress's solution has been to tax only that portion of SSB that exceeds a base amount related to other sources of income. SSB are calculated as follows:

       1) PI = Adjusted gross income (AGI) + Tax-exempt interest (excluded foreign income) + 50% of SSB.

       2) Base amount (BA) is $32,000 if married filing jointly (MFJ), $0 if married filing separately and having lived with spouse at any time during the tax year (MFSLT), or $25,000 for all others.

       3) Adjusted base amount (ABA) is $44,000 if MFJ, $0 if MFSLT, or $34,000 for all others.

       4) If PI < BA, there is no inclusion. If PI falls between BA and ABA, up to 50% of SSB will be included. If PI > ABA, up to 85% of SSB will be included.

EXAMPLE

Mr. and Mrs. Slom, both over 65 and filing jointly, received $20,000 in Social Security benefits. Additionally, they reported $30,000 of taxable interest, $15,000 of tax-exempt interest, $18,000 in dividends, and a taxable pension of $16,000. Therefore, their AGI, excluding Social Security benefits, is $64,000 ($30,000 taxable interest + $18,000 dividends + $16,000 taxable pension payments).

- Provisional income is $89,000 [$64,000 AGI + $15,000 tax-exempt interest + 50% of SS benefits ($10,000)].
- The adjusted base amount is $44,000.
- The amount of $17,000 (85% of SS benefits) will be included in gross income since it is less than 85% of the excess of PI over the ABA plus the lesser of 50% of the incremental BA ($6,000) or 50% of SS benefits.
- Calculation of included Social Security benefits is as follows:

1)	AGI, excluding SS benefits		$64,000
2)	+ Tax-exempt interest (excluded foreign income)	+	15,000
3)	= Modified AGI	=	$79,000
4)	+ 50% of SS benefits	+	10,000
5)	= Provisional income (PI)	=	$89,000
6)	− BA ($32,000, $25,000, or $0)	−	32,000
7)	= Excess PI (If < $0, then $0 inclusion)	=	$57,000
8)	− Incremental base amount ($12,000, $9,000, or $0)	−	12,000
9)	= Excess PI	=	$45,000
10)	Smaller of amount in line 7 or 8		$12,000
11)	50% of line 10		6,000
12)	Smaller of amount in line 4 or 11		6,000
13)	Multiply line 9 by 85%		38,250
14)	Add lines 12 and 13		44,250
15)	SS benefits × 85%		17,000
16)	Taxable benefits = Smaller of amount in line 14 or 15		17,000

NOTE: SSB is listed on Form SSA-1099 and reported on Form 1040.

FORM SSA-1099 – SOCIAL SECURITY BENEFIT STATEMENT

[Year]	• PART OF YOUR SOCIAL SECURITY BENEFITS SHOWN IN BOX 5 MAY BE TAXABLE INCOME. • SEE THE REVERSE FOR MORE INFORMATION.

Box 1. Name	Box 2. Beneficiary's Social Security Number

Box 3. Benefits Paid in Year	Box 4. Benefits Repaid to SSA in Year	Box 5. Net Benefits for Year *(Box 3 minus Box 4)*

DESCRIPTION OF AMOUNT IN BOX 3	DESCRIPTION OF AMOUNT IN BOX 4
	Box 6. Voluntary Federal Income Tax Withheld
	Box 7. Address
	Box 8. Claim Number *(Use this number if you need to contact SSA.)*

Form **SSA-1099-SM**   **DO NOT RETURN THIS FORM TO SSA OR IRS**

11. Other Income

From Form 1040

21	Other income. List type and amount		21	

a. **Gambling winnings** are gross income and can be offset by gambling losses (e.g., non-winning lottery tickets) only to the extent of winnings and only as a miscellaneous itemized deduction. However, gambling losses over winnings for the taxable year cannot be used as a carryover or carryback to reduce gambling income from other years.

b. **Prizes or awards** in a form other than money are included in gross income at the FMV of the property.

　　1) The honoree may avoid inclusion by rejecting the prize or award.

　　2) Some prizes and awards are excludable (e.g., transfers to charities, employee achievement).

c. **Business inducements** transfer value (even as "gifts") in exchange for past or anticipated economic benefits.

　　1) The FMV of the inducement is income to the recipient.

d. Gross income includes the **Recovery of Tax Benefit** items in a prior year.

EXAMPLE

Taxpayer writes off bad debt in Year 1. In Year 7, the debtor pays Taxpayer the principal of the debt written off, which must be included in GI since the deduction in Year 1 reduced the tax liability.

---

e. **Treasure troves** that are undisputedly in the taxpayer's possession are gross income for the tax year.

EXAMPLE

Rich purchased an old piano for $500 last year. In the current year, Rich finds $10,000 hidden in the piano. Rich must report the $10,000 as gross income in the current year.

---

f. Income from **illegal activities**, such as money from dealing illegal drugs, must be included in the taxpayer's income on Form 1040 or on Schedule C (Form 1040) if from the taxpayer's self-employment activity.

g. Gross income includes **discharge (cancellation) of indebtedness** when a debt is canceled in whole or part for consideration.

　　1) If a debtor performs services to satisfy a debt, the debtor must recognize the amount of the debt as income.

　　2) If a creditor gratuitously cancels a debt, the amount forgiven is treated as a gift.

　　3) Gross income **does not include** discharges that

　　　　a) Occur in bankruptcy (except a stock for debt transfer).

　　　　b) Occur when the debtor is insolvent but not in bankruptcy.

　　　　　　i) The maximum amount that can be excluded is the amount by which liabilities exceed the FMV of assets.

　　　　c) Are related to qualified farm indebtedness.

　　　　d) Are related to principal residence indebtedness. The basis of the residence is reduced by the excluded income.

　　　　NOTE: This exception expired December 31, 2016, but is likely to be renewed and applicable retroactively for 2017. Therefore, this course covers it as if it has been extended for 2017.

      e)   Are related to a purchase-money debt reduction in which a seller reduces the debt and the debtor is not in bankruptcy and is not insolvent. The discharge is treated as a purchase price adjustment.

    4)   When a taxpayer excludes discharge of indebtedness under 1), 2), or 3) above and on the previous page, the taxpayer must reduce his or her tax attributes in the following order:

        a)   NOLs
        b)   General business credit
        c)   Capital loss carryovers
        d)   Basis reductions

        NOTE: However, the taxpayer may first elect to decrease the basis in depreciable property.

    5)   Generally, the creditor will send the taxpayer Form 1099-C listing the amount of cancellation of debt to be reported.

   h.   **Subpart F income** provisions were enacted to prevent U.S. persons from deferring income recognition by shifting income to low- or no-tax jurisdictions.

    1)   In general, qualified income from controlled foreign corporations (CFC) is included in income for the U.S. shareholder. The following defines the key terms for understanding what is qualified income:

        a)   CFC: A foreign corporation owned more than 50% by U.S. shareholders.
        b)   U.S. Shareholder: A U.S. person with 10% or more voting-ownership in the CFC.
        c)   U.S. Person: A U.S. citizen, resident alien, domestic corporation, partnership, estate, or trust.

    2)   Qualified income includes a variety of sources; however, the most significant and only source covered in this review is foreign-based-company income (FBCI). FBCI consists of

        a)   Foreign-personal-holding-company income,
        b)   Foreign-based-company sales income, and
        c)   Foreign-based-company services income.

    3)   The sales income does not qualify if the item sold was manufactured or sold within the country of the CFC.

        a)   The service income only qualifies if the service is performed outside the country of the CFC.

    4)   The provisions of Subpart F are exceedingly intricate and contain numerous general rules, special rules, definitions, exceptions, exclusions, and limitations, which require careful consideration. Only the basics required for the CPA exam are covered in this course.

The AICPA has regularly tested candidates' knowledge of what types of income constitute gross income. Both theoretical and calculation questions have covered this topic.

Stop and review! You have completed the outline for this subunit. Study multiple-choice questions 6 through 13 beginning on page 115.

4.3 EXCLUSIONS

1. **Specifically Stated**

    a. An item of income generally constitutes gross income unless a provision of the IRC **specifically states** that all or part of it is not treated as income.

2. **Not Specifically Stated**

    a. Certain items are not treated as income for federal income tax purposes even though no IRC section specifically excludes them. The following are examples:

        1) **Unrealized income.** Income must be realized before it constitutes gross income. Generally, a gain is not realized until the property is sold or disposed. Mere fluctuations in market value are not treated as income for tax purposes.

        2) **Return of capital.** An amount invested in an asset is generally not treated as income for tax purposes upon an otherwise taxable disposition of the asset. Receipt of payment of debt principal is return of capital and not income. The value of one's own services, however, is not treated as capital invested.

        3) **Cost of goods sold.** This is considered a return of capital.

        4) **Loans.** Receipt of loan funds does not give rise to income.

        5) **Intra-family services.** The value of services rendered by a person for himself or herself is not treated as income for tax purposes. The same applies for gratuitous services performed by one member of a family for another.

        6) **Use of one's own property.** Income is not imputed for the economic benefit of the use of property owned by oneself.

        7) **Survivor benefits for public safety officers killed in the line of duty.** The annuity must be a result of a governmental plan meeting certain requirements and is attributable to the officer's service as a public safety officer.

3. **Life Insurance Proceeds**

    a. In general, proceeds of a life insurance policy paid by reason of the death of the insured are excluded from gross income.

    NOTE: Benefits from "employer-owned" life insurance contracts are to be included in gross income to the extent they exceed premiums paid "effective for contracts issued after August 17, 2006."

    b. The exclusion is allowed regardless of form of payment or recipient. Interest earned on proceeds (after death of the insured) is gross income to the beneficiary.

    c. The amount of each payment in excess of the death benefit principal amount is interest income.

EXAMPLE

A $75,000 policy pays off in $6,000 installments over 15 years. The principal amount per installment, $5,000 ($75,000 ÷ 15 years), is excluded. The remaining $1,000 ($6,000 − $5,000) is taxable interest income.

---

    d. If the owner of a policy transfers the policy to another person for consideration, the proceeds are taxable. However, amounts paid to acquire the policy and subsequent premium payments are treated as return of investment capital.

e. Any amounts received as accelerated death benefits under a life insurance contract for individuals who are either terminally ill (certified by a physician that death can be reasonably expected to result within 24 months) or chronically ill are excluded from gross income.

f. Dividends paid on insurance policies are excluded from gross income to the extent cumulative dividends do not exceed cumulative premiums and provided the cash value does not exceed the net investment, which it normally does not.

   1) Interest on Veterans Administration insurance dividends left on deposit with the VA is excluded from gross income.

4. **Annuity Contracts**

a. Taxpayers are permitted to recover the cost of the annuity (the price paid) tax-free (e.g., dividends from life insurance policy up to the amount of premiums paid). The nontaxable portion of an annuity is determined as follows:

   1) Calculate the expected return, which is equal to the annual payment multiplied by the expected return multiple (life expectancy determined from an actuarial table).

   2) The exclusion ratio is equal to the investment in the contract (or its cost) divided by the expected return.

   3) The current exclusion is calculated by multiplying the exclusion ratio by the amount received during the year.

EXAMPLE

Xavier, age 56, purchased an annuity contract to provide monthly payments of $150 until his death. The annuity cost is $35,000. The annual exclusion is calculated as follows:

Annual payment	$ 1,800
Exclusion multiple	× 27.7
Expected return	$49,860

Age	Exclusion Multiple
55	28.6
56	27.7
57	26.8

Exclusion ratio $\dfrac{35,000}{49,860} = 70\%$

Annual exclusion = $1,260

---

   4) A simplified method is required for retirement plan (employee) annuities with starting dates after November 18, 1996. The nontaxable portion is calculated by dividing the investment in the contract, as of the annuity starting date, by the number of anticipated monthly payments.

Age of Primary Annuitant on the Annuity Starting Date	Number of Anticipated Monthly Payments
55 and under	360
56-60	310
61-65	260
66-70	210
71 and over	160

   a) If the annuity has a fixed number of payments, use that number instead.

5. **Gifts**

    a.   A gift is a transfer for less than full or adequate consideration. The IRC excludes from the gross income of the recipient the value of property acquired by gift.

        1)   Voluntary transfers from employer to employee are presumed to be compensation, not gifts.

6. **Prizes and Awards**

    a.   A prize or award may qualify for exclusion as a scholarship. Additionally, a recipient may exclude the FMV of the prize or award if

        1)   The amount received is in recognition of religious, scientific, charitable, or similar meritorious achievement;

        2)   The recipient is selected without action on his or her part;

        3)   The receipt of the award is not conditioned on substantial future services; and

        4)   The amount is paid by the organization making the award to a tax-exempt organization (including a governmental unit) designated by the recipient.

    b.   A qualified employee achievement plan award is provided under an established written program that does not discriminate in favor of highly compensated employees.

        1)   Employee achievement awards may qualify for exclusion from the recipient employee's gross income if they are awarded as part of a meaningful presentation for safety achievement or length of service and

            a)   The awards do not exceed $400 for all nonqualified plan awards or

            b)   The awards do not exceed $1,600 for all qualified plan awards.

7. **Scholarships and Tuition Reduction**

    a.   Amounts received by an individual as scholarships or fellowships are excluded from gross income to the extent that the individual is a candidate for a degree from a qualified educational institution and the amounts are used for required tuition or fees, books, supplies, or equipment (not personal expenses).

    b.   Gross income includes any amount received, e.g., as tuition reduction, in exchange for the performance of such services as teaching or research.

    c.   Generally, a reduction in undergraduate tuition for an employee of a qualified educational organization does not constitute gross income.

        1)   The exclusion is not allowed for amounts representing payments for services (e.g., research, teaching) performed by the student as a condition for receiving the qualified scholarship.

8. **Student Loan Forgiveness**

    a.   Federal, state, and/or local government student loan indebtedness may be discharged and excluded from income if the former student engages in certain employment (e.g., in a specified location, for a specified period, or for a specified employer).

9. **Redemption of U.S. Savings Bonds to Pay Educational Expenses**

    a.   If a taxpayer pays qualified higher education expenses during the year, a portion of the interest on redemption of a Series EE U.S. Savings Bond is excluded.

    b.   The exclusion rate equals qualified expenses divided by the total of principal and interest (not to exceed 100% or 1.0).

   c.   The amount of qualified expenses is reduced by the total of qualified scholarships (excluded from income), employer-provided educational assistance, expenses for American Opportunity and Lifetime Learning credits, and other higher education related benefits. In order to qualify,

       1)   The bond must have been issued to the taxpayer after December 31, 1989, at a discount.

       2)   The taxpayer, the taxpayer's spouse, or a dependent incurs tuition and fees to attend an eligible educational institution.

       3)   The taxpayer's modified AGI must not exceed a certain limit. For 2017, the exclusion is reduced when MAGI exceeds a threshold of $78,150 ($117,250 if a joint return). The amount at which the benefit is completely phased out is $93,150 ($147,250 if a joint return).

       4)   The purchaser of the bonds must be the sole owner of the bonds (or joint owner with his or her spouse).

       5)   The issue date of the bonds must follow the 24th birthday(s) of the owner(s).

10. Interest on State and Local Government Obligations

From Form 1040

b	Tax-exempt interest. Do not include on line 8a . . .	8b				

   a.   Payments to a holder of a debt obligation incurred by a state or local governmental entity are generally exempt from federal income tax.

Background

Historically, this exemption has been extremely important to state and local governments. It allows them to offer their debt at lower interest rates, thereby lowering their cost of capital.

---

   b.   Exclusion of interest received is allowable even if the obligation is not evidenced by a bond, is in the form of an installment purchase agreement, or is an ordinary commercial debt.

   c.   These obligations must be in registered form.

   d.   The exclusion applies to obligations of states, the District of Columbia, U.S. possessions, and political subdivisions of each of them.

   e.   The interest on certain private activity bonds and arbitrage bonds is not excluded.

       1)   Private activity bonds are bonds of which more than 10% of the proceeds are to be used in a private business and more than 10% of the principal or interest is secured or will be paid by private business property or more than 5% or $5 million of the proceeds are to be used for private loans.

       2)   Interest on private activity bonds can still be excluded if the bond is for residential rental housing developments, public facilities (such as airports or waste removal), or other qualified causes.

11. Compensation for Injury or Sickness

   a.   Gross income does not include benefits specified that might be received in the form of disability pay, health or accident insurance proceeds, workers' compensation awards, or other "damages" for personal physical injury or physical sickness.

    b.   Specifically **excluded** from gross income are amounts received

        1)   By employees as reimbursement for medical care and payments for permanent injury or loss of bodily function under an employer-financed accident or health plan. If the employer contributed to the coverage (employer contributions are excluded), then the amount received must be prorated into taxable and nontaxable amounts. Payments made from a qualified trust on behalf of a self-employed person are considered employer contributions.

        2)   Under workers' compensation acts as compensation for personal injuries or illness.

        3)   Under an accident and health insurance policy purchased by the taxpayer even if the benefits are a substitute for lost income.

        4)   As a pension, annuity, or similar allowance for personal injuries or sickness resulting from active service in the armed forces of any country.

        5)   As wrongful death damages to the extent they were received due to personal injury or sickness.

        6)   As damages for personal injury or physical sickness.

        7)   For emotional distress if an injury has its origin in a physical injury or sickness.

    c.   Specifically **included** in gross income are

        1)   Compensation for slander of reputation.

        2)   Damages for lost profits in a business.

        3)   Punitive damages received.

            a)   If a judgment results in both actual and punitive damages, the judgment must be allocated.

        4)   Damages received **solely** for emotional distress.

    d.   Interest earned on an award for personal injuries is not excluded from gross income.

    e.   Recovery of deductions

        1)   If the taxpayer incurred medical expenses in Year 1, deducted these expenses on his or her Year 1 tax return, and received reimbursement for the same medical expenses in Year 2, the reimbursement is included in gross income on the Year 2 return in an amount equal to the previous deduction.

12. **Recovery of Tax Benefit Item**

    a.   Amounts recovered during the tax year that did not provide a tax benefit in the prior year are excluded.

EXAMPLE

Taxpayer pays state income tax in excess of the standard deduction and itemizes deductions. Subsequent refunds in excess of the applicable standard deduction must be included in gross income. However, if Taxpayer filed Form 1040 EZ, which does not allow for itemizing deductions, and therefore must use the standard deduction, the refund would not be included because no tax benefit was realized.

---

    b.   A similar rule applies to credits.

13. **Gain on Sale of Principal Residence**

    a.   A taxpayer may exclude up to $250,000 ($500,000 for married taxpayers filing jointly) of realized gain on the sale of a principal residence.

14. **Stock Dividends**

    a.   Generally, a shareholder does not include in gross income the value of a stock dividend (or right to acquire stock) declared on its own shares unless one of the following exceptions applies:

        1)   Any shareholder can elect to receive cash or other property.

        2)   Some common stock shareholders receive preferred stock, while other common stock shareholders receive common stock.

3) The distribution is on preferred stock (but a distribution on preferred stock merely to adjust conversion ratios as a result of a stock split or dividend is excluded).

4) If a shareholder receives common stock and cash for a fractional portion of stock, then only the cash received for the fractional portion is included in gross income.

15. **Foreign-Earned Income Exclusion**

a. U.S. citizens may exclude up to $102,100 (in calendar year 2017) of foreign-earned income and a statutory housing cost allowance from gross income.

b. **To qualify for exclusion**, the taxpayer must either be a resident of one or more foreign countries for the entire taxable year or be present in one or more foreign countries for 330 days during a consecutive 12-month period.

c. The $102,100 limitation must be prorated if the taxpayer is not present in (or a resident of) the foreign country for the entire year.

d. This exclusion is in lieu of the foreign tax credit.

e. Deductions attributed to the foreign-earned income (which is excluded) are disallowed.

16. **Lease Improvements**

a. The value of improvements made by the real property lessee, including buildings erected, is excludable by the lessor unless the lessee provided the improvements in lieu of rent. Income realized by the lessor from the improvements subsequent to termination of the lease is included.

b. Amounts received by a retail lessee as cash or rent reductions are not included in gross income if used for qualified construction or improvements to the retail space.

17. **Insurance Payments for Living Expenses**

a. If an individual's principal residence is damaged by casualty or the individual is denied access by governmental authorities to the casualty, then amounts paid to reimburse for living expenses are excluded from gross income. The exclusion is limited to actual living expenses incurred less the normal living expenses the taxpayer would have incurred during the period.

18. **Rental Value of Parsonage**

a. Ministers may exclude from gross income the rental value of a home or a rental allowance to the extent the allowance is used to provide a home. However, for self-employment tax purposes, income is calculated without regard to the housing allowance for nonretired ministers.

19. **Combat Zone Compensation**

a. Military officers may exclude compensation up to an amount equal to the highest rate of basic pay at the highest pay grade that enlisted personnel may receive (plus any hostile fire or imminent danger pay).

b. The exclusion applies only to compensation received while serving in a combat zone or while hospitalized as a result of duty in a combat zone.

c. Military personnel below officer level are allowed the same exclusion without the cap.

20. **Foster Care**

a. Amounts received in return for foster care are excluded.

Candidates should expect to see questions testing exclusions from gross income on the exam and may see questions that give a list of items and ask for the amount of those items excluded from gross income.

Stop and review! You have completed the outline for this subunit. Study multiple-choice questions 14 through 20 beginning on page 118.

QUESTIONS

4.1 Accounting Methods

1. Aviary Corp. sold a building for $600,000. Aviary received a down payment of $120,000, as well as annual principal payments of $120,000 for each of the subsequent 4 years. Aviary purchased the building for $500,000 and claimed depreciation of $80,000. What amount of gain should Aviary report in the year of sale using the installment method?

A. $180,000

B. $120,000

C. $54,000

D. $36,000

Answer (D) is correct.

REQUIRED: The amount of gain reported under the installment method.

DISCUSSION: Under the installment method, the gain recognized is equal to the proceeds received in the current year multiplied by the gross profit percentage. The gross profit percentage is the gross profit divided by the sales price. The gross profit of $180,000 is the sales price less the AB. The AB of the asset is the $500,000 initial cost reduced by the $80,000 depreciation, or $420,000. Thus, the gross profit percentage is equal to 30% ($180,000 gross profit ÷ $600,000 sales price). The only installment received this period is the down payment of $120,000, which is multiplied by the gross profit percentage (30%) for a reported gain of $36,000 currently.

Answer (A) is incorrect. The entire gross profit is not reported in the current period under the installment method. Answer (B) is incorrect. The entire $120,000 down payment should not be reported as a gain in the current period. The reported gain must consider the gross profit percentage, which is multiplied by the current proceeds. Answer (C) is incorrect. Multiplying the gross profit percentage by the gross profit equals $54,000; however, the gain reported in the current period is the gross profit percentages multiplied by the installments received currently.

2. A taxpayer is **not** required to obtain the permission of the Commissioner of Internal Revenue to change from the

A. LIFO method to the FIFO method of valuing inventories.

B. Units-of-production method to the straight-line method of computing depreciation.

C. Cash basis to the accrual basis of reporting income.

D. Accrual method to the installment method of reporting income.

Answer (D) is correct.

REQUIRED: The change that does not require the permission of the IRS.

DISCUSSION: The general rule is that to change an accounting method the taxpayer must obtain the permission of the IRS. In general, the installment method of reporting income may be used by a taxpayer without the permission of the IRS.

Answer (A) is incorrect. A change from LIFO to FIFO requires permission from the IRS. A change from FIFO to LIFO does not require permission. Answer (B) is incorrect. A change from units-of-production to straight-line depreciation requires permission from the IRS. Answer (C) is incorrect. A change from the cash basis to the accrual basis requires permission from the IRS.

3. Soma Corp. had $600,000 in compensation expense for book purposes in Year 1. Included in this amount was a $50,000 accrual for Year 1 nonshareholder bonuses. Soma paid the actual Year 1 bonus of $60,000 on March 1, Year 2. In its Year 1 tax return, what amount should Soma deduct as compensation expense?

A. $600,000

B. $610,000

C. $550,000

D. $540,000

Answer (B) is correct.

REQUIRED: The amount of compensation expense deductible when paid.

DISCUSSION: A deduction is allowed for all ordinary and necessary business expenses paid or incurred during the taxable year, including a reasonable allowance for salaries or other compensation for personal services actually rendered. Because the bonuses were compensation to unrelated parties, Soma accrues and deducts $50,000 of them in Year 1 and an additional $10,000 in Year 2 because the payment in Year 2 was attributable to the Year 1 tax year of an accrual-method taxpayer.

Answer (A) is incorrect. The additional $10,000, although paid in Year 2, was attributable to services rendered in a prior tax year to an accrual-method taxpayer. Answer (C) is incorrect. The amount of $550,000 results from subtracting the accrued nonshareholder bonuses from compensation expense. Answer (D) is incorrect. The amount of $540,000 results from subtracting the actual Year 1 bonuses paid in Year 2 from compensation expense.

4. A cash-basis taxpayer should report gross income

A. Only for the year in which income is actually received in cash.

B. Only for the year in which income is actually received whether in cash or in property.

C. For the year in which income is either actually or constructively received in cash only.

D. For the year in which income is either actually or constructively received, whether in cash or in property.

Answer (D) is correct.
REQUIRED: The time for a cash-basis taxpayer to report gross income.
DISCUSSION: A cash-basis taxpayer should report gross income for the year in which income is either actually or constructively received in cash or property. Constructive receipt is when the payment is made available to the taxpayer or when the taxpayer has economic benefit of the funds.
Answer (A) is incorrect. Gross income is reported by a cash-basis taxpayer when actually or constructively received in cash. Answer (B) is incorrect. Gross income is reported by a cash-basis taxpayer when actually or constructively received in cash or property. Answer (C) is incorrect. Gross income is not limited to cash.

5. Nare, an accrual-basis taxpayer, owns a building which was rented to Mott under a 10-year lease expiring August 31, Year 4. On January 2, Year 1, Mott paid $30,000 as consideration for canceling the lease. On November 1, Year 1, Nare leased the building to Pine under a 5-year lease. Pine paid Nare $10,000 rent for the 2 months of November and December, and an additional $5,000 for the last month's rent. What amount of rental income should Nare report in its Year 1 income tax return?

A. $10,000
B. $15,000
C. $40,000
D. $45,000

Answer (D) is correct.
REQUIRED: A landlord's rental income from various types of payments.
DISCUSSION: Both cash- and accrual-basis taxpayers must include amounts in gross income upon actual or constructive receipt if the taxpayer has an unrestricted claim to such amounts. Since Nare has an unrestricted claim to the $5,000 of rent paid in advance, it is included in his rental income. The amounts received by a lessee to cancel a lease are treated as an amount realized on a disposition of property. However, value received by a lessor to cancel a lease is gross income from rent as if received in lieu of rent.
Answer (A) is incorrect. Money paid as consideration for canceling a lease is also included in rental income. The $5,000 payment by Pine for the last month's rent is also included in rental income for Year 1. Answer (B) is incorrect. The amount of $15,000 does not include the money paid as consideration for canceling the lease. Answer (C) is incorrect. Prepaid income is rent when received even if the lessor uses the accrual method of accounting.

4.2 Gross Income

6. Which of the following conditions must be present in a post-1984 divorce agreement for a payment to qualify as deductible alimony?

I. Payments must be in cash.
II. The payments must end at the recipient's death.

A. I only.
B. II only.
C. Both I and II.
D. Neither I nor II.

Answer (C) is correct.
REQUIRED: The conditions required in a post-1984 divorce agreement for payments to qualify as deductible alimony.
DISCUSSION: In order for payments to qualify as deductible alimony, they must meet all of the following requirements:

1) Paid in cash
2) Paid pursuant to a written divorce or separation instrument
3) Not designated as other than alimony
4) Terminated at death of recipient
5) Not paid to a member of the same household
6) Not paid to a spouse with whom the taxpayer is filing a joint return

7. Pierce Corp., an accrual-basis, calendar-year C corporation, had the following 2017 receipts:

2018 advance rental payments for a lease ending in 2019	$250,000
Lease cancelation payment from a 5-year lease tenant	100,000

Pierce had no restrictions on the use of the advance rental payments and renders no services in connection with the rental income. What amount of gross income should Pierce report on its 2017 tax return?

A. $350,000

B. $250,000

C. $100,000

D. $0

8. Darr, an employee of Source C corporation, is not a shareholder. Which of the following should be included in Darr's gross income?

A. Employer-provided medical insurance coverage under a health plan.

B. A $15,000 gift from the taxpayer's grandparents.

C. The fair market value of land that the taxpayer inherited from an uncle.

D. The dividend income on shares of stock that the taxpayer received for services rendered.

9. An individual received $50,000 during the current year pursuant to a divorce decree. A check for $25,000 was identified as annual alimony, checks totaling $10,000 were identified as annual child support, and a check for $15,000 was identified as a property settlement. What amount should be included in the individual's gross income?

A. $50,000

B. $40,000

C. $25,000

D. $0

Answer (A) is correct.

REQUIRED: The amount of gross income for the current year.

DISCUSSION: Both cash- and accrual-basis taxpayers must include rental payments in gross income upon actual or constructive receipt if the taxpayer has an unrestricted claim to the amount. A lease cancelation payment is in lieu of rent and is included in income like rent. Because Pierce had no restrictions on the use of the payments, the entire amount of the payments is included in income.

Answer (B) is incorrect. A lease cancelation payment is a payment made in lieu of rent and is included in income like rent. Answer (C) is incorrect. Without restrictions on the use, prepaid rent is income when received even if the lessor uses the accrual method of accounting. Answer (D) is incorrect. Without restrictions on the use, prepaid rent is income when received, and lease cancelation payments are made in lieu of rent and are included in income like rent.

Answer (D) is correct.

REQUIRED: The item included in the gross income of an employee.

DISCUSSION: The dividend income as well as the FMV of the stock would be included in Darr's gross income. The FMV of the stock is classified as compensation.

Answer (A) is incorrect. Employer-provided medical coverage is excluded from an employee's gross income. However, any benefits (reimbursement) from the employer-provided plan in excess of expenses should be included. Answer (B) is incorrect. Gifts are excluded from gross income. Answer (C) is incorrect. Land acquired by inheritance is excluded.

Answer (C) is correct.

REQUIRED: The amount included in an individual's gross income.

DISCUSSION: Alimony is gross income to the recipient and deductible by the payor. Alimony is payment in cash, paid pursuant to a written divorce decree, not designated as other than alimony (e.g., child support), terminated at death of recipient, not paid to a member of the same household, and not paid to a spouse with whom the taxpayer is filing a joint return. Child support and property settlement payments are not alimony. Thus, the $25,000 of alimony is included in gross income.

Answer (A) is incorrect. Child support payments are an exclusion from gross income of the recipient and are not deductible by the payor. These payments are not alimony. Property settlement payments are not treated as alimony. They are treated as a transfer by gift, which is specifically excluded from gross income. Answer (B) is incorrect. Property settlement payments are not treated as alimony. They are treated as a transfer by gift, which is specifically excluded from gross income. Answer (D) is incorrect. Alimony is gross income to the recipient and deductible by the payor. Thus, $25,000 of alimony is included in gross income.

10. Easel Co. has elected to reimburse employees for business expenses under a nonaccountable plan. Easel does not require employees to provide proof of expenses and allows employees to keep any amount not spent. Under the plan, Mel, an Easel employee for a full year, gets $400 per month for business automobile expenses. At the end of the year, Mel informs Easel that the only business expense incurred was for business mileage of 8,411 at a rate of 53.5 cents per mile, the IRS standard mileage rate at the time of travel. Mel encloses a check for $300 to refund the overpayment to Easel. What amount should be reported in Mel's gross income for the year?

A. $0

B. $300

C. $4,500

D. $4,800

Answer (D) is correct.

REQUIRED: The gross income reported for reimbursements from a nonaccountable plan.

DISCUSSION: In a nonaccountable plan, the reimbursements are included in the employee's gross income, and all the expenses are deducted from AGI (below-the-line-deductions). These expenses are a miscellaneous itemized deduction subject to the 2% floor. Since the employee accounted to the employer and returned the excess reimbursement, this could have qualified as an "accountable plan." Under an accountable plan, the employee would include nothing in income and take no deduction. However, the company uses a nonaccountable plan, and Mel must include $4,800 ($400 × 12 months) in his gross income.

Answer (A) is incorrect. Under a nonaccountable plan, Mel must include all reimbursements in gross income ($4,800). Answer (B) is incorrect. With a nonaccountable plan, the amount included in gross income is the total reimbursement (not limited to overpayment of the reimbursement). Answer (C) is incorrect. Under a nonaccountable plan, Mel must include all reimbursements in gross income ($4,800).

11. In 2017, Emil Gow won $10,000 in a state lottery and spent $800 for the purchase of lottery tickets. Emil elected the standard deduction on his 2017 income tax return. The amount of lottery winnings that should be included in Emil's 2017 gross income is

A. $0

B. $2,850

C. $3,650

D. $10,000

Answer (D) is correct.

REQUIRED: The amount of state lottery winnings included in gross income.

DISCUSSION: Gambling winnings (whether legal or illegal) are included in gross income. Therefore, Emil must include the full $10,000 in gross income. Gambling losses, i.e., amounts spent on nonwinning tickets, may be deductible but only as an itemized deduction to the extent of gambling winnings.

Answer (A) is incorrect. All gambling winnings constitute gross income. Answer (B) is incorrect. If the standard deduction is claimed, itemized deductions are not allowed. In addition, the standard deduction reduces AGI, not the amount included in gross income. Answer (C) is incorrect. Although the standard deduction may reduce taxable income, it does not reduce the amount of gambling winnings included in gross income.

12. Porter was unemployed for part of the year. Porter received $35,000 of wages, $4,000 from a state unemployment compensation plan, and $2,000 from his former employer's company-paid supplemental unemployment benefit plan. What is the amount of Porter's gross income?

A. $35,000

B. $37,000

C. $39,000

D. $41,000

Answer (D) is correct.

REQUIRED: The total amount of gross income.

DISCUSSION: Gross income is all income from whatever source derived except as otherwise provided. All compensation (wages) for personal services is gross income. Unemployment benefits received under a federal or state program are gross income. Supplemental unemployment is included in gross income as wages (not under unemployment). Porter's total gross income is $41,000 ($35,000 wages + $4,000 state unemployment + $2,000 supplemental unemployment).

Answer (A) is incorrect. Although the $35,000 he received as wages is included in gross income, so are the $4,000 of state unemployment and the $2,000 of supplemental unemployment, for a total of $41,000. Answer (B) is incorrect. Although both the $35,000 of wages and $2,000 of supplemental unemployment are included in gross income, so is the $4,000 of state unemployment. Answer (C) is incorrect. Although both the $35,000 of wages and $4,000 of state unemployment are included in gross income, so is the $2,000 of supplemental unemployment.

13. Paul Crane, age 25, is single with no dependents and had an adjusted gross income of $30,000 in 2017, exclusive of $2,000 in unemployment compensation benefits received in 2017. The amount of Crane's unemployment compensation benefits taxable for 2017 is

- A. $2,000
- B. $1,000
- C. $500
- D. $0

Answer (A) is correct.

REQUIRED: The amount of taxable unemployment compensation.

DISCUSSION: All unemployment compensation constitutes gross income. The IRC does not allow exclusion or deduction of any of it.

4.3 Exclusions

14. Klein, a master's degree candidate at Briar University, was awarded a $12,000 scholarship from Briar in Year 1. The scholarship was used to pay Klein's Year 1 university tuition and fees. Also in Year 1, Klein received $5,000 for teaching two courses at a nearby college. What amount must be included in Klein's Year 1 gross income?

- A. $0
- B. $5,000
- C. $12,000
- D. $17,000

Answer (B) is correct.

REQUIRED: The amount of scholarship received that is includible in gross income.

DISCUSSION: Scholarships may be excluded from gross income provided a student is enrolled in a degree-seeking program and that the scholarship is used for qualified expenses such as tuition and fees. However, amounts received for services such as teaching must be included in gross income.

Answer (A) is incorrect. Klein must include the $5,000 received for teaching the two courses. Answer (C) is incorrect. Klein may exclude the $12,000 scholarship but must include the $5,000 for teaching. Answer (D) is incorrect. Klein may exclude the $12,000 scholarship.

15. Sam and Ann Hoyt filed a joint federal income tax return for the calendar year 2017. Among the Hoyts' cash receipts during 2017 was the following: $6,000 first installment on a $75,000 life insurance policy payable to Ann in annual installments of $6,000 each over a 15-year period, as beneficiary of the policy on her uncle, who died in 2016. What portion of the $6,000 installment on the life insurance policy is excludable from 2017 gross income in arriving at the Hoyts' adjusted gross income?

- A. $0
- B. $1,000
- C. $5,000
- D. $6,000

Answer (C) is correct.

REQUIRED: The life insurance proceeds excluded from gross income.

DISCUSSION: Proceeds under a life insurance contract paid by reason of death of the insured are excluded from gross income. But the amount of each payment in excess of the death benefit prorated over the period of payment ($75,000 ÷ 15 years = $5,000 per year) is interest income ($6,000 – $5,000), which is included in gross income.

Answer (A) is incorrect. The portion paid by reason of death, i.e., the amount of coverage, is excluded. Answer (B) is incorrect. The amount of interest included in gross income is $1,000. Answer (D) is incorrect. Only the portion paid by reason of death, i.e., the amount of coverage, is excluded.

16. Clark filed Form 1040EZ for the 2016 taxable year. In July 2017, Clark received a state income tax refund of $900, plus interest of $10, for overpayment of 2016 state income tax. What amount of the state tax refund and interest is taxable in Clark's 2017 federal income tax return?

A. $0

B. $10

C. $900

D. $910

Answer (B) is correct.

REQUIRED: The amount of a recovered item that produced no tax benefit, and interest, includible in gross income.

DISCUSSION: If a taxpayer obtains a deduction for an item that reduces taxes in one year and later recovers all or a portion of the prior deduction, the recovery is included in gross income in the year it is received. To the extent the expense did not reduce federal income taxes in the earlier year, the recovery is excluded from income. A taxpayer who files Form 1040EZ may claim no deductions other than the standard deduction and one personal exemption. Thus, the state tax paid produced no tax benefit and is excluded from gross income. Interest on state income tax refunds is not excludable. It is expressly included in gross income.

Answer (A) is incorrect. The interest on the tax refund is not excludable. Answer (C) is incorrect. The state income tax paid was not deducted on the Form 1040EZ and is thus excluded from gross income. Furthermore, the interest on the tax refund is not excludable. Answer (D) is incorrect. The state income tax paid was not deducted on the Form 1040EZ and is thus excluded from gross income.

17. DAC Foundation awarded Kent $75,000 in recognition of lifelong literary achievement. Kent was not required to render future services as a condition to receive the $75,000. What condition(s) must have been met for the award to be excluded from Kent's gross income?

I. Kent was selected for the award by DAC without any action on Kent's part.

II. Pursuant to Kent's designation, DAC paid the amount of the award either to a governmental unit or to a charitable organization.

A. I only.

B. II only.

C. Both I and II.

D. Neither I nor II.

Answer (C) is correct.

REQUIRED: The conditions under which an award may be excluded from a taxpayer's gross income.

DISCUSSION: Prizes and awards made primarily in recognition of charitable, scientific, educational, etc., achievement are excluded from gross income only if the recipient was selected without any action on his or her part, is not required to render substantial future services as condition of receiving the prize or award, and assigns it to charity.

Answer (A) is incorrect. Kent must also assign the award to charity. Answer (B) is incorrect. Kent must have been selected without any action on his or her part. Answer (D) is incorrect. Prizes and awards made primarily in recognition of charitable, scientific, educational, etc., achievement are excluded from gross income only if the recipient was selected without any action on his or her part, is not required to render substantial future services as condition of receiving the prize or award, and assigns it to charity.

18. Charles and Marcia are married cash-basis taxpayers. In 2017, they had interest income as follows:

- $500 interest on federal income tax refund
- $600 interest on state income tax refund
- $800 interest on federal government obligations
- $1,000 interest on state government obligations

What amount of interest income is taxable on Charles and Marcia's 2017 joint income tax return?

A. $500

B. $1,100

C. $1,900

D. $2,900

Answer (C) is correct.

REQUIRED: The amount of interest income included in gross income.

DISCUSSION: Unless otherwise excluded in another section, the IRC includes interest in gross income. The IRC excludes from gross income interest on most obligations of states or political subdivisions of a state (e.g., municipal bonds). This exclusion does not apply to the obligations of the United States (with the exception of EE bonds used for qualifying education expenses) or interest on state income tax overpayments. Interest income is taxable unless specifically excluded from gross income.

19. During 2017, Adler had the following cash receipts:

Wages	$18,000
Interest income from investments in municipal bonds	400
Unemployment compensation	1,500

What is the total amount that must be included in gross income on Adler's 2017 income tax return?

- A. $18,000
- B. $18,400
- C. $19,500
- D. $19,900

Answer (C) is correct.

REQUIRED: The amount included in gross income on a taxpayer's income tax return.

DISCUSSION: The IRC specifically includes wages and unemployment compensation as gross income. Furthermore, the IRC excludes from gross income interest on most obligations of states or political subdivisions of a state (e.g., municipal bonds).

Answer (A) is incorrect. Unemployment compensation is also included in gross income. Answer (B) is incorrect. Interest on state and local government obligations is specifically excluded from gross income, and unemployment compensation is included in gross income. Answer (D) is incorrect. Interest on state and local government obligations is specifically excluded from gross income.

20. Cassidy, an individual, reported the following items of income and expense during the current year:

Salary	$50,000
Alimony paid to a former spouse	10,000
Inheritance from a grandparent	25,000
Proceeds of a lawsuit for physical injuries	50,000

What is the amount of Cassidy's adjusted gross income?

- A. $40,000
- B. $50,000
- C. $115,000
- D. $125,000

Answer (A) is correct.

REQUIRED: The taxpayer's adjusted gross income, including determining which items are gross income and which items are deducted from gross income.

DISCUSSION: A taxpayer's adjusted gross income equals all gross income items, as defined by Sec. 61 of the Internal Revenue Code, less any available deductions from gross income, as defined by the Internal Revenue Code.

Salary	$ 50,000
Alimony Paid	(10,000)
AGI	$ 40,000

The inheritance and proceeds for physical injury are excluded from gross income.

Answer (B) is incorrect. A deduction is allowed for alimony paid to a former spouse. Answer (C) is incorrect. Inheritances are excluded from the gross income of the recipient as gifts, and proceeds of a lawsuit for physical injuries, provided they are for actual damages, are specifically excluded from gross income as compensation for injury or sickness. Answer (D) is incorrect. Only one item is includible in gross income, and a deduction is allowed for alimony paid to a former spouse.

STUDY UNIT FIVE
SELF-EMPLOYMENT AND FARMING

(23 pages of outline)

Gross income is reduced by deductions to compute taxable income. No amount can be deducted from gross income unless allowed by the Internal Revenue Code (IRC). Deductible business expenses apply to sole proprietorships as well as other business entities. Employers who pay wages are required to pay employment taxes based on the employee's pay. These taxes include Social Security tax, Medicare tax, and Unemployment tax. Not all payments made to employees are includible in their gross income.

Deductions to compute taxable income are heavily tested on the CPA exam. The business expense deductions explained in this study unit are also tested in the corporate context. The CPA exam has decreased its testing of exact amounts of limits. Nevertheless, you should be familiar with limit and threshold amounts.

Some candidates find it helpful to have the entire tax form side-by-side with our Knowledge Transfer Outline when studying. The full versions of the most up-to-date forms are easily accessible at www.gleim.com/taxforms. These forms and the form excerpts used in our outline are periodically updated as the latest versions are released by the IRS.

5.1 BUSINESS INCOME AND EXPENSES

1. **Self-Employment Income**

   a. A sole proprietor generally reports all self-employment income and expense on Schedule C.

   b. Gross income (GI) includes all income from a trade or business.

      1) GI from a business that sells products or commodities is

         Gross sales (receipts)
         – Cost of goods sold
         + Other GI (e.g., rentals)
         = **GI from the business**

      2) Cost of goods sold (COGS) is treated as a return of capital, which is not income for tax purposes. COGS for a tax year, typically, is

         Beginning inventory
         + Inventory purchased during year
         – Year-end inventory
         = **COGS**

      3) COGS should be determined in accordance with the accounting method consistently used by the business. In general, COGS is computed by starting with the beginning inventory, adding the cost of materials purchased during the year and the cost of production, and subtracting the ending inventory.

SCHEDULE C
(Form 1040)

Department of the Treasury
Internal Revenue Service (99)

Profit or Loss From Business
(Sole Proprietorship)

▶ **Information about Schedule C and its separate instructions is at** *www.irs.gov/schedulec.*
▶ **Attach to Form 1040, 1040NR, or 1041; partnerships generally must file Form 1065.**

OMB No. 1545-0074

[Year]

Attachment
Sequence No. **09**

Name of proprietor	Social security number (SSN)

A Principal business or profession, including product or service (see instructions)

B Enter code from instructions ▶

C Business name. If no separate business name, leave blank.

D Employer ID number (EIN), (see instr.)

E Business address (including suite or room no.) ▶

City, town or post office, state, and ZIP code

F Accounting method: **(1)** ☐ Cash **(2)** ☐ Accrual **(3)** ☐ Other (specify) ▶

G Did you "materially participate" in the operation of this business during [Year]? If "No," see instructions for limit on losses . ☐ Yes ☐ No

H If you started or acquired this business during [Year], check here . . . . ▶ ☐

I Did you make any payments in [Year] that would require you to file Form(s) 1099? (see instructions) . . . . ☐ Yes ☐ No

J If "Yes," did you or will you file required Forms 1099? . . . . ☐ Yes ☐ No

Part I   Income

1	Gross receipts or sales. See instructions for line 1 and check the box if this income was reported to you on Form W-2 and the "Statutory employee" box on that form was checked . . . . ▶ ☐	**1**	
2	Returns and allowances	**2**	
3	Subtract line 2 from line 1	**3**	
4	Cost of goods sold (from line 42)	**4**	
5	**Gross profit.** Subtract line 4 from line 3	**5**	
6	Other income, including federal and state gasoline or fuel tax credit or refund (see instructions) . . .	**6**	
7	**Gross income.** Add lines 5 and 6 . . . . ▶	**7**	

Part II   Expenses. Enter expenses for business use of your home **only** on line 30.

8	Advertising	**8**		**18**	Office expense (see instructions)	**18**	
9	Car and truck expenses (see instructions).	**9**		**19**	Pension and profit-sharing plans	**19**	
10	Commissions and fees .	**10**		**20**	Rent or lease (see instructions):		
11	Contract labor (see instructions)	**11**		**a**	Vehicles, machinery, and equipment	**20a**	
12	Depletion	**12**		**b**	Other business property . . .	**20b**	
13	Depreciation and section 179 expense deduction (not included in Part III) (see instructions)	**13**		**21**	Repairs and maintenance . .	**21**	
				22	Supplies (not included in Part III) .	**22**	
				23	Taxes and licenses	**23**	
				24	Travel, meals, and entertainment:		
14	Employee benefit programs (other than on line 19) . .	**14**		**a**	Travel	**24a**	
15	Insurance (other than health)	**15**		**b**	Deductible meals and entertainment (see instructions)	**24b**	
16	Interest:			**25**	Utilities	**25**	
a	Mortgage (paid to banks, etc.)	**16a**		**26**	Wages (less employment credits) .	**26**	
b	Other	**16b**		**27a**	Other expenses (from line 48) .	**27a**	
17	Legal and professional services	**17**		**b**	**Reserved for future use** . . .	**27b**	

28	**Total expenses** before expenses for business use of home. Add lines 8 through 27a . . . . . ▶	**28**	
29	Tentative profit or (loss). Subtract line 28 from line 7	**29**	
30	Expenses for business use of your home. Do not report these expenses elsewhere. Attach Form 8829 unless using the simplified method (see instructions). **Simplified method filers only:** enter the total square footage of: (a) your home: _____ and (b) the part of your home used for business: _____ . Use the Simplified Method Worksheet in the instructions to figure the amount to enter on line 30	**30**	
31	**Net profit or (loss).** Subtract line 30 from line 29. • If a profit, enter on both **Form 1040, line 12** (or **Form 1040NR, line 13**) and on **Schedule SE, line 2.** (If you checked the box on line 1, see instructions). Estates and trusts, enter on **Form 1041, line 3.** • If a loss, you **must** go to line 32.	**31**	
32	If you have a loss, check the box that describes your investment in this activity (see instructions). • If you checked 32a, enter the loss on both **Form 1040, line 12,** (or **Form 1040NR, line 13**) and on **Schedule SE, line 2.** (If you checked the box on line 1, see the line 31 instructions). Estates and trusts, enter on **Form 1041, line 3.** • If you checked 32b, you **must** attach **Form 6198.** Your loss may be limited.	**32a** ☐ All investment is at risk. **32b** ☐ Some investment is not at risk.	

For Paperwork Reduction Act Notice, see the separate instructions.   Cat. No. 11334P   **Schedule C (Form 1040) [Year]**

2. **Ordinary and Necessary Expense**

   a. A deduction from gross income is allowed for all ordinary and necessary expenses paid or incurred during a tax year in carrying on a trade or business.

   b. These deductions apply to sole proprietors as well as other business entities.

3. **Trade/Business and Expenses Defined**

   a. A trade or business is a regular and continuous activity that is entered into with the expectation of making a profit.

      1) "Regular" means the taxpayer devotes a substantial amount of business time to the activity.

   b. An activity that is not engaged in for a profit is a hobby (personal).

      1) An activity that results in a profit in any 3 of 5 consecutive tax years (2 of 7 for the breeding and racing of horses) is presumed not to be a hobby.

   c. An expense must be **both** ordinary and necessary to be deductible.

      1) "Ordinary" implies that the expense normally occurs or is likely to occur in connection with businesses similar to the one operated by the taxpayer claiming the deduction.

         a) The expenditures need not occur frequently.

      2) "Necessary" implies that an expenditure must be appropriate and helpful in developing or maintaining the trade or business.

      3) Implicit in the "ordinary and necessary" requirement is the requirement that the expenditures be reasonable.

4. **Compensation**

   a. Cash and the FMV of property paid to an employee are deductible by the employer.

5. **Rent**

   a. Advance rental payments may be deducted by the lessee only during the tax periods to which the payments apply.

   b. Generally, even a cash-method taxpayer must amortize prepaid rent expense over the period to which it applies. The exception to this rule is if the payments do not extend beyond a year.

6. **Entertainment and Meals**

   a. Entertainment includes recreation, e.g., entertaining guests at a nightclub or theater, or by vacations, trips, etc., and furnishing a hotel suite, food and beverages, or the like to a customer or a member of his or her family.

      1) Club dues for social gatherings are not deductible, e.g., country club membership dues.

      2) Dues paid to professional clubs are deductible if they are paid for business reasons and the principal purpose is professional, i.e., not for entertainment.

   b. The expense must be **directly related** or **associated with** the active conduct of a trade or business. The predominant purpose must be the furthering of the trade or business of the taxpayer incurring the expense.

      1) **"Directly related"** means that business is actually conducted during the entertainment period.

      2) **"Associated with"** means that the entertainment must occur directly before or after a business discussion.

    c.   Meal expenses are not deductible if neither the taxpayer nor an employee of the taxpayer is present at the meal.

    d.   There is a 50% limit to deductible amounts for allowable meal and entertainment expenses and related expenses, such as taxes, tips, and parking fees.

        1)   No deduction is allowed for meal and entertainment expenses (or any portion thereof) that are lavish or extravagant under the circumstances.

        2)   Transportation to and from a business meal is not limited.

        3)   The IRS has denied deductions for any meal or entertainment expense over $75 for which the claimant did not provide substantiating evidence.

When Are Entertainment Expenses Deductible?

General rule	The taxpayer can deduct ordinary and necessary expenses to entertain a client, customer, or employee if the expenses meet the directly related test or the associated test.
Definitions	• **Entertainment** includes any activity generally considered to provide entertainment, amusement, or recreation and includes meals provided to a customer or client. • An **ordinary** expense is one that is common and accepted in the taxpayer's field of business, trade, or profession. • A **necessary** expense is one that is helpful and appropriate, although not necessarily required, for the taxpayer's business.

Tests to be met	**Directly related test**
	• Entertainment took place in a clear business setting, **or**
	• Main purpose of entertainment was the active conduct of business, **and**
	   The taxpayer did engage in business with the person during the entertainment period, **and**
	   The taxpayer had more than a general expectation of getting income or some other specific business benefit.
	
	Associated test
	• Entertainment is associated with the taxpayer's trade or business, **and**
	• Entertainment directly precedes or follows a substantial business decision.

Other rules	• The taxpayer cannot deduct the cost of the taxpayer's meal as an entertainment expense if the taxpayer is claiming the meal as a travel expense. • The taxpayer cannot deduct expenses that are lavish or extravagant under the circumstances. • The taxpayer generally can deduct only 50% of the taxpayer's unreimbursed entertainment expenses.

    7.   **Travel**

        a.   While away from home overnight on business, travel expenses are deductible. Travel expenses include transportation, lodging, and meal expenses in an employment-related context.

        b.   No deduction is allowed for

            1)   Travel that is primarily personal in nature

            2)   The travel expenses of the taxpayer's spouse unless

               a)   There is a bona fide business purpose for the spouse's presence,

               b)   The spouse is an employee, and

               c)   The expenses would be otherwise deductible.

            3)   Commuting between home and work

            4)   Attending investment meetings

            5)   Travel as a form of education

c. A rule allows for lodging deductions when not traveling away from home (e.g., a conference or trade show held at a local hotel with evening events), if qualified under one of two tests or rules.

1) The deduction is allowed if all the facts and circumstances indicate the lodging is for carrying on a taxpayer's trade or business. One factor under this test is whether the taxpayer incurs an expense because of a bona fide condition or requirement of employment imposed by the taxpayer's employer.

2) A safe harbor rule applies if

a) The lodging is necessary for the individual to participate fully in, or be available for, a bona fide business meeting, conference, training activity, or other business function;

b) The lodging is for a period that does not exceed 5 calendar days and does not recur more frequently than once per calendar quarter;

c) The employee's employer requires the employee to remain at the activity or function overnight (if the individual is an employee); and

d) The lodging is not lavish or extravagant under the circumstances and does not provide any significant element of personal pleasure, recreation, or benefit.

8. **Foreign Travel**

a. Traveling expenses of a taxpayer who ventures outside of the United States away from home must be allocated between time spent on the trip for business and time spent for pleasure.

EXAMPLE

Scott's foreign trip is for more than a week, and he spends most of his time as a personal vacation. However, he spends some time at a business-related conference.

Only the expenses related to the conference, including lodging, local travel, etc., may be deducted.

---

b. No allocation is required when

1) The trip is for no more than 1 week and

2) A personal vacation was not the major consideration or

3) The personal time spent on the trip is less than 25% of the total time away from home.

9. **Automobile Expenses**

a. Actual expenses for automobile use are deductible (e.g., services, repairs, gas).

b. Alternatively, the taxpayer may deduct the standard mileage rate ($0.535 per mile for 2017), plus parking fees, tolls, etc.

10. **Taxes**

a. Taxes paid or accrued in a trade or business are deductible.

b. Taxes paid or accrued to purchase property are treated as part of the cost of the property.

c. Sales tax is treated as part of the property's cost.

1) If capitalized, the sales tax may be recoverable as depreciation.

2) If the cost of the property is currently expensed and deductible, so is the tax.

d. Occupational license taxes are deductible.

e.   Property tax.

1)   Tax on real and personal property is an itemized deduction for individuals.

2)   Tax on business property is a business expense (i.e., deducted on a business return, for example, Schedule C or E).

3)   Local improvements.

a)   Taxes assessed for local benefit that tend to increase the value of real property are added to the property's adjusted basis and are not currently deductible as tax expense.

f.   Income taxes.

1)   State and local taxes imposed on net income of an individual are NOT deductible on Schedule C.

a)   They are deductible as a personal, itemized deduction not subject to the 2% exclusion.

b)   They are not a business expense of a sole proprietorship.

2)   Federal income taxes generally are not deductible.

3)   Individual taxpayers may claim an itemized deduction for either general state and local sales taxes or state income taxes, but not both.

g.   Employment taxes.

1)   An employer may deduct the employer portion of FICA and FUTA taxes.

2)   An employee may not deduct FICA tax.

3)   A self-employed person is allowed a deduction for the employer's portion of the FICA taxes paid to arrive at his or her AGI. For 2017, this equals

a)   6.2% of the first $127,200 of net self-employment income plus
b)   1.45% of net self-employment income (no cap).

4)   The employee portion includes an additional 0.9% for high-income earnings, i.e., earnings in excess of $200,000 ($250,000 MFJ, $125,000 MFS).

11.   **Insurance Expense**

a.   Trade or business insurance expense paid or incurred during the tax year is deductible.

b.   A cash-method taxpayer may not deduct a premium before it is paid.

c.   Prepaid insurance must be apportioned over the period of coverage.

12.   **Bad Debts**

a.   A bad debt deduction is allowed only for a bona fide debt arising from a debtor-creditor relationship based upon a valid and enforceable obligation to pay a fixed or determinable sum of money.

b.   Worthless debt is deductible only to the extent of adjusted basis in the debt.

1)   A cash-basis taxpayer has no basis in accounts receivable and generally has no deduction for bad debts.

c.   A **business bad debt** is one incurred or acquired in connection with the taxpayer's trade or business.

1)   Partially worthless business debts may be deducted to the extent they are worthless and specifically written off.

2)   A business bad debt is treated as an ordinary loss.

    d. A **nonbusiness bad debt** is a debt other than one incurred or acquired in connection with the taxpayer's trade or business.

        1) Investments are not treated as a trade or business.
        2) A partially worthless nonbusiness bad debt is not deductible.
        3) A wholly worthless nonbusiness debt is treated as a short-term capital loss.

    e. Worthless corporate securities are not considered bad debts. They are generally treated as a capital loss.

    f. The **specific write-off method** must be used for tax purposes. The allowance method is used only for financial accounting purposes.

13. **Loan Costs**

    a. Costs of business borrowing are generally deductible.

    b. Costs of obtaining a loan, other than interest, are deductible over the period of the loan. Examples of such costs are recording fees and mortgage commissions.

    c. Interest is deductible when paid, as are payments in lieu of interest.

        1) Prepayment penalties are treated as interest and are deductible when paid.
        2) Points are treated as interest. They must be amortized.

            a) However, ordinary points on acquisition indebtedness of a principal residence may be treated as currently deductible loan costs.

            b) Points paid on refinancing must be amortized.

        3) Prepaid interest in any form must be amortized over the period of the loan.

            a) Any undeducted balance is deductible in full when the loan is paid off.

14. **Business Gifts**

    a. Expenditures for business gifts are deductible. They must be ordinary and necessary.

    b. Deduction is limited to $25 per recipient per year for excludable items.

        1) The $25 limit does not apply to incidental items costing (the giver) $4 each or less.
        2) A husband and wife are treated as one taxpayer, even if they file separate returns and have independent business relationships with the recipient.

    c. In the case of a gift (e.g., tickets to an event) that appears to qualify as a gift or a more tax friendly entertainment expense, the defining factor is attendance by the taxpayer.

Allowed Treatment

	Gift	Entertainment
Taxpayer **does not** attend with customer	X	X
Taxpayer **does** attend with customer		X

15. **Employee Achievement Awards**

    a. Up to $400 of the cost of employee achievement awards is deductible by an employer for all nonqualified plan awards.

        1) An employee achievement award is tangible personal property awarded as part of a meaningful presentation for safety achievement or length of service.

    b. Deduction of qualified plan awards is limited to $1,600 per year.

        1) A qualified plan award is an employee achievement award provided under an established written program that does not discriminate in favor of highly compensated employees.

        2) If the average cost of all employee achievement awards is greater than $400, then it is not a qualified plan award.

16. **Start-Up and Organization Costs**

   a. Taxpayers can deduct up to $5,000 of start-up costs and $5,000 of organizational costs in the taxable year in which the business begins.

      1) Examples of start-up costs are costs incurred to prepare to enter into the trade or business, to secure suppliers and customers, and to obtain certain supplies and equipment (noncapital).

      2) Examples of organizational costs are legal and accounting fees; costs of state filings; and expenses of meetings with directors, shareholders, or partners.

      3) Any start-up or organizational costs in excess of $5,000 are capitalized and amortized proportionally over a 180-month period beginning with the month in which the active trade or business begins.

         a) These amounts are reduced, but not below zero, by the cumulative cost of the start-up costs or organizational costs that exceed $50,000.

      4) Taxpayers are not required to file a separate election statement. The taxpayer needs only to expense or capitalize the cost; from there, the election is irrevocable.

17. **Vacant Land**

   a. Interest and taxes on vacant land are deductible.

18. **Medical Reimbursement Plans**

   a. The cost of such a plan for employees is deductible by the employer.

19. **Political Contributions and Lobbying Expenses**

   a. Contributions to a political party or candidate and, generally, lobbying expenses are not deductible.

20. **Intangibles**

   a. The cost of intangibles must generally be capitalized.
   b. Amortization is allowed if the intangible has a determinable useful life.

21. **Tax-Exempt Income**

   a. An expenditure related to producing tax-exempt income is not deductible, e.g., interest on a loan used to purchase tax-exempt bonds.

22. **Public Policy**

   a. A trade or business expenditure that is ordinary, necessary, and reasonable may be nondeductible if allowing the deduction would frustrate public policy.

   b. Examples are

      1) Fines and penalties paid to the government for violation of the law
      2) Illegal bribes and kickbacks
      3) Two-thirds of damages for violation of federal antitrust law
      4) Expenses of dealers in illegal drugs (as determined at the federal level)

         a) However, adjustment to gross receipts is permitted for the cost of merchandise.

23. **Miscellaneous Ordinary and Necessary Business Expenses**

   a. Miscellaneous ordinary and necessary business expenses are deductible.
   b. Examples include costs of advertising, bank fees, depreciation, amortization, office supplies, etc.

24. **Capital Expenditures**

    a.   Capital expenditures are made in acquiring or improving property that will have a useful life of longer than 1 year.

        1)   For example, replacing machinery is generally a capital expenditure. Also, wages paid to employees for constructing a new building to be used in the business are capitalized.

    b.   If the property is a depreciable asset, the cost is recovered through depreciation.

    c.   If the property is not a depreciable asset, the amount of the capital expenditure might be recovered at the time of disposition.

25. **Business Use of Home**

    a.   Expenses incurred for the use of a person's home for business purposes are deductible only if strict requirements are met.

        1)   The portion of the home must be used exclusively and regularly as

            a)   The principal place of business for any trade or business of the taxpayer;

            b)   A place of business that is used by patients, clients, or customers in the normal course of the taxpayer's trade or business; or

            c)   A separate structure that is not attached to the dwelling unit that is used in the taxpayer's trade or business.

        2)   If the taxpayer is an employee, the business use of the home must also be for the convenience of the employer.

    b.   The exclusive-use test is strictly applied. Any personal use of the business portion of the home by anyone results in complete disallowance of the deductions. There are two exceptions to the exclusive-use test:

        1)   Retail/wholesale. A retailer or wholesaler whose **sole** location of his or her business is his or her home need not meet the exclusive-use test.

            a)   The ordinary and necessary business expenses allocable to an identifiable space used regularly for inventory or product sample storage by a taxpayer in the active pursuit of his or her trade or business are deductible.

        2)   Day care. If the business portion of a home is used to offer qualifying day care, the exclusive-use test need not be met.

    c.   If the taxpayer has more than one business location, the primary factor in determining whether a home office is a taxpayer's principal place of business is the relative importance of the activities performed at each business location.

        1)   If the primary location cannot be determined by the relative importance test, then the amount of time spent at each location will be used.

    d.   A home office qualifies as a "principal place of business" if used by the taxpayer to conduct administrative or management activities of the taxpayer's trade or business and there is no other fixed location where the taxpayer conducts such activities.

    e.   Deduction for business use is limited to

        1)   Gross income derived from the use, minus

        2)   Deductions related to the home, allowed regardless of business or personal use, e.g., mortgage interest or real estate taxes, minus

        3)   Business expenses that are not home office expenses, e.g., employee compensation, minus

        4)   Home office expense other than depreciation (limited to remaining gross income), minus

        5)   Depreciation related to the home office (limited to remaining gross income).

NOTE: Keep in mind the Schedule C deduction is still only the portion allocated to the business use of the home. The remaining expense is an itemized deduction on Schedule A.

EXAMPLE

Tammy has $30,000 of gross income from a business activity conducted in a home office. Of mortgage interest and property taxes allocable to the home office, $10,000 is deductible as personal expenses. Tammy has $20,000 of home office expenses and $15,000 of business deductions that are not home office expenses. Only $5,000 [$30,000 − ($10,000 + $15,000)] is deductible as home office expenses.

---

f.   Any currently disallowed amount is deductible in succeeding years, subject to the same limitations.

g.   A simplified option allows taxpayers to claim a deduction of $5 per square foot of home office space, up to 300 square feet, for a maximum deduction of $1,500. This option eliminates depreciation recordkeeping and recapture.

Business Use of the Home Deductible Expense Decision Chart

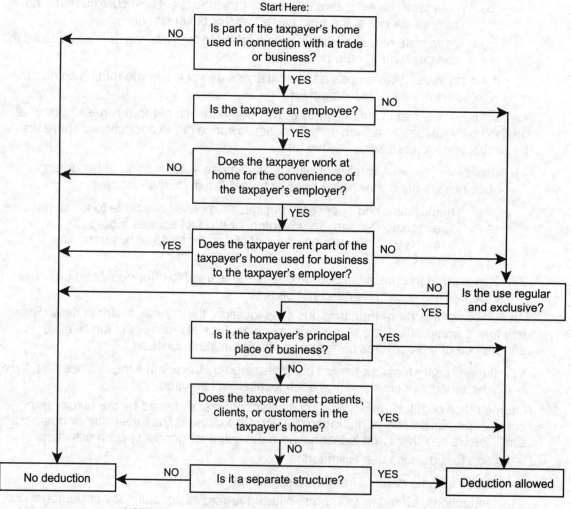

NOTE: Do not use this chart if the taxpayer uses the taxpayer's home for the storage of inventory or product samples or to operate a daycare facility.

26. **Rental Property Income and Expense**

   a. Generally, rental property activity is **reported on Schedule E** for individuals.
   b. Expenses related to the production of rental income are generally deductible to arrive at adjusted gross income.
   c. Rental property expenditures may be deducted by depreciation. Generally, a Sec. 179 deduction (i.e., "bonus depreciation") is not allowed for rental property. (Study Unit 8, Subunit 2, "Depreciation and Amortization," has more detail on the Sec. 179 deduction.) The exceptions to this include a deduction for leasehold improvement property (not residential), restaurant property, and retail improvement property.
   d. Special rules limit deductions on the rental of a residence or a vacation home.

   1) **Minimum rental use.** The property must be rented for more than 14 days during the year for deductions to be allowable.
   2) **Minimum personal use.** The vacation-home rules apply when the taxpayer uses the residence for personal purposes for the greater of (a) more than 14 days or (b) more than 10% of the number of days for which the residence is rented.

   a) When the residence is rented for less than 15 days, the rental income does not need to be reported. Any corresponding rental expenses cannot be deducted.

   e. A residence is deemed to have been used by the taxpayer for personal purposes if the home is used by

   1) The taxpayer for personal purposes, by any other person who owns an interest in the rental property, or by the relatives of either

   a) However, if the taxpayer rented or tried to rent the property for 12 or more consecutive months, the days during which (s)he used the property as a main home do not count as personal days.

   2) Any individual under a reciprocal arrangement, whether or not rent is charged
   3) Any individual, unless a fair rental is charged

   f. If the taxpayer spends substantially full-time repairing or maintaining the rental property, such time does not count toward the personal use test.
   g. If the property passes the minimum rental-use test but fails the minimum personal-use test, the property is considered a vacation home, and rental deductions may not exceed the gross income derived from rental activities.

   1) When deductions are limited to gross income, the order of deductions is

   a) The allocable portion of expenses deductible regardless of rental income (e.g., mortgage interest and property taxes)
   b) Deductions that do not affect basis (e.g., ordinary repairs and maintenance)
   c) Deductions that affect basis (e.g., depreciation)

   2) Expenses must be allocated between the personal use and the rental use based on the number of days of use of each.

   h. If the property passes both the minimum rental-use test and the minimum personal-use test, then all deductions may be taken and a loss may occur, subject to the passive loss limits.

	Minimum Use Tests	
	Rental Use	Personal Use
Pass	> 14 days	≤ 14 days or < 10%
Fail	≤ 14 days	greater of > 14 days or > 10%

27. **Domestic Production Activities Deduction**

a. **Domestic production gross receipts** (DPGR) are defined by Section 199 as gross receipts that are derived from

1) The sale, exchange, or other disposition; or any rental, lease, or licensing of

a) Qualified production property that is manufactured, produced, grown, or extracted in the United States by the taxpayer in whole or in significant part

b) Any qualified film produced by the taxpayer in the United States

c) Electricity, natural gas, or potable water produced by the taxpayer in the United States

2) Construction performed in the United States

3) Engineering and architectural services performed in the United States for a construction project located in the United States

b. Qualified **production property** generally includes tangible personal property, computer software, and sound recordings.

c. Gross receipts from the sale or lease of **personal property** that is manufactured in the United States are considered DPGR.

1) The gross receipts from the lease, rental, or license of property to a related party do not qualify as DPGR.

a) Employees are considered related parties to an employer.

b) All employees of a company and its subsidiaries are considered to be employed by a single employer.

d. When determining the income attributable to **domestic activities**, a company does not include any gross receipts from nondomestic production in the calculation of DPGR.

1) If nondomestic production gross receipts are less than 5% of the total gross receipts for the company, the company may treat all gross receipts as though they are DPGR.

e. The deduction applies to taxpayers that perform manufacturing, production, or extraction activities in the United States. The deduction for income attributable to domestic gross income is equal to the lesser of the following:

1) 9% of the qualified production activities income (QPAI),

a) QPAI is calculated by taking the DPGR and subtracting the sum of the following from it:

i) The cost of goods sold attributable to DPGR;

ii) Other deductions, expenses, or losses that are directly attributable to DPGR; and

iii) A proper share of other deductions, expenses, or losses that are not directly allocable to DPGR or another class of income.

2) 9% of the taxable income of the taxpayer, or

3) 50% of the W-2 wages for the year allocable only to qualified production activities income instead of all wages.

Stop and review! You have completed the outline for this subunit. Study multiple-choice questions 1 through 6 beginning on page 144.

5.2 FICA AND FUTA TAXES

1. **Federal Insurance Contributions Act (FICA) -- Social Security & Medicare Tax**

   a. Employers are required to pay employment tax based on the employee's pay.

   b. The **employer** must pay

      1) 6.2% of the first $127,200 (2017) of wages paid for Social Security tax plus
      2) 1.45% of all wages for Medicare tax. There is no cap on this tax.

   c. The Additional Medicare Tax on earned income is a 0.9% tax on wages and net self-employment income in excess of a threshold.

      1) This additional tax applies to earned income exceeding $200,000 for single, head-of-household, or surviving spouse; $250,000 for married filing jointly; and $125,000 for married filing separately. Employers withhold an additional 0.9% for income beyond $200,000 regardless of filing status.

   d. The employer must withhold the following amounts from the **employee's** wages:

      1) Tier 1 – From $0 to $127,200; 7.65% × Employee's wages (Social Security + Medicare)
      2) Tier 2 – From $127,200 to $200,000 or $250,000; 1.45% × Employee's wages (Medicare)
      3) Tier 3 – Above $200,000 of earned income; 2.35% × Employee's wages (Medicare + Additional Medicare)
      4) Overwithholding is alleviated as a credit against the income tax if the overwithholding resulted from multiple employer withholding.

   e. Contributions made by the employee are not tax deductible by the employee, while those made by the employer are deductible by the employer.

   f. An employer must pay FICA taxes for all household employees who are paid more than $2,000 during the year 2017.

2. **Net Investment Income Tax (NIIT)**

   a. All investment income in excess of deductions allowable for such income and income from passive activities are subject to a 3.8% **net investment income tax**. This tax essentially applies FICA taxes to income that previously was not subject to the taxes.

   b. The tax is imposed on the lesser of an individual's net investment income or any excess of modified adjusted gross income (MAGI) for the tax year over a specified threshold.

Filing Status	Threshold Amount
Married filing jointly, surviving spouse	$250,000
Single, head of household	$200,000
Married filing separately	$125,000

   c. MAGI is the sum of AGI and excludable foreign earned income/housing costs after any deductions, exclusions, or credits applicable to the foreign earned income.

   d. Net investment income tax does not apply to non-resident aliens.

3. **Self-Employment Tax**

   a. Self-employment taxes are paid through estimated payments, not withholding.

   b. The FICA tax liability is imposed on net earnings from self-employment at the employer rate plus the employee rate as follows:

      1) Tier 1 – From $0 to $127,200; 15.3% × Net self-employment income
      2) Tier 2 – From $127,200 to $200,000 or $250,000; 2.9% × Net self-employment income
      3) Tier 3 – Above $200,000 or $250,000; 3.8% × Net self-employment income

   c.   NI from self-employment − (.0765 × NI from self-employment) = Net Earnings from Self-Employment.

   d.   Net income from self-employment does not include the following:

       1)   Rents
       2)   Gain or loss from disposition of business property
       3)   Capital gain or loss
       4)   Nonbusiness interest
       5)   Dividends
       6)   Income or expenses related to personal activities
       7)   Wages, salaries, or tips received as an employee

   e.   A self-employed person is allowed a deduction for the employer's portion of the FICA taxes paid to arrive at his or her AGI. For 2017, this equals

       1)   6.2% of the first $127,200 of net self-employment income plus
       2)   1.45% of net self-employment income (no cap).

   f.   The additional 0.9% Medicare tax is only imposed on the employee portion of self-employment tax. Therefore, it is not deductible.

       1)   Individuals with wages and self-employment income calculate their liabilities in three steps:

           a)   Calculate the tax on any wages in excess of the applicable threshold without regard to any withholding;

           b)   Reduce the applicable threshold by the total amount of Medicare wages received, but not below zero; and

           c)   Calculate the tax on any self-employment income in excess of the reduced threshold.

EXAMPLE

C, a single filer, has $130,000 in wages and $145,000 in self-employment income. C's wages are not in excess of the $200,000 threshold for single filers, so C is not liable for the surtax on these wages. Before calculating the tax on self-employment income, the $200,000 threshold for single filers is reduced by C's $130,000 in wages, resulting in a reduced self-employment threshold of $70,000. C is liable to pay the additional 0.9% tax on $75,000 of self-employment income ($145,000 − $70,000).

---

   g.   The employee's portion of the FICA taxes is not deductible.

   h.   The income inclusion for self-employment taxes **differs from gross income** inclusion in the case of ministers and/or clergymen.

       1)   A minister may exclude the rental value of his or her home or parsonage if it is not connected with the performance of religious duties.

       2)   The rental value is not excluded from the income used to compute self-employment taxes.

       3)   Any wages received by ministers and/or clergymen on a W-2 are not subject to Social Security but are included in self-employment income unless one of the following applies:

           a)   The minister and/or clergyman is a member of a religious order and has taken a vow of poverty.

           b)   The minister and/or clergyman requests and is granted an exemption from self-employment tax by the IRS.

           c)   The minister and/or clergyman is subject only to the Social Security laws of a foreign country under the provisions of a Social Security agreement between the United States and that country.

4. **Federal Unemployment Taxes (FUTA)**

   a. This tax is imposed on employers. The tax is 6.0% of the first $7,000 of wages paid to each employee. The employee does not pay any portion of FUTA.

   b. If state unemployment tax is paid, a credit is available that reduces the FUTA tax rate by up to 5.4%. So, the lowest possible FUTA rate is .6% (6% − 5.4% max credit).

5. Taxpayers have different reporting responsibilities for payments to employees than to independent contractors. The basic differences are covered in the following chart.

FICA and FUTA Reporting Requirement Chart

Employee	Independent Contractor
The employer must withhold federal income tax and the employee's half of FICA.	Generally the contractor is responsible for federal income taxes and FICA.
The employer must pay the employer's half of FICA, as well as FUTA.	Generally the contractor is responsible for federal income taxes and FICA. No FUTA responsibility.
The employer must issue Form W-2, *Wage and Tax Statement*, to the employee and send copies to the IRS.	The taxpayer must issue the contractor Form 1099-MISC and file copies with the IRS if the taxpayer pays the contractor $600 or more during the year.

Stop and review! You have completed the outline for this subunit. Study multiple-choice questions 7 and 8 beginning on page 145.

5.3 EMPLOYEE BENEFITS

1. **Fringe Benefits**

   a. An employee's GI does not include the cost of any qualified fringe benefit supplied or paid for by the employer.

2. **Employee Discounts**

   a. Certain employee discounts on the selling price of qualified property or services of their employer are excluded from GI.

   b. The employee discount may not exceed

      1) The gross profit percentage normally earned on merchandise or
      2) 20% of the price offered to customers in the case of qualified services.

3. **Working Condition**

   a. Benefits provided to an employee by his or her employer are excludable if such benefits are provided as a working condition fringe benefit.

EXAMPLE

Jamaal, a pharmaceutical salesperson, spends most of his day driving to various medical facilities. He was provided a vehicle as a fringe benefit. The business use of the vehicle is not included in GI. However, any personal use would be included in GI.

---

4. **De Minimis**

    a. The value of property or services (not cash) provided to an employee is excludable as a de minimis fringe benefit if the value is so minimal that accounting for it would be unreasonable or impracticable.

    b. The following are examples of de minimis fringe benefits. The list is not exhaustive.

        1) Occasional use of company copy machines
        2) Occasional company parties or picnics
        3) Occasional tickets to entertainment/sporting events (not season tickets)
        4) Occasional taxi fare or meal money due to overtime work
        5) Traditional noncash holiday gifts with a small FMV

        NOTE: Use of an employer-provided car more than once a month for commuting and membership to a private country club or athletic facility are never excludable as de minimis fringe benefits.

    c. An eating facility for employees is treated as a de minimis fringe benefit if

        1) It is located on or near the business premises of the employer and
        2) The facility's revenue normally equals or exceeds its operating costs.

        NOTE: The excess value of the meals over the fees charged to employees is excluded from employees' income.

    d. The value of an on-premises athletic facility provided by an employer is generally excluded from GI of employees.

5. **Qualified Transportation Fringe Benefits**

    a. Up to $255 a month may be excluded for the value of employer-provided transit passes and transportation in an employer-provided "commuter highway vehicle."

    b. Additionally, an exclusion of up to $255 per month is available for employer-provided parking.

    c. Employees may use both of these exclusions.

6. **Moving Reimbursements**

    a. Qualified moving reimbursements are excludable amounts received from an employer that would be deductible if paid by the individual.

7. **Employer-Provided Educational Assistance**

    a. Up to $5,250 may be excluded by the employee for employer-provided educational assistance.

    b. Excludable assistance payments may not include the cost of meals, lodging, transportation, tools, or supplies that the employee retains after the course.

8. **Employer-Provided Life Insurance**

    a. Proceeds of a life insurance policy for which the employer paid the premiums may be excluded from the employee's GI.

    b. The cost of group term life insurance up to a coverage amount of $50,000 is excluded from the employee's GI.

EXAMPLE

Janet, who is 40 years old, is provided with $150,000 of nondiscriminatory group term life insurance by her employer. Based on the IRS uniform premium cost table, the total annual cost of a policy of this type is $1.20 per $1,000 of coverage. Janet contributed $50 toward the policy. Janet should include $70 in GI.

Amount in excess of $50,000:	$100,000
Cost of $100,000 policy:	120
– Janet's contribution:	50
GI to Janet:	$70

    c.   Premiums paid by the employer for excess coverage (coverage over $50,000) are included in GI.

    d.   The employer must report the amount taxable to the employee on Form W-2.

    e.   The exclusion applies only to coverage of the employee. Payments for coverage of an employee's spouse or dependent are included as GI.

9. **Accident and Health Plans**

    a.   Benefits received by an employee under an accident and health plan under which the employer paid the premiums or contributed to an independent fund are excluded from GI of the employee.

    b.   The benefits must be either

        1)   Payments made due to permanent injury or loss of bodily functions or

        2)   Reimbursement paid to the employee for medical expenses of the employee, spouse, or dependents. Any reimbursement in excess of medical expenses is included in income.

10. **Death Benefits**

    a.   All death benefits received by the beneficiaries or the estate of an employee from or on behalf of an employer are included in GI.

        1)   This is for employer paid death benefits, not to be confused with death benefits of a life insurance plan provided by an employer.

11. **Dependent Care Assistance**

    a.   An employee may exclude costs incurred by an employer for care of dependents who are under the age of 13 or disabled that allow the employee's gainful employment.

    b.   The maximum amount of the exclusion is the lesser of

        1) $5,000 ($2,500 if married filing separately) or

        2)   The lesser of the earned income for the taxable year of the employee or the employee's spouse, if married.

    c.   The value of dependent care provided by an employer at an on-site facility is based on the value of services provided and not the actual cost.

12. **Meals and Lodging**

    a. The value of meals furnished to an employee by or on behalf of the employer is excluded from the employee's GI if the meals are furnished on the employer's business premises and for the employer's convenience. The exclusion does not cover meal allowances.

    b. The value of lodging is excluded from GI if the lodging is on the employer's premises, is for the convenience of the employer, and must be accepted as a condition of employment.

13. **Incentive Stock Options**

    a. An employee may not recognize income when an incentive stock option is granted or exercised depending upon certain restrictions.

    b. The employee recognizes long-term capital gain if the stock is sold 2 years or more after the option was granted and 1 year or more after the option was exercised.

       1) The employer is not allowed a deduction.

    c. Otherwise, the excess of the stock's FMV on the date of exercise over the option price is ordinary income to the employee when the stock is sold.

       1) The employer may deduct this amount.
       2) The gain realized is short-term or long-term capital gain.

    d. Nonqualified stock option

       1) An employee stock option is not qualified if it does not meet numerous technical requirements to be an incentive stock option.

       2) If the option's FMV is ascertainable on the grant date,

          a) The employee has GI equal to the FMV of the option.
          b) The employer is allowed a deduction.
          c) There are no tax consequences when the option is exercised.
          d) Capital gain or loss is reported when the stock is sold.

       3) If the option's FMV is not ascertainable on the grant date,

          a) The excess of FMV over the option price is GI to the employee when the option is exercised.
          b) The employer is allowed a corresponding compensation deduction.
          c) The employee's basis in the stock is the exercise price plus the amount taken into ordinary income.

14. **Cafeteria Plans**

    a. A cafeteria plan is a benefit plan under which all participants are employees, and each participant has the opportunity to select between cash and nontaxable benefits.

       1) If the participant chooses cash, such cash is GI.
       2) If qualified benefits are chosen, they are excludable to the extent permitted by the IRC.

    b. The employee must choose the benefit before the tax year begins.

    c. Any unused benefit is forfeited.

    d. Self-employed individuals are not included.

    e. Employers **may** offer participation in a cafeteria plan to an employee on the employee's first day of employment, but employers **must** offer participation after the employee completes 3 years of employment.

f. The plan cannot discriminate in favor of highly compensated employees.

g. Every employer maintaining a cafeteria plan must file an information return, reporting the number of eligible and participating employees, the total cost of the plan for the tax year, and the number of highly compensated employees.

h. Nontaxable benefits include

   1) Dependent care assistance
   2) Group term life insurance coverage up to $50,000
   3) Disability benefits
   4) Accident and health benefits
   5) Group legal services

i. Plans may not offer scholarships, educational assistance, or meals and lodging (for the convenience of the employer).

j. Deferred compensation plans other than 401(k) plans do not qualify for exclusion under a cafeteria plan.

k. Nonemployee beneficiaries (e.g., spouses) may not participate in a cafeteria plan. They might benefit, however, depending on the plan selection.

Stop and review! You have completed the outline for this subunit. Study multiple-choice questions 9 through 14 beginning on page 146.

5.4 FARM INCOME AND EXPENSES

1. **Farm Income**

   a. Income from farming activity is reported in Part I of Schedule F (Form 1040). In addition to Part I, accrual method taxpayers must use Part III for reporting income.

   b. **Gains from Sales**

      1) In general, gains from the sale of livestock, produce, and grains are reported on Schedule F.

         a) Gains from the sale of livestock used for draft (hauling), dairy, breeding, or sporting purposes generally result in capital gains and are not reported on Schedule F.

   c. **Distributions from a Cooperative**

      1) All distributions from a farm cooperative must be reported.

   d. **Payments from Agricultural Programs**

      1) Government payments for these programs are usually reported to the farmer on Form 1099-G.

      2) The amount reported on Schedule F includes direct, counter-cyclical, price support, diversion, and cost-share payments, along with payments in the form of materials or services.

   e. **Commodity Credit Corporation (CCC) Loans**

      1) Farmers may choose to treat CCC loans secured by pledged crops as taxable income in the year the loan proceeds are received.

         a) If the pledged crops are later forfeited to the CCC in full payment of the loan, any outstanding loan amount is taxable income.

    f.   **Crop Insurance Proceeds**

        1) Payments received for losses to crops are income in the year received.

            a) A 1-year deferment of income is allowed if the payment was received in the year of the damage.

        2) Federal crop disaster payments are treated the same as crop insurance proceeds.

    g.   **Custom Hire (Machine Work)**

        1) Payment received for contract work or custom work performed off the taxpayer's own farm for others or for the use of the taxpayer's property or machines is income regardless of the form of payment.

    h.   Other income includes tax credits, bartering income, discharge of indebtedness, excess depreciation recapture, prizes, etc.

    i.   **Farm Income Averaging**

        1) If a taxpayer is engaged in a farming or fishing business, (s)he may be able to average all or some of his or her current year's farm income by shifting it to the 3 prior years (base years).

        2) An individual, a partner in a partnership, or a shareholder in an S corporation may elect farm income averaging on a timely filed return (including extensions) or later if the IRS approves.

        3) The taxpayer need not have engaged in a farming business in any base year.

        4) Corporations, partnerships, S corporations, estates, and trusts cannot use farm income averaging.

        5) To elect farm income averaging as a tax computation method, the taxpayer must file a Schedule J with his or her income tax return for the election year. This includes late or amended returns if the period of limitations on filing a claim for credit or refund has not expired.

    j.   **Special Circumstances**

        1) The gain from sales of livestock caused by drought, flood, or other weather-related conditions can be postponed for 4 years. If, because of the weather-related conditions, a farmer who uses the cash method of accounting sells more livestock (including poultry) than (s)he would have sold under normal business conditions, the farmer may choose to include the gain from the sale of the additional livestock in income next year instead of the current year.

            a) The election applies to all livestock, whether held for resale or other purposes. It applies even if the livestock was not actually raised or sold within an area designated for federal assistance, as long as the weather-related condition forced the sale.

SCHEDULE F
(Form 1040)

Department of the Treasury
Internal Revenue Service (99)

Profit or Loss From Farming

▶ Attach to Form 1040, Form 1040NR, Form 1041, Form 1065, or Form 1065-B.
▶ Information about Schedule F and its separate instructions is at *www.irs.gov/schedulef*.

OMB No. 1545-0074

[Year]

Attachment
Sequence No. **14**

Name of proprietor

Social security number (SSN)

A Principal crop or activity	B Enter code from Part IV ▶	C Accounting method: ☐ Cash ☐ Accrual	D Employer ID number (EIN), (see instr)

E Did you "materially participate" in the operation of this business during [current year]? If "No," see instructions for limit on passive losses ☐ Yes ☐ No

F Did you make any payments in [current year] that would require you to file Form(s) 1099 (see instructions)? . . . . ☐ Yes ☐ No

G If "Yes," did you or will you file required Forms 1099? . . . . ☐ Yes ☐ No

Part I   Farm Income—Cash Method. Complete Parts I and II (Accrual method. Complete Parts II and III, and Part I, line 9.)

1a	Sales of livestock and other resale items (see instructions) . . .	**1a**	
b	Cost or other basis of livestock or other items reported on line 1a . . .	**1b**	
c	Subtract line 1b from line 1a		**1c**
2	Sales of livestock, produce, grains, and other products you raised		**2**
3a	Cooperative distributions (Form(s) 1099-PATR) .	**3a**	**3b** Taxable amount	**3b**
4a	Agricultural program payments (see instructions) .	**4a**	**4b** Taxable amount	**4b**
5a	Commodity Credit Corporation (CCC) loans reported under election		**5a**
b	CCC loans forfeited	**5b**	**5c** Taxable amount	**5c**
6	Crop insurance proceeds and federal crop disaster payments (see instructions)		
a	Amount received in [current year]	**6a**	**6b** Taxable amount	**6b**
c	If election to defer to [next year] is attached, check here ▶ ☐		**6d** Amount deferred from [prior year]	**6d**
7	Custom hire (machine work) income		**7**
8	Other income, including federal and state gasoline or fuel tax credit or refund (see instructions)		**8**
9	**Gross income.** Add amounts in the right column (lines 1c, 2, 3b, 4b, 5a, 5c, 6b, 6d, 7, and 8). If you use the accrual method, enter the amount from Part III, line 50 (see instructions) . . . . ▶		**9**

Part II   Farm Expenses—Cash and Accrual Method. Do not include personal or living expenses (see instructions).

10	Car and truck expenses (see instructions). Also attach **Form 4562**	**10**		23	Pension and profit-sharing plans	**23**
11	Chemicals	**11**		24	Rent or lease (see instructions):	
12	Conservation expenses (see instructions)	**12**		a	Vehicles, machinery, equipment	**24a**
13	Custom hire (machine work) .	**13**		b	Other (land, animals, etc.) . .	**24b**
14	Depreciation and section 179 expense (see instructions) .	**14**		25	Repairs and maintenance . .	**25**
				26	Seeds and plants	**26**
15	Employee benefit programs other than on line 23 . . .	**15**		27	Storage and warehousing . .	**27**
				28	Supplies	**28**
16	Feed	**16**		29	Taxes	**29**
17	Fertilizers and lime . . .	**17**		30	Utilities	**30**
18	Freight and trucking . . .	**18**		31	Veterinary, breeding, and medicine	**31**
19	Gasoline, fuel, and oil . . .	**19**		32	Other expenses (specify):	
20	Insurance (other than health)	**20**		a	_____	**32a**
21	Interest:			b	_____	**32b**
a	Mortgage (paid to banks, etc.)	**21a**		c	_____	**32c**
b	Other	**21b**		d	_____	**32d**
22	Labor hired (less employment credits)	**22**		e	_____	**32e**
				f	_____	**32f**

33	**Total expenses.** Add lines 10 through 32f. If line 32f is negative, see instructions . . . . ▶		**33**
34	**Net farm profit or (loss).** Subtract line 33 from line 9		**34**

If a profit, stop here and see instructions for where to report. If a loss, complete lines 35 and 36.

35 Did you receive an applicable subsidy in [current year]? (see instructions) . . . . ☐ Yes ☐ No

36 Check the box that describes your investment in this activity and see instructions for where to report your loss.

a ☐ All investment is at risk.   b ☐ Some investment is not at risk.

For Paperwork Reduction Act Notice, see the separate instructions.   Cat. No. 11346H   Schedule F (Form 1040) [Year]

2. **Farm Expenses**

   a. Farmers are allowed to deduct any ordinary and necessary costs of operating a farm for profit.

   b. Payments or portions thereof used by a farmer for personal or living expenses do not qualify as farm expenses and are not reported on Schedule F; however, they may be deductible and reported elsewhere on Form 1040 and related schedules.

   c. Generally, farming deductions are claimed in Part II of Schedule F.

   d. **Part I**

   1) **Cost of Sales**

   a) The cost of livestock and other resale purchases are deductible as COGS on line 1b.

   b) These are the only expenses reported in Part I.

   e. **Part II**

   1) **Car and Truck Expenses**

   a) The actual expenses or standard mileage rate may be deducted.

   b) If the actual expenses are used, then the amounts for depreciation and rent/lease are reported on separate lines of the return.

   2) **Conservation**

   a) Expenses paid to conserve soil and water, or to prevent erosion of land used for farming, may be deducted.

   b) The deduction is limited to 25% of gross farm income, and the expenses must be consistent with an approved conservation plan.

   3) **Custom Hire/Machine Work**

   a) Expenses for equipment rental with an operator.

   b) Expenses for rentals without an operator are deductible, but on a separate line of the schedule.

   4) **Depreciation/Section 179**

   a) Only allowed for farm equipment. In other words, there is no deduction for home (except for business portion), personal items, land, livestock for resale, or other inventory.

   5) **Employee Benefit Programs**

   a) Examples include health and pension plans.

   b) Pension and profit-sharing plan expenses are reported on a separate line from other programs.

   6) **Feed**

   a) In general, cash basis taxpayers can deduct prepaid livestock feed only in the year the feed is consumed.

   i)   An exception allows feed not used until the following year to be deducted up to 50% of other farm expenses.

   7) **Freight/Trucking**

   a) Transportation cost associated with the purchase of livestock for resale is not freight expense. Instead the cost is added to the cost of the livestock and deducted when the livestock is sold.

8) **Insurance**

    a)   Premiums for farm business insurance and employee accident and health insurance are deductible, although separately reported.

    b)   Amounts credited to a reserve for self-insurance or premiums paid for lost earnings coverage due to sickness or disability are not deductible.

9) **Interest**

    a)   Business mortgage interest and other business interest (e.g., investment) are deductible but are separately stated on the return.

10) **Labor Hired**

    a)   Deductible amounts for farm labor include boarding cost but not the value of farm products used by farm labor.

11) **Rental/Leases**

    a)   In addition to deducting machine rentals, mentioned under "Custom Hire/ Machine Work" on the previous page, land and animal rentals or leases are deductible.

12) **Repairs and Maintenance**

    a)   Incidental repair and maintenance costs of farm assets are deductible.

    b)   The work must not add value to or appreciably prolong the life of the asset (those costs would be capitalized and depreciated).

    c)   Repairs or maintenance on the farmer's home are personal expenses and not deductible.

13) **Taxes**

    a)   Deductible taxes include real estate and personal property taxes on farm business assets, FICA taxes to match employee withholding, FUTA tax, and federal highway use tax.

    b)   Taxes not included on Schedule F are federal income, estate, gift, improvement (e.g., paving, sewers), personal use property (e.g., home), and sales taxes.

14) **Utilities**

    a)   Deductible utilities are those for business use on the farm.

    b)   Only the business percentage of charges of a second phone line (including the base rate) are deductible.

    c)   The first phone line is considered 100% personal.

15) **Miscellaneous**

    a)   Chemicals; fertilizers and lime; gasoline, fuel, and oil; seeds and plants; storage and warehousing; supplies; and veterinary, breeding, and medicine each have their own return line for reporting.

16) **Other Expenses**

    a)   Other expenses include carryover of at-risk loss; bad debts; start-up costs; business use of home; forestation costs; legal and professional fees; travel, meals, and entertainment; and reproductive period expenses.

17) Farmers must **withhold federal income, Social Security, and Medicare taxes** from the salaries and wages of farm employees.

Stop and review! You have completed the outline for this subunit. Study multiple-choice questions 15 through 20 beginning on page 148.

QUESTIONS

5.1 Business Income and Expenses

1. On December 1, 2017, Krest, a self-employed cash-basis taxpayer, borrowed $200,000 to use in her business. The loan was to be repaid on November 30, 2018. Krest paid the entire interest amount of $24,000 on December 1, 2017. What amount of interest was deductible on Krest's 2017 income tax return?

A. $0

B. $2,000

C. $22,000

D. $24,000

Answer (B) is correct.
    REQUIRED: The amount of prepaid interest deductible on Krest's tax return for the current year.
    DISCUSSION: Costs of business borrowing are generally deductible, but prepaid interest in any form must be amortized over the period of the loan. Only 1 month of the loan has expired, so $2,000 [$24,000 × (1 ÷ 12)] is deductible.
    Answer (A) is incorrect. The interest related to the expired portion of the loan is deductible. Answer (C) is incorrect. The amount of $22,000 is the prepaid interest that should be amortized in 2018. Answer (D) is incorrect. Only one month of interest is deductible, not the entire interest amount of $24,000.

2. Mock operates a retail business selling illegal narcotic substances. When Mock calculates business income, he may adjust for

I.   Cost of merchandise

II.   Business expenses other than the cost of merchandise

A. I only.

B. II only.

C. Both I and II.

D. Neither I nor II.

Answer (A) is correct.
    REQUIRED: The deductible items allowed to arrive at business income.
    DISCUSSION: An adjustment to gross receipts is permitted for the cost of merchandise related to the selling of illegal narcotic substances (Sec. 280E), even if the narcotics are listed in the Controlled Substances Act. However, all other business expenses related to the sales are not deductible.
    Answer (B) is incorrect. Business expenses for the sale of narcotics are not deductible. Answer (C) is incorrect. An adjustment for cost of merchandise is allowed, but business expenses associated with the sale of narcotics are not deductible. Answer (D) is incorrect. An adjustment to gross receipts is permitted for the cost of merchandise related to the selling of illegal narcotic substances.

3. Phil Armonic is actively engaged in the oil business and owns numerous oil leases in the Southwest. During 2017, he made several trips to inspect oil wells on the leases. As a result of these overnight trips, he paid the following

Plane fares	$4,000
Hotels	1,000
Meals	800
Entertaining lessees	500

Of the $6,300 in expenses incurred, he can claim as deductible expenses

A. $6,300

B. $5,650

C. $5,000

D. $4,650

Answer (B) is correct.
    REQUIRED: The deductible amount of expenses incurred on overnight trips.
    DISCUSSION: A deduction is allowed for travel expenses while away from home in the pursuit of a trade or business. Both meal and entertainment expenses are limited to 50% of their cost. Assuming that Armonic's expenses meet the business relation requirements, his total deduction is

Plane fares	$4,000
Hotels	1,000
Meals ($800 × 50%)	400
Entertainment ($500 × 50%)	250
Total deduction	$5,650

    Answer (A) is incorrect. Only part of the expenses may be deducted. Answer (C) is incorrect. Meal and entertainment expenses are deductible but limited to 50%. Answer (D) is incorrect. The cost of lodging is deductible as travel expense.

4. The following 2017 information pertains to Sam and Ann Hoyt, who filed a joint federal income tax return for the calendar year 2017:

Adjusted gross income -- $34,000
$100 contribution to a recognized political party

The Hoyts itemized their deductions. What amount of the $100 political contribution were the Hoyts entitled to claim as a credit against their 2017 tax?

A. $0

B. $25

C. $50

D. $100

Answer (A) is correct.
    REQUIRED: The amount taxpayers are entitled to claim as a credit for political contributions.
    DISCUSSION: Contributions to a political party or candidate are not deductible.

5. Recasto owns a second residence that is used for both personal and rental purposes. During 2017, Recasto used the second residence for 50 days and rented the residence to Louis for 200 days. Which of the following statements is true?

A. Depreciation may not be deducted on the property under any circumstances.

B. A rental loss may be deducted if rental-related expenses exceed rental income.

C. Utilities and maintenance on the property must be divided between personal and rental use.

D. All mortgage interest and taxes on the property will be deducted to determine the property's net income or loss.

Answer (C) is correct.

REQUIRED: The true statement regarding Recasto's second residence.

DISCUSSION: The expenses for rental property must be allocated between personal and rental use. Deductions are only allowed for those expenses related to the rental expense. In order to qualify to deduct these amounts, the taxpayer must pass the "Minimum Rental Use" test, which states that the property must be rented for at least 15 days to qualify as business use. In addition, if the taxpayer uses the residence for personal use more than either 14 days or 10% of the days it is rented, the deductions are further limited.

Answer (A) is incorrect. Expenses allocable to the rental use are deductible. Answer (B) is incorrect. Although the minimum rental use test was passed, the residence failed the minimum personal use test. Therefore, it cannot qualify for any passive activity loss deduction. Answer (D) is incorrect. The expenses must be allocated between personal and rental use.

6. Basic Partnership, a cash-basis, calendar-year entity, began business on February 1, 2017. Basic incurred and paid the following in 2017:

Filing fees incident to the creation of the partnership	$ 3,600
Accounting fees to prepare the representations in offering materials	12,000

Basic elected to amortize costs. What is the maximum amount that Basic may deduct on the 2017 partnership return?

A. $5,000

B. $3,300

C. $0

D. $3,600

Answer (D) is correct.

REQUIRED: The amount of organizational costs that is deductible in the current tax year.

DISCUSSION: A partnership may elect to deduct up to $5,000 of any qualified organizational expenses (in addition to $5,000 of any startup costs) it incurs in the tax year in which it begins business. The $5,000 deducted for organizational expenses must be reduced by the amount by which the expenses exceed $50,000. Any remaining balance of organizational expenditures that are not immediately deductible must be amortized over a 15-year period. Organizational costs include costs associated with the formation of the partnership. They do not include syndication fees. Thus, the filing fees are the only fees that may be deducted. The maximum amount that Basic may deduct is $3,600.

Answer (A) is incorrect. A $5,000 deduction includes the syndication fees. Answer (B) is incorrect. The amount of $3,300 is the result of amortizing the organizational costs over 11 months. Answer (C) is incorrect. The amount of $0 does not include the filing fees.

5.2 FICA and FUTA Taxes

7. Michael operates his health food store as a sole proprietorship out of a building he owns. Based on the following information regarding Year 6, compute his net self-employment income (for SE tax purposes) for Year 6.

Gross receipts	$100,000
Cost of Goods Sold	49,000
Utilities	6,000
Real estate taxes	1,000
Gain on sale of business truck	2,000
Depreciation expense	5,000
Section 179 expense	1,000
Mortgage interest on building	7,000
Contributions to Keogh retirement plan	2,000
Net operating loss (NOL) from Year 5	10,000

A. $14,000

B. $16,000

C. $24,000

D. $31,000

Answer (D) is correct.

REQUIRED: The sole proprietor's net self-employment income.

DISCUSSION: Net earnings from self employment are gross income derived from a trade or business, less allowable deductions attributable to the trade or business. Capital gains and losses and contributions to retirement plans are not considered income or expenses for self-employment purposes. In addition, net operating losses are not considered for self-employment purposes. Michael's net self-employment income is computed as follows:

Gross receipts	$100,000
Cost of goods sold	(49,000)
Utilities	(6,000)
Real estate taxes	(1,000)
Depreciation expense	(5,000)
Section 179 expense	(1,000)
Mortgage interest	(7,000)
Net self-employment income	$ 31,000

Answer (A) is incorrect. The NOL is not considered when computing self-employment income. Answer (B) is incorrect. The NOL is not considered when computing self-employment income. Answer (C) is incorrect. The gain on the sale of the business truck, contributions to the Keogh retirement plan, and the NOL are not considered when computing self-employment income.

8. The self-employment tax is

   A. Fully deductible as an itemized deduction.

   B. Fully deductible in determining net income from self-employment.

   C. Partially deductible from gross income in arriving at adjusted gross income.

   D. Not deductible.

Answer (C) is correct.
REQUIRED: The true statement concerning deductibility of the self-employment tax.
DISCUSSION: To arrive at AGI, a self-employed person is allowed a deduction for the employer's portion of the self-employment tax paid. This is an above-the-line deduction.
Answer (A) is incorrect. Only a portion of the self-employment tax may be deducted, and the deduction is above-the-line. Answer (B) is incorrect. Only a portion of the self-employment tax may be deducted to arrive at AGI. Answer (D) is incorrect. A deduction for self-employment tax is available.

5.3 Employee Benefits

9. Under a "cafeteria plan" maintained by an employer,

   A. Participation must be restricted to employees and their spouses and minor children.

   B. At least 3 years of service are required before an employee can participate in the plan.

   C. Participants may select their own menu of benefits.

   D. Provision may be made for deferred compensation other than 401(k) plans.

Answer (C) is correct.
REQUIRED: The true statement about a maintained by an employer.
DISCUSSION: Section 125 defines a cafeteria plan as a written plan under which all participants are employees and the participants may choose among benefits consisting of cash and qualified benefits. Participation is restricted to the employee. There is no minimum period of employment required. Benefits that do not qualify include (1) deferred compensation plans other than Sec. 401(k) plans, (2) scholarships and fellowship grants or tuition reductions, (3) educational assistance, and (4) other fringe benefits.
Answer (A) is incorrect. Spouses and other nonemployee beneficiaries may not participate in a cafeteria plan. Answer (B) is incorrect. No minimum period of employment is required. The maximum period of employment an employer may require is 3 years. Answer (D) is incorrect. Deferred compensation plans other than Sec. 401(k) plans do not qualify for exclusion under a cafeteria plan.

10. John Budd files a joint return with his wife. Budd's employer pays 100% of the cost of all employees' group term life insurance under a qualified plan. Under this plan, the maximum amount of tax-free coverage that may be provided for Budd by his employer is

   A. $100,000

   B. $50,000

   C. $10,000

   D. $5,000

Answer (B) is correct.
REQUIRED: The maximum amount of employer-paid group term life insurance cost excludable by the employee.
DISCUSSION: Benefits received from an employer are compensation for services and are included in gross income unless provided otherwise. Included in gross income is the cost of group term life insurance paid by the employer, but only to the extent that such cost exceeds the cost of $50,000 of such insurance. The plan cannot discriminate in favor of highly-compensated employees.

11. Howard, an employee of Ogden Corporation, died on June 30, 2017. During July, Ogden made employee death payments of $10,000 to his widow and $10,000 to his 15-year-old son. What amounts should be included in gross income by the widow and son in their respective tax returns for 2017?

	Widow	Son
A.	$0	$0
B.	$10,000	$10,000
C.	$5,000	$5,000
D.	$7,500	$7,500

Answer (B) is correct.
REQUIRED: The employee death benefits a widow and son should each include in gross income.
DISCUSSION: All death benefits received by the beneficiaries or the estate of an employee from or on behalf of an employer are included in gross income. Therefore, the widow and the son should each include the full $10,000 received as employee death benefits.

12. In 2013, Ross was granted an incentive stock option (ISO) by his employer as part of an executive compensation package. Ross exercised the ISO in 2015 and sold the stock in 2017 at a gain. Ross's profit was subject to the income tax for the year in which the

A. ISO was granted.

B. ISO was exercised.

C. Stock was sold.

D. Employer claimed a compensation deduction for the ISO.

Answer (C) is correct.

REQUIRED: The year in which the taxpayer's profit on an ISO is subject to the income tax.

DISCUSSION: According to the Internal Revenue Code, an employee will have no income tax consequences on the grant date or the exercise date of an incentive stock option if that employee meets two requirements. First, the employee cannot dispose of the stock within 2 years after the grant date or within 1 year after the exercise date. Second, the employee must be employed by the company on the grant date until 3 months prior to the exercise date. Since Ross meets these requirements, he is not subject to any tax on the grant or exercise dates. Ross did, however, recognize a capital gain when he sold the stock in 2017.

Answer (A) is incorrect. There are no income tax consequences on the grant date. Answer (B) is incorrect. There are no income tax consequences on the exercise date. Answer (D) is incorrect. An employer may not take a deduction for the amount of the profit on an incentive stock option.

13. Frank Clarke, an employee, was covered under a noncontributory pension plan. Frank died on April 15, 2017, at age 64 and, pursuant to the plan, his widow received monthly pension payments of $500 beginning May 1, 2017. Mrs. Clarke also received an employee death payment of $10,000 in May 2017. How much should she include in her gross income for 2017?

A. $5,000

B. $9,000

C. $10,000

D. $14,000

Answer (D) is correct.

REQUIRED: The amount of monthly pension payments and/or the amount of a lump-sum death benefit that is included in gross income.

DISCUSSION: All death benefits received by the beneficiaries or the estate of an employee from, or on behalf of, an employer are included in gross income. The pension payments must be included unless Frank made contributions to the pension plan.

14. Which of the following fringe benefits is **not** excludable from an employee's wages?

A. Qualified employee discount.

B. Educational assistance expenses of $5,250 provided through an educational assistance program.

C. $2,500 of group term life insurance covering the death of an employee's spouse or dependent.

D. Dependent care assistance of $5,000 provided through a dependent care assistance program.

Answer (C) is correct.

REQUIRED: The fringe benefit not excludable from an employee's wages.

DISCUSSION: Under the IRC, the cost of qualified group term life insurance paid by an employer is included in the employee's gross income to the extent that such cost exceeds the cost of $50,000 of such insurance. The exclusion only applies to coverage of the employee. Payments for coverage of an employee's spouse or dependent are included in an employee's wages.

Answer (A) is incorrect. Qualified employee discounts are excludable. Answer (B) is incorrect. Under an employer's educational assistance program, the employee may exclude up to $5,250 from his or her gross income. Answer (D) is incorrect. Dependent care assistance of $5,000 is excludable.

5.4 Farm Income and Expenses

15. Jon, a cash-basis taxpayer, is the sole proprietor of a deer farm. Part of his farm land was transferred to the bank for partial payment of a loan. The remaining loan balance was discharged. He received the following amounts during 2017:

Deer sales	$100,000
Alimony	5,000
Debt discharge	9,000

Each of the deer had been purchased 2 years earlier for $5,000 and sold this year for $10,000. One of the deer sales was a buck that Jon had purchased and used for breeding. What amount does Jon report on Schedule F as gross income?

- A. $50,000

- B. $54,000

- C. $109,000

- D. $114,000

Answer (B) is correct.
REQUIRED: The calculated gross income for Form 1040 Schedule F.
DISCUSSION: Most farm-related income is reported in Part 1 of Form 1040 Schedule F; however, one exception to that is the reporting of capital gains. Capital assets include livestock used for breeding and are reported on Schedule D. The cost of livestock purchased for resale is calculated in to arrive at gross income. Jon's gross income includes the gain from nine deer ($100,000 ÷ $10,000 – 1 capital asset) and the debt discharge. The gross income is $54,000 ($90,000 of sales – $45,000 COGS + $9,000 debt discharge). Alimony received is reported on line 11 of Form 1040, not on Schedule F.
Answer (A) is incorrect. The deer used for breeding is a capital asset and reported on Schedule D (not Schedule F). In addition, gross income includes the $9,000 from the discharge of debt. Answer (C) is incorrect. The deer used for breeding is a capital asset and reported on Schedule D (not Schedule F). In addition, the cost of the sales is calculated in to arrive at gross income. Answer (D) is incorrect. Alimony and capital gains are reported on Form 1040 and Schedule D, respectively, and the cost of sales is calculated in arriving at gross farm income.

16. Farmer Jane received the following income during the current year:

Materials as a direct payment from agricultural program	$30,000
Insurance proceeds for crop losses last year	50,000
Rental of spare rooms attached to residence	14,400
Discharge of loan for farming property	2,500

What is Jane's gross income reported on Schedule F?

- A. $30,000

- B. $32,500

- C. $82,500

- D. $96,900

Answer (C) is correct.
REQUIRED: The calculated gross income for Form 1040 Schedule F.
DISCUSSION: Only farm-related income is reported on Schedule F. In general, any income or expenses related to Jane's personal residence is not farm related; therefore, the rental income is not farm related and not reported on Schedule F but would instead be reported on Schedule E. Farm income this year does include crop insurance proceeds since the loss was last year and deferment is only allowed for payments in the year of the damage. Payments from agricultural programs are farm income regardless of whether paid in cash, materials, or services. Discharge of indebtedness for farm assets is farm income. Jane's gross farm income is $82,500 ($30,000 + $50,000 + $2,500).
Answer (A) is incorrect. Crop insurance proceeds along with any discharge of farm indebtedness are reported on Schedule F. Answer (B) is incorrect. Crop insurance proceeds are reported on Schedule F. Answer (D) is incorrect. Only farm-related income is reported on Schedule F. Income related to the personal residence (e.g., rent) is not farm related.

17. A cash-basis farmer with gross farm income of $95,000 incurred the following expenses:

Feed for the current year	$ 5,000
Combine rental with an operator	1,500
Auger rental without an operator	50
Phone line installation	65
Farm labor	30,000

The phone installation expense is for a first line into the home of the farmer. The line is used 20% for business. The farm labor cost includes $15,000 for wages, $12,000 for boarding, and $3,000 for farm products used by the labor. What is the net farm profit?

- A. $58,385

- B. $58,450

- C. $61,450

- D. $64,885

Answer (C) is correct.
REQUIRED: The net farm profit.
DISCUSSION: Farmers may deduct any ordinary and necessary costs of operating a farm for profit. Only feed expense for the amount consumed during the current tax year may be deducted by a cash basis taxpayer. Both farm-related rentals (i.e., with or without an operator) are deductible. Farmers may only deduct the business portion of phone installations for other than the first line. Farm labor and labor boarding costs are deductible, but not the value of farm products used by farm labor. The net farm profit is $61,450 [$95,000 – $5,000 – $1,500 – $50 – ($30,000 – $3,000)].
Answer (A) is incorrect. Installation cost of a first line in a home is a personal expense, even if the farmer uses it for business. In addition, the value of farm products used by hired labor is not deductible. Answer (B) is incorrect. The value of farm products used by hired labor is not deductible. Answer (D) is incorrect. The feed and rentals are all deductible. In addition, the cost of installing the phone line (first line) and the value of farm products used by hired labor are not deductible.

18. Which of the following may use income averaging for farming?

    A. Corporations.

    B. Partnerships.

    C. Trusts.

    D. S corporation shareholder.

Answer (D) is correct.
    REQUIRED: The entity or individual allowed to use income averaging for farming.
    DISCUSSION: Individuals, partners, and S corporation shareholders are allowed to average all or some of his or her current year's farm income by shifting it to the 3 prior years (base years).
    Answer (A) is incorrect. Neither a corporation nor its shareholders may average their farm income. Answer (B) is incorrect. A partner may use farm income averaging but not the partnership. Answer (C) is incorrect. Individuals, not trusts, may use farm income averaging.

19. During the current year, a farmer paid $20,000 for an approved conservation plan to prevent erosion of farm land. If the farmer had gross receipts of $80,000 and $20,000 in costs of livestock sold, what is the farmer's net farm profit?

    A. $40,000

    B. $45,000

    C. $60,000

    D. $80,000

Answer (B) is correct.
    REQUIRED: The net farm profit (Schedule F).
    DISCUSSION: Net farm profit equals gross farm income less applicable expenses. Gross farm income equals total sales less the cost of livestock sold ($60,000). The conservation cost deduction is limited to 25% of gross farm income ($15,000). The net farm profit is $45,000 ($60,000 – $15,000).
    Answer (A) is incorrect. The conservation cost deduction is limited to 25% of gross farm income. Answer (C) is incorrect. The farmer is allowed a limited deduction for the cost of the conservation plan. Answer (D) is incorrect. The farmer is allowed a deduction for the cost of the livestock sold and a limited deduction for the cost of the conservation plan.

20. In June of Year 1, a farmer paid a premium of $3,000 for tornado insurance on the barn. The policy will cover a period of 3 years beginning on July 1, Year 1. During the same year, the farmer spent $5,000 to repair the barn roof and another $5,000 to repair the house roof, which were damaged by a tornado in April. The farmer has dedicated 1/5 of the house as an office for operating the farm. How much may be deducted in Year 1 for insurance and repairs/maintenance?

	Insurance	Repairs/Maintenance
A.	$1,000	$10,000
B.	$3,000	$8,000
C.	$1,000	$1,000
D.	$500	$6,000

Answer (D) is correct.
    REQUIRED: The amount of the deduction for prepaid insurance premium and repairs/maintenance.
    DISCUSSION: Advanced payments of insurance premiums are deductible, but only in the year to which they apply, regardless of the accounting method used. Coverage of the barn is a farm business expense. The portion of the premium that is currently deductible is $500 [$3,000 × (6 ÷ 36 months)]. The repair/maintenance expenses must be separated into business use and personal use. Only the business use expenses are deductible. The barn repair expense is 100% business, but the house repair is only 1/5 business. The repair/maintenance deduction is $6,000 [$5,000 barn + ($5,000 × 20%)].
    Answer (A) is incorrect. The premiums only cover 6 months of Year 1. In addition, the repair/maintenance expense must be apportioned between business and personal. Answer (B) is incorrect. Advanced payments of insurance premiums are only deductible in the year to which they apply. Also, only 20% of the repair to the roof of the house is a business expense. Answer (C) is incorrect. The premiums only cover 6 months of Year 1. Also, 100% of the repair to the barn is deductible.

STUDY UNIT SIX
ADJUSTMENTS AND DEDUCTIONS FROM AGI

(25 pages of outline)

Above-the-line deductions are adjustments deducted from gross income to arrive at adjusted gross income (AGI).

Taxpayers are allowed to take certain deductions from AGI, including the greater of the standard or itemized deductions. The following are common deductions tested on the CPA exam:

Adjustments to Gross Income	Itemized Deductions
• Educator expenses • Certain business expenses of reservists, performing artists, etc. • Health savings account deduction • Moving expenses • Deductible part of self-employment tax • Self-employed SEP, SIMPLE, and qualified plans • Self-employed health insurance deduction • Penalty on early withdrawal of savings • Alimony paid • IRA deduction • Student loan interest deduction • Domestic production activities deduction • Jury duty repayments	• Medical and dental expenses • Taxes paid • Interest paid • Gifts to charity • Casualty and theft losses • Job expenses and certain miscellaneous deductions • Unreimbursed employee expenses • Tax preparation fees • Other expenses (e.g., investment fees, safe deposit box, etc.) • Other miscellaneous deductions

The CPA exam tests the method of computing income tax liability. In the past, however, candidates have generally not been required to memorize the tax rates for each bracket for each filing status. The computation questions have generally provided brackets and rates to be applied for specific questions. Nevertheless, candidates should be prepared to answer questions on the current rate-bracket structure (e.g., what is the highest marginal rate?).

2017 Individual Income Tax Rates and Brackets						
Rate	10%	15%	25%	28%	33%	35%	39.6%
Taxable Income		From 10%	From 15%	From 25%	From 28%	From 33%	From 35%
Filing Status	The First	Max. up to	Max. up to	Max. up to	Max. up to	Max. up to	Max. up to
Married Filing Jointly and Qualifying Widow(er)	$18,650	$75,900	$153,100	$233,350	$416,700	$470,700	$Balance
Head of Household	$13,350	$50,800	$131,200	$212,500	$416,700	$444,550	$Balance
Single	$9,325	$37,950	$91,900	$191,650	$416,700	$418,400	$Balance
Married Filing Separately	$9,325	$37,950	$76,550	$116,675	$208,350	$235,350	$Balance

Some candidates find it helpful to have the entire tax form side-by-side with our Knowledge Transfer Outline when studying. The full versions of the most up-to-date forms are easily accessible at www.gleim.com/taxforms. These forms and the form excerpts used in our outline are periodically updated as the latest versions are released by the IRS.

6.1 ABOVE-THE-LINE DEDUCTIONS

1.   Overview

a.   Above-the-line deductions are deducted from gross income to arrive at adjusted gross income (AGI).

Gross income – Above-the-line deductions = Adjusted gross income (AGI)

    1)   "Above-the-line deductions" is a term used in our materials, but they can also be referred to as "adjustments," "deductions to arrive at AGI," and "deductions for AGI."

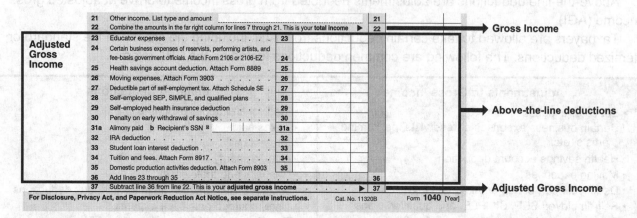

NOTE: This section of Form 1040 is condensed to help you conceptualize the difference between Gross Income and Adjusted Gross Income. Because the deductions are above line 37, they are referred to as above-the-line.

2.   Educator Expenses

From Form 1040

| 23 | Educator expenses . . . . | 23 | | |

a.   Primary and secondary school educators may claim an above-the-line deduction for unreimbursed expenses paid or incurred for books and supplies used in the classroom up to $250 annually. Each taxpayer (educator) on a joint return may deduct up to the maximum amount.

    1)   Books, supplies, computer equipment (including related software and services) and other equipment, and supplementary materials used in the classroom qualify for the deduction.

    2)   An eligible educator is an individual who, for at least 900 hours during a school year, is a kindergarten through grade 12 teacher, instructor, counselor, principal, or aide.

    3)   The term "school" is defined as one that provides elementary or secondary education, as determined under state law.

3. **Certain business expenses of reservists, performing artists, and fee-basis government officials.**

   From Form 1040

24	Certain business expenses of reservists, performing artists, and fee-basis government officials. Attach Form 2106 or 2106-EZ	24		

   a. Expenses reported on line 24 include

      1) Certain business expenses of National Guard and reserve members who traveled more than 100 miles from home to perform services as a National Guard or reserve member.
      2) Performing-arts-related expenses.
      3) Business expenses of fee-basis state or local government officials.

4. **Health Savings Account Deduction**

   From Form 1040

25	Health savings account deduction. Attach Form 8889	25		

   a. **Archer MSAs**

      1) Archer MSAs (previously called Medical Savings Accounts) allow individuals who are self-employed or employed by a small employer and covered by a high deductible health insurance plan to make tax-deductible contributions to pay medical expenses.
      2) The deduction for an Archer MSA is not included with other medical expenses and is not subject to the 10% limitation.
      3) The following are nontaxable:

         a) Earnings generated by the plan
         b) Distributions from an Archer MSA used to pay medical expenses
         c) Distributions made after the age of 65
         d) Distribution made upon death or disability

      4) Distributions that do not meet any criteria above are subject to a 20% penalty tax.
      5) Contributions are limited to a percentage of the deductible of the required high-deductible health plan (i.e., varies per health plan).
      6) An Archer MSA can be rolled into a Health Savings Account tax-free.

   b. **Health Savings Account**

      1) A Health Savings Account is a tax-exempt account the taxpayer sets up with a U.S. financial institution to save money used exclusively for future medical expenses.

         a) This account must be used in conjunction with a High Deductible Health Plan.

      2) The amount that may be contributed to a taxpayer's Health Savings Account depends on the nature of his or her coverage and his or her age.

         a) For self-only coverage, the taxpayer or his or her employer can contribute up to $3,400 ($4,400 for taxpayers who have reached age 55).
         b) For family coverage, the taxpayer or his or her employer can contribute up to $6,750 ($8,750 for taxpayers who have both reached age 55).

      3) The taxpayer must have the insurance for the whole year to contribute the full amount.

         a) For each month that (s)he did not have a High Deductible Health Plan, (s)he must reduce the amount that can be contributed by one-twelfth.

      4) Contributions to a Health Savings Account for 2017 may include contributions made until April 15, 2018.

5.   **Moving Expenses**

From Form 1040

26	Moving expenses. Attach Form 3903	26		

a.   Deduction for job-related relocation.

b.   Moving expenses are deductible to arrive at AGI to the extent the expenses are not reimbursed or paid for by the taxpayer's employer.

    1)   If expenses exceed reimbursements, only the qualified expenses in excess of the reimbursement are deductible.

    2)   If reimbursements exceed expenses, the excess is included in income.

c.   Qualifications

    1)   The individual's new principal place of work is at least **50 miles farther from the former residence than was the former principal place of work**. Measurement is by the shortest possible commonly traveled route.

Distance Test

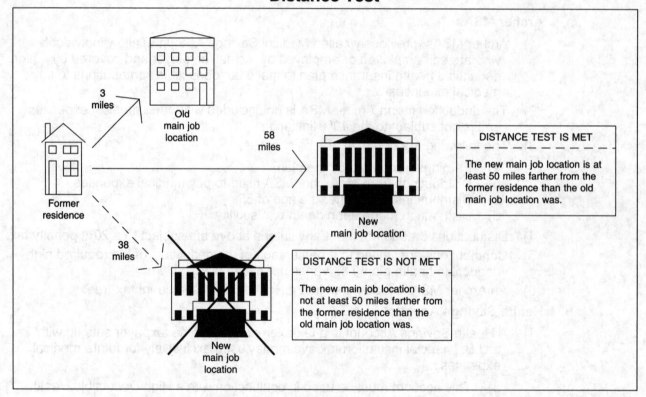

Figure 6-1

    2)   If the individual did not have a former principal place of work, the new principal place of work must be at least 50 miles from the taxpayer's former residence.

    3)   The individual is **employed full time in the new location during at least 39 weeks in the 12-month period immediately following the move**.

        a)   If the individual is self-employed, the above 39-week requirement must be met, and full-time employment during at least 78 weeks of the 24-month period immediately following the move is required.

    4)   Moving expenses may be deducted in the year in which they were incurred even if the 39- or 78-week employment requirement has not yet been satisfied.

        a)   If the time requirements are subsequently not met, an amended return must be filed or the amount of the deduction must be reported as gross income in the following year.

d. Direct expenses

1) Are deductible to arrive at AGI

2) Include the expenses of actually moving a taxpayer and his or her household goods and personal effects and travel (including lodging) from the former residence to the new residence

   a) Instead of actual expenses, a mileage rate of $.17 per mile in 2017 can be used for driving one's own automobile.

   b) The cost of meals en route is not deductible as a direct moving expense.

   c) Expenses incurred by members of the taxpayer's household are deductible.

e. Indirect expenses

1) Are not deductible

2) Include house hunting; temporary living expenses; and expenses related to the sale, purchase, or lease of a residence

6. **Self-Employment**

From Form 1040

27	Deductible part of self-employment tax. Attach Schedule SE .	27	
28	Self-employed SEP, SIMPLE, and qualified plans . .	28	
29	Self-employed health insurance deduction	29	

a. **Self-Employment Tax**

1) A self-employed person is allowed a deduction for the employer's portion of the FICA taxes paid to arrive at his or her AGI. The deduction for the employer's share is equal to 50% of the self-employment tax. For 2017, the deduction equals

   a) 6.2% of the first $127,200 of net self-employment income plus

   b) 1.45% of net self-employment income (no cap).

2) The 0.9% additional Medicare tax is on the employee's portion of FICA taxes. Therefore, the 0.9% tax is not deductible.

b. **Self-Employed SEP, SIMPLE, and Qualified Plans**

1) A self-employed individual can deduct specified amounts paid on his or her behalf to a qualified retirement or profit-sharing plan, such as a SEP or SIMPLE plan.

2) The most common self-employed retirement plan used is a SEP (Keogh) plan.

   a) The maximum annual contribution is limited to the lesser of 25% of the self-employed earnings or $54,000 (indexed for inflation).

   b) Self-employed earnings are reduced by the deductible part of self-employment taxes.

   c) Contributions to the plan are subtracted from net earnings to calculate self-employed earnings, creating a circular computation. For convenience, a standard rate of 20% is used to calculate the allowed deduction.

EXAMPLE

Alice has business income of net self-employed earnings of $125,000 before the deductible part of self-employment taxes of $25,000. The maximum annual deduction is calculated as follows:

($125,000 − $25,000) × 20% = $20,000

3) Another option for a self-employed taxpayer is a Savings Incentive Match Plan for Employees (SIMPLE).

a) Self-employed taxpayers may make both employer contributions and elective employee contributions.

b) Employee contributions are considered deferred compensation and are limited to $12,500 in 2017.

c) An employer match of up to 3% of self-employed earnings may be deducted as an above-the-line deduction.

c. **Self-Employed Health Insurance Deduction**

1) Self-employed individuals can deduct 100% of payments made for health insurance coverage for the individual, his or her spouse, and dependents.

2) The deduction is limited to the taxpayer's earned income derived from the business for which the insurance plan was established.

7. **Penalty on Early Withdrawal of Savings**

From Form 1040

30	Penalty on early withdrawal of savings	30	

a. Deduction is allowable for penalties from an early withdrawal of funds from certificates of deposit or other time savings accounts.

b. The deduction is taken in the year the penalty is incurred.

8. **Alimony**

From Form 1040

31a	Alimony paid **b** Recipient's SSN ▶		31a	

a. Alimony is gross income to the recipient and deductible by the payor.

b. Alimony payments may not extend past the death of the payee spouse.

c. Child support is neither gross income to the recipient nor deductible by the payor.

9. **IRA Deduction**

From Form 1040

32	IRA deduction	32	

a. **Individual Retirement Arrangement (IRA) Contributions**

1) For 2017, contributions are fully deductible (subject to certain qualifying rules and limitations) up to the lesser of $5,500 ($6,500 for taxpayers age 50 and over) or 100% of includible compensation. Because contributions are deducted from gross income, all distributions are included as ordinary gross income.

2) To qualify for the return year, contributions must be made by the due date of the return without regard to extensions.

3) Compensation includes alimony and earned income but not pensions, annuities, or other deferred compensation distributions.

4) An additional $5,500 ($6,500 for taxpayers age 50 and over) may be contributed to the IRA for the taxpayer's nonworking spouse if a joint return is filed.

a) The combined IRA contributions by both spouses cannot exceed their combined compensation for the year.

5) If the taxpayer is an active participant in an employer-sponsored retirement plan and has earned income of over $99,000 [married filing jointly or qualifying widow(er)] in 2017 ($62,000 in 2017 for head of household or single taxpayers, and $0 for married filing separate), the IRA deduction is proportionately reduced over a phaseout range.

   a) An individual is not labeled an active plan participant due to the status of that individual's spouse.

   b) If an individual's spouse is an active plan participant, that individual's deductible contribution will be phased out when AGI is between $186,000 and $196,000.

6) Excessive contributions may be subject to a 6% excise tax.

7) The owner of an IRA must begin receiving distributions by April 1 of the calendar year following the later of the calendar year in which the employee attains age 70 1/2 or the calendar year in which the employee retires.

8) IRA distributions made before age 59 1/2 are subject to regulation taxation plus a 10% penalty tax. Some exceptions to the penalty include distributions for

   a) Death or disability
   b) Medical expenses in excess of 10% of AGI
   c) Qualified higher education expenses
   d) The purchase of a first home (up to $10,000)

b. **Roth IRAs and Roth 401(k)s**

1) The Roth IRA is a **nondeductible** IRA.

2) Earnings on contributions are not taxed, provided they meet certain requirements to be considered a qualified distribution. To be a qualified distribution, the distribution must

   a) Satisfy the 5-year holding period.

      i) The distribution may not be made before the end of the 5-tax-year period.
      ii) The holding period begins with the tax year to which the contribution relates, not the year of contribution.

EXAMPLE

A contribution made on April 6, 2013, designated as a 2012 contribution, may be withdrawn tax-free in 2017 if it is otherwise a qualified distribution.

---

   b) Meet one of four other requirements. It must be

      i) Made on or after the date on which the individual attains age 59 1/2,
      ii) Made to a beneficiary or the individual's estate on or after the individual's death,
      iii) Attributed to the individual's disability, or
      iv) To pay for qualified first-time homebuyer expenses.

3) Distributions are treated as made from contributions first; thus, no portion of a distribution is treated as attributable to earnings or includible in gross income until the total of all distributions from the Roth IRA exceeds the amount of contributions.

   a) Nonqualified distributions are included in income after recovery of contribution, and they are subject to the 10% early withdrawal penalty.

EXAMPLE

John made $5,500 in contributions to his Roth IRA over the last decade. The value of John's Roth IRA is now $8,500. If the $8,500 is distributed and the distribution is qualified, John will not owe any tax or 10% penalty. If the distribution is unqualified, John will owe taxes at his marginal tax rate on the $3,000 in earnings and will owe a penalty ($300) of 10% of the earnings.

---

4) The overall limit for contributions to IRAs, both deductible and nondeductible, is $5,500 ($6,500 for taxpayers age 50 and over).

5) Contributions to a Roth IRA may continue past the age of 70 1/2.

6) Contributions to Roth IRAs are phased out when AGI is between $118,000 and $133,000 (between $186,000 and $196,000 for joint filers and $0 and $10,000 for married filing separate).

10. Education

NOTE: The above-the-line tuition and fees deduction expired at the end of 2016 and is not available for tax years 2017 or later.

a. Student Loan Interest Deduction

From Form 1040

33	Student loan interest deduction	33	

1) Taxpayers may deduct $2,500 of interest paid on qualified educational loans in 2017. This deduction is available for each year interest is paid.

2) The deduction is subject to income limits.

   a) The phaseout range begins when AGI exceeds $65,000 ($135,000 for joint filers) and ends at $80,000 ($165,000 for joint filers).

   b) The amount of reduction in the deduction can be calculated as follows:

$$\$2,500 \times \frac{(AGI - \$65,000)}{\$15,000 \text{ phaseout range}}$$

b. Coverdell Education Savings Accounts (CESA)

1) Taxpayers may make **nondeductible contributions** of $2,000 per child (beneficiary) to a CESA.

2) Contributions to CESAs are phased out when AGI is between $95,000 and $110,000 (between $190,000 and $220,000 for joint filers).

3) The earnings may be distributed tax free, provided they are used for qualified education expenses.

4) This income exclusion is not available for any year in which the American Opportunity Credit or Lifetime Learning Credit is claimed.

11. Domestic Production Activities Deduction

From Form 1040

35	Domestic production activities deduction. Attach Form 8903	35		

a. Generally, up to 9% of income derived from qualified production activities within the U.S. may be deducted. Refer to Study Unit 5, Subunit 1, "Business Income and Expenses," for details.

12. Jury Duty Pay

From Form 1040

36	Add lines 23 through 35	36		
37	Subtract line 36 from line 22. This is your **adjusted gross income** . . . . . ▶	37		

a. Jury duty pay is included in gross income.
b. However, jury duty pay remitted to an employer in exchange for regular pay is an above-the-line deduction.
c. Jury duty pay is considered a "write-in" adjustment, with the description and amount required to be entered on the dotted portion of line 36.

Stop and review! You have completed the outline for this subunit. Study multiple-choice questions 1 through 6 beginning on page 176.

6.2 STANDARD AND ITEMIZED DEDUCTIONS

1. Taxable Income

a. Taxable income is adjusted gross income (AGI) minus the greater of itemized deductions or the standard deduction, minus the deduction for personal exemptions.
b. Below-the-line deductions are all the deductions that may be subtracted from AGI to arrive at taxable income.

Taxable income = Adjusted gross income – Greater of allowable itemized deductions on Schedule A or the standard deduction – Personal exemptions

2. Itemized vs. Standard

a. The taxpayer itemizes deductions if the total amount of allowable itemized deductions, after all limits have been applied, is greater than the amount of the standard deduction. Otherwise, the taxpayer claims the standard deduction. A taxpayer must elect to itemize, or no itemized deductions will be allowed.

1) Election is made by filing Schedule A of Form 1040.
2) Election made in any other taxable year is not relevant.
3) Election may be changed by filing an amended return (Form 1040X).
4) A person who itemizes may not file either Form 1040EZ or Form 1040A.

3. Standard Deduction Unavailable

a. The following taxpayers are **not allowed** the standard deduction:

1) Persons who itemize deductions
2) Nonresident alien individuals
3) Individuals who file a "short period" return
4) A married individual who files a separate return and whose spouse itemizes
5) Partnerships, estates, and trusts

4.   **Standard Deduction**

STANDARD DEDUCTION AMOUNTS -- 2017

Filing Status	Basic	Additional Age 65/Blind
Married Filing Jointly (MFJ)	$12,700	$1,250
Qualifying Widow(er)	12,700	1,250
Head of Household (HH)	9,350	1,550
Single (other than above)	6,350	1,550
Married Filing Separately (MFS)	6,350	1,250

a.   The standard deduction is the sum of the basic standard deduction and the additional standard deductions.

b.   The **basic standard deduction** amount (shown in the table above) depends on filing status and dependency status on another's return.

1)   The basic standard deduction amount of a child under age 19 or a student under age 24 who can be claimed as a dependent on another individual's income tax return is limited to the greater of either

a) $1,050 or

b)   Earned income for the year plus $350 up to the otherwise applicable standard deduction.

i)   Earned income does not include either dividends or capital gains from the sale of stock.

c.   **Additional standard deduction** amounts, indexed for inflation, appear in the table above.

1)   An individual who has reached age 65 or is blind is entitled to the amount.

2)   An individual who both has reached age 65 and is blind is entitled to twice the amount.

3)   The individual is entitled to the amount if (s)he reaches age 65 before the end of the tax year

a)   Even if (s)he dies before the end of the year, but

b)   Not if (s)he dies before reaching age 65 even if (s)he would have otherwise reached age 65 before year's end.

4)   A person who becomes blind on or before the last day of the taxable year is entitled to the amount.

5)   Once qualified, the standard deduction is allowed in full.

a)   It is not prorated if a person dies during a tax year.

d.   As mentioned in Study Unit 3, Subunit 2 under Filing Requirements, the threshold requiring a tax return to be filed is generally the sum of the standard deduction (excluding any amount for being blind) plus personal exemptions (excluding dependency exemptions).

Traditionally, the AICPA has heavily tested itemized deductions, mostly with questions requiring calculations. Always read the questions very carefully. A question may contain one small, easily missed detail that changes the amount of the deduction.

5. **Itemized Deductions**

    a. Schedule A is the form where itemized deductions are reported.
    b. Itemized deductions include

        1) Medical and dental expenses
        2) Taxes paid
        3) Interest paid
        4) Charitable contributions
        5) Casualty and theft losses
        6) Other miscellaneous deductions
        7) Job expenses (covered in Subunit 6.3 and subject to 2% of AGI floor)

6. **Medical and Dental Expenses**

    From Form 1040 Schedule A

Medical and Dental Expenses	**Caution:** Do not include expenses reimbursed or paid by others.		
	1 Medical and dental expenses (see instructions)	**1**	
	2 Enter amount from Form 1040, line 38 **2**		
	3 Multiply line 2 by 10% (0.10).		
		3	
	4 Subtract line 3 from line 1. If line 3 is more than line 1, enter -0-		**4**

    a. Amounts paid for qualified medical expenses that exceed 10% of AGI may be
        deducted.

    NOTE: The disparity in the threshold percentage between taxpayers 65 or older and
    taxpayers under 65 ended starting with the 2017 tax year.

    b. To qualify for a deduction, an expense must be paid during the taxable year for the
        taxpayer, the taxpayer's spouse, or a dependent and must not be compensated for
        by insurance or otherwise during the taxable year.
    c. Deductible medical expenses are amounts paid for

        1) Diagnosis, cure, mitigation, treatment or prevention of disease, or for the
            purpose of affecting any structure or function of the body
        2) Transportation primarily for and essential to medical care
        3) Medical insurance
        4) Qualified long-term care premiums and services

    d. A medical expense deduction is not allowed for amounts paid for any activity or
        treatment designed merely to improve an individual's general health or sense of
        wellness, even if recommended by a physician.

        1) Examples include participation in a health club, a stop-smoking clinic, or a
            weight-loss institute.

            a) Such expenses may be deductible if the services are prescribed by a
                physician who provides a written statement that they are necessary to
                alleviate a physical or mental defect or illness.

e.   The cost of in-patient hospital care (including meals and lodging) is deductible as a medical expense.

1)   If the principal reason an individual is in an institution (e.g., nursing home, rehabilitation facility, or disability-specific school) other than a hospital is the need for and availability of the medical care furnished by the institution, the full costs of meals, lodging, and other services necessary (including special schooling) for furnishing the medical care are all deductible.

f.   Only drugs that require a prescription are qualified medical expenses.

g.   The following are also considered deductible medical expenses:

1)   Eyeglasses
2)   A guide dog
3)   Wheelchair, crutches, or artificial limbs
4)   Special beds
5)   Air conditioning
6)   Dehumidifying equipment

h.   Expenditures for new building construction or for permanent improvements to existing structures may be deductible in part.

1)   The excess of the cost of a permanent improvement over the increase in value of the property is a deductible medical expense.

a)   Even when the cost of the capital asset is not deductible, the cost of operating and maintaining the asset may be deductible when the asset is operated primarily for medical care.

2)   Construction of ramps for the disabled, installation of elevators, widening of doorways, or lowering of kitchen cabinets or equipment may each qualify.

i.   Travel

1)   Amounts paid for transportation essential to (and primarily for) medical care are deductible.

a)   This includes the transportation cost of traveling on a doctor's order to alleviate a specific chronic ailment.

2)   The taxpayer may choose between actual expenditures (e.g., taxis, air fare) or $.17 per mile for 2017 (plus the cost of tolls and parking).

3)   Expenditures for lodging are deductible up to $50 per night per individual.

j.   Insurance

1)   Premiums paid for medical insurance that provides for reimbursement of medical care expenses are deductible.

2)   Self-employed health insurance payments may be deducted as an above-the-line deduction.

7. **Taxes Paid**

From Form 1040 Schedule A

Taxes You Paid	5 State and local **(check only one box):**
	  a ☐ Income taxes, **or**
	  b ☐ General sales taxes
			5		

	6 Real estate taxes (see instructions)		6		
	7 Personal property taxes		7		
	8 Other taxes. List type and amount ▶ _____ _____		8		
	9 Add lines 5 through 8			9	

a. A taxpayer who itemizes deductions is permitted to deduct the full amount of certain taxes that are paid and incurred during the taxable year, subject to the limit on aggregate itemized deductions.

b. Recovery of a tax benefit item is generally included in gross income.

   1) The recovered amount is included in income to the extent total allowable itemized deductions (for the applicable year) exceed the standard deduction (for the same year).

c. Real Property

   1) The owner may deduct state, local, and foreign real property taxes.

   2) If real property is bought or sold during the year, the real property tax is apportioned between the buyer and the seller on the basis of the number of days each one held the property during the real property tax year (regardless of nonproration agreements between buyers and sellers).

      a) The purchaser is presumed to own the property on the date of sale.

   3) Special assessments for local improvements increase the basis of the property and are not deductible.

d. Ad Valorem, Personal Property Taxes

   1) These taxes are deductible, but only if the tax is

      a) Substantially in proportion to the value of the property,

      b) Imposed on an annual basis, and

      c) Actually imposed.

e. Income Taxes

   1) State income taxes are deductible.

   2) Foreign income taxes paid are deductible, unless the foreign tax credit is claimed.

   3) Individual taxpayers may claim an itemized deduction for general state and local sales tax in lieu of state income tax.

f. The following taxes are not deductible:

   1) Federal taxes on income, estates, gifts, inheritances, legacies, and successions

   2) State taxes on cigarettes and tobacco, alcoholic beverages, gasoline, registration, estates, gifts, inheritances, legacies, and successions

   3) Licensing fees of highway motor vehicles (if based on the weight of the vehicle)

8.   Interest Paid

From Form 1040 Schedule A

Interest You Paid	10	Home mortgage interest and points reported to you on Form 1098	**10**			
	11	Home mortgage interest not reported to you on Form 1098. If paid to the person from whom you bought the home, see instructions and show that person's name, identifying no., and address ▶				
Note: Your mortgage interest deduction may be limited (see instructions).		-- --	**11**			
	12	Points not reported to you on Form 1098. See instructions for special rules	**12**			
	13	Mortgage insurance premiums (see instructions)	**13**			
	14	Investment interest. Attach Form 4952 if required. (See instructions.)	**14**			
	15	Add lines 10 through 14			**15**	

a.   Qualified Residence Interest

1)   Qualified residence interest is deductible on no more than $1 million of acquisition indebtedness ($500,000 if married filing separately) and $100,000 of home equity indebtedness (aggregate amount) ($50,000 if married filing separately).

2)   It is interest paid or accrued during the tax year on acquisition or home equity indebtedness that is secured by a qualified residence.

3)   A qualified residence includes the principal residence of the taxpayer and one other residence owned by the taxpayer.

4)   A taxpayer who has more than two residences may select, each year, the residences used to determine the amount of qualified residence interest.

5)   Acquisition indebtedness is debt incurred in acquiring, constructing, or substantially improving a qualified residence. The debt must be secured by the residence.

6)   Home equity indebtedness is all debt other than acquisition debt that is secured by a qualified residence to the extent it does not exceed the fair market value of the residence reduced by any acquisition indebtedness.

7)   Points paid by the borrower are prepaid interest, which is typically deductible over the term of the loan.

   a)   Amounts paid as points may be deducted in the year paid if

      i)   The loan is used to buy or improve a taxpayer's principal home and is secured by that home;

      ii)   Payment of points is an established business practice in the area where the loan is made; and

      iii)   The points paid do not exceed points generally charged in the area.

8)   Points paid by the seller are a selling expense that reduces the amount realized on the sale.

   a)   The purchaser can elect to deduct points on the acquisition indebtedness of a principal residence by reducing the basis.

b. **Investment Interest Expense**

1) The IRC allows the deduction of a limited amount of investment interest as an itemized deduction.
2) Investment interest is interest paid or incurred (on debt) to purchase or carry property held for investment.
3) Investment interest does **not** include qualified residence interest or passive activity interest.

   a) Passive activity interest is includible with passive activities and deductible within the passive loss rules.

4) Limit

   a) Investment interest may be deducted only to the extent of net investment income, which is any excess of investment income over investment expense.

   b) Investment income is

      i) Non-trade or nonbusiness income from (a) interest; (b) dividends not subject to the capital gains tax; and (c) annuities, royalties, and other gross income from property held for investment.

      ii) Net gain on the disposition of property held for investment. A taxpayer may elect to treat all or a portion of long-term capital gains and qualified dividends as investment income.

      iii) Income treated as gross portfolio income under the PAL rules.

      iv) Income from interests in activities that involve a trade or business in which the taxpayer does not materially participate, if the activity is not treated as passive activity under the PAL rules.

   c) Investment income is **not**

      i) From rental real estate activity in which the taxpayer actively participates

5) Disallowed investment interest is carried forward indefinitely. It is deductible to the extent of investment income in a subsequent tax year.
6) Interest related to producing tax-exempt income is not deductible.

c. **Personal Interest Expense**

1) The general rule is that personal interest expense may **not** be deducted.
2) This includes interest on credit card debt, revolving charge accounts and lines of credit, car loans, medical fees, premiums, etc.
3) Personal interest expense does not include

   a) Interest on trade or business debt
   b) Investment interest
   c) Passive activity interest
   d) Qualified residence interest
   e) Interest on the unpaid portion of certain estate taxes
   f) Student loan interest

9.   Charitable Contributions

From Form 1040 Schedule A

Gifts to Charity	16	Gifts by cash or check. If you made any gift of $250 or more, see instructions	16				
If you made a gift and got a benefit for it, see instructions.	17	Other than by cash or check. If any gift of $250 or more, see instructions. You **must** attach Form 8283 if over $500 . . .	17				
	18	Carryover from prior year	18				
	19	Add lines 16 through 18				19	

a.   Charitable contributions are deductible only if they are made to qualified organizations.

b.   Qualified organizations can be either public charities or private foundations.

1)   Generally, a public charity is one that derives more than one-third of its support from its members and the general public.

c.   Donations can be made in the form of cash or noncash property.

d.   Individuals may carry forward excess contributions for 5 years.

e.   All rights and interest to the donation must be transferred to the qualified organization.

f.   Additional donation requirements:

1)   Clothing and household items donated must be in good or better condition.

a)   The exception to this rule is that a single item donation in less than good condition but still a $500 value or more is deductible with a qualified appraisal.

2)   Cash or cash equivalent donations require a bank record alone or a receipt, letter, etc., from the donee regardless of the amount. The receipt, etc., must

a)   Be provided at the time of donation

b)   State the name of the organization

c)   Include the date and amount of the donation

3)   Donations of $250 or more continue to require substantiation by a written receipt from the organization (the bank record alone is insufficient).

4)   A qualified appraisal for real property donations is required to be attached to the tax return for property valued over $5,000.

g.   If a donation is in the form of property, the amount of the donation depends upon the type of property and the type of organization that receives the property.

1)   Capital gain property is property on which a long-term capital gain would be recognized if it were sold on the date of the contribution.

2)   Ordinary income property is property on which ordinary income or short-term capital gain would be recognized if it were sold on the date of the contribution.

Examples of Charitable Contributions

Deductible as Charitable Contributions	Not Deductible As Charitable Contributions
Qualified donations to: <ul><li>Churches, synagogues, temples, mosques, and other religious organizations</li><li>Federal, state, and local governments, if the taxpayer's contribution is solely for public purposes (for example, a gift to reduce the public debt or maintain a public park)</li><li>Nonprofit schools and hospitals</li><li>The Salvation Army, American Red Cross, CARE, Goodwill Industries, United Way, Boy Scouts of America, Girl Scouts of America, Boys and Girls Clubs of America, etc.</li><li>War veterans groups</li></ul>	Qualified donations to: <ul><li>Civic leagues, social and sports clubs, labor unions, and chambers of commerce</li><li>Foreign organizations (exceptions exist)</li><li>Groups that are run for personal profit</li><li>Groups whose purpose is to lobby for law changes</li><li>Homeowners' associations</li><li>Individuals</li><li>Political groups or candidates for public office</li></ul>
Expenses paid for a student living with the taxpayer, sponsored by a qualified organization	Cost of raffle, bingo, or lottery tickets
	Dues, feed, or bills paid to country clubs, lodges, fraternal orders, or similar groups
Out-of-pocket expenses when the taxpayer serves a qualified organization as a volunteer	Tuition
	Value of the taxpayer's time or services
	Value of blood given to a blood bank

h. There are basically two types of charitable organizations: those classified as **50% limit organizations** and those classified as **non-50% limit organizations**.

1) 50% limit organizations, which encompass the majority of qualified charitable organizations, are generally public organizations. The following list represents some 50% organizations (IRS Publication 526 contains a complete, detailed list):

   a) Churches

   b) Educational organizations

   c) Hospitals and certain medical research organizations

   d) Organizations that are operated only to receive, hold, invest, and administer property and to make expenditures to or for the benefit of state and municipal colleges and universities

   e) The United States or any state, the District of Columbia, a U.S. possession (including Puerto Rico), a political subdivision of a state or U.S. possession, or an Indian tribal government

   f) Private operating foundations

   g) Private nonoperating foundations that make qualifying distributions of 100% of contributions within 2 1/2 months following the year they receive the contribution

2) Non-50% limit organizations are all qualified charities that are not designated as 50% limit organizations.

   a) They are generally other private organizations.

    i.   Charitable contribution deductions are subject to limitations.

        1)   The overall limitation on charitable deductions is 50% of AGI without regard to any net operating loss carry back (simply referred to as AGI through the rest of item 9's coverage of charitable contributions) (applicable to the total of all charitable contributions during the year), but certain contributions may be further limited to 30% or 20% of AGI, depending on the type of contribution given and the type of organization to which it is given (refer to the table on the next page).

        2)   Any donations that exceed this limitation can be carried forward and potentially deducted in the next 5 tax years.

        3)   Further limitations:

            a)   30% limitation. This 30% limit applies to gifts to all qualified charitable organizations other than 50% limit organizations.

            b)   Special 30% limitation for capital gain property. (Refer to Study Unit 8, Subunit 3, "Capital Gains and Losses," for the definition of a capital asset.) A special 30% limitation applies to gifts of capital gain property given to 50% limit organizations.

                i)   It is only applicable if the donor elects NOT to reduce the fair market value of the donated property by the amount that would have been long-term capital gain if (s)he had sold the property.

                ii)   If the reduction is elected, then only the 50% limitation applies.

            c)   20% limitation. This limitation applies to capital gain property donated to non-50% limit charities. The limit is actually the lesser of 20% of AGI or 30% of AGI minus capital gain contributions to public charities.

            d)   In accounting for the different limitations, all donations subject to the 50% limit are considered before the donations subject to the 30% limit.

            e)   In carrying over excess contributions to subsequent tax years, the excess must be carried over to the appropriate limitation categories. If a contribution in the 30% category is in excess of the limit, the excess is carried over and subject to the 30% limitation in the next year.

    j.   The value of services provided to a charitable organization is not deductible.

        1)   However, out-of-pocket, unreimbursed expenses incurred in rendering the services are deductible.

    k.   The value of a ticket to a charitable event is a deductible contribution to the extent the purchase price exceeds the FMV of the event's admission.

    l.   Generally, a deduction is allowed in the year the contribution is paid, including amounts charged to a bank credit card.

    m.   Up to $50 per month of actual expenses incurred for maintaining a qualified student may be deducted if there is a written agreement with the sponsoring charitable organization.

Form of Property	Amount of Donation	Limitation
50% Limit Organizations (Mainly Public)		
Cash	Cash amount	50% AGI
Capital Gain Property	FMV (elect not to reduce FMV by potential long-term capital gain)	30% AGI (special limit)
• Tangible personal property unrelated to donee's purpose	Lower of FMV or AB	50% AGI
• Election to reduce property to adjusted basis	Lower of FMV or AB	50% AGI
Ordinary Income Property	Lower of FMV or AB	50% AGI
Services	Unreimbursed expenses	50% AGI
Non-50% Limit Organizations (Mainly Private)		
Cash	Cash amount	30% AGI (regular limit)
Capital Gain Property	Lower of FMV or AB	Lesser of: 20% AGI or excess of 30% AGI over contributions to public charities
Ordinary Income Property	Lower of FMV or AB	30% AGI (regular limit)
Services	Unreimbursed expenses	30% AGI (regular limit)

10. Casualty and Theft Losses

From Form 1040 Schedule A

Casualty and Theft Losses	20	Casualty or theft loss(es). Attach Form 4684. (See instructions.)	**20**

a. Taxpayers who itemize may deduct a limited amount for losses to nonbusiness property that arise from theft, fire, or other casualty.

b. In general, the loss amount is the lesser of the decline in FMV or the AB minus insurance reimbursements.

c. Limitation.

   1) Only the amount of each loss over $100 is deductible.

   2) Only the aggregate amount of all losses in excess of 10% of AGI is deductible.

   3) If the loss was covered by insurance, timely filing of an insurance claim is prerequisite to deduction.

d. If the net amount of all personal casualty gains and losses after applying the $100 limit (but before the 10%-of-AGI threshold) is positive, each gain or loss is treated as a capital gain or loss.

e. If the net amount is negative, the excess over 10% of AGI is deductible as an itemized deduction.

f. The cost of appraising a casualty loss is treated as a cost to determine tax liability (a miscellaneous itemized deduction subject to the 2%-of-AGI exclusion).

g. The cost of insuring a personal asset is a nondeductible personal expense.

11. Other Miscellaneous Deductions

From Form 1040 Schedule A

| Other Miscellaneous Deductions | 28 | Other—from list in instructions. List type and amount ▶ _____ _____ | | | 28 | | |

a. The following expenses are deductible as miscellaneous itemized deductions (not subject to 2% limit):

    1) Amortizable premium on taxable bonds
    2) Casualty and theft losses from income-producing property
    3) Federal estate tax on income in respect of a decedent
    4) Gambling losses up to the amount of gambling winnings
    5) Impairment-related work expenses of persons with disabilities
    6) Repayments of more than $3,000 under a claim of right
    7) Unrecovered investment in a pension

Stop and review! You have completed the outline for this subunit. Study multiple-choice questions 7 through 17 beginning on page 178.

6.3 JOB EXPENSES AND CERTAIN MISCELLANEOUS DEDUCTIONS

From Form 1040 Schedule A

Job Expenses and Certain Miscellaneous Deductions	21	Unreimbursed employee expenses—job travel, union dues, job education, etc. Attach Form 2106 or 2106-EZ if required. (See instructions.) ▶ _____		21				
	22	Tax preparation fees		22				
	23	Other expenses—investment, safe deposit box, etc. List type and amount ▶ _____ _____		23				
	24	Add lines 21 through 23		24				
	25	Enter amount from Form 1040, line 38	25					
	26	Multiply line 25 by 2% (0.02)		26				
	27	Subtract line 26 from line 24. If line 26 is more than line 24, enter -0-				27		

1. **Overview**

a. These itemized deductions are subject to a 2%-of-AGI exclusion.

b. Only that portion of the aggregate amount of these deductions that exceeds the threshold amount of 2% of AGI may be deducted from AGI.

c. Any surplus cannot be carried forward to a succeeding year.

d. The three categories of these itemized deductions are unreimbursed employee expenses, tax preparation fees, and other expenses.

2. **Unreimbursed Employee Expenses**

   a.   Employee expenditures **not reimbursed** by the employer are itemized deductions. These expenses are deductible because services as an employee are considered trade or business.

NOTE: Remember that Study Unit 4, Subunit 3, explained reimbursements under a nonaccountable plan, e.g., expense advance. The advance is income to the employee and the expense deductions are itemized as explained below and on the following pages.

      1) Employee travel away from home (including meals and lodging)

         a) **Travel expenses** include transportation, lodging, and meal expenses incurred in an employment-related context. To qualify for a deduction, the taxpayer must be away from his or her tax home overnight, and the purpose of the trip must be connected with the taxpayer's business.

         b) Only 50% of meals are deductible.

         c) If the employee's meal expenses are reimbursed by his or her employer and the reimbursement is not treated as compensation, the employer's deduction is limited to 50% of the expenses.

         d) If the employee's meal expenses are reimbursed by his or her employer and treated as compensation, the employee's deduction is limited to 50% of the expenses.

            i) Employers are not subject to the 50% limit to the extent they treat the reimbursement as compensation to employees.

      2) A new rule allows for lodging deductions when not traveling away from home, if qualified under one of two tests or rules.

         a) The deduction is allowed if all the facts and circumstances indicate the lodging is for carrying on a taxpayer's trade or business. One factor under this test is whether the taxpayer incurs an expense because of a bona fide condition or requirement of employment imposed by the taxpayer's employer.

         b) A safe harbor rule applies if

            i) The lodging is necessary for the individual to participate fully in, or be available for, a bona fide business meeting, conference, training activity, or other business function;

            ii) The lodging is for a period that does not exceed 5 calendar days and does not recur more frequently than once per calendar quarter;

            iii) The employee's employer requires the employee to remain at the activity or function overnight (if the individual is an employee); and

            iv) The lodging is not lavish or extravagant under the circumstances and does not provide any significant element of personal pleasure, recreation, or benefit.

IF there are expenses for . . .	THEN the taxpayer can deduct the cost of . . .
transportation	travel by airplane, train, bus, or car between the home and the business destination. If the taxpayer was provided with a free ticket or the taxpayer was riding free as a result of a frequent traveler or similar program, the cost is zero. Travel by ship (e.g., cruise ships) for Conventions has additional rules and limits.
taxi, commuter bus, and airport limousine	fares for these and other types of transportation that take the taxpayer between <ul><li>The airport or station and the hotel, and</li><li>The hotel and the work location of the customers or clients, the business meeting place, or the temporary work location.</li></ul>
baggage and shipping	sending baggage and sample or display material between the regular and temporary work locations.
car	operating and maintaining the car when traveling away from home on business. The taxpayer can deduct the actual expenses or the standard mileage rate, as well as business-related tolls and parking. If the taxpayer rents a car while away from home on business, (s)he can deduct only the business-use portion of the expenses.
lodging and meals	lodging and meals if the business trip is overnight or long enough to require a stop for sleep or rest to properly perform duties. Meals include amounts spent for food, beverages, taxes, and related tips and have additional rules and limits.
cleaning	dry cleaning and laundry.
telephone	business calls while on the business trip. This includes business communication by fax machine or other communication devices.
tips	tips paid for any expenses in this chart.
other	other similar ordinary and necessary expenses related to the business travel. These expenses might include transportation to or from a business meal, public stenographer's fees, computer rental fees, and operating and maintaining a house trailer.

3)   Employee transportation expenses

   a)   **Transportation expenses** include taxi fares, automobile expenses, tolls and parking fees, and airfare.

   b)   These expenses are treated as travel expenses if the employee is away from home overnight. Otherwise, they are transportation expenses.

   c)   Commuting costs are nondeductible.

   d)   Actual automobile expenses may be used for the deduction, or the taxpayer may use the standard mileage rate.

      i)   The standard mileage rate is $.535 per mile for 2017, plus parking fees and tolls.

      ii)   Actual expenses must be allocated between business use and personal use of the automobile. A deduction is allowed only for the business use.

e) Reimbursements for transportation from an employer not exceeding $.535 per mile for 2017 must be adequately substantiated by a record of time, place, and business purpose.

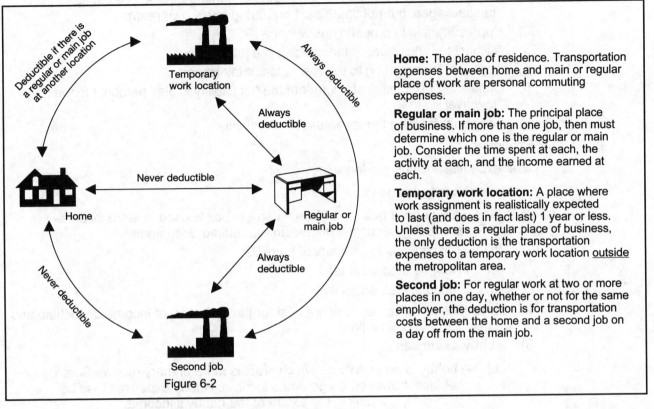

Home: The place of residence. Transportation expenses between home and main or regular place of work are personal commuting expenses.

Regular or main job: The principal place of business. If more than one job, then must determine which one is the regular or main job. Consider the time spent at each, the activity at each, and the income earned at each.

Temporary work location: A place where work assignment is realistically expected to last (and does in fact last) 1 year or less. Unless there is a regular place of business, the only deduction is the transportation expenses to a temporary work location <u>outside</u> the metropolitan area.

Second job: For regular work at two or more places in one day, whether or not for the same employer, the deduction is for transportation costs between the home and a second job on a day off from the main job.

Figure 6-2

4) Outside salesperson expenses

5) Employee entertainment expenses

a) **Entertainment expenses** are subject to the 50% limitation and are deductible only if they are directly related to or associated with the taxpayer's employment.

6) Employee home office expenses

7) Employee uniforms (provided they are not usable away from work)

8) Union dues and initiation fees

9) Professional dues and memberships

10) Subscriptions to business journals

11) Job-seeking expenses (in the same business)

12) Education expenses

a) **Education expenses** may be deductible only if incurred to maintain or improve skills that are required in the taxpayer's current employment context or if incurred to meet legal requirements or employer requirements.

b) In contrast, the expense of education to enter a trade, business, or profession or to meet the minimum education requirements is not deductible, even if state law requires the education.

3. **Tax Preparation Fees**

    a. Tax preparation expenses include the following:

        1) Return preparation: manuals, legal and accounting advice, preprinted forms or tax packages, but not time spent preparing one's own return
        2) Representation in proceedings with the IRS
        3) Accountant and attorney fees to obtain a letter ruling
        4) Appraisal fees relating to the resolution of tax issues
        5) Contesting tax liability of another (if the tax liability is also personal to the taxpayer)
        6) Fees paid for filing the tax return electronically

4. **Other Expenses**

    a. Other expenses include the following:

        1) **Investment expenses**

            a) Safe-deposit box rental fees when the box is used to store income-producing securities or investment-related documents
            b) Subscriptions to investment journals
            c) Investment counsel fees
            d) Custodial fees on an IRA

        2) Legal fees to collect alimony are cost for the collection of income deductible and subject to 2%-of-AGI floor.

        3) **Hobby expenses**

            a) A hobby is an activity for which profit is not a primary motive. Some hobbies, however, do generate income. Hobby expenses may be deducted, but only to the extent of the hobby's income.
            b) If expenses exceed the income of a hobby, the expenses must be deducted in the following order:

                i)   Expenses that are deductible even if not incurred in a trade, business, or investment activity (e.g., taxes, interest)
                ii) Expenses that do not reduce the tax basis of any of the hobby's assets (e.g., utilities)
                iii) Expenses that reduce the tax basis of the hobby's assets (e.g., depreciation)

            c) The amount of expenses that do not exceed the hobby's gross income are deductions from AGI. Items ii) and iii) above are miscellaneous itemized deductions subject to the 2%-of-AGI floor.

5. **Summary of Itemized Deductions Subject to 2%-of-AGI Exclusion**

    a. Hobby expenses (other than taxes and interest)
    b. Unreimbursed employee expenses
    c. Tax preparation fees
    d. Investment expenses

    NOTE: A convenient mnemonic to help remember the itemized deductions subject to 2%-of-AGI exclusion is Harry Uses Tax Information.

6. **Summary of Employee Expenditures Subject to 2%-of-AGI Exclusion**

   a. <u>H</u>ome office expenses
   b. <u>U</u>nion dues
   c. <u>P</u>rofessional dues and memberships
   d. <u>U</u>niforms
   e. <u>J</u>ob-seeking expenses (in the same business)
   f. <u>E</u>ntertainment expenses
   g. <u>T</u>ransportation expenses
   h. <u>S</u>ubscriptions to business journals
   i. <u>T</u>ravel expenses
   j. <u>O</u>utside salesperson expenses
   k. <u>E</u>ducation expenses

   NOTE: A mnemonic to help remember the employee expenditures subject to 2%-of-AGI exclusion is <u>H</u>arry <u>U</u>sually <u>P</u>refers <u>U</u>sing <u>J</u>ournal <u>E</u>ntries <u>T</u>o <u>S</u>how <u>T</u>otal <u>O</u>perating <u>E</u>xpenses.

7. **Overall Limitation**

   From Form 1040 Schedule A

Total Itemized Deductions	**29**	Is Form 1040, line 38, over [threshold]? ☐ **No.** Your deduction is not limited. Add the amounts in the far right column for lines 4 through 28. Also, enter this amount on Form 1040, line 40. ☐ **Yes.** Your deduction may be limited. See the Itemized Deductions Worksheet in the instructions to figure the amount to enter.	} . .	**29**	
	30	If you elect to itemize deductions even though they are less than your standard deduction, check here . . . . ▶ ☐			

   a. In 2017, married taxpayers filing a joint return with AGI that exceeds $313,800 ($287,650 if head of household, $261,500 if single, and $156,900 if married filing separately) must reduce the aggregate amount of their itemized deductions. The amount of the reduction is the lesser of 80% of otherwise allowable itemized deductions or 3% of the amount by which AGI exceeds the threshold.

   b. The overall limitation does **not** apply to deductions for the following:

      1) Medical expenses
      2) Investment interest expenses
      3) Casualty or theft losses
      4) Gambling losses (to the extent of gains)

8. **Recovery of Tax Benefits**

   a. Recovery of a tax benefit item is generally included in gross income.
   b. The recovered amount is included in income to the extent total allowable itemized deductions (for the applicable year) exceed the standard deduction (for the same year).

Stop and review! You have completed the outline for this subunit. Study multiple-choice questions 18 through 20 on page 181.

QUESTIONS

6.1 Above-the-Line Deductions

1. In 2017, a self-employed taxpayer had gross income of $57,000. The taxpayer paid self-employment tax of $8,000, health insurance of $6,000, and $5,000 of alimony. The taxpayer also contributed $2,000 to a traditional IRA. What is the taxpayer's adjusted gross income?

A. $55,000

B. $50,000

C. $46,000

D. $40,000

Answer (D) is correct.

REQUIRED: The taxpayer's AGI.

DISCUSSION: In 2017, self-employed individuals can deduct 50% of FICA taxes paid and 100% of payments made for health insurance coverage for the individual and his or her family. Alimony is gross income to the recipient and deductible by the payor. Contributions of up to $5,500 to an individual retirement account are deductible. The taxpayer's AGI is $40,000 ($57,000 GI – $4,000 SE tax paid – $6,000 health insurance – $5,000 alimony – $2,000 contribution to IRA).

Answer (A) is incorrect. Self-employment taxes and health insurance, along with alimony paid, also reduce GI to arrive at AGI. Answer (B) is incorrect. Self-employment taxes and health insurance paid also reduce GI to arrive at AGI. Answer (C) is incorrect. Self-employment health insurance paid also reduces GI to arrive at AGI.

2. A 33-year-old taxpayer withdrew $30,000 (pretax) from a traditional IRA. The taxpayer has a 33% effective tax rate and a 35% marginal tax rate. What is the total tax liability associated with the withdrawal?

A. $10,000

B. $10,500

C. $13,000

D. $13,500

Answer (D) is correct.

REQUIRED: The tax liability associated with an early distribution from a traditional IRA.

DISCUSSION: IRA distributions made before age 59 1/2 are subject to taxation as well as a 10% penalty. Each amount is calculated based on the distribution. No penalty is applied if it is for reason of death or disability, use of medical expenses in excess of 10% limitation, or up to $10,000 use of purchase of a first home. None of these circumstances are applicable; therefore, tax and penalty apply to the entire $30,000. The applicable tax rate is 35% for a tax liability of $10,500 ($30,000 × 35%), which is added to the penalty of $3,000 ($30,000 × 10%), for a total of $13,500.

Answer (A) is incorrect. Early distributions from a traditional IRA must be taxed as well as penalized. Answer (B) is incorrect. In addition to the tax at a rate of 35%, a 10% penalty is also applicable. Answer (C) is incorrect. The tax rate used should be the marginal rate, not the effective rate.

3. In 2017, Barlow moved from Chicago to Miami to start a new job, incurring costs of $1,200 to move household goods and $2,500 in temporary living expenses. Barlow was not reimbursed for any of these expenses. What amount should Barlow deduct as an above-the-line deduction for moving expense?

A. $1,200

B. $2,700

C. $3,000

D. $3,700

Answer (A) is correct.

REQUIRED: The allowable moving expense deduction.

DISCUSSION: A deduction for moving expenses paid or incurred in connection with the commencement of work by the taxpayer at a new place of work is allowed. The expenses of actually moving the taxpayer, family, and household goods are deductible above-the-line. Indirect moving expenses, including house-hunting trips, temporary living expenses, and expenses related to the sale, purchase, or lease of a residence are not deductible.

Answer (B) is incorrect. Even a small percentage of indirect moving expenses is not deductible. Answer (C) is incorrect. Even a percentage of temporary living expenses is not deductible. Answer (D) is incorrect. Indirect moving expenses, including temporary living expenses, are not deductible.

4. With regard to tax recognition of alimony in connection with a 2017 divorce, which one of the following statements is true?

A. The divorced couple may be members of the same household when payments are made.

B. Payments may be made in cash or property.

C. If the payor spouse pays premiums for insurance on his life as a requirement under the divorce agreement, the premiums are alimony if the payor spouse owns the policy.

D. Payments must terminate at the death of the payee spouse.

Answer (D) is correct.
 REQUIRED: The amounts deductible as alimony.
 DISCUSSION: Only amounts that are required to be included as gross income of the recipient as alimony are deductible by the payor in calculating AGI. A component of the alimony definition is that the payor has no liability to make the payment for any period after the death of the payee spouse.
 Answer (A) is incorrect. Alimony consists of payments when the payor and payee are not members of the same household. Answer (B) is incorrect. Alimony payments must be made in cash. Answer (C) is incorrect. The payments are not made to the payee spouse (the payor spouse owns the policy).

5. In the current year, an unmarried individual with modified adjusted gross income of $25,000 paid $1,000 interest on a qualified education loan entered into on July 1. How may the individual treat the interest for income tax purposes?

A. As a $500 deduction to arrive at AGI for the year.

B. As a $1,000 deduction to arrive at AGI for the year.

C. As a $1,000 itemized deduction.

D. As a nondeductible item of personal interest.

Answer (B) is correct.
 REQUIRED: The treatment of interest paid for qualified higher education loans.
 DISCUSSION: Taxpayer may deduct up to $2,500 of interest paid on qualified educational loans. The deduction is subject to income limits. The phaseout range begins when AGI exceeds $65,000 for unmarried individuals and ends at $80,000. The deduction is taken above-the-line to arrive at AGI for the year.
 Answer (A) is incorrect. The reduction in the deduction does not begin until AGI exceeds $65,000. Answer (C) is incorrect. The deduction is taken above-the-line to arrive at AGI for the year. Answer (D) is incorrect. Taxpayers may take an above-the-line deduction up to $2,500 of interest paid on qualified educational loans.

6. Dale received $1,000 in 2017 for jury duty. In exchange for regular compensation from her employer during the period of jury service, Dale was required to remit the entire $1,000 to her employer in 2017. In Dale's 2017 income tax return, the $1,000 jury duty fee should be

A. Claimed in full as an itemized deduction.

B. Claimed as an itemized deduction to the extent exceeding 2% of adjusted gross income.

C. Deducted from gross income in arriving at adjusted gross income.

D. Included in taxable income without a corresponding offset against other income.

Answer (C) is correct.
 REQUIRED: The deductibility of jury duty pay.
 DISCUSSION: Pay for jury duty is compensation gross income. Jury duty pay remitted to an employer (in return for being paid during the duty) is deductible for AGI.

6.2 Standard and Itemized Deductions

7. Which of the following requirements must be met in order for a single individual to qualify for an additional standard deduction?

	Must Be Age 65 or Older or Blind	Must Support Dependent Child or Aged Parent
A.	Yes	Yes
B.	No	No
C.	Yes	No
D.	No	Yes

Answer (C) is correct.

REQUIRED: The requirement for a single individual to qualify for the additional standard deduction.

DISCUSSION: An additional standard deduction is allowed for a taxpayer if, during the year, the taxpayer is age 65 or over or blind. The respective amounts are doubled if the taxpayer is both elderly and blind. Support of a dependent is a condition of an additional personal exemption amount, not an increase to the standard deduction.

Answer (A) is incorrect. The additional standard deduction amount is not available to single individuals merely supporting a dependent child or aged parent. Answer (B) is incorrect. The additional standard deduction amount is available to individuals 65 (or over) or blind. Answer (D) is incorrect. The additional standard deduction amount is available for taxpayers who are age 65 or over or blind.

8. Moore, a single taxpayer, had $50,000 in adjusted gross income for 2017. During 2017, she contributed $18,000 to her church. She had a $10,000 charitable contribution carryover from her 2016 church contribution. What was the maximum amount of properly substantiated charitable contributions that Moore could claim as an itemized deduction for 2017?

- A. $10,000
- B. $18,000
- C. $25,000
- D. $28,000

Answer (C) is correct.

REQUIRED: The amount of deductible charitable contributions.

DISCUSSION: Properly substantiated cash contributions by individuals to qualified charities are limited to 50% of the taxpayer's AGI, or $25,000 in this case. The carryover is deductible this year to the extent that the total deduction does not exceed the 50%-of-AGI limit, or $7,000 ($25,000 − $18,000).

Answer (A) is incorrect. The contribution made this year is fully deductible. The carryover is deductible to the extent that the total charitable contribution deduction does not exceed 50% of AGI. Answer (B) is incorrect. The carryover is deductible to the extent that the total charitable contribution deduction does not exceed 50% of AGI. Answer (D) is incorrect. The total charitable contribution is limited to 50% of a taxpayer's AGI.

9. The Browns borrowed $20,000, secured by their home, to pay their son's college tuition. At the time of the loan, the fair market value of their home was $400,000, and it was unencumbered by other debt. The interest on the loan qualifies as

- A. Deductible personal interest.
- B. Deductible qualified residence interest.
- C. Nondeductible interest.
- D. Investment interest expense.

Answer (B) is correct.

REQUIRED: The nature and deductibility of interest.

DISCUSSION: Qualified residence interest is deductible. It is interest paid or accrued during the tax year on home acquisition or home equity indebtedness. Home equity indebtedness is all debt other than acquisition debt that is secured by a qualified residence to the extent it does not exceed the fair market value of the residence, reduced by any acquisition indebtedness.

Answer (A) is incorrect. Personal interest is generally not deductible. Answer (C) is incorrect. The interest is deductible. Answer (D) is incorrect. It is qualified residence interest, not investment interest.

10. In 2017, Smith paid $6,000 to the tax collector of Big City for realty taxes on a two-family house owned by Smith's mother. Of this amount, $2,800 covered back taxes for 2016, and $3,200 covered 2017 taxes. Smith resides on the second floor of the house, and his mother resides on the first floor. In Smith's itemized deductions on his 2017 return, what amount was Smith entitled to claim for realty taxes?

- A. $6,000
- B. $3,200
- C. $3,000
- D. $0

Answer (D) is correct.

REQUIRED: The amount of deductible property taxes.

DISCUSSION: Taxes may be deducted only by the person on whom they are legally levied. Smith does not own the house, therefore none of the taxes paid can be deducted on his tax return and the payment is treated as a gift to Smith's mother. Smith's mother is entitled to the deduction only if she pays the taxes.

Answer (A) is incorrect. The total amount of taxes are not levied on Smith. Answer (B) is incorrect. Had Smith owned the property, the deduction would not have been limited to current taxes. Assuming he is a cash-basis taxpayer, the deductions are taken when amounts are paid. Answer (C) is incorrect. The IRC generally does not allow a deduction for paying the liability of another. It is treated as a gift.

11. In 2017, Joan Frazer's residence was totally destroyed by fire. The property had an adjusted basis and a fair market value of $130,000 before the fire. During 2017, Frazer received insurance reimbursement of $120,000 for the destruction of her home. Frazer's 2017 adjusted gross income was $70,000. Frazer had no casualty gains during the year. What amount of the fire loss was Frazer entitled to claim as an itemized deduction on her 2017 tax return?

    A. $2,900

    B. $3,000

    C. $9,900

    D. $10,000

Answer (A) is correct.
    REQUIRED: The amount of the deductible casualty loss.
    DISCUSSION: A personal casualty loss is limited to the amount of the loss exceeding 10% of AGI and a $100 nondeductible floor. The casualty loss is $10,000 ($130,000 FMV – $120,000 reimbursement). The itemized deduction is $2,900 ($10,000 loss – $7,000 10% of AGI limit – $100 floor).
    Answer (B) is incorrect. It does not take into account the nondeductible floor. Answer (C) is incorrect. The loss can only be deducted to the extent that it exceeds 10% of AGI. Answer (D) is incorrect. It ignores the AGI limit and floor.

12. In 2017, Welch paid the following expenses:

Premiums on an insurance policy against loss of earnings due to sickness or accident	$3,000
Physical therapy after spinal surgery	2,000
Premium on an insurance policy that covers reimbursement for the cost of prescription drugs	500

In 2017, Welch recovered $1,500 of the $2,000 that she paid for physical therapy through insurance reimbursement from a group medical policy paid for by her employer. Disregarding the adjusted gross income percentage threshold, what amount could be claimed on Welch's 2017 income tax return for medical expenses?

    A. $4,000

    B. $3,500

    C. $1,000

    D. $500

Answer (C) is correct.
    REQUIRED: The amount of deductible medical expenses.
    DISCUSSION: Medical expenses are deductible to the extent they exceed 10% of AGI. Medical care expenses include amounts paid for the diagnosis, cure, medication, treatment, or prevention of a disease or physical handicap or for the purpose of affecting any structure or function of the body. The term medical care also includes amounts paid for insurance covering medical care. However, the amount deductible for expenses incurred for medical care is reduced by the amount of reimbursements. The cost of insurance against loss of earnings is not deductible. Therefore, deductible medical expenses are $1,000 [($2,000 – $1,500 reimbursement) + $500].
    Answer (A) is incorrect. The cost of insurance against loss of earnings is not deductible. Answer (B) is incorrect. The cost of insurance against loss of earnings is not deductible. The cost of insurance for medical care, which includes the cost of prescription drugs, is deductible. Answer (D) is incorrect. The cost of insurance covering medical expenses is deductible.

13. In 2017, Wood's residence had an adjusted basis of $150,000, and it was destroyed by a tornado. An appraiser valued the decline in market value at $175,000. Later that same year, Wood received $130,000 from his insurance company for the property loss and did not elect to deduct the casualty loss in an earlier year. Wood's 2017 adjusted gross income was $60,000, and he did not have any casualty gains. What total amount can Wood deduct as a 2017 itemized deduction for the casualty loss, after the application of the threshold limitations?

    A. $39,000

    B. $38,900

    C. $19,900

    D. $13,900

Answer (D) is correct.
    REQUIRED: The amount of casualty loss deduction.
    DISCUSSION: The amount of a personal casualty loss is equal to the lesser of adjusted basis or the decline in FMV due to the casualty. Therefore, Wood's loss is equal to $150,000. Additionally, several limits apply. First, the loss must be reduced by any insurance recovery. Additionally, the loss must be reduced by $100 per casualty and is only deductible to the extent that it exceeds 10% of AGI. Therefore, Wood's deductible loss is

Adjusted basis	$150,000
Less: Insurance	(130,000)
$100 floor	(100)
10% of AGI	(6,000)
Deductible loss	$ 13,900

    Answer (A) is incorrect. The deductible loss is based on the lesser of adjusted basis and FMV and must be reduced by $100. Answer (B) is incorrect. The deductible loss is based on the lesser of adjusted basis and the decline in FMV. Answer (C) is incorrect. The loss must be reduced by 10% of AGI.

14. The 2017 deduction by an individual taxpayer for interest on investment indebtedness is

- A. Limited to investment interest paid in 2017.
- B. Limited to the taxpayer's 2017 interest income.
- C. Limited to the taxpayer's 2017 net investment income.
- D. Not limited.

Answer (C) is correct.

REQUIRED: The true statement concerning limits on deductibility of interest on investment indebtedness.

DISCUSSION: The deduction for interest on investment indebtedness is limited to the amount of net investment income for the taxable year. Any disallowed investment interest may be carried over and treated as investment interest paid or accrued in the succeeding taxable year.

Answer (A) is incorrect. Interest on investment indebtedness is deductible only to the extent of net investment income for the taxable year, not investment interest paid. Answer (B) is incorrect. The deduction for interest on investment indebtedness is not tied to general interest income. Answer (D) is incorrect. The deduction for interest on investment indebtedness is limited.

15. Jimet, an unmarried taxpayer, qualified to itemize 2017 deductions. Jimet's 2017 adjusted gross income was $30,000, and he made a $2,000 cash donation directly to a needy family. In 2017, Jimet also donated stock, valued at $3,000, to his church. Jimet had purchased the stock 4 months earlier for $1,500. What was the maximum amount of the charitable contribution allowable as an itemized deduction on Jimet's 2017 income tax return?

- A. $0
- B. $1,500
- C. $2,000
- D. $5,000

Answer (B) is correct.

REQUIRED: The maximum allowed charitable contribution deduction.

DISCUSSION: A deduction is allowed for contributions to a qualified organization. Therefore, no deduction is allowed for the contribution to the family. However, a deduction is available for the donation of stock in the amount of $1,500. Since the stock has not been held long term, it is ordinary income property, and the deduction is equal to the lesser of FMV or AB.

Answer (A) is incorrect. A deduction is allowed. Answer (C) is incorrect. The cash may not be deducted. Answer (D) is incorrect. Only the stock is allowed as a deduction, and the deduction amount is $1,500.

16. Smith paid the following unreimbursed medical expenses:

Dentist and eye doctor fees	$ 5,000
Contact lenses	500
Facial cosmetic surgery to improve Smith's personal appearance (surgery is unrelated to personal injury or congenital deformity)	10,000
Premium on disability insurance policy to pay him if he is injured and unable to work	2,000

What is the total amount of Smith's tax-deductible medical expenses before the adjusted gross income limitation?

- A. $17,500
- B. $15,500
- C. $7,500
- D. $5,500

Answer (D) is correct.

REQUIRED: The amount of deductible medical expenses.

DISCUSSION: Medical expenses are deductible to the extent they exceed 10% of AGI. Medical care expenses include amounts paid for the diagnosis, cure, medication, treatment, or prevention of a disease or physical handicap or for the purpose of affecting any structure or function of the body. Therefore, $5,500 ($5,000 dentist and eye doctor fees + $500 contact lenses) qualifies for the deduction before the AGI limitation.

Answer (A) is incorrect. Cosmetic surgery is not deductible unless it corrects a congenital deformity. Furthermore, only premiums paid for medical insurance that provides for reimbursement of medical care expenses is deductible. Answer (B) is incorrect. Cosmetic surgery is not deductible unless it corrects a congenital deformity. Answer (C) is incorrect. Only premiums paid for medical insurance that provides for reimbursement of medical care expenses is deductible.

17. How may taxes paid by an individual to a foreign country be treated?

- A. As an itemized deduction subject to the 2% floor.
- B. As a credit against federal income taxes due.
- C. As an adjustment to gross income.
- D. As a nondeductible.

Answer (B) is correct.

REQUIRED: The treatment of taxes paid to a foreign country.

DISCUSSION: A taxpayer may elect either a credit or an itemized deduction for taxes paid to other countries or U.S. possessions.

Answer (A) is incorrect. If treated as an itemized deduction, it is not subject to the 2% floor. Answer (C) is incorrect. The foreign tax can be treated as a credit or deduction, not an adjustment. Answer (D) is incorrect. Foreign taxes paid can be deductible.

6.3 Job Expenses and Certain Miscellaneous Deductions

18. Which expense, both incurred and paid in 2017, can be claimed as an itemized deduction subject to the 2%-of-AGI floor?

    A. Employee's unreimbursed business car expense.

    B. One-half of the self-employment tax.

    C. Employee's unreimbursed moving expense.

    D. Self-employed health insurance.

Answer (A) is correct.
    REQUIRED: The expense that is an itemized deduction subject to the 2%-of-AGI floor.
    DISCUSSION: Unreimbursed employee expenses, including car expenses, are deductible as itemized deductions subject to the 2%-of-AGI floor.
    Answer (B) is incorrect. One-half of the self-employment tax is an above-the-line deduction. Answer (C) is incorrect. An employee's unreimbursed direct moving expenses are available as an above-the-line deduction. Answer (D) is incorrect. Self-employed health insurance is an above-the-line deductible expense equal to 100% of the actual amount paid during the taxable year.

19. Hall, a divorced person and custodian of her 12-year-old child, filed her 2017 federal income tax return as head of household. She submitted the following information to the CPA who prepared her 2017 return:

- The divorce agreement, executed in 2006, provides for Hall to receive $3,000 per month, of which $600 is designated as child support. After the child reaches 18, the monthly payments are to be reduced to $2,400 and are to continue until remarriage or death. However, for 2017, Hall received a total of only $5,000 from her former husband. Hall paid an attorney $2,000 in 2017 in a suit to collect the alimony owed.

The $2,000 legal fee that Hall paid to collect alimony should be treated as a(n)

    A. Deduction in arriving at AGI.

    B. Itemized deduction subject to the 2%-of-AGI floor.

    C. Itemized deduction not subject to the 2%-of-AGI floor.

    D. Nondeductible personal expense.

Answer (B) is correct.
    REQUIRED: The deductible amount of a fee paid to collect alimony.
    DISCUSSION: Fees to collect alimony are considered expenditures for the production of income, deductible as a miscellaneous itemized deduction subject to the 2%-of-AGI exclusion.
    Answer (A) is incorrect. The fee is not listed in the IRC as a deduction for AGI. Answer (C) is incorrect. The fee is not listed as not subject to the 2%-of-AGI exclusion. Answer (D) is incorrect. The fee is treated as paid or incurred to produce income.

20. Which of the following is a miscellaneous itemized deduction subject to the 2% of adjusted gross income floor?

    A. Gambling losses up to the amount of gambling winnings.

    B. Medical expenses.

    C. Real estate tax.

    D. Employee business expenses.

Answer (D) is correct.
    REQUIRED: Identify the itemized deduction subject to the 2% of AGI floor.
    DISCUSSION: Miscellaneous itemized deductions are subject to a 2%-of-AGI exclusion. Only that portion of the aggregate amount of allowable second-tier itemized deductions that exceeds the threshold amount of 2% of AGI may be deducted from AGI. Any surplus cannot be carried forward to a succeeding year. The three categories of miscellaneous itemized deductions are employee expenses, tax determination expenses, and other expenses.
    Answer (A) is incorrect. Gambling losses up the amount of gambling winnings are reported on Schedule A after itemized deductions that are subject to the 2% of AGI floor. Answer (B) is incorrect. Medical expenses are subject to a 10% of AGI floor and not part of the deductions subject to the 2% of AGI floor. Answer (C) is incorrect. Real estate taxes are itemized deductions but are reported above those subject to the 2% of AGI floor.

STUDY UNIT SEVEN
CREDITS, AMT, AND LOSSES

(20 pages of outline)

Tax credits, dollar for dollar, are a greater benefit to taxpayers than deductions, which depend on individual income tax rates and brackets.

The basics of the alternative minimum tax (AMT), an additional income tax, are presented in Subunit 7.2. AMT has been tested more often in the corporate context and is explained further in Study Unit 10, "Corporate Tax Computations."

The various loss deductions available are always subject to some limiting amount or qualification. This study unit analyzes available losses and the applicable limitations of each.

Some candidates find it helpful to have the entire tax form side-by-side with our Knowledge Transfer Outline when studying. The full versions of the most up-to-date forms are easily accessible at www.gleim.com/taxforms. These forms and the form excerpts used in our outline are periodically updated as the latest versions are released by the IRS.

7.1 TAX CREDITS

1. **Overview**

   a. Tax credits are used to achieve policy objectives, such as encouraging energy conservation or providing tax relief to low-income taxpayers. A $1 credit reduces gross tax liability by $1. Most credits are nonrefundable, meaning that once tax liability reaches zero, no more credits can be taken to produce refunds. However, there are several refundable credits, including taxes withheld and the Earned Income Credit.

2. **Nonrefundable Personal Credits**

   a. These credits include the

      1) Foreign Tax Credit
      2) Child and Dependent Care Credit
      3) Lifetime Learning Credit
      4) Retirement Savings Contribution Credit
      5) Child Tax Credit
      6) Credit for the Elderly or the Disabled
      7) General Business Credit
      8) Adoption Credit

   b. **Foreign Tax Credit.** This is an alternative to deduction of the tax. The credit is equal to the lesser of

      1) Foreign taxes paid/accrued during the tax year or
      2) The portion of U.S. tax liability (before credits) attributed to all foreign-earned income.

$$FTC = U.S.\ income\ tax^1 \times \frac{Foreign\text{-}earned\ taxable\ income^2}{Worldwide\ taxable\ income}$$

[1] Before the FTC
[2] Not more than worldwide TI

      a) If the credit is limited to the amount in 2) above, unused foreign tax credits will equal the difference between 1) and 2).
      b) The unused credits can be carried back for 1 year and then carried forward for 10 years.

c.   **Child and Dependent Care Credit.** A taxpayer is eligible for this credit only if 1) and
      2) below are satisfied.

1)   Child and dependent care expenses are incurred to enable a taxpayer to
      maintain gainful employment.

      a)   The expenses may be incurred when the taxpayer is employed or actively
            seeking employment.

2)   The taxpayer provides more than half the cost of maintaining a household for a
      dependent under age 13 or an incapacitated spouse or dependent.

      a)   Qualifying expenses include household services such as babysitting,
            housekeeping, and nursing. Outside services, such as day care facilities,
            must be in qualified facilities. Outside expenses for the care of an
            incapacitated spouse or dependent qualify only if the individual spends
            more than 8 hours a day in the taxpayer's home.

      b)   Total child and dependent care expenses cannot exceed the taxpayer's
            earned income. For married taxpayers, the income for this limitation is the
            smaller income of the two.

EXAMPLE

The taxpayer remarried on December 3 and the taxpayer's earned income for the year was $18,000. The taxpayer's new
spouse's earned income for the year was $2,000. The taxpayer paid work-related expenses of $3,000 for the care of
the taxpayer's 5-year-old child and qualified to claim the credit. The amount of expenses the taxpayer uses to figure the
taxpayer's credit cannot be more than $2,000 (i.e., the smaller of the taxpayer's earned income or that of the taxpayer's
spouse).

---

      i)   If one of the spouses is a full-time student at an educational
            institution or is unable to care for himself or herself, (s)he is
            considered to have earned $250 per month if there is one qualifying
            individual and $500 per month if there are two or more qualifying
            individuals.

      c)   Child and dependent care expenses are limited to $3,000 for one qualifying
            individual and $6,000 for two or more individuals.

      d)   The credit is equal to 35% of the child and dependent care expenses.
            This rate is reduced by 1% (but not below 20%) for each $2,000 (or part
            thereof) by which AGI exceeds $15,000. Therefore, taxpayers with AGI
            over $43,000 will have a credit of 20%.

d.   **Lifetime Learning Credit.** This credit is 20% of qualified tuition expenses paid by the
      taxpayer. The maximum credit allowed per year is $2,000 and is limited to 20% of the
      first $10,000 of expenses. The Lifetime Learning Credit

1)   Phases out for AGI between $56,000 and $66,000 for singles and between
      $112,000 and $132,000 on a joint return.

2)   Is available in years that the American Opportunity Credit is not claimed with
      respect to the same student.

3)   Is available for an unlimited number of years and can be used for both graduate-
      and undergraduate-level courses.

NOTE: The tuition statement (Form 1098) provided to the taxpayer must include the name, address, and TIN (Taxpayer Identification Number) of the student.

EXAMPLE

Weasley and Brandy Kat, who file a joint tax return, have an adjusted gross income (AGI) of $110,000 for 2017. Their daughter, Honey, began her first year of graduate school on July 21, 2016. The Kat's expenses incurred in 2017 were $12,000 for tuition.

A Lifetime Learning Credit is limited to the amount of 20% of the first $10,000 of tuition paid. The Lifetime Learning Credit is available in years the American Opportunity Credit is not claimed. The Kat's credit for 2017 will be $2,000 ($10,000 × 20%). There is no phaseout of the Lifetime Learning Credit for the Kat's since the credit phaseout for married taxpayers filing jointly commences when modified AGI is $112,000 and ends at $132,000.

---

e. **Retirement Savings Contribution Credit.** Unlike most other tax topics allowing a credit or deduction, this credit is in addition to the exclusion or deduction from GI for qualified contributions. In general, a taxpayer may claim a credit for an eligible contribution to an eligible retirement plan.

    1) The credit is a percentage based on AGI on a retirement contribution of up to $2,000 ($4,000 if married filing jointly). The following table provides the 2017 AGI thresholds and corresponding percentages:

AGI		Filing Status		
Over–	But not over–	MFJ	HH	Other
---	$18,500	50%	50%	50%
$18,500	$20,000	50%	50%	20%
$20,000	$27,750	50%	50%	10%
$27,750	$30,000	50%	20%	10%
$30,000	$31,000	50%	10%	10%
$31,000	$37,000	50%	10%	0%
$37,000	$40,000	20%	10%	0%
$40,000	$46,500	10%	10%	0%
$46,500	$62,000	10%	0%	0%
$62,000	---	0%	0%	0%

f. **Child Tax Credit**

    1) Taxpayers who have qualifying children are entitled to the Child Tax Credit of $1,000 per child.

        a) **Qualifying child** is defined as the taxpayer's child, stepchild, sibling, step-sibling, or a descendant of any of these, or an eligible foster child (1) who is a U.S. citizen or resident alien, (2) for whom the taxpayer may claim a dependency exemption, and (3) who is less than 17 years old as of the close of the tax year.

        b) The credit is allowed only for tax years consisting of 12 months.

    2) The credit begins to phase out when modified AGI reaches $110,000 for joint filers, $55,000 for married filing separately, and $75,000 for single filers. The credit is reduced by $50 for each $1,000 of modified AGI above the thresholds.

g. **Elderly or Disabled Credit.** An individual may be eligible for this credit if (s)he was age 65 before the close of the tax year or retired before the close of the tax year due to a total and permanent disability.

1) The credit is equal to 15% multiplied by the initial base amount, which is

a) $5,000 for single filers and married filing jointly with only one qualified spouse

b) $7,500 for married filing jointly (both aged 65 or older)

c) $3,750 for married filing separately

2) The initial base amount is reduced by the following:

a) Tax-exempt Social Security benefits
b) Pension or annuity benefits excluded from gross income
c) Disability income if under 65
d) One-half the excess of AGI over

i) $7,500 for single
ii) $10,000 for married filing jointly
iii) $5,000 for married filing separately

3) A married person filing separately who lives with the spouse at any time during the year may not claim the credit.

Elderly or Disabled Credit Eligibility Decision Chart

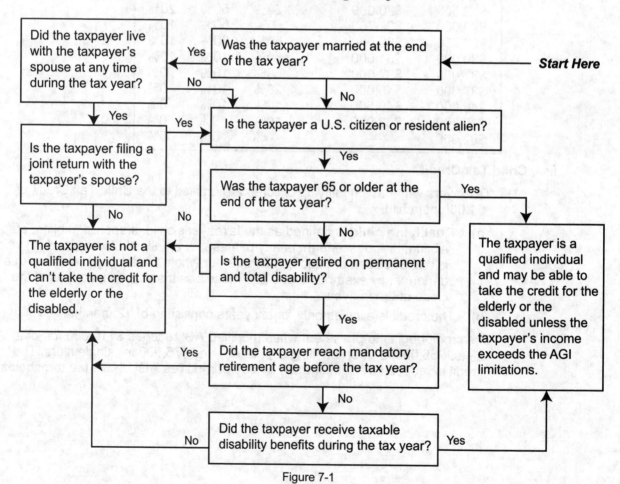

Figure 7-1

h. **General Business Credit.** The General Business Credit (GBC) is a set of more than thirty credits commonly available to businesses. The GBC includes credits for investment, research, work opportunity, low-income housing, and alternative motor vehicles, among others.

   1) Overall limit. The GBC is limited to net income tax minus the greater of the tentative minimum tax or 25% of net regular tax over $25,000.

      a) On Form 1040, the regular tax (line 44) is the tax computed on taxable income. The income tax (line 47) is the regular tax (line 44) plus the AMT (line 45) plus excess advance premium tax credit repayment (line 46). The net income tax is the income tax (line 47) minus the nonrefundable credits other than the General Business Credit. The General Business Credit will not be available when the alternative minimum tax exceeds the regular tax.

EXAMPLE

The taxpayer has a regular tax of $60,000 and a tentative minimum tax of $57,000. The taxpayer also has $10,000 of potential general business credits. Since the regular tax exceeds the tentative minimum tax, there is no alternative minimum tax. The taxpayer is allowed a General Business Credit computed as follows:

$60,000	Regular tax
(0)	Alternative minimum tax
$60,000	Income tax
(0)	Nonrefundable credits other than General Business Credit
$60,000	Net income tax
(57,000)	Greater of tentative minimum tax or 25% of net regular tax over $25,000
$ 3,000	General Business Credit

---

      b) Tentative minimum tax is an amount used in computing the alternative minimum tax.

      c) Net regular tax is the taxpayer's regular income tax liability (i.e., without alternative minimum tax) reduced by nonrefundable credits.

      d) Excess over the limit may be allowable as a current deduction to the extent it is attributable to the Work Opportunity Tax Credit, among others.

      e) Any excess of the combined GBC over the limit (and not allowed as a current deduction) may be carried back 1 year and forward 20 as a credit. It is carried to the earliest year to which it could be used, then to the next, and so on.

2) **Work Opportunity Tax Credit (WOTC).** Employers may take a credit equal to 40% (reduced to 25% for employment of more than 120 hours but less than 400) of the first $6,000 paid to employees from certain targeted groups who work at least 400 hours ($10,000 for LT Family Assistance Recipients and $3,000 for Qualified Summer Youth Employees).

    a) Generally, the maximum credit is $2,400 ($6,000 × 0.40) [$4,000 for LT Family Assistance Recipients ($10,000 × 0.40) and $1,200 for Qualified Summer Youth Employees ($3,000 × 0.40)] per non-veteran groups ($9,600 per veteran groups).

    b) The credit is not available for an individual with less than 120 hours of service performed for the employer.

    c) The second-year credit allowed only for LT Family Assistance Recipients is 50% of the first $10,000. The maximum credit for both years is $9,000 ($4,000 + $5,000).

        i) Qualified wages include

- Remuneration for employment
- Amount received under accident and health plans
- Contributions by employers to accident and health plans
- Educational assistance
- Dependent care expenses

3) **Research Credit.** A credit is allowed for 20% of the amount by which the taxpayer's qualified research expenditures for a tax year exceed its base-period amount. Taxpayers may elect an alternative simplified credit equal to 14% of expenses in excess of 50% of the average expense for the preceding 3 years.

i. **Adoption Credit.** A credit is allowed for qualified adoption expenses incurred by the taxpayer.

1) Qualified adoption expenses are reasonable and necessary adoption expenses, including adoption fees, court costs, attorney fees, and other directly related expenses.

2) The maximum credit is $13,570 per qualified child, including a special-needs adoption.

    a) The maximum credit amount is allowed for the adoption of a child with special needs regardless of the actual expenses paid or incurred in the year the adoption becomes final.

    b) The amount of the credit allowable for any tax year is phased out for taxpayers with modified adjusted gross income (MAGI) in excess of $203,540 and is fully eliminated when MAGI reaches $243,540.

3) Any unused credit may be carried forward for up to 5 years and is not subject to the MAGI phaseout.

3.   **Refundable Credits**

    a.   A refundable credit is payable as a refund to the extent the credit amount exceeds tax otherwise due. Refundable credits include credits for the following:

        1)   Taxes withheld
        2)   Earned Income Credit
        3)   Additional Child Tax Credit
        4)   American Opportunity Credit

    b.   Withholdings from employee wages for income tax are treated as refundable credit. Withholdings from wages for Social Security (FICA) tax are also refundable but only if an aggregate is withheld in excess of the maximum by two or more employers.

    c.   **Earned Income Credit (EIC)**

        1)   To qualify for EIC, the taxpayer and spouse (if married and filing a joint return), must meet all of the following criteria:

            a)   Have a valid Social Security number

            b)   Have earned income from employment, self-employment, or another source

            c)   Cannot use the married filing separately filing status

            d)   Must be a U.S. citizen or resident alien all year or a nonresident alien married to a U.S. citizen or resident alien and choose to file a joint return and be treated as a resident alien

            e)   Cannot be the qualifying child (QC) of another person

            f)   Have adjusted gross income and earned income less than the thresholds in item 6) on page 191.

            g)   Have investment income less than $3,450 for 2017

        2)   Earned income includes wages, salaries, tips, and net earnings from self-employment. Disqualified income includes interest, dividends, capital gain net income, net passive income, unemployment compensation, and any compensation that is not taxable (other than excluded combat-zone pay).

        3)   An individual without a QC must have his or her principal residence in the U.S. for more than half of the tax year, be at least 25 but not over 64 years old, and not be a dependent of another.

        4)   Taxpayers with one or more QCs are eligible for a higher applicable percentage and more lenient phase-out amounts. In order for a child to be a QC, three tests must be met:

            a)   Relationship. The child must be related by birth or adoption or be an eligible foster child or stepchild.

            b)   Residency. The taxpayer must provide the child's principal place of abode for more than half of the year.

            c)   Age. The child must be under age 19 at the close of the tax year, be permanently disabled, or be a student under the age of 24.

Tests for Qualifying Child

Relationship

A qualifying child who is the taxpayer's . . .

Son, daughter, stepchild, foster child, or a descendant of any of them (for example, the taxpayer's grandchild)

OR

Brother, sister, half brother, half sister, stepbrother, stepsister, or a descendant of any of them (for example, the taxpayer's niece or newphew)

AND

Age

was . . .

Under age 19 at the end of the tax year and younger than the taxpayer (or taxpayer's spouse, if filing jointly)

OR

Under age 24 at the end of the tax year, a student, and younger than the taxpayer (or the taxpayer's spouse, if filing jointly)

OR

Permanently and totally disabled at any time during the year, regardless of age

AND

Residency

Who lived with the taxpayer in the United States for more than half of the tax year

Figure 7-2

5) Calculation of EIC. Multiply the individual's earned income by the applicable percentage.

EIC: Maximum Amounts, 2017

Type of Taxpayer	Applicable Percentage	Earned Income Amount	Maximum EIC
0 QC	7.65%	$ 6,670	$ 510
1 QC	34%	$10,000	$3,400
2 QC	40%	$14,040	$5,616
3 or more QC	45%	$14,040	$6,318

6) Phaseout of EIC. Decrease the maximum EIC by any phaseout, which is determined by multiplying the applicable phaseout percentage by the excess of the amount of the individual's AGI (or earned income, if greater) over the beginning amount. No EIC is available when AGI or earned income exceeds the completed phaseout amount.

EIC: Phaseout Amounts, 2017

Type of Taxpayer	Applicable Phaseout Percentage	Beginning Phaseout Amount	Beginning Phaseout Amt. for Joint Filers	Completed Phaseout Amount	Completed Phaseout Amt. for Joint Filers
0 QC	7.65%	$ 8,340	$13,930	$15,010	$20,600
1 QC	15.98%	$18,340	$23,930	$39,617	$45,207
2 QC	21.06%	$18,340	$23,930	$45,007	$50,597
3 or more QC	21.06%	$18,340	$23,930	$48,340	$53,930

d. **Additional Child Tax Credit**

1) This credit is available for certain taxpayers who get less than the full amount of the Child Tax Credit.

2) The credit is refundable up to the lesser of 15% of earned income in excess of $3,000 or the unclaimed portion of the nonrefundable credit. The refund is capped at the per child credit amount.

e. **American Opportunity Credit.** This credit provides a maximum allowed credit of $2,500 per student per year for the first 4 years of post-secondary education. The credit may be used for qualified tuition and expenses.

1) The credit is computed as 100% of the first $2,000 of expenses and 25% of the second $2,000 of expenses.

2) Qualified expenses include required tuition, fees, and course materials. The credit is not allowed for room and board, activity fees, and any other fees or expenses not related to the student's academic course of instruction.

3) The credit phases out for AGI between $80,000 ($160,000 for joint filers) and $90,000 ($180,000 for joint filers). The amount of reduction in credit can be calculated as follows:

$$\text{Amount of credit allowed} \times \frac{AGI - \$80,000 \ (\text{or} \ \$160,000 \ \text{for joint filers})}{\$10,000 \ (\text{or} \ \$20,000 \ \text{for joint filers})}$$

4) Up to 40% of the credit is refundable.

5) The American Opportunity Credit is allowed per student, whereas the Lifetime Learning Credit is calculated per taxpayer without reference to the number of students.

NOTE: The tuition statement (Form 1098) provided to the taxpayer must include the name, address, and TIN (Taxpayer Identification Number) of the student.

Stop and review! You have completed the outline for this subunit. Study multiple-choice questions 1 through 7 beginning on page 202.

7.2 ALTERNATIVE MINIMUM TAX

1. The alternative minimum tax (AMT) is applied only if the tentative minimum tax exceeds the taxpayer's regular tax liability. Individuals use Form 6251 to calculate AMT. The formula below is an overview of the AMT.

AMT FORMULA

Taxable income
+   Tax preferences
+   Personal exemptions
+   Standard deduction if taxpayer does not itemize
+/– Certain other adjustments
=   **Alternative minimum taxable income (AMTI)**

– Exemption amount	2017	25% phaseout for excess over
Married filing jointly	$84,500	$160,900
Single	$54,300	$120,700
Married filing separately	$42,250	$ 80,450

=   **Alternative minimum tax base**

× Rate	2017
AMT base (married filing jointly)	
First $187,800 ($93,900 MFS)	26%
Excess	28%

=   **Tentative minimum tax**
–   Regular income tax
=   **Alternative minimum tax**

2. Tax **preference** items receive favorable treatment in computing regular income tax, e.g., tax-exempt interest on private activity bonds (issued after 1986 but excluding those issued in 2009 and 2010), excess depletion, intangible drilling cost, small business stock exclusion (purchased prior to September 28, 2010).

    a. Small business stock. When computing taxable income, noncorporate taxpayers may exclude up to 50% (100% for stock purchased after September 27, 2010) of gain realized on the sale or exchange of qualified small business stock held more than 5 years.

        1) Generally, 7% of the excluded gain is added as an AMT tax preference item. However, stock purchased after September 27, 2010, is excluded from tax preference treatment.

3. AMT **adjustments** represent either a limitation on itemized deductions or timing differences.

    a. Only certain itemized deductions are allowed in calculating the AMT. The following are not allowed and must be added back for AMT if deducted for regular tax:

        1) Miscellaneous itemized deductions (only the allowed regular tax deduction subject to 2% of AGI floor is an adjustment)
        2) State, local, and foreign income taxes
        3) Real and personal property taxes

b. Medical expense deduction is allowed subject to the same 10%-of-AGI floor as regular tax. Therefore, the prior adjustment for the 7.5% AGI regular tax and 10% AGI for AMT discrepancy is no longer applicable.

c. The standard deduction and personal exemptions are not allowed.

d. Timing differences may permit the taxpayer to defer income temporarily or to accelerate deductions. Appropriate adjustments are made, taking into account the timing of different accounting methods.

1) For example, the installment method is not allowed for sales of dealer property. Another example is when depreciation is taken under MACRS using the 200%-declining-balance method, and 150%-declining-balance method for AMT.

e. Interest from refinancing in excess of the acquisition amount is not allowed (i.e., interest on loan amount qualified for regular itemized tax deduction, in excess of acquisition amount).

1) Interest from home equity indebtedness may only be deducted if the indebtedness was incurred to acquire, construct, or substantially improve a qualified residence. Transient homes (e.g., motor homes) do not qualify.

4. **Minimum Tax Credit (MTC)**

a. A credit is allowed for AMT paid in a tax year against regular tax liability in 1 or more subsequent tax years.

b. The MTC amount is the AMT that would have been computed if the only adjustments made to TI in computing AMTI were those for (tax-favored) items that result in deferral, as opposed to exclusion, of income. To compute the MTC amount, recompute the most recent year's AMT without adjustment for the following (exclusion) items and add carryover MTC:

1) Standard deduction
2) Personal exemptions deduction
3) Miscellaneous itemized deductions
4) Tax-exempt interest on private activity bonds (not necessary for bonds issued in 2009 or 2010)
5) Qualified interest expense (qualified mortgage interest, investment interest, etc.)
6) Charitable contributions of appreciated property
7) Medical expenses
8) Depletion
9) Taxes

c. Form 8801, *Credit for Prior Year Minimum Tax – Individuals, Estates, and Trusts*, is used to figure the minimum tax credit, if any, for AMT incurred in prior tax years and to figure any credit carryforward to 2017.

Form **6251**	**Alternative Minimum Tax – Individuals**	OMB No. 1545-0074
Department of the Treasury Internal Revenue Service (99)	▶ Information about Form 6251 and its separate instructions is at *www.irs.gov/form6251*. ▶ Attach to Form 1040 or Form 1040NR.	**[Year]** Attachment Sequence No. **32**

Name(s) shown on Form 1040 or Form 1040NR | Your social security number

Part I   Alternative Minimum Taxable Income (See instructions for how to complete each line.)

1	If filing Schedule A (Form 1040), enter the amount from Form 1040, line 41, and go to line 2. Otherwise, enter the amount from Form 1040, line 38, and go to line 7. (If less than zero, enter as a negative amount.)	**1**
2	Medical and dental. If you or your spouse was 65 or older, enter the **smaller** of Schedule A (Form 1040), line 4, **or** 2.5% (0.025) of Form 1040, line 38. If zero or less, enter -0-	**2**
3	Taxes from Schedule A (Form 1040), line 9	**3**
4	Enter the home mortgage interest adjustment, if any, from line 6 of the worksheet in the instructions for this line	**4**
5	Miscellaneous deductions from Schedule A (Form 1040), line 27.	**5**
6	If Form 1040, line 38, is $155,650 or less, enter -0-. Otherwise, see instructions	**6** ( )
7	Tax refund from Form 1040, line 10 or line 21	**7** ( )
8	Investment interest expense (difference between regular tax and AMT).	**8**
9	Depletion (difference between regular tax and AMT)	**9**
10	Net operating loss deduction from Form 1040, line 21. Enter as a positive amount	**10**
11	Alternative tax net operating loss deduction	**11** ( )
12	Interest from specified private activity bonds exempt from the regular tax	**12**
13	Qualified small business stock, see instructions	**13**
14	Exercise of incentive stock options (excess of AMT income over regular tax income)	**14**
15	Estates and trusts (amount from Schedule K-1 (Form 1041), box 12, code A)	**15**
16	Electing large partnerships (amount from Schedule K-1 (Form 1065-B), box 6)	**16**
17	Disposition of property (difference between AMT and regular tax gain or loss)	**17**
18	Depreciation on assets placed in service after 1986 (difference between regular tax and AMT)	**18**
19	Passive activities (difference between AMT and regular tax income or loss)	**19**
20	Loss limitations (difference between AMT and regular tax income or loss).	**20**
21	Circulation costs (difference between regular tax and AMT)	**21**
22	Long-term contracts (difference between AMT and regular tax income)	**22**
23	Mining costs (difference between regular tax and AMT)	**23**
24	Research and experimental costs (difference between regular tax and AMT)	**24**
25	Income from certain installment sales before January 1, 1987	**25** ( )
26	Intangible drilling costs preference	**26**
27	Other adjustments, including income-based related adjustments	**27**
28	**Alternative minimum taxable income.** Combine lines 1 through 27. (If married filing separately and line 28 is more than $247,450, see instructions.)	**28**

Part II   Alternative Minimum Tax (AMT)

29 Exemption. (If you were under age 24 at the end of [Year], see instructions.)

IF your filing status is . . .	AND line 28 is not over . . .	THEN enter on line 29 . . .	
Single or head of household	$119,700	$53,900	
Married filing jointly or qualifying widow(er)	159,700	83,800	
Married filing separately	79,850	41,900	

If line 28 is **over** the amount shown above for your filing status, see instructions. | **29** |

30	Subtract line 29 from line 28. If more than zero, go to line 31. If zero or less, enter -0- here and on lines 31, 33, and 35, and go to line 34	**30**
31	• If you are filing Form 2555 or 2555-EZ, see instructions for the amount to enter. • If you reported capital gain distributions directly on Form 1040, line 13; you reported qualified dividends on Form 1040, line 9b; **or** you had a gain on both lines 15 and 16 of Schedule D (Form 1040) (as refigured for the AMT, if necessary), complete Part III on the back and enter the amount from line 64 here. • **All others:** If line 30 is $186,300 or less ($93,150 or less if married filing separately), multiply line 30 by 26% (0.26). Otherwise, multiply line 30 by 28% (0.28) and subtract $3,726 ($1,863 if married filing separately) from the result.	**31**
32	Alternative minimum tax foreign tax credit (see instructions)	**32**
33	Tentative minimum tax. Subtract line 32 from line 31	**33**
34	Add Form 1040, line 44 (minus any tax from Form 4972), and Form 1040, line 46. Subtract from the result any foreign tax credit from Form 1040, line 48. If you used Schedule J to figure your tax on Form 1040, line 44, refigure that tax without using Schedule J before completing this line (see instructions)	**34**
35	**AMT.** Subtract line 34 from line 33. If zero or less, enter -0-. Enter here and on Form 1040, line 45	**35**

For Paperwork Reduction Act Notice, see your tax return instructions.   Cat. No. 13600G   Form **6251** [Year]

Part III Tax Computation Using Maximum Capital Gains Rates

Complete Part III only if you are required to do so by line 31 or by the Foreign Earned Income Tax Worksheet in the instructions.

36	Enter the amount from Form 6251, line 30. If you are filing Form 2555 or 2555-EZ, enter the amount from line 3 of the worksheet in the instructions for line 31	**36**
37	Enter the amount from line 6 of the Qualified Dividends and Capital Gain Tax Worksheet in the instructions for Form 1040, line 44, or the amount from line 13 of the Schedule D Tax Worksheet in the instructions for Schedule D (Form 1040), whichever applies (as refigured for the AMT, if necessary) (see instructions). If you are filing Form 2555 or 2555-EZ, see instructions for the amount to enter	**37**
38	Enter the amount from Schedule D (Form 1040), line 19 (as refigured for the AMT, if necessary) (see instructions). If you are filing Form 2555 or 2555-EZ, see instructions for the amount to enter	**38**
39	If you did not complete a Schedule D Tax Worksheet for the regular tax or the AMT, enter the amount from line 37. Otherwise, add lines 37 and 38, and enter the **smaller** of that result or the amount from line 10 of the Schedule D Tax Worksheet (as refigured for the AMT, if necessary). If you are filing Form 2555 or 2555-EZ, see instructions for the amount to enter	**39**
40	Enter the **smaller** of line 36 or line 39	**40**
41	Subtract line 40 from line 36	**41**
42	If line 41 is $186,300 or less ($93,150 or less if married filing separately), multiply line 41 by 26% (0.26). Otherwise, multiply line 41 by 28% (0.28) and subtract $3,726 ($1,863 if married filing separately) from the result . . . ▶	**42**
43	Enter: • $75,300 if married filing jointly or qualifying widow(er), • $37,650 if single or married filing separately, or • $50,400 if head of household. }	**43**
44	Enter the amount from line 7 of the Qualified Dividends and Capital Gain Tax Worksheet in the instructions for Form 1040, line 44, or the amount from line 14 of the Schedule D Tax Worksheet in the instructions for Schedule D (Form 1040), whichever applies (as figured for the regular tax). If you did not complete either worksheet for the regular tax, enter the amount from Form 1040, line 43; if zero or less, enter -0-. If you are filing Form 2555 or 2555-EZ, see instructions for the amount to enter	**44**
45	Subtract line 44 from line 43. If zero or less, enter -0-	**45**
46	Enter the **smaller** of line 36 or line 37	**46**
47	Enter the **smaller** of line 45 or line 46. This amount is taxed at 0%	**47**
48	Subtract line 47 from line 46	**48**
49	Enter: • $415,050 if single • $233,475 if married filing separately • $466,950 if married filing jointly or qualifying widow(er) • $441,000 if head of household }	**49**
50	Enter the amount from line 45	**50**
51	Enter the amount from line 7 of the Qualified Dividends and Capital Gain Tax Worksheet in the instructions for Form 1040, line 44, or the amount from line 19 of the Schedule D Tax Worksheet, whichever applies (as figured for the regular tax). If you did not complete either worksheet for the regular tax, enter the amount from Form 1040, line 43; if zero or less, enter -0-. If you are filing Form 2555 or Form 2555-EZ, see instructions for the amount to enter	**51**
52	Add line 50 and line 51	**52**
53	Subtract line 52 from line 49. If zero or less, enter -0-	**53**
54	Enter the smaller of line 48 or line 53	**54**
55	Multiply line 54 by 15% (0.15) . . . . ▶	**55**
56	Add lines 47 and 54	**56**
	If lines 56 and 36 are the same, skip lines 57 through 61 and go to line 62. Otherwise, go to line 57.	
57	Subtract line 56 from line 46	**57**
58	Multiply line 57 by 20% (0.20) . . . . ▶	**58**
	If line 38 is zero or blank, skip lines 59 through 61 and go to line 62. Otherwise, go to line 59.	
59	Add lines 41, 56, and 57	**59**
60	Subtract line 59 from line 36	**60**
61	Multiply line 60 by 25% (0.25) . . . . ▶	**61**
62	Add lines 42, 55, 58, and 61	**62**
63	If line 36 is $186,300 or less ($93,150 or less if married filing separately), multiply line 36 by 26% (0.26). Otherwise, multiply line 36 by 28% (0.28) and subtract $3,726 ($1,863 if married filing separately) from the result	**63**
64	Enter the **smaller** of line 62 or line 63 here and on line 31. If you are filing Form 2555 or 2555-EZ, do not enter this amount on line 31. Instead, enter it on line 4 of the worksheet in the instructions for line 31 . .	**64**

EXAMPLE

A taxpayer with AGI of $100,000 and taxable income excluding personal exemptions of $94,000 has the following return items:

- $11,000 medical expenses
- $5,000 mortgage interest paid
- $2,000 municipal bond interest received

This taxpayer's AMTI is calculated as follows:

Taxable Income before deduction for personal exemptions	$94,000
Exempt interest	2,000
AMTI	$96,000

Stop and review! You have completed the outline for this subunit. Study multiple-choice questions 8 through 12 beginning on page 204.

7.3 LOSSES AND LIMITS

1. **Casualty and Theft Losses**

    a. The IRC allows deduction for losses caused by theft or casualties, whether business or personal.

    b. A casualty loss arises from a sudden, unexpected, or unusual event caused by an external force, such as fire, storm, shipwreck, earthquake, sonic boom, etc.

    1) Losses resulting from ordinary accidents are not deductible. Examples of these include dropping a vase or progressive deterioration, such as rust or insect damage.

    c. Theft includes robbery, larceny, etc. It may also include loss from extortion, blackmail, etc.

    1) Misplacing or losing items or having them confiscated by a foreign government is not considered theft.

    d. In general, the loss amount is the lesser of the decline in FMV or the AB minus insurance reimbursements.

    1) However, if business or investment property is completely lost or stolen, FMV is disregarded and AB is used to compute the loss.

EXAMPLE

Kaitlyn is a veterinarian. She had business equipment with a FMV of $15,000 and adjusted basis of $20,000 and had a business computer with a FMV of $1,000 and adjusted basis of $500. Both the equipment and computer were completely destroyed by a storm. She did not have insurance on these assets. Kaitlyn is able to deduct a loss of the combined adjusted bases since the assets are business assets equal to $20,500 ($20,000 + $500). If the same assets were personal-use assets and not business assets, the loss would have been the lower of the decline in adjusted basis and fair market value. Since there was one event, look at the items' combined value.

---

    e. Reimbursement

    1) Only the amount of loss not compensated by insurance is deductible.
    2) Any excess recovered over the amount of property basis is gain.

    f. Timing

    1) A casualty loss is deductible in the tax year in which it occurs.
    2) A theft loss is deductible when it is discovered.

    g. Inventory

    1) The normal casualty and theft loss rules do not apply to inventory. The loss is accounted for by increasing COGS.
    2) Any insurance reimbursement is gross income.

    h.   Business casualty losses are taken above-the-line; personal casualty losses are taken below-the-line.

2.   **Disaster Areas**

    a.   A taxpayer is subject to a special rule if (s)he sustains a loss from a federally declared disaster area.

    b.   Disaster loss treatment is available when a personal residence is rendered unsafe due to the disaster in the area and is ordered to be relocated or demolished by the state or local government.

    c.   The taxpayer has the option of deducting the loss on

        1)   The return for the year in which the loss actually occurred or

        2)   The preceding year's return (by filing an amended return).

    d.   Revocation of the election may be made before the expiration of time for filing the return for the year of loss.

    e.   A disaster loss deduction is computed the same as a casualty loss.

        1)   If the disaster loss is claimed on the preceding year's return, the AGI limitation is based on the prior year's AGI.

    f.   The loss is calculated on Form 4684, *Casualties and Thefts*, and carried over to Schedule A, *Itemized Deductions*.

3.   **Capital Losses**

    a.   Capital gain or loss realized on the sale or exchange of a capital asset is discussed in Study Unit 8, Subunit 3.

        1)   An individual taxpayer may deduct net capital losses to the extent that they do not exceed the lesser of ordinary income or $3,000 ($1,500 if married filing separately).

        2)   The individual may carry forward any excess capital losses indefinitely.

    b.   Capital Losses per Corporations

        1)   The amount of capital loss (CL) included in the NOL of a noncorporate taxpayer is limited.

        2)   Before the limit is applied, the CL must be separated into business CL and nonbusiness CL.

        3)   Capital losses are included in the NOL only as follows:

            a)   Nonbusiness CL is deducted to the extent of nonbusiness capital gain (CG).

                i)   Any excess nonbusiness CL is not deductible.

            b)   If nonbusiness CG exceeds nonbusiness CL [in a) above], then such excess is applied against any excess of nonbusiness deductions over nonbusiness income.

            c)   If nonbusiness CG exceeds excess nonbusiness deductions [in b) above], then the excess nonbusiness CG may offset business CL.

                i)   Business CL may also be deducted to the extent of business CG.

            d)   A corporation may use capital losses only to offset capital gains each year. A corporation must carry the excess capital loss back 3 years and forward 5 years and characterize all carryovers as short-term capital losses (regardless of character).

4. **Net Operating Loss (NOL)**

    a. A net operating loss occurs when business expenses exceed business income.
    b. The NOL is deductible when carried to a year in which there is taxable income.

        1) NOLs are first carried back for 2 years. Any remaining NOL is carried forward up to 20 years.
        2) The taxpayer can elect to forgo the carryback and start with the carryforward period.

    c. Although NOLs are typically business deductions, an individual may have an NOL.

        1) NOLs relating to casualty and theft losses for an individual may be carried back for 3 years.
        2) NOLs associated with federally declared disaster areas and incurred by a small business or a farmer may be carried back 3 years.
        3) NOLs attributable to farming business may be carried back for 5 years.

    d. To calculate NOL, start with taxable income (a negative amount) and make the following adjustments:

        1) Add back NOLs either carried forward or back into the current tax year.
        2) Add back personal exemptions.
        3) Add back excess of nonbusiness deductions over nonbusiness income.

            a) For this purpose, nonbusiness deductions are

                i)   Alimony,
                ii)   Contributions to self-employed retirement plans,
                iii) Loss from the sale of investment property, and
                iv)   Either the standard deduction or all itemized deductions.

                NOTE: Business deductions include all (even personal) casualty losses.

            b) Nonbusiness income includes

                i)   Interest,
                ii)   Dividends,
                iii) Gain on the sale of investment property, and
                iv)   Treasure trove.

            c) Rents and wages are business income.

EXAMPLE

For 2017, Sally realized a $30,000 net loss (sales of $200,000 less expenses of $230,000) from operating a sole proprietorship without regard to dispositions of property other than inventory. Other than this, the income tax return showed gross income of $10,000 ($4,500 of wages, $1,000 interest on personal savings, and a $4,500 long-term capital gain on business property). The excess of deductions over income was $30,400 ($10,000 gross income – $30,000 loss from business operations – $6,350 standard deduction – $4,050 personal exemption).

To compute Sally's NOL,
(1) Add back the $4,050 personal exemption amount and
(2) Add the $5,350 excess of nonbusiness deductions over nonbusiness income ($6,350 standard deduction – $1,000 interest).

Thus, Sally's NOL for the current tax year is $21,000 [$(30,400) "negative taxable income" + $4,050 + $5,350].

---

    e. If the NOL is carried back, the taxpayer files for a tax refund, which may require a recomputation of taxable income.
    f. An NOL carried forward is a deduction to arrive at AGI.

5. **At-Risk Rules**

   a. The amount of a loss allowable as a deduction is limited to the amount a person has at risk in the activity.

   b. A loss is the excess of deductions over gross income attributable to the activity.

   c. The amount at risk and any deductible loss are calculated on Form 6198.

   d. The rules apply to individuals, partners in partnerships, members in limited liability companies, shareholders of S corporations, trusts, estates, and certain closely held C corporations.

   e. The rules are applied separately to each trade, business, or income-producing activity.

   f. A person's amount at risk in an activity is determined at the close of the tax year.

      1) A person's initial at-risk amount includes money contributed, the adjusted basis of property contributed, and borrowed amounts.

      2) Recourse debt

         a) A person's at-risk amount includes amounts borrowed only to the extent that, for the debt, the person has either personal liability or pledged property as security.

         b) The at-risk amount does not include debt if one of the following applies:

            i) Property pledged as security is used in the activity.

            ii) Personal liability is protected against by insurance, guarantees, stop-loss agreements, or similar arrangements.

            iii) The creditor is a person with an interest in the activity or one related to the taxpayer.

      3) Nonrecourse debt is generally excluded from the amount at risk.

         a) The amount at risk in the activity of holding real property includes qualified nonrecourse financing (QNRF).

         b) In qualified nonrecourse financing, the taxpayer is not personally liable, but the financing is

            i) Incurred in a real estate activity;

            ii) Secured by the real property;

            iii) Not convertible to an ownership interest; and

            iv) Either from an unrelated third party, from a related party but on commercially reasonable terms, or guaranteed by a governmental entity.

   g. Adjustments to an at-risk amount are made for events that vary the investors' economic risk of loss.

      1) Add contributions of money and property (its AB), recourse debt increases, QNRF increase, and income from the activity.

      2) Subtract distributions, liability reductions, and tax deductions allowable (at year end), but only to the extent they reduce the at-risk amount to zero.

         a) If the amount at risk decreases below zero, previously allowed losses must be recaptured as income.

   h. Disallowed losses are carried forward.

   i. If a deduction would reduce basis in property and part or all of the deduction is disallowed by the at-risk rules, the basis is reduced anyway.

6. **Passive Activity Loss (PAL) Limitation Rules**

   a. The amount of a loss attributable to a person's passive activities is allowable as a deduction or credit only against, and to the extent of, gross income or tax attributable to those passive activities (in the aggregate).

      1) The excess is deductible or creditable in a future year, subject to the same limits.

EXAMPLE

A wealthy taxpayer invested in an architecture partnership as a passive investor. Because the taxpayer does not engage in the business outside of occasional business consulting, any income or loss derived from the business is passive in nature. Therefore, any losses derived from the partnership may only offset passive activity gains.

---

   b. The passive activity rules apply to individuals, estates, trusts (other than grantor trusts), personal service corporations, and closely held corporations.

      1) Although passive activity rules do not apply to grantor trusts, partnerships, and S corporations directly, they do apply to the owners of these entities.

   c. A passive activity is either a trade or business in which the person does not materially participate or a rental activity.

      1) A taxpayer materially participates in an activity during a tax year if (s)he satisfies one of the following tests:

         a) Participates more than 500 hours.

         b) The taxpayer's participation constitutes substantially all of the participation in the activity.

         c) Participates more than 100 hours and exceeds the participation of any other individual.

         d) Materially participated in the activity for any 5 years of the preceding 10 years before the year in question.

         e) Materially participated in a personal service activity for any 3 years preceding the year in question.

         f) Participates in the activity on a regular, continuous, and substantial basis.

   d. Passive activity rules do not apply to

      1) Active income/loss/credit

      2) Portfolio income/loss/credit

      3) Casualty and theft losses, vacation home rental, qualified home mortgage interest, business use of home, or a working interest in an oil or gas well held through an entity that does not limit the person's liability

   e. Rental Real Estate

      1) All rental activity is passive.

      2) However, a person who actively participates in rental real estate activity is entitled to deduct up to $25,000 of losses from the passive activity from other than passive income.

      3) This exception to the general PAL limitation rule applies to a person who

         a) Actively participates in the activity

         b) Owns 10% or more of the activity (by value) for the entire year

         c) Has MAGI of less than $150,000 [phaseout begins at $100,000; shown in 4)a) on the next page]

4) $25,000 of a tax year loss from rental real estate activities in excess of passive activity gross income is deductible against portfolio or active income.

   a) The $25,000 limit is reduced by 50% of the person's MAGI [i.e., AGI without regard to PALs, Social Security benefits, and qualified retirement contributions (e.g., IRAs)] over $100,000.

   b) Excess rental real estate PALs are suspended. They are treated as other PALs carried over.

5) Active participation is a less stringent requirement than material participation.

   a) It is met with participation in management decisions or arranging for others to provide services (such as repairs).

   b) There will not be active participation if at any time during the period there is ownership of less than 10% of the interest in the property (including the spouse's interest).

6) Real property trades or businesses

   a) The passive activity loss rules do not apply to certain taxpayers who are involved in real property trades or businesses.

   b) An individual may avoid passive activity loss limitation treatment on a rental real estate activity if two requirements are met:

      i) More than 50% of the individual's personal services performed during the year are performed in the real property trades or businesses in which the individual materially participates.

      ii) The individual performs more than 750 hours of service in the real property trades or businesses in which the individual materially participates.

   c) This provision also applies to a closely held C corporation if 50% of gross receipts for the tax year are from real property trades or businesses in which the corporation materially participated.

   d) Any deduction allowed under this rule is not taken into consideration in determining the taxpayer's AGI for purposes of the phaseout of the $25,000 deduction.

   e) If 50% or less of the personal services performed are in real property trades or businesses, the individual will be subject to the passive activity limitation rules.

EXAMPLE

Lynne, a single taxpayer, has $70,000 in wages, $15,000 income from a limited partnership, and a $26,000 loss from rental real estate activities in which she actively participated and is not subject to the modified adjusted gross income phaseout rule. She can use $15,000 of her $26,000 loss to offset her $15,000 passive income from the partnership. She actively participated in her rental real estate activities, so she can use the remaining $11,000 rental real estate loss to offset $11,000 of her nonpassive income (wages).

   f.   **Suspension**

        1)   A PAL not allowable in the current tax year is carried forward indefinitely and
             treated as a deduction in subsequent tax years.

   g.   PALs continue to be treated as PALs even after the activity ceases to be passive in a
        subsequent tax year, except that it may also be deducted against income from that
        activity.

   h.   Disposition of a Passive Activity

        1)   Suspended (and current-year) losses from a passive activity become deductible
             in full in the year the taxpayer completely disposes of all interest in the passive
             activity.

        2)   The loss is deductible first against net income or gain from the taxpayer's
             other passive activities. The remainder of the loss, if any, is then treated as
             nonpassive.

7.   **Hobby Losses**

     a.   Hobby expenses can be deducted to the extent the hobby generates income.

**Stop and review! You have completed the outline for this subunit. Study multiple-choice
questions 13 through 20 beginning on page 206.**

QUESTIONS

7.1 Tax Credits

1. Karen, filing as head of household, and her son
James and daughter Julia are all in graduate school.
James and Julia are not dependents on Karen's
return, although they live with her and she pays all
of their education expenses. Karen paid $6,000 in
qualified tuition expenses for herself in January 2017
for the term starting in January 2017. She also paid
$2,500 in qualified tuition expenses for James and
another $2,500 for Julia in July 2017 for the terms
starting in July 2017. Her adjusted gross income is
$67,000. Which of the following is true for tax year
2017?

A.   Karen may claim no American Opportunity
     Credit and $2,000 Lifetime Learning Credit.

B.   Karen may claim $5,000 American Opportunity
     Credit and $1,000 Lifetime Learning Credit.

C.   Karen may claim neither the American
     Opportunity nor the Lifetime Learning Credit.

D.   Karen may claim no American Opportunity
     Credit and $1,000 Lifetime Learning Credit.

Answer (C) is correct.
   REQUIRED: The amount of American Opportunity Credit
and Lifetime Learning Credit a taxpayer may claim.
   DISCUSSION: The American Opportunity Credit and
Lifetime Learning Credit may not be claimed at the same time.
The American Opportunity Credit is available during a student's
first 4 years in college. Since Karen is in graduate school,
she does not qualify for the American Opportunity Credit. The
Lifetime Learning Credit is available in years that the American
Opportunity Credit is not taken (for example, graduate school).
However, the Lifetime Learning Credit phases out for single
filers whose AGI is between $56,000 and $66,000 in 2017.
Since Karen's AGI is $67,000, the Lifetime Learning Credit is
completely phased out.

2. Which of the following credits is a combination of
several tax credits to provide uniform rules for the
current and carryback-carryover years?

A.   General Business Credit.

B.   Foreign Tax Credit.

C.   Minimum Tax Credit.

D.   Research Credit.

Answer (A) is correct.
   REQUIRED: The credit that is actually a combination of
several credits.
   DISCUSSION: The General Business Credit is a set of
several credits commonly available to businesses, including
credits for investment, research, and work opportunity jobs,
among others.
   Answer (B) is incorrect. The Foreign Tax Credit is a specific,
individual credit. Answer (C) is incorrect. The Minimum Tax
Credit is a specific, individual credit. Answer (D) is incorrect.
The Research Credit is a specific, individual credit.

3. To qualify for the Child Care Credit on a joint return, at least one spouse must

	Have an Adjusted Gross Income of $15,000 or Less	Be Gainfully Employed when Related Expenses Are Incurred
A.	Yes	Yes
B.	No	No
C.	Yes	No
D.	No	Yes

Answer (B) is correct.

REQUIRED: The requirement(s) to qualify for the Child Care Credit on a joint return.

DISCUSSION: The IRC allows a nonrefundable credit to a provider of care to dependents for a limited portion of expenses necessary to enable gainful employment. The credit claimant must have qualified child care expenses when the claimant is employed or actively seeking gainful employment. The credit amount is not eliminated when AGI exceeds $15,000, only phased down from 35% to 20% in increments of 1% for each $2,000 AGI exceeds $15,000.

Answer (A) is incorrect. Qualifying expenses may be incurred when the claimant is actively seeking gainful employment, and the credit is not eliminated by reference to AGI. The credit is phased from 35% to 20%. Answer (C) is incorrect. The credit is not eliminated when AGI exceeds a cap amount. The credit is phased from 35% to 20%. Answer (D) is incorrect. Qualifying expenses may be incurred when the claimant is actively seeking gainful employment.

4. Which of the following credits can result in a refund even if the individual had **no** income tax liability?

A. Foreign Tax Credit.

B. Elderly and Permanently and Totally Disabled Credit.

C. Earned Income Credit.

D. Child and Dependent Care Credit.

Answer (C) is correct.

REQUIRED: The credit that is refundable.

DISCUSSION: A refundable credit is payable as a refund to the extent the credit amount exceeds tax otherwise due. Some of the refundable credits are credits for taxes withheld, overpayments of income tax, and the Earned Income Credit.

Answer (A) is incorrect. The credit for foreign taxes paid is not refundable. Answer (B) is incorrect. The Elderly and Disabled Credit is not refundable. Answer (D) is incorrect. The Child and Dependent Care Credit is not refundable.

5. Which of the following disqualifies an individual from the Earned Income Credit?

A. The taxpayer's qualifying child is a 17-year-old grandchild.

B. The taxpayer has earned income of $5,000.

C. The taxpayer's 5-year-old child lived in the taxpayer's home for only 8 months.

D. The taxpayer has a filing status of married filing separately.

Answer (D) is correct.

REQUIRED: The situation that disqualifies an individual from the EIC.

DISCUSSION: The Earned Income Credit is unavailable to taxpayers filing married filing separately.

Answer (A) is incorrect. The child must be under age 19 at the close of the tax year, or 24 if a student. Answer (B) is incorrect. The phaseout thresholds for the EIC vary depending on number of children and filing status. However, all thresholds exceed $5,000. Answer (C) is incorrect. The child needs only to live with the taxpayer for more than 6 months.

6. Which of the following statements about the Child and Dependent Care Credit is correct?

A. The credit is nonrefundable.

B. The child must be under the age of 18 years.

C. The child must be a direct descendant of the taxpayer.

D. The maximum credit is $600.

Answer (A) is correct.

REQUIRED: The true statement about the Child and Dependent Care Credit.

DISCUSSION: A nonrefundable tax credit is allowed for child and dependent care expenses incurred to enable the taxpayer to be gainfully employed. To qualify, the taxpayer must provide more than half the cost of maintaining a household for a dependent under age 13 or an incapacitated spouse or dependent. The maximum credit is equal to 35% of up to $3,000 of child and dependent care expenses for one qualifying individual ($6,000 for two or more individuals).

Answer (B) is incorrect. A child who is not incapacitated must be under the age of 13. Dependents who are incapacitated do not have an age restriction. Answer (C) is incorrect. Direct "descendant" is not a requirement (e.g., incapacitated spouse). Answer (D) is incorrect. The maximum credit is $1,050 ($3,000 expense limit × 35%) for one qualifying individual and $2,100 ($6,000 expense limit × 35%) for two or more qualifying individuals.

7. All of the following qualify as work-related expenses for computing the Child and Dependent Care Credit **except**

   A. The parent-employer's portion of Social Security tax paid on wages for a person to take care of dependent children while the parents work.

   B. Payments to a nursery school for the care of dependent children while the parents work.

   C. The cost of meals for a housekeeper who provides necessary care for a dependent child while the parents work.

   D. Payments to a housekeeper who provides dependent care while the parent is off from work because of illness.

Answer (D) is correct.

REQUIRED: The child or dependent care expense that does not qualify as employment-related.

DISCUSSION: Employment-related expenses are paid for household services and for the care of a qualifying individual. Expenses are classified as work-related only if they are incurred to enable the taxpayer to be gainfully employed. An expense is not considered to be work-related merely because it is incurred while the taxpayer is gainfully employed.

Answer (A) is incorrect. The parent-employer's portion of Social Security tax paid on wages for a person to take care of dependent children while the parents work is an expense incurred to enable the taxpayer to be gainfully employed. Answer (B) is incorrect. Payments to a nursery school for the care of dependent children while the parents work is an expense incurred to enable the taxpayer to be gainfully employed. Answer (C) is incorrect. The cost of meals for a housekeeper who provides necessary care for a dependent child while the parents work is an expense incurred to enable the taxpayer to be gainfully employed.

7.2 Alternative Minimum Tax

8. The alternative minimum tax (AMT) is computed as the

   A. Excess of the regular tax over the tentative AMT.

   B. Excess of the tentative AMT over the regular tax.

   C. Tentative AMT plus the regular tax.

   D. Lesser of the tentative AMT or the regular tax.

Answer (B) is correct.

REQUIRED: The correct computation of the AMT.

DISCUSSION: The alternative minimum tax is the excess of the minimum tax over the regular tax. The AMT is payable in addition to the regular tax.

Answer (A) is incorrect. AMT is an additional tax. Answer (C) is incorrect. AMT equals tentative AMT minus regular tax. Answer (D) is incorrect. AMT equals the difference, and not the lesser, of tentative AMT and regular tax.

9. Alternative minimum tax preferences include

	Tax-Exempt Interest from Private Activity Bonds Issued during 2017	Charitable Contributions of Appreciated Capital Gain Property
A.	Yes	Yes
B.	Yes	No
C.	No	Yes
D.	No	No

Answer (B) is correct.

REQUIRED: The AMT preference items.

DISCUSSION: AMT preferences are items that are allowed relatively favorable treatment in determining regular taxable income. These preferences are added back to TI to find AMTI. Tax-exempt interest from private activity bonds is an AMT preference item. A charitable contribution of appreciated capital gain property is not an AMT preference item.

Answer (A) is incorrect. A charitable contribution of capital gain property is not an alternative minimum tax preference. Answer (C) is incorrect. Tax-exempt interest from private activity bonds is an AMT preference item, but a charitable contribution of capital property is not. Answer (D) is incorrect. Tax-exempt interest from private activity bonds is an AMT preference item.

10. In 2017, Don Mills, a single taxpayer, had $70,000 in taxable income before personal exemptions. Mills had no tax preferences. His itemized deductions were as follows:

State and local income taxes	$5,000
Home mortgage interest on loan to acquire residence	6,000
Miscellaneous deductions that exceed 2% of adjusted gross income	2,000

What amount did Mills report as alternative minimum taxable income before the AMT exemption?

- A. $72,000
- B. $75,000
- C. $77,000
- D. $83,000

Answer (C) is correct.
REQUIRED: The adjustments made to TI to reach AMTI.
DISCUSSION: The itemized deduction for state and local income taxes and miscellaneous itemized deductions exceeding the 2%-of-AGI floor are AMT adjustment items that must be added back to TI to find AMTI. Therefore, AMTI is $77,000 ($70,000 TI + $5,000 + $2,000).
Answer (A) is incorrect. The itemized deduction for state and local income taxes is an AMT adjustment item that should also be added back. Answer (B) is incorrect. The miscellaneous itemized deductions exceeding the 2%-of-AGI floor are an AMT adjustment item that should also be added back. Answer (D) is incorrect. Qualified home mortgage interest is not an AMT adjustment item.

11. Generally, in computing the alternative minimum tax for individuals, which one of the following is **not** an adjustment or tax preference for alternative minimum tax purposes?

- A. Personal exemptions.
- B. Tax-exempt interest on certain private activity bonds.
- C. Standard deduction.
- D. Contributions to an Individual Retirement Arrangement (IRA).

Answer (D) is correct.
REQUIRED: The item that is not an adjustment or a tax preference for arriving at alternative minimum taxable income.
DISCUSSION: Taxable income must be adjusted to arrive at alternative minimum taxable income (AMTI). The adjustments are described in Secs. 56 and 58 with tax preferences in Sec. 57. The adjustments with respect to itemized deductions of an individual are contained in Sec. 56(b)(1). Contributions to an IRA have no effect on AMTI.
Answer (A) is incorrect. Personal exemptions are not allowed as deductions in arriving at alternative minimum taxable income under Sec. 56(b) and, therefore, must be added back as adjustments to taxable income for arriving at alternative minimum taxable income. Answer (B) is incorrect. It is a tax preference item. Answer (C) is incorrect. The standard deduction is not allowed as a deduction in arriving at alternative minimum taxable income under Sec. 56(b) and, therefore, must be added back as an adjustment to taxable income for arriving at alternative minimum taxable income.

12. Alternative minimum tax for individuals requires certain adjustments and preferences. Generally, which of the following is a preference or adjustment item for noncorporate taxpayers?

- A. Personal exemptions.
- B. Incentive stock options.
- C. Tax-exempt interest on certain private activity bonds.
- D. All of the answers are correct.

Answer (D) is correct.
REQUIRED: The item that is a preference or adjustment item for noncorporate taxpayers.
DISCUSSION: Several adjustments affect only noncorporate taxpayers. Personal exemptions, tax-exempt interest on private activity bonds (which is included in investment income), and incentive stock options are examples of these adjustments.
Answer (A) is incorrect. Incentive stock options and tax-exempt interest on certain private activity bonds are also preference or adjustment items for noncorporate taxpayers when determining the alternative minimum tax. Answer (B) is incorrect. Personal exemptions and tax-exempt interest on certain private activity bonds are also preference or adjustment items for noncorporate taxpayers when determining the alternative minimum tax. Answer (C) is incorrect. Personal exemptions and incentive stock options are also preference or adjustment items for noncorporate taxpayers when determining the alternative minimum tax.

7.3 Losses and Limits

13. Lee qualified as head of a household for 2017 tax purposes. Lee's 2017 taxable income was $100,000, exclusive of capital gains and losses. Lee had a net long-term capital loss of $8,000 in 2017. What amount of this capital loss can Lee offset against 2017 ordinary income?

- A. $0
- B. $3,000
- C. $4,000
- D. $8,000

Answer (B) is correct.

REQUIRED: The deductible amount of a net capital loss.

DISCUSSION: Capital losses offset capital gains. Excess of capital losses over capital gains (net capital loss) is deductible against ordinary income, but only up to $3,000 in the current tax year.

Answer (A) is incorrect. Lee may offset part of the capital loss. Answer (C) is incorrect. The offset is limited to $3,000. Answer (D) is incorrect. The whole amount of the loss may not be offset in the current year.

14. Don Wolf became a general partner in Gata Associates on January 1, 2017, with a 5% interest in Gata's profits, losses, and capital. Gata is a distributor of auto parts. Wolf does not materially participate in the partnership business. For the year ended December 31, 2017, Gata had an operating loss of $100,000. In addition, Gata earned interest of $20,000 on a temporary investment while awaiting delivery of equipment that is presently on order. The principal will be used to pay for this equipment. Wolf's passive loss for 2017 is

- A. $0
- B. $4,000
- C. $5,000
- D. $6,000

Answer (C) is correct.

REQUIRED: The amount treated as a passive loss.

DISCUSSION: In general, losses arising from one passive activity may be used to offset income from other passive activities but may not be used to offset active or portfolio income. Wolf's $5,000 operating loss ($100,000 × 5%) may not be used to offset his $1,000 portfolio income ($20,000 × 5%); i.e., interest and dividends are portfolio income. Therefore, his passive loss for 2017 is his $5,000 operating loss. The losses may be carried forward indefinitely or until the entire interest is disposed of.

Answer (A) is incorrect. The operating losses are passive since Wolf does not materially participate. Answer (B) is incorrect. The interest income is classified as portfolio income and is not offset by passive losses. Answer (D) is incorrect. The $1,000 interest constitutes income, not loss.

15. In computing an individual's net operating loss, which of the following is **not** considered business income or deduction(s)?

- A. Wages.
- B. Personal casualty loss.
- C. Gain on sale of investment property.
- D. Gain on sale of business property.

Answer (C) is correct.

REQUIRED: The item not considered business income or deductions in computing an individual's NOL.

DISCUSSION: Business and nonbusiness income and deductions need to be distinguished because nonbusiness deductions are deductible in computing a NOL only to the extent of nonbusiness income. Nonbusiness deductions and income are those that are not attributable to, or derived from, a taxpayer's trade or business. Also, capital losses are only deductible to the extent of capital gains. A gain on the sale of investment property is a capital gain and not business income.

Answer (A) is incorrect. Employment is considered a trade or business; therefore, wages are business income. Answer (B) is incorrect. A personal casualty loss is treated as a business deduction. Answer (D) is incorrect. A gain on the sale of business property is considered business income.

16. Greg and Reni, who are married, file joint income tax returns. In 2017, they paid $90 to repair a glass vase accidentally broken in their home by their pet dog. The vase cost $500 in 2017. Its FMV was $600 before the accident and $200 after the accident. Without regard to the $100 "floor" and the adjusted gross income percentage threshold, what amount should Greg and Reni deduct for the casualty loss in their itemized deductions on Schedule A for 2017?

- A. $0
- B. $90
- C. $300
- D. $400

Answer (A) is correct.

REQUIRED: The deductible amount of a casualty loss.

DISCUSSION: A casualty is defined as the complete or partial destruction of property arising from a sudden, unexpected, or unusual event caused by an external force. Nondeductible casualty losses include casualty losses caused by the taxpayer's willful negligence or act, those caused by gradual wearing away, and those due to accidental breakage of articles, such as glassware or china, under normal conditions. No part of the loss is deductible.

17. Which of the following statements is **false** regarding individual taxpayers and allowed losses?

A. Net capital loss deductions are limited by ordinary income and $3,000 maximum ($1,500 if married filing separately).

B. A disaster loss may be taken on the prior year's return but still subject to current year AGI limitations.

C. Loss deductions are limited to the amount a person has at risk in the activity.

D. Hobby expense deductions are limited to hobby income.

Answer (B) is correct.
    REQUIRED: The false statement regarding allowed losses.
    DISCUSSION: Taxpayers have the option of deducting a disaster loss on the return for the year in which the loss actually occurred or the preceding year's return. The AGI limitation is based on the AGI of the return year. In this case, it would be the AGI of the prior year.
    Answer (A) is incorrect. Capital losses are deductible in excess of capital gains, but this excess is limited to the lessor of ordinary income or $3,000 ($1,500 if married filing separately). Answer (C) is incorrect. The at-risk rules limit the amount of a deductible loss to the amount a person has at risk in the activity. Answer (D) is incorrect. Hobby expenses can be deducted to the extent the hobby generates income.

18. If an individual taxpayer's passive losses and credits relating to rental real estate activities **cannot** be used in the current year, then they may be carried

A. Back 2 years, but they cannot be carried forward.

B. Forward up to a maximum period of 20 years, but they cannot be carried back.

C. Back 2 years or forward up to 20 years, at the taxpayer's election.

D. Forward indefinitely or until the property is disposed of in a taxable transaction.

Answer (D) is correct.
    REQUIRED: The correct statement concerning the carryover or carryback of unused passive losses and credits.
    DISCUSSION: Disallowed passive activity losses (and credits) are carried forward and used to offset passive activity income (and taxes) in later years. This applies to passive losses and credits from rental real estate activities or from any other passive activity. The carryover is accomplished by treating the disallowed loss from each activity as a deduction for the activity in the following year. In this manner, the carryforward is indefinite. If the entire interest in a passive activity is disposed of in a taxable transaction in a later year, the passive loss may be used at that time.

19. Which of the following statements about losses in federally declared disaster areas is **false**?

A. The taxpayer has the option of deducting the loss on the return for the year immediately preceding the year in which the disaster actually occurred.

B. If the taxpayer's home is located in a federally declared disaster area, and the state government orders that it be torn down, the taxpayer may be able to treat the loss in value as a casualty loss from a disaster.

C. Disaster area loss deductions are figured using the usual rules for casualty losses.

D. Once made, the election to deduct the loss on the prior-year return cannot be revoked.

Answer (D) is correct.
    REQUIRED: The false statement about losses in federally declared disaster areas.
    DISCUSSION: If a taxpayer sustains a loss from a disaster in an area subsequently designated as a federal disaster area, a special rule may help the taxpayer to cushion his or her loss. Disaster loss treatment is available with respect to a personal residence declared unsafe and ordered to be demolished by the state or local government. The taxpayer also has the option of deducting the loss on his or her return for the year in which the loss occurred or on the return for the previous year. Revocation of the election to deduct the loss on the preceding year's tax return may be made before the expiration of time for filing the return for the year of loss. The calculation of the deduction for a disaster loss follows the same rules as those for nonbusiness casualty losses.
    Answer (A) is incorrect. It is a true statement about losses in federally declared disaster areas. Answer (B) is incorrect. It is a true statement about losses in federally declared disaster areas. Answer (C) is incorrect. It is a true statement about losses in federally declared disaster areas.

20. The at-risk rules

A. Limit a taxpayer's deductible losses from investment activities.

B. Limit the type of deductions in income-producing activities.

C. Apply to business and income-producing activities on a combined basis.

D. Apply at the entity level for partnerships and S corporations.

Answer (A) is correct.
    REQUIRED: The correct statement concerning the at-risk rules.
    DISCUSSION: The at-risk rules limit a taxpayer's deductible losses from each business and income-producing activity to the amount for which the taxpayer is at risk with respect to that activity.
    Answer (B) is incorrect. The losses from each activity, not the type of deductions, are limited. Answer (C) is incorrect. The at-risk rules apply to each business and income-producing activity separately. Answer (D) is incorrect. The at-risk rules apply at the partner or shareholder level for these pass-through entities.

STUDY UNIT EIGHT
PROPERTY TRANSACTIONS

(33 pages of outline)

The tax treatment of property transactions is integrated with that of other transactions on the CPA exam. Visualize the following steps to analyze the income tax consequences of property transactions.

1. Determine gain or loss realized.
2. Apply related party sales rules.
3. Apply nonrecognition rules.
4. Apply Sec. 1245 and 1250 recapturing rules.
5. Characterize gains and losses under Sec. 1231.
6. Apply capital loss rules.
7. Apply other loss limits.

    a. At-risk rules
    b. Passive activity loss rules
    c. Net operating loss rules

8. Report gross income, claim deductions, and compute taxable income and tax liability in accordance with other rules. For example,

    a. Apply installment sales rules.
    b. Deduct allowable capital losses.
    c. Phase out personal exemptions with capital gains included in taxable income.
    d. Apply tax rates separately to capital gains and other income.

The sale of a business requires special attention. When more than one asset of a business is transferred in bulk (total consideration exchanged for assets in combination), including all the assets of a sole proprietorship, gain or loss must be accounted for separately for each asset transferred. Allocation among assets of consideration paid or to be paid is by agreement of parties, by relative FMV of assets, or by the residual method. Also note the following:

1. Capital gain or loss might arise from assets that have no fixed or determinable useful life, such as goodwill that was not amortized (self-created goodwill) under Sec. 197 or an exclusive franchise.
2. Ordinary income or loss might arise from the following assets:

    a. Inventory
    b. Accounts receivable
    c. Covenants not to compete (all ordinary)
    d. Section 1245 property, e.g., equipment
    e. Section 1250 property, i.e., depreciable realty
    f. Section 1231 property, e.g., depreciable trade or business property

Some candidates find it helpful to have the entire tax form side-by-side with our Knowledge Transfer Outline when studying. The full versions of the most up-to-date forms are easily accessible at www.gleim.com/taxforms. These forms and the form excerpts used in our outline are periodically updated as the latest versions are released by the IRS.

8.1 BASIS

1. **Overview**

    a. When a taxpayer acquires property, his or her basis in the property is initially cost, transferred, or exchanged basis.

    1) **Cost basis** is the sum of capitalized acquisition costs.

        a) Cost basis includes the fair market value (Sec. 1245 ordinary income) of property given up. If it is not determinable with reasonable certainty, use FMV of property received.

        b) A rebate to the purchaser is treated as a reduction of the purchase price. It is not included in basis nor in gross income.

    2) **Transferred basis** is computed by reference to basis in the property in the hands of another.

    3) **Exchanged basis** is computed by reference to basis in other property previously held.

        a) The basis of property converted into business use is the lesser of the FMV of the property at the conversion date or the adjusted basis at conversion.

2. **Unit of Property**

    a. The determination of whether tangible property costs are deducted or capitalized is determined by examining the unit of property. The unit of property is a group of functionally interdependent components and can either be an asset, group of assets, or a defined portion of an asset.

    1) Non-building property generally remains subject to the functional interdependence test.

        a) In the case of personal or real property other than a building, all the components that are functionally interdependent comprise a single unit of property.

        b) Components of property are functionally interdependent if the placing in service of one component by the taxpayer is dependent on the placing in service of the other component by the taxpayer. The following are included in this classification of unit of property:

            i)   Personal and other real property,
            ii) Improvements to a unit of property,
            iii) Components with different property classes,
            iv) Plant property, and
            v)   Network assets.

    b. Taxpayers must further divide the identified units of property into major components and substantial structural parts. Absent an available exception, costs to replace a major component or substantial structural part must be capitalized.

3. **Capitalized Costs**

    a. Initial basis in purchased property is the cost of acquiring it. Only capital costs are included.

    1) Capital expenditures may be made by cash, by cash equivalent, in property, with liability, or by services.

    b. An improvement expenditure must be capitalized if it (1) results in a betterment to the unit of property, (2) adapts the unit of property to a new or different use, or (3) results in a restoration of the unit of property.

    1) An expenditure is a **betterment** if it ameliorates a condition or defect that existed before acquisition of the property or arose during the production of the property; is for a material addition to the property; or increases the property's productivity, efficiency, strength, etc.

    2) An expenditure is an **adaptation** to a new or different use if it adapts the unit of property to a use inconsistent with the taxpayer's intended ordinary use at the time the taxpayer originally placed the property into service.

    3) An expenditure is a **restoration** if it

        a) Restores a basis that has been taken into account,

        b) Returns the unit of property to working order from a state of nonfunctional disrepair,

        c) Results in a rebuilding of the unit of property to a like-new condition after the end of the property's alternative depreciation system class life, or

        d) Replaces a major component or substantial structural part of the unit of property.

Common Capitalized Costs (for Sec. 1012)

Purchase Price (Stated)
NOTE: Not unstated interest
Liability to which property is subject

Closing Costs
Brokerage commissions
Pre-purchase taxes
Sales tax on purchase
Excise taxes
Title transfer taxes
Title insurance
Recording fees
Attorney fees
Document review, preparation

Miscellaneous Costs
Appraisal fees
Freight
Installation
Testing

Major Improvements
New roof
New gutters
Extending water line to property
Demolition costs and losses
New electrical wiring

EXAMPLE

If an individual buys a building for $20,000 cash and assumes a mortgage of $80,000 on it, his or her basis is $100,000.

---

    4) In the case of repainting a building's exterior, the basic rules are

        a) If painting is the only thing being done, the painting costs are expensed or

        b) If painting is part of a larger project that includes capital improvements to the building's structure, the painting costs are capitalized.

  c. A taxpayer must capitalize amounts paid to **facilitate** the acquisition of real or personal property. This treatment applies when the amount is paid in the process of investigating or otherwise pursuing the acquisition.

    1) Facilitative (i.e., capitalized) costs do not include amounts paid to determine whether to acquire real property or which real property to acquire. Such amounts are current deductions.

    2) Amounts paid for employee compensation and overhead are treated as amounts that do not facilitate the acquisition of real or personal property.

EXAMPLE

Dolores is a manager of a family-owned grocery store and is assigned to determine where to open a second location. The compensation for Dolores' time is deducted, not capitalized, by the grocery store as a facilitative cost. If the work had been performed by a real estate professional and paid as commission, the amount would have to be capitalized because it was paid to facilitate the acquisition of real property.

---

  d. **Expenses not properly chargeable to a capital account.** Costs of maintaining and operating property are not added to basis.

4. **Uniform Capitalization Rules**

    a. Costs for construction (manufacture) of real or tangible personal property to be used in trade or business and costs of producing or acquiring property for sale to customers (retail) are capitalized.

        1) Capitalize all costs necessary to prepare it for its intended use, both direct and most allocable indirect costs, e.g., engineering, permit, material, storage, and equipment rent.

            a) Costs and losses associated with demolishing a structure are allocated to the **land**. The basis of any new building constructed on the land is its original cost (not FMV).

        2) Construction period interest and taxes must be capitalized as part of building cost.

        3) Indirect costs not capitalized include, among others, marketing, selling, advertising, distribution, research, experimental, Sec. 179, strike, warranty, unsuccessful bid, and deductible service costs.

    b. Uniform capitalization rules do not apply if property is acquired for resale and the company's annual gross receipts (for the past 3 years) do not exceed $10 million.

5. **De Minimis Expense**

    a. Taxpayers can make an election to deduct a de minimis amount for each transaction relating to tangible property with an economic useful life of at least 12 months.

        1) A **de minimis amount** is a cost that is so small that it is not worth tracking. Taxpayers may expense any purchased assets with a cost of less than $2,500 provided they also use this policy for financial accounting purposes.

            a) If the taxpayer has audited or other approved financial statements, assets up to $5,000 may be expensed.

            b) The determination of the value of an asset includes all capitalized costs but the limit is applied on a per unit basis.

EXAMPLE

Henry, a business owner who does not have his financial statements audited, purchases 2 computers for $3,000 and pays $500 to have them installed. The cost per computer is $1,750 [($3,000 + $500) ÷ 2], which allows the computers to be expensed as a de minimis expense.

---

6. **Lump-Sum Assets**

    a. When more than one asset is purchased for a lump sum, the basis of each is computed pro rata by apportioning the total cost based on the relative FMV of each asset.

$$Allocable\ cost\ (basis) = \frac{FMV\ of\ asset}{FMV\ of\ all\ assets\ purchased} \times Lump\ sum\ purchase\ price$$

    b. Alternatively, the transferor and transferee may agree in writing as to the allocation of consideration or the FMV of any assets. The agreement is binding unless the IRS deems it improper.

    c. The residual method must be used for any transfers of a group of assets that constitutes a trade or business and for which the buyer's basis is determined only by the amount paid for the assets.

d. The **residual method** allocates purchase price for both transferor and transferee to asset categories up to FMV in the following order:

1) Cash and cash equivalents

2) Near-cash items, such as CDs, U.S. government securities, foreign currency, and other marketable securities

3) Accounts receivable, mortgages, and credit card receivables acquired in the ordinary course of business

4) Property held primarily for sale to customers in the ordinary course of a trade or business or stocks included in dealer inventory

5) Assets not listed in 1) through 4) above

6) Section 197 intangibles, such as patents and covenants not to compete except goodwill and going-concern value

7) Goodwill and going-concern value

NOTE: When the purchase price is lower than the aggregate FMV of the assets other than goodwill/going-concern value, the price is allocated first to the face amount of cash and then to assets 2) through 6) above, according to relative FMVs.

EXAMPLE

Bennett Industries just purchased Beard Nation, Inc., for $450,000. All of the liabilities were paid off at the date of purchase. The assets of Beard Nation are as follows:

Cash	$ 50,000
Marketable securities	150,000
Accounts receivable	125,000
Inventory	100,000
Equipment	75,000
Land	50,000
FMV of all assets	$550,000

The basis of cash is the face value of $50,000, which reduces the outstanding basis to $400,000. Next, the fair market value is assigned to Class 2 assets, so the basis for marketable securities is $150,000, which reduces the remaining basis to $250,000. Accounts receivable are Class 3 assets and are assigned the fair market value of $125,000, reducing the remaining basis to $125,000. Inventory is a Class 4 asset and receives the fair market value of $100,000, reducing the remaining allocable basis to $25,000. The land and equipment are both Class 5 assets, but the fair market value of these assets is less than the remaining basis. The basis needs to be allocated between these two assets based upon the relative fair market values. The equipment receives a basis of $15,000 ($25,000 × $75,000 ÷ $125,000), and the basis receives a $10,000 basis ($25,000 × $50,000 ÷ $125,000).

EXAMPLE

The same as above, except Bennett Industries purchases Beard Nation, Inc., for $650,000.

The basis of the assets acquired from Beard Nation are their FMVs because the purchase price exceeds the FMV of all assets. The remaining $100,000 ($650,000 purchase price – $550,000 FMV of all assets) is classified as goodwill and going concern value.

---

7. **Property for Services**

a. The FMV of property received in exchange for services is income (compensation) to the provider when it is not subject to a substantial risk of forfeiture and not restricted as to transfer. The property acquired has a tax cost basis equal to the FMV of the property.

EXAMPLE

Jim's neighbor needs his fence painted and offers to give Jim a rare baseball card if Jim paints his fence. The baseball card has a fair market value of $500. If Jim paints the fence, he has a $500 basis in the baseball card.

---

b. Sale of restricted stock to an employee is treated as gross income to the extent the FMV exceeds the price paid. This amount is included in gross income in the first taxable year in which the property is unrestricted.

8. **Gifts**

a. The donee's basis in property acquired by gift is the donor's basis, increased for any gift tax paid attributable to appreciation. The donee's basis is increased by

$$\text{Gift tax paid} \times \left[\frac{\text{FMV (at time of gift)} - \text{Donor's basis}}{\text{FMV (at time of gift)} - \text{Annual exclusion}} \right]$$

NOTE: The 2017 annual exclusion is $14,000.

b. If the FMV on the date of the gift is less than the donor's basis, the donee has a dual basis for the property.

1) **Loss basis.** The FMV at the date of the gift is used if the property is later transferred at a loss.

2) **Gain basis.** The donor's basis is used if the property is later transferred at a gain.

3) If the property is later transferred for more than FMV at the date of the gift but for less than the donor's basis at the date of the gift, no gain (loss) is recognized.

c. Depreciable basis is transferred basis adjusted for gift taxes paid. If converted from personal to business use, it is the lesser of FMV on the date of conversion or the transferor's adjusted basis.

EXAMPLE

Bobby received a house as a gift from his father. At the time of the gift, the house had a FMV of $80,000 and the father's adjusted basis was $100,000. If no events occurred that changed the basis and Bobby sells the house for $120,000, Bobby will have a $20,000 gain because he must use the father's adjusted basis ($100,000) at the time of the gift to figure his gain. If he sells the house for $70,000, he will have a $10,000 loss because he must use the FMV ($80,000) at the time of the gift to figure his loss.

If the sale was between $80,000 and $100,000, Bobby would not recognize a gain or a loss.

---

9. **Inherited Property**

a. Basis is the FMV on the date of death or 6 months after if the executor elects the alternate valuation date for the estate tax return. The FMV basis rule also applies to the following property:

1) Property received prior to death without full and adequate consideration (if a life estate was retained in it) or subject to a right of revocation. Reduce basis by depreciation deductions allowed the donee.

2) One-half of community property interests.

3) Property acquired by form of ownership, e.g., by right of survivorship, except if consideration was paid to acquire the property from a nonspouse.

10. Adjusted Basis

a. Initial basis is adjusted consistent with tax-relevant events. Adjustments include the following:

   1) Certain expenditures subsequent to acquisition are property costs, and they increase basis, e.g., legal fees to defend title or title insurance premiums.

   2) Basis must be increased for expenditures that prolong the life of the property by at least 1 year or materially increase its value, i.e., improve the unit of property. Assessments/improvements that increase the value of property should be capitalized.

      a) Examples include major improvements (e.g., new roof, addition to building, etc.) and zoning changes.

EXAMPLE

In order to save money on their utility bills, Mr. and Mrs. Thrifty paid to replace their old roof with a new one with better insulation. The new roof materially increased the value of the house, so the cost of the roof should be added to the basis of the house.

---

   3) Generally, repairs and maintenance expenses are considered a current-period deduction. However, certain repairs may be classified as an improvement, which must be capitalized. There are multiple safe harbors that allow repairs and maintenance to always be classified as a current-period expense instead of capitalized.

      a) Taxpayers who have elected to use the de minimis expense treatment must expense all repairs up to the de minimis amount (i.e., $2,500, or $5,000 for taxpayers with audited or other approved financial statements).

      b) The costs of performing certain routine maintenance activities for property may result in an improvement to the unit of property, i.e., capitalized costs. However, a safe harbor allows routine repairs and maintenance to be expensed. This safe harbor applies to actions that maintain the asset and is reasonably expected to be performed more than once for the asset's class life under the alternative depreciation system.

   4) An increase to basis may result from liability to the extent it is secured by real property and applied to extend its life.

   5) Basis must be reduced by the larger of the amount of depreciation allowed or allowable (even if not claimed). Unimproved land is not depreciated.

   6) A shareholder does not recognize gain on the voluntary contribution of capital to a corporation. The shareholder's stock basis equals his or her basis in the contributed property. The corporation has a transferred basis in the property.

      a) A return of capital distribution reduces basis and becomes a capital gain when the shareholder's basis in the stock reaches zero.

   7) The basis of stock acquired in a nontaxable distribution (e.g., stock rights) is allocated a portion of the basis of the stock upon which the distribution was made.

      a) If the new shares and old shares are not identical, the basis is allocated in proportion to the FMV of the original stock and the distribution as of the date of distribution.

      b) If the new and old shares are identical (e.g., stock splits) the old basis is simply divided among the new total of shares.

      c) If the FMV of the stock rights is less than 15% of the FMV of the stock upon which it was issued, the rights have a basis of zero (unless an election is made to allocate basis).

8) Basis adjustment is required for certain specific items that represent a tax benefit. Three examples follow:

 a) Casualty losses reduce basis by the amount of the loss, by any amounts recovered by insurance, and by any amounts for which no tax benefit was received, e.g., $100 floor for individuals.

 b) Debt discharge. Specific exclusion from gross income is allowed to certain insolvent persons for debt discharged. Taxpayers may elect to reduce basis in depreciable assets by the amount of the exclusion. If an election is not made, they must reduce certain tax attributes.

 c) Credit for building rehabilitation. The full amount of the credit must be deducted from the basis.

Common Examples of Decreases to Basis

Exclusion from income of subsidies for energy conservation measures

Casualty or theft loss deductions and insurance reimbursements

Certain vehicle credits

Section 179 deduction

Deductions previously allowed (or allowable) for amortization, depreciation, and depletion

Depreciation

Nontaxable corporate distributions

Rebates treated as adjustments to the sales price

Stop and review! You have completed the outline for this subunit. Study multiple-choice questions 1 through 3 on page 242.

8.2 DEPRECIATION AND AMORTIZATION

Candidates should expect to be tested on capital cost recovery for corporations, including depreciation, Sec. 179 expense, and amortization.

1. **Accelerated Cost Recovery (ACR)**

 From Form 4562

| 16 | Other depreciation (including ACRS) . . . . | 16 | |

 a. Tax accounting methods of depreciation that allow a deduction in excess of a current year's decline in economic value are accelerated cost recovery methods.

 b. Property subject to the allowance for depreciation is tangible property used in trade, in business, or for production of income and has a determinable, limited useful life.

 c. The amount of a current depreciation deduction is computed by applying a rate to depreciable basis.

2. **General Information**

Background

Accelerated depreciation is a tax relief measure highly desired by businesses. Quickly expensing the cost of investment in plant and equipment for tax purposes allows businesses to significantly reduce their tax liability. In 1971, Congress regularized the haphazard use of accelerated depreciation by introducing the Asset Depreciation Range (ADR) system. Assets of a similar nature or use could be classed together, thereby simplifying the calculation of depreciation expense.

---

a. The IRS has published a list of acceptable useful life ranges by types of asset: the **asset depreciation range (ADR)**.

b. Straight-line (SL) depreciation. The annual amount allowable is the depreciable basis reduced for salvage value (SV) and divided by the useful life of the asset.

$$(Basis - SV) \div Useful\ life$$

c. 150% declining balance (DB). Basis (not reduced by SV) minus previously allowable deductions, which is adjusted basis (AB), is multiplied by 150% of the straight-line rate.

$$AB \times (150\% \div Useful\ life)$$

   1) The rate is constant. It is applied to declining basis. It is generally applicable to used property with a useful life of at least 3 years and used depreciable real property.

d. 200% declining balance. The constant rate is 200% of the straight-line rate.

$$AB \times (200\% \div Useful\ life)$$

   1) It is generally allowable for property with a useful life of at least 3 years and new residential rental property.

e. Unit of Production Method

$$(Basis - SV) \times \left(\frac{\#\ of\ units\ produced\ during\ tax\ year}{Estimated\ total\ of\ units\ asset\ will\ produce} \right)$$

f. Operating Days Method

$$(Basis - SV) \times \left(\frac{\#\ of\ days\ used\ during\ tax\ year}{Estimated\ total\ of\ days\ asset\ can\ be\ used} \right)$$

g. Income Forecast Method

$$(Basis - SV) \times \left(\frac{Income\ generated\ by\ the\ property\ during\ tax\ year}{Estimated\ total\ of\ income\ from\ the\ property\ during\ its\ useful\ life} \right)$$

   1) The income forecast method is limited to film, videotapes, sound recordings, copyrights, books, and patents.

   2) The estimated total of income to be produced from the asset must include all income forecasted to be earned before the close of the 10th year following the tax year in which the property was placed in service.

3.   **MACRS: 1987 and After**

From Form 4562

Part III	MACRS Depreciation (**Don't** include listed property.) (See instructions.)

Section A

17 MACRS deductions for assets placed in service in tax years beginning before [Year] . . . . | 17 |

18 If you are electing to group any assets placed in service during the tax year into one or more general asset accounts, check here . . . . ▶ ☐

Section B—Assets Placed in Service During [Year] Tax Year Using the General Depreciation System

(a) Classification of property	(b) Month and year placed in service	(c) Basis for depreciation (business/investment use only—see instructions)	(d) Recovery period	(e) Convention	(f) Method	(g) Depreciation deduction
19a 3-year property						
b 5-year property						
c 7-year property						
d 10-year property						
e 15-year property						
f 20-year property						
g 25-year property			25 yrs.		S/L	
h Residential rental property			27.5 yrs.	MM	S/L	
			27.5 yrs.	MM	S/L	
i Nonresidential real property			39 yrs.	MM	S/L	
				MM	S/L	

Section C—Assets Placed in Service During [Year] Tax Year Using the Alternative Depreciation System

20a Class life					S/L	
b 12-year			12 yrs.		S/L	
c 40-year			40 yrs.	MM	S/L	

Background

The deliberations leading up to the passage of the Tax Reform Act of 1986, including the intense discussions around reconciling the House and Senate versions, were heavily reported in the news media. One of the Act's provisions was the creation of the Modified Accelerated Cost Recovery System (MACRS).

---

a.   The Modified Accelerated Cost Recovery System (MACRS) is used to recover the basis of most business and investment property placed in service after 1986.

b.   MACRS consists of two depreciation systems, the **General Depreciation System (GDS)** and the **Alternative Depreciation System (ADS)**. Generally, GDS must be used unless the taxpayer is specifically required by law to use ADS or the taxpayer elects to use ADS. Election must be made by the due date, including extensions, for the tax return of the year in which the property was placed in service.

1)   A switch is made to straight-line on adjusted (reduced for allowable depreciation) basis when it yields a higher amount.

2)   Real property costs are recovered using a straight-line rate on unadjusted basis.

3)   Salvage value is ignored.

4)   The 200%-declining-balance method is used for MACRS recovery periods of 3, 5, 7, and 10 years (except farm property).

5)   150% is used for 15- and 20-year property and farm personal property.

6)   ADS utilizes a straight-line rate based on longer recovery periods. Examples of ADS recovery periods follow:

# Years	Items
5	Cars, light trucks, certain technological equipment
12	Personal property with no class life
15	Agricultural structures (single-purpose)
40	Residential rental and nonresidential real estate

c.   Mid-year (personal property) and mid-month (real property) conventions apply.

1)   Under the mid-year convention, each asset is treated as placed into service at the midpoint of the year in which it was actually placed into service.

2)   Under the mid-month convention, each asset is treated as placed into service at the midpoint of the month in which it was actually placed into service.

3)   A mid-quarter convention applies when asset acquisition is bunched at the end of the year.

   a)   Each asset is treated as placed in service at the midpoint of the quarter in which it actually was placed in service.

   b)   Apply the convention to all depreciable property acquired during the tax year when the sum of the bases of all depreciable personal property placed in service during the last quarter of the year exceeds 40% of those placed in service during the entire year.

   c)   The first year depreciation is calculated by multiplying the full-year amount by the following percentages based on the quarter placed in service:

87.5% for the first quarter
62.5% for the second quarter
37.5% for the third quarter
12.5% for the fourth quarter

EXAMPLE

The formula for 3-year property placed in service in the third quarter is AB × (200% ÷ Useful life) × 37.5%.

---

d.   IRS tables provide rates to be applied to the unadjusted basis (except for Sec. 179 expense) for each year of service. The rate incorporates applicable methods, applicable recovery periods, and conventions.

e.   Depreciation is allowed during a disposition year.

f.   Personal property is assigned a recovery period of either 3, 5, 7, 10, 15, or 20 years, according to the midpoint of the ADR class life applicable to the type of property. The half-year or mid-quarter convention is applied.

MACRS Recovery Period (# of Years)	Midpoint of ADR for Class (# of Years)	DB Rate Applicable Percent	Examples
3	4 or less	200	Special tools, e.g., for rubber manufacturing
5	>4, <10	200	Computers, office machinery (e.g., copier) Cars, trucks R&E equipment
7	≥10, <16	200	Most machinery Office furniture and equipment Agricultural structures (single-purpose) Property without ADR midpoint & not otherwise classified
10	≥16, <20	200	Water vessels, e.g., barge Petroleum processing equipment Food & tobacco manufacturing
15	≥20, <25	150	Data communication plants, e.g., for phone Sewage treatment plants Billboards
20	≥25	150	Utilities, e.g., municipal sewers Not real property with ADR midpoint 27.5 years

MACRS Recovery Periods (Personal Property)

g. Real property. The straight-line method and the mid-month convention apply.

1) Residential rental property. The straight-line rate is based on a 27 1/2-year recovery period.

   a) It is real property with at least 80% of gross rents coming from dwelling units. Partial use by the owner is included. Transient use of more than half the units excludes the property, e.g., a motel.

2) Nonresidential real estate is assigned a 39-year recovery period.

   a) It is real property that is not residential rental property.

   b) It also includes real property with an ADR midpoint of less than 27 1/2 years.

3) Some realty has a recovery period less than 27 1/2 years, e.g., specified farm buildings.

4) The following three types of real property qualify for 15-year, straight-line depreciation:

   a) Qualified leasehold improvement property
   b) Qualified restaurant property
   c) Qualified retail improvement property

Depreciation Methods

Method		Type of Property	Benefit
GDS	200% DB	• Nonfarm 3-, 5-, 7-, and 10-year property	• Provides a greater deduction during the earlier recovery years • Changes to SL when that method provides an equal or greater deduction
	150% DB	• All farm property (except real property) • All 15- and 20-year property (except qualified leasehold improvement property, qualified restaurant property, and qualified retail improvement property) • Nonfarm 3-, 5-, 7-, and 10-year property	• Provides a greater deduction during the earlier recovery years • Changes to SL when that method provides an equal or greater deduction
	SL	• Nonresidential real property • Qualified leasehold improvement property • Qualified restaurant property • Qualified retail improvement property • Residential rental property • Trees or vines bearing fruit or nuts • Water utility property • All 3-, 5-, 7-, 10-, 15-, and 20-year property electing SL	• Provides for equal yearly deductions (except for the first and last years)
ADS	SL	• Listed property used 50% or less for business • Property used predominantly outside the U.S. • Tax-exempt property • Tax-exempt bond-financed property • Farm property used when an election not to apply the uniform capitalization rules is in effect • Imported property from trade-discriminating countries • Any property for which you elect to use this method	• Provides for equal yearly deductions (except for the first and last years)

4. Section 179 Expense

From Form 4562

Part I	Election To Expense Certain Property Under Section 179				
	Note: If you have any listed property, complete Part V before you complete Part I.				
1	Maximum amount (see instructions)			**1**	
2	Total cost of section 179 property placed in service (see instructions)			**2**	
3	Threshold cost of section 179 property before reduction in limitation (see instructions)			**3**	
4	Reduction in limitation. Subtract line 3 from line 2. If zero or less, enter -0-			**4**	
5	Dollar limitation for tax year. Subtract line 4 from line 1. If zero or less, enter -0-. If married filing separately, see instructions			**5**	
6	**(a)** Description of property	**(b)** Cost (business use only)	**(c)** Elected cost		
7	Listed property. Enter the amount from line 29	**7**			
8	Total elected cost of section 179 property. Add amounts in column (c), lines 6 and 7			**8**	
9	Tentative deduction. Enter the **smaller** of line 5 or line 8			**9**	
10	Carryover of disallowed deduction from line 13 of your [prior year] Form 4562			**10**	
11	Business income limitation. Enter the smaller of business income (not less than zero) or line 5 (see instructions)			**11**	
12	Section 179 expense deduction. Add lines 9 and 10, but don't enter more than line 11			**12**	
13	Carryover of disallowed deduction to [next year]. Add lines 9 and 10, less line 12 ▶	**13**			

Note: Don't use Part II or Part III below for listed property. Instead, use Part V.

a. A person may elect to deduct all or part of the cost of Sec. 179 property acquired during the year as an expense rather than a capital expenditure.

   1) Section 179 expense is treated as depreciation.

      a) It must be elected by the taxpayer.

      b) It reduces basis in the property (but not below zero) prior to computation of any other depreciation deduction allowable for the first year.

      c) It is subject to depreciation recapture under Sec. 1245.

b. Section 179 property is depreciable personal property used in the active conduct of a trade or business.

   1) Section 179 property must be acquired by purchase from an unrelated party.

   NOTE: Specifically excluded from the Sec. 179 election are air-conditioning and heating units, property used for lodging, property used by tax-exempt organizations, and property used outside the United States.

c. For 2017, a deduction may be for no more than either

   1) The amount of $510,000 minus the excess of Sec. 179 costs for the year over $2.03 million or

   2) Taxable income from the active conduct of any trade or business during the tax year.

      a) Current-year excess over TI may be carried forward and treated as Sec. 179 cost in a subsequent year subject to the overall limitation.

EXAMPLE

In 2017, Diana's Corner Stores upgraded various equipment and computers at a total cost of $2,260,000. All assets purchased are eligible for Sec. 179 treatment. The Sec. 179 deduction is phased out dollar for dollar once the minimum threshold for purchases is exceeded. Therefore, the maximum Sec. 179 deduction Diana's Corner Stores can take is $280,000 [$510,000 maximum deduction – ($2,260,000 purchases – $2,030,000 phaseout)].

d. Apply the following limits in the order presented:

1) Pass-through entities. Apply each limit on Sec. 179 expense first at the entity level and then at the partner/shareholder level.

2) Trusts and estates may not claim a Sec. 179 deduction.

3) Only the business-use portion of the cost of Sec. 179 property may be expensed.

4) Cost of Sec. 179 property does not include the basis determined by reference to other property held by the taxpayer.

5) No more than the statutory amount may be deducted as depreciation on cars and certain luxury items. Excess over the limit may not be expensed under Sec. 179.

6) The limit described in item c. on the previous page.

e. Recapture. Section 179 property need not be used to elect the deduction. The amount of allowed Sec. 179 deduction may be allocated to Sec. 179 property as desired. But if Sec. 179 property is disposed of prior to the end of the MACRS recovery period, gross income includes any

1) Excess of Sec. 179 deduction over

2) MACRS deductions allowable, notwithstanding Sec. 179.

NOTE: Recapture also applies when the business use of the Sec. 179 property changes to less than 50% of total use.

5. **Bonus Depreciation**

From Form 4562

Part II	Special Depreciation Allowance and Other Depreciation (Don't include listed property.) (See instructions.)
14	Special depreciation allowance for qualified property (other than listed property) placed in service during the tax year (see instructions) **14**

a. A first-year depreciation (also called bonus depreciation) of 50% (40% in 2018, 30% in 2019) of the adjusted basis is allowed for qualified property.

1) This is in addition to the Section 179 deduction.

2) Qualifying property must be new, generally have a 20-year or less recovery period, and be acquired by the taxpayer after December 31, 2007, and before January 1, 2020, and placed in service before January 1, 2020 (or before January 1, 2021, in the case of property with a longer production period and certain noncommercial aircraft). Qualifying property includes leasehold improvements.

3) First-year depreciation of 100% was allowed for assets placed in service between September 8, 2010, and January 1, 2012.

4) The deduction is permitted for both regular and AMT purposes.

6. **Amortization**

From Form 4562

Part VI	Amortization				
(a) Description of costs	(b) Date amortization begins	(c) Amortizable amount	(d) Code section	(e) Amortization period or percentage	(f) Amortization for this year
42 Amortization of costs that begins during your [Year] tax year (see instructions):					
43 Amortization of costs that began before your [Year] tax year				**43**	
44 **Total.** Add amounts in column (f). See the instructions for where to report				**44**	

a. Amortization accounts for recovery of capital (e.g., intangible assets, Sec. 197) in a similar manner as straight-line depreciation. Intangible assets make up the majority of amortizable assets and are recovered over the asset's useful life or, in the case of Sec. 197 intangibles, 15 years. Other items are amortized over a period specified for that item.

b. Any start-up costs or organizational expenses after the allowed $5,000 immediate deduction are amortized over 15 years. The $5,000 deduction is reduced by the amount of the total costs exceeding $50,000. Amortization starts with the month the active trade or business begins.

c. Costs of acquiring a lease are amortized over the lease term.

   1) Renewal options are included in the term if less than 75% of the cost is attributable to the period prior to renewal. Allocate the cost over the original and renewal term, unless the contract (reasonably) specifies otherwise.

   2) Improvements by the lessee are deducted under the MACRS method.

      a) For a lease entered into before September 26, 1985, the lessee could elect to recover the costs over the remaining lease term.

d. Intangibles. The cost of certain intangibles acquired (not created) in connection with the conduct of a trade or business or income-producing activity is amortized over a 15-year period, beginning with the later of the month in which the intangible is acquired or business begins.

   1) Qualified intangibles do not include intangibles that result from the taxpayer's own efforts, unless in connection with the acquisition of a trade or business.

   2) Qualified intangibles include the following:

      a) Acquired goodwill and going-concern value
      b) The work force, information base, patent, copyright, know-how, customers, suppliers, or similar items
      c) Licenses, permits, or other rights granted by governmental units
      d) Covenants not to compete
      e) Any franchise, trademark, or trade name

   3) Excluded from intangible amortization treatment are the following:

      a) Interests in corporations, partnerships, trusts, estates
      b) Interests in land
      c) Most financial instruments and contracts
      d) Leases of intangible personal property
      e) Professional sports franchises

EXAMPLE

EMEN Corp. purchased all the assets of a sole proprietorship, including the following intangible assets:

Goodwill	$98,000
Copyright	71,000
Interest in land	12,000
Covenant not to compete	13,000

The cost of certain intangibles acquired (not created) in connection with the conduct of a trade or business or income-producing activity is amortized over a 15-year period. Qualified intangibles include acquired goodwill, copyrights, and covenants not to compete. Therefore, EMEN should amortize $182,000 ($98,000 goodwill + $71,000 copyright + $13,000 covenant not to compete) over the 15-year period.

---

   4) Loss realized on disposition of a qualified intangible is disallowed if the taxpayer retains other qualified intangibles acquired in the same (set of) transaction(s). The amount disallowed is added to the basis of the intangibles retained.

e.   Reforestation costs not immediately deductible are amortized over 7 years. Amortization starts the sixth month of the year costs are incurred.

f.   The cost of geological and geophysical expenses related to domestic oil and gas exploration or development are amortized over 2 years. Like reforestation cost, amortization begins on the mid-point of the year costs are paid or incurred.

g.   Pollution control facility costs are amortized over 5 years, with an exception of 7 years for atmospheric facilities.

h.   Research and experimentation costs have a 5-year amortization period.

7.   **Depletion**

From Form 1040 Schedule E

18	Depreciation expense or depletion	18						

a.   Depletion accounts for recovery of investment in natural resources property.

b.   Only a person who has an economic interest in a (mineral) property is entitled to deductions for depletion.

1)   A person has an economic interest if (s)he

a)   Acquires by investment an interest in the mineral in place
b)   Derives income from extraction of the mineral
c)   Looks to the extracted mineral for return of capital

2)   Investment need not be in cash and could be in, for example,

a)   Land that ensures control over access to the mineral
b)   Stationary equipment used to extract and produce the mineral

c.   Cost depletion is computed as follows:

$$\frac{Adjusted\ basis\ in\ mineral\ property}{Estimated\ mineral\ units\ available\ at\ year's\ start} \times Mineral\ units\ sold\ during\ year$$

NOTE: The total deductions are limited to unrecovered capital investment.

1)   Percentage depletion, which allows deduction in excess of capital investment, is the lower of

a)   50% of the person's TI before depletion (100% in some cases)
b)   A percentage (specified by statute) of gross income from the property less related rents or royalties paid or incurred

Stop and review! You have completed the outline for this subunit. Study multiple-choice questions 4 through 6 on page 243.

8.3 CAPITAL GAINS AND LOSSES

1.   **Capital Assets**

a.   All property is characterized as a capital asset, unless expressly excluded.

b.   The following types of property are not capital assets:

1)   Inventory (or stock in trade) -- property held primarily for sale to customers in the ordinary course of a trade or business

2)   Real or depreciable property used in a trade or business

3)   Accounts or notes receivable acquired in the ordinary course of trade or business for services rendered or for 1) or 2) above

4)   Copyrights and artistic compositions held by the person who composed them

5)   Certain U.S. government publications acquired at reduced cost

c. Property held either for personal use or for the production of income is a capital asset, but dealer property (i.e., property held primarily for sale to customers in the ordinary course of trade or business) is not.

1) Stocks, bonds, commodities, and the like are capital assets unless they are dealer property.

2) Land held primarily for investment (capital asset), which is then subdivided, may be treated as converted to property held for sale in a trade or business.

d. Goodwill is a capital asset when generated within the business. If a business sells its assets and receives more than the FMV of those assets, the remainder is considered a capital gain from the sale of goodwill.

2. **Gain (Loss) Realized and Recognized**

a. Generally, all gains (losses) are realized on the sale or other disposition of property. This includes sales or exchanges that are required in characterizing a realized gain or loss as capital. For capital assets that become wholly worthless during the year, the sale or disposition date is considered to be the last day of the year.

1) For real property, a sale or exchange occurs on the earlier of the date of conveyance or the date that the burdens of ownership pass to the buyer.

2) Also, liquidating distributions and losses on worthless securities are treated as sales or exchanges.

3) The transfer of a franchise is not treated as a sale or exchange of a capital asset if the transferor retains significant power, rights, or continuing interest with respect to the franchise.

b. The following formula shows computation of gain or loss realized:

	Money received (or to be received)		
+	FMV of other property received [1]		
+	Liability relief [2]		
−	Money or other property given up		
−	Selling expenses [3]		**Amount realized**
−	Liabilities assumed [2]	−	Adjusted basis
=	**Amount realized**	=	**Gain (loss) realized**

[1] If FMV of other property received is not determinable with reasonable certainty, FMV of the property given up is used.

[2] Whether recourse or nonrecourse.

[3] Selling expenses are subtracted from gross receivables to yield the amount realized.

EXAMPLE

The purchase price of a building was $400,000 ($100,000 cash + $300,000 mortgage). Two years later, improvements of $80,000 were made to the building. The building sold for $700,000 ($600,000 cash + $100,000 mortgage balance). A total of $180,000 depreciation had been taken as of the date sold. The adjusted basis is $300,000 ($400,000 original basis + $80,000 improvements − $180,000 depreciation taken). The realized gain is $400,000 ($700,000 cash and liability relief − $300,000 adjusted basis).

---

c. All realized gains must be recognized unless the IRC expressly provides otherwise. Conversely, no deduction is allowed for a realized loss unless the IRC expressly provides for it.

NOTE: Though personal-use property is a capital asset and gains from such property are recognized, a loss is not deductible.

3. **Holding Period**

a. The holding period of an asset is measured in calendar months, beginning on the day after acquisition and including the disposal date.

Acquisition by or of	Holding Period -- Starts or by reference to
Sale or exchange	Acquisition [1]
Gift: For gain	Donor's acquisition
For loss	Acquisition
Inheritance	Automatic LT
Nontaxable exchanges	
Like-kind (Sec. 1031)	Include HP of exchanged asset [2]
Corporate stock (Sec. 351)	Include HP of contributed asset
Property in entity	Include transferor's HP
Partnership interest (Sec. 721)	Include HP of contributed asset [2]
Property in entity	Include transferor's HP [2]
Ordinary income property	Exchange
Involuntary conversion (Sec. 1033)	Include HP of converted asset
Residence (Sec. 1034)	Include HP of old home
Use conversion (T/B & personal)	Include period of prior use
Optioned property	Exclude option period
Securities	Trading date
Short sales (Ss)	Earlier of Ss closing or property sale date
Commodity futures	LT after 6-month HP

[1] *Always start computation using day after date of applicable acquisition.*

[2] *If capital asset or Sec. 1231 property; otherwise, the holding period starts the day after date of exchange.*

b. Long-term capital gain or loss (LTCG or LTCL) is realized from a capital asset held for more than 1 year. Short-term capital gain or loss (STCG or STCL) is realized if the asset was held 1 year or less.

c. For individuals, net capital gain (NCG) is the excess of net LTCG over net STCL. Net STCG is not included in NCG. Do not confuse it with capital gain net income.

d. Net STCG is treated as ordinary income for individuals. Net capital gain rates do not apply to net STCG.

    1) Net STCG = STCG – STCL.

    2) But net STCG may be offset by net LTCL.

4. **Taxation**

a. For individuals, net short-term capital gain is taxed as ordinary income.

b. For individuals, capital transactions involving **long-term holding periods** (assets held for over 12 months) are grouped by tax rates. The maximum capital gains rates are 0%, 15%, 20%, 25%, or 28%. These capital transaction groups are combined into "baskets."

    1) **15/20% Basket**

        a) The capital gains rate is **0%** if the taxpayer is in the 10% or 15% income tax brackets.

        b) The capital gains rate is **15%** if the taxpayer is in the 25%, 28%, 33%, or 35% income tax brackets.

        c) The capital gains rate is **20%** if the taxpayer is in the 39.6% tax bracket.

2) **25% Basket**

a) The capital gains rate is **25%** on unrecaptured Sec. 1250 gains (discussed further in Subunit 8.7).

3) **28% Basket**

a) The capital gains rate is **28%** on gains and losses from the sale of collectibles and gains from Sec. 1202 stock (certain small business stock).

c. After gains and losses are classified in the appropriate baskets, losses for each long-term basket are first used to offset any gains within that basket.

d. If a long-term basket has a net loss, the loss will be used first to offset net gain for the highest long-term rate basket, then to offset the next highest rate basket and so on.

EXAMPLE

A taxpayer realizes a $10,000 net loss in the 15/20% basket, a $5,000 net gain in the 25% basket, and an $8,000 net gain in the 28% basket. The taxpayer will first apply the net loss against the gain in the 28% basket, reducing the gain in this basket to zero. Then, the remaining $2,000 loss is applied against the gain in the 25% basket, leaving a $3,000 net capital gain in the 25% basket.

---

e. A carryover of a net long-term capital loss from a prior year is used first to offset any net gain in the 28% basket, then to offset any net gain in the 25% basket, and finally to offset any net gain in the 15/20% basket. Likewise, net STCL is also used first to offset net gain for the highest long-term basket and so on.

EXAMPLE

A taxpayer has a $1,000 long-term capital loss carryover, a net short-term capital loss of $2,000, a $1,000 net gain in the 28% basket, and a $5,000 net gain in the 15/20% basket. Both losses are first applied to offset the 28% rate gain, using the $1,000 loss carryover first until completely exhausted. Since no gain exists in the 28% basket after applying the carryover, the net STCL is then applied against the next highest gain in the 15/20% basket. As a result, only a $3,000 net capital gain remains in the 15/20% basket.

---

f. An individual may deduct a net capital loss in the current year up to the lesser of $3,000 ($1,500 if MFS) or ordinary income.

1) An individual may carry forward any excess CLs indefinitely.

2) The carryforward is treated as a CL incurred in the subsequent year.

3) Net STCL is treated as having been deductible in the preceding year before net LTCL.

4) No carryover is allowed from a decedent to their estate.

g. Schedule D (Form 1040) is used to compute and summarize capital gains and/or losses on the sale or disposition of capital assets listed on Form 8949, and the summary combines the long-term gains (losses) with the short-term gains (losses). When these capital gains and losses all net to a gain, it is called capital gain net income.

h. For corporations, all capital gain is taxed at the corporation's regular tax rate.

i. A corporation may use CLs only to offset CGs each year. A corporation must carry the excess CL back 3 years and forward 5 years and characterize all carryovers as STCLs (regardless of character).

5. **Return of Capital**

    a.   The amount of a distribution is a dividend to the extent of earnings and profits. Dividends do not reduce the shareholder's basis in the stock.

    b.   A shareholder treats the amount of a distribution in excess of earnings and profits (E&P) as tax-exempt return of capital to the extent of his or her basis. A distribution in excess of basis is a capital gain.

6. **Wash Sales**

    a.   A current loss realized on a wash sale of securities is not recognized. A wash sale occurs when substantially the same securities are purchased within 30 days before or after being sold at a loss.

        1)   The disallowed loss is added to the basis of the stock purchased in the wash sale.

        2)   The holding period includes that of the originally purchased stock.

        3)   Spouses are treated as one person.

EXAMPLE

Taxpayer sells 100 shares of ABC stock for $400, a loss of $200. Within 30 days, Taxpayer purchases an identical 100 shares of ABC for $500 and sells all 100 shares two months later for $900. Taxpayer recognizes no loss (i.e., $200) on first sale and only $200 gain ($900 sale price – $500 cost – $200 basis adjustment due to loss) on subsequent sale of stock.

---

7. **Small Business Stock**

    a.   Section 1244 stock is stock (common or preferred, voting or nonvoting) of a small business corporation held since its issuance (e.g., not acquired by gift) and issued for money or other property (not stock or securities).

    b.   Up to $50,000 ($100,000 if MFJ) of loss realized on disposition or worthlessness of Sec. 1244 stock is treated as an ordinary loss.

        1)   The limit applies to Sec. 1244 stock held in all corporations.

        2)   The limit is applied at a partner level, if applicable.

        3)   The loss is considered to be from a trade or business for NOL purposes.

    c.   To be classified as a small business corporation, the aggregate amount of money and property received by the corporation for stock cannot exceed $1 million.

        1)   Even if the contributions exceed $1 million, part of the stock (up to $1 million) may be designated by the corporation as qualifying for Sec. 1244 ordinary loss treatment.

    d.   If the basis of property contributed in exchange for Sec. 1244 stock exceeds its FMV, the excess is treated as capital loss before any other realized loss may be treated as ordinary.

        1)   Basis in the stock is equal to the property's basis in the hands of the transferor when contributed.

    e.   Additional investment without issuance of additional shares of Sec. 1244 stock increases original basis; however, any resulting loss must be apportioned between the qualifying Sec. 1244 stock and the nonqualifying additional capital interest.

8. **Small Business Stock Exclusion**

   a. Under Section 1202, taxpayers may exclude 50% of the gain from the sale or exchange of small business stock. The stock must have been issued after August 10, 1993, and held for more than 5 years. The exclusion increases to 75% for stock acquired after February 17, 2009, and before September 28, 2010. The exclusion increases to 100% for stock acquired after September 27, 2010.

> Capital gains and losses has been a heavily tested topic on CPA exams, with both conceptual and calculation questions being used to test this area.

9. **Nonbusiness Bad Debt**

   a. A business bad debt is deductible to arrive at AGI (above-the-line) as ordinary loss. A nonbusiness bad debt is treated as a STCL.

10. **Business Start-up Costs**

    a. Capitalized amounts not yet amortized upon disposition of the business are treated as a capital loss.

11. **Short Sales**

    a. Property held long-term substantially identical to property sold short (at that time) results in any loss on the short sale being treated as long-term.

12. **Casualties**

    a. Casualty losses on personal-use capital assets are itemized deductions.

13. **Market Discount Bonds**

    a. Gain on sale is treated as ordinary income to the extent the market discount could have accrued as interest.

$$\text{Taxable accrued market discount} = \text{Market discount} \times \frac{\text{\# of days security held}}{\text{\# of days from acquisition to maturity}}$$

EXAMPLE

John purchases a $100, 360-day bond for $90. The market discount equals $10. If John sells the bond 180 days later, he must recognize $5 (half of the discount) as ordinary income (interest).

---

14. **Bond Premium Treatment**

    a. The bondholder may either (1) elect to amortize the premium until bond maturity and reduce the basis or (2) elect not to amortize and treat the premium as bond basis.

Stop and review! You have completed the outline for this subunit. Study multiple-choice questions 7 through 10 beginning on page 244.

8.4 RELATED PARTY SALES

1. **Limited Tax Avoidance**

    a. These rules limit tax avoidance between related parties.

    b. Gain recognized on an asset transfer to a related person in whose hands the asset is depreciable is ordinary income.

    c. Loss realized on sale or exchange of property to a related person is not deductible. The transferee takes a cost basis. There is no adding of holding periods.

      1) Gain realized on a subsequent sale to an unrelated party is recognized only to the extent it exceeds the previously disallowed loss.

         a) If the gain realized on the sale to an unrelated third party is less than the amount of disallowed loss, no gain is recognized.

EXAMPLE

Taxpayer A sells stock with a basis of $100,000 to a related person, Taxpayer B, for $80,000, creating a $20,000 disallowed loss for Taxpayer A. If Taxpayer B then sells the stock to an unrelated party for $130,000, the realized gain will be $50,000 ($130,000 sale price – $80,000 basis) and Taxpayer B will recognize a $30,000 gain ($50,000 realized gain – $20,000 disallowed loss from original transaction between A and B).

However, if the sale to an unrelated party were for $90,000, the resulting $10,000 gain ($90,000 sale price – $80,000 basis) would not be recognized. The $10,000 gain is offset by $10,000 of the $20,000 disallowed loss.

Finally, if the unrelated sale had been for $65,000 (creating an additional $15,000 loss), Taxpayer B could only recognize a $15,000 loss, not a $35,000 loss ($20,000 disallowed loss + $15,000 unrelated-sale loss).

---

      2) Loss realized on a subsequent sale to a third party is recognized, but the previously disallowed loss is not added to it.

    d. For property purchased on or after January 1, 2016, a new rule precludes the above recognition of the disallowed loss when later sold to an unrelated party if the original transferor (e.g., Taxpayer A in the prior example) is a tax-indifferent party.

      1) Tax-indifferent parties are those not subject to federal income tax or to whom an item would have no substantial impact on its income tax. Examples of tax-indifferent parties include non-U.S. persons, tax-exempt organizations, and government entities.

EXAMPLE

If we use the details from the previous example but change Taxpayer A to a tax-indifferent party, the disallowed loss will still be $20,000 when the stock sells for $80,000 to Taxpayer B; however, on the sale from Taxpayer B to an unrelated party for $130,000, the realized and recognized gain is $50,000 ($130,000 – $80,000). The $50,000 gain is not offset by the disallowed loss.

---

    e. For purposes of these provisions, related parties generally include

      1) Ancestors (parents, grandparents, etc.), descendants (children, grandchildren, etc.), spouses, and siblings

      2) Trusts and beneficiaries of trusts

      3) Controlled entities (50% ownership)

      NOTE: Constructive ownership rules between family members apply.

    f. Loss on sale or exchange of property between a partnership and a person owning more than 50% of the capital or profit interests in the partnership is not deductible.

Stop and review! You have completed the outline for this subunit. Study multiple-choice questions 11 through 13 on page 245.

8.5 INSTALLMENT SALES

1. **Overview**

   a. An installment sale is a disposition of property in which at least one payment is to be received after the close of the tax year of the disposition.

   b. The installment method must be used to report installment sales unless election is made not to apply the method.

2. **Excluded Dispositions**

   a. Installment sales do not apply to the following dispositions:

      1) Inventory personal property sales

      2) Revolving credit personal property sales

      3) Dealer dispositions, including dispositions of

         a) Personal property of a type regularly sold by the person on the installment plan

         b) Real property held for sale to customers in the ordinary course of trade or business

      4) Securities, generally, if publicly traded

      5) Sales on agreement to establish an irrevocable escrow account

3. **Specific Dispositions Not Excluded**

   a. Not excluded from installment sale deferral are certain sales of residential lots or timeshares subject to interest on the deferred tax and property used or produced in a farming business.

4. **Recognized Gain**

   a. The amount of realized gain to be recognized in a tax year is equal to the gross profit multiplied by the ratio of payments received in the current year divided by the total contract price.

   $$Realized\ gain = Gross\ profit \times \frac{Payments\ received\ in\ the\ current\ year}{Total\ contract\ price}$$

   b. Recognize, as income, payments received multiplied by the gross profit ratio.

   $$Recognized\ gain = Gross\ profit\ ratio \times Payments\ received$$

      1) A payment is considered paid in full if the balance is placed into an irrevocable escrow account (i.e., amounts that cannot revert to the purchaser) at a later date.

   c. The gross profit is the sales price minus selling expenses (including debt forgiveness) and adjusted basis. It includes the unrecognized gain on sale of a personal residence.

      1) The sales price is the sum of any cash received, liability relief, and installment notes from the buyer. It does not include imputed interest.

      2) Gross profit includes the unrecognized gain on sale of a personal residence.

   d. The total contract price is the sales price minus liabilities assumed by the buyer (that does not exceed the seller's basis in the property).

      1) Contract price includes the excess of liability assumed over AB and selling expenses.

         a) When the liability exceeds AB and selling expenses, the gross profit percentage is 100%.

e.   The gross profit ratio is the ratio of the gross profit to the total contract price.

$$Gross\ profit\ ratio = \frac{Gross\ profit}{Contract\ price} = \frac{Selling\ price - Selling\ expense - Adjusted\ basis}{Amount\ to\ be\ collected}$$

1)   When the selling price is reduced in a future year, the gross profit on the sale also will be reduced. Therefore, the gross profit ratio must be recalculated for the remaining periods by using the reduced sales price and subtracting the gross profit already recognized.

5.   **Repossession**

a.   The seller recognizes as gain or loss any difference between the FMV of repossessed personal property and the AB of an installment sale obligation satisfied by the repossession. If real property, recognize the lesser of

1)   Cash and other property (FMV) received in excess of gain already recognized or
2)   Gross profit in remaining installments less repossession costs.

b.   Interest is imposed on deferred tax on obligations from nondealer installment sales (of more than $150,000) outstanding at the close of the tax year. This interest is applied if the taxpayer has nondealer installment receivables of over $5 million at the close of the tax year from installment sales of over $150,000 that occurred during the year.

1)   This interest is not applied to the following:

a)   Personal-use property
b)   Residential lots and time shares
c)   Property produced or used in the farming business

6.   **Disposition of Installment Obligations**

a.   Excess of the FMV over the AB of an installment obligation is generally recognized if it is transferred. FMV is generally the amount realized. If a gift, use the face amount of the obligation.

b.   Exceptions. Disposition of obligations by the following events can result in the transferee treating payments as the transferor would have:

1)   Transfers to a controlled corporation
2)   Corporate reorganizations and liquidations
3)   Contributions to capital of, or distributions from, partnerships
4)   Transfer between spouses incident to divorce
5)   Transfer upon death of the obligee

c.   The date the installment payment is received determines the capital gains rate to be applied rather than the date the asset was sold under an installment sales contract.

7.   **Character**

a.   Character of gain recognized depends on the nature of the property in the transferor's hands.

b.   The full amount of Secs. 1245 and 1250 ordinary gain ("depreciation recapture") must be recognized in the year of sale, even if it is more than payments received. The gain is added to basis before further applying the installment method.

c.   An anti-avoidance rule applies to an installment sale of property to a related party. On a second disposition (by the related party transferee in the first sale), payments received must be treated as a payment received by the person who made the first (installment) sale to a related party.

1)   A second disposition by gift is included. The FMV is treated as the payment.
2)   Death of the first disposition seller or buyer does not accelerate recognition.

Stop and review! You have completed the outline for this subunit. Study multiple-choice question 14 on page 246.

8.6 NONRECOGNITION TRANSACTIONS

1. **General Rule**

   a. The general rule is to recognize all gain realized during the tax year. This topic discusses some transactions for which the IRC requires or permits exclusion or deferral of all or part of the gain realized in the current tax year.

2. **Like-Kind Exchanges**

   a. Section 1031 defers recognizing gain or loss to the extent that property productively used in a trade or business or held for the production of income (investment) is exchanged for property of like kind.

   b. Like-kind property is alike in nature or character but not necessarily in grade or quality.

      1) Properties are of like kind if each is within a class of like nature or character, without regard to differences in use (e.g., business or investment), improvements (e.g., bare land or house), location, or proximity.

General Asset Classes	
Office furniture, fixtures, and equipment (asset class 00.11)	Light general-purpose trucks (asset class 00.241)
Information systems (computers and peripheral equipment) (asset class 00.12)	Heavy general-purpose trucks (asset class 00.242)
Data handling equipment, except computers (asset class 00.13)	Railroad cars and locomotives, except those owned by railroad transportation companies (asset class 00.25)
Airplanes (airframes and engines), except those used in commercial or contract carrying of passengers or freight, and all helicopters (airframes and engines) (asset class 00.21)	Tractor units for use over-the-road (asset class 00.26)
Automobiles, taxis (asset class 00.22)	Trailers and trailer-mounted containers (asset class 00.27)
Buses (asset class 00.23)	Vessels, barges, tugs, and similar water transportation equipment, except those used in marine construction (asset class 00.28)
Industrial steam and electric generation and/or distribution systems (asset class 00.4)	

EXAMPLE

Taxpayer C transfers a railroad car (asset class 00.25) to D in exchange for a tractor-trailer container (asset class 00.27). The properties exchanged are not of a like class because they are within different General Asset Classes. Because each of the properties is within a General Asset Class, the properties may not be classified within a Product Class. The airplane and heavy general-purpose truck are also not of a like kind. Therefore, the exchange does not qualify for nonrecognition of gain or loss under Section 1031.

      2) Real property is of like kind to other real property, except foreign property.
      3) Personal property and real property are not of like kind.
      4) A lease of real property for 30 or more years is treated as real property.

   c. The following property types do not qualify for Sec. 1031 nonrecognition:

      1) Money
      2) Liabilities
      3) Inventory
      4) Partnership interest in different partnerships, e.g., general for general
      5) Securities and debt instruments, e.g., stocks, bonds

    d.   Boot is all nonqualified property transferred in an exchange transaction.

    e.   **Gain is recognized** equal to the lesser of gain realized or boot received.

        1)   Boot received includes cash, net liability relief, and other nonqualified property (its FMV).

            a)   If each party assumes a liability of the other, only the net liability given or received is treated as boot.

    f.   Basis. Qualified property received in a like-kind exchange has an exchanged basis adjusted for boot and gain recognized.

            AB of property given
        + Gain recognized
        + Boot given (cash, liability incurred, other property)
        – Boot received (cash, liability relief, other property)
        = **Basis in acquired property**

    g.   If some qualified property is exchanged, loss realized with respect to qualified or other property is not recognized. However, excess mortgage incurred cannot be netted against cash received.

3.   **Involuntary Conversions**

    a.   A taxpayer may elect to defer recognition of gain if property is involuntarily converted into money or property that is similar or related in service or use under Sec. 1033.

        1)   An involuntary conversion of property results from destruction, theft, seizure, requisition, condemnation, or the threat of imminent requisition or condemnation.

        2)   Section 1033 does not apply to any realized losses.

            a)   Loss from condemnation or requisition of a personal-use asset is not deductible. But certain casualty losses are deductible.

            b)   When loss is realized, basis is determined independently of Sec. 1033.

    b.   Similar or related in service or use means that the property has the qualities outlined in items 1) and 2) below:

        1)   For an **owner-user**, functional similarity, i.e., meets a functional use test that requires that the property

            a)   Have similar physical characteristics
            b)   Be used for the same purpose

        2)   For an **owner-investor**, a close relationship to the service or use the previous property had to the investor, such that the owner-investor's

            a)   Risks, management activities, services performed, etc., continue without substantial change.

        3)   Generally, if property held for investment or for productive use in a trade or business is involuntarily converted due to a **federally declared disaster**, the tangible replacement property will be deemed similar or related in service or use. Any tangible property acquired and held for productive use in a trade or business is treated as similar or related in service or use to property that was

            a)   Held for investment or for productive use in a trade or business and
            b)   Involuntarily converted as a result of a federally declared disaster.

    c. **Direct conversion.** Conversion into property similar or related in service or use to the converted property.

        1) Nonrecognition is mandatory, not elective, on direct conversion to the extent of any amount realized in the form of qualified replacement property.

        2) Basis in the proceeds (property) is exchanged, i.e., equal to the basis in the converted property.

    d. **Indirect conversion.** Acquiring control of a corporation that owns similar or related-in-service-or-use property is treated as acquiring qualified property. Control is ownership of at least 80% of the voting stock and 80% of any other stock.

        1) Recognized gain is limited to any excess of any amount realized over any cost of qualified property.

    e. When property is converted involuntarily into nonqualified proceeds and qualified property is purchased within the replacement period, an election may be made to defer realized gain.

        1) The deferral is limited to the extent that the amount realized is reinvested in qualified replacement property.

        2) Basis in the qualified replacement property is the cost of such property decreased by the amount of any unrecognized gain.

    f. The replacement period begins on the earlier of the date of disposition or the threat of condemnation and ends 2 years after the close of the first tax year in which any part of the gain is realized.

        1) If real property used in business or held for investment (not inventory, dealer property, or personal-use property) is converted by condemnation or requisition, or threat thereof, 3 years is allowed.

        2) Construction of qualified property must be complete before the end of the replacement period for its cost to be included.

    g. For real property used in business or held for investment (not inventory, dealer property, personal-use property, etc.), if conversion is by condemnation, like-kind property qualifies as replacement. This standard is less stringent.

        1) Conversion must be direct. There is no indirect ownership allowance.

    h. To recap, on a Sec. 1033 involuntary conversion, realized gain is generally recognized only to the extent that any amount realized exceeds the cost of the similar or related-in-service property.

        1) The gain recognized is classified as ordinary income under Sec. 1245 or Sec. 1250.

4. **Sale of Principal Residence**

    a. Section 121 provides an exclusion upon the sale of a principal residence. No loss may be recognized on the sale of a personal residence.

    b. A taxpayer may exclude up to $250,000 ($500,000 for married taxpayers filing jointly) of realized gain on the sale of a principal residence.

  c. The individual must have owned and used the residence for an aggregate of 2 of the 5 prior years.

    1) For married taxpayers, the $500,000 exclusion is available if

      a) Either spouse meets the ownership requirement

      b) Both spouses meet the use requirement

      c) Neither spouse is ineligible for the exclusion by virtue of a sale or an exchange of a residence within the last 2 years

    2) However, if one spouse fails to meet these requirements, the other qualifying spouse is not prevented from claiming a $250,000 exclusion.

  d. The exclusion may be used only once every 2 years.

  e. The exclusion amount may be prorated if the use and ownership tests are not met. The exclusion is based on the ratio of months used to 24 months and is a proportion of the total exclusion.

    1) The pro rata exclusion is allowed if the sale is due to a change in the place of employment, health, or unforeseen circumstances.

  f. The gain on the sale of the residence must be prorated between qualified and nonqualified use.

    1) Nonqualified use includes periods that the residence was not used as the principal residence of the taxpayer.

    2) Nonqualified use does not include use before 2009.

  g. Gain must be recognized to the extent of any depreciation adjustments with respect to the rental or business use of a principal residence after May 6, 1997.

  h. Basis in a new home is its cost.

5. **Section 1202 Qualified Small Business Stock**

  a. When a taxpayer sells or exchanges Sec. 1202 small business stock that the taxpayer has held for more than 5 years, 50% of the gain may be excluded from the taxpayer's gross income.

    1) If the small business stock qualifies for this 50% exclusion, any recognized gain from the sale or exchange of the stock is subject to a maximum capital gains rate of 28%.

  b. The general requirements for stock to be treated as Sec. 1202 qualified small business stock are as follows:

    1) The stock is received after August 10, 1993.

    2) The issuing corporation is a domestic C corporation.

    3) The seller is the original owner of the stock.

    4) The corporation's gross assets do not exceed $50 million at the time the stock was issued.

  c. If the stock is acquired after February 17, 2009, and before September 28, 2010, 75% of the gain may be excluded. The exclusion increases to 100% for stock acquired after September 27, 2010.

Stop and review! You have completed the outline for this subunit. Study multiple-choice questions 15 through 17 beginning on page 246.

8.7 BUSINESS PROPERTY RECHARACTERIZATION

Author's note: Because the concepts in this subunit are challenging, we have included four examples, beginning on page 240, to provide additional context. Read through the outline and be sure to pay close attention to the examples in order to see the rules in practice.

1. **Overview**

   a. Sections 1231, 1245, and 1250 recharacterize gain or loss.

Overview of Business Property Recharacterization
(i.e., depreciation recapture)

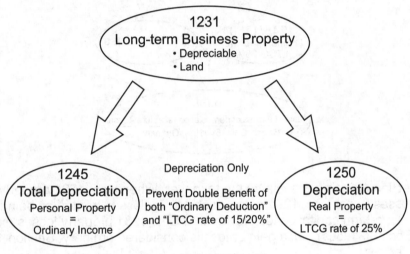

Figure 8-1

2. **Section 1231 Property**

Background
Before 1938, productive assets used in business were treated as capital property. As the Great Depression dragged on, however, it became clear that relief was needed–businesses struggling to sell their outmoded equipment found themselves subject to the limitations on recognizing capital losses. Thus, the Revenue Act of 1938 carved out an exception to capital gain-and-loss treatment for business property. By 1942, however, another change was called for, since the treatment needed during a depression was not appropriate for a wartime economy. Firms making large profits selling to the government needed lower rates on capital gains, so Sec. 117 (forerunner of the current Sec. 1231) was modified once again to provide special treatment for capital gains.

---

   a. Section 1231 property is property held for more than 1 year and includes

   1) All real or depreciable property used in a trade or business

   2) Involuntarily converted capital assets held in connection with a trade or business or in a transaction entered into for a profit

   b. Examples of Sec. 1231 property include apartment buildings, parking lots, manufacturing equipment, and involuntarily converted investment artwork.

   c. Examples of property that is not Sec. 1231 property include personal-use property and inventory.

Overview of Business Property Gains & Losses
(i.e., Beyond Depreciation Recapture)

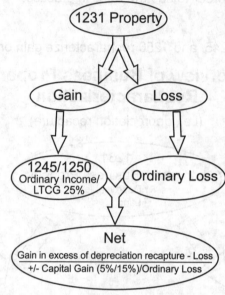

Figure 8-2

d. Section 1231 is beneficial to the taxpayer. When Sec. 1231 property gains exceed losses (a net Sec. 1231 gain), each gain or loss is treated as being from the sale of a long-term capital asset. However, if Sec. 1231 property losses exceed gains (a net Sec. 1231 loss), each gain or loss is considered ordinary. Section 1231 has a two-step test.

   1) Step 1: Determine net gain or loss from all casualties or thefts of Sec. 1231 property for the tax year. Gain or loss from involuntary conversions by other than casualty or theft is included in Step 2 but not Step 1.

      a) If the result is a net loss, each gain or loss is treated as ordinary income or loss.

      b) If the result is a net gain, each gain or loss is included in Step 2.

   2) Step 2: Determine net gain or loss from all dispositions of Sec. 1231 property for the year, including the property included in Step 1 only if Step 1 resulted in a net gain.

      a) If the result is a net loss, each gain or loss is treated as ordinary income or loss.

      b) If the result is a net gain, each gain or loss is treated as a long-term capital gain or loss.

e. Recapture. Net gain on Sec. 1231 property is treated as ordinary income to the extent of unrecaptured net Sec. 1231 losses from preceding tax years.

   1) Unrecaptured net Sec. 1231 losses are the total of net Sec. 1231 losses for the last 5 tax years, reduced by net Sec. 1231 gains characterized as ordinary income under Sec. 1231(c).

   2) Sections 1245 and 1250 recapture is computed before Sec. 1231 recapture, but Sec. 1231 recapture is computed before Steps 1 and 2 above.

f. The installment method can apply to Sec. 1231 property. Section 1231 merely characterizes gain or loss. Any Sec. 1231 gain that is recharacterized as capital gain will first consist of 28% gain, then 25% gain, and finally, 15/20% gain.

g. Allocation is required when Sec. 1245 or Sec. 1250 property is also Sec. 1231 property and only a portion of gain recognized is Sec. 1245 or Sec. 1250 OI.

h. Sections 1245 and 1250 only involve gains. If disposition of business property results in a loss then the loss is a 1231 loss.

3. **Section 1245 Ordinary Income**

a. Section 1245 property generally is depreciable personal property (tangible/intangible) used in a trade or business for over 12 months.

b. Gain on the disposition of Sec. 1245 property is ordinary income to the extent of the lesser of all depreciation taken (including amounts expensed under Sec. 179) or gain recognized.

1) If gain realized is not recognized (like-kind exchanges, involuntary conversions, etc.), Sec. 1245 ordinary income is limited to the sum of the following:

a) Gain recognized

b) FMV of property acquired that is not Sec. 1245 property and is not included in computing the recognized gain

2) The recognized gain in excess of the depreciation taken may be treated as a gain from the sale or exchange of Sec. 1231 property.

c. Intangible amortizable personal Sec. 1245 property examples include

1) Leaseholds of Sec. 1245 property
2) Professional athletic contracts, e.g., baseball
3) Patents
4) Goodwill acquired in connection with the acquisition of a trade or business
5) Covenants not to compete

4. **Section 1250 Ordinary Income**

a. Section 1250 property is all depreciable real property, such as a building or its structural components.

1) Examples of Sec. 1250 property include shopping malls, an apartment or office building, low-income housing, rented portions of residences, and escalators or elevators (placed in service after 1986).

2) Land is not Sec. 1250 property, but leases of land are Sec. 1250 intangible properties. Certain improvements to land may be treated as land, e.g., dams and irrigation systems.

b. Section 1250 property is subject to its own recapture rules. For the three items listed below, the aggregate gain recognized on the sale or disposition of Sec. 1250 property is ordinary income.

1) The excess of accelerated depreciation taken over S-L depreciation is ordinary income to the extent of gain recognized. This applies to purchases made before 1987.

2) For property held less than 1 year, the remaining depreciation is recaptured.

NOTE: Partial reduction of excess depreciation is provided for under Sec. 1250 for low-income housing and rehabilitated structures.

3) For corporations, the gain must be computed under both Sec. 1245 and 1250. If Sec. 1245 gain is larger than Sec. 1250 gain, 20% of the difference is characterized as ordinary income.

c. If gain realized is not recognized (like-kind exchanges, involuntary conversions, etc.), Sec. 1250 ordinary income is limited to the greater of the following:

1) Recognized gain

2) Excess of the potential Sec. 1250 ordinary income over the FMV of Sec. 1250 property received

5. **Gift Property**

    a. Neither Sec. 1245 nor Sec. 1250 applies to a gift disposition.
    b. Any gain realized by the donee upon a subsequent taxable disposition is subject to Sec. 1245 and Sec. 1250 characterization up to the sum of

        1) Potential Sec. 1245 and Sec. 1250 OI at the time of the gift
        2) Potential Sec. 1245 and Sec. 1250 OI arising between gift and subsequent disposition

6. **Inherited Property**

    a. Neither Sec. 1245 nor Sec. 1250 applies to a disposition by bequest, devise, or intestate succession.
    b. Exceptions: Sec. 1245 and Sec. 1250 OI are recognized for a transfer at death to the extent of any income in respect of a decedent (IRD). Section 1245 OI potential also results from depreciation allowed to a decedent because the depreciation does not carry over to the transferee.

7. **Installment Sales**

    a. All gain realized and recharacterized as ordinary income from a disposal of recaptured Sec. 1245 or Sec. 1250 property in an installment sale must be recognized in the period of sale.

        1) Any excess gain over Sec. 1245 or Sec. 1250 OI is accounted for by the installment method.

8. **Income for Multiple Assets**

    a. Income received or accrued for more than one asset is allocated to each asset by agreement, by FMV, or by the residual method.

        1) To compute Sec. 1245 and Sec. 1250 ordinary income, an amount realized allocable to an asset must be further allocated to each use of a mixed use asset for each tax year.

9. **Section 351 Exchange for Stock**

    a. Generally, no gain is recognized upon an exchange of property for all the stock of a newly formed corporation.
    b. Section 1245 and Sec. 1250 OI is limited to any amount of gain recognized in a Sec. 351 transaction.

 The topic of business property gain (loss) recharacterization often intimidates CPA candidates as they study for the exam due to the different rules applied under Secs. 1231, 1245, and 1250. Because the AICPA has tested this area relatively often, you should have a solid understanding of these rules. Take the time necessary to understand the outline and answer the multiple-choice questions to reinforce your knowledge of this area.

EXAMPLE 1

On January 17, Year 1, Relief Corp. purchased and placed into service 7-year MACRS tangible property costing $100,000. On December 21, Year 4, Relief Corp. sold the property for $105,000 (selling price 1) after taking $60,000 in MACRS depreciation deductions.

The adjusted basis of the property is $40,000 ($100,000 historical cost – $60,000 depreciation); therefore, Relief will recognize a gain of $65,000 ($105,000 selling price 1 – $40,000 adjusted basis). Since this property qualifies for Sec. 1245 recapture, the gain will be recaptured as ordinary income to the extent of the lesser of all depreciation taken or gain realized. Thus, Relief will have $60,000 of Sec. 1245 (ordinary) gain. The remaining $5,000 of gain is Sec. 1231 (capital) gain.

EXAMPLE 2

The facts from the previous example apply, except Relief sold the property for $95,000 (selling price 2).

Relief will recognize a gain of $55,000 ($95,000 selling price 2 – $40,000 adjusted basis). Since this property qualifies for Sec. 1245 recapture, the gain will be recaptured as ordinary income to the extent of the lesser of all depreciation taken or gain realized. Thus, Relief will have $55,000 of Sec. 1245 (ordinary) gain.

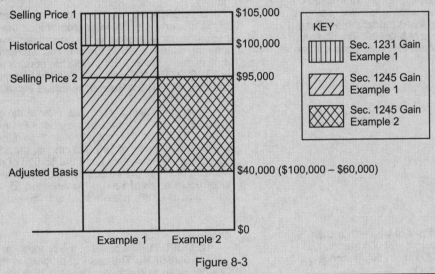

Figure 8-3

EXAMPLE 3

Martha purchased and placed into service Sec. 1250 property costing $600,000. After 5 years, the property was sold for $650,000 (selling price 1) after having taken $300,000 in MACRS depreciation deductions. Straight-line depreciation would have been $100,000.

The adjusted basis of the property is $300,000 ($600,000 historical cost – $300,000 MACRS depreciation); therefore, Martha will recognize a gain of $350,000 ($650,000 selling price 1 – $300,000 adjusted basis). Since this property is subject to Sec. 1250 recapture, the excess of accelerated depreciation taken over S-L depreciation is ordinary income to the extent of gain recognized. Thus, Martha will have $200,000 ($300,000 MACRS depreciation – $100,000 S-L depreciation) of Sec. 1250 (ordinary) gain. The remaining $150,000 ($350,000 gain recognized – $200,000 Sec. 1250 gain) is Sec. 1231 (capital) gain.

EXAMPLE 4

The facts from the previous example apply, except Martha sold the property for $400,000 (selling price 2).

Martha will recognize a gain of $100,000 ($400,000 selling price 2 – $300,000 adjusted basis). Since this property qualifies for Sec. 1250 recapture, the excess of accelerated depreciation taken over S-L depreciation is ordinary income to the extent of gain recognized, i.e., $200,000 limited to $100,000. Thus, Martha will have $100,000 of Sec. 1250 (ordinary) gain.

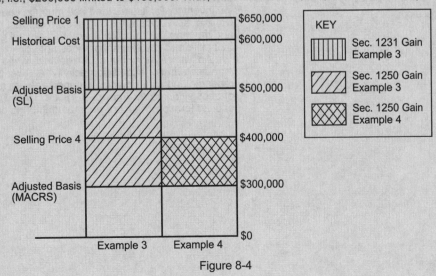

Figure 8-4

Stop and review! You have completed the outline for this subunit. Study multiple-choice
questions 18 through 20 beginning on page 247.

QUESTIONS

8.1 Basis

1. Bluff purchased equipment for business use for $35,000 and made $1,000 of improvements to the equipment. After deducting depreciation of $5,000, Bluff gave the equipment to Russett for business use. At the time the gift was made, the equipment had a fair market value of $32,000. Ignoring gift tax consequences, what is Russett's basis in the equipment?

A. $31,000

B. $32,000

C. $35,000

D. $36,000

Answer (A) is correct.

REQUIRED: The basis of an asset that was received as a gift.

DISCUSSION: According to IRS Publication 551, if the FMV of the property is equal to or greater than the donor's adjusted basis, the donee's basis is the donor's adjusted basis at the time the donee received the gift. The fair market value at the date of the gift is $32,000, while the donor's adjusted basis is $31,000 ($35,000 cost + $1,000 improvements – $5,000 depreciation). Thus, Russett's basis is equal to Bluff's adjusted basis of $31,000.

Answer (B) is incorrect. The FMV at the date of the gift is $32,000. The FMV is used only if the FMV is less than the donor's basis and the property is later sold for a loss. Answer (C) is incorrect. A basis of $35,000 ignores the $1,000 improvement that should be capitalized and the $5,000 of depreciation that reduces Bluff's adjusted basis in the equipment. Answer (D) is incorrect. A basis of $36,000 ignores the $5,000 of depreciation that reduces Bluff's adjusted basis in the equipment.

2. Fred Berk bought a plot of land with a cash payment of $40,000 and a $50,000 mortgage. In addition, Berk paid $200 for a title insurance policy. Berk's basis in this land is

A. $40,000

B. $40,200

C. $90,000

D. $90,200

Answer (D) is correct.

REQUIRED: The basis of the property acquired.

DISCUSSION: The basis of property is its cost. Cost includes cash paid and any debt to which the property is subject, regardless of whether the debt is recourse or nonrecourse. In addition, basis includes expenditures for major improvements and costs to acquire title.

Answer (A) is incorrect. Basis includes acquisition debt and costs. Answer (B) is incorrect. Basis includes acquisition debt to which the property is subject. Answer (C) is incorrect. The cost to acquire property, such as title insurance, is part of its cost basis.

3. Which of the following is subject to the Uniform Capitalization Rules of Code 263A?

A. Editorial costs incurred by a freelance writer.

B. Research and experimental expenditures.

C. Mine development and exploration costs.

D. Warehousing costs incurred by a manufacturing company with $12 million in annual gross receipts.

Answer (D) is correct.

REQUIRED: The uniform capitalization rules.

DISCUSSION: The uniform capitalization rules require the costs for construction (manufacture) of real or tangible personal property to be used in trade or business and costs of producing or acquiring property for sale to customers (retail) to be capitalized. The uniform capitalization rules do not apply if property is acquired for resale and the company's annual gross receipts (for the past 3 years) do not exceed $10 million. Both direct and most allocable indirect costs necessary to prepare the inventory for its intended use must be capitalized. The warehousing costs are direct costs that must be capitalized and the manufacturing company has annual gross receipts of $12 million so the exemption does not apply.

Answer (A) is incorrect. A freelance writer is not a manufacturing or acquisition activity. Answer (B) is incorrect. The research and experimental expenditures are not manufacturing or acquisition costs. Answer (C) is incorrect. Mine development and exploration costs are not manufacturing or acquisition costs.

8.2 Depreciation and Amortization

4. On August 1 of the current year, Graham purchased and placed into service an office building costing $264,000, including $30,000 for the land. What was Graham's MACRS deduction for the office building in the current year?

A. $9,600

B. $6,000

C. $3,600

D. $2,250

Answer (D) is correct.

REQUIRED: The amount of MACRS depreciation deduction.

DISCUSSION: Under MACRS, an office building is nonresidential real estate having a 39-year recovery period and is depreciated using the straight-line depreciation method. The land is not depreciable. The cost of the office building ($234,000) is divided by 39 years to yield $6,000. Because of the mid-month convention, 4.5 months of depreciation, or $2,250, is deductible in the year of purchase.

Answer (A) is incorrect. The $30,000 attributable to the land is not depreciable; nonresidential real property uses a 39-year, not a 27.5-year, recovery period; and only 4.5 months of depreciation can be expensed in the year of purchase. Answer (B) is incorrect. Only 4.5 months of depreciation can be expensed in the year of purchase. Answer (C) is incorrect. The $30,000 attributable to the land is not depreciable, and nonresidential real property uses a 39-year, not a 27.5-year, recovery period.

5. Browne, a self-employed taxpayer, had 2017 business taxable income of $505,000 prior to any expense deduction for equipment purchases. In 2017, Browne purchased and placed into service, for business use, office machinery costing $508,000. This was Browne's only 2017 capital expenditure. Browne's business establishment was not in an economically distressed area. Browne made a proper and timely expense election to deduct the maximum amount. Browne was not a member of any pass-through entity. What is Browne's deduction under the election?

A. $505,000

B. $508,000

C. $510,000

D. $2,030,000

Answer (A) is correct.

REQUIRED: The maximum amount of Sec. 179 deduction in 2017.

DISCUSSION: Tangible and depreciable personal property can be expensed by up to $510,000 in 2017, the year of acquisition. This amount is reduced when the amount of Sec. 179 property placed in service in a given year exceeds $2,030,000. Since this limit does not apply, the maximum deduction would be $510,000; however, there are other limits. Section 179(b)(3)(A) limits the deduction to taxable income derived from the active conduct of any trade or business. In this case, the maximum deduction is $505,000.

Answer (B) is incorrect. The Sec. 179 deduction is limited to taxable income. Answer (C) is incorrect. The maximum Sec. 179 deduction of $510,000 for 2017 ignores the taxable income limit. Answer (D) is incorrect. The amount of $2,030,000 is the threshold at which the deduction is reduced dollar-for-dollar, ignoring the taxable income limit in this case.

6. Which of the following conditions must be satisfied for a taxpayer to expense, in the year of purchase, under Internal Revenue Code Section 179, the cost of new or used tangible depreciable personal property?

I. The property must be purchased for use in the taxpayer's active trade or business.

II. The property must be purchased from an unrelated party.

A. I only.

B. II only.

C. Both I and II.

D. Neither I nor II.

Answer (C) is correct.

REQUIRED: The conditions that must be satisfied under Sec. 179 to expense property.

DISCUSSION: In order for a property to be expensed under Sec. 179, it must be both purchased for use in the taxpayer's active trade or business as well as be purchased from an unrelated party.

Answer (A) is incorrect. The property must also be purchased from an unrelated party. Answer (B) is incorrect. The property must also be purchased for use in the taxpayer's active trade or business. Answer (D) is incorrect. At least one of the conditions must be satisfied.

8.3 Capital Gains and Losses

7. Which of the following is a capital asset?

A. Inventory held primarily for sale to customers.

B. Accounts receivable.

C. A computer system used by the taxpayer in a personal accounting business.

D. Land held as an investment.

Answer (D) is correct.

REQUIRED: The property classified as a capital asset.

DISCUSSION: All property is classified as a capital asset unless specifically excluded. Accounts receivable, inventory, and depreciable property or real estate used in a business are not capital assets. Land held as an investment, however, is a capital asset unless it is held by a dealer (the general rule and not an exception is being tested).

Answer (A) is incorrect. Inventory held primarily for sale to customers is not included in the capital assets classification. Answer (B) is incorrect. Accounts receivable are specifically excluded as capital assets. Answer (C) is incorrect. A computer system is amortized over its useful life (i.e., depreciable property used in a trade or business) and is not considered a capital asset.

8. In the current year, Susan sold an antique that she bought 6 years ago to display in her home. Susan paid $800 for the antique and sold it for $1,400. Susan chose to use the proceeds to pay a court-ordered judgment. The $600 gain that Susan realized on the sale of the antique should be treated as

A. Ordinary income.

B. Long-term capital gain.

C. An involuntary conversion.

D. A nontaxable transaction.

Answer (B) is correct.

REQUIRED: The treatment of gain on a property sale.

DISCUSSION: The antique is a capital asset. A capital asset must be held for more than 1 year for gain or loss on its sale or exchange to be treated as long-term.

Answer (A) is incorrect. The facts do not indicate that Susan held the asset as a dealer. Unless an exception applies, sale of a capital asset gives rise to capital gain or loss. Answer (C) is incorrect. How proceeds of an asset sale are used defines neither an involuntary conversion nor a capital asset. Answer (D) is incorrect. The IRC contains no provision excepting from recognition gain realized on this transaction.

9. Sand purchased 100 shares of Eastern Corp. stock for $18,000 on April 1 of the prior year. On February 1 of the current year, Sand sold 50 shares of Eastern for $7,000. Fifteen days later, Sand purchased 25 shares of Eastern for $3,750. What is the amount of Sand's recognized gain or loss?

A. $0

B. $500

C. $1,000

D. $2,000

Answer (C) is correct.

REQUIRED: The recognized gain or loss on a wash sale of stock.

DISCUSSION: A current loss realized on a wash sale of securities is not recognized. A wash sale occurs when substantially the same securities are purchased within 30 days before or after being sold at a loss. Although Sand sold 50 shares of Eastern on February 1, it reacquired 25 more shares of Eastern less than 30 days later. Thus, the 25 shares that Sand reacquired 15 days later do not contribute to the recognized loss on February 1. If the total realized loss on February 1 is $2,000 ($9,000 basis of shares sold – $7,000 sales price), only half is recognized because only half is not subsequently reacquired.

Answer (A) is incorrect. Sand may recognize a $1,000 loss equal to the shares of stock sold on February 1 not subsequently reacquired 15 days later. Answer (B) is incorrect. The realized loss on February 1 is related to 50 shares. If 25 shares are subsequently reacquired, half the loss must not be recognized, not 75% of it. Answer (D) is incorrect. Half of the shares sold on February 1 are reacquired within the 30-day wash sale period. Thus, the realized loss of $2,000 must be reduced by the 25 shares reacquired 15 days later.

10. During the current year, all of the following events occurred: On June 1, Ben Rork sold 500 shares of Kul Corp. stock. Rork had received this stock on May 1 as a bequest from the estate of his uncle, who died on March 1. Rork's basis was determined by reference to the stock's fair market value on March 1. Rork's holding period for this stock was

A. Short-term.

B. Long-term.

C. Short-term if sold at a gain; long-term if sold at a loss.

D. Long-term if sold at a gain; short-term if sold at a loss.

Answer (B) is correct.

REQUIRED: The holding period for property acquired from a decedent.

DISCUSSION: Under Sec. 1223(11), if property acquired from a decedent is sold or otherwise disposed of by the recipient within 12 months of the decedent's death, then the property is considered to have been held for more than 12 months. Therefore, under Sec. 1223(3), it is long-term and subject to the maximum preferential tax rate of 15% (0% if the individual is in the 10% or 15% tax bracket).

8.4 Related Party Sales

Questions 11 and 12 are based on the following information. Conner purchased 300 shares of Zinco stock for $30,000 in 1999. On May 23, 2017, Conner sold all the stock to his daughter Alice for $20,000, its fair market value at the time. Conner realized no other gain or loss during 2017. On July 26, 2017, Alice sold the 300 shares of Zinco for $25,000.

11. What amount of the loss from the sale of Zinco stock can Conner deduct in 2017?

A. $0

B. $3,000

C. $5,000

D. $10,000

Answer (A) is correct.

REQUIRED: The amount of deductible loss in a related party sale.

DISCUSSION: The $10,000 realized loss ($20,000 proceeds – $30,000 basis) on the sale of the stock from father to daughter is disallowed. The daughter takes a cost basis of $20,000 in the stock as well as a new holding period. Related parties include ancestors, descendants, spouses, and siblings.

12. What was Alice's recognized gain or loss on her sale?

A. $0

B. $5,000 long-term gain.

C. $5,000 short-term loss.

D. $5,000 long-term loss.

Answer (A) is correct.

REQUIRED: The amount of gain recognized when stock acquired from a related party is sold to an unrelated third party.

DISCUSSION: The $5,000 realized gain ($25,000 proceeds – $20,000 basis) is recognized only to the extent it exceeds the previously disallowed loss of $10,000. Since the realized gain on the sale to an unrelated third party is less than the amount of disallowed loss, no gain is recognized.

13. Among which of the following related parties are losses from sales and exchanges **not** recognized for tax purposes?

A. Father-in-law and son-in-law.

B. Brother-in-law and sister-in-law.

C. Grandfather and granddaughter.

D. Ancestors, lineal descendants, and all in-laws.

Answer (C) is correct.

REQUIRED: The identification of the related party.

DISCUSSION: Losses are not allowed on sales or exchanges of property between related parties. Related parties include ancestors (grandfather), descendants (granddaughter), spouses, and siblings.

8.5 Installment Sales

14. The following data pertain to installment sales of personal property made by Fred Dale, an accrual-method taxpayer, in his retail furniture store:

Year of Sale	Installment Sales	Profit	Collections in Year 3
Year 1	$ 50,000	$15,000	$10,000
Year 2	100,000	40,000	30,000
Year 3	150,000	75,000	40,000

These sales were not under a revolving credit plan. Under the installment method, Dale should report gross profit for Year 3 of

- A. $35,000
- B. $75,000
- C. $80,000
- D. $130,000

Answer (B) is correct.
REQUIRED: The amount collected that is reported as gross profit.
DISCUSSION: The installment method is usually disallowed for dispositions of property by dealers. This includes any disposition of (1) personal property, if the person regularly sells such personal property on the installment plan, and (2) real property held by the taxpayer for sale to customers in the ordinary course of his or her trade or business. Exceptions are made for property used or produced in the trade or business of farming and, if so elected, sales of residential lots or timeshares, subject to interest payments on the deferred tax. Dale is excluded from installment sale deferral because the disposition of his property falls under "personal property of a type regularly sold by the person on the installment plan." Because he does not qualify, he must recognize all of his profit in Year 3, which is stated in the question as $75,000.
Answer (A) is incorrect. The amount of $35,000 results from subtracting the collections in Year 3 from the installment sale profits. Answer (C) is incorrect. The amount of $80,000 results from adding all the collections in Year 3. Answer (D) is incorrect. The amount of $130,000 results from adding the profits from installment sales in all 3 years.

8.6 Nonrecognition Transactions

15. A heavy-equipment dealer would like to trade some business assets in a nontaxable exchange. Which of the following exchanges would qualify as nontaxable?

- A. The company jet for a large truck to be used in the corporation.
- B. Investment securities for antiques to be held as investments.
- C. A road grader held in inventory for another road grader.
- D. A corporate office building for a vacant lot.

Answer (D) is correct.
REQUIRED: The transaction qualifying as a like-kind exchange.
DISCUSSION: Property qualifying for a like-kind treatment under IRC Sec. 1031 depends on the property's nature or character, but not necessarily in grade or quality. Real property is of like kind to other real property, except foreign property. Thus, the corporate office building and vacant lot qualify as a nontaxable exchange even though they are not used for the same purpose.
Answer (A) is incorrect. Personal properties are of like kind if they are of a like class. Airplanes (class 00.21) and trucks (class 00.24) are not of a like class. Answer (B) is incorrect. Securities and debt instruments do not qualify for Sec. 1031 nonrecognition. Thus, the investment securities disqualify the transaction as like-kind. Answer (C) is incorrect. Inventory is specifically excluded from like-kind exchange treatment.

16. Wynn, a 60-year old single individual, sold his personal residence for $450,000. Wynn had owned his residence, which had a basis of $250,000, for 6 years. Within 8 months of the sale, Wynn purchased a new residence for $400,000. What is Wynn's recognized gain from the sale of his personal residence?

- A. $0
- B. $50,000
- C. $75,000
- D. $200,000

Answer (A) is correct.
REQUIRED: The amount of recognized gain from sale of a personal residence.
DISCUSSION: Wynn will realize a $200,000 ($450,000 sales price – $250,000 adjusted basis) gain on the sale of the residence. Section 121, as amended by the Taxpayer Relief Act of 2000, allows an exclusion of up to $250,000 for single taxpayers on the sale of a principal residence. Therefore, Wynn's recognized gain is $0 ($200,000 realized gain – up to $250,000 exclusion).
Answer (B) is incorrect. The purchase price of the new residence does not calculate into the gain of the old residence. Answer (C) is incorrect. The amount of gain to be recognized is equal to the realized gain on the sale of the residence, $200,000, less the exclusion amount of up to $250,000. Answer (D) is incorrect. This is the amount of realized gain on the sale of Wynn's principal residence. The exclusion amount of up to $250,000 from Sec. 121 offsets this amount so that the recognized gain is $0.

17. On October 1, 2017, Donald Anderson exchanged an apartment building, having an adjusted basis of $375,000 and subject to a mortgage of $100,000, for $25,000 cash and another apartment building with a fair market value of $550,000 and subject to a mortgage of $125,000. The property transfers were made subject to the outstanding mortgages. What amount of gain should Anderson recognize in his tax return for 2017?

   A. $0

   B. $25,000

   C. $125,000

   D. $175,000

Answer (B) is correct.
   REQUIRED: The gain recognized in a like-kind exchange of properties subject to mortgages.
   DISCUSSION: Anderson's realized gain is

Fair market value of building received		$ 550,000
Mortgage on old building		100,000
Cash received		25,000
Total amount realized		$ 675,000
Less: Basis of old building	$375,000	
Mortgage on new building	125,000	(500,000)
Realized gain (only $25,000 recognized)		$ 175,000

Under Reg. 1.1031(d)-2, excess mortgage incurred cannot be netted against cash received to reduce the amount of boot received.
   Answer (A) is incorrect. The $25,000 cash boot received by Anderson is recognized gain. Answer (C) is incorrect. The mortgages are netted. Thus, Anderson is considered to have given $25,000 boot by taking the larger mortgage and not to have received another $100,000 boot. Answer (D) is incorrect. Gain realized is recognized only to the extent of boot received in a like-kind exchange.

8.7 Business Property Recharacterization

18. On January 2, Year 1, Bates Corp. purchased and placed into service 7-year MACRS tangible property costing $100,000. On December 31, Year 3, Bates sold the property for $102,000, after having taken $47,525 in MACRS depreciation deductions. What amount of the gain should Bates recapture as ordinary income?

   A. $0

   B. $2,000

   C. $47,525

   D. $49,525

Answer (C) is correct.
   REQUIRED: The amount of gain recaptured as ordinary income in Sec. 1245.
   DISCUSSION: Depreciable tangible property used in a trade or business is Sec. 1245 property. Section 1245 states that gain realized on the disposition of this property is recaptured as ordinary income to the extent of the lesser of depreciation taken or realized gain.
   Answer (A) is incorrect. Section 1245 recaptures as ordinary income the realized gain to the extent of the depreciation taken. Answer (B) is incorrect. The amount of Sec. 1231 gain is $2,000. Answer (D) is incorrect. The realized gain is $49,525. Section 1245 states that realized gain up to the amount of depreciation taken is reclassified as ordinary income.

19. Platt owns land that is operated as a parking lot. A shed was erected on the lot for the related transactions with customers. With regard to capital assets and Sec. 1231 assets, how should these assets be classified?

	Land	Shed
A.	Capital	Capital
B.	Sec. 1231	Capital
C.	Capital	Sec. 1231
D.	Sec. 1231	Sec. 1231

Answer (D) is correct.
   REQUIRED: The classification of property as a Sec. 1231 or capital asset.
   DISCUSSION: Capital assets are any property not excluded by IRC definition. Real property used in a trade or business is excluded. Section 1231 property includes all real or depreciable property used in the taxpayer's trade or business and held more than 1 year.

20. Mary Brown purchased an apartment building on January 1, 2008, for $200,000. The building was depreciated using the straight-line method. On December 31, 2017, the building was sold for $210,000 when the asset basis net of accumulated depreciation was $160,000. On her 2017 tax return, Brown should report

    A. Section 1231 gain of $10,000 and ordinary income of $40,000.

    B. Section 1231 gain of $40,000 and ordinary income of $10,000.

    C. Ordinary income of $50,000.

    D. Section 1231 gain of $50,000.

Answer (D) is correct.

REQUIRED: The amount and character of gain that should be recognized.

DISCUSSION: When depreciable property used in a trade or business is sold at a gain, first Sec. 1245 and Sec. 1250 are applied; then the balance of the gain not recaptured as ordinary income is Sec. 1231 gain. In this case, Sec. 1245 does not apply, and Sec. 1250 recapture is limited to the excess of accelerated depreciation over straight-line depreciation. Since the building was depreciated on the straight-line method, the entire $50,000 gain ($210,000 – $160,000) is Sec. 1231 gain.

STUDY UNIT NINE
CORPORATE TAXABLE INCOME

(21 pages of outline)

Corporate taxable income computations generally parallel those for individuals. Federal tax is determined by applying applicable tax rates to taxable income. Shareholders are then subject to federal income tax on distributions out of corporate earnings and profits (dividends). In addition to regular income tax, a C corporation may also be subject to the AMT (alternative minimum tax), the AET (accumulated earnings tax), and the PHC (personal holding company) tax. A corporation is required to make payments of estimated income tax and for FICA tax on wages paid.

Some candidates find it helpful to have the entire tax form side-by-side with our Knowledge Transfer Outline when studying. The full versions of the most up-to-date forms are easily accessible at www.gleim.com/taxforms. These forms and the form excerpts used in our outline are periodically updated as the latest versions are released by the IRS.

9.1 DEFINITION AND ACCOUNTING

1. **General Classification**

   a. If no election is made for a newly formed domestic entity, an entity with two or more members will be classified as a partnership, and an entity with a single member will be disregarded as an entity separate from the owner. A newly formed foreign entity with limited liability will be classified as an association taxed as a corporation.

   b. Certain businesses must be classified as corporations for federal tax purposes. Among the entities treated as corporations are ones incorporated under state or federal law, associations, joint stock companies, insurance companies, certain banks, state-owned organizations, certain foreign organizations, and publicly traded partnerships.

   c. **C corporations** are corporations other than S corporations.

   d. An **S corporation** is a pass-through entity that is not subject to the regular corporate income tax. Qualified corporations that elect subchapter S status are treated similarly to partnerships.

   e. **Partnerships, trusts, and estates** are generally not treated as corporations.

   f. **Publicly traded partnerships** are ineligible entities and must generally be taxed as corporations.

   g. **Limited Liability Company (LLC).** Normally, an LLC would elect partnership status to avoid being taxed as a corporation. This election allows for limited liability of the owners while at the same time retaining the single taxation. The owners are allowed to participate in the operations of the business, and there are no restrictions on the type of owners.

   h. **Professional Association (PA).** An association of professionals, e.g., accountants, doctors, or lawyers, is treated as a corporation for tax purposes if it is both organized under a state's Professional Association Act and operated as a corporation. One individual may be a professional association.

i.   **Personal Service Corporation (PSC).** The corporate rates do not apply to PSCs. These corporations are taxed at a flat rate of 35%.

    1)   A PSC's principal activity is performing personal services, substantially by employee-owners. An employee-owner owns more than 10% of the stock.

    2)   The IRS may allocate income, deductions, credits, exclusions, and other allowances between a PSC and its employee-owners if substantially all the PSC's services are performed for one other corporation, partnership, or entity, and the principal purpose of the PSC is tax avoidance.

j.   **Personal Holding Company (PHC).** Any nonexempt closely held corporation is classified as a PHC if a significant portion of its income is passive in nature. PHCs are subject to a penalty tax on excess personal holding company income.

2.   **Check-the-Box**

a.   The "check-the-box" regulations apply to business entities other than trusts that are separate for federal tax purposes. The regulations allow an eligible entity to decide whether it will be taxed as a corporation or a partnership. An eligible entity is a business that is not required to be treated as a corporation under federal tax law.

3.   **Single vs. Multi-Member Entities**

a.   An eligible entity with a single member can elect to be taxed as a corporation or disregarded as an entity separate from its owner (sole proprietorship).

b.   An eligible entity with two or more members can elect to be taxed as either a partnership or a corporation.

4.   **Tax Year**

a.   The separate nature of the entity from its owners also requires a separate income tax form, Form 1120, *U.S. Corporation Income Tax Return*, for C corporations.

    1)   Profits are taxed once at the corporate level and then again when profits are distributed to the owners. This is known as double taxation.

EXAMPLE

Peter and Paul each own 50% of AZY Company. Assume AZY had gross income of $500,000 and no deductions. If AZY is a C corporation, AZY will be taxed on this income on its Corporation Income Tax Return (Form 1120). Assuming a rate of 35%, AZY will pay $175,000 in taxes and have net income of $325,000. If AZY chooses to distribute this income to its shareholders ($162,500 each), the income will be included on Peter and Paul's returns as dividend income and will be taxed once again. Assuming Peter and Paul qualify for a 15% tax rate on dividends, they will each incur an additional $24,375 in tax. Due to this double taxation, the total tax levied on the income is $223,750 ($175,000 + $24,375 + $24,375).

---

b.   Generally, a corporation may elect either a calendar or fiscal tax year.

    1)   A PSC is required to use a calendar tax year.

        a)   An exception exists for a valid business purpose or a PSC that makes "minimum distributions."

    2)   A C corporation's tax return is due on or before the 15th day of the 4th month following the close of the tax year (e.g., April 15 for a calendar year corporation).

        a)   A corporation that files Form 7004 and pays its estimated unpaid tax liability is allowed an extension of up to 6 months for calendar year and fiscal year C corporations other than June 30 fiscal year C corporations.

        b)   C corporations with a June 30 fiscal year will continue to have a due date of the 15th day of the 3rd month following the close of the tax year. This will continue until tax years beginning after December 31, 2025. The extension date is April 15, resulting in a 7-month extension until tax year 2026.

5. **Accounting Method**

   a. No formal election is required for the accounting method of a newly incorporated C corporation. Any method allowed by the C corporation may be "elected" by using that method on its initial return. For example, a newly formed C corporation that chooses to use the accrual method must only use this method on its initial return in order to elect the method.

   b. The cash method may be used only by PSCs, S corporations, certain farming corporations, and C corporations that have average annual gross receipts of no more than $5 million in the 3 preceding tax years. Tax shelters may not use the cash method. A newly incorporated C corporation makes its initial accounting method selection simply by using the chosen method on its initial return.

6. **Corporation Income Tax Formula**

	Income
–	Exclusions
=	**Gross income**
–	Deductions
=	**Taxable income**
×	Tax rate
=	**Gross regular tax liability**
–	Credits
=	**Net regular tax liability or refund receivable**
+	AMT
+	FICA taxes
+	Special taxes
=	**Tax liability or refund receivable**

Stop and review! You have completed the outline for this subunit. Study multiple-choice questions 1 through 3 on page 270.

9.2 GROSS INCOME OF A CORPORATION

1. **Scope**

   a. Gross income of a corporation, similar to individual taxation, is all income from whatever source derived unless specifically excluded.

2. **Excluded Items**

   a. **Capital contributions** are excluded from a corporation's gross income.

      1) Gifts from a nonshareholder. Property other than money gifted from a nonshareholder has a zero basis. When money is contributed instead of property, it is given a basis equal to the value of the money and the basis of other property is reduced. First, reduce basis in property acquired within 1 year after the gift, then in all depreciable property, if any, and then in any remaining property, in proportion to the relative basis of any property in each of these categories.

EXAMPLE

Alpha Corporation receives $100,000 from the local government as an inducement gift to locate. Alpha purchases a piece of land for its future location for $450,000. The basis of the land will be $350,000 ($450,000 – $100,000). No gain is recognized on the receipt of land.

EXAMPLE

Assume the cost of the purchased land in the previous example was only $80,000. The basis in the land would be $0. Then, if any other property is purchased within the year, the basis of Alpha Corporation's other depreciable assets will be reduced by up to $20,000. If any of the $20,000 remains unused, the balance will be applied to any remaining (i.e., nondepreciable) assets.

---

    2) Pro rata contributions by shareholders, whether voluntary or by assessment, are not deductible by the shareholders. Instead, their individual basis in the stock is increased. The corporation may take a transferred basis in the property.

  b. **Treasury stock.** No gain or loss is recognized by a corporation on the sale or exchange of its own stock (including treasury stock).

3. **Included Items**

  a. **Life insurance income.** Proceeds received due to the death of the insured are generally excluded from gross income.

    1) If an employer purchases a policy that covers an employee and is issued after August 17, 2006, the proceeds from the policy are taxable to the extent proceeds exceed premiums paid. An exception is made for key employees, for whom the full amount of life insurance proceeds is excluded from gross income.

    2) Proceeds received under a policy transferred for consideration (e.g., secured debt) are income to the recipient only to the extent that the proceeds exceed the consideration.

  b. **Discharge of debt.** Except in stock-for-debt exchanges, income from cancelation of a corporation's debt at less than the outstanding carrying amount is excluded to the extent the corporation is insolvent. When the exclusion applies, the following tax attributes of the corporation must be reduced (dollar for dollar) in the order listed.

    1) NOLs and NOL carryovers
    2) The general business credit
    3) Capital loss carryovers
    4) Basis in property of the corporation
    5) Foreign tax credit carryovers

    NOTE: An election to first reduce basis is available.

  c. **Bond repurchase.** A corporation's income includes the issue price of its own bond minus the repurchase price and any premium it has already recognized. Subunit 9.3 discusses repurchase at a premium.

  d. **Sinking-fund income.** Interest or other income from property (including money) in a sinking fund to satisfy an obligation is income (even if in the hands of a trustee).

  e. **Unrestrained claim.** Both cash- and accrual-basis taxpayers must include in gross income, in the year of receipt, amounts actually or constructively received if the taxpayer has an unrestrained claim to the amounts (e.g., prepaid rent).

  f. **Refunds.** As with individuals, a refund of state taxes deducted for a prior year is included in income for the current year, to the extent that the deduction in the prior year generated a tax benefit. If the deduction generated no tax benefit, the refund is not included.

Stop and review! You have completed the outline for this subunit. Study multiple-choice questions 4 through 6 on page 271.

9.3 DEDUCTIONS OF A CORPORATION

> Deductions of a corporation have been regularly tested on the CPA exam. You should be familiar with calculating both corporate book income and corporate taxable income. In a question testing corporate deductions, you may be given corporate book income, along with other information, and asked to calculate corporate taxable income.

NOTE: This subunit covers deductions with special rules. Ordinary deductions without restrictions (e.g., utilities) are not specifically addressed.

1. **Overview**

    a. Theoretically, all corporate expenditures have a business objective. Deductions from corporate gross income for ordinary and necessary business expenses are allowed. Differences from deductions for individuals are discussed below.

        1) Organizational expenditures are allowed an immediate expense and amortization of balance.
        2) Deduction is allowed for dividends received from corporations.
        3) Interest on a corporation's own debt is generally deductible.
        4) AGI and limits based on it do not apply to a corporation.
        5) Personal deductions, e.g., the standard deduction, are not allowed.
        6) Passive activity loss rules do not apply to C corporations.

2. **Organizational Expense and Start-Up Costs**

    a. Costs of organizing a corporation are properly chargeable to a capital account. They generally are not deductible as a current expense because they benefit more than one tax period.

        1) However, a corporation may elect to expense up to $5,000 of qualified organizational expenses and $5,000 of start-up costs in the taxable year in which the business begins.

            a) The amount expensed is reduced by the costs exceeding $50,000.
            b) The remaining balance is amortized over a 15-year (180-month) period beginning with the month business began.
            c) Only expenditures incurred before the end of the tax year in which the corporation commences business may be expensed (amortized). When they are paid is irrelevant.
            d) The election is irrevocable.

    b. **Qualifying organizational expenditures** are ones incurred incidental to formation of the corporation and are distinct from start-up costs. Examples are legal fees for drafting the charter, incorporation fees, expenses for temporary directors, and organizational meeting costs.

    c. Organizational expenditures that are not qualified are costs related to the transfer of assets to the corporation or the issuance and sale of stock. Examples are printing stock certificates; professional fees for issuing stock; and costs incurred in the marketing, advertising, or promoting of stock issuances.

    d. Examples of start-up costs are costs incurred to prepare to enter into the trade or business, to secure suppliers and customers, and to obtain certain supplies and equipment.

3. **Charitable Contributions**

   a. A corporation's charitable contribution is deductible only if it is made to a qualified organization.

   b. Deductible amounts must be paid during the tax year. An accrual method corporation may elect to deduct an amount authorized by the board during the current tax year and paid not later than 2 1/2 months after the close of the tax year.

   c. A corporation may deduct the adjusted basis of inventory and other ordinary income property contributed.

   d. A corporation is allowed a deduction for the donation of qualified food and book inventory.

      1) The deduction is equal to basis plus one-half of the gain that would have been recognized if the asset were sold at FMV.

      2) The deduction may not exceed two times the asset's basis.

EXAMPLE

Corcory's Bakery only sells food prepared within the last 2 days to ensure customers receive products at peak freshness. However, since the food is edible for a full week, the bakery donates the unsold food to the local food bank, which qualifies as a donation of inventory to the needy. If, on a given day, Corcory donates food that would have sold for $100 and cost $50 to make, Corcory could take a donation of $75 [$50 + .5 × ($100 − $50)] for the inventory plus any additional costs to provide the food to the food bank.

---

   e. In general, the deduction for the contribution of capital gain property is the property's FMV.

   f. The property must be used in a manner related to the organization's exempt purpose. It must not be disposed of for value.

   g. Deductions are limited to 10% of taxable income (TI) before any

      1) Charitable contributions
      2) Dividends-received deduction
      3) Domestic production activities deduction
      4) NOL carryback
      5) Capital loss carryback
      6) Deduction allowed under IRC Sec. 249 for bond premium

   h. Excess over the TI limit is deductible during the succeeding 5 tax years.

      1) No carryback is allowed.
      2) Current-year contributions are deducted first.
      3) FIFO treatment applies to carryforwards.

4. **Dividends-Received Deduction (DRD)**

   a. A special corporate deduction for dividends received from domestic taxable corporations is allowed.

   b. Amounts deductible vary with the percentage of the stock of the distributing corporation (by voting and value) owned by the recipient.

Percent of Ownership	Percent of Dividends Deductible	Limit: Percent of TI of Recipient
< 20%	70%	70%
≥ 20%, < 80%	80%	80%
≥ 80% & affiliated	100%	100%

      1) Members of an affiliated group of corporations may deduct 100% of the dividends received from a member of the same affiliated group.

EXAMPLE

Alpha Corporation owns 10% of Beta Corporation. Alpha Corporation has $200,000 of ordinary income plus $100,000 in dividend income from Beta Corporation. Alpha Corporation has a $70,000 dividends-received deduction.

  c.   To be eligible for the DRD, a corporation must hold the stock at least 46 days during the 90-day period that begins 45 days before the stock becomes ex-dividend with respect to the dividend.

  d.   A corporation cannot take a DRD if it holds a short position in substantially similar or related property.

  e.   The DRD may be reduced when the investment company receives substantial amounts of income from sources other than dividends from domestic corporations eligible for the DRD.

  f.   The DRD is limited by the recipient corporation's adjusted taxable income. The TI limit amount varies with the recipient's stock ownership of the corporation.

    1)   To compute the limit, use TI before any of the following:

      a)   Dividends-received deduction
      b)   Domestic production activities deduction
      c)   NOL deduction
      d)   Capital loss carryback
      e)   Certain extraordinary dividend adjustments

    2)   First, compute the limit with respect to 20%-and-more-owned corporate dividends.

    3)   The TI limit does not apply if a current NOL exists or an NOL results from the DRD.

EXAMPLE

A corporation has taxable income of $1,000, including $10,000 in dividends received from a less-than-20%-owned domestic taxable corporation but before DRD. The DRD before applying the TI limit is $7,000 ($10,000 × 70%). Because the DRD produces an NOL, it is not limited to 70% of taxable income before the deduction ($700).

  g.   The DRD is allowable for dividends received from foreign corporations if the following are met:

    1)   The distributing foreign corporation is at least 10% owned by the recipient domestic corporation,

    2)   The foreign corporation is subject to U.S. federal income tax,

    3)   The foreign corporation has income effectively connected with a trade or business in the U.S., and

    4)   The foreign corporation is not a foreign personal holding company.

  h.   The DRD is allowable only on the portion of the dividends attributable to the effectively connected income.

  i.   Credit for foreign taxes deemed paid by the corporation on the dividend producing earnings and profit (E&P) may be allowable.

  j.   An S corporation may not claim the DRD.

  k.   Disqualified dividends. No deduction is allowed, or it is further restricted, for dividends received from the following:

    1)   Mutual savings banks (they are like interest)
    2)   Real estate investment trusts
    3)   Domestic international sales corporations, generally
    4)   Public utilities, on preferred stock
    5)   A corporation exempt from tax during the distribution year

5. **Gifts**

    a. Distinguish gifts from charitable contributions, which are made to qualified organizations. A deduction for business gifts is allowable only to the extent of $25 per donee per year. The following are not treated as gifts for this limit:

        1) Signs or promotional materials used on the recipient's business premises

        2) An item costing less than $4 having a permanent imprint of the donor's name

6. **Compensation**

    a. Compensation, e.g., salary, wages, or bonuses, is a deductible business expense unless the services are capital in nature.

    b. Unreasonable compensation to a shareholder is generally treated as a distribution, characterized as a dividend, to the extent of earnings and profits.

    c. Compensation by an accrual taxpayer (corporation) to a cash-basis taxpayer (employee) is not deductible by the corporation until the period in which the cash-basis taxpayer receives the payment and recognizes the income.

    d. Payments made by March 15 of the succeeding year may be accrued and expensed in a prior year if related to services rendered in that prior year.

    e. Deduction is disallowed to a publicly held corporation for compensation in excess of $1 million paid in any tax year to certain employees.

        1) The limit applies to compensation paid to the chief operating officer and to the four other officers whose compensation must be reported to shareholders under the Securities Exchange Act of 1934.

            a) No amount of a "parachute payment" made to an officer, shareholder, or highly compensated person is deductible.

        2) The following forms of remuneration are not included in the $1 million limit:

            a) Income from pension plans, annuity plans, and specified employer trusts

            b) Benefits that are tax-free under the Code

            c) Commissions based on income generated by the individual performance of the employee

            d) Compensation based on performance goals

        3) The disallowance of the deduction for the compensation payment does not change the employee's reporting of the compensation for income tax purposes.

            a) The $1 million and any excess is generally compensation gross income.

            b) The salary, bonus, or other payment is not required to be treated as a dividend.

            c) Dividend reporting for compensation may be required if part or all of the compensation is unreasonable.

EXAMPLE

David Davidson is the Chief Executive Officer (CEO) for publicly held Davidson & Sons, Inc. David is paid a $3 million cash salary, $500,000 in bonuses tied to performance, and $10,000 in tax-free fringe benefits that are accessible to all employees. David includes $3.5 million in income ($3,000,000 salary + $500,000 bonuses). Davidson & Sons can deduct $1,510,000 ($1,000,000 maximum deductible salary + $500,000 performance-based pay not subject to limitations + $10,000 fringe benefits).

---

    f. Stock. FMV of property received for services is gross income when it is not subject to a substantial risk of forfeiture and its value can be ascertained with reasonable certainty. Deduction of the compensation is allowed when the amount is included as gross income but only if federal income tax on the compensation is withheld.

EXAMPLE

Employee purchases stock (FMV = $1,000) in Year 1 for $500. In Year 8, when its FMV is $2,000, Employee's rights in it are no longer subject to a substantial risk of forfeiture. Employee includes $1,500 in gross income in Year 8. Employer may deduct $1,500 in Year 8.

---

    1)   Sale prior to vesting in a non-arm's-length transaction results in gross income computed from the current FMV of the property. Further, gross income is includible upon a subsequent arm's-length sale.

EXAMPLE

In the example above, Employee sold the stock to Spouse in Year 2 for $750 when its FMV was $1,500. The sale in Year 8 was by Spouse. Employee includes and Employer deducts $1,000 in Year 2 and $500 in Year 8.

---

    g.   Education. An employer's expenditures for employee education are deductible as a business expense. An individual, in contrast, may deduct only educational expenses required to maintain or improve skills in a present position.

7. **Travel and Meals**

    a.   Travel and meals are deductible business expenses. Meals bought while traveling or served on the business premises are deductible by 50% of the amount incurred.

        1)   All meals served on the business premises are fully deductible if provided to more than half of the employees for the convenience of the employer.

        2)   Expenses for **entertainment** that are ordinary and necessary to the business are deductible by up to 50% of the amount incurred.

EXAMPLE

Joe is an employee of ARC. He invited several of ARC's top clients to a presentation on new product lines. ARC often uses these presentations to entice clients to place orders. After the presentation, Joe took the clients out to dinner and a show at a cost of $1,000. ARC may deduct $500 of this expense ($1,000 × 50%) since the amount paid is ordinary, necessary, and associated with the active conduct of trade or business.

---

    b.   Limitation of deduction

        1)   If the employee's meal and entertainment expenses are reimbursed by his or her employer and the reimbursement is not treated as compensation, the employer's deduction is limited to 50% of the expenses.

        2)   If the employee's meal expenses are reimbursed by his or her employer and the reimbursement is treated as compensation, the employee's deduction is limited to 50% of the expenses.

            a)   Employers are not subject to the 50% limit to the extent they treat the reimbursement as compensation to employees.

8. **Insuring an Employee**

    a.   Reasonable amounts of expenditures to promote employee health, goodwill, and welfare are deductible. Reasonable amounts paid or incurred for employee life insurance are included.

    b.   Key employee. Premiums for life insurance covering an officer or employee are not deductible if the corporation is a direct or indirect beneficiary.

    c.   A deduction is denied for interest expense incurred with respect to corporate-owned life insurance policies, or endowment or annuity contracts.

9. **R&E Expenditures**

a. Qualified research and experimental expenditures may be capitalized, amortized, or currently deducted.

1) Generally, costs incidental to development of a model, process, or similar property are included.

2) Not included are costs of market research, sociological research, or development of art.

3) Purchase of equipment and land receives its regular treatment and may not be deducted immediately.

10. **Fines**

a. Fines and penalties paid to a governmental entity are not deductible.

11. **Bad Debts**

a. For cash-basis taxpayers, income is only recognized when actually received. Therefore, any bad debt will not be included as part of income since the cash is never received. Accrual-basis taxpayers, however, do recognize the income and are allowed a bad debt deduction.

b. The allowance method is not allowed (except for financial institutions).

1) A corporation must use the direct charge-off method or the nonaccrual-experience method.

2) The nonaccrual-experience method is a procedure for not recognizing income if it is expected to be uncollectible. This is similar to treatment by cash-basis taxpayers in that the income is never recognized and therefore there is no need for a deduction.

12. **Worthless Securities**

a. Loss incurred when a security becomes worthless is generally treated as a capital loss subject to the capital loss limitations. Loss incurred when a security of an affiliated corporation becomes worthless may be treated as an ordinary loss.

13. **Stock Redemptions**

a. Generally, deduction of amounts paid or incurred with respect to a stock redemption or the redemption of the stock of any related person is not allowed. An exception to the general rule is the allowance for deductions for interest paid or accrued within the tax year on indebtedness.

14. **Original Issue Discount (OID)**

a. OID is treated as deductible interest expense.

b. Constant yield method. OID is deductible as interest, using the yield method to amortize the discount.

1) Constant yield to maturity is computed and applied to adjusted issue price (AIP) to compute deductible interest.

2) The OID portion does not include cash interest payments made to the holder during the period.

3) AIP is the original issue price adjusted for OID previously taken into account.

4) Yield to maturity is determined on the basis of compounding at the end of each (typically 6-month) accrual period.

a) Daily portions of OID must be computed. It is the ratable daily portion of the excess of AIP multiplied by yield to maturity over cash interest payable for the bond year.

EXAMPLE

Consider a 5-year 10% bond issued on June 30, Year 1, with a $10,000 face, a $9,250 original issue price, and 12% yield.

Year 1 amortization of interest:

$$\$9{,}250 \text{ price} \times 12\% \text{ yield} \times \frac{6 \text{ months}}{12 \text{ months}}$$

$$= \$555 - \$500 \left(\$10{,}000 \text{ face} \times 10\% \times \frac{6 \text{ months}}{12 \text{ months}}\right) \text{ cash paid}$$

$$= \$55 \text{ interest}$$

Year 2 amortization of interest:

$$(\$9{,}250 \text{ price} + \$55 \text{ interest}) \times 12\% \text{ yield}$$

$$= \$1{,}116.60 - \$1{,}000 \ (\$10{,}000 \text{ face} \times 10\%) \text{ cash paid}$$

$$= \$116.60 \text{ interest}$$

---

15. **Repurchase at Premium**

   a. A corporation that repurchases its own bonds may deduct as interest expense the excess of the repurchase price over the issue price.

   1) Issue price is adjusted for OID deducted.
   2) No more than the normal call premium on nonconvertible debt is allowable, unless the corporation can show that the excess is not attributed to a conversion feature.
   3) A call premium not exceeding 1 year's interest at the rate stated in the bond is considered normal.

16. **Interest Expense**

   a. Interest expense incurred in a trade or business is generally deductible from gross income.
   b. Interest expense incurred on borrowings used to repurchase stock is deductible in the period in which it is paid or incurred. However, other expenses related to a stock purchase on reorganization are generally not deductible.

17. **Casualty Losses**

   a. Casualty losses are deductible. When business property is partially destroyed, the deductible amount is the lesser of the decline in FMV or the property's adjusted basis (prior to the loss).

   1) When business property is completely destroyed, the deductible amount is the property's adjusted basis (prior to the loss).
   2) Unlike individuals, there is no $100-per-loss or 10%-of-AGI floor for corporations.

18. **Taxes**

   a. State income taxes based on gross income are deductible. However, federal income taxes are not.

Form 1120 pages 1 and 2 are reproduced below and on the following page to illustrate the sections of the tax return used to report income and deduction items.

Form **1120**		**U.S. Corporation Income Tax Return**			OMB No. 1545-0123

Form **1120**
Department of the Treasury
Internal Revenue Service

U.S. Corporation Income Tax Return

For calendar year [Year] or tax year beginning _____ , [Year], ending _____ , 20 _____

▶ Information about Form 1120 and its separate instructions is at *www.irs.gov/form1120.*

OMB No. 1545-0123

[Year]

A Check if:
1a Consolidated return (attach Form 851) . . ☐
b Life/nonlife consolidated return . . ☐
2 Personal holding co. (attach Sch. PH) . . ☐
3 Personal service corp. (see instructions) . . ☐
4 Schedule M-3 attached ☐

TYPE OR PRINT

Name
REG, Inc.
Number, street, and room or suite no. If a P.O. box, see instructions.
987 Duece Street
City or town, state, or province, country, and ZIP or foreign postal code
Oldsville, NM 01239

B Employer identification number
98-7654321
C Date incorporated
1-1-2006
D Total assets (see instructions)
$ 10,000,000

E Check if: **(1)** ☐ Initial return **(2)** ☐ Final return **(3)** ☐ Name change **(4)** ☐ Address change

Income

1a	Gross receipts or sales	**1a**	
b	Returns and allowances	**1b**	
c	Balance. Subtract line 1b from line 1a	**1c**	
2	Cost of goods sold (attach Form 1125-A)	**2**	
3	Gross profit. Subtract line 2 from line 1c	**3**	
4	Dividends (Schedule C, line 19)	**4**	
5	Interest	**5**	
6	Gross rents	**6**	
7	Gross royalties	**7**	
8	Capital gain net income (attach Schedule D (Form 1120)) . . .	**8**	
9	Net gain or (loss) from Form 4797, Part II, line 17 (attach Form 4797) .	**9**	
10	Other income (see instructions—attach statement)	**10**	
11	**Total income.** Add lines 3 through 10 . . . . . . ▶	**11**	

Deductions (See instructions for limitations on deductions.)

12	Compensation of officers (see instructions—attach Form 1125-E) . ▶	**12**	
13	Salaries and wages (less employment credits)	**13**	
14	Repairs and maintenance	**14**	
15	Bad debts	**15**	
16	Rents	**16**	
17	Taxes and licenses	**17**	
18	Interest	**18**	
19	Charitable contributions	**19**	
20	Depreciation from Form 4562 not claimed on Form 1125-A or elsewhere on return (attach Form 4562) . .	**20**	
21	Depletion	**21**	
22	Advertising	**22**	
23	Pension, profit-sharing, etc., plans	**23**	
24	Employee benefit programs	**24**	
25	Domestic production activities deduction (attach Form 8903) . .	**25**	
26	Other deductions (attach statement)	**26**	
27	**Total deductions.** Add lines 12 through 26 . . . . ▶	**27**	
28	Taxable income before net operating loss deduction and special deductions. Subtract line 27 from line 11.	**28**	
29a	Net operating loss deduction (see instructions) . .	**29a**	
b	Special deductions (Schedule C, line 20) . .	**29b**	
c	Add lines 29a and 29b	**29c**	

Tax, Refundable Credits, and Payments

30	**Taxable income.** Subtract line 29c from line 28. See instructions .	**30**	
31	Total tax (Schedule J, Part I, line 11)	**31**	
32	Total payments and refundable credits (Schedule J, Part II, line 21) .	**32**	
33	Estimated tax penalty. See instructions. Check if Form 2220 is attached . ▶ ☐	**33**	
34	**Amount owed.** If line 32 is smaller than the total of lines 31 and 33, enter amount owed	**34**	
35	**Overpayment.** If line 32 is larger than the total of lines 31 and 33, enter amount overpaid	**35**	
36	Enter amount from line 35 you want: **Credited to [next year] estimated tax** ▶ _____ **Refunded** ▶	**36**	

Sign Here

Under penalties of perjury, I declare that I have examined this return, including accompanying schedules and statements, and to the best of my knowledge and belief, it is true, correct, and complete. Declaration of preparer (other than taxpayer) is based on all information of which preparer has any knowledge.

▶ _____
Signature of officer   Date

▶ _____
Title

May the IRS discuss this return with the preparer shown below? See instructions. ☐ Yes ☐ No

Paid Preparer Use Only

Print/Type preparer's name	Preparer's signature	Date	Check ☐ if self-employed	PTIN

Firm's name ▶
Firm's address ▶

Firm's EIN ▶
Phone no.

For Paperwork Reduction Act Notice, see separate instructions.   Cat. No. 11450Q   Form **1120** [Year]

Form 1120 [Year]   Page **2**

Schedule C	**Dividends and Special Deductions** (see instructions)	**(a)** Dividends received	**(b)** %	**(c)** Special deductions (a) × (b)
1	Dividends from less-than-20%-owned domestic corporations (other than debt-financed stock) . . .		70	
2	Dividends from 20%-or-more-owned domestic corporations (other than debt-financed stock) . . .		80	
3	Dividends on debt-financed stock of domestic and foreign corporations		*see instructions*	
4	Dividends on certain preferred stock of less-than-20%-owned public utilities . . .		42	
5	Dividends on certain preferred stock of 20%-or-more-owned public utilities		48	
6	Dividends from less-than-20%-owned foreign corporations and certain FSCs . . .		70	
7	Dividends from 20%-or-more-owned foreign corporations and certain FSCs . . .		80	
8	Dividends from wholly owned foreign subsidiaries		100	
9	**Total.** Add lines 1 through 8. See instructions for limitation			
10	Dividends from domestic corporations received by a small business investment company operating under the Small Business Investment Act of 1958		100	
11	Dividends from affiliated group members		100	
12	Dividends from certain FSCs		100	
13	Dividends from foreign corporations not included on line 3, 6, 7, 8, 11, or 12 . . .			
14	Income from controlled foreign corporations under subpart F (attach Form(s) 5471) .			
15	Foreign dividend gross-up			
16	IC-DISC and former DISC dividends not included on line 1, 2, or 3			
17	Other dividends			
18	Deduction for dividends paid on certain preferred stock of public utilities			
19	**Total dividends.** Add lines 1 through 17. Enter here and on page 1, line 4 . . . ▶			
20	**Total special deductions.** Add lines 9, 10, 11, 12, and 18. Enter here and on page 1, line 29b . . . . ▶			

Form **1120** [Year]

Stop and review! You have completed the outline for this subunit. Study multiple-choice questions 7 through 14 beginning on page 271.

9.4 LOSSES OF A CORPORATION

1. The following rules apply only for corporations, not individuals.

2. **Net Operating Loss (NOL)**

    a. An NOL is any excess of deductions over gross income.

    b. Modified deductions for some items are used in computing an NOL.

        1) An NOL carried over from other tax years is not allowed in computing a current NOL.

        2) A dividends-received deduction (DRD) may produce or increase an NOL.

            a) A corporation is entitled to disregard the limitations on a DRD when calculating an NOL. The DRD would increase the NOL.

        3) Charitable contributions are not allowed in computing a current NOL.

        4) The allowable depreciation may not create or increase an NOL.

    c. Applying NOLs as a deduction. Generally, a corporation's NOL is carried back to each of the 2 preceding tax years and forward to the 20 succeeding tax years.

EXAMPLE

Assume a corporation is moving from the growth stage to the established stage. In the previous year, the corporation had a small income of $25,000 (which is taxed at the 15% rate). In the current year, the corporation has invested in capital expansion, advertising, and other costs that created a loss. As a result of the expenses in the current year, the corporation is expected to earn $1,000,000 subject to the maximum rate of 34% next year. This is an example where the election to forgo the carryback would be beneficial since the carryback will generate a 15% refund whereas carrying forward the NOL will result in a 34% decrease in taxes in future years.

---

        1) A corporation may elect to forgo carryback and only carry the NOL forward.

        2) The NOL must be applied to the earliest tax year to which it can be carried and used to the fullest extent possible in that year.

        3) The NOL reduces TI, but not below zero, for that year.

        4) TI for the carryover year is adjusted TI.

            a) A charitable contribution allowable in a carryback year remains deductible because the charitable contribution 10%-of-TI limit is applied before an NOL carryback.

            b) Applying an NOL as a deduction in a subsequent tax year and computing excess NOL carryover from the subsequent year are complex when the charitable contribution 10%-of-TI limit applies.

    d. Carryback procedure. Carryback of an NOL results in overpayment in a prior tax year.

        1) Claiming a refund requires filing an amended return (Form 1120X), which must be filed during the statute of limitations period.

        2) Application for quick refund of tax as a result of an NOL carryback is permitted (Form 1139).

        3) The application window is the date the loss year return is due until 12 months from the close of the tax year.

3. **Capital Gain and Loss**

    a.   Capital gain net income (CGNI) occurs when net short-term capital gain (net STCG) exceeds net long-term capital loss (net LTCL).

    b.   Net capital gains (NCGs) constitute gross income.

    c.   Net capital gains (net LTCG – net STCL) are currently taxed as ordinary income.

        1)   The 35% alternative tax on NCGs does not apply at current rates.

        2)   Net STCGs (STCGs – STCLs) are treated as ordinary income (OI) unless offset by LTCLs.

    d.   A corporation's capital losses are deductible only to the extent of capital gains, whether they are short- or long-term.

        1)   A net capital loss (NCL) is not deductible against OI in the tax year incurred.

          NCL = Excess of CLs (ST & LT) over CG (ST & LT)

        2)   It cannot produce or increase an NOL.

        3)   When figuring a current-year net capital loss, capital losses carried from other years are not included.

        4)   A corporation may not carry a capital loss from, or to, a year during which it is an S corporation.

    e.   A corporation's NCL for a particular tax year may be carried back to each of the 3 preceding tax years and forward to the 5 succeeding tax years.

        1)   No election to forgo carryback is provided.

        2)   The NCL must be used to the extent possible in the earliest applicable tax year.

        3)   The oldest unused NCL is applied first.

    f.   The NCL is treated as an STCL in a carryover tax year. It offsets only a net capital gain before the carryover, but it may not produce or increase an NOL.

4. **Passive Activity Loss (PAL)**

    a.   The passive activity loss limitation rules explained in Study Unit 7, Subunit 3, apply to individuals, estates, and trusts (other than grantor trusts). Special PAL rules apply to closely held corporations and personal service corporations. Even though the PAL rules do not apply to grantor trusts, partnerships, and S corporations directly, they do apply to the owners of these entities.

Stop and review! You have completed the outline for this subunit. Study multiple-choice questions 15 through 17 on page 274.

9.5 RECONCILING BOOK AND TAXABLE INCOME

Background

The divergence of tax accounting from financial accounting has received the stamp of approval of the U.S. Supreme Court. In the case *Thor Power Tool Company v. Commissioner* (1979), the Court noted that "the primary goal of financial accounting is to provide useful information to management, shareholders, creditors, and other properly interested . . . the primary goal of the income tax system is the equitable collection of revenue."

1. **Reconciliation**

    a. Corporations file federal returns using Form 1120. Reconciliation of income per books of the corporation with income per tax is reported on Schedule M-1. It addresses differences, both permanent and temporary, for general financial reporting and tax accounting. Schedule M-3 is required for corporations with total assets of $10 million or more.

2. **Temporary and Permanent Differences**

    a. Temporary differences are timing differences and occur because tax laws require the recognition of some income and expenses in a different period than that required for book purposes. These differences originate in one period and reverse or terminate in one or more subsequent periods. Accelerated depreciation is an example of a temporary difference, as tax depreciation is greater than book in the beginning.

    b. Permanent differences result from transactions that will not be offset by any corresponding differences in other periods. The tax exempt income from municipal bonds interest is an example of a permanent difference, as it will not be taxable in a later period.

3. **Calculation**

    a. To reconcile income per books with income per tax, the following adjustments are made to net income (loss) per books (similar to Schedule M-1).

    Net income (loss) per books
    + Federal income tax
    + Excess of capital losses over capital gains
    + Income subject to tax not recorded on books
    + Expenses recorded on books not deducted on the tax return
    − Income recorded on books not subject to tax
    − Deductions on this return not charged against book income (e.g., depreciation)

    = **Taxable income**

b. Examples of expenses recorded on books that are not deductible include contributions in excess of 10% taxable income limitation, book depreciation expense in excess of allowable tax depreciation, disallowed travel and entertainment costs (50% of meals and entertainment expenses are nondeductible), life insurance premiums on key personnel when the corporation is the beneficiary, political contributions, interest expense to carry tax-free interest instruments (e.g., municipal bonds), and bad debt allowances.

c. Examples of nontaxable income include prepaid rent or interest previously received and recorded for tax purposes but not earned until the current year, life insurance proceeds received on the death of key personnel, and tax-exempt interest.

From Form 1120

Schedule M-1	**Reconciliation of Income (Loss) per Books With Income per Return**
	Note. The corporation may be required to file Schedule M-3 (see instructions).

1	Net income (loss) per books		7	Income recorded on books this year not included on this return (itemize):	
2	Federal income tax per books				
3	Excess of capital losses over capital gains		a	Tax-exempt interest $	
4	Income subject to tax not recorded on books this year (itemize):		b	Other (itemize):	
			8	Deductions on this return not charged against book income this year (itemize):	
5	Expenses recorded on books this year not deducted on this return (itemize):		a	Depreciation . . $	
a	Depreciation . . . . $		b	Charitable contributions $	
b	Charitable contributions $		c	Other (itemize):	
c	Travel and entertainment $				
d	Other (itemize):		9	Add lines 7 and 8	
6	Add lines 1 through 5		10	Income—line 6 less line 9	

EXAMPLE

The following information comes from Fern Corporation's financial statements:

- Fern's net income per books (after tax expenses) is $150,000.
- The federal income tax expense per Fern's books is $24,580.
- Fern received $40,000 of interest income of which $24,000 relates to municipal bonds owned.
- Fern received $2,000 in prepaid rent in the current year.
- Fern's books showed a $4,000 short-term capital gain distribution from a mutual fund corporation and a $5,000 loss on the sale of Retro stock that was purchased 3 years ago. The stock was an investment in an unrelated corporation. There were no other gains or losses and no loss carryovers from prior years.
- Fern's distributions included reimbursed employee expenses for travel of $100,000 and business meals of $30,000. The reimbursed expenses met the conditions of deductibility and were properly substantiated under an accountable plan. The reimbursement was not treated as employee compensation.
- Fern expensed $7,000 for the term life insurance premiums on the corporation officers. Fern was the policy owner and the beneficiary.
- Book depreciation on computers purchased was $10,000. Tax depreciation was $25,000 for the purchased computers.

-- Continued on next page --

EXAMPLE -- Continued

The following is the completed M-1, which shows the reconciliation from net income to taxable income. The explanations showing how each number was determined are given below by number.

| **Schedule M-1** | **Reconciliation of Income (Loss) per Books With Income per Return** Note: The corporation may be required to file Schedule M-3 (see instructions). |

1	Net income (loss) per books	[1]	150,000	7	Income recorded on books this year not included on this return (itemize):		
2	Federal income tax per books	[2]	24,580				
3	Excess of capital losses over capital gains	[3]	1,000	a	Tax-exempt interest $ [9] 24,000		
4	Income subject to tax not recorded on books this year (itemize):			b	Other (itemize):		
						[10]	24,000
	Prepaid Rent	[4]	2,000	8	Deductions on this return not charged against book income this year (itemize):		
5	Expenses recorded on books this year not deducted on this return (itemize):						
a	Depreciation . . . . . $ ____0			a	Depreciation . . $ [11] 15,000		
b	Charitable contributions $			b	Charitable contributions $		
c	Travel and entertainment $ [5] 15,000			c	Other (itemize):		
d	Other (itemize):					[12]	15,000
	Life Insurance Premiums [6] 7,000	[7]	22,000	9	Add lines 7 and 8	[13]	39,000
6	Add lines 1 through 5	[8]	199,580	10	Income—line 6 less line 9	[14]	160,580

1) Fern reports net income per books (after tax expenses) as $150,000.

2) $24,580 is the federal income tax expense reported on Fern's books for the year.

3) For federal income tax, a corporation's capital losses are limited to capital gains. Thus, any excess loss must be added back to the net income per books in order to arrive at taxable income.

4) The $2,000 prepaid rent collected in the current year is subject to tax and must be added to net income per books in order to arrive at taxable income.

5) Only one-half of the business meals are deductible for tax purposes. Therefore, a $15,000 adjustment is required to increase taxable income.

6) Key-person life insurance premiums paid by an employer are not deductible for tax purposes if the employer is a beneficiary under the policy. Thus, a $7,000 adjustment is required to increase taxable income.

7) The total amount of expenses recorded on Fern's books and not deductible on its tax return is $22,000.

8) The sum of lines 1 through 5 of Schedule M-1 is $199,580.

9) The $24,000 interest received relating to municipal bonds held is tax exempt. Thus, a $24,000 adjustment is required to decrease taxable income.

10) The total amount of income recorded on Fern's books but not included in its tax return is $24,000.

11) Tax depreciation was $15,000 greater than book depreciation ($25,000 tax depreciation – $10,000 book depreciation). Since tax depreciation is greater, it goes on line 8a. If book depreciation were greater, the amount would have been listed on line 5a.

12) The total amount of deductions on Fern's tax return but not expensed on its books is $15,000.

13) The sum of lines 7 and 8 of Schedule M-1 is $39,000.

14) The difference of line 6 over line 9 is $160,580. This is the amount of Fern's taxable income and should be the same as that reported on line 28 of page 1 of Form 1120 for the current year.

4.   **Schedule M-3**

a.   In an effort to increase transparency and provide the IRS with more detail about book income and tax differences, Schedule M-3 is required for large entities. The schedule shows the differences by category, dollar amount, and status as permanent or temporary. Part I asks certain questions about the financial statements and reconciles book net income to net income for tax purposes. Parts II and III reconcile book net income to taxable income, indicating temporary and permanent differences. Carefully review the Form 1120 Schedule M-3 on the following pages.

Stop and review! You have completed the outline for this subunit. Study multiple-choice questions 18 through 20 on page 275.

SCHEDULE M-3 **(Form 1120)** Department of the Treasury Internal Revenue Service	**Net Income (Loss) Reconciliation for Corporations** **With Total Assets of $10 Million or More** ▶ **Attach to Form 1120 or 1120-C.** ▶ **Information about Schedule M-3 (Form 1120) and its** **separate instructions is available at** *www.irs.gov/form1120.*	OMB No. 1545-0123 **[Year]**

Name of corporation (common parent, if consolidated return) | Employer identification number

Check applicable box(es):   (1) ☐ Non-consolidated return   (2) ☐ Consolidated return (Form 1120 only)

(3) ☐ Mixed 1120/L/PC group   (4) ☐ Dormant subsidiaries schedule attached

Part I   **Financial Information and Net Income (Loss) Reconciliation** (see instructions)

1a Did the corporation file SEC Form 10-K for its income statement period ending with or within this tax year?
  ☐ **Yes.** Skip lines 1b and 1c and complete lines 2a through 11 with respect to that SEC Form 10-K.
  ☐ **No.** Go to line 1b. See instructions if multiple non-tax-basis income statements are prepared.

b Did the corporation prepare a certified audited non-tax-basis income statement for that period?
  ☐ **Yes.** Skip line 1c and complete lines 2a through 11 with respect to that income statement.
  ☐ **No.** Go to line 1c.

c Did the corporation prepare a non-tax-basis income statement for that period?
  ☐ **Yes.** Complete lines 2a through 11 with respect to that income statement.
  ☐ **No.** Skip lines 2a through 3c and enter the corporation's net income (loss) per its books and records on line 4a.

2a Enter the income statement period: Beginning   MM/DD/YYYY   Ending   MM/DD/YYYY

b Has the corporation's income statement been restated for the income statement period on line 2a?
  ☐ **Yes.** (If "Yes," attach an explanation and the amount of each item restated.)
  ☐ **No.**

c Has the corporation's income statement been restated for any of the five income statement periods immediately preceding the period on line 2a?
  ☐ **Yes.** (If "Yes," attach an explanation and the amount of each item restated.)
  ☐ **No.**

3a Is any of the corporation's voting common stock publicly traded?
  ☐ **Yes.**
  ☐ **No.** If "No," go to line 4a.

b Enter the symbol of the corporation's primary U.S. publicly traded voting common stock . . . .

c Enter the nine-digit CUSIP number of the corporation's primary publicly traded voting common stock . . . .

4a Worldwide consolidated net income (loss) from income statement source identified in Part I, line 1 .	**4a**	
b Indicate accounting standard used for line 4a (see instructions): (1) ☐ GAAP (2) ☐ IFRS (3) ☐ Statutory (4) ☐ Tax-basis (5) ☐ Other (specify) _____		
5a Net income from nonincludible foreign entities (attach statement)	**5a**	( )
b Net loss from nonincludible foreign entities (attach statement and enter as a positive amount) . . .	**5b**	
6a Net income from nonincludible U.S. entities (attach statement)	**6a**	( )
b Net loss from nonincludible U.S. entities (attach statement and enter as a positive amount)	**6b**	
7a Net income (loss) of other includible foreign disregarded entities (attach statement)	**7a**	
b Net income (loss) of other includible U.S. disregarded entities (attach statement)	**7b**	
c Net income (loss) of other includible entities (attach statement)	**7c**	
8 Adjustment to eliminations of transactions between includible entities and nonincludible entities (attach statement)	**8**	
9 Adjustment to reconcile income statement period to tax year (attach statement)	**9**	
10a Intercompany dividend adjustments to reconcile to line 11 (attach statement)	**10a**	
b Other statutory accounting adjustments to reconcile to line 11 (attach statement)	**10b**	
c Other adjustments to reconcile to amount on line 11 (attach statement)	**10c**	
11 **Net income (loss) per income statement of includible corporations.** Combine lines 4 through 10 .	**11**	

Note: Part I, line 11, must equal Part II, line 30, column (a) or Schedule M-1, line 1 (see instructions).

12 Enter the total amount (not just the corporation's share) of the assets and liabilities of all entities included or removed on the following lines.

	Total Assets	Total Liabilities
a Included on Part I, line 4 . . . . ▶		
b Removed on Part I, line 5 . . . . ▶		
c Removed on Part I, line 6 . . . . ▶		
d Included on Part I, line 7 . . . . ▶		

For Paperwork Reduction Act Notice, see the Instructions for Form 1120.   Cat. No. 37961C   **Schedule M-3 (Form 1120) [Year]**

Schedule M-3 (Form 1120) [Year]   Page **2**

Name of corporation (common parent, if consolidated return)	Employer identification number

Check applicable box(es): **(1)** ☐ Consolidated group   **(2)** ☐ Parent corp   **(3)** ☐ Consolidated eliminations   **(4)** ☐ Subsidiary corp   **(5)** ☐ Mixed 1120/L/PC group

Check if a sub-consolidated: **(6)** ☐ 1120 group   **(7)** ☐ 1120 eliminations

Name of subsidiary (if consolidated return)	Employer identification number

Part II **Reconciliation of Net Income (Loss) per Income Statement of Includible Corporations With Taxable Income per Return** (see instructions)

Income (Loss) Items (Attach statements for lines 1 through 12)	(a) Income (Loss) per Income Statement	(b) Temporary Difference	(c) Permanent Difference	(d) Income (Loss) per Tax Return
1 Income (loss) from equity method foreign corporations				
2 Gross foreign dividends not previously taxed . . .				
3 Subpart F, QEF, and similar income inclusions . .				
4 Section 78 gross-up				
5 Gross foreign distributions previously taxed . . .				
6 Income (loss) from equity method U.S. corporations				
7 U.S. dividends not eliminated in tax consolidation .				
8 Minority interest for includible corporations . . .				
9 Income (loss) from U.S. partnerships				
10 Income (loss) from foreign partnerships				
11 Income (loss) from other pass-through entities . .				
12 Items relating to reportable transactions				
13 Interest income (see instructions)				
14 Total accrual to cash adjustment				
15 Hedging transactions				
16 Mark-to-market income (loss)				
17 Cost of goods sold (see instructions)	( )			( )
18 Sale versus lease (for sellers and/or lessors) . .				
19 Section 481(a) adjustments				
20 Unearned/deferred revenue				
21 Income recognition from long-term contracts . .				
22 Original issue discount and other imputed interest .				
23a Income statement gain/loss on sale, exchange, abandonment, worthlessness, or other disposition of assets other than inventory and pass-through entities				
b Gross capital gains from Schedule D, excluding amounts from pass-through entities				
c Gross capital losses from Schedule D, excluding amounts from pass-through entities, abandonment losses, and worthless stock losses				
d Net gain/loss reported on Form 4797, line 17, excluding amounts from pass-through entities, abandonment losses, and worthless stock losses				
e Abandonment losses				
f Worthless stock losses (attach statement)				
g Other gain/loss on disposition of assets other than inventory				
24 Capital loss limitation and carryforward used . . .				
25 Other income (loss) items with differences (attach statement)				
26 **Total income (loss) items.** Combine lines 1 through 25				
27 **Total expense/deduction items** (from Part III, line 38)				
28 Other items with no differences				
29a Mixed groups, see instructions. All others, combine lines 26 through 28				
b PC insurance subgroup reconciliation totals . . .				
c Life insurance subgroup reconciliation totals . .				
30 **Reconciliation totals.** Combine lines 29a through 29c				

Note: Line 30, column (a), must equal Part I, line 11, and column (d) must equal Form 1120, page 1, line 28.

Schedule M-3 (Form 1120) [Year]

Schedule M-3 (Form 1120) [Year]

Page **3**

Name of corporation (common parent, if consolidated return)	Employer identification number

Check applicable box(es): **(1)** ☐ Consolidated group   **(2)** ☐ Parent corp   **(3)** ☐ Consolidated eliminations   **(4)** ☐ Subsidiary corp   **(5)** ☐ Mixed 1120/L/PC group

Check if a sub-consolidated: **(6)** ☐ 1120 group   **(7)** ☐ 1120 eliminations

Name of subsidiary (if consolidated return)	Employer identification number

Part III   **Reconciliation of Net Income (Loss) per Income Statement of Includible Corporations With Taxable Income per Return—Expense/Deduction Items** (see instructions)

Expense/Deduction Items	(a) Expense per Income Statement	(b) Temporary Difference	(c) Permanent Difference	(d) Deduction per Tax Return
1 U.S. current income tax expense				
2 U.S. deferred income tax expense				
3 State and local current income tax expense				
4 State and local deferred income tax expense				
5 Foreign current income tax expense (other than foreign withholding taxes)				
6 Foreign deferred income tax expense				
7 Foreign withholding taxes				
8 Interest expense (see instructions)				
9 Stock option expense				
10 Other equity-based compensation				
11 Meals and entertainment				
12 Fines and penalties				
13 Judgments, damages, awards, and similar costs				
14 Parachute payments				
15 Compensation with section 162(m) limitation				
16 Pension and profit-sharing				
17 Other post-retirement benefits				
18 Deferred compensation				
19 Charitable contribution of cash and tangible property				
20 Charitable contribution of intangible property				
21 Charitable contribution limitation/carryforward				
22 Domestic production activities deduction				
23 Current year acquisition or reorganization investment banking fees				
24 Current year acquisition or reorganization legal and accounting fees				
25 Current year acquisition/reorganization other costs				
26 Amortization/impairment of goodwill				
27 Amortization of acquisition, reorganization, and start-up costs				
28 Other amortization or impairment write-offs				
29 Reserved				
30 Depletion				
31 Depreciation				
32 Bad debt expense				
33 Corporate owned life insurance premiums				
34 Purchase versus lease (for purchasers and/or lessees)				
35 Research and development costs				
36 Section 118 exclusion (attach statement)				
37 Other expense/deduction items with differences (attach statement)				
38 **Total expense/deduction items.** Combine lines 1 through 37. Enter here and on Part II, line 27, reporting positive amounts as negative and negative amounts as positive				

QUESTIONS

9.1 Definition and Accounting

1. In Year 1, Brun Corp. properly accrued $10,000 for an income item on the basis of a reasonable estimate. In Year 2, Brun determined that the exact amount was $12,000. Which of the following statements is true?

A. Brun is required to file an amended return to report the additional $2,000 of income.

B. Brun is required to notify the IRS within 30 days of the determination of the exact amount of the item.

C. The $2,000 difference is includible in Brun's Year 2 income tax return.

D. The $2,000 difference of income must be included when the reasonable estimate amount is determined.

Answer (C) is correct.

REQUIRED: The true statement about accrual of a reasonable estimate when the exact amount is greater than the estimate.

DISCUSSION: Under the accrual method of accounting, income is includible in gross income when all the events have occurred that fix the right to receive the income and the amount can be determined with reasonable accuracy. If an amount of income is properly accrued on the basis of a reasonable estimate and the exact amount is subsequently determined, the difference, if any, shall be taken into account for the taxable year in which such determination is made.

Answer (A) is incorrect. The excess is reported as gross income in the tax year in which the exact amount is determined, in this case, in Year 2. Answer (B) is incorrect. Notification is not necessary. Answer (D) is incorrect. The taxpayer cannot include an amount (s)he is not aware of. The additional amount of $12,000 was determined later.

2. An S corporation engaged in manufacturing has a year end of June 30. Revenue consistently has been more than $10 million under both cash and accrual basis of accounting. The stockholders would like to change the tax status of the corporation to a C corporation using the cash basis with the same year end. Which of the following statements is correct if it changes to a C corporation?

A. The year end will be December 31, using the cash basis of accounting.

B. The year end will be December 31, using the accrual basis of accounting.

C. The year end will be June 30, using the accrual basis of accounting.

D. The year end will be June 30, using the cash basis of accounting.

Answer (C) is correct.

REQUIRED: The appropriate year end for a C corporation.

DISCUSSION: C corporations that are not personal service corporations, S corporations, or small C corporations (less than an average of $5 million in revenues per year over the past 3 years) must use the accrual basis of accounting. A corporation can use a fiscal year end; June 30 is therefore allowed.

Answer (A) is incorrect. C corporations that are not personal service corporations, S corporations, or small C corporations (less than an average of $5 million in revenues per year over the past 3 years) must use the accrual basis of accounting. A corporation is not required to use a calendar year end; it can use a fiscal year end. Answer (B) is incorrect. The corporation does not need to change its tax year to a calendar year end. The C corporation can keep the fiscal year end of June 30. Answer (D) is incorrect. C corporations that are not personal service corporations or small C corporations must use the accrual basis of accounting.

3. In which type of business entity is the entire ownership interest most freely transferable?

A. General partnership.

B. Limited partnership.

C. Corporation.

D. Limited liability company.

Answer (C) is correct.

REQUIRED: The business entity in which the entire ownership interest is most freely transferable.

DISCUSSION: Simply acquiring a corporation's stock gives an individual an ownership interest. Shares can be freely bought and sold, usually without any restriction.

Answer (A) is incorrect. An ownership interest in a general partnership is not easily transferable. An interest can be assigned, but an assignee does not have the rights of a general partner. Moreover, the other partners must approve the admission of a new partner. Answer (B) is incorrect. An ownership interest in a limited partnership is not easily transferable. The partnership may impose restraints on assignability, for example, to qualify for an exemption from registration under federal securities law. Answer (D) is incorrect. An ownership interest in a limited liability company is not easily transferable. A transferee does not become a member absent consent of all members or a provision in their agreement.

9.2 Gross Income of a Corporation

4. The following information pertains to treasury stock sold by Lee Corporation to an unrelated broker in the current year:

Proceeds received	$50,000
Cost	30,000
Par value	9,000

What amount of capital gain should Lee recognize in the current year on the sale of this treasury stock?

A. $0

B. $20,000

C. $21,000

D. $41,000

Answer (A) is correct.
    REQUIRED: The gain a corporation should report as a result of the sale of treasury stock.
    DISCUSSION: A corporation does not recognize gain or loss on the receipt of money or other property in exchange for its stock, including treasury stock. Therefore, no gain or loss is recognized by Lee as a result of the treasury stock sale.

5. For the year ended December 31, 2017, Kell Corp.'s book income, before income taxes, was $70,000. Included in the computation of this $70,000 was $10,000 of proceeds of a life insurance policy, representing a lump-sum payment in full as a result of the death of Kell's controller. Kell was the owner and beneficiary of this policy since 2005. In its income tax return for 2017, Kell should report taxable life insurance proceeds of

A. $10,000

B. $8,000

C. $5,000

D. $0

Answer (D) is correct.
    REQUIRED: The extent to which proceeds of a life insurance policy constitute gross income.
    DISCUSSION: For employer-owned policies issued prior to August 17, 2006, proceeds of a life insurance policy paid by reason of death of the insured are excluded by the beneficiary. Since no part of the $10,000 represents interest on proceeds retained by the insurance company, no part of it is reported as gross income.

6. Sanders Corporation purchased a $1 million 10-year debenture for $1.2 million on January 1, 2010. In 2017, how much amortization of bond premium must Sanders report on its 2017 income tax return from purchase of this bond?

A. $240,000

B. $200,000

C. $20,000

D. $0

Answer (C) is correct.
    REQUIRED: The income reported from the issuance of a 10-year debenture.
    DISCUSSION: In the case of a bond, the amount of amortizable bond premium for the taxable year shall be allowed as a reduction of interest income. The amount is amortized over the life of the bond. Thus, Sanders must report $20,000 [($1,200,000 – $1,000,000) ÷ 10].
    Answer (A) is incorrect. Incorrectly amortizing the issue price over 5 years results in $240,000. Answer (B) is incorrect. The total premium is $200,000. Answer (D) is incorrect. The premium may be amortized over the life of the bond.

9.3 Deductions of a Corporation

7. Which of the following costs are amortizable organizational expenditures?

A. Professional fees to issue the corporate stock.

B. Printing costs to issue the corporate stock.

C. Legal fees for drafting the corporate charter.

D. Commissions paid by the corporation to an underwriter.

Answer (C) is correct.
    REQUIRED: The costs amortizable as organizational expenditures.
    DISCUSSION: A corporation may elect to amortize qualified organizational expenses over a period of not less than 180 months. Expenditures associated with the formation of the corporation, including legal fees for drafting the corporate charter, are amortizable.

8. In 2017, Kara Corp. incurred the following expenditures in connection with the repurchase of its stock from shareholders:

Interest on borrowings used to repurchase stock	$100,000
Legal and accounting fees in connection with the repurchase	400,000

The total of the above expenditures deductible in 2017 is

    A. $0

    B. $100,000

    C. $400,000

    D. $500,000

Answer (B) is correct.
    REQUIRED: The amount that a corporation may deduct for expenses related to the repurchase of its stock.
    DISCUSSION: Interest expense incurred on business borrowings is deductible in the period in which it is paid or accrued. However, other expenses related to a stock repurchase or reorganization are capitalized.
    Answer (A) is incorrect. Interest expense incurred on business borrowings is deductible. Answer (C) is incorrect. Amounts paid or incurred in connection with a stock redemption are not deductible. Answer (D) is incorrect. The interest is deductible, but the costs associated with the repurchase are not.

9. Placebo Corp. is an accrual-basis, calendar-year corporation. On December 13, 2017, the board of directors declared a 2%-of-profits bonus to all employees for services rendered during 2017 and notified them in writing. None of the employees own stock in Placebo. The amount represents reasonable compensation for services rendered and was paid on March 13, 2018. Placebo's bonus expense may

    A. Not be deducted on Placebo's 2017 tax return because the per-share employee amount cannot be determined with reasonable accuracy at the time of the declaration of the bonus.

    B. Be deducted on Placebo's 2017 tax return.

    C. Be deducted on Placebo's 2018 tax return.

    D. Not be deducted on Placebo's tax return because payment is a disguised dividend.

Answer (B) is correct.
    REQUIRED: The treatment of bonus compensation.
    DISCUSSION: Under Sec. 404, certain contributions paid by an employer are subject to being treated as deferred compensation and are deductible in the year of payment. This limitation is applicable if the deduction would otherwise be allowed under Sec. 162(a). The deduction is required in the payment year unless distributed prior to March 15. Because the present amount was paid on March 13, the time of receipt was within the allocated period of time, and the compensation can be deducted as a business expense under Sec. 162 in 2017.
    Answer (A) is incorrect. This determination is not required by Sec. 404. Answer (C) is incorrect. Section 404 is not applicable due to the timely payment of the bonus. Answer (D) is incorrect. The facts of the problem provide that the amount of the bonus represents reasonable compensation and not a disguised dividend.

10. John Budd is the sole shareholder of Ral Corp., an accrual-basis taxpayer engaged in wholesaling operations. Ral's retained earnings at January 1, 2017, amounted to $1 million. For the year ended December 31, 2017, Ral's book income, before federal income tax, was $300,000. Included in the computation of this $300,000 were the following:

Key employee insurance premiums paid on Budd's life (Ral is the beneficiary of this policy.)	$3,000
Group term insurance premiums paid on $10,000 life insurance policies for each of Ral's four employees (The employees' spouses are the beneficiaries.)	4,000

What amount should Ral deduct for key employee and group life insurance premiums in computing taxable income for 2017?

    A. $0

    B. $3,000

    C. $4,000

    D. $7,000

Answer (C) is correct.
    REQUIRED: The amount that a corporation may deduct for payment of life insurance premiums.
    DISCUSSION: Ral Corp. may deduct the premiums paid for group term life insurance. However, no deduction is allowed for premiums paid for life insurance for which the corporation is the beneficiary.
    Answer (A) is incorrect. Premiums paid for group term life insurance are deductible. Answer (B) is incorrect. Premiums paid for life insurance for which the corporation is the beneficiary are not deductible. Answer (D) is incorrect. The group term life premiums are deductible, but the key employee insurance premiums are not.

11. If a corporation's charitable contributions exceed the limitation for deductibility in a particular year, the excess

   A. Is not deductible in any future or prior year.

   B. May be carried back or forward for 1 year at the corporation's election.

   C. May be carried forward to a maximum of 5 succeeding years.

   D. May be carried back to the preceding year.

Answer (C) is correct.
   REQUIRED: The treatment of a corporation's excess charitable contributions.
   DISCUSSION: A corporation may carry unused charitable contributions forward for 5 years. Current contributions are deducted before carryovers. Carryovers are applied on a FIFO basis. Carrybacks of excess charitable contributions are not permitted.

12. Pope, a C corporation, owns 15% of Arden Corporation. Arden paid a $3,000 cash dividend to Pope. What is the amount of Pope's dividends-received deduction?

   A. $3,000

   B. $2,400

   C. $2,100

   D. $0

Answer (C) is correct.
   REQUIRED: The DRD for a 15% owner.
   DISCUSSION: The DRD is available only to corporations. The deduction is based on the distributee corporation's percentage ownership of the distributing corporation and may be limited to taxable income. The deduction percentage is 70% for corporations with less than 20% ownership in the distributing corporation. Pope's deduction is $2,100 ($3,000 dividend × 70%).
   Answer (A) is incorrect. The deduction is limited based on Pope's ownership percentage of Arden. Pope must own 80% or more of Arden to take a 100% DRD. Answer (B) is incorrect. An 80% deduction requires 20% to 79% ownership of the distributing corporation. Answer (D) is incorrect. Corporations are allowed a deduction based on ownership. The minimum deduction is 70%.

13. The costs of organizing a corporation in 2017

   A. May be deducted in full in the year in which these costs are incurred even if paid in later years.

   B. May be deducted only in the year in which these costs are paid.

   C. May be amortized over a period of not less than 180 months, even if these costs are capitalized on the company's books.

   D. Are nondeductible capital expenditures.

Answer (C) is correct.
   REQUIRED: The deductibility of a corporation's organization costs.
   DISCUSSION: A corporation may elect to amortize the expenditures over a period of not less than 180 months, beginning with the month in which the corporation starts business.

14. In 2017, Pine Corporation had losses of $20,000 from operations. It received $180,000 in dividends from a 25%-owned domestic corporation. Pine's taxable income is $160,000 before the dividends-received deduction. What is the amount of Pine's dividends-received deduction?

   A. $0

   B. $144,000

   C. $128,000

   D. $180,000

Answer (C) is correct.
   REQUIRED: The dividends-received deduction of a corporation.
   DISCUSSION: A corporate deduction for dividends received from domestic taxable corporations is allowed. Pine Corporation may deduct 80% of dividends received from a domestic corporation in which Pine owned between 20% and 80% of the stock. This dividends-received deduction is limited to 80% of taxable income. Without regard to the limitation, Pine could deduct $144,000 ($180,000 × 80%). Pine, however, is limited to a $128,000 deduction ($160,000 taxable income × 80%). Thus, Pine's dividends-received deduction is $128,000.
   Answer (A) is incorrect. Pine is entitled to a dividends-received deduction. Answer (B) is incorrect. Pine's dividends-received deduction is limited to 80% of taxable income. Answer (D) is incorrect. Pine may not deduct all of the dividends received.

9.4 Losses of a Corporation

15. For each of the years 2014 through 2016, Geyer, Inc., a calendar-year corporation, had net income (loss) per books as follows:

2014	$ 15,000
2015	10,000
2016	(60,000)

Included in Geyer's gross revenues for 2016 were taxable dividends of $20,000 received from an unrelated 20%-owned domestic corporation. If Geyer elects to give up the carryback period, what is its NOL that may be carried forward to 2017?

A. $35,000

B. $51,000

C. $60,000

D. $76,000

Answer (D) is correct.

REQUIRED: The net operating loss (NOL) carryover.

DISCUSSION: Barring any allowable special election, an NOL may be carried back to each of the 2 preceding taxable years and forward to the 20 succeeding taxable years. The NOL must be carried to the earliest possible year, unless an election is made to give up the 2-year carryback. Because Geyer made this election, the 2016 net operating loss is a carryforward to 2017. In computing the net operating loss, the dividends-received deduction (DRD) is computed without regard to the 80%-of-taxable-income limitation.

Net loss per books	$(60,000)
Allowable DRD ($20,000 × 80%)	(16,000)
NOL carryover	$(76,000)

Answer (A) is incorrect. The amount of $35,000 is merely the sum of net income (loss) per books for 2014, 2015, and 2016. Answer (B) is incorrect. The corporation elected to forgo the carryback of the NOL. Answer (C) is incorrect. In computing the NOL, the dividends-received deduction is computed without regard to the 80%-of-taxable-income limitation.

16. A C corporation has gross receipts of $150,000, $35,000 of other income, and deductible expenses of $95,000. In addition, the corporation incurred a net long-term capital loss of $25,000 in the current year. What is the corporation's taxable income?

A. $65,000

B. $87,000

C. $90,000

D. $115,000

Answer (C) is correct.

REQUIRED: The correct calculation of corporate taxable income.

DISCUSSION: Net capital gains (NCGs) constitute gross income. However, a corporation's capital losses are deductible only to the extent of capital gains, whether they are short- or long-term. Therefore, a net capital loss is not deductible against ordinary income in the tax year incurred. The corporation has taxable income of $90,000 ($150,000 + $35,000 – $95,000).

Answer (A) is incorrect. Capital losses are deductible only to the extent of capital gains; therefore, a net capital loss is not deductible against ordinary income in the tax year incurred. Answer (B) is incorrect. Only individuals (not corporations) are allowed to deduct up to $3,000 of net capital losses in the current year. Corporations may only deduct capital losses up to the amount of capital gains. Answer (D) is incorrect. Both gross receipts and other income are additions (increases) to taxable income. In addition, there are other reductions to taxable income to consider in this problem.

17. Wonder, Inc., had 2017 taxable income of $200,000 exclusive of the following:

Gain on sale of land used in business	$25,000
Loss on sale of machinery used in business	(13,000)
Loss on sale of securities held 3 years	(4,000)
Loss on sale of securities held 3 months	(3,000)

On what amount of taxable income should Wonder compute tax?

A. $200,000

B. $202,500

C. $205,000

D. $212,000

Answer (C) is correct.

REQUIRED: The taxable income of a corporation with both capital and Sec. 1231 gains and losses.

DISCUSSION: The sale of the land and the sale of machinery used in the business are Sec. 1231 transactions, if held more than 1 year. Since the gain and loss net to a gain of $12,000, they are a long-term capital gain and loss. The capital losses on the securities are fully deductible because they do not exceed the $12,000 net Sec. 1231 gain.

Answer (A) is incorrect. Net capital gain constitutes taxable income. Answer (B) is incorrect. The Code allows no deduction for net capital gains. Answer (D) is incorrect. The net Sec. 1231 gain is treated as capital gain and is already included in taxable income.

9.5 Reconciling Book and Taxable Income

18. In the current year, Starke Corp., an accrual-basis, calendar-year corporation, reported book income of $380,000. Included in that amount was $50,000 municipal bond interest income, $170,000 for federal income tax expense, and $2,000 interest expense on the debt incurred to carry the municipal bonds. What amount should Starke's taxable income be as reconciled on Starke's Schedule M-1 of Form 1120, *U.S. Corporation Income Tax Return*?

- A. $330,000
- B. $500,000
- C. $502,000
- D. $550,000

Answer (C) is correct.
  REQUIRED: The corporation's taxable income given book income and some of its components.
  DISCUSSION: The municipal bond income and the related interest expenses are not considered for tax purposes. The federal tax expense is not deductible for federal income tax purposes. Therefore, the net Schedule M-1 adjustment of $122,000 ($2,000 + $170,000 – $50,000) results in taxable income of $502,000 ($380,000 + $122,000).
  Answer (A) is incorrect. The $170,000 income tax expense and the $2,000 interest expense on the municipal bonds are positive adjustments to book income. Answer (B) is incorrect. Interest expense on tax-exempt investments is not deductible. Answer (D) is incorrect. The $50,000 of municipal bond interest is a negative adjustment, and $2,000 of related interest expense is a positive adjustment.

19. Would the following expense items be reported on Schedule M-1 of the corporation income tax return showing the reconciliation of income per books with income per return?

	Interest Incurred on Loan to Carry U.S. Obligations	Provision for State Corporation Income Tax
A.	Yes	Yes
B.	No	No
C.	Yes	No
D.	No	Yes

Answer (B) is correct.
  REQUIRED: The item reported on Schedule M-1.
  DISCUSSION: Items treated differently in computing income per books and taxable income are reported and reconciled on Schedule M-1. Items treated the same for financial and tax purposes are not reported on the schedule. Both interest to carry U.S. obligations and state income tax are deducted in computing book income and taxable income.

20. In the reconciliation of income per books with income per return,

- A. Only temporary differences are considered.
- B. Only permanent differences are considered.
- C. Both temporary and permanent differences are considered.
- D. Neither temporary nor permanent differences are considered.

Answer (C) is correct.
  REQUIRED: The differences included in the reconciliation of income per books with income per return.
  DISCUSSION: Reconciling income per books with income per return considers both temporary differences (i.e., differences expected to be eliminated in the future, such as an accelerated method of depreciation for tax purposes and a straight-line method for financial reporting purposes) and permanent differences (i.e., differences not expected to be eliminated in the future, such as that caused by the deduction of federal income tax for financial reporting purposes).
  Answer (A) is incorrect. Permanent differences must be reconciled. Answer (B) is incorrect. Temporary differences must be reconciled. Answer (D) is incorrect. Both temporary and permanent differences must be reconciled.

STUDY UNIT TEN
CORPORATE TAX COMPUTATIONS

(20 pages of outline)

The only credits explained in the corporate tax study unit are the foreign tax credit and the minimum tax credit. Like the alternative minimum tax, these credits also apply to individuals. The subject matter appears here because it has been tested most commonly in the corporate context. Candidates should also review the general business credit and its limits discussed in Study Unit 7, Subunit 1, which also apply to corporations.

Some candidates find it helpful to have the entire tax form side-by-side with our Knowledge Transfer Outline when studying. The full versions of the most up-to-date forms are easily accessible at www.gleim.com/taxforms. These forms and the form excerpts used in our outline are periodically updated as the latest versions are released by the IRS.

10.1 REGULAR INCOME TAX

1. **Tax Brackets**

   a. Section 11 imposes tax on the taxable income of most corporations using a multi-bracket graduated rate system.

   If Taxable Income Is

Over	But Not Over	The Tax Is	Of the Amount Over
$ 0	$ 50,000	15%	$ 0
50,000	75,000	$ 7,500 + 25%	50,000
75,000	100,000	13,750 + 34%	75,000
100,000	335,000	22,250 + 39%	100,000
335,000	10,000,000	113,900 + 34%	335,000
10,000,000	15,000,000	3,400,000 + 35%	10,000,000
15,000,000	18,333,333	5,150,000 + 38%	15,000,000
18,333,333		6,416,667 + 35%	18,333,333

2. **Surtax**

   a. Two of the rate brackets include surtaxes.

   b. A surtax of 5% is charged on taxable income (TI) between $100,000 and $335,000, which eliminates the tax savings on the first $100,000 of taxable income from the benefits of 15% and 25% rates.

   c. A 3% surtax is charged on TI between $15,000,000 and $18,333,333, which recaptures the tax savings from $335,000 to $10,000,000 by phasing out the 34% rate.

EXAMPLE

Little Corporation had $175,000 of taxable income in the ordinary course of business that does not include a $30,000 capital gain. The tax on the taxable income is $51,500 {$22,250 + [($175,000 – $100,000) × 39%]} and the tax on the capital gain is $11,700 [$30,000 × (35% tax rate + 4% surtax)]. Little Corporation's total regular federal income tax is $63,200 ($51,500 + $11,700).

3. **Top Rate**

   a.   All TI of a corporation with TI over $18,333,333 is taxed at a flat rate of 35%.

   b.   The alternative tax on a corporation's net capital gain (when regular rates exceed 35%) is not applicable (currently). Thus, long-term capital gain of a corporation does not receive preferred treatment. The two surtaxes apply.

   c.   Personal service corporations are taxed at a flat rate of 35% on all taxable income.

   d.   A controlled group of corporations (which is discussed in Subunit 10.4) must allocate a single application of reduced rates for lower brackets between them. Rates are applied to the aggregate TI of the group as if the group were a single corporation.

4. **Disallowed Corporate Credits**

   a.   Most tax credits are allowable to corporations. However, the following are not permitted:

   1)   Earned Income Credit
   2)   Child and Dependent Care Credit
   3)   Elderly and Disabled Credit
   4)   Child Tax Credit
   5)   Adoption Credit
   6)   American Opportunity Credit
   7)   Lifetime Learning Credit

Stop and review! You have completed the outline for this subunit. Study multiple-choice questions 1 and 2 on page 296.

10.2 FOREIGN TAX CREDIT (FTC)

1. **Election Options**

   a.   A taxpayer may elect either a credit or a deduction for taxes paid to other countries or U.S. possessions.

2. **Credit Application**

   a.   Generally, the FTC is applied against gross tax liability after the AMT (alternative minimum tax) but before all other credits.

3. **Other Taxes**

   a.   The FTC may offset **AMT** liability. However, the FTC is not creditable against the **AET (accumulated earnings tax)** or the **PHC (personal holding company) tax**.

4. **Pass-Through Entities**

   a.   Pass-through entities apportion the foreign taxes among the partners, shareholders (of an S corporation), or beneficiaries (of an estate). The individuals elect and compute a credit or deduction on their personal returns.

5. **Non-U.S. Taxpayer**

   a.   For a non-U.S. taxpayer, the FTC is allowed only for foreign taxes paid on income effectively connected with conduct of a trade or business in the U.S. and against U.S. tax on the effectively connected income.

6. **Qualified Foreign Taxes**

   a.   Qualified foreign taxes (QFTs) include foreign taxes on income, war profits, and excess profits.

   b.   QFTs must be analogous to the U.S. income tax.

   1)   They must be based on a form of net annual income, including gain.
   2)   Concepts such as realization should be incorporated into the tax structure.

    c.   Foreign taxes paid on foreign earned income or housing costs excluded as excessive may neither be credited nor deducted.

    d.   Deemed QFT. A domestic corporation that owns at least 10% (voting) of a foreign corporation is deemed to have paid foreign taxes paid by the foreign corporation on income that it distributed to the domestic corporation as a dividend.

7.   **FTC Limit**

    a.   The maximum amount of tax that may be credited is computed using the following formula:

$$FTC = U.S.\ income\ tax^1 \times \frac{Foreign\ source\ taxable\ income^2}{Worldwide\ taxable\ income}$$

       [1] *Before the FTC*
       [2] *Not more than total TI*

    b.   The limit must be applied separately to nonbusiness interest income and all other income.

    c.   The amount used for TI in the numerator and denominator is regular TI with adjustments. For example, an individual must add back personal exemptions.

    d.   The current allowance of FTC is the lesser of (1) foreign tax paid or (2) maximum amount of tax allowed (FTC limit).

8.   **Carryover**

    a.   Foreign tax paid in excess of the FTC limit may be carried back 1 year and forward 10 years in chronological order.

        1)   The carryover is treated as foreign tax paid subject to the FTC limit.

        2)   The carryover may not be applied in any year when a deduction for foreign taxes is taken (in lieu of the FTC).

EXAMPLE

A client paid $400,000 in qualified foreign taxes. The corporation had $1,000,000 in foreign source taxable income and $10,000,000 in worldwide taxable income. If the corporation had a $3,400,000 U.S. income tax liability before the FTC, its FTC limit would be calculated as follows:

           FTC Limit = $3,400,000 × ($1,000,000 ÷ $10,000,000)

           FTC Limit = $340,000

Thus, the client's FTC is $340,000, the lesser of foreign taxes paid and the FTC limit. The client may carry the remaining $60,000 ($400,000 in foreign taxes paid – $340,000 allowed credit) FTC back 1 year and any unused amount is then carried forward for up to 10 years.

Stop and review! You have completed the outline for this subunit. Study multiple-choice questions 3 and 4 on page 297.

10.3 CONSOLIDATED RETURNS

1.   **Overview**

    a.   A single federal income tax return may be filed by two or more includible corporations that are members of an affiliated group.

2. **Includible corporations** are all corporations **except** the following:

    a. Tax-exempt corporations
    b. S corporations
    c. Foreign sales corporations (FSCs)
    d. Insurance corporations
    e. REITs (real estate investment trusts)
    f. Regulated investment companies
    g. DISCs (domestic international sales corporations)
    h. Corporations that claim Sec. 936 possessions tax credit

3. **Affiliated Groups**

    a. An affiliated group includes each corporation in a chain of corporations under the following conditions:

        1) The other group members must directly own stock in the corporation that represents both

            a) 80% or more of total voting power **and**
            b) 80% or more of total value outstanding.

        2) A parent corporation must directly own stock as outlined in 1) above (80% voting and value) of at least one includible corporation.

4. **Election**

    a. Election to file a consolidated return is made by the act of filing a consolidated return.
    b. Consent of each included corporation is required.
    c. Consolidated financial statements or IRS approval is not required to file a consolidated return.
    d. Consent of the IRS is required to terminate an election.
    e. Controlled group restrictions (mandatory rules for certain related companies) apply without regard to some of its members filing a consolidated return.

5. **Tax Year**

    a. Each subsidiary included in a consolidated return must adopt the parent's tax year.

6. **Accounting Methods**

    a. One or more members of a controlled group filing a consolidated return may use the cash method, and one or more others may use the accrual method.

7. **Consolidation**

    a. The corporations remove from taxable income (TI) items that are separately consolidated or that are treated specially. Net TI is consolidated and then adjusted for the items removed after separate consolidation.
    b. **Items that are consolidated separately** include the following:

        1) Charitable contribution deductions
        2) Dividends received and paid deductions
        3) Percentage depletion of mineral properties
        4) NOL deductions
        5) Section 1231 gains and losses
        6) Capital gains and losses

8. **Dividends on a Consolidated Return**

    a. A dividend distributed by one consolidated corporation to another is eliminated.
    b. The dividends-received deduction (DRD) is not allowed for such dividends.
    c. A deduction for dividends received from corporations outside the consolidating group is computed on a consolidated basis.

9.   **Losses**

   a.   Losses of one consolidating corporation may offset TI of another. Consolidated NOL is computed using consolidated items (aggregate of consolidating corporations' separate items) as follows:

>   **TI (Separate net TI)**
>   + Net capital gain
>   − Section 1231 net loss
>   − Charitable contribution deduction
>   − Dividends-received deduction
>   − Dividends-paid deduction
>   = **Consolidated NOL**

   b.   Carryover of a consolidated NOL is allowed only to a prior or subsequent year of a consolidation election. Special rules apply when members change.

10. **Intercompany Transactions**

   a.   An intercompany transaction is a transaction between corporations that are members of the same consolidated group. In the consolidated tax return, any gain or loss realized on the intercompany transaction is deferred.

   b.   A single-entity approach is used to resolve the deferred gain or loss.

   c.   For consolidation purposes, the buyer in the intercompany transaction assumes the same basis and holding period as the selling member. The consolidated gain or loss is recognized upon the happening of an event such as

   1)   The acquiring corporation claiming depreciation
   2)   One of the members leaving the consolidated group
   3)   Disposition of the property outside of the consolidated group

   d.   The character of the recognized gain or loss is determined with reference to the consolidated group member holding the property immediately before the recognition event.

EXAMPLE

P and S are two affiliated corporations that file consolidated tax returns. P sells an asset held for investment (i.e., a capital asset) to S at a gain of $10,000. S holds the property as inventory and sells to an unrelated party at an additional gain of $5,000. Under the single-entity approach, the consolidated entity recognizes $15,000 of ordinary income upon the sale to the outside party.

---

   e.   In certain other intercompany transactions, the income and expense items net each other out.

 The AICPA has tested candidates' knowledge of the rules and regulations for filing consolidated returns. Most of the released AICPA questions test the theory and do not require calculations.

Stop and review! You have completed the outline for this subunit. Study multiple-choice questions 5 through 7 beginning on page 297.

10.4 CONTROLLED GROUPS

1. **Definition**

    a. A controlled group of corporations includes corporations with a specified degree of relationship by stock ownership.

2. **Parent-Subsidiary Controlled Group**

    a. This type of controlled group consists of

    1) Two corporations if one of the corporations owns stock that represents

        a) 80% or more of total voting power **or**
        b) 80% or more of total value outstanding of the stock of the other

    2) Any other corporation that meets the requirements in 1) above (if the two corporations discussed there and others in the group own stock in it)

    b. A member of a controlled group need not use a parent's tax year.

EXAMPLE

Each corporation has a single class of stock. P owns 80% of S stock. P and S each own 40% of O stock. P, S, and O each own 30% of T stock. P, S, O, and T are a controlled group.

---

3. **Brother-Sister Controlled Group**

    a. Any two or more corporations are considered a brother-sister controlled group if the stock of each is owned by the same five or fewer persons (only individuals, trusts, or estates)

    1) Represents either

        a) 80% or more of voting power of all classes or
        b) 80% or more of value of all classes and

    2) Represents either (counting for each person only the smallest amount owned by that person in any of the corporations)

        a) More than 50% of voting power of all classes or
        b) More than 50% of value of all classes.

EXAMPLE

Alpha, Bravo, and Charley Corporations, each with one class of stock, have the following ownership:

	80% Test			
Shareholders	Alpha	Bravo	Charley	50% Test
Mike	45%	5%	30%	5%
Sierra	30%	65%	10%	10%
Oscar	25%	30%	60%	25%
	100%	100%	100%	40%

Alpha, Bravo, and Charley passed the 80% test but not the 50% test and therefore are not a controlled brother-sister group.

---

4. **Rights** to acquire stock are treated as the stock would be.

5. **Constructive Ownership**

    a. Stock both actually and constructively owned is counted. Generally, a person constructively owns stock owned by a

    1) Family member [spouse (not legally separated), child, grandchild, parent, or grandparent] and

    2) Corporation, partnership, estate, or trust

        a) In which (s)he has a 5% or more interest
        b) In proportion to that interest

6. **Limit on Tax Benefits**

    a.   Each of the following is an example of tax benefit items of which only one must be shared by the members of a controlled group:

        1)   Tax brackets
        2)   Section 179 expensing maximum of $510,000
        3)   AMT exemption base of $40,000
        4)   General business credit $25,000 offset
        5)   AET $250,000 presumed deduction base

    NOTE: A controlled group generally may choose any method to allocate the amounts among themselves. By default, an item is divided equally among members.

EXAMPLE

Brother Bill, Inc., and Sister Suzie, Inc., are brother-sister corporations. Before considering the impact of the controlled group, Brother Bill has a tax liability of $40,000 and is eligible for a $15,000 general business credit, and Sister Suzie has a tax liability of $100,000 and is eligible for a $20,000 general business credit. Controlled groups must split the $25,000 general business credit among the members. By default, both corporations receive a $12,500 general business credit. However, Brother Bill and Sister Suzie may allocate the general business credit in any manner that is agreed upon.

---

7. **Intergroup Transactions**

    a.   Anti-avoidance rules apply to transactions between members of a controlled group.

    b.   Loss is not recognized when property is sold by one member of a controlled group to another.

        1)   The loss may be recognized on a subsequent sale to an unrelated third party.

    c.   Expenditure to a controlled group member is not deductible before being included in the income of the payee.

    d.   Gain on sale or exchange of property by a controlled group member to a member in whose hands the property is depreciable is treated as ordinary income.

    e.   The IRS is authorized to redetermine the price for property transferred between members of a controlled group.

        1)   To reflect income clearly or to prevent tax evasion, the price may be redetermined to reflect an arm's-length price.

        2)   Three methods to determine an arm's-length price are by reference to

            a)   Comparable uncontrolled prices
            b)   Resale prices
            c)   Cost plus return

Stop and review! You have completed the outline for this subunit. Study multiple-choice questions 8 and 9 beginning on page 298. Note that these are questions on consolidated returns as well as controlled groups.

10.5 ALTERNATIVE MINIMUM TAX (AMT)

1. **AMT Formula**

    a.   The alternative minimum tax is an income tax in addition to the regular income tax. The formula for computing AMT is illustrated within the example at the end of this subunit.

    b.   Use Form 4626, *Alternative Minimum Tax – Corporations*, to determine the AMT for a corporation.

        1)   **Consolidated returns.** For an affiliated group filing a consolidated return, AMT must be figured on a consolidated basis.

Form 4626

Department of the Treasury
Internal Revenue Service

Alternative Minimum Tax—Corporations

▶ Attach to the corporation's tax return.
▶ Information about Form 4626 and its separate instructions is at *www.irs.gov/form4626*.

OMB No. 1545-0123

[Year]

Name

Employer identification number

Note: *See the instructions to find out if the corporation is a small corporation exempt from the alternative minimum tax (AMT) under section 55(e).*

1	Taxable income or (loss) before net operating loss deduction	**1**
2	**Adjustments and preferences:**	
a	Depreciation of post-1986 property	**2a**
b	Amortization of certified pollution control facilities.	**2b**
c	Amortization of mining exploration and development costs	**2c**
d	Amortization of circulation expenditures (personal holding companies only)	**2d**
e	Adjusted gain or loss	**2e**
f	Long-term contracts	**2f**
g	Merchant marine capital construction funds.	**2g**
h	Section 833(b) deduction (Blue Cross, Blue Shield, and similar type organizations only)	**2h**
i	Tax shelter farm activities (personal service corporations only)	**2i**
j	Passive activities (closely held corporations and personal service corporations only)	**2j**
k	Loss limitations	**2k**
l	Depletion	**2l**
m	Tax-exempt interest income from specified private activity bonds	**2m**
n	Intangible drilling costs	**2n**
o	Other adjustments and preferences	**2o**
3	Pre-adjustment alternative minimum taxable income (AMTI). Combine lines 1 through 2o.	**3**
4	**Adjusted current earnings (ACE) adjustment:**	
a	ACE from line 10 of the ACE worksheet in the instructions	**4a**
b	Subtract line 3 from line 4a. If line 3 exceeds line 4a, enter the difference as a negative amount. See instructions	**4b**
c	Multiply line 4b by 75% (0.75). Enter the result as a positive amount.	**4c**
d	Enter the excess, if any, of the corporation's total increases in AMTI from prior year ACE adjustments over its total reductions in AMTI from prior year ACE adjustments. See instructions. **Note:** *You **must** enter an amount on line 4d (even if line 4b is positive).*	**4d**
e	ACE adjustment.	
	• If line 4b is zero or more, enter the amount from line 4c	**4e**
	• If line 4b is less than zero, enter the **smaller** of line 4c or line 4d as a negative amount	
5	Combine lines 3 and 4e. If zero or less, stop here; the corporation does not owe any AMT	**5**
6	Alternative tax net operating loss deduction. See instructions	**6**
7	**Alternative minimum taxable income.** Subtract line 6 from line 5. If the corporation held a residual interest in a REMIC, see instructions	**7**
8	**Exemption phase-out** (if line 7 is $310,000 or more, skip lines 8a and 8b and enter -0- on line 8c):	
a	Subtract $150,000 from line 7 (if completing this line for a member of a controlled group, see instructions). If zero or less, enter -0-	**8a**
b	Multiply line 8a by 25% (0.25)	**8b**
c	Exemption. Subtract line 8b from $40,000 (if completing this line for a member of a controlled group, see instructions). If zero or less, enter -0-	**8c**
9	Subtract line 8c from line 7. If zero or less, enter -0-	**9**
10	Multiply line 9 by 20% (0.20)	**10**
11	Alternative minimum tax foreign tax credit (AMTFTC). See instructions	**11**
12	Tentative minimum tax. Subtract line 11 from line 10	**12**
13	Regular tax liability before applying all credits except the foreign tax credit	**13**
14	**Alternative minimum tax.** Subtract line 13 from line 12. If zero or less, enter -0-. Enter here and on Form 1120, Schedule J, line 3, or the appropriate line of the corporation's income tax return	**14**

For Paperwork Reduction Act Notice, see separate instructions.   Cat. No. 12955I   Form **4626** [Year]

    2) The generalized structure is presented below.

  c. AMT income (AMTI) is based on taxable income (TI).

    1) AMTI is TI after amounts are added or subtracted for tax preferences, adjustments, and loss limitations.

    2) The AMT base is AMTI reduced by an exemption amount and any AMT NOL carryover.

  d. Tentative AMT is determined by first multiplying a rate times the AMT base and then subtracting the AMT foreign tax credit.

    1) For corporations, a 20% rate applies.

    2) For individuals, a two-tiered graduated rate schedule applies.

      a) A 26% rate applies to the first $187,800 ($93,900 if married filing separately) of AMTI (net of the exemption amount).

      b) A 28% rate applies to any excess.

  e. AMT is the excess tentative AMT over regular income tax.

  f. AMT must be reported and paid at the same time as regular tax liability.

  g. Estimated payments of AMT are required.

2. **Tax Preference Items**

  a. These items generate tax savings by reducing the taxpayer's taxable income. Therefore, they must be added back to taxable income when computing AMTI.

    1) Private activity bonds (other than those **issued** in 2009 and 2010). Add any tax-exempt interest minus expenses (including interest) attributable to earning it.

    2) Percentage depletion. Add any excess of deduction claimed over adjusted basis.

    3) Intangible drilling costs (IDC). Add any excess of IDC amortized over 10 years over 65% of net income from oil, gas, and geothermal properties.

3. **Adjustments**

  a. Usually, adjustments eliminate "time value" tax savings from accelerated deductions or deferral of income. An adjustment is an increase or a decrease to TI in computing AMTI.

  b. Adjustments affecting corporate and noncorporate taxpayers:

    1) Accelerated depreciation

      a) Real property. The AMT allowable amount is computed using a straight-line method, 40-year recovery period, and the mid-month convention.

      b) Personal property. Generally, the AMT allowable amount is computed using the 150%-declining-balance method and changing to the straight-line method when it yields a larger amount.

      c) Section 1250 property placed in service after December 31, 1998, does not require an adjustment, as all of it is depreciated using a straight-line method.

    2) Installment sales. The installment method is not allowed for a disposition of stock in trade in the ordinary course of business (e.g., inventory). Add any balance (+ or −) of current-year gain recognized, disregarding the installment method, minus gain recognized under the installment method.

    3) Long-term contracts. The percentage-of-completion method must be used to determine AMTI. Add any balance (+ or −) if the completed-contract or cash-basis method is normally used.

      a) The same percentage of completion must be used for AMT and regular tax.

          b)   Small construction contracts require a simplified method of allocating costs in applying the percentage-of-completion method. The contract's estimated duration must be less than 2 years.

          c)   No AMT adjustment is made for home construction contracts.

    4)   Pollution control facilities (certified). For facilities placed in service after 1998, calculate the amortization deduction for AMT under MACRS using the straight-line method. Add any balance (+ or −).

    5)   Mining exploration and development. If these expenditures were expensed for regular tax purposes, the expenditures must be capitalized and amortized over a 10-year period for AMT. Add any balance for the difference.

          a)   Tax loss. If a worthless mine is abandoned, expenditures capitalized but unamortized can be deducted from AMTI.

    6)   Net operating loss adjustments. To determine the NOL amount for AMT,

          a)   Subtract all amounts added to TI as tax preference amounts, to the extent they increased the regular tax NOL.

          b)   Tax adjustments made for the AMTI calculation must be made for the NOL calculation.

  c.   Adjustments affecting only noncorporate taxpayers:

    1)   Research and experimental expenditures. Add any balance (+ or −) of regular tax deduction claimed for the year (normally expensed), minus expenditures capitalized and amortized over 10 years (beginning in year made).

    2)   Circulation expenditures. Add any balance (+ or −) of regular tax deduction for the year (normally expensed), minus the expenditures capitalized and amortized over 3 years (beginning in year made).

    3)   Incentive stock option (ISO). Add any balance (+ or −) of the FMV of the stock when exercised, minus the amount paid for stock.

  d.   Adjustments affecting only corporate taxpayers:

    1)   ACE adjustment (covered below).

4. **ACE Adjustment**

  a.   A corporation must make an additional adjustment (upward or downward) to TI, the adjusted current earnings (ACE) adjustment, in computing AMTI.

    1)   When computing ACE for AMTI, the AMTI amount is gross of the ACE adjustment and the AMT NOL deduction.

    2)   ACE is not the same as earnings and profits but is based on undistributed corporate earnings.

  b.   Adjustments to AMTI to compute ACE include the following:

    1)   Organizational expenditures amortized and deducted (Sec. 248) are added.

    2)   The 70% dividends-received deduction attributable to < 20%-owned corporations is added.

    3)   Life insurance proceeds on a corporate officer are added.

    4)   The installment method on nondealer sales is disregarded unless interest is paid.

    5)   LIFO recapture must be recorded for the excess of FIFO inventory valuation over LIFO inventory valuation.

    6)   Depreciation is computed using the alternative depreciation system method. AMT basis is used.

          a)   For corporations, this adjustment is not required for property placed in service after 1993.

    7)   Tax exempt interest.

    c.   Not requiring adjustment for ACE are the following:

        1)   Long-term capital gains
        2)   DRD of 80% or 100% of dividends received
        3)   Discharge of debt income excluded by Sec. 108 (state and local bonds)
        4)   Tax-exempt interest from state and local bonds issued in 2009 and 2010

    d.   Amount of ACE adjustment = (ACE − AMTI) × 75%.

        1)   AMTI is gross of the ACE adjustment and NOL deduction.
        2)   Add the ACE adjustment amount if ACE > AMTI.
        3)   Subtract the ACE adjustment amount if ACE < AMTI.

            a)   Limit negative ACE adjustments to prior years'

                i)   Aggregate positive ACE adjustments, minus
                ii) Aggregate negative ACE adjustments.

EXAMPLE

From its Form 4626, Corporation A has an ACE of $25,000. If Corporation A has pre-adjustment AMTI in the three scenario amounts shown below, the difference between ACE and AMTI amounts is calculated as follows to determine the amount to be multiplied by 75%.

	Scenario 1	Scenario 2	Scenario 3
ACE	$25,000	$25,000	$25,000
Pre-adjustment AMTI	10,000	30,000	(50,000)
Difference to be multiplied by 75%	$15,000	$ (5,000)	$75,000

---

5. **AMT NOL**

    a.   The alternative minimum tax net operating loss (AMT NOL) is technically an adjustment to taxable income (TI). After tax preferences have been computed and added to TI and all other adjustments have been computed and made, one of the two AMT NOL adjustment steps is performed.

    b.   NOL year. Compute the AMT NOL. It is carried back or forward to another tax year.

        1)   The AMT NOL is modified for each of the tax preferences and other adjustments for the current tax year.

    c.   Profit year. An AMT NOL is a final adjustment to TI in computing AMTI in a tax year in which (before reduction by part or all of unused AMT NOLs) there is AMT base.

        1)   Limit: 90% of AMTI. Alternative NOL may not offset more than 90% of the AMTI (computed without the alternative NOL deduction).

6. **AMT Exemption**

    a.   An exemption is allowed that reduces AMTI to produce the AMTI base.

        1)   The basic exemption is phased out at $0.25 for each dollar of AMTI above a threshold.
        2)   All members of a controlled group must share the exemption amount.
        3)   The basic exemption for a corporation is $40,000.
        4)   The AMT exemption is phased out beginning when AMTI is $150,000 and is fully phased out when AMTI is $310,000.

7. **AMT FTC**

    a.   Only one credit is allowed in computing AMT: the AMT foreign tax credit (FTC). The AMT FTC is the lower of

        1)   The FTC or
        2)   90% of gross tentative AMT computed before any AMT NOL deduction and FTC.

8. **Minimum Tax Credit (MTC)**

a. A credit is allowed for AMT paid in a tax year against regular tax liability in 1 or more subsequent tax years.

b. **Individuals.** The MTC amount is the AMT that would have been computed if the only adjustments made to TI in computing AMTI were those for (tax-favored) items that result in deferral, as opposed to exclusion, of income. To compute the MTC amount, recompute the most recent year's AMT without adjustment for the following (exclusion) items and add carryover MTC:

1) Standard deduction
2) Personal exemptions deduction
3) Miscellaneous itemized deductions
4) Tax-exempt interest on private activity bonds (not necessary for bonds issued in 2009 or 2010)
5) Qualified interest expense (qualified mortgage interest, investment interest, etc.)
6) Charitable contributions of appreciated property
7) Medical expenses
8) Depletion
9) Taxes

c. **Corporations.** A corporation's credit for AMT is for both deferred items and exclusion items.

d. The MTC allowable is limited to current-year gross regular tax (reduced by certain credits) minus current-year tentative minimum tax.

> **Gross regular tax**
> – Credits
> – Tentative minimum tax (for current year)
> = **MTC maximum allowable**

1) The current-year gross regular tax amount is reduced by the amount currently allowable for each of the following:

   a) Refundable credits
   b) Nonrefundable personal credits
   c) Foreign tax, drug testing, nonconventional source fuel credits
   d) General business credit

e. Any MTC amount beyond the current limit may be carried forward indefinitely.

EXAMPLE

Corc Corporation has a minimum tax credit from Year 1 of $98,000. For Year 2, it had a total tax liability of $70,000, including $63,000 tentative minimum tax. For Years 3 and 4, it had losses and no tentative minimum tax or regular corporate tax liability. The Year 5 tax liability is undetermined. Corc Corporation is not exempt from alternative minimum tax.

Corporations are allowed a credit for the full amount of AMT paid in a tax year against regular tax liability in one or more subsequent tax year(s). Any minimum tax credit amount is carried forward indefinitely.

Year 2		
Available MTC (from Year 1)		$98,000
Total tax liability (regular tax)	$70,000	
Tentative minimum tax	(63,000)	
Maximum MTC allowed		7,000
MTC carryforward		$91,000
Years 3-4		
MTC available	$91,000	
MTC used	0	
MTC available for Year 5	$91,000	

9.   **Small Corporations**

 a.   Certain "small corporations" are exempt from the AMT.

  1) A corporation will initially qualify as a small corporation if it had average gross receipts of $5 million or less for the 3 years that ended with its first tax year beginning after December 31, 1996.

  2) Small corporation status is maintained as long as average gross receipts for the prior 3 years do not exceed $7.5 million.

 b.   If a small corporation has average gross receipts exceeding $7.5 million, it will lose its small corporation status and be liable for the AMT.

COMPUTATIONAL EXAMPLE

AMT COMPUTATIONS

Taxable income (for regular tax)			$200,000
Tax preference items (+)			
Excess depletion	$15,000		
Tax-exempt bonds [1]	25,000	$ 40,000	
Adjustment items (+/−)			
Depreciation on machinery			
($150 − $105)	$45,000		
Mining exploration costs	15,000	60,000	
Pre-adjustment AMTI		$300,000	
ACE adjustment (see computation at right)		60,000	
AMT NOL deduction		(20,000)	
AMTI		$340,000	
Less: AMT exemption (see computation at right)		0	
AMTI (the base)		$340,000	
Rate for AMT		× .20	
Gross tentative AMT		$ 68,000	
Foreign tax credit (AMT)		0	
Tentative minimum tax		$ 68,000	
Less: Regular tax		(62,500)	
AMT		**$ 5,500**	

ACE Adjustment

Pre-adjustment AMTI	$300,000
Installment sales	80,000
ACE	$380,000
Pre-adjustment AMTI	300,000
Difference	$ 80,000
Times: Percentage	× .75
ACE adjustment	$ 60,000

AMT Exemption

Basic exemption		$ 40,000
Less:		
AMTI	$340,000	
Threshold	(150,000)	
Excess	$190,000	
Times: Percentage	× .25	
Phaseout amount		47,500
AMT exemption		$ 0

[1] No adjustment for amounts attributed to bonds issued in 2009 and 2010.

Stop and review! You have completed the outline for this subunit. Study multiple-choice questions 10 and 11 on page 299.

10.6 ESTIMATED TAX

1. **Due Dates**

 a.   A corporation is required to make estimated tax payments on the 15th day of the 4th, 6th, 9th, and 12th months of the tax year.

 b.   Any difference between the estimated tax and actual tax is due with the return by the 15th day of the 4th month following the end of the tax year (April 15 for calendar-year C corporations). The change from the 3rd month to the 4th first applied to C corporations whose tax year began after December 31, 2015.

 c.   An extension of time to file the tax return does not provide an extension of time to pay the tax liability without incurring interest and/or penalty.

2. **Estimated Payments**

 a.   Tax includes the regular income tax and the AMT, net of credits and payments.

 b.   Each quarterly estimated tax payment required is 25% of the lesser of

  1) 100% of the prior year's tax (provided a tax liability existed and the preceding tax year was 12 months) or

  2) 100% of the current year's tax.

NOTE: Any increase in estimated tax during the year should be reconciled and paid on the next estimated payment.

    c.   A corporation with uneven income flows can make its estimated tax payments by annualizing its income.

        1)   A corporation has the option of annualizing income and paying its estimated taxes accordingly.

        2)   If income in later quarters is greater than in prior quarters, the estimated tax payments must be increased so that 100% of the shortfall is covered.

    d.   Paying 100% of the prior year's tax is not an option for a large corporation.

        1)   A large corporation may make its first quarter estimated tax payment based on the preceding year's tax liability and make up any difference in its second quarter payment.

            a)   A large corporation is one with taxable income of $1 million or more during any of the 3 preceding years.

3.   **Penalty**

    a.   A penalty is imposed in the amount by which any required installment exceeds estimated tax paid multiplied by the federal short-term rate plus 5% (3% for individuals).

    b.   The penalty accrues from the installment due date until the underpayment is paid or, if earlier, the due date for filing the tax return.

    c.   The penalty is not allowed as an interest deduction.

    d.   If any underpayment of estimated tax is indicated by the tax return, Form 2220 should be submitted with the return.

EXAMPLE

Fad Corporation paid $4 million in taxes in Year 1, causing it to be considered a large corporation. In Year 2, Fad had a tax liability of $10 million. Incorrectly relying on its Year 1 tax liability, Fad paid the Year 2 quarterly estimated taxes of $1 million on April 15, June 15, September 15, and December 15, Year 2. Assuming income was not seasonal, each payment fell short by $1.5 million [($10 million ÷ 4 quarters) – $1 million]. Assuming a 0.5% short-term federal interest rate, interest of 5.5% accrues from each of the payment dates until Fad pays the outstanding taxes on March 31, Year 3. To have avoided the penalty, Fad should have made an adjustment following the first quarter, paying the difference in the second quarter.

---

    e.   **No** estimated tax penalty is imposed if

        1)   Tax liability shown on the return for the tax year is less than $500
        2)   The IRS waives all or part of the penalty for good cause
        3)   An erroneous IRS notice to a large corporation is withdrawn by the IRS

4.   **Refund**

    a.   A corporation may obtain a quick refund of estimated tax paid, but adjustment is allowed only if the overpayment is both ≥ $500 and ≥ 10% of the corporation's estimate of its tax liability.

    b.   Application is filed (Form 4466) after the close of the tax year but before the return due date (without extensions).

Stop and review! You have completed the outline for this subunit. Study multiple-choice questions 12 and 13 beginning on page 299.

10.7 ACCUMULATED EARNINGS TAX (AET)

1.   **Application**

    a.   The AET is imposed only on a corporation that, for the purpose of avoiding income tax at the shareholder level, allows earnings and profits to accumulate instead of distributing them to shareholders.

    b.   A corporation is presumed to have the avoidance purpose or intent to the extent it accumulates (does not distribute) earnings beyond its (reasonable) business needs.

2. **Reasonable Needs of the Business**

    a.   AET is based on the excess of undistributed current earnings over the increase in the reasonable needs of the business.

        1)   Reasonable needs of a business include only those items required to meet future needs and for which there are specific, foreseeable plans for use.

        NOTE: Most businesses are able to avoid the AET by documenting reasonable needs of the business periodically.

    b.   Reasonable needs might include the following:

        1)   Raw materials purchase
        2)   Equipment update
        3)   Expansion of production facilities
        4)   Retirement of business debt
        5)   Redeeming stock in gross estate of a shareholder
        6)   Product liability loss reserves
        7)   Realistic business contingencies
        8)   Acquiring a related business
        9)   Investments or loans to suppliers or customers
        10) Working capital

    c.   The following are **not** considered reasonable needs of a business. Any of them may trigger determination of AET liability.

        1)   Funding plans to

            a)   Declare a stock dividend or
            b)   Redeem stock of a shareholder

        2)   Unrealistic business hazard protection
        3)   Investment property unrelated to business activities of the corporation
        4)   Loans to shareholders

3. **Penalty**

    a.   The tax of 20% imposed on accumulated taxable income is a penalty tax in addition to the regular income tax and AMT.

    b.   No offsetting credit or deduction is allowed for either the corporation or its shareholders, not even upon subsequent distribution of the earnings.

    c.   Excess undistributed earnings of preceding tax years are excluded from the AET base.

4. **Determination of Liability**

    a.   AET liability is generally determined by the IRS only on an audit. A corporation does not file a form to compute AET with its annual income tax return.

5. **Exempt Entities**

    a.   AET liability is incurred only by a corporation that unreasonably accumulates current earnings. But every corporation may incur AET, even if publicly held, unless the corporation is expressly exempt. No AET liability is incurred by the following:

        1)   S corporations
        2)   Tax-exempt corporations
        3)   PHCs (personal holding companies)
        4)   FPHCs (foreign personal holding companies)
        5)   PFICs (passive foreign investment companies)

6. **Accumulated Taxable Income (ATI)**

   a.   ATI is the AET base. ATI is a measure of the corporation's ability to distribute dividends from current-year earnings. ATI is taxable income, net of specific adjustments, a dividends-paid deduction, and the accumulated earnings credit (AEC). Specific adjustments to TI include

   1) NOLs. Add any deduction that reduced TI.
   2) DRD. Add dividends-received deductions that reduced TI.
   3) Charitable contributions. Adjust TI by

      a) Subtracting excess over 10% of TI disallowed
      b) Adding carryover applied to reduce TI for the year

   4) Federal income tax accrued.

      a) Subtract it from TI
      b) Do not subtract AET or PHC tax

   5) Capital gains. Adjust TI by

      a) Subtracting net capital gains for the tax year
      b) Adding federal income tax on the gain

   6) Capital losses. Adjust TI by

      a) Subtracting excess of net capital losses over net capital gains
      b) Adding amounts carried back or forward to the year
      c) Adding the lesser of

         i) Accumulated E&P
         ii) Net capital gains subtracted in prior years but not yet added back to TI in prior years

7. **Dividends-Paid Deduction**

   a.   A deduction from TI in computing ATI is allowed for four types of distributions attributable to E&P. Only differences with dividends deducted in computing PHC tax liability are discussed below.

   1) Dividends are distributions treated as ordinary dividend income.
   2) Throwback dividends are deductible with the appropriate election.
   3) Consent dividends are deducted.
   4) Distributions in complete liquidation are deducted (to the extent of current E&P).
   5) Preferential dividends are not allowed.

8. **Accumulated Earnings Credit (AEC)**

   a.   The AEC is a deduction for ATI. Generally, the AEC is the increased amount of reasonable needs of the business during the tax year.

   b.   The AEC is the greater of

   1) The general credit -- the portion of retained current E&P for reasonable needs of the business less capital gain adjustments, or
   2) The minimum floor -- the statutory amount (generally, $250,000) less accumulated E&P at the close of the preceding year. The minimum floor cannot be lower than zero.

   c.   In calculating the minimum floor, the statutory amount above is lowered to $150,000 for certain service corporations whose principal function is service in such fields as health, law, engineering, or accounting.

EXAMPLE

Calendar Corp., AEC for 2017

The general credit		
Current E&P (2017)	$225,000	
Less: Dividends-paid deduction	(0)	
Retained current E&P	$225,000	
Reasonable needs (given)		$535,000
Less: Accumulated E&P (12/31/16)		(415,000)
Retained current E&P to meet reasonable needs		120,000
Less: Net capital gain adjustments		
Capital gain	$ 10,000	
Less: Tax on the gain	(3,400)	(6,600)
The general credit		$113,400
The minimum floor		
Statutory amount		$250,000
Less: Accumulated E&P (12/31/16)		(415,000)
The minimum floor		$ 0
AEC (greater of the general credit or the minimum floor)		$113,400

Stop and review! You have completed the outline for this subunit. Study multiple-choice questions 14 through 16 on page 300.

10.8 PERSONAL HOLDING COMPANY (PHC) TAX

1. **Penalty**

    a. The tax of 20% imposed on undistributed PHC income is a penalty in addition to regular income tax and AMT.

    b. No offsetting credit or deduction is allowed for either the corporation or its shareholders, not even upon subsequent distribution of the earnings.

2. **Self-Assessment**

    a. Self-assessment of PHC tax liability is required. Schedule PH is filed with Form 1120 by a PHC. There is a 6-year statute of limitations if the schedule is not filed.

3. **Objective Tests**

    a. Every corporation that is not exempt and meets two objective tests (with respect to stock ownership distribution and the nature of its income) is a PHC subject to PHC tax.

        1) **Stock ownership test.** 50% or more by value of the corporation's shares are owned, directly or indirectly, by five or fewer shareholders at any time during the last half of the year.

        2) **Nature of income test.** Sixty percent or more of adjusted ordinary gross income (AOGI) of the corporation is personal holding company income (PHCI).

4. **Exempt Entities**

    a. No PHC tax liability is incurred by the following:

        1) S corporations
        2) Tax-exempt corporations
        3) FPHCs (foreign personal holding companies)
        4) Banks
        5) Insurance companies

5. **Income**

    a. PHC status is limited to corporations with personal holding company income (PHCI) of at least 60% of adjusted ordinary gross income (AOGI).

    b. Ordinary gross income (OGI) is GI for regular tax adjusted for property disposition transactions.

    > **GI**
    > + Losses on property dispositions that reduced GI
    > = **GI for PHC tax**
    > − Gains on disposition of Sec. 1231 property
    > − Gains on disposition of capital assets
    >
    > = **OGI**

    c. AOGI is OGI reduced by certain items related to rentals and other activities.

    > **OGI**
    > − Rental property items
    >   (only property tax interest, depreciation, rent paid)
    > − Interest on tax refunds, judgments, condemnation awards
    > − Interest (to a dealer) on U.S. obligations
    > − Some mining property expenses
    >
    > = **AOGI**

    1) The following items attributable to rental property income are deducted for AOGI. Adjusted income from rents (AIR) refers to rental income net of these items.

        a) Property taxes
        b) Interest
        c) Depreciation
        d) Rent paid

    2) No deduction for other rental property expenses is made, including

        a) Maintenance
        b) Administration
        c) Other expenses

    d. PHCI is generally passive-type income.

    e. PHCI includes the following:

        1) Interest, unless exempt from GI
        2) Dividends, i.e., taxable distributions from E&P
        3) Annuity proceeds, to the extent included in gross income
        4) Royalties (special rules apply)
        5) Rental income, unless excepted
        6) Personal services income, if conditions are met
        7) Distributions from estates or trusts

    f. AIR is PHCI only if

        1) AIR is less than 50% of AOGI.
        2) Distributions from E&P equal or exceed the amount by which PHCI, excluding rental income, is more than 10% of OGI.

        NOTE: AIR does not include rental income from leasing property to a more-than-25% shareholder.

g. Personal service income is PHCI only if

1) It is earned by a 25%-or-more shareholder,
2) It is from a personal services contract, and
3) Either some person other than the corporation is entitled to perform the services, or the contract designates who will.

NOTE: Unless the services are unique such that no one other than the 25%-or-more shareholder can perform them, the income is not PHCI.

The AICPA has tested candidates' knowledge of the personal holding company tax. Remember that one income amount, personal holding company income, is used to determine whether or not a corporation meets the nature of income test. If the corporation is a personal holding company, then another income amount, undistributed personal holding company income, is used to calculate the amount of personal holding company tax owed by the corporation. Be careful not to confuse these two amounts.

6. **Tax**

a. The PHC tax is 20% of the undistributed personal holding company income (UPHCI) of a PHC. PHCI for determining the base, UPHCI, is not the same as PHCI for determining if a corporation is a PHC. UPHCI is taxable income, net of specific adjustments and a dividends-paid deduction. Specific adjustments include

1) NOLs. Add any deduction that reduced TI in the present year.

a) Subtract an NOL from the preceding tax year in full,
b) Less any dividends-received deduction for that year.

2) DRD. Add dividends received deducted in computing TI.

3) Charitable contributions. Adjust TI by

a) Subtracting excess over 10% of TI disallowed
b) Adding carryover applied to reduce TI for the year

4) Federal income tax accrued.

a) Subtract this tax from TI.
b) Do not subtract PHC tax.

5) Capital gains. Adjust TI by

a) Subtracting net capital gains for the year
b) Adding federal income tax on the gain (tax – tax without NCG)

6) Excess rental deductions. Add to TI any excess of

a) Deductions claimed on rental property over
b) Income from the property.

NOTE: This adjustment does not apply if the corporation can prove that

i) The rental activity was bonafide,
ii) It produced the highest obtainable rent, and
iii) There was a reasonable expectation of profit or the property was necessary to conduct the business.

7. **Dividends-Paid Deduction**

a. A deduction from TI in computing UPHCI is allowed for five types of distributions attributable to E&P.

1) Dividends. Distributions are treated as ordinary dividend income to the extent of E&P.

a) This includes dividend income received in redemption of stock or in partial liquidation.
b) If property other than money is distributed, its AB is used.

2) Throwback dividends. Dividends paid during the 2 1/2 months following the close of the tax year are treated as paid on the last day of the (preceding) tax year.

a) Election is required for a PHC deduction.

b) Limit. No more is allowed than the lesser of 20% of dividends paid for the year or UPHCI before throwback dividends.

3) Consent dividends. This type of dividend addresses a situation of current accumulated earnings with insufficient liquidity to distribute dividends.

a) Shareholders on the last day of the tax year must consent to treat an amount as a currently taxable dividend (to them) even though no distribution was made.

b) Only ordinary dividend income is deductible.

4) Complete liquidation. The dividends-paid deduction includes the amount of distributions within the 24 months after adopting a plan of complete liquidation to the extent of any current E&P for the tax year of the distribution minus any capital loss deduction.

5) Deficiency dividend. A corporation is allowed 90 days to pay a deficiency dividend after a determination of PHC tax liability is made.

a) It must be paid in cash.

b) The corporation must elect to apply it to the year of liability.

c) Interest and penalties otherwise imposed still apply.

b. Preferential dividends are **not** allowed to be deducted. The entire amount of a distribution is considered to be preferential if

1) The distribution is not pro rata to the shareholders or

2) For a particular class of stock, the distribution is greater or less than the amount to which that class of stock is otherwise entitled.

c. Dividend carryover. Excess dividends paid (over UPHCI before the DPD) may be treated as a DPD for UPHCI for the following 2 tax years only.

Stop and review! You have completed the outline for this subunit. Study multiple-choice questions 17 through 20 beginning on page 301.

QUESTIONS

10.1 Regular Income Tax

1. A corporation may reduce its regular income tax by taking a tax credit for

A. Dividends-received exclusion.

B. Foreign income taxes.

C. State income taxes.

D. Accelerated depreciation.

Answer (B) is correct.
  REQUIRED: The available tax credit.
  DISCUSSION: A credit is available for certain foreign income taxes paid or accrued. Note that credits are more valuable than deductions since they reduce the tax on a dollar-for-dollar basis.
  Answer (A) is incorrect. The dividends-received exclusion is a deduction. Answer (C) is incorrect. State income taxes are deductible but do not give rise to a tax credit. Answer (D) is incorrect. Accelerated depreciation is a tax deduction, not a tax credit.

2. Which of the following tax credits **cannot** be claimed by a corporation?

A. Foreign Tax Credit.

B. Earned Income Credit.

C. Alternative Fuel Production Credit.

D. General Business Credit.

Answer (B) is correct.
  REQUIRED: The tax credit that cannot be claimed by a corporation.
  DISCUSSION: Most tax credits are allowable to corporations, but certain personal credits are not permitted. They include the Earned Income Credit, the Child and Dependent Care Credit, and the Elderly and Disabled Credit.

10.2 Foreign Tax Credit (FTC)

3. Sunex Co., an accrual-basis, calendar-year domestic C corporation, is taxed on its worldwide income. In the current year, Sunex's U.S. tax liability on its domestic and foreign source income is $60,000, and no prior-year foreign income taxes have been carried forward. Which factor(s) may affect the amount of Sunex's Foreign Tax Credit available in its current-year corporate income tax return?

	Income Source	The Foreign Tax Rate
A.	Yes	Yes
B.	Yes	No
C.	No	Yes
D.	No	No

Answer (A) is correct.
REQUIRED: The factor(s) that may affect the amount of the Foreign Tax Credit.
DISCUSSION: The Foreign Income Tax Credit is equal to the lesser of the actual foreign tax paid or the Foreign Tax Credit limit. The Foreign Tax Credit limit is the proportion of the taxpayer's tentative income tax (before the Foreign Tax Credit) that the taxpayer's foreign source taxable income bears to his or her worldwide taxable income for the year.
Answer (B) is incorrect. The Foreign Income Tax Credit is equal to the lesser of the actual foreign tax paid or the Foreign Tax Credit limit. Answer (C) is incorrect. The Foreign Tax Credit limit is the proportion of the taxpayer's tentative income tax (before the Foreign Tax Credit) that the taxpayer's foreign source taxable income bears to his or her worldwide taxable income for the year. Answer (D) is incorrect. The Foreign Income Tax Credit is equal to the lesser of the actual foreign tax paid or the Foreign Tax Credit limit. The Foreign Tax Credit limit is the proportion of the taxpayer's tentative income tax (before the Foreign Tax Credit) that the taxpayer's foreign source taxable income bears to his or her worldwide taxable income for the year.

4. The following information pertains to Wald Corp.'s operations for the year ended December 31, 2017:

Worldwide taxable income	$300,000
U.S. source taxable income	180,000
U.S. income tax before Foreign Tax Credit	96,000
Foreign nonbusiness-related interest earned	30,000
Foreign income taxes paid on nonbusiness-related interest earned	12,000
Other foreign source taxable income	90,000
Foreign income taxes paid on other foreign source taxable income	27,000

What amount of Foreign Tax Credit may Wald claim for 2017?

A. $28,800

B. $36,600

C. $38,400

D. $39,000

Answer (B) is correct.
REQUIRED: The Foreign Tax Credit amount.
DISCUSSION: The Foreign Tax Credit limit is the proportion of the taxpayer's tentative U.S. income tax (before the Foreign Tax Credit) that the taxpayer's foreign taxable income bears to his or her worldwide taxable income for the year. The limit must be applied separately to nonbusiness interest income.

Nonbusiness interest income computation:

$$(\$30,000 \div \$300,000) \times \$96,000 = \$9,600$$

Other foreign source taxable income computation:

$$(\$90,000 \div \$300,000) \times \$96,000 = \$28,800$$

Foreign taxes paid on the other income is less than the limit and fully creditable. The total credit is $36,600 ($9,600 + $27,000).
Answer (A) is incorrect. Foreign taxes paid on the other income is less than the limit and fully creditable. Furthermore, foreign taxes paid on nonbusiness-related interest earned is limited. Answer (C) is incorrect. The limit must be applied separately to nonbusiness interest income and other income. Answer (D) is incorrect. Qualified foreign taxes creditable are limited to the proportion of the taxpayer's tentative U.S. income tax (before the Foreign Tax Credit) that the taxpayer's foreign taxable income bears to his or her worldwide taxable income for the year.

10.3 Consolidated Returns

5. Tech Corp. files a consolidated return with its wholly owned subsidiary, Dow Corp. During 2017, Dow paid a cash dividend of $20,000 to Tech. What amount of this dividend is taxable on the 2017 consolidated return?

A. $20,000

B. $14,000

C. $6,000

D. $0

Answer (D) is correct.
REQUIRED: The taxable amount of a dividend distributed by a wholly owned subsidiary to its parent when a consolidated return is filed.
DISCUSSION: A dividend distributed by one member of a group filing a consolidated tax return to another member of that group is eliminated. The recipient of the dividend makes an adjustment to its separate taxable income that eliminates the dividend from the affiliated group's consolidated taxable income. Note that the dividends-received deduction (DRD) does not apply to intergroup dividends of affiliated groups that file a consolidated tax return.

6. With regard to consolidated tax returns, which of the following statements is true?

    A. Operating losses of one group member may be used to offset operating profits of the other members included in the consolidated return.

    B. Only corporations that issue their audited financial statements on a consolidated basis may file consolidated returns.

    C. Of all intercompany dividends paid by the subsidiaries to the parent, 70% are excludable from taxable income on the consolidated return.

    D. The common parent must directly own 51% or more of the total voting power of all corporations included in the consolidated return.

Answer (A) is correct.

    REQUIRED: The true statement regarding consolidated tax returns.

    DISCUSSION: Operating losses of one group member must be used to offset current-year operating profits of other group members before a net operating loss carryback or carryforward can occur.

    Answer (B) is incorrect. There is no such requirement. Answer (C) is incorrect. A dividend distributed by one member of a group filing a consolidated tax return to another member of that same group is completely eliminated. There is no dividends-received deduction. Answer (D) is incorrect. A corporation must own 80% of the total voting power and 80% of the total value of the stock in order to file a consolidated return.

7. Which of the following groups may elect to file a consolidated corporate return?

    A. A brother/sister-controlled group.

    B. A parent corporation and all more-than-10%-controlled partnerships.

    C. A parent corporation and all more-than-50%-controlled subsidiaries.

    D. Members of an affiliated group.

Answer (D) is correct.

    REQUIRED: The groups includible in a consolidated corporate return.

    DISCUSSION: A single federal income tax return may be filed by two or more includible corporations that are members of an affiliated group. Includible corporations are all corporations except (1) tax-exempt corporations, (2) S corporations, (3) foreign sales corporations, (4) insurance corporations, (5) REITs, (6) regulated investment companies, (7) domestic international sales corporations, and (8) corporations claiming Sec. 936 possessions tax credit. An affiliated group includes each corporation in a chain of corporations under the following conditions:

1. The other group members must directly own stock in the corporation that represents 80% or more of both total voting power and total value outstanding.
2. A parent corporation must directly own stock under the 80% rules of at least one includible corporation.

    Answer (A) is incorrect. A brother/sister-controlled group possession requirement is only 50% of total combined voting stock or 50% of total value of all stock. An affiliated group requires a higher percentage. Answer (B) is incorrect. An affiliated group must meet an 80% requirement for total voting power and total value outstanding. Answer (C) is incorrect. To be a member of an affiliated group, the group members must directly own stock in the corporation representing both 80% or more of total voting power and 80% or more of total value outstanding.

10.4 Controlled Groups

8. Consolidated returns may be filed

    A. Either by parent-subsidiary corporations or by brother-sister corporations.

    B. Only by corporations that formally request advance permission from the IRS.

    C. Only by parent-subsidiary affiliated groups.

    D. Only by corporations that issue their financial statements on a consolidated basis.

Answer (C) is correct.

    REQUIRED: The requirement for corporations to file consolidated tax returns.

    DISCUSSION: Corporations must be members of an affiliated group to file a consolidated tax return. An affiliated group consists of one or more chains of includible corporations that are connected through stock ownership with a common parent corporation. There is an 80% ownership requirement. Only parent-subsidiary affiliated groups will meet this requirement of having a common parent corporation.

    Answer (A) is incorrect. Brother-sister corporations exist if two corporations are owned by five or fewer persons with certain stock ownership requirements. They must not have a common parent corporation; one (or more) individual(s) may own the stock. Answer (B) is incorrect. There is no requirement that formal advance permission be obtained from the IRS. Answer (D) is incorrect. Corporations are not required to issue financial statements on a consolidated basis in order to file tax returns on a consolidated basis.

9. Prin Corp., the parent corporation, and Strel Corp., both accrual-basis, calendar year C corporations, file a consolidated return. During the current year, Strel made dividend distributions to Prin as follows:

	Adjusted tax basis	FMV
Cash	$4,000	$4,000
Land	2,000	9,000

What amount of income should be reported in Prin and Strel's consolidated income tax return for the current year?

A. $13,000

B. $11,000

C. $6,000

D. $0

Answer (D) is correct.

REQUIRED: The amount of income to include in dividends of a consolidated entity.

DISCUSSION: Dividends paid from one member of a consolidated group to another member are eliminated. None of the dividends, whether in cash or property, are included in the consolidated income tax return for the current year. The DRD is not allowed for such dividends.

10.5 Alternative Minimum Tax (AMT)

10. If a corporation's tentative minimum tax exceeds the regular tax, the excess amount is

A. Carried back to the first preceding taxable year.

B. Carried back to the third preceding taxable year.

C. Payable in addition to the regular tax.

D. Subtracted from the regular tax.

Answer (C) is correct.

REQUIRED: The application of the alternative minimum tax.

DISCUSSION: The excess of the tentative minimum tax over the regular tax is payable in addition to the regular tax. This excess is called the alternative minimum tax and is due on the same date as the regular tax.

Answer (A) is incorrect. The excess is not carried back to the preceding taxable year, but is payable currently. Answer (B) is incorrect. The excess is payable currently, not carried back 3 years. Answer (D) is incorrect. The excess is the AMT, payable in addition to regular income tax.

11. The credit for prior-year alternative minimum tax liability may be carried

A. Forward for a maximum of 5 years.

B. Back to the 3 preceding years or carried forward for a maximum of 5 years.

C. Back to the 3 preceding years.

D. Forward indefinitely.

Answer (D) is correct.

REQUIRED: The true statement regarding the AMT credit.

DISCUSSION: The minimum tax credit can be carried forward indefinitely. It may be used to offset regular tax liabilities in future years to the extent the regular tax liability exceeds the corporation's tentative minimum tax in the carryforward year.

Answer (A) is incorrect. The minimum tax credit is not limited to 5 years carryforward. Answer (B) is incorrect. The minimum tax credit is not limited by such a scheme. Answer (C) is incorrect. The minimum tax credit cannot be carried back to preceding years.

10.6 Estimated Tax

12. Blink Corp., an accrual-basis, calendar-year corporation, carried back a net operating loss for the tax year ended December 31, Year 1. Blink's gross revenues have been under $500,000 since inception. Blink expects to have profits for the tax year ending December 31, Year 2. Which method(s) of estimated tax payment can Blink use for its quarterly payments during the Year 2 tax year to avoid underpayment of federal estimated taxes?

I. 100%-of-the-preceding-tax-year method
II. Annualized income method

A. I only.

B. Both I and II.

C. II only.

D. Neither I nor II.

Answer (C) is correct.

REQUIRED: The acceptable method(s) of estimating quarterly tax payments.

DISCUSSION: Blink Corp. qualifies as a small corporation because it has not had taxable income exceeding $1 million during any of the 3 preceding years. However, it must have shown a tax liability in the previous year in order to use the 100%-of-the-preceding-tax-year method. Since the previous year generated an NOL, this method cannot be used. The annualized income method is available in this situation.

Answer (A) is incorrect. The 100%-of-the-preceding-tax-year method cannot be used since the preceding tax year generated an NOL. Answer (B) is incorrect. The 100%-of-the-preceding-tax-year method cannot be used since the preceding tax year generated an NOL. However, the annualized income method is available in this situation. Answer (D) is incorrect. The annualized income method is available in this situation.

13. No penalty will be imposed on a corporation for underpayment of estimated tax for a particular year if

    A. The tax for that year is less than $500.

    B. Estimated tax payments for the year equal at least 80% of the tax shown on the return for that year.

    C. The corporation is a personal holding company.

    D. The alternative minimum tax is at least $1,000.

Answer (A) is correct.
    REQUIRED: The condition under which a corporation is not liable for the penalty on underpayment of estimated tax.
    DISCUSSION: No estimated tax underpayment penalty is imposed on a corporation if actual tax liability shown on the return for the tax year is less than $500.
    Answer (B) is incorrect. The applicable percentage is 100%. Answer (C) is incorrect. No exception exempts PHCs from the penalty. Answer (D) is incorrect. The code requires estimated tax payments of AMT.

10.7 Accumulated Earnings Tax (AET)

14. The accumulated earnings tax

    A. Should be self-assessed by filing a separate schedule along with the regular tax return.

    B. Applies only to closely held corporations.

    C. Can be imposed on S corporations that do not regularly distribute their earnings.

    D. Cannot be imposed on a corporation that has undistributed earnings and profits of less than $150,000.

Answer (D) is correct.
    REQUIRED: The entities subject to, the limits on, and the procedural characteristics of the AET.
    DISCUSSION: The Accumulated Earnings Credit (AEC) is deducted from taxable income (TI) to determine accumulated taxable income (ATI), the AET base. The minimum credit base is $250,000. However, the minimum credit base is $150,000 for certain service corporations. The AET base is not less than any excess of the minimum credit base ($150,000) over accumulated E&P. Thus, AET is not imposed on a corporation that has undistributed earnings and profits of less than $150,000.
    Answer (A) is incorrect. AET is not self-assessed. It is assessed, if at all, on an IRS audit. Filing a separate return reporting AET is not required. Answer (B) is incorrect. AET can apply to publicly held corporations. Answer (C) is incorrect. An S corporation is expressly exempt from AET. Its shareholders are currently subject to tax on its earnings.

15. In determining whether a corporation is subject to the accumulated earnings tax, which of the following items is **not** a subtraction in arriving at accumulated taxable income?

    A. Federal income tax.

    B. Capital loss carryback.

    C. Dividends-paid deduction.

    D. Accumulated Earnings Credit.

Answer (B) is correct.
    REQUIRED: The item that does not reduce ATI.
    DISCUSSION: The accumulated earnings tax is applied to accumulated taxable income, which is taxable income, subject to certain adjustments. Capital loss carrybacks and carryforwards are not allowed. Instead, capital losses are deductible in full in the year incurred (but must be reduced by prior net capital gain deductions).
    Answer (A) is incorrect. Federal income taxes are deducted as an adjustment to taxable income. Answer (C) is incorrect. The dividends-paid deduction is subtracted from adjusted taxable income. Answer (D) is incorrect. The Accumulated Earnings Credit is subtracted from adjusted taxable income.

16. The accumulated earnings tax can be imposed

    A. On both partnerships and corporations.

    B. On companies that make distributions in excess of accumulated earnings.

    C. On personal holding companies.

    D. Regardless of the number of shareholders in a corporation.

Answer (D) is correct.
    REQUIRED: The characteristic of the accumulated earnings tax.
    DISCUSSION: The accumulated earnings tax (AET) is imposed only on a corporation that, for the purpose of avoiding income tax at the shareholder level, allows earnings and profits to accumulate instead of being distributed. The AET will be imposed regardless of the number of shareholders, provided the corporation does not qualify as a personal holding company.
    Answer (A) is incorrect. Partnerships, along with any other entities that are not corporations, are not subject to the AET. Answer (B) is incorrect. Distributions in excess of accumulated earnings are the opposite of accumulated earnings. ATI, the AET base, will be zero in such a case. Answer (C) is incorrect. Personal holding companies are excluded from the AET. They are subject to tax on undistributed PHC income.

10.8 Personal Holding Company (PHC) Tax

17. Edge Corp. met the stock ownership requirements of a personal holding company. What sources of income must Edge consider to determine if the income requirements for a personal holding company have been met?

I. Interest earned on tax-exempt obligations

II. Dividends received from an unrelated domestic corporation

A. I only.

B. II only.

C. Both I and II.

D. Neither I nor II.

Answer (B) is correct.

REQUIRED: The items included in personal holding company income.

DISCUSSION: A personal holding company tax is assessed on the undistributed personal holding company income (PHCI) of many C corporations. This tax is self-assessed when 50% or more of the value of the corporation's shares are owned by five or fewer shareholders at any time during the last half of the fiscal year, and 60% or more of AGI is PHCI. PHCI includes taxable interest and dividends but not tax-exempt interest.

Answer (A) is incorrect. Tax-exempt interest is not a type of PHCI since it is exempt from gross income. Answer (C) is incorrect. Only one option is a type of PHCI. Answer (D) is incorrect. Dividends received from unrelated domestic corporations are included in PHCI.

18. Zero Corp. is an investment company authorized to issue only common stock. During the last half of the current year, Edward owned 450 of the 1,000 outstanding shares of stock in Zero. Zero would **not** be subject to the personal holding company (PHC) penalty tax if the remaining 550 shares of common stock were owned by

A. An estate in which Edward is the beneficiary.

B. Edward's brother.

C. Fifty-five shareholders who are related neither to each other nor to Edward, in equal lots of 10 shares each.

D. Edward's grandmother.

Answer (C) is correct.

REQUIRED: The ownership requirements of a personal holding company.

DISCUSSION: One of the tests used to determine if a company is subject to the personal holding company (PHC) penalty tax is the stock ownership test. More than 50% of the value of the outstanding stock must be owned by five or fewer individuals at some time during the last 6 months of the tax year. However, if 10 or more unrelated taxpayers own equal shares, the ownership requirement cannot be met. Therefore, if 55 taxpayers own equal lots of 10 shares each, Zero will not be subject to the personal holding company penalty tax.

Answer (A) is incorrect. Stock owned by an estate is considered under the constructive ownership rules as being owned by its beneficiaries, pushing Zero over the 50%-ownership limit for a PHC. Answer (B) is incorrect. Ownership of stock by a brother is considered under the constructive ownership rules as being owned by Edward, pushing Zero over the 50%-ownership limit for a PHC. Answer (D) is incorrect. Ownership of stock by a grandmother is considered under the constructive ownership rules as being owned by Edward, pushing Zero over the 50%-ownership limit for a PHC.

19. Kane Corp. is a calendar-year domestic personal holding company. Which deduction(s) must Kane make from current year taxable income to determine undistributed personal holding company income prior to the dividends-paid deduction?

	Federal Income Taxes	Net Long-Term Capital Gain Less Related Federal Income Taxes
A.	Yes	Yes
B.	Yes	No
C.	No	Yes
D.	No	No

Answer (A) is correct.

REQUIRED: The determination of undistributed personal holding company income.

DISCUSSION: Undistributed personal holding company income is taxable income net of specific adjustments and the dividends-paid deduction. Federal income taxes accrued and capital gains (net of related federal taxes) are subtracted from taxable income.

Answer (B) is incorrect. Capital gains are deducted. Answer (C) is incorrect. Federal income taxes accrued are deducted to arrive at undistributed personal holding company income. Answer (D) is incorrect. Both deductions are necessary to arrive at undistributed personal holding company income.

20. Benson, a singer, owns 100% of the outstanding capital stock of Lund Corporation. Lund contracted with Benson, specifying that Benson was to perform personal services for Magda Productions, Inc., in consideration of which Benson was to receive $50,000 a year from Lund. Lund contracted with Magda, specifying that Benson was to perform personal services for Magda, in consideration of which Magda was to pay Lund $1 million a year. Personal holding company income will be attributable to

A. Benson only.

B. Lund only.

C. Magda only.

D. All three contracting parties.

Answer (B) is correct.

REQUIRED: The corporation to which the personal holding company income will be attributed.

DISCUSSION: Amounts received by corporations under personal service contracts involving a 25%-or-more shareholder are personal holding company income if the contract designates specifically that only the shareholder will provide the services. As such, Lund has personal service income of $1 million a year.

Answer (A) is incorrect. Benson is an individual, and personal holding company income applies only to corporations. Answer (C) is incorrect. Magda is paying the income, not receiving it. Answer (D) is incorrect. Not all parties will have personal holding company income.

Online is better! To best prepare for the CPA exam, access **thousands** of exam-emulating MCQs and TBSs through Gleim CPA Review online courses with SmartAdapt technology. Learn more at www.gleimcpa.com or contact our team at 800.874.5346 to upgrade.

STUDY UNIT ELEVEN
CORPORATE TAX SPECIAL TOPICS

(22 pages of outline)

This study unit addresses the federal income tax aspects of utilizing the corporate structure. This study unit will help develop an understanding of the fundamental general rules: nonrecognition on contributions by shareholders in the control group, recognition of gain on distributions of appreciated property by the corporation, shareholder dividend treatment of distributions to the extent of earnings and profits, and nonrecognition by parties to a reorganization.

Corporations have tax procedures that are specific to that type of entity.

Taxpayers who operate or otherwise have a presence in more than one tax jurisdiction are subject to tax laws that are distinct for each jurisdiction.

11.1 FORMATION

1. **Overview**

   a. Without Sec. 351, any gain realized on the transfer of property to a corporation in exchange for stock of the corporation would be recognized.

EXAMPLE

A taxpayer transfers property with a basis of $10,000 and an FMV of $20,000 for a corporation's stock with an FMV of $20,000. The taxpayer realizes and recognizes a $10,000 gain ($20,000 FMV – $10,000 basis).

---

   b. Section 351 requires that no gain or loss be recognized if property is transferred to a corporation by one or more persons solely in exchange for stock in the corporation and, immediately after the exchange, such person or persons control the corporation. This nonrecognition treatment is mandatory, not elective.

2. **Section 351**

   a. **Control** is ownership of 80% or more of the voting power of stock and 80% or more of the shares of each class of nonvoting stock of the corporation.

      1) Stock exchanged for services is not counted toward the 80%.

         a) The FMV of the stock is gross income to the shareholder.
         b) The shareholder's basis in the stock exchanged for services is its FMV.

      2) Nonqualified preferred stock is treated as boot received and is not counted as stock toward the 80%-ownership test.

b. **Solely for stock.** To the extent the shareholder receives the corporation's stock in exchange for property, nonrecognition is required. This is so even if the shareholder receives some boot (money or other property) in the exchange.

EXAMPLE

Taxpayer transfers an asset to the corporation in a Sec. 351 exchange. The asset has a basis of $10,000. Taxpayer receives $3,000 in cash and stock worth $15,000. Taxpayer has a realized gain of $8,000 and a recognized gain of $3,000.

---

1) **Disparate value.** Inequality of FMV of the stock and property exchanged is not relevant in itself.

   a) The shareholder may have gross income if the disparity represents an (unstated) additional transaction, e.g., payment of compensation, a constructive dividend.

2) Section 351 may apply to an exchange after formation.

3) Section 351 can apply to contributions of property even if the corporation issues no stock in the exchange, e.g., a capital contribution by a sole shareholder who receives no stock in exchange for the contribution.

4) Section 351 may also apply when the corporation exchanges treasury stock.

c. **Boot.** The shareholder recognizes gain realized to the extent of money and the FMV of other property (except the stock of the corporation) received in the exchange.

1) FMV of property given up is used if FMV of property received cannot be ascertained.

2) Character of the gain depends on the property contributed.

3) No loss is recognized on the receipt of boot.

d. **Liabilities.** Section 351 applies even if the corporation assumes the shareholder's liability or takes property subject to a liability in the exchange.

1) The amount of the liabilities is treated as recognized gain from the sale or exchange of an asset only to the extent it exceeds the AB of all property contributed by the shareholder.

EXAMPLE

A taxpayer transfers an asset with a basis of $60,000 and a fair market value of $100,000 to a corporation for all of its stock. The asset has a liability attached of $70,000. The taxpayer must recognize $10,000 of income, the excess of the liability ($70,000) over the basis of the asset ($60,000).

---

2) If tax avoidance was a purpose or if no business purpose was present for the assumption or transfer, the full amount of gain is recognized.

e. The corporation recognizes no gain on exchange of its stock for property (including money).

1) Treasury stock is included.

2) The corporation recognizes gain on exchanging other property (neither money nor its stock), even with a shareholder, unless an exception applies.

3. **Basis of Shareholder in Stock**

a. A control group shareholder's basis in the stock of the corporation is the adjusted basis in contributed property adjusted for the boot received and the gain recognized.

AB in contributed property
– Boot received
Money, including
Liability relief (corporation assumes or takes subject to)
Property received FMV (other than above and the corporation's stock)
+ Gain recognized (by shareholder)
= **Basis in stock of issuing corporation**

    b.   All liability is treated as boot when computing stock basis.

    c.   Holding period is generally tacked; i.e., the holding period of the property exchanged for stock is added to the holding period of the stock.

    d.   **Sole proprietor.** If a capital asset and other assets (e.g., Sec. 1231 property) are contributed when incorporating a business, each share received in the exchange has a split holding period.

4.   **Basis of Shareholder in Boot**

    a.   Boot generally has a basis equal to fair market value.

5.   **Basis of Corporation in Property**

    a.   The corporation's initial carryover basis in property exchanged by a control group shareholder for its stock is an adjusted carryover basis.

>   **AB in property to shareholder**
> \+ Gain recognized by shareholder
> = **Basis in property to corporation**

    b.   This basis also applies when the shareholder receives nothing in return.

    c.   This basis is also the corporation's initial depreciable basis in the property.

        1)   Allowable depreciation is apportioned based on the number of months the corporation owned the asset.

    d.   Holding period is tacked.

Stop and review! You have completed the outline for this subunit. Study multiple-choice questions 1 through 3 beginning on page 324.

11.2 CURRENT EARNINGS AND PROFITS

1.   **Definition**

    a.   The term "earnings and profits" (E&P) is the federal tax accounting version of financial accounting's retained earnings. Though similar in purpose, they are not the same amount. E&P determines whether corporate distributions are taxable dividends.

        1)   There are two types of E&P, current and accumulated. A corporation first determines its current E&P, which is the E&P for the current year. Then any excess current E&P after making distributions is added to the accumulated E&P balance, and any distributions in excess of current E&P reduce the accumulated E&P balance.

>   **Current E&P**
> − Distributions
> = **Increase (decrease) to accumulated E&P**

2.   **Calculation**

    a.   Calculating current E&P starts with the current-year taxable income or loss and then makes various positive and negative adjustments.

        1)   The positive adjustments include some exempt income, deductions, and deferred income. Examples include interest from municipal bonds, injury compensation, life insurance proceeds, DRD, capital and NOL carryover, depreciation in excess of straight-line, income per completed-contract method, and deferred income from an installment sale.

        2)   The negative adjustments include some nondeductible items for taxable income and recognized deferred income. Examples include life insurance premiums, penalties, fines, municipal bond expense, excessive compensation, federal income taxes, portions of meals and entertainment, charitable contributions in excess of the 10% AGI limit, and prior-year(s) installment sales.

3)   Transactions excluded from both E&P and taxable income do not require any adjustment. Examples include unrealized gains and losses, gifts, state tax refunds, and contributions to capital.

EXAMPLE

NEEM Co. had taxable income of $20,000 that included the following unadjusted items:

Meals and entertainment	$ 400
Capital loss carried over from prior year	5,000

Current E&P is the current-year taxable income adjusted for specific items. Positive adjustments include loss carryovers, as they were negative adjustments in the year they occurred. Negative adjustments include the nondeductible portion of meals and entertainment. Corporations are allowed to deduct 50% of qualifying meals and entertainment expenses. The corporation's current E&P is $24,800 [$20,000 + $5,000 − ($400 × 50%)].

Stop and review! You have completed the outline for this subunit. Study multiple-choice question 4 on page 325.

11.3 DISTRIBUTIONS

1.   **Definition**

   a.   A **distribution** is any transfer of property by a corporation to any of its shareholders with respect to the shareholder's shares in the corporation. Property is defined as money, bonds or other obligations, stock in other corporations, and other property, including receivables.

2.   **Distribution Amount**

> Money
> + Obligations (FMV), e.g., a bond
> + Property (FMV), other
> − Related liabilities, recourse or not
> = Distribution amount

3.   **Corporate Treatment**

   a.   A corporation is required to file a Form 1099-DIV no later than February 28 of the following year for each shareholder if the corporation did any of the following at the shareholder level:

   1)   Paid gross dividends of $10 or more during the calendar year
   2)   Withheld any federal income taxes under the backup withholding rules
   3)   Made payments of $600 or more as part of a liquidation

   b.   **Corporate loss unrecognized.** No loss realized on an ordinary distribution of property (AB > FMV) may be recognized. The shareholder takes a FMV basis in the property.

   1)   Loss on a sale to a more-than-50% shareholder is not recognized.

      a)   Stock owned by related parties is attributed to the shareholder.
      b)   The shareholder takes a FMV basis in the property.
      c)   Gain realized on a subsequent taxable disposition to an unrelated party is recognized only to the extent it exceeds the previously disallowed loss.

   c.   **Corporate gain recognized.** Gain realized on distributed property must be recognized by the corporation as if the property were sold to the distributee at its FMV. But no gain is recognized to the corporation on distribution of money or obligations it issues, e.g., bonds.

EXAMPLE

Kyle Corp. owned 200 shares of Honey Corp. stock that it bought 19 years ago for $10 per share. This year, when the fair market value of the Honey stock was $14 per share, Kyle distributed this stock to a noncorporate shareholder. Because a corporation must recognize gains realized on distributions of property and the stock involved is not issued by Kyle, Kyle must recognize a gain of $800 ($2,800 FMV – $2,000 basis) on this distribution.

---

    1)   Liabilities. FMV is conclusively presumed to be no less than liabilities related to the property subject to which the shareholder assumes or takes the property, whether with recourse or not.

    2)   The character of recognized gain is determined by treating the distribution as a sale to the shareholder.

        a)   Gain recognized on depreciable property in the hands of a more-than-50% shareholder distributee is ordinary income (OI).

    3)   Earnings and profits (E&P). Recognized gains increase E&P. Tax on the gain and FMV reduce E&P.

4.   **Shareholder Treatment**

 The CPA exam has often contained questions regarding shareholder treatment of corporate distributions. A common question format has asked for the distribution amount that is taxable as dividend income to the shareholder.

    a.   **Dividend.** The amount of a distribution is a dividend to the extent, first, of any current E&P and then of any accumulated E&P (AE&P).

        1)   When distributions during the year exceed current E&P, pro rata portions of each distribution are deemed to be from current E&P.

            a)   If the current E&P balance is positive, the positive balance is computed as of the close of the taxable year, without regard to the amount of E&P at the time of the distribution.

            b)   If the current E&P balance is negative, prorate the negative balance to the date of each distribution made during the year.

        2)   Treatment of a distribution is determined by reference to AE&P only after any current E&P have been accounted for.

            a)   AE&P constitute the remaining balance of E&P from prior tax years.

            b)   Deficit in AE&P never results from a distribution. It results from any aggregate excess of current E&P deficits over unused positive AE&P. Deficit in AE&P does not offset current E&P.

            c)   Current E&P are added to AE&P after determining treatment of distributions.

        3)   Distributions > AE&P. When distributions exceed both current E&P and AE&P, allocate AE&P to distributions in their chronological order.

        4)   Distributions from current E&P are first allocated to preferred stock, and any excess is then allocated to common stock.

EXAMPLE

Impartial, Inc., has a zero balance in AE&P but $25,000 in current E&P. Impartial makes a distribution of $20,000 to its preferred shareholders and a distribution of $10,000 to its common shareholders. The preferred shareholders will report the $20,000 as dividend income. The common shareholders will report $5,000 as dividend income and $5,000 as a return of capital.

---

5) To determine E&P from taxable income, adjustments similar to those used to reconcile income per books with taxable income must be made. For example, tax-exempt interest would be added to taxable income because, although it is excluded from gross income, it represents earnings available for distribution as dividends.

   a) Gain recognized on distribution of appreciated property increases E&P.
   b) E&P are determined at the end of the tax year.

      i) They are then reduced for money and the greater of FMV or AB of other property (net of liabilities) distributed during the year.
      ii) If E&P remain for the current year, they increase a positive AE&P balance or reduce a negative AE&P balance.

6) **Constructive dividends** are treated the same as other dividends.

   a) Constructive dividends are undeclared distributions to shareholders.

      i) Examples include the use of corporate vehicles or money borrowed from the corporation to purchase personal items.

   b) Like other dividends, constructive dividends may not be deducted by the company, creating double taxation of that income (corporate level and shareholder level).
   c) To the extent the distribution exceeds current and accumulated earnings and profits, it is treated as a return of capital to the shareholder.

      i) Once the basis of the stock has been reduced to zero, any distributions received are treated as a gain from the sale of the stock.

b. **Capital recovery.** A shareholder treats the amount of a distribution in excess of dividends as tax-exempt return of capital to the extent of his or her basis.

   1) Basis in the stock is reduced (but not below zero).
   2) Apportion the distribution among the shares if they have different bases.

c. **Gain on sale.** Any excess of the amount of a distribution over E&P and basis is treated as gain on the sale of the stock (e.g., the $2,000 in the example below).

   1) Character of the gain is determined by the nature of the property in the hands of the shareholder (e.g., a capital asset or dealer property).
   2) Loss may be recognized only if the stock becomes worthless or is redeemed.

EXAMPLE

Corporation distributes $90,000 when E&P are $60,000. Shareholder N receives $30,000 of the distribution, of which $20,000 is a dividend (2/3).

	# of Shares	Basis	Dividend	Capital Recovery	Gain
Block 1	1,000	$ 3,000	$10,000	$3,000	$2,000
Block 2	1,000	$15,000	$10,000	$5,000	0

---

d. **Basis in distributed property.** The shareholder's basis in property received in a nonliquidating distribution is generally its FMV at the time of the distribution.

   1) The FMV is used for obligations of the distributing corporation.
   2) If liabilities assumed or liabilities of property taken are

      a) < FMV, then the shareholder's basis in the property is its FMV.
      b) > FMV and the distributee shareholder assumes personal liability, then the shareholder's basis should equal the liability.

EXAMPLE

Gabrielle, the sole shareholder in Kleen, a C corporation, has a tax basis of $71,000. Kleen has $50,000 of accumulated positive earnings and profits at the beginning of the year and $9,000 of current positive earnings and profits for the current year. At year end, Kleen distributed land with an adjusted basis of $28,000 and a fair market value (FMV) of $46,000 to Gabrielle. The land has an outstanding mortgage of $10,000 that Gabrielle must assume.

Because the distribution is nonliquidating and the assumed liability is less than the FMV of the land, Gabrielle's basis in the land is equal to the $46,000 FMV. Had the liability assumed exceeded the FMV, then the basis would be the amount of the liability.

---

5. **Extraordinary Dividend**

   a. Additional gain may be recognized by a shareholder who sells stock on which an extraordinary dividend was received.

   b. An extraordinary dividend is a dividend on stock held 2 years or less that exceeds 10% (5% for preferred stock) of either the basis or the FMV of the stock.

   c. Basis in the stock is reduced by the nontaxed portion of the extraordinary dividend, i.e., the amount of a DRD (dividends-received deduction).

   d. If the nontaxed portion of the dividend exceeds the stock's basis, the excess is treated as a gain from the sale or exchange of such stock in the year the extraordinary dividend is received.

6. **Stock Distributions**

   a. A corporation recognizes no gain or loss on distribution of its own stock. Generally, a shareholder does not include a distribution of stock or rights to acquire stock in gross income unless it is a

      1) Distribution in lieu of money (treated as a dividend)
      2) Disproportionate distribution
      3) Distribution on preferred stock
      4) Distribution of convertible preferred stock
      5) Distribution of common and preferred stock, resulting in receipt of preferred stock by some shareholders and common stock by other shareholders

   b. A **proportionate distribution** of stock issued by the corporation is generally not gross income to the shareholders.

      1) A shareholder allocates the aggregate basis (AB) in the old stock to the old stock and new stock in proportion to the FMV of the old and new stock.

         a) Basis is apportioned by relative FMV to different types (e.g., common, preferred) of stock if applicable.

EXAMPLE

Company A distributed two shares of preferred stock for each share of its common stock in a nontaxable distribution. On the day of distribution, Company B had 100 shares of Company A common stock. The fair market value of common stock on the day of distribution was $80 per share, and the value of the preferred stock was $60 per share. Company B would therefore allocate 3/5 of the basis in Company A common stock to the 200 (100 shares of common stock × 2) shares of distributed preferred stock, calculated as follows:

(200 preferred × $60 FMV) ÷ [(200 preferred × $60 FMV) + (100 common × $80 FMV)] = 0.6 or 3/5

The remaining 2/5 would stay allocated to the common stock.

---

      2) The holding period of the distributed stock includes that of the old stock.
      3) E&P are not altered for a tax-free stock dividend.

    c.   **Stock rights.** Treat a distribution of stock rights as a distribution of the stock.

        1)   Basis is allocated based on the FMV of the rights.

            a)   Basis in the stock rights is zero if their aggregate FMV is less than 15% of the FMV of the stock on which they were distributed, unless the shareholder elects to allocate.

        2)   Basis in the stock, if the right is exercised, is any basis allocated to the right, plus the exercise price.

        3)   Holding period of the stock begins on the exercise date.

        4)   No deduction is allowed for basis allocated to stock rights that lapse. Basis otherwise allocated remains in the underlying stock.

7.   **Taxable Stock Distribution**

    a.   Distributions of stock described in 1) through 6) below are subject to tax. Unless otherwise stated in 1) through 6) below, the amount of a distribution subject to tax is the FMV of distributed stock or stock rights.

        1)   Any shareholder has an option to choose between a distribution of stock or a distribution of other property. The amount of the distribution is the greater of

            a)   The FMV of stock or
            b)   The cash or FMV of other property.

        2)   Some shareholders receive property, and other shareholders receive an increase in their proportionate interests.

        3)   Some common shareholders receive common stock; others receive preferred stock.

        4)   Distribution is on preferred stock.

        5)   Convertible preferred stock is distributed, and the effect is to change the shareholder's proportionate stock ownership.

        6)   Constructive stock distributions change proportionate interests resulting from, e.g., a change in conversion ratio or redemption price.

    b.   E&P are reduced by the FMV of stock and stock rights distributed.

    c.   Basis in the underlying stock does not change. Basis in the new stock or stock rights is their FMV.

    d.   The holding period for the new stock begins on the day after the distribution date.

    e.   If a distribution of a stock dividend or stock right is taxable when received, the basis is the FMV on the date of acquisition.

        1)   When the dividend is taxable, there is no tacking on of the holding period for the underlying stock.

        2)   The holding period begins the day following the acquisition date.

8.   **Stock Split**

    a.   A stock split is not a distribution.

    b.   Basis in the old stock is also "split" and allocated to the new stock.

    c.   The holding period of the new stock includes that of the old stock.

Stop and review! You have completed the outline for this subunit. Study multiple-choice questions 5 through 8 beginning on page 325.

11.4 REDEMPTIONS

1. **Overview**

   a. Stock is redeemed when a corporation acquires its own stock from a shareholder in exchange for property, regardless of redeemed stock being canceled, retired, or held as treasury stock.

   b. A shareholder is required to treat amounts realized on a redemption (not in liquidation) either as a distribution (a corporate dividend) or as a sale of stock redeemed.

2. **Dividend or Sale Treatment**

   a. Redemptions of stock by a corporation are treated as dividends unless certain conditions are met. If any of the following conditions are met, the exchange is treated as a sale, and the gains or losses are capital gains and losses.

      1) The redemption is not essentially equivalent to a dividend.
      2) The redemption is substantially disproportionate.
      3) The distribution is in complete redemption of all of a shareholder's stock.
      4) The distribution is to a noncorporate shareholder in partial liquidation.
      5) The distribution is received by an estate.

3. **Gain Recognition**

   a. A **corporation** recognizes gain realized on a distribution

      1) As if the property distributed were sold at FMV to the distributee immediately prior to the distribution
      2) Even if stock is redeemed by the distribution

4. **Loss Recognition**

   a. No recognition of loss realized is allowed by the corporation, unless the redemption is

      1) In complete liquidation of the corporation or
      2) Of stock held by an estate (to pay death taxes).

5. **Recognition of Depreciated Property Distribution**

   a. A corporation recognizes ordinary income on the distribution of depreciated property to the extent of depreciation or amount realized, whichever is less.

6. **Shareholder Treatment**

   a. A **shareholder** treats a redemption in the same manner as a regular distribution. The amount is a dividend to the extent of E&P. Any unrecovered basis in the redeemed stock is added to the shareholder's basis in stock retained.

EXAMPLE

Since 2011, Paige has owned all 1,010 outstanding shares of E and E Corporation's stock. Paige's basis for the stock is $10,100. In 2017, E and E has earnings and profits of $110,000. The corporation redeemed 450 shares of Paige's stock for $98,000 in 2017. Because Paige owns 100% of the stock before and after the redemption, the transaction is a dividend to the extent that E and E has earnings and profits. Since the distribution ($98,000) is less than earnings and profits ($110,000), the entire amount is taxable as a dividend.

NOTE: Do not confuse this with noncorporate shareholder treatment of a partial liquidation. (Details of partial liquidation requirements are covered later in Subunit 11.6.)

---

7. **Stock Reacquisition**

   a. The expenses incurred in connection with any reacquisition by a corporation of its own stock or the stock of a related person (50% relationship test) are not deductible. An exception exists for any cost allocable to an indebtedness and amortized over the life of the indebtedness (e.g., financial advisory costs).

8. **Sale Treatment**

   a. The shareholder treats qualifying redemptions as if the shares redeemed were sold to a third party.

   b. Gain or loss is any spread between AB of the shares and the FMV of property received.

   c. The character of gain or loss depends on the nature of the stock in the shareholder's hands.

   d. The basis in distributed property is its FMV.

   e. The holding period for the property starts the day after the redemption exchange.

   f. This treatment applies only to redemptions that

      1) Terminate a shareholder's interest
      2) Are substantially disproportionate between shareholders
      3) Are not essentially equivalent to a dividend
      4) Are received by an estate
      5) Are from a shareholder, other than a corporation, in partial liquidation

   g. Treatment of a redemption as a sale is determined separately for each shareholder.

9. **Termination of Interest**

   a. Termination of a shareholder's interest must be complete to qualify. All the corporation's stock owned by the shareholder must be redeemed in the exchange for the property.

      1) Family attribution rules apply but may be waived if the following three requirements are met:

         a) The shareholder may not retain any interest, except as a creditor, in the corporation.

         b) The shareholder may not acquire any interest, except by bequest or inheritance, for 10 years.

         c) A written agreement must be filed with the IRS stating that the IRS will be notified if a prohibited interest is acquired.

10. **Substantially Disproportionate**

    a. Substantially disproportionate means that the amount received by shareholders is not in the same proportion as their stock holdings.

    b. It is tested by determining the shareholders' applicable ownership percentages (including constructive ownership) both before and after redemption.

    c. A redemption is substantially disproportionate with respect to a shareholder if, immediately after the redemption, the shareholder owns

       1) Less than 50% of the voting power of outstanding stock and
       2) Less than 80% each of the interest in the

          a) Voting stock owned before the redemption
          b) Common stock owned before the redemption

EXAMPLE

Carol, an individual shareholder, owns 275 shares of Allegiance Corporation. Allegiance has 1,000 shares of common stock outstanding and redeems 200 shares of common stock from its shareholders. The least number of Carol's shares that will need to be redeemed in order for the redemption to be substantially disproportionate to Carol is determined as follows:

Carol owned 27.5% of Allegiance Corporation before the redemption (275 shares ÷ 1,000 shares). Carol must reduce her interest to below 22% for the redemption to be substantially disproportionate (80% × 27.5%). Carol needs to own less than 176 shares after the redemption [22% × (1,000 shares − 200 shares)]. Thus, more than 99 shares (275 shares − 176 shares) need to be redeemed to reduce Carol's interest below 22%. Accordingly, Carol needs to have a minimum of 116 shares redeemed for the redemption to be substantially disproportionate.

11. **Not Essentially Equivalent to a Dividend**

   a. Not essentially equivalent to a dividend means that there is a meaningful reduction in the shareholder's proportionate interest in the corporation. Reduction in voting power is generally required for a redemption.

12. **Estate**

   a. An estate may treat a qualifying redemption (e.g., to pay death taxes) as a sale.

      1) Redeemed stock must be valued at more than 35% of the gross estate net of deductions allowed.
      2) Deductions allowed are administration expenses, funeral expenses, claims against the estate (including death taxes), and unpaid mortgages.

13. **Partial Liquidations**

   a. Partial liquidations are one type of redemption.

14. **Constructive Ownership**

   a. The (redeemed) shareholder is treated as owning shares owned by certain related parties, e.g., family members (excluding siblings and grandparents).

Stop and review! You have completed the outline for this subunit. Study multiple-choice questions 9 and 10 on page 327.

11.5 COMPLETE LIQUIDATION

1. **Defined**

   a. Under a plan of complete liquidation, a corporation redeems all of its stock in a series of distributions.

2. **Corporate Gains**

   a. A corporation recognizes any gain or loss realized on distributions in complete liquidation as if the property were sold at its FMV to the shareholder immediately before its distribution.
   b. Gain or loss is computed on an asset-by-asset basis.
   c. FMV of distributed property is treated as not less than the related liabilities that the shareholder assumes or to which the property is subject.
   d. The character of amounts recognized depends on the nature of the asset in the hands of the distributing corporation, e.g., Secs. 1245 and 1250.

EXAMPLE

Under a plan of complete liquidation, Zaige Corporation distributed land having an adjusted basis to Zaige of $19,000 to its sole shareholder. The land was subject to a liability of $98,000, which the shareholder assumed for legitimate business purposes. The fair market value of the land on the date of distribution was $71,000.

Generally, the FMV of $71,000 would be used to determine any gain; however, because the liability relief of $98,000 is greater than the FMV, Zaige's recognized gain is $79,000 ($98,000 liability relief – $19,000 AB).

---

3. **Corporate Losses**

   a. A corporation generally recognizes any losses realized on liquidating distributions.
   b. Certain realized losses are not recognized when the distributee shareholder is related to the corporation. A more-than-50% shareholder, actually or constructively, is a typical related distributee.

      1) Applicable distributions are of assets non-pro rata or acquired within 5 years by a contribution to capital or a Sec. 351 exchange.
      2) Permanent disallowance results, even if post-contribution.

c. Precontribution loss. The amount of a loss inherent on a contribution reduces loss recognized on distribution.

1) Applicable dispositions are of assets a liquidating corporation distributes, sells, or exchanges that were acquired by a contribution to capital or by a Sec. 351 exchange when its AB exceeded FMV for the principal purpose of recognizing the loss on liquidation.

2) The loss limit operates by requiring that basis for computing the amount of loss be reduced by loss inherent on contribution.

d. Carryovers. Unused, unexpired NOLs, capital losses, and charitable contribution carryover amounts are lost.

4. **Shareholder Treatment**

a. A shareholder treats amounts distributed in complete liquidation as realized in exchange for stock.

b. Capital recovery to the extent of basis is permitted before recognizing gain or loss.

c. The holding period will not include that of the liquidated corporation.

d. Amounts realized include money and the FMV of other distributed property received.

1) Liabilities to which property is subject reduce the amount realized.

2) Allocation of amounts realized to each block of stock is required.

EXAMPLE

Consider a single liquidating distribution to Shareholder S on February 1, 2017, of $70 cash and a car ($25 × FMV) subject to a liability of $15. S's amount realized is $80 [$70 + ($25 − $15)].

Block	Shares	Acquired	Basis	Amount Realized	Gain (Loss) Realized
A	1	5/14	$10	$20	$10
B	3	10/15	90	60	(30)

---

e. Character of recognized gain or loss depends on the nature of each block of the stock in the hands of the shareholder.

EXAMPLE

If S in the previous example held the stock for investment, S would recognize LTCG on Block A and STCL on Block B.

---

f. Basis in distributed property is its FMV, but only after gain or loss on its receipt has been recognized.

5. **Reporting**

a. A corporation must file an information return (Form 966, *Corporation Dissolution or Liquidation*) reporting adoption of a plan or resolution for its dissolution, or partial or complete liquidation, within 30 days of adoption.

1) The IRS requires a corporation to file Form 1099-DIV for each calendar year it makes partial distribution(s) of $600 or more under a plan of complete liquidation.

2) Liquidation expenses incurred are deductible by the dissolved corporation.

Stop and review! You have completed the outline for this subunit. Study multiple-choice questions 11 and 12 beginning on page 327.

11.6 PARTIAL LIQUIDATION

1. **Noncorporate Shareholder**

a. A noncorporate shareholder treats a distribution as a sale to the extent it is (in redemption) in partial liquidation of the corporation.

2. **Corporate Distributor**

   a. The corporation making the distribution recognizes gain but not loss.

3. **Corporate Distributee**

   a. A corporation that receives a distribution in redemption for partial liquidation of another corporation treats the distribution as a dividend to the extent of E&P of the distributing corporation. The distributee corporation is eligible for the dividends-received deduction.

4. **Contraction of the Corporation**

   a. Partial liquidation refers to contraction of the corporation. Focus is not on the shareholders but on genuine reduction in size of the corporation.

   b. Partial liquidation must be pursuant to a plan. The partial liquidation must be complete within either the tax year of plan adoption or the succeeding tax year.

   c. Pro rata distributions do not preclude partial liquidation sale treatment, and shareholders are not required to surrender stock to the corporation.

   d. Safe harbor. Noncorporate shareholders apply partial liquidation sale treatment to distributions received if the following conditions are satisfied:

      1) The distribution is attributable to the corporation ceasing to conduct a trade or business that it actively conducted for at least 5 years ending with the date of the distribution.

      2) Immediately after the distribution, the corporation continues to conduct at least one active trade or business it has conducted for 5 years.

Stop and review! You have completed the outline for this subunit. Study multiple-choice question 13 on page 328.

11.7 SUBSIDIARY LIQUIDATION

1. **Nonrecognition**

   a. Neither the parent corporation nor a controlled subsidiary recognizes gain or loss on a liquidating distribution to the parent.

2. **Control**

   a. Control means the parent owns 80% or more of both the voting power and total value of the stock of the liquidating corporation.

3. **Basis**

   a. Basis in property distributed to the parent is transferred to the parent, and basis in stock in the subsidiary disappears.

4. **Liabilities**

   a. No gain is recognized on distributions that satisfy obligations of the subsidiary to the parent.

5. **Tax Attributes**

   a. Tax attributes of the subsidiary, such as NOLs and capital losses, carry over to the parent. The holding period will include that of the subsidiary.

6. **Minority Shareholders**

   a. Complete liquidation rules apply to distributions made to shareholders other than the parent. The subsidiary recognizes gain but not losses. The shareholder recognizes gain or loss and takes FMV basis in the property.

Stop and review! You have completed the outline for this subunit. Study multiple-choice questions 14 and 15 on page 328.

11.8 REORGANIZATIONS

1. **Overview**

   a. For federal tax purposes, a qualified reorganization of one or more corporations is considered a mere change in form of investment rather than a disposition of assets. For this reason, a general rule of nonrecognition applies to qualifying reorganizations. However, gain is recognized to the extent of boot.

2. **Shareholders**

   a. In a reorganization, a shareholder recognizes no gain or loss on an exchange of stock or securities solely for stock or securities in the same or another corporation that is a party to the reorganization.

   b. **Boot.** Gain on nonqualifying property (generally, property other than stock or securities in a corporation that is a party to the reorganization) is recognized.

      1) The amount recognized is the lesser of gain realized or FMV of nonqualifying property.

      2) Securities received when none are surrendered are nonqualifying property.

         a) The FMV of any excess of face value received over that given up is boot.

      3) **Character.** The shareholder is deemed to have received only stock and then to have redeemed the stock for cash.

         a) Gain is treated as a dividend (OI) to the extent of E&P, if the exchange has the effect of a dividend distribution.

   c. Loss. No loss is recognized.

   d. Basis in stock or qualified securities received is exchanged.

      1) Basis in boot is (tax) cost.

3. **Transferor Corporation (Acquired or Purchased)**

   a. A corporation that is a party to a reorganization generally recognizes no gain or loss on exchange of property solely for stock or securities of another corporate party.

   b. Gain is recognized only on boot not distributed (by the transferee). Liability relief is not boot unless it was for a nonbusiness or tax-avoidance purpose.

   c. The transferor (acquired) corporation recognizes gain realized if it distributes property other than stock or securities of another corporate party.

      1) The amount of liability in excess of basis is treated as the FMV of the property.
      2) No loss is recognized unless distribution is to a creditor.

   d. The transferor (acquired) corporation, finally, recognizes no gain or loss on distribution (even if the distribution is to a creditor) of

      1) Stock or securities it received from a party to the reorganization
      2) Boot received, except for post-acquisition gain realized

4. **Transferee Corporation (Acquiring or Purchasing)**

   a. The transferee corporation recognizes gain only on appreciated property (but not its own stock or securities) exchanged.

   b. Basis in property acquired from the transferor is transferred, i.e., the basis of the property

      1) In the hands of the transferor corporation, plus
      2) Gain recognized by the transferor corporation.

The CPA exam has required candidates to determine from a series of facts whether a qualified reorganization has occurred. It also has tested candidates on the basic characteristics of the types of reorganizations.

5. **Reorganization Types**

a. Nonrecognition treatment applies only if the change in corporate structure fits within the definition of one of the following specific reorganization types.

1) **Type A: Statutory merger or consolidation.** Under state law, two corporations merge into one. Stock in the non-surviving corporation is canceled. In exchange, its shareholders receive stock in the surviving corporation.

a) Merger. One of the corporations remains, while the other is no longer in existence.

b) Consolidation. Existing corporations are combined into a newly formed corporation.

2) **Type B: Stock-for-stock.** Shareholders acquire stock of a corporation solely for part or all of the voting stock of the acquiring corporation or its parent.

a) No boot is allowed.

b) The acquiring corporation must control the acquired corporation after the exchange; i.e., it must own 80% of the stock (voting and all other).

3) **Type C: Stock-for-assets.** One corporation acquires substantially all the assets of another in exchange for its voting stock (or its parent's). The transferor (sale of assets) corporation must liquidate.

a) Only 20% of the assets acquired may be exchanged for other than voting stock of the acquiring corporation. Limited amounts of boot are thus allowable.

b) "Substantially all assets" means ≥ 90% of the FMV of net assets and ≥ 70% of gross assets.

4) **Type D: Division**

a) A corporation transfers all or part of its assets to another in exchange for the other's stock.

b) The transferor or its shareholders must control the transferee after the exchange. Control means owning 80% of voting power and 80% of each class of nonvoting stock.

c) The stock or securities of the controlled corporation must be distributed to shareholders of the corporation that transferred assets to the controlled corporation.

d) Distribution of the stock need not be pro rata among the shareholders of the corporation that transferred assets to the controlled corporation. Thus, division of the original corporation may result.

5) **Type E: Recapitalization.** The capital structure of the corporation is modified by exchanges of stock and securities between the corporation and its shareholders.

6) **Type F: Reincorporation.** Stock and securities are exchanged upon a mere change in the name, form, or place of incorporation.

7) **Type G: Bankruptcy reorganization.** Stock, securities, and property are exchanged pursuant to a court-supervised bankruptcy proceeding.

6. **Nonrecognition Requirements**

a. Nonrecognition applies only to the extent each of several statutory and judicially sourced requirements are met.

1) The reorganization must be pursuant to a plan, a copy of which is filed with the tax return of each participating corporation.

2) Nonrecognition treatment applies only with respect to distributions in exchange for stock or securities of a corporation that is a party to the reorganization.

3) Business purpose, other than tax avoidance, must be present.

4) Owners of the reorganized enterprise(s) must retain an interest in the continuing enterprise. At least 40% continuity of equity interest by value is a benchmark.

5) Continuity of business enterprise. The acquiring corporation must continue either operating the historic business of the acquired corporation or using a significant portion of the acquired corporation's historic business assets. Continuing a significant line of business is sufficient if there was more than one.

Stop and review! You have completed the outline for this subunit. Study multiple-choice questions 16 through 18 on page 329.

11.9 MULTIPLE JURISDICTIONS

1. **Multijurisdictional Issues for State Taxes**

   a. A tax jurisdiction is a geographic area with its own distinct set of tax rules and regulations, e.g., a municipality, county, state, or country. When a taxable transaction has occurred across multiple jurisdictions, authoritative guidance must be established in order to reconcile or override the distinct sets of tax rules that may apply.

      1) The foreign tax credit presented in Study Unit 7, Subunit 1, is an example of a multijurisdictional issue.

   b. This subunit explains two of the longest-standing rules for interstate taxation: Public Law (PL) 86-272 and the Uniform Division of Income for Tax Purposes Act (UDITPA). Although the applicable taxes are state (not federal) taxes, these rules are tested as federal taxation by the AICPA because they are established at the federal level.

2. **Cross-Boundary Taxation**

   a. In general, a **nexus** (also called sufficient physical presence) is a connection. In tax law, a "foreign" entity (not a citizen of a given tax jurisdiction, e.g., city, county, state, nation) is required to have a nexus to the tax jurisdiction before a sales tax or income tax may be imposed on the activities of that entity.

      1) For example, Internet sales by Amazon and other online retailers resulted in no sales or income taxes being paid on sales made within the borders of many taxing authorities. States have been trying to capture revenue from online sales made inside their states. Foreign companies have also tried to recapture sales, income, and value-added taxes.

3. **Sales Tax**

   a. In 1967 and 1992, the U.S. Supreme Court ruled that states cannot collect sales taxes on retailers unless there is a physical presence (nexus) within the state. Consequently, some states are replacing "nexus" with "economic nexus," emphasizing financial dealings over physical presence. The definition continues to evolve and differs from state to state.

   b. For sales taxes, a business might have nexus if it has

      1) A physical location in the state,
      2) Resident employees working in the state,
      3) Real or intangible property (owned or rented) within the state, or
      4) Employees who regularly solicit business within the state.

   c. Forwarding services in states without sales taxes (e.g., Oregon) have been used to avoid the sales tax; however, if that occurs, the sale may be traced back up the distribution chain.

d.   An entity is generally allowed to offset taxes paid to another jurisdiction either by a direct tax credit for U.S. taxes or a deduction of the foreign taxes paid.

1)   For the tax credit, the payer must not receive a specific benefit from paying the tax. The right to engage in business is not considered a benefit for this purpose.

4.   **Income Tax**

a.   The form of organization may influence how cross-border events and transactions are taxed.

1)   A **branch** is not a separate legal entity of the parent company, but is a legal extension of the head office. The parent company is subject to taxes on all income, not just branch income.

2)   A **subsidiary** is a separate legal entity owned by a parent company. The most common are limited liability corporations (LLCs), which are pass-through entities in which the owner pays the income tax. However, a subsidiary may be set up so the income does not pass through to the owner.

5.   **Public Law 86-272**

a.   Before a state can tax a nonresident (e.g., a resident of another state), a minimum presence in the taxing state by the nonresident must be established. As mentioned on the previous page, sufficient presence to tax the nonresident is nexus.

b.   Public Law 86-272 limits the state's ability to tax the net income of nonresidents by establishing the following nexus rules:

1)   Nexus is not established if

a)   Activity is limited to solicitation of orders for tangible personal property,

b)   The orders are sent out of state for approval or rejection, and

c)   The orders are filled by shipment or delivery from a point outside the state if approved.

c.   The Multistate Tax Commission's (MTC's) "Statement of Information Concerning Practices of Multistate Tax Commission and Signatory States Under Public Law 86-272" lists the following as **protected in-state activities** (i.e., they will not establish nexus):

1)   Soliciting orders for sales by any type of advertising

2)   Soliciting of orders by an in-state resident with only an "in-home" office

3)   Carrying free samples and promotional materials for display or distribution

4)   Furnishing display racks and advising customers of the products without charge

5)   Providing automobiles for conducting protected activities

6)   Passing orders, inquiries, and complaints on to the home office

7)   Missionary sales activities

a)   For example, a manufacturer's solicitation of retailers to buy the manufacturer's goods from the manufacturer's wholesale customers

8)   Coordinating shipment/delivery and providing related information without charge

9)   Checking customers' inventories (e.g., reorder, but not quality control)

10) Maintaining a sample/display room at one location for less than 14 days during the tax year

11) Recruiting, training, and evaluating sales personnel

12) Mediating customer complaints solely for ingratiating the sales personnel with the customer and facilitating order request

13) Owning, leasing, using, or maintaining personal property for use in the employee's "in-home" office or automobile that is solely limited to the conducting of protected activities

d. The MTC's statement lists the following as **unprotected in-state activities** (i.e., they create nexus):

1) Making repairs to or performing maintenance or service on the property sold or to be sold
2) Collecting on accounts
3) Investigating creditworthiness
4) Installing a product at or after shipment or delivery
5) Conducting training courses, seminars, or lectures for non-soliciting personnel
6) Providing technical assistance or service for purposes other than the facilitation of the solicitation of orders

    a) For example, engineering assistance or design service

7) Investigating, handling, or otherwise assisting in resolving customer complaints, other than mediating direct customer complaints with the sole purpose of ingratiating the sales personnel with the customer
8) Approving or accepting orders
9) Repossessing property
10) Securing deposits on sales
11) Picking up or replacing damaged or returned property
12) Hiring, training, or supervising personnel (other than personnel involved only in solicitation)
13) Using agency stock checks or any other instrument or process by which sales are made within the home state by sales personnel
14) Maintaining a sample or display room at any one location in excess of 14 days during the tax year
15) Carrying samples for sale, exchange, or distribution in any manner for consideration or other value
16) Owning, leasing, using, or maintaining any of the following facilities or property in-state:

    a) Repair shop
    b) Parts department
    c) Office other than "in-home" office
    d) Warehouse
    e) Meeting place for directors, officers, or employees
    f) Stocks of goods other than samples
    g) Telephone-answering service publicly attributed to the company/ representative
    h) Mobile stores
    i) Real property or fixtures to real property of any kind

17) Consigning stock of goods or other tangible personal property for sale
18) Maintaining, by the employee or other representative, an office or place of business of any kind other than a qualified "in-home" office

NOTE: Generally, telephone or other public listings indicating company/employee contact at a specific location creates nexus; however, normal distribution of business cards/stationery does not create nexus.

19) Entering into or disposing of a franchise or licensing agreement or transferring related tangible personal property
20) Conducting any activity not listed as protected that is not entirely ancillary to requests for orders, even if such activity helps to increase purchases

6. **The Uniform Division of Income for Tax Purposes Act (UDITPA)**

   a. The UDITPA was drafted by the National Conference of Commissioners on Uniform State Laws and is recommended for enactment in all states. Each state decides whether or not to adopt the act.

   b. Once nexus is established, net income must be accurately allocated or apportioned among the various jurisdictions. The UDITPA provides a uniform method for allocating and apportioning a business's income. The rules for the business's nonbusiness income are different than those for the business's business income.

   c. **Allocation** is used to identify nonbusiness income to a specific state or local taxing authority for income derived solely from assets held for investment purposes.

   d. **Apportionment** uses a formula to calculate the average amount of business income a company brings in by conducting operations within that state.

      1) Apportionment of business income to the taxing state is determined by the following equation:

      $$\frac{Property\ factor\ +\ Payroll\ factor\ +\ Sales\ factor}{3}$$

      NOTE: Some states only use the sales (gross receipts) factor.

      a) The property factor determines the in-state use of real and tangible personal business property.

      $$\frac{Avg.\ value\ of\ in\text{-}state\ real\ and\ tangible\ personal\ property\ used}{Avg.\ value\ of\ all\ real\ and\ tangible\ personal\ property\ used}$$

         i) Property owned by the taxpayer is valued at its original cost, not the AB (i.e., no depreciation reduction).

         ii) Property rented by the taxpayer is valued at eight times the net annual rental rate (rate paid minus rate received from sub-rentals).

      b) The payroll factor uses amounts determined by the accounting methods of the business so that accruals are treated as paid.

      $$\frac{In\text{-}state\ compensation\ paid}{Total\ compensation\ paid}$$

         i) Payroll attributed to management or maintenance or otherwise allocable to nonbusiness property should be excluded from the formula.

      c) The sales factor is only for business income. Capital gains are nonbusiness income and are allocated, not apportioned.

      $$\frac{In\text{-}state\ sales}{Total\ sales}$$

         i) Sales means net sales after discounts and returns.

         ii) Sales shipped to a state with no taxation of the taxpayer (i.e., no nexus) may be thrown back and taxed by the shipped-from state. If neither state taxes the taxpayer, the state in which the order was taken may be apportioned the sale.

e. Nonbusiness income is all income other than business income. It is allocated, not apportioned. Specific rules apply to nonbusiness income from rents, royalties, capital gains, interest, dividends, patents, and copyrights as follows:

Property Type		Allocation based on:
Net Rents & Royalties	Real	Location of property
	Tangible Personal	Proportional use[1] or commercial domicile[2]
Capital Gains & Losses	Real	Location of property
	Tangible Personal	Location of property[3] or commercial domicile[4]
	Intangible Personal	Commercial domicile
Interest & Dividends		Commercial domicile
Patent & Copyright Royalties		Proportional use[1] or commercial domicile[2]

[1] Proportional use within the taxing state

[2] The taxpayer's commercial domicile (i.e., home state) if the taxpayer is not organized or taxed in the state the property is used

[3] Location of property at time of sale

[4] The taxpayer's commercial domicile if the taxpayer is not taxed in the state the property is located at time of sale

f. If the allocation and apportionment provisions do not fairly represent the taxpayer's in-state activity, the taxpayer may request or the state may require (1) separate accounting (typically costly and difficult to carry out), (2) the exclusion of any one or more factors, (3) the inclusion of one or more additional factors, or (4) the employment of any other method to equitably allocate and apportion the income.

7. **Multijurisdictional Issues for Multinational Transactions**

a. U.S. taxpayers (individuals or business entities) are subject to tax on world-wide income. This may result in the income being subject to double-taxation. In an effort to mitigate double-taxation, various allowances have been made (e.g., foreign earned income exclusion, foreign tax credit). These allowances, to varying degrees, give up U.S. jurisdiction over foreign income.

1) Nonresident aliens are usually only subject to U.S. income tax on U.S. source income. The table on the next page shows the general rules for determining U.S. source income of nonresident aliens.

General Rules for Income Source	
Item of Income	Factor Determining Source
Salaries, wages, other compensation	Where services performed

Business Income:
  Personal services
  Sale of inventory – purchased
  Sale of inventory – produced
	Where services performed
	Where sold
	Where produced (Allocation may be necessary)

Interest	Residence of payer
Dividends	Whether a U.S. or foreign corporation*
Rents	Location of property

Royalties:
  Natural resources
  Patents, copyrights, etc.
	Location of property
	Where property is used

Sale of real property	Location of property
Sale of personal property	Generally seller's tax home
Pension distributions attributable to contributions	Where services were performed that earned the pension
Investment earnings on pension contributions	Location of pension trust
Sale of natural resources	Allocation based on fair market value of product at export terminal
Scholarships Fellowships	Generally, the residence of the payer

*Exceptions include
  Part of a dividend paid by a foreign corporation is U.S. source income if at least 25% of the corporation's gross income for the preceding 3 tax years before the year in which the dividends are declared is effectively connected with a U.S. trade or business.

    b. U.S. tax law attempts to reclaim some of the lost income due to the surrendering of jurisdiction, especially when the taxpayer's accounting practices are perceived as simply a means to avoid U.S. tax law. Generally, the rules attempt to capture the income when the income is repatriated to the U.S. taxpayer. Controlled foreign corporation (CFC) and subpart F income were covered in item 11. of Study Unit 4, Subunit 2.

    c. Transfer pricing is an accounting practice used to avoid proper tax treatment. Transfer pricing reallocates items of income and deduction among entities under common control. Reallocation of the income and deduction results in minimizing the U.S. tax of foreign corporations' U.S. affiliates. Since the foreign parent corporations do not normally do business in the U.S., their income is free from U.S. tax. To prevent evasion, the IRS reallocates items affecting taxable income as if the transactions were conducted in an arm's-length transaction between uncontrolled parties.

8. **Federal Filing Requirements for Cross-Border Business Investments**

    a. A tax return must be filed if a foreign corporation is engaged in a trade or business in the U.S.

    b. U.S. citizens and residents are taxed on world-wide income regardless of where they live. The income that needs to be reported on a U.S. tax return includes, but is not limited to, earned and unearned income, such as wages, salary and tips, interest, dividends, capital gains, pensions, rents, and royalties. This is true even if the income is nontaxable under Internal Revenue Code or treaty.

    c. Nonresident aliens are generally subject to U.S. income taxes only on their U.S.-source income. Passive income (e.g., interest, dividends, rents, and royalties) is generally taxed at a flat rate of 30% unless a tax treaty specifies a lower rate.

9.   **Tax Withholding in the U.S.**

a.   Three types of tax withholding are imposed in the U.S., depending on the payment source:

1)   Wages earned, e.g., income tax, Social Security, and Medicare

2)   Payments to foreign persons, including nonresident aliens, foreign corporations, foreign partnerships, and foreign partners in U.S. partnerships

3)   Backup withholding on dividends and interest if

a)   A person fails to provide a tax identification number to the payer or

b)   The IRS has notified the payer that the payer must withhold taxes.

b.   The payer must send the withheld amounts to the IRS, and excess withholding is refunded to the payee after an annual tax return has been filed.

Stop and review! You have completed the outline for this subunit. Study multiple-choice questions 19 and 20 on page 330.

QUESTIONS

11.1 Formation

1. Ames and Roth form Homerun, a C corporation. Ames contributes several autographed baseballs to Homerun. Ames purchased the baseballs for $500, and they have a total fair market value of $1,000. Roth contributes several autographed baseball bats to Homerun. Roth purchased the bats for $5,000, and they have a fair market value of $7,000. What is Homerun's basis in the contributed bats and balls?

A. $0

B. $5,500

C. $6,000

D. $8,000

Answer (B) is correct.

REQUIRED: The basis in property contributed to a corporation.

DISCUSSION: The basis of property acquired by a corporation in connection with a Sec. 351 transaction is the same as the basis in the hands of the transferor (shareholder), increased by the amount of gain recognized by the transferor on such transfer. Since neither shareholder received any boot, no gain was recognized. Thus, the corporation's total basis in the transferred assets is the same as that in the shareholder's hands, or $5,500 ($500 + $5,000).

Answer (A) is incorrect. The basis of property acquired by a corporation in connection with a Sec. 351 transaction is the same as the basis in the hands of the transferor (shareholder), increased by the amount of gain recognized by the transferor on such transfer. Answer (C) is incorrect. The $6,000 takes a basis equal to the fair market value of Ames's contribution and the adjusted basis of Roth's contribution. The basis of property acquired by a corporation in connection with a Sec. 351 transaction is the same as the basis in the hands of the transferor (shareholder), increased by the amount of gain recognized by the transferor on such transfer. Answer (D) is incorrect. A basis of $8,000 is equal to the fair market value of each of the contributions. The basis of property acquired by a corporation in connection with a Sec. 351 transaction is the same as the basis in the hands of the transferor (shareholder), increased by the amount of gain recognized by the transferor on such transfer.

2. In April, A and B formed X Corp. A contributed $50,000 cash, and B contributed land worth $70,000 (with an adjusted basis of $40,000). B also received $20,000 cash from the corporation. A and B each receive 50% of the corporation's stock. What is the tax basis of the land to X Corp.?

A. $40,000

B. $50,000

C. $60,000

D. $70,000

Answer (C) is correct.

REQUIRED: The tax basis of land transferred to X Corp.

DISCUSSION: The basis of land to X Corp. is the adjusted basis to B ($40,000) increased by B's recognized gain ($20,000). B's realized gain is $30,000. Recognized gain is the lesser of boot received ($20,000) and realized gain.

Answer (A) is incorrect. A $40,000 basis would be the applicable tax basis to X Corp. if B did not recognize any gain on the transfer. Answer (B) is incorrect. Neither the use of the FMV of the property nor a reduction equal to the boot received is how X Corp. calculates the basis of the land ($50,000 is the FMV of the property transferred to X Corp. reduced by the boot received by B). Answer (D) is incorrect. The inclusion of gain realized in the basis of the land is limited to the boot received by B.

3. On July 1 of the current year, Rich, sole proprietor of Kee Nail, transferred all of Kee's assets to Merit, Inc., a new corporation, solely for a certain percentage of Merit's stock. Dee, who is not related to Rich, also bought some of Merit's stock on July 1. Merit's outstanding capital stock consisted of 1,000 shares of common stock with a par value of $100 per share. For the transfer of Kee Nail's assets to be tax-free, what is the minimum number of shares of Merit's stock that must be owned by Rich and Dee immediately after the exchange?

A. 500

B. 501

C. 800

D. 801

Answer (C) is correct.

REQUIRED: The minimum number of shares of stock that must be owned by two transferors immediately after the exchange for the transfer to be tax-free.

DISCUSSION: A transfer of assets for stock of a corporation is tax-free if the transferors are in control of the corporation immediately after the exchange. A person who transfers appreciated property will receive the benefit if another transferor transfers property and together they meet the control test. Property includes money. Control is ownership of stock possessing at least 80% of the total combined voting power of all classes of stock entitled to vote and at least 80% of the total number of shares of all other classes of stock of the corporation. At a minimum, Rich and Dee must own 800 shares (1,000 shares × 80%).

Answer (A) is incorrect. The number 500 results from multiplying the 1,000 shares of common stock by 50%. Answer (B) is incorrect. The number 501 results from a greater than 50% ownership. Transferors must own a minimum of 80% of the common shares. Answer (D) is incorrect. A total of 801 shares is greater than the 80% minimum number of shares of ownership to receive tax-free treatment.

11.2 Current Earnings and Profits

4. What is the current earnings and profits (E&P) of a corporation with taxable income of $10,000 that included the following unadjusted items:

Meals and entertainment	$ 200
Capital loss carried over from prior year	3,000

A. $7,100

B. $10,000

C. $12,800

D. $12,900

Answer (D) is correct.

REQUIRED: The current E&P of the corporation.

DISCUSSION: Current E&P is the current-year taxable income adjusted for specific items. Positive adjustments include loss carryovers, as they were negative adjustments in the year they occurred. Negative adjustments include the nondeductible portion of meals and entertainment. Corporations are allowed to deduct 50% of qualifying meals and entertainment expenses. The corporation's current E&P is $12,900 [$10,000 + $3,000 – ($200 × 50%)].

Answer (A) is incorrect. The loss carryover is a positive adjustment, and the excess portion of deductible meals and entertainment is a negative adjustment. Answer (B) is incorrect. Taxable income is only the starting point for calculating current E&P. Both positive and negative adjustments must be made in order to arrive at current E&P. Answer (C) is incorrect. Only the nondeductible portion of meals and entertainment for taxable income is adjusted for current E&P.

11.3 Distributions

5. Fox, the sole shareholder in Fall, a C corporation, has a tax basis of $60,000. Fall has $40,000 of accumulated positive earnings and profits at the beginning of the year and $10,000 of current positive earnings and profits for the current year. At year end, Fall distributed land with an adjusted basis of $30,000 and a fair market value (FMV) of $38,000 to Fox. The land has an outstanding mortgage of $3,000 that Fox must assume. What is Fox's tax basis in the land?

A. $38,000

B. $35,000

C. $30,000

D. $27,000

Answer (A) is correct.

REQUIRED: The shareholder basis of property received in a nonliquidating distribution.

DISCUSSION: In a nonliquidating distribution, the shareholder's basis in property received is the FMV at the date of distribution. If the shareholder also assumes a liability with the property distribution, it must be compared to the property's FMV. In the event the liability exceeds the FMV, the liability is the shareholder's basis in the property. If the liability is less, as this situation indicates ($3,000 < $38,000), the basis will remain equal to the FMV.

Answer (B) is incorrect. The property's FMV is not reduced by the liability assumed. If the liability exceeds the FMV of the property assumed, the liability is the basis. Otherwise, it does not affect basis. Answer (C) is incorrect. The shareholder's basis in the property distribution is equal to the FMV at the date of distribution, not the adjusted basis under the corporation. Answer (D) is incorrect. The beginning amount for the shareholder's basis is not the corporation's adjusted basis. The FMV at the time of distribution is the shareholder's basis. Additionally, there is no adjustment for a liability assumed by the shareholder unless the liability exceeds the FMV of the property.

6. Nyle Corp. owned 100 shares of Beta Corp. stock that it bought 16 years ago for $9 per share. This year, when the fair market value of the Beta stock was $20 per share, Nyle distributed this stock to a noncorporate shareholder. Nyle's recognized gain on this distribution was

A. $2,000

B. $1,100

C. $900

D. $0

Answer (B) is correct.

REQUIRED: The amount of gain recognized by a corporation on distribution of stock.

DISCUSSION: A corporation must recognize gain realized on distributions of property. The definition of property excludes stock, but only if issued by the corporation. Thus, Nyle Corp. must recognize gain of $1,100 ($2,000 FMV – $900 basis).

Answer (A) is incorrect. The FMV of the stock is $2,000. Answer (C) is incorrect. The basis of the stock is $900. Answer (D) is incorrect. A corporation recognizes gain or loss on distribution of stock that is not issued by the corporation.

7. Brisk Corp. is an accrual-basis, calendar-year C corporation with one individual shareholder. At year end, Brisk had $600,000 accumulated and current earnings and profits as it prepared to make its only dividend distribution for the year to its shareholder. Brisk could distribute either cash of $200,000 or land with an adjusted tax basis of $75,000 and a fair market value of $200,000. How would the taxable incomes of both Brisk and the shareholder change if land were distributed instead of cash?

	Brisk's taxable income	Shareholder's taxable income
A.	No change	No change
B.	Increase	No change
C.	No change	Decrease
D.	Increase	Decrease

Answer (B) is correct.

REQUIRED: The effect of a property distribution on a corporation's and shareholder's taxable income.

DISCUSSION: The shareholder will include the cash or the FMV of the property in their income regardless of the two distributions. Each will also be dividend income because Brisk has sufficient E&P. Brisk's taxable income will increase, based on the gain from the property's excess FMV over its adjusted basis.

Answer (A) is incorrect. Even though the shareholder's taxable income will not change based on the cash or property distribution, Brisk's taxable income will increase as a result of the property distribution gain. Answer (C) is incorrect. Brisk's taxable income should increase as a result of the property distribution, and the shareholder's taxable income will not change if property is distributed. Answer (D) is incorrect. Brisk's taxable income will increase, yet the shareholder's taxable income will not decrease. The shareholder will include the FMV of the property in income, not the corporation's adjusted basis.

8. A corporation that has both preferred and common stock has a deficit in accumulated earnings and profits at the beginning of the year. The current earnings and profits are $25,000. The corporation makes a dividend distribution of $20,000 to the preferred shareholders and $10,000 to the common shareholders. How will the preferred and common shareholders report these distributions?

A. Preferred - $20,000 dividend income; common - $10,000 dividend income.

B. Preferred - $20,000 dividend income; common - $5,000 dividend income, $5,000 return of capital.

C. Preferred - $15,000 dividend income; common - $10,000 dividend income.

D. Preferred - $20,000 return of capital; common - $10,000 return of capital.

Answer (B) is correct.

REQUIRED: The amount and character of dividends distributed to preferred and common shareholders.

DISCUSSION: The amount of a distribution is a dividend to the extent, first, of any current E&P and, then, of any accumulated E&P. To the extent current E&P are sufficient to cover a distribution, the distribution is treated as a taxable dividend, even if there is a deficit in the accumulated E&P. The amount of a distribution in excess of dividends is treated as tax-exempt return of capital to the extent of the shareholder's basis. Distributions are first allocated to the preferred shareholders and then to the common shareholders.

Answer (A) is incorrect. Only $5,000 of the distribution to common shareholders is dividend income, while the other $5,000 is treated as a return of capital since there is no accumulated E&P remaining. Answer (C) is incorrect. There is a $20,000 distribution to the preferred shareholders, and $5,000 of the distribution to common shareholders must be treated as a return of capital. Answer (D) is incorrect. Distributions are not treated as a return of capital until there is no current and accumulated E&P remaining.

11.4 Redemptions

9. Elm Corp. is an accrual-basis, calendar-year C corporation with 100,000 shares of voting common stock issued and outstanding as of December 30, Year 1. On December 31, Year 1, Hall surrendered 2,000 shares of Elm stock to Elm in exchange for $33,000 cash. Hall had no direct or indirect interest in Elm after the stock surrender. Additional information follows:

Hall's adjusted basis in 2,000 shares of Elm on December 31, Year 1 ($8 per share)	$16,000
Elm's accumulated earnings and profits at January 1, Year 1	25,000
Elm's Year 1 net operating loss	(7,000)

What amount of income did Hall recognize from the stock surrender?

- A. $33,000 dividend.
- B. $25,000 dividend.
- C. $18,000 capital gain.
- D. $17,000 capital gain.

Answer (D) is correct.
   REQUIRED: The income recognized from a stock redemption.
   DISCUSSION: In the case of a stock redemption in complete liquidation of a shareholder's interest, the redemption is treated as a sale or exchange of a capital asset. Therefore, Hall's income from the redemption is a $17,000 capital gain ($33,000 – $16,000 basis).
   Answer (A) is incorrect. The amount of cash exchanged for the Elm stock is $33,000. Answer (B) is incorrect. The amount of Elm's accumulated earnings and profits at January 1, Year 1, is $25,000. Answer (C) is incorrect. The difference between Elm's accumulated earnings and profits and Elm's Year 1 net operating loss is $18,000.

10. Zeb, an individual shareholder, owned 25% of Towne Corporation stock. Pursuant to a series of stock redemptions, Towne redeemed 10% of the shares of stock Zeb owned in exchange for land having a fair market value of $30,000 and an adjusted basis of $10,000. Zeb's basis for all of his Towne stock was $200,000. Zeb reported the redemption transaction as if it were a dividend. Zeb's basis in the land and his Towne stock (immediately after the redemption) is

- A. Land, $30,000; stock, $200,000.
- B. Land, $30,000; stock, $180,000.
- C. Land, $10,000; stock, $200,000.
- D. Land, $20,000; stock, $200,000.

Answer (A) is correct.
   REQUIRED: The basis in land received in a redemption of stock treated as a dividend, and the basis in the stock after the redemption.
   DISCUSSION: If a redemption of shares does not qualify as a sale or exchange, it is treated as a dividend. The amount of a dividend distribution is the amount of money received plus the fair market value of the property received. Zeb has a $30,000 dividend. The basis of property received in a distribution is the FMV of such property. Therefore, Zeb's basis in the land is $30,000. A dividend distribution does not affect the basis in a shareholder's stock, so Zeb's stock basis remains $200,000.

11.5 Complete Liquidation

11. Krol Corporation distributed marketable securities in redemption of its stock in a complete liquidation. On the date of distribution, these securities had a basis of $100,000 and a fair market value of $150,000. What gain does Krol have as a result of the distribution?

- A. $0
- B. $50,000 capital gain.
- C. $50,000 Sec. 1231 gain.
- D. $50,000 ordinary gain.

Answer (B) is correct.
   REQUIRED: The gain to a corporation on distribution of property in redemption of its stock in a complete liquidation.
   DISCUSSION: Gain or loss is recognized when a corporation distributes property as part of a complete liquidation. Krol recognizes a $50,000 gain ($150,000 FMV – $100,000 AB). It is a capital gain because the marketable securities are a capital asset.
   Answer (A) is incorrect. A corporation must recognize any gain it realizes on distribution of property in redemption of its stock in a complete liquidation. Answer (C) is incorrect. The transaction results in a capital gain. Section 1231 property is property held for more than 1 year. It includes real or depreciable property used in a trade or business and involuntarily converted capital assets. Answer (D) is incorrect. The transaction results in a capital gain.

12. A corporation was completely liquidated and dissolved during the current year. The filing fees, professional fees, and other expenditures incurred in connection with the liquidation and dissolution are

    A. Deductible in full by the dissolved corporation.

    B. Deductible by the shareholders and not by the corporation.

    C. Treated as capital losses by the corporation.

    D. Not deductible by either the corporation or the shareholders.

Answer (A) is correct.
    REQUIRED: The tax treatment for expenses incurred in connection with a corporate liquidation.
    DISCUSSION: The filing fees, professional fees, and other liquidation-related expenses are deductible in the final tax return of the corporation.
    Answer (B) is incorrect. The expense is not incurred by the shareholders. Therefore, the shareholders cannot deduct them. Answer (C) is incorrect. The expenses are deductible as trade or business expenses. Answer (D) is incorrect. The expenses are deductible by the corporation.

11.6 Partial Liquidation

13. How does a noncorporate shareholder treat the gain on a redemption of stock that qualifies as a partial liquidation of the distributing corporation?

    A. Entirely as capital gain.

    B. Entirely as a dividend.

    C. Partly as capital gain and partly as a dividend.

    D. As a tax-free transaction.

Answer (A) is correct.
    REQUIRED: The treatment of a partially liquidating distribution received by a noncorporate shareholder.
    DISCUSSION: A redemption made in partial liquidation of an interest held by a noncorporate shareholder is treated as a distribution in exchange for the stock, i.e., a sale. The shareholder will treat any gain on the redemption as a capital gain. The amount of the distribution is the FMV of the property.

11.7 Subsidiary Liquidation

14. Forrest Corp. owned 100% of both the voting stock and total value of Diamond Corp. Both corporations were C corporations. Forrest's basis in the Diamond stock was $200,000 when it received a lump sum liquidating distribution of property as a result of the redemption of all of Diamond stock. The property had an adjusted basis of $270,000 and a fair market value of $500,000. What amount of gain did Forrest recognize on the distribution?

    A. $0

    B. $70,000

    C. $270,000

    D. $500,000

Answer (A) is correct.
    REQUIRED: The recognized gain of a liquidating distribution to a parent corporation.
    DISCUSSION: Neither the parent corporation nor a controlled subsidiary recognizes gain or loss on a liquidating distribution to the parent. Control means the parent owns 80% or more of both the voting power and total value of the stock of the liquidating corporation. Forrest Corp. controls Diamond Corp. because it owns 100% of both the voting stock and total value of Diamond Corp. Therefore, Forrest does not recognize any gain on the liquidating distribution.
    Answer (B) is incorrect. The amount of $70,000 uses the AB to calculate a gain. Special rules apply to complete liquidations between parent and controlled corporations. Answer (C) is incorrect. The amount of $270,000 is the AB of the distribution; however, in a complete liquidation, the amount realized is the FMV. In addition, special rules apply to complete liquidations between parent and controlled corporations. Answer (D) is incorrect. The amount of $500,000 is the realized gain (not recognized gain) in a complete liquidation between noncontrolling corporations. Special rules apply to complete liquidations between parent and controlled corporations.

15. When a parent corporation completely liquidates its 80%-owned subsidiary, the parent (as shareholder) will ordinarily

    A. Be subject to capital gains tax on 80% of the long-term gain.

    B. Be subject to capital gains tax on 100% of the long-term gain.

    C. Have to report any gain on liquidation as ordinary income.

    D. Not recognize gain or loss on the liquidating distribution(s).

Answer (D) is correct.
    REQUIRED: The correct statement about a complete liquidation of a subsidiary under Sec. 332.
    DISCUSSION: When a subsidiary corporation is liquidated into the parent corporation in a Sec. 332 transaction, no gain or loss is recognized on the liquidation.
    Answer (A) is incorrect. The parent corporation will not be subject to capital gains tax on 80% of the long-term gain. Answer (B) is incorrect. The parent corporation will not be subject to capital gains tax on 100% of the long-term gain. Answer (C) is incorrect. The parent corporation will not have to report any gain on liquidations as ordinary income.

11.8 Reorganizations

16. Jaxson Corp. has 200,000 shares of voting common stock issued and outstanding. King Corp. has decided to acquire 90% of Jaxson's voting common stock solely in exchange for 50% of its voting common stock and retain Jaxson as a subsidiary after the transaction. Which of the following statements is true?

A. King must acquire 100% of Jaxson stock for the transaction to be a tax-free reorganization.

B. The transaction will qualify as a tax-free reorganization.

C. King must issue at least 60% of its voting common stock for the transaction to qualify as a tax-free reorganization.

D. Jaxson must surrender assets for the transaction to qualify as a tax-free reorganization.

Answer (B) is correct.

REQUIRED: The requirements of a stock-for-stock acquisition.

DISCUSSION: A Type B, or stock-for-stock, acquisition qualifies as a tax-free reorganization if the shareholders of one company acquire the stock of the target company solely in exchange for stock of their company. The acquiring company must control at least 80% of the stock of the target company after the exchange.

Answer (A) is incorrect. Only 80% or more of the target company's stock must be acquired. Answer (C) is incorrect. There is no such requirement for a stock-for-stock reorganization. Answer (D) is incorrect. Assets need not be surrendered for qualification as a tax-free reorganization.

17. Pursuant to a plan of corporate reorganization adopted in July Year 1, Gow exchanged 500 shares of Lad Corp. common stock that he had bought in January Year 1 at a cost of $5,000 for 100 shares of Rook Corp. common stock having a FMV of $6,000. Gow's recognized gain on this exchange was

A. $1,000 long-term capital gain.

B. $1,000 short-term capital gain.

C. $1,000 ordinary income.

D. $0

Answer (D) is correct.

REQUIRED: The amount of gain recognized in a corporate reorganization.

DISCUSSION: The exchange of stock for stock in obtaining control of a corporation qualifies as a reorganization. No gain or loss is recognized in a reorganization if stock or securities are exchanged solely for stock or securities in the same corporation or in another corporation that was a party to the reorganization. For Gow, since no boot was received, no gain is recognized.

Answer (A) is incorrect. The amount of $1,000 is the difference between the $6,000 of Rook Corp. common stock and $5,000 of Lad Corp. common stock. No capital gain is recognized. Long-term capital gain occurs for capital property held longer than 1 year. Answer (B) is incorrect. The amount of $1,000 is the difference between the $6,000 of Rook Corp. common stock and $5,000 of Lad Corp. common stock. This transaction is tax-free, and no gain is recognized. Answer (C) is incorrect. The amount of $1,000 is the difference between the $6,000 of Rook Corp. common stock and $5,000 of Lad Corp. common stock. No gain is recognized because the transaction is a stock-for-stock reorganization.

18. Ace Corp. and Bate Corp. combine in a qualifying reorganization and form Carr Corp., the only surviving corporation. This reorganization is tax-free to the

	Shareholders	Corporation
A.	Yes	Yes
B.	Yes	No
C.	No	Yes
D.	No	No

Answer (A) is correct.

REQUIRED: The taxability of reorganization.

DISCUSSION: This exchange represents a Type A statutory consolidation wherein neither the shareholders nor the corporations involved will recognize income, provided no boot is exchanged.

11.9 Multiple Jurisdictions

19. What is the general term for a single geographic area that has its own distinct set of tax rules and regulations?

- A. Municipality.
- B. Interstate commerce.
- C. Tax jurisdiction.
- D. Multijurisdictional.

Answer (C) is correct.

REQUIRED: The general term for an area with its own tax rules.

DISCUSSION: A tax jurisdiction is a geographic area that has its own distinct set of tax rules and regulations. Specific examples of tax jurisdictions include a municipality, county, state, or country.

Answer (A) is incorrect. A municipality is a specific example of a tax jurisdiction. Answer (B) is incorrect. Interstate commerce is commercial activity involving multiple states, each with its own distinct set of tax rules and regulations. A state is a specific example of a tax jurisdiction. Answer (D) is incorrect. Multijurisdictional describes issues involving more than one jurisdiction.

20. In accordance with the UDITPA, which of the following is correct for allocating interest and dividends?

- A. Allocate based on the location of the property.
- B. Allocate based on the commercial domicile of the taxpayer.
- C. Allocate based on proportional use within the taxing state.
- D. Not allocated, but apportioned with other business income.

Answer (B) is correct.

REQUIRED: The correct statement regarding allocation of interest and dividends.

DISCUSSION: Nonbusiness income means all income other than business income. It is allocated, not apportioned. Specific rules apply to nonbusiness income from rents, royalties, capital gains, interest, dividends, patents, and copyrights. Interest and dividends are allocated based on the taxpayer's commercial domicile; i.e., they are taxed by the company's "home state."

Answer (A) is incorrect. There is no physical location for interest and dividends. Answer (C) is incorrect. Proportional use applies to tangible personal property. Interest and dividends do not have physical characteristics to be used in any particular location. Answer (D) is incorrect. The UDITPA specifically classifies interest and dividends as nonbusiness property and subject to allocation.

STUDY UNIT TWELVE
S CORPORATIONS AND EXEMPT ORGANIZATIONS

(19 pages of outline)

An S corporation is generally not subject to a federal tax on its income. Its items of income, loss, deduction, and credit are passed through to its shareholders on a per-day and per-share basis. Each shareholder is taxed on his or her share of the S corporation's income as it is earned. Distributions of cash or property generally are not income to its shareholders.

Certain organizations may qualify for exemption from federal income tax under Sec. 501(a). They are referred to as nonprofit organizations. Most organizations seeking recognition of exemption from federal income tax must use application forms specifically prescribed by the IRS.

Some candidates find it helpful to have the entire tax form side-by-side with our Knowledge Transfer Outline when studying. The full versions of the most up-to-date forms are easily accessible at www.gleim.com/taxforms. These forms and the form excerpts used in our outline are periodically updated as the latest versions are released by the IRS.

12.1 ELIGIBILITY AND ELECTION

1. **Overview**

   a. A corporation is treated as an S corporation only for those days for which each specific eligibility requirement is met and the required election is effective.

2. **Eligibility**

   a. Eligibility depends on the nature of the corporation, its shareholders, and its stock.

   b. An S corporation must have only one class of stock.

      1) Variation in voting rights of that one class of stock is permitted.
      2) Rights to profits and assets on liquidation must be identical.
      3) Debt may be treated as a disqualifying second class of stock.

   c. Issuance of debt does not disqualify S corporation status. A conversion feature or some other provision that would entitle the debtholder to control of the corporation is generally needed to disqualify S corporation status.

   d. The number of shareholders may not exceed 100.

      1) A husband and wife are considered a single shareholder for this purpose.
      2) Family members in a six-generation range are considered one shareholder.
      3) A nonresident alien (NRA) may not own any shares.
      4) Each shareholder must be either an individual, an estate, a single-member LLC, or a qualified trust.

         a) Certain small business trusts and tax-exempt organizations can be shareholders.
         b) Partnerships, Charitable Remainder Unitrusts, and Charitable Remainder Annuity Trusts may not be shareholders.

      5) Domestic partnerships are not eligible to be a shareholder.

      6)   The following is a list of qualified trusts that are allowed as shareholders of an S corporation:

          a)   A trust, all of which is treated as owned by an individual who is a citizen or resident of the United States.

          b)   A trust described in item a) immediately before the death of the deemed owner that continues in existence after such death.

              i)   This provision lasts for 2 years, beginning on the day of the deemed owner's death.

          c)   A trust that receives a stock transfer pursuant to the terms of a will.

              i)   This provision lasts for 2 years, beginning on the day of the stock transfer.

          d)   A trust created primarily to exercise the voting power of stock transferred to it. This does not apply to any foreign trust.

    e.   Certain entities cannot elect S status. These include some insurance companies, possession corporations, domestic international sales corporations (DISC) and former DISCs, and some institutions using the reserve method of accounting for bad debts.

      1)   However, domestic building and loan associations, mutual savings banks, and a cooperative bank--without capital stock organized and operated for mutual purposes and without profit--are all able to elect S status.

    f.   The corporation must be domestic and eligible.

      1)   Ineligible corporations include financial institutions, such as banks (that use the allowance method of accounting) and insurance companies.

    g.   S corporations can own C corporations or Qualified Subchapter S Subsidiaries (QSSS).

      1)   A QSSS is an electing domestic corporation that qualifies as an S corporation and is 100% owned by an S corporation parent.

3.   **Election**

    a.   An eligible corporation must make the election for S corporation status by filing Form 2553.

    b.   All shareholders at the time the election is made must file a consent.

      1)   Each person who was a shareholder at any time during the part of the tax year before the election is made must also consent.

      2)   If any former shareholders do not consent, the election is considered made for the following year.

    c.   Election made within the first 2 1/2 months of the beginning of the corporation's tax year is effective from the first day of that tax year.

    d.   Election made after the first 2 1/2 months of the corporation's tax year will become effective on the first day of the following tax year.

    e.   The IRS can treat a late-filed election as timely filed if it determines that reasonable cause existed for failing to file the election in a timely manner.

    f.   After revocation or termination of an election, a new election cannot be effectively made for 5 years without the consent of the IRS.

    g.   The IRS can waive the effect of an invalid election resulting from failure to qualify as an S corporation and/or failing to obtain the necessary shareholder consents.

4. **Termination**

    a. Upon the occurrence of a terminating event, an S corporation becomes a C corporation.

        1) The IRS may waive termination.

            a) The terminating event must be inadvertent and corrected within a reasonable time.

    b. An S corporation election is terminated by any of the following:

        1) An effective revocation. A majority of the shareholders (voting and nonvoting) must consent.

        2) Any eligibility requirement not being satisfied on any day.

        3) Passive investment income (PII) termination.

    c. The termination is effective as of the date the disqualifying event, other than a PII termination, occurs.

    d. **PII termination** occurs when, for 3 consecutive tax years, the corporation has both Subchapter C E&P on the last day and PII that is greater than 25% of gross receipts.

        1) An S corporation does not have E&P unless it was formerly a C corporation or acquired E&P in a tax-free reorganization, e.g., a merger.

        2) Gross receipts are gross receipts of the S corporation for the tax year.

            a) This amount is reduced by capital losses (other than on stock and securities) to the extent of capital gains.

        3) PII consists of gross receipts from dividends, interest, royalties, rents, and annuities, reduced by

            a) Interest on accounts receivable (notes) for inventory sold in the ordinary course of trade or business

            b) Rents from a lease under which significant services are rendered to the lessee (those not customarily rendered)

        4) Interest includes tax-exempt interest.

        5) Termination is effective at the beginning of the following tax year.

        6) Receipts from sales and exchanges of stock and securities are not considered PII.

The AICPA has used theoretical questions to test candidates' knowledge of requirements for S corporation eligibility, election, and termination.

5. **Accounting Method**

    a. An S corporation is not required to use the accrual method.

    b. Accounting method election is generally made by the S corporation.

    c. Shareholders, however, personally elect

        1) Credit or a deduction for foreign income taxes

        2) Percentage or cost depletion for oil and gas properties

        3) Treatment of mining exploration expenditures

6.   **Tax Year**

a.   An S corporation generally must adopt a calendar tax year.

b.   With IRS consent, it may adopt a fiscal year, if it establishes a valid business purpose for doing so, that

1)   Does not result in deferral of income to shareholders but
2)   Coincides with a natural business year.

a)   A natural business year may end with or after the end of the peak period of a cyclical business.

c.   An S corporation that deposits the equivalent amount of the deferred tax may elect a fiscal year.

1)   A new S corporation is limited to no more than 3 months' deferral of income to its shareholders.

2)   An existing S corporation may continue to use the fiscal year previously adopted.

d.   To change its tax year other than by a Sec. 444 election, an S corporation should file Form 1128 by the 15th day of the 3rd month of the new tax year.

e.   When S status is terminated, creating a short year, nonseparately computed income is allocated on a pro rata basis unless certain exceptions apply or an election is made.

7.   **Administration**

a.   The tax treatment of S corporation items of income, loss, deduction, and credit is determined at the corporate level.

b.   The S corporation files a tax return (Form 1120S). The due date is the 15th day of the 3rd month following the close of the tax year (e.g., March 15 for calendar-year taxpayers).

c.   Each shareholder must report a pro rata share of income and expenses on his or her personal tax return.

1)   The shareholder's reporting must be consistent with the corporate return.

a)   An exception applies if the shareholder notifies the IRS of the inconsistency.

2)   A shareholder's pro rata share of items is reported on his or her tax return for his or her tax year in which the S corporation tax year ends.

EXAMPLE

Compliance Corporation is a calendar-year S corporation. Compliance has two shareholders: Shelly, with a year end of June 30 of the current year, and Julie, with a year end of December 31 of the current year. Because Julie is a calendar-year taxpayer, she will report any current-year income from Compliance on her current-year return. Shelly, on the other hand, will report any current-year income from Compliance on her return for the following year.

---

d.   Administrative and judicial proceedings to determine proper treatment of items are unified at the level of the S corporation.

Stop and review! You have completed the outline for this subunit. Study multiple-choice questions 1 through 4 beginning on page 349.

12.2 OPERATIONS

1. **Exempt Taxes**

   a. Provisions that govern taxation of C corporations also govern taxation of S corporations unless a specific exception applies. S corporations are expressly exempt from the following taxes:

      1) Corporate income tax
      2) AMT (alternative minimum tax)
      3) AET (accumulated earnings tax)
      4) PHC (personal holding company) tax

2. **Reported Items**

   a. The items of income, deduction (including losses), and credit of an S corporation are reported by the corporation.

From Form 1120S

Income	**1a**	Gross receipts or sales	**1a**		
	b	Returns and allowances	**1b**		
	c	Balance. Subtract line 1b from line 1a		**1c**	
	2	Cost of goods sold (attach Form 1125-A)		**2**	
	3	Gross profit. Subtract line 2 from line 1c		**3**	
	4	Net gain (loss) from Form 4797, line 17 (attach Form 4797)		**4**	
	5	Other income (loss) (see instructions—attach statement)		**5**	
	6	**Total income (loss).** Add lines 3 through 5 . . . . ▶		**6**	
Deductions (see instructions for limitations)	**7**	Compensation of officers (see instructions—attach Form 1125-E) . . .		**7**	
	8	Salaries and wages (less employment credits)		**8**	
	9	Repairs and maintenance		**9**	
	10	Bad debts		**10**	
	11	Rents		**11**	
	12	Taxes and licenses		**12**	
	13	Interest		**13**	
	14	Depreciation not claimed on Form 1125-A or elsewhere on return (attach Form 4562)		**14**	
	15	Depletion **(Do not deduct oil and gas depletion.)**		**15**	
	16	Advertising		**16**	
	17	Pension, profit-sharing, etc., plans		**17**	
	18	Employee benefit programs		**18**	
	19	Other deductions (attach statement)		**19**	
	20	**Total deductions.** Add lines 7 through 19 . . . . ▶		**20**	
	21	**Ordinary business income (loss).** Subtract line 20 from line 6 . . .		**21**	
Tax and Payments	**22a**	Excess net passive income or LIFO recapture tax (see instructions) . .	**22a**		
	b	Tax from Schedule D (Form 1120S)	**22b**		
	c	Add lines 22a and 22b (see instructions for additional taxes) . . .		**22c**	
	23a	2016 estimated tax payments and 2015 overpayment credited to 2016	**23a**		
	b	Tax deposited with Form 7004	**23b**		
	c	Credit for federal tax paid on fuels (attach Form 4136)	**23c**		
	d	Add lines 23a through 23c . . . . ▶		**23d**	
	24	Estimated tax penalty (see instructions). Check if Form 2220 is attached . . . . . . ▶ ☐		**24**	
	25	**Amount owed.** If line 23d is smaller than the total of lines 22c and 24, enter amount owed . .		**25**	
	26	**Overpayment.** If line 23d is larger than the total of lines 22c and 24, enter amount overpaid . .		**26**	
	27	Enter amount from line 26 **Credited to 2017 estimated tax ▶**		**Refunded ▶**	**27**	

b.   A shareholder computes taxable income by taking into account the pro rata share of items passed through from the S corporation. The shareholder reports his or her pro rata share in the tax year within which the tax year of the S corporation ended.

EXAMPLE

Super, Inc., an S corporation, properly reported nonseparately stated net income from operations of $100,000 for its tax year ending November 30, Year 1. Sheldon, a calendar-year taxpayer who owns 5% of the shares of Super, Inc., must include $5,000 of ordinary income in his tax return for Year 1, which is due on or before April 15, Year 2.

---

3.   **Items Separately Stated**

a.   S corporation items of income, deduction, and credit, which could alter the tax liability of shareholders if taken into account by them on their personal returns, are required to be stated and passed through separately. Separately stated items include

1)   Section 1231 gains and losses
2)   Net short-term capital gains and losses
3)   Net long-term capital gains and losses
4)   Dividends
5)   Charitable contributions
6)   Taxes paid to a foreign country or to a U.S. possession
7)   Tax-exempt interest and related expense
8)   Investment income and related expense
9)   Amounts previously deducted (e.g., bad debts)
10) Real estate activities
11) Section 179 deduction (immediate expensing of new business equipment)
12) Credits
13) Deductions disallowed in computing S corporation income

Form 1120S   Page **3**

Schedule K		Shareholders' Pro Rata Share Items		Total amount	
Income (Loss)	**1**	Ordinary business income (loss) (page 1, line 21)	**1**		
	2	Net rental real estate income (loss) (attach Form 8825)	**2**		
	3a	Other gross rental income (loss) . . . . `3a`			
	b	Expenses from other rental activities (attach statement) . . `3b`			
	c	Other net rental income (loss). Subtract line 3b from line 3a	**3c**		
	4	Interest income	**4**		
	5	Dividends: **a** Ordinary dividends	**5a**		
		b Qualified dividends . . . . `5b`			
	6	Royalties	**6**		
	7	Net short-term capital gain (loss) (attach Schedule D (Form 1120S))	**7**		
	8a	Net long-term capital gain (loss) (attach Schedule D (Form 1120S))	**8a**		
	b	Collectibles (28%) gain (loss) . . . . `8b`			
	c	Unrecaptured section 1250 gain (attach statement) . . . . `8c`			
	9	Net section 1231 gain (loss) (attach Form 4797)	**9**		
	10	Other income (loss) (see instructions) . . Type ▶	**10**		
Deductions	**11**	Section 179 deduction (attach Form 4562)	**11**		
	12a	Charitable contributions	**12a**		
	b	Investment interest expense	**12b**		
	c	Section 59(e)(2) expenditures **(1)** Type ▶ _____ **(2)** Amount ▶	**12c(2)**		
	d	Other deductions (see instructions) . . Type ▶	**12d**		
Credits	**13a**	Low-income housing credit (section 42(j)(5))	**13a**		
	b	Low-income housing credit (other)	**13b**		
	c	Qualified rehabilitation expenditures (rental real estate) (attach Form 3468, if applicable)	**13c**		
	d	Other rental real estate credits (see instructions) Type ▶	**13d**		
	e	Other rental credits (see instructions) . . . Type ▶	**13e**		
	f	Biofuel producer credit (attach Form 6478)	**13f**		
	g	Other credits (see instructions) . . . . . Type ▶	**13g**		
Foreign Transactions	**14a**	Name of country or U.S. possession ▶			
	b	Gross income from all sources	**14b**		
	c	Gross income sourced at shareholder level	**14c**		
		Foreign gross income sourced at corporate level			
	d	Passive category	**14d**		
	e	General category	**14e**		
	f	Other (attach statement)	**14f**		
		Deductions allocated and apportioned at shareholder level			
	g	Interest expense	**14g**		
	h	Other	**14h**		
		Deductions allocated and apportioned at corporate level to foreign source income			
	i	Passive category	**14i**		
	j	General category	**14j**		
	k	Other (attach statement)	**14k**		
		Other information			
	l	Total foreign taxes (check one): ▶ ☐ Paid ☐ Accrued	**14l**		
	m	Reduction in taxes available for credit (attach statement)	**14m**		
	n	Other foreign tax information (attach statement)			
Alternative Minimum Tax (AMT) Items	**15a**	Post-1986 depreciation adjustment	**15a**		
	b	Adjusted gain or loss	**15b**		
	c	Depletion (other than oil and gas)	**15c**		
	d	Oil, gas, and geothermal properties—gross income	**15d**		
	e	Oil, gas, and geothermal properties—deductions	**15e**		
	f	Other AMT items (attach statement)	**15f**		
Items Affecting Shareholder Basis	**16a**	Tax-exempt interest income	**16a**		
	b	Other tax-exempt income	**16b**		
	c	Nondeductible expenses	**16c**		
	d	Distributions (attach statement if required) (see instructions)	**16d**		
	e	Repayment of loans from shareholders	**16e**		

Form **1120S**

Form 1120S   Page **4**

Schedule K		Shareholders' Pro Rata Share Items (continued)		Total amount	
Other Information	**17a**	Investment income	**17a**		
	b	Investment expenses	**17b**		
	c	Dividend distributions paid from accumulated earnings and profits	**17c**		
	d	Other items and amounts (attach statement)			
Recon-ciliation	**18**	**Income/loss reconciliation.** Combine the amounts on lines 1 through 10 in the far right column. From the result, subtract the sum of the amounts on lines 11 through 12d and 14l	**18**		

4. **Corporate Level Items**

   a. Items not required to be separately stated, such as organizational costs (e.g., utilities, noninvestment interest expense, and other ordinary items of income and expense) are combined at the corporate level, and the net amount of ordinary income or loss is passed through to shareholders.

5. **Amortizable Items**

   a. Shareholders (who are individuals) may elect to deduct ratably the expenses incurred during the tax year for

      1) Research and experimentation costs (over a 10-year period)
      2) Mining exploration and development costs (over a 10-year period)
      3) Increasing the circulation of a periodical (over a 3-year period)
      4) Intangible drilling costs (over a 5-year period)

6. **Allocation**

   a. The amount of each item that each shareholder takes into account is computed on a per-day and then a per-share basis. A shareholder's holding period does not include the date of acquisition but does include the date of disposition. All allocations are made on a per-share, per-day basis.

EXAMPLE

Axel transfers 100 shares of GNR Corp., an S Corporation, to fellow shareholder Duff on March 14. Therefore, Axel is allotted 73 days of ownership (January 1 – March 14) amounting to 20% (73 days ÷ 365 days) of each stock, or 20 shares combined. Duff will receive the other 80% (292 days ÷ 365 days) of each stock, or 80 shares combined.

---

   1) Upon a termination of a shareholder's interest during the tax year, an election is available to allocate items according to the books and records of the corporation (its accounting methods) instead of by daily proration.

7. **IRS Reallocation**

   a. Pro rata shares of S corporation items passed through may be reallocated by the IRS among shareholders who are members of the same family.
   b. Distributive shares must reflect reasonable compensation for services or capital furnished to the corporation by family members.
   c. The IRS may disregard a stock transfer (by gift or sale) motivated primarily by tax avoidance.

8. **Character**

   a. The shareholder characterizes each item as the corporation would.

9. **Disallowed Deductions**

   a. An S corporation is not allowed certain deductions.

      1) These are deductions for items that must be separately stated.
      2) Each shareholder may be allowed deductions for his or her pro rata share of the items passed through.

10. **Carryovers**

   a. Carryovers (e.g., NOL) between S and C corporations are permitted with limitations. This applies to corporations that change their status from C to S or from S to C.

      NOTE: Do not confuse this rule with the carryover rules for built-in gains tax explained in Subunit 12.4.

11. **Employee Fringe Benefits**

    a. A person who directly or by attribution owns more than 2% of the stock of an S corporation (voting power or amount) on any day during its tax year is not considered an employee entitled to employee benefits (i.e., they are employee-owners, not employees).

    b. The S corporation must treat an amount paid for fringe benefits as deductible compensation, and the shareholder must include the amount in gross income.

    c. This rule does not apply to pension and profit-sharing plans.

    d. This rule precludes

        1) Payments to accident and health plans
        2) Group-term life insurance coverage up to $50,000
        3) Medical reimbursement plans and disability plans
        4) Meals and lodging furnished for the convenience of the employer
        5) Cafeteria plans
        6) Qualified transportation benefits
        7) Personal use of employer-provided property or services
        8) Adoption assistance program
        9) Employment achievement award

    e. Fringe benefits available to 2% shareholders include the following:

        1) Dependent care assistance program
        2) Educational assistance program
        3) Compensation for injury and sickness
        4) No additional-cost service
        5) Qualified employee discount
        6) Working condition fringe
        7) De minimis fringe
        8) On-premises athletic facilities

    f. Accident and health insurance premiums paid by an S corporation are considered for services rendered.

        1) The premiums are deductible by the S corporation and includible in the shareholder's W-2.

        2) The premiums are excludable for Social Security and Medicare if the payments are made under a "qualified plan," such as a cafeteria plan.

        3) Qualified plans are those that treat all employees uniformly and do not give preferential treatment to key employees.

    g. The medical insurance deduction is available for 2% shareholders of S corporations for amounts paid by their corporation for health insurance on their behalf.

        1) The premiums must be included in income by the 2% shareholder.

            a) A deduction is allowed above-the-line on Form 1040 if the taxpayer has self-employment earnings at least equal to the deduction.

12. **Stock Basis**

    a. An individual is considered as owning the stock directly by or for

        1) The individual's spouse (other than a legally separated spouse)
        2) The individual's children, grandchildren, and parents

b. Generally, if a shareholder purchases stock, the shareholder's original basis in the stock is its cost.

1) If a shareholder receives stock in exchange for property, the basis is the same as the property's basis.

2) If a shareholder lends money to the S corporation, the basis is usually the amount of the loan.

3) If a shareholder guarantees a third-party loan to an S corporation, the loan does not increase the shareholder's basis. Two exceptions apply:

a) The shareholder makes payments on the loan.

b) The shareholder is the primary signer on the note, and the S corporation is the guarantor.

c. The adjusted basis of the shareholder's stock is calculated at year end with increases for the shareholder's pro rata share of the following:

1) All income items of the S corporation, including tax-exempt income, that are separately stated

2) Any nonseparately stated income of the S corporation

3) The amount of the deduction for depletion (other than oil and gas) that is more than the basis of the property being depleted

---

EXAMPLE

The taxpayer's basis in the S corporation is $12,000 at the beginning of the year. The corporation has ordinary income of $6,000, tax-exempt interest of $2,000, and a long-term capital gain of $1,500. The taxpayer's basis will be increased by $9,500 ($6,000 + $2,000 + $1,500) to $21,500 at the end of the year.

---

d. The adjusted basis of the shareholder's stock must also be decreased by the shareholder's pro rata share of the following:

1) Distributions by the S corporation that were not included in income (done before determining the allowable loss deduction)

2) All separately stated loss and deduction items

3) Any nonseparately stated loss of the S corporation

4) Any expenses of the S corporation that are not deductible in figuring its taxable income or are not properly capitalized

5) The shareholder's deduction for depletion of oil and gas property held by the S corporation to the extent it is not more than the shareholder's share of the adjusted basis of the property

---

EXAMPLE

The taxpayer's basis at the beginning of the year is $22,000. The taxpayer withdraws $16,000 during the year, and the corporation has an ordinary loss of $9,000. Basis in the corporation is first reduced by the $16,000 distribution to $6,000. Only $6,000 of the loss is deductible by the shareholder, limited to basis.

---

e. After basis in the shareholder's S corporation stock has been reduced to zero, the shareholder's basis in debt of the S corporation to that shareholder is reduced (but not below zero) by his or her share of items of loss and deduction.

1) In a subsequent tax year, items passed through must restore the basis in the debt before basis in the stock.

2) **Limit.** A shareholder's share of loss and deduction items in excess of basis in the debt is not deductible.

a) The excess is suspended and carried over indefinitely.

b) It may be deducted in a subsequent tax year in which basis is restored to debt or to stock.

EXAMPLE

The taxpayer's basis in the corporation is made up of $19,500 stock basis and $2,500 debt basis. The stock basis is first reduced by the $16,000 distribution to $3,500. Then, the stock basis is reduced to zero by the loss passthrough. Next, the debt basis is reduced to zero by the loss passthrough, with $3,000 of the loss carried forward ($9,000 – $3,500 – $2,500).

---

13. **At-Risk Rules**

    a. At-risk rules are applied at the shareholder level.

        1) If the shareholder's pro rata share of passed-through losses exceeds his or her amount at risk at the close of his or her tax year, the excess is not deductible.

            a) The excess is suspended and carried forward indefinitely.

            b) It is deductible when the shareholder's amount at risk has increased.

    b. Each shareholder's at-risk amount equals, basically, the sum of the following:

        1) Money and the adjusted basis of property contributed to the corporation

        2) Amounts borrowed and lent to the corporation to the extent the shareholder has personal liability for repayment or (s)he has pledged as security for repayment property not used in the activity (of the corporation)

            a) However, it does not include other debts of the corporation to third parties, even if the repayment is guaranteed by the shareholder.

            b) The shareholder's amount at risk is increased or decreased by the shareholder's pro rata share of passed-through income and deduction (tax-exempt related also) and by distributions to the shareholder.

    c. The shareholder's basis in his or her stock and debt of the corporation is reduced (subject to prior application of the basis loss limitation), even if current deductibility of the loss is prohibited by the at-risk rules.

14. **Passive Activity Loss Rules**

    a. Current deductibility of any passive activity losses passed through is limited, at the shareholder level, to passive activity income.

        1) Passive activity includes rental activity or any activity of the corporation in which the shareholder does not materially participate.

            a) Material participation by the S corporation is not sufficient.

    b. A shareholder's amount at risk must be reduced by the full amount allowable as a current deduction after application of the at-risk rules, even if part of it must be suspended by the passive loss rules.

15. **Failure to File Penalty**

    a. The penalty is imposed in the amount of the number of persons who were shareholders during any part of the year, multiplied by $200 for each of up to 12 months (including a portion of one) that the return was late or incomplete.

 Past CPA exams have contained questions asking for calculations of both a shareholder's adjusted basis in S corporation stock and a shareholder's share of net income from the S corporation.

Stop and review! You have completed the outline for this subunit. Study multiple-choice questions 5 through 12 beginning on page 350.

12.3 DISTRIBUTIONS

1. **Overview**

   a. Distributions include nonliquidating and liquidating distributions of money or other property but not of the S corporation's own stock or obligations. The amount of a particular distribution is the sum of any money plus the FMV of property distributed.

2. **Shareholder Accounts**

   a. S corporations are required to maintain records, with respect to each shareholder, referred to as

      1) Accumulated adjustments account (AAA)
      2) Other adjustments account (OAA)
      3) Previously taxed income account (PTI account)

      These records, along with the shareholder's basis in his or her stock and any Subchapter C E&P, are used to determine the shareholder's tax treatment of distributions.

   b. Distributions from an S corporation reduce the retained earnings in the following order:

      1) AAA
      2) PTI
      3) AE&P
      4) OAA
      5) Stock basis

   c. Note that AAA, OAA, and PTI records and information are needed by S corporations only for purposes of helping shareholders determine taxability of distributions when the S corporation has E&P.

   d. Subchapter C E&P. An S corporation does not have E&P unless it was formerly a C corporation or acquired E&P in a tax-free reorganization, e.g., a merger.

   e. The accumulated adjustments account (AAA) represents the current cumulative balance of the S corporation.

      1) It is calculated without regard to any net negative adjustments (excess of losses and deductions over income and gains).

      2) AAA is not affected by any transactions related to when it was a C corporation (e.g., federal income taxes).

      3) Expenditures that are not deductible by the S corporation decrease basis in stock and the AAA.

      4) Adjustment is not made to the AAA for tax-exempt income (which increases basis) or related nondeductible expenses (which reduce basis). These adjustments are made to OAA.

      5) The AAA balance can be reduced below zero. (Basis may not.)

   f. The OAA represents a cumulative balance of tax-exempt interest earned and life insurance proceeds, reduced by expenses incurred in earning it.

   g. The PTI account represents a balance of undistributed net income on which the shareholders were already taxed prior to 1983.

3. **Distributions of Property**

   a. An S corporation recognizes gain realized on the distribution of appreciated property (FMV > basis).

   b. The amount and character of the gain and its treatment are determined as if the distributed property were sold to the shareholder at its FMV.

      1) Ordinary income results if the property is depreciable in the hands of a more-than-50% shareholder.

    c.   The gain is passed through pro rata to each shareholder.

        1)   The shareholder's basis in his or her stock and the AAA is increased by his or her shares as if the S corporation had sold the property.

        2)   The distributee (recipient) shareholder must determine the proper treatment of the distribution.

EXAMPLE

The S corporation sells an investment asset with a basis of $15,000 for $23,000. The corporation reports an $8,000 gain, which flows through to the shareholders.

---

    d.   When loss property (basis > FMV) is distributed, no loss may be recognized by the S corporation.

        1)   The loss is passed through to the shareholders and is nondeductible.

            a)   Each shareholder must reduce the basis in his or her stock in the S corporation and take a FMV basis in the property distributed.

            b)   The distributee (recipient) shareholder must determine the proper treatment of the distribution.

        2)   Sale instead of distribution results in pass-through of loss.

EXAMPLE

The S corporation has a capital asset with a basis of $7,000 and a FMV of $5,000, which it distributes to the sole shareholder. The corporation has a nondeductible loss of $2,000. The shareholder reduces basis by $7,000 and has a $5,000 basis in the asset. If the corporation sold the asset and distributed the proceeds, the shareholder would have a $2,000 deductible loss.

---

    e.   An S corporation is not required to recognize gain on the liquidating distributions of certain installment obligations.

        1)   The shareholder treats each payment as a passed-through item.

4.   **Shareholder Treatment of Distributions**

    a.   Shareholder treatment of distributions from the S corporation is determined at the end of the S corporation's tax year.

        1)   The AAA, OAA, bases in shareholders' stock, and basis in corporate-shareholder debt must be adjusted for the S corporation's items of income, deduction, etc., before each shareholder determines the proper treatment of his or her distributions.

    b.   No E&P. Shareholder treatment of distributions is straightforward when the S corporation has no Subchapter C E&P.

        1)   That portion of distributions that does not exceed the basis in the shareholder's stock is treated as tax-free return of capital.

        2)   Excess over basis is treated as gain on sale of the stock.

            a)   The character depends on the nature of the stock in the hands of the shareholder and his or her holding period.

    c.   If there are Subchapter C E&P, the distribution is first treated as return of capital (tax-free) to the extent of the shareholder's AAA balance and then to PTI (up to any basis in the shareholder's stock).

        1)   Excess distribution beyond AAA and PTI is dividend income to the extent of Subchapter C E&P in the corporation.

        2)   Excess distribution beyond Subchapter C E&P is return of capital to the extent of OAA.

    3)   Excess distribution beyond OAA is return of capital to the extent of any remaining basis in the stock.

    4)   Any excess distribution over remaining basis distributed is treated as gain from the sale of the stock.

S Corporation without Subchapter C E&P

Shareholder Distribution	Tax Result
To extent of basis in stock	Not subject to tax; reduces basis in stock
In excess of basis of stock	Taxed as capital gain

S Corporation with Subchapter C E&P

Shareholder Distribution	Tax Result
To extent of AAA	Not subject to tax; reduces AAA and basis in stock
To extent of PTI	Already taxed previously; reduces PTI and basis in stock
To extent of C corporation E&P	Taxed as a dividend; reduces E&P, but not basis in stock
To extent of OAA	Not subject to tax; reduces OAA and basis in stock
To extent of basis in stock	Not subject to tax; reduces basis in stock
In excess of basis	Taxed as capital gain

NOTE: In the above determination of shareholder treatment of distributions, any amount to be treated as tax-free return of capital reduces the shareholder's basis in his or her stock.

EXAMPLE

A single-owner S corporation has AAA of $12,000, PTI of $4,000, and E&P of $8,000. The shareholder's basis is $25,000. The first $12,000 of any distribution reduces AAA and shareholder basis by $12,000 and is nontaxable. The next $4,000 of distributions reduces PTI and shareholder basis by $4,000 and is nontaxable. The next $8,000 of distributions is classified as dividend income and reduces E&P. The next $9,000 of distributions is a tax-free reduction of basis ($25,000 − $12,000 − $4,000) and is classified as return of capital. Any distributions above $33,000 will be taxed as capital gain income.

---

    d.   An election may be made to treat distributions as coming first from Subchapter C E&P.

        1)   This results in ordinary dividend income to the distributee (recipient) to the extent of the E&P.

        2)   Any excess distribution is treated as in 4.b. on the previous page.

    e.   Cash distributions within a relatively short transition period subsequent to termination of an S election are treated as a return of capital to the extent of the AAA.

        1)   Basis in shareholder stock is reduced.

    f.   Form 1099-DIV is used to report any distribution that is in excess of the accumulated adjustments account and that is treated as a dividend to the extent of accumulated earnings and profits.

From Form 1120S

Schedule M-2	Analysis of Accumulated Adjustments Account, Other Adjustments Account, and Shareholders' Undistributed Taxable Income Previously Taxed (see instructions)		
	(a) Accumulated adjustments account	(b) Other adjustments account	(c) Shareholders' undistributed taxable income previously taxed
1 Balance at beginning of tax year			
2 Ordinary income from page 1, line 21 . . .			
3 Other additions			
4 Loss from page 1, line 21	( )		
5 Other reductions	( )	( )	
6 Combine lines 1 through 5			
7 Distributions other than dividend distributions			
8 Balance at end of tax year. Subtract line 7 from line 6			

Form **1120S** [Year]

Stop and review! You have completed the outline for this subunit. Study multiple-choice questions 13 and 14 beginning on page 352.

12.4 SPECIAL TAXES

1. **Overview**
   a. Although S corporations are not generally subject to income tax, the following four special taxes are imposed on S corporations.

2. **Passive Investment Income (PII) Tax**
   a. An S corporation with Subchapter C E&P at the close of its tax year and PII of more than 25% of its gross receipts is subject to a tax of 35% of excess net passive income.
   b. Gross receipts (GR) and PII are defined in item 4.d. of Subunit 12.1.
   c. Net passive income (NPI) is PII reduced by expenses directly attributable to its production.
   d. PII tax liability is allocated to the PII items and reduces the amount of the item passed through to shareholders.
   e. S corporations are required to make estimated payments of PII tax.

3. **Built-In Gains (BIG) Tax**
   a. An S corporation that, upon conversion from C to S status, had net appreciation inherent in its assets is subject to tax of 35% on net gain recognized (up to the amount of built-in gain on conversion) during the recognition period.
   b. For conversions made after the 2010 tax year, the recognition period is the 5-year period beginning on the date the S election became effective.
      1) Thus, the conversion must have taken place effective 2012 for 2017 disposals.
   c. The tax liability is passed through, as a loss, pro rata to its shareholders.
      1) It reduces basis in each shareholder's stock and any AAA balance.
      2) Subchapter C E&P are not reduced by BIG tax liability.
   d. S corporations are required to make estimated payments of BIG tax.
   e. Any net operating or capital loss carryover arising in a tax year in which the S corporation was a C corporation can offset the built-in gain for the tax year.

4. **LIFO Recapture**
   a. Any excess of the FIFO inventory value over the LIFO inventory value at the close of the last tax year of C corporation status is gross income to a corporation that used the LIFO method to inventory goods.
   b. Basis of the inventory is increased by the amount on which the recapture tax is imposed.
   c. The recapture income is spread over 4 years: the last C corporation year and the first 3 years of the S corporation.

EXAMPLE

Miles, Inc., switched from a C Corporation to an S Corporation at the beginning of the current year. Miles had used the LIFO inventory valuation method during its existence as a C Corporation. Miles's inventory for the previous year was $2,750,000, and if it used the FIFO method, its inventory would be valued at $3,000,000. Therefore, for the previous year's tax return, Miles must include an additional $250,000 of gross income due to the LIFO recapture, and the tax associated with this additional gross income will be paid over four equal annual installments beginning with the previous year.

5. **General Business Credit Recapture**
   a. An S corporation remains liable for any recapture attributable to credits during C corporation tax years.

Stop and review! You have completed the outline for this subunit. Study multiple-choice questions 15 and 16 on page 353.

12.5 EXEMPT ORGANIZATIONS

1. **Exempt Status**

   a. Exempt status generally depends on the nature and purpose of an organization.

      1) An organization is tax-exempt only if it is of a class specifically described by the IRC as one on which exemption is conferred.

      2) It may be organized as a corporation, trust, foundation, fund, community chest, society, etc.

      3) An organization operated for the primary purpose of carrying on a trade or business for profit is generally not tax-exempt.

   b. Examples of organization types that may be exempt are religious or apostolic organizations, political organizations, social clubs, athletic clubs, fraternal beneficiary associations, chambers of commerce, real estate boards, labor organizations, civic welfare associations, and certain domestic and foreign corporations.

   c. Organizations that foster national or international amateur sports competition may be exempt if they do not provide athletic facilities or equipment.

   d. Fraternal beneficiary associations that operate under the lodge system and provide payment of life, sick, accident, or other benefits to members and their dependents are an exempt class.

   e. Social clubs organized for pleasure, recreation, and other nonprofitable purposes, substantially all of the activities of which are for such purposes, are an exempt class.

      1) No part of net earnings may inure to the benefit of any private shareholder.

      2) Exempt status is lost if 35% or more of its receipts are from sources other than membership fees, dues, and assessments.

   f. **Prohibited Transactions**

      1) Certain employee trusts lose exempt status if they engage in prohibited transactions, e.g., lending without adequate security or reasonable interest, or paying unreasonable compensation for personal services.

   g. **Religious, Charitable, Scientific, Educational, Literary**

      1) Organizations formed and operated exclusively for religious, charitable, scientific, educational, literary, or similar purposes are a broad class of exempt organizations.

      2) No part of net earnings may inure to the benefit of any private shareholder or individual.

      3) No substantial part of its activities may attempt to influence legislation or a political candidacy (e.g., Political Action Committees).

      4) In general, if a substantial part of the activities of an organization consists of attempting to influence legislation, the organization will lose its exempt status. However, most organizations can elect to replace the substantial part of activities test with a lobbying expenditure limit.

      5) If an election for a tax year is in effect for an organization and that organization exceeds the lobbying expenditure limits, an excise tax of 25% will be imposed on the excess amount.

      6) Exempt status will be lost if the organization directly participates in a political campaign.

   h. **Private Foundations**

      1) Each domestic or foreign exempt organization is a private foundation unless, generally, it receives more than a third of its support (annually) from its members and the general public. In this case, the private foundation status terminates, and the organization becomes a public charity.

2) Exempt status of a private foundation is subject to statutory restrictions, notification requirements, and excise taxes.

3) A charitable, religious, or scientific organization is presumed to be a private foundation unless it either

a) Is a church or has annual gross receipts under $5,000 or

b) Notifies the IRS that it is not a private foundation (on Form 1023) within 15 months from the end of the month in which it was organized.

i. **Feeder Organization**

1) An organization must independently qualify for exempt status. It is not enough that all of its profits are paid to exempt organizations.

j. **Homeowners' Association**

1) It is treated as a tax-exempt organization.

2) A homeowners' association is one organized for acquisition, construction, management, maintenance, etc., of residential real estate or condominiums. A cooperative housing corporation is excluded.

3) A condominium management association, to be treated as a tax-exempt housing association, must file a separate election for each tax year by the return due date of the applicable year.

Tax-Exempt Organization Internal Revenue Code Chart

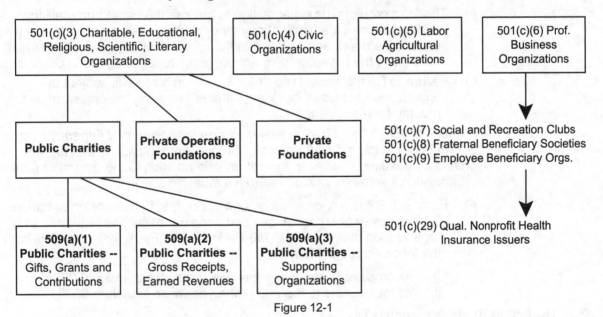

Figure 12-1

2. **Requirements for Exemption**

a. An organization, other than a church or an employees' qualified pension or profit-sharing trust, must apply in writing to its IRS district director for a ruling or a determination that it is tax-exempt.

1) To establish its exemption, an organization must file a **written application** with the key director for the district in which the principal place of business or principal office of the organization is located.

a) Religious, charitable, scientific, educational, etc., organizations (public charities) use Form 1023. Form 1024 is used by most others.

b) If filed within the 15-month period, retroactive treatment is available.

b.   **Annual Information Return**

1) Exempt organizations generally are required to file annual information returns on or before the 15th day of the 5th month following the close of the taxable year.

2) Exempt status may be denied or revoked for failure to file.

3) The organization reports all gross income, receipts, and disbursements.

   a) The amount of contributions received is reported.
   b) All substantial contributions are identified.

4) Some organizations exempted from the requirement include a(n)

   a) Church or church-affiliated organization
   b) Exclusively religious activity or any religious order
   c) Organizations (other than a private foundation) having annual gross receipts that are not more than $50,000
   d) Stock bonus, pension, or profit-sharing trust that qualified under Sec. 401

5) Private foundations are required to file annual information returns on Form 990 or Form 990-PF, regardless of the amounts of their gross receipts.

6) Organizations with under $50,000 in gross receipts that do not have to file an annual notice will be required to file a Form 990-N.

   a) The form is due by the 15th day of the 5th month following the close of the tax year.
   b) The form requires the organization to provide the name and mailing address of the organization, any other names used, a web address (if one exists), the name and address of the principal officer, and a statement confirming the organization's annual gross receipts are $50,000 or less.
   c) Failure to file the annual report for 3 years in a row will subject the organization to loss of its exempt status, requiring the organization to reapply for recognition.

7) A central or parent organization may file Form 990, *Return of Organizations Exempt from Income Tax*, for two or more local organizations that are not private foundations. However, this return is in addition to the central or parent organization's separate annual return if it must file one.

   a) Form 990-EZ is a shortened version of Form 990. It is designed for use by small exempt organizations and nonexempt charitable trusts. An organization may file Form 990-EZ instead of Form 990 if it meets both of the following requirements:

      i)   Its gross receipts during the year were less than $200,000.
      ii) Its total assets at the end of the year were less than $500,000.

3.   **Unrelated Business Income Tax**

a.   Tax-exempt organizations are generally subject to tax on income from unrelated business income (UBI).

b.   An unrelated business is a trade or business activity regularly carried on for the production of income (even if a loss results) that is not substantially related to performance of the exempt purpose or function, i.e., that does not contribute more than insubstantial benefits to the exempt purposes.

c.   Certain qualified sponsorship payments received by an exempt organization have not been subject to unrelated business income tax.

1) A qualified sponsorship payment is one from which the payor does not expect any substantial return or benefit other than the use or acknowledgment of the payor's name or logo.

2) The payor may not receive a substantial return.

d. Exempt organizations subject to tax on UBI are required to comply with the Code provisions regarding installment payments of estimated income tax by corporations [Sec. 6655(g)(3)].

e. An unrelated business income (UBI) tax return (Form 990-T) is required of an exempt organization with at least $1,000 of gross income used in computing the UBI tax for the tax year [Reg. 1.6012-2(e)].

4. **Charitable Deduction**

a. Solicitations for contributions or other payments by tax-exempt organizations must include a statement if payments to that organization are not deductible as charitable contributions for federal income tax purposes. Donations to the following organizations are tax deductible:

1) Corporations organized under an Act of Congress
2) All 501(c)(3) organizations except those testing for public safety
3) Cemetery companies
4) Cooperative hospital service organizations
5) Cooperative service organizations of operating educational organizations
6) Child-care organizations

Stop and review! You have completed the outline for this subunit. Study multiple-choice questions 17 through 20 beginning on page 353.

QUESTIONS

12.1 Eligibility and Election

1. Bristol Corp. was formed as a C corporation on January 1, 1985, and elected S corporation status on January 1, 1991. At the time of the election, Bristol had accumulated C corporation earnings and profits that have not been distributed. Bristol has had the same 25 shareholders throughout its existence. In 2017, Bristol's S election will terminate if it

A. Increases the number of shareholders to 50.

B. Adds a decedent's estate as a shareholder to the existing shareholders.

C. Takes a charitable contribution deduction.

D. Has passive investment income exceeding 90% of gross receipts in each of the 3 consecutive years ending December 31, 2017.

Answer (D) is correct.
    REQUIRED: The S corporation termination event.
    DISCUSSION: An S corporation's status will terminate if (1) it has C corporation earnings and profits at the close of 3 consecutive years, and (2) during those 3 years, over 25% of the gross receipts of the S corporation was due to passive investment income. First, the existence of the undistributed earnings and profits satisfies the first test. Second, with 90% passive investment income within the gross receipts, the termination is effective.
    Answer (A) is incorrect. An S corporation is limited to a maximum of 100 shareholders. Answer (B) is incorrect. An estate is an eligible shareholder. Answer (C) is incorrect. A charitable contribution deduction will not terminate the election.

2. Which of the following conditions will prevent a corporation from qualifying as an S corporation?

A. The corporation has both common and preferred stock.

B. The corporation has one class of stock with different voting rights.

C. One shareholder is an estate.

D. One shareholder is a grantor trust.

Answer (A) is correct.
    REQUIRED: The condition that will prevent a corporation from qualifying as an S corporation.
    DISCUSSION: An S corporation may have only one class of stock.
    Answer (B) is incorrect. An S corporation may have only one class of (common) stock, but shares of that class may have different voting rights. Answer (C) is incorrect. A decedent's estate may be a shareholder. Answer (D) is incorrect. A grantor trust may be a shareholder for a 2-year period following the death of a grantor.

3. On February 10, 2017, Ace Corp., a calendar-year corporation, elected S corporation status, and all shareholders consented to the election. There was no change in shareholders in 2017. Ace met all eligibility requirements for S status during the pre-election portion of the year. What is the earliest date on which Ace can be recognized as an S corporation?

A. February 10, 2017.

B. February 10, 2018.

C. January 1, 2018.

D. January 1, 2017.

Answer (D) is correct.

REQUIRED: The effective date of an S corporation election.

DISCUSSION: The S corporation election is effective for the current tax year if it is made on or before March 15 for calendar-year corporations, subject to certain exceptions relating to ineligibility and complete consent. Since this election was made on February 10 and no exceptions applied, the election will be effective for the entire taxable year in which it was made.

4. An S corporation has 30,000 shares of voting common stock and 20,000 shares of nonvoting common stock issued and outstanding. The S election can be revoked voluntarily with the consent of the shareholders holding, on the day of the revocation,

	Shares of Voting Stock	Shares of Nonvoting Stock
A.	0	20,000
B.	7,500	5,000
C.	10,000	16,000
D.	20,000	0

Answer (C) is correct.

REQUIRED: The number of shares required to consent to a voluntary revocation of an S election.

DISCUSSION: An S corporation election may be terminated by revocation. A revocation may be made only with the consent of shareholders who, at the time the revocation is made, hold more than one-half of the number of issued and outstanding shares of stock (including both voting and nonvoting stock) of the corporation.

12.2 Operations

5. Bern Corp., an S corporation, had an ordinary loss of $36,500 for the year ended December 31, 2017. On January 1, 2017, Meyer owned 50% of Bern's stock. Meyer held the stock for 40 days in 2017 before selling the entire 50% interest to an unrelated third party. Meyer's basis for the stock was $10,000. Meyer was a full-time employee of Bern until the stock was sold. Meyer's share of Bern's 2017 loss was

A. $0

B. $2,000

C. $10,000

D. $18,250

Answer (B) is correct.

REQUIRED: The allocable share of an S corporation item when a shareholder's interest changes during the tax year.

DISCUSSION: The amount of each S corporation item, which each shareholder takes into account, is computed on a per-day and per-share basis. The portion of the loss passed through to Meyer is

$$\$36,500 \times 50\% \times \frac{40}{365} = \$2,000$$

Answer (A) is incorrect. Each shareholder's allocable portion is determined on a per-day and a per-share basis. Answer (C) is incorrect. Each shareholder's allocable portion is determined on a per-day and a per-share basis. Meyer's basis in Bern Corp. was $10,000 before the sale. Answer (D) is incorrect. Each shareholder's allocable portion is determined on a per-day and a per-share basis. The amount of $18,250 represents 50% of the loss and is not allocated between the two owners.

6. A shareholder's basis in the stock of an S corporation is increased by the shareholder's pro rata share of income from

	Tax-Exempt Interest	Taxable Interest
A.	No	No
B.	No	Yes
C.	Yes	No
D.	Yes	Yes

Answer (D) is correct.

REQUIRED: The item(s) that increase(s) a shareholder's basis in S corporation stock.

DISCUSSION: Interest income received by an S corporation, whether taxable or nontaxable, increases the basis of an S corporation shareholder's stock.

7. Bow, Inc., an S corporation, has three equal shareholders. For the year ended December 31, 2017, Bow had taxable income and current earnings and profits of $300,000. Bow made cash distributions totaling $120,000 during 2017. For 2017, what amount from Bow should be included in each shareholder's gross income?

A. $140,000

B. $100,000

C. $60,000

D. $40,000

Answer (B) is correct.

REQUIRED: The gross income of a shareholder of an S corporation with current earnings that made distributions.

DISCUSSION: Each shareholder includes in his or her personal gross income his or her share of ordinary income and separately stated items of the S corporation on a per-day and per-share basis. Each shareholder's share is 1/3 of $300,000. Shareholder inclusion will be $100,000 each. Excess distributions are treated as tax-free return of capital.

8. Bob and Sally, unmarried taxpayers, each owned 50% of Lostalot, Inc., an S corporation. The corporation had a $50,000 operating loss for the tax year ending December 31, 2017. As of December 31, 2016, Bob's basis in his stock was $15,000 and Sally's was $5,000. During the 2017 tax year, Sally mortgaged her home for $25,000 and loaned the money to the corporation. Although not personally liable, Bob told her not to worry and that if anything happened, he would help pay the mortgage debt. Calculate the amount of allowable loss deduction each shareholder would be able to recognize on their individual 2017 tax returns.

A. Bob: $25,000, and Sally: $25,000.

B. Bob: $15,000, and Sally: $5,000.

C. Bob: $15,000, and Sally: $30,000.

D. Bob: $15,000, and Sally: $25,000.

Answer (D) is correct.

REQUIRED: The loss deduction that may be recognized on a shareholder's individual return.

DISCUSSION: Bob and Sally's share of the loss is $25,000 each. However, the deduction for each is limited to their basis in the S corporation. Bob's deduction is limited to his $15,000 basis in the stock. Sally's basis consists of her $5,000 stock basis and her $25,000 debt basis. Sally has enough basis to cover her share of the loss.

Answer (A) is incorrect. Bob's basis is not large enough to cover the $25,000 share of the loss. Answer (B) is incorrect. Sally's basis is larger than $5,000. Answer (C) is incorrect. Sally's share of the loss is not $30,000.

9. Sandy is the sole shareholder of Swallow, an S corporation. Sandy's adjusted basis in Swallow stock is $60,000 at the beginning of the year. During the year, Swallow reports the following income items:

Ordinary income	$30,000
Tax-exempt income	5,000
Capital gains	10,000

In addition, Swallow makes a nontaxable distribution to Sandy of $20,000 during the year. What is Sandy's adjusted basis in the Swallow stock at the end of the year?

A. $60,000

B. $70,000

C. $80,000

D. $85,000

Answer (D) is correct.

REQUIRED: Shareholder's adjusted basis in the stock of an S corporation.

DISCUSSION: The adjusted basis of the shareholder's stock is figured at year end with increases for the shareholder's pro rata share of all income items, including tax-exempt income, that are separately stated and any nonseparately stated income. Also, all separately and nonseparately stated losses, distributions, and deduction items decrease the basis of the shareholder's stock on a pro rata basis. Sandy's stock basis on January 1, Year 1, is $60,000.

Original basis	$60,000
Ordinary income	30,000
Tax-exempt income	5,000
Capital gains	10,000
Nontaxable distribution	(20,000)
Adjusted basis	$85,000

Answer (A) is incorrect. A $60,000 adjusted basis ignores the effects of the income items and the nontaxable distribution. Answer (B) is incorrect. A $70,000 adjusted basis excludes the effects of the tax-exempt income and the capital gains. Answer (C) is incorrect. An $80,000 adjusted basis does not include the effects of the tax-exempt income.

10. As of January 1, 2017, Kane owned all 100 issued shares of Manning Corp., a calendar-year S corporation. On the 41st day of 2017, Kane sold 25 of the Manning shares to Rodgers. For the year ended December 31, 2017 (a 365-day calendar year), Manning had $73,000 in nonseparately stated income and made no distributions to its shareholders. What amount of nonseparately stated income from Manning should be reported on Kane's 2017 tax return?

A. $56,800

B. $54,750

C. $16,250

D. $0

Answer (A) is correct.
REQUIRED: The shareholder's income from an S corporation when shares are transferred during the year.
DISCUSSION: Each shareholder shall include in gross income the pro rata share of the S corporation's income. The pro rata share is the taxpayer's share of the corporation's income after assigning an equal portion of the income to each day of the taxable year and then dividing that portion pro rata among the shares outstanding on each day. Therefore, each day of the year will be assigned $200 of income ($73,000 ÷ 365). Kane's share will be $56,800 [$8,200 (41 days × $200 × 100% ownership) plus $48,600 (324 days × $200 × 75% ownership)].
Answer (B) is incorrect. The figure of $54,750 applies Kane's end-of-year ownership percentage to the entire year's income instead of on a pro rata basis for the shares outstanding on each day. Answer (C) is incorrect. The figure of $16,250 is Rodgers's pro rata share. Answer (D) is incorrect. Each shareholder must include in taxable income the pro rata share of the S corporation's income.

11. Which of the following items is **not** a separately stated item for Form 1120S shareholders?

A. Charitable contributions made by the corporation.

B. Sec. 179 deduction.

C. Depreciation.

D. Tax-exempt interest.

Answer (C) is correct.
REQUIRED: The item that is not a separately stated item for Form 1120S shareholders.
DISCUSSION: An S corporation passes a pro rata share of its total income (loss) through to the individual shareholders except for items that require separate treatment by the shareholder. Charitable contributions made by the corporation, Sec. 179 deduction, and tax-exempt interest must be separately stated. Depreciation, however, is combined with other nonseparately stated income or loss.
Answer (A) is incorrect. Charitable contributions made by the corporation are separately stated for Form 1120S shareholders. Answer (B) is incorrect. A Sec. 179 deduction is an item that is separately stated for Form 1120S shareholders. Answer (D) is incorrect. Tax-exempt interest is an item that is separately stated for Form 1120S shareholders.

12. Tap, a calendar-year S corporation, reported the following items of income and expense in the current year:

Revenue	$44,000
Operating expenses	20,000
Long-term capital loss	6,000
Charitable contributions	1,000
Interest expense	4,000

What is the amount of Tap's ordinary income?

A. $13,000

B. $19,000

C. $20,000

D. $24,000

Answer (C) is correct.
REQUIRED: The amount of Tap's ordinary income.
DISCUSSION: The items of income, deduction, and credit of an S corporation are reported by the corporation; however, an S corporation is not allowed deductions for items that must be separately stated, which include long-term capital losses and charitable contributions. Therefore, Tap's ordinary income equals $20,000 ($44,000 revenue – $20,000 operating expenses – $4,000 interest expense).
Answer (A) is incorrect. The long-term capital loss and charitable contribution must be stated separately and are therefore not deductible by the S corporation. Answer (B) is incorrect. The charitable contribution must be stated separately and is therefore not deductible by the S corporation. Answer (D) is incorrect. The S corporation may deduct the $4,000 of interest expense.

12.3 Distributions

13. If an S corporation has no accumulated earnings and profits, the amount distributed to a shareholder

A. Must be returned to the S corporation.

B. Increases the shareholder's basis in the stock.

C. Decreases the shareholder's basis in the stock.

D. Has no effect on the shareholder's basis in the stock.

Answer (C) is correct.
REQUIRED: The true statement regarding a distribution by an S corporation that has no accumulated earnings and profits.
DISCUSSION: Distribution from an S corporation with no Subchapter C earnings and profits is treated as a tax-free return of capital to the extent of a shareholder's basis in his or her stock of the corporation, decreasing the stock's basis. Excess is treated as gain or loss on the sale of the stock.

14. Jenny Corporation (an S corporation) is owned entirely by Craig. At the beginning of 2017, Craig's adjusted basis in his Jenny Corporation stock was $20,000. Jenny reported ordinary income of $5,000 and a capital loss of $10,000. Craig received a cash distribution of $35,000 in November 2017. What is Craig's gain from the distribution?

    A. $0

    B. $10,000

    C. $20,000

    D. $35,000

Answer (B) is correct.

    REQUIRED: The sole shareholder's gain from the distribution of an S corporation.

    DISCUSSION: The basis is increased by the ordinary income to $25,000. The $35,000 distribution is taken next and, since it exceeds the basis, there is a $10,000 gain. The capital loss is nondeductible because there is no basis left after the deduction from the distribution for Craig and it is carried over.

    Answer (A) is incorrect. If the distribution is greater than the basis, the excess is taxable as a sale or an exchange of property (a taxable capital gain). Answer (C) is incorrect. The distribution is taken before the deduction for the capital loss. Answer (D) is incorrect. The entire distribution is not taxable, only the difference between the distribution and the basis.

12.4 Special Taxes

15. Tax Corp. converted from C to S status in 2017. The net appreciation inherent in its assets is subject to a tax on net gain recognized

    A.   At the time of the conversion.

    B.   During a recognition period of 2 years.

    C.   With no effect on any shareholder's basis in the stock.

    D.   Up to the amount of built-in gain on conversion.

Answer (D) is correct.

    REQUIRED: The true statement about the built-in gains tax.

    DISCUSSION: An S corporation that, upon conversion from C to S status after 1986, had net appreciation inherent in its assets is subject to a tax of 35% on net gain recognized (up to the amount of built-in gain on conversion) during the recognition period.

    Answer (A) is incorrect. The net appreciation inherent in its assets is subject to a tax on net gain recognized during the recognition period. Answer (B) is incorrect. For conversions made after the 2010 tax year, the recognition period is a 5-year period beginning on the date the S election became effective. Answer (C) is incorrect. The tax liability is passed through, as a loss, pro rata to its shareholders, and it reduces each shareholder's basis in the stock.

16. Magic Corp., a regular C corporation, elected S corporation status at the beginning of the current calendar year. It had an asset with a basis of $40,000 and a fair market value (FMV) of $85,000 on January 1. The asset was sold during the year for $95,000. Magic's corporate tax rate was 35%. What was Magic's tax liability as a result of the sale?

    A. $0

    B. $3,500

    C. $15,750

    D. $19,250

Answer (C) is correct.

    REQUIRED: The gain on a sale reported by a C corporation that elected to be a S corporation.

    DISCUSSION: An S corporation that, upon conversion from C to S status, had net appreciation inherent in its assets is subject to a built-in gains tax of 35% on net gain recognized (up to the amount of built-in gain on conversion) during the recognition period. Magic had $45,000 ($85,000 FMV in January 1 – $40,000 basis) of built-in gains at the time that Magic elected to be an S corporation. The tax on the $45,000 is $15,750 ($45,000 × 35%).

    Answer (A) is incorrect. A gain on the sale is recognized by Magic. Answer (B) is incorrect. The figure of $3,500 is the corporate tax on the gain that occurred after the S corporation election. Answer (D) is incorrect. The figure of $19,250 is the corporate tax on the entire gain of $55,000 ($95,000 amount realized – $40,000 basis).

12.5 Exempt Organizations

17. Which of the following is **not** an exempt organization?

    A.   American Society for Prevention of Cruelty to Animals.

    B.   Red Cross.

    C.   State-chartered credit unions.

    D.   Privately owned nursing home.

Answer (D) is correct.

    REQUIRED: The organization that does not qualify as exempt.

    DISCUSSION: Exempt status generally depends on the nature and purpose of an organization. Among the types of organizations that may qualify as exempt are corporations, trusts, foundations, funds, community funds, etc. A more complete list can be found in Sec. 501(c) along with the permitted stated purposes and requirements.

    Answer (A) is incorrect. The American Society for Prevention of Cruelty to Animals is an exempt organization according to Sec. 501(c). Answer (B) is incorrect. The Red Cross is an exempt organization according to Sec. 501(c). Answer (C) is incorrect. State-chartered credit unions are exempt organizations.

18. Which of the following statements is true with respect to tax-exempt organizations?

    A. A foundation may qualify for exemption from federal income tax if it is organized for the prevention of cruelty to animals.

    B. A partnership may qualify as an organization exempt from federal income tax if it is organized and operated exclusively for one or more of the purposes found in Sec. 501(c)(3).

    C. An individual can qualify as an organization exempt from federal income tax.

    D. In order to qualify as an exempt organization, the organization must be a corporation.

Answer (A) is correct.
REQUIRED: The true statement with respect to tax-exempt organizations.
DISCUSSION: Exempt status generally depends on the nature and purpose of an organization. Among the types of organizations that may qualify as exempt are corporations, trusts, foundations, funds, community funds, etc. A more complete list can be found in Sec. 501(c) along with the permitted stated purposes and requirements.
Answer (B) is incorrect. A partnership is, by definition, a for-profit association. Also, a partnership is not listed as a type of organization that may qualify for exempt status in Sec. 501(c) or (d). Answer (C) is incorrect. An individual is not an organization described in Sec. 501(c) or (d) that may qualify for exempt status. Answer (D) is incorrect. Other types of organizations listed in Sec. 501(c) or (d) may also qualify.

19. An incorporated exempt organization subject to tax on its current-year unrelated business income (UBI)

    A. Must make estimated tax payments if its tax can reasonably be expected to be $100 or more.

    B. Must comply with the Code provisions regarding installment payments of estimated income tax by corporations.

    C. Must pay at least 70% of the tax due as shown on the return when filed, with the balance of tax payable in the following quarter.

    D. May defer payment of tax for up to 9 months following the due date of the return.

Answer (B) is correct.
REQUIRED: The timing of payment obligations with respect to UBI tax.
DISCUSSION: Exempt organizations subject to tax on UBI are required to comply with the Code provisions regarding installment payments of estimated income tax by corporations [Sec. 6655(g)(3)].
Answer (A) is incorrect. Like a corporation, quarterly payments of estimated tax are required of an exempt organization that expects estimated tax on UBI to equal or exceed $500 for the tax year. Answer (C) is incorrect. Tax on UBI is due in full when the UBI return and annual information return are due. Answer (D) is incorrect. Tax on UBI is due in full when the UBI return and annual information return are due.

20. Which of the following organizations exempt from federal income tax must generally file an annual information report?

    A. An organization, other than a private foundation, with annual gross receipts that normally are not more than $50,000.

    B. A private foundation.

    C. A church.

    D. A religious order.

Answer (B) is correct.
REQUIRED: The organization that must file an annual information return.
DISCUSSION: Most organizations exempt from tax under Sec. 501(a) must file annual information returns on Form 990, *Return of Organization Exempt from Income Tax*. Those excepted from the requirement are

1. A church or church-affiliated organization
2. An exclusively religious activity or religious order
3. An organization (other than a private foundation) having annual gross receipts that are not more than $50,000
4. A stock bonus, pension, or profit-sharing trust that qualified under Sec. 401
5. A Keogh plan whose total assets are less than $100,000

Answer (A) is incorrect. Such an organization is specifically exempt from filing annual information returns. Answer (C) is incorrect. A church is specifically exempt from filing annual information returns. Answer (D) is incorrect. A religious order is specifically exempt from filing annual information returns.

STUDY UNIT THIRTEEN
PARTNERSHIPS

(21 pages of outline)

A partnership is a business organization other than a corporation, trust, estate, or qualified joint venture co-owned by two or more persons and operated for a profit. The partnership, as an untaxed flow-through entity, reports taxable income or loss and separately stated items. For the computation of personal income tax liability, each partner considers his or her distributive share of the partnership's taxable income or loss and each of the partnership's separately stated items, whether or not any distributions are made from the partnership to the partner. Federal income tax rules for partnerships are similar to those for S corporations. Nonseparately and separately stated partnership items are currently taxed to the partners, but distributions are generally received tax-free.

Some candidates find it helpful to have the entire tax form side-by-side with our Knowledge Transfer Outline when studying. The full versions of the most up-to-date forms are easily accessible at www.gleim.com/taxforms. These forms and the form excerpts used in our outline are periodically updated as the latest versions are released by the IRS.

13.1 PARTNERSHIP FORMATION AND TAX YEAR

1. **Overview**

   a. Realized gain or loss is not generally recognized by a partner when a partnership interest is received in exchange for property contributed to the partnership unless boot is received.

EXAMPLE

In 2017, Albert acquired a 20% interest in a partnership by contributing a parcel of land and $10,000 in cash. At the time of Albert's contribution, the land had a fair market value of $50,000, an adjusted basis to Albert of $20,000, and was subject to a mortgage of $70,000. Albert's relinquished liability is a gain. When Albert became a 20% partner, he was relieved of 80% of the mortgage debt. Thus, 80% of his $70,000 mortgage, or $56,000, is a benefit to Albert because the other partners are assuming part of the mortgage obligation. Therefore, Albert has a gain of $26,000 ($56,000 benefit – $10,000 cash – $20,000 AB of property).

	Cash contributed	$ 10,000
+	AB of property contributed	20,000
+	Any gain recognized on contributed property or services	26,000
+	Share of partnership liabilities	14,000
–	Partner's liability assumed by partnership	(70,000)
=	**Basis in partnership interest**	$ 0

---

2. **Contributed Property**

a. A **partner's basis** in contributed items is exchanged for basis in the partnership interest received, adjusted for gain recognized and liabilities. The formula to calculate basis in a partnership is as follows:

> Cash contributed
> + AB of property contributed
> + Any gain recognized on contributed property or services
> + Share of partnership liabilities
> − Partner's liability assumed by partnership
> = **Basis in partnership interest**

b. When a partner contributes **property subject to a liability**, or the partnership assumes a liability of the contributing partner, the partner is treated as receiving a distribution of money from the partnership in the amount of the liability. A distribution reduces the partner's basis in the partnership interest.

c. Recognized gain. To the extent liabilities assumed by the partnership exceed the partner's aggregate AB in all property contributed, the partner recognizes gain.

1) Note that a partner still bears responsibility for his or her share of the liabilities assumed by the partnership. Basis of other partners also increases by their share of assumed liability.

2) The gain recognized may be characterized as ordinary income by Secs. 1245 and 1250.

a) Ordinary income recapture potential in excess of the amount of gain recognized remains with the property in the hands of the partnership.

The AICPA has tested on the calculation of the initial basis of a partner's interest in a partnership. Questions have described the various items contributed by a partner and asked for the amount of the contributing partner's basis in the partnership.

---

3. **Contributed Services**

a. A partner who receives a partnership interest in exchange for services recognizes compensation income equal to the FMV of the partnership interest.

1) Gross income must be reported when an interest received is subject to neither substantial risk of forfeiture nor restrictions on transfer.

2) The income reported is ordinary.

b. A partner's interest has ascertainable FMV if sold shortly after receipt.

4. **Partnership's Gain**

a. The partnership realizes neither gain nor loss when it receives contributions of money or property in exchange for partnership interests.

5. **Partnership's Basis in Contributed Property**

a. The partnership's basis in contributed property is equal to the contributing partner's AB in the property immediately before contribution increased by any gain recognized by the partner and is not adjusted for liabilities.

EXAMPLE

In 2017, Albert provided services to Jim's Sole Proprietorship in exchange for a 20% share of the newly created partnership. If the FMV of the assets equals $500,000 and the liabilities equal $100,000, Albert recognizes $80,000 as compensation income ($400,000 × 20%). Albert's basis in the partnership is equal to the compensation income recognized; in this case, it is $80,000.

---

6. **Holding Periods**

   a. The holding period (HP) of the partner's interest includes the HP of contributed capital and Sec. 1231 assets.

      1) If the interest was received in exchange for ordinary income property or services, the HP starts the day following the exchange.

      2) The partnership's HP in contributed property includes the partner's HP even if the partner recognized gain.

7. **Partner-Purchased Interest**

   a. The basis in a partnership interest purchased from a partner is its cost, which is the sum of the purchase price and the partner's share of partnership liabilities.

   b. The partnership may elect to adjust the basis in its assets by the difference between the transferee's basis in his or her partnership interest and his or her proportionate share of the partnership's adjusted basis (AB) in its assets. This is referred to as a Sec. 754 election.

      1) The difference is allocated first to Sec. 1231 property and capital assets and then to other partnership property. Finally, allocation is made to assets within each of the two classes.

         a) For upward adjustment, allocation is on the basis of relative appreciation of classes and assets. No adjustment is made to a depreciated class or asset.

         b) For downward adjustment, allocation is on the basis of relative depreciation of classes and assets. No allocation is made to an appreciated class or asset.

8. **Partners' Capital Accounts**

   a. A capital account is maintained for each partner at the partnership level.

      1) A partner's initial capital account balance is the FMV of the assets (net of liabilities) (s)he contributed to the partnership.

      2) It is separate from the partner's AB in his or her partnership interest.

      3) Basis in partnership interest vs. capital account.

EXAMPLE

Taxpayer contributes property that has an adjusted basis of $400 and a FMV of $1,000. Taxpayer's partner contributes $1,000 cash. While each has increased his or her capital account by $1,000, the adjusted basis of Taxpayer's partnership interest is only $400 and the adjusted basis of Taxpayer's partner's partnership interest is $1,000.

---

9. **Partnership Tax Year**

    a. The partnership's tax year is determined with respect to the partners' tax years.

        1) Unless an exception applies, the partnership must use a required tax year. A required tax year is the first of a), b), or c) below that applies.

            a) **Majority interest tax year.** It is the tax year of partners owning more than 50% of partnership capital and profits if they have the same year as determined on the first day of the partnership's tax year.

            b) **Principal partners' tax year.** It is the same tax year of all principal partners, i.e., partners owning 5% or more of capital and profits.

            c) Least aggregate deferral tax year.

                i)   Multiply each partner's ownership percentage by the number of months of income deferral for each possible partnership tax year.

                ii) Select the tax year that produces the smallest total tax deferral.

                iii) The deferral period begins with the possible partnership tax-year end date and extends to the partner's tax-year end date.

EXAMPLE

Test 12/31	Year End	Ownership	×	Months Deferred	=	Deferral
Tom Barnes	12/31	50%		0		0.0
Jerry Corp	11/30	50%		11		5.5
				Total Deferral		5.5
Test 11/30						
Tom Barnes	12/31	50%		1		0.5
Jerry Corp	11/30	50%		0		0.0
				Total Deferral		0.5

The least aggregate deferral tax year is 11/30.

---

        2) Any time there is a change in partners or a partner changes his or her tax year, the partnership may be required to change its tax year.

    b. When each partner includes his or her pro rata share of partnership income depends on both the partnership tax year and the individual's tax year.

        1) If the partner's tax year coincides with the partnership's, the partner reports his or her distributive share of partnership items, including guaranteed payments, in that year.

        2) If the partner's tax year does not coincide with the partnership's, the partner reports his or her distributive share of partnership items, including guaranteed payments, in the tax year in which the partnership's tax year ends.

    c. A year other than one required may be adopted for a business purpose, with IRS approval. Income deferral is not a business purpose.

        1) Natural business year. Accounting for a natural business year, e.g., in a seasonal line of business, can be an acceptable business purpose.

            a) The business is considered seasonal if, in any 12-month period, at least 25% of annual gross receipts were received during the last 2 months of the year in each of the preceding 3 years.

        2) Fiscal year. A partnership may elect a tax year that is neither the required year nor a natural business year.

            a) The year elected may result in no more than 3 months' deferral (between the beginning of a tax year elected and the required tax year).

            b) The partnership must pay an amount approximating the amount of additional tax that would have resulted had the election not been made.

10. **Partnership Elections**

    a. **Elections** are generally made by the partnership.

        1) Partnership-level election examples are accounting methods, tax year, inventory methods, start-up costs, installment sales, and depreciation methods.

        2) Each partner makes certain elections for his or her distributive share, e.g., deduction (credit) for foreign tax expense of the partnership or the order of reducing tax attributes upon forgiveness of partnership debt.

Stop and review! You have completed the outline for this subunit. Study multiple-choice questions 1 through 3 beginning on page 375.

13.2 PARTNER'S TAXABLE INCOME

1. **Overview**

    a. A partner's taxable income may be affected by his or her interest in a partnership in several ways, e.g., as a result of his or her distributive share of partnership taxable income and separately stated items, from sale of his or her partnership interest, and from dealings with the partnership.

    b. Partnership taxable income is determined in the same way as for individuals, except that certain deductions are not allowed for a partnership, and other items are required to be separately stated.

2. **Separately Stated Items**

    a. Each partnership item of income, gain, deduction, loss, or credit that may vary the tax liability of any partner must be separately stated. Items that must be separately stated include the following:

        1) Ordinary income (loss)
        2) Rental activities and related expenses
        3) Guaranteed payments
        4) Interest and dividend income
        5) Royalties
        6) Net short- and long-term capital gain or loss from the sale or exchange of capital assets
        7) Section 1231 gain and loss
        8) Other income

            a) Portfolio income
            b) Cancelation of debt
            c) Recovery items (e.g., prior taxes, bad debts, etc.)
            d) Investment income

        9) Section 179 deductions
      10) Other deductions

            a) Charitable contributions
            b) Investment expense
            c) Depletion on oil and gas wells

      11) Foreign income taxes paid or accrued
      12) Tax-exempt income and related expenses
      13) Distributions

From Form 1065 Schedule K-1

Part III	Partner's Share of Current Year Income, Deductions, Credits, and Other Items		
1 Ordinary business income (loss)		**15** Credits	
2 Net rental real estate income (loss)			
3 Other net rental income (loss)		**16** Foreign transactions	
4 Guaranteed payments			
5 Interest income			
6a Ordinary dividends			
6b Qualified dividends			
7 Royalties			
8 Net short-term capital gain (loss)			
9a Net long-term capital gain (loss)		**17** Alternative minimum tax (AMT) items	
9b Collectibles (28%) gain (loss)			
9c Unrecaptured section 1250 gain			
10 Net section 1231 gain (loss)		**18** Tax-exempt income and nondeductible expenses	
11 Other income (loss)			
		19 Distributions	
12 Section 179 deduction			
13 Other deductions			
		20 Other information	
14 Self-employment earnings (loss)			

3. **Ordinary Income (Loss)**

   a.   Generally, this includes taxable items of income, gain, loss, or deduction that are not separately stated.

   1)   Ordinary income is different from taxable income, which is the sum of all taxable items, including the separately stated items and the partnership ordinary income or loss.

   a)   Ordinary income includes such items as gross profit, administrative expenses, and employee salaries.

b) **Exception:** Guaranteed payments are subtracted as expenses for computing taxable income but are separately stated as income to the recipient partner.

From Form 1065

Income	1a	Gross receipts or sales	**1a**		
	b	Returns and allowances	**1b**		
	c	Balance. Subtract line 1b from line 1a		**1c**	
	2	Cost of goods sold (attach Form 1125-A)		**2**	
	3	Gross profit. Subtract line 2 from line 1c		**3**	
	4	Ordinary income (loss) from other partnerships, estates, and trusts (attach statement) . .		**4**	
	5	Net farm profit (loss) (attach Schedule F (Form 1040))		**5**	
	6	Net gain (loss) from Form 4797, Part II, line 17 (attach Form 4797)		**6**	
	7	Other income (loss) (attach statement)		**7**	
	8	**Total income (loss).** Combine lines 3 through 7		**8**	
Deductions (see the instructions for limitations)	9	Salaries and wages (other than to partners) (less employment credits)		**9**	
	10	Guaranteed payments to partners		**10**	
	11	Repairs and maintenance		**11**	
	12	Bad debts		**12**	
	13	Rent		**13**	
	14	Taxes and licenses		**14**	
	15	Interest		**15**	
	16a	Depreciation (if required, attach Form 4562)	**16a**		
	b	Less depreciation reported on Form 1125-A and elsewhere on return	**16b**	**16c**	
	17	Depletion (**Do not deduct oil and gas depletion.**)		**17**	
	18	Retirement plans, etc.		**18**	
	19	Employee benefit programs		**19**	
	20	Other deductions (attach statement)		**20**	
	21	**Total deductions.** Add the amounts shown in the far right column for lines 9 through 20 .		**21**	
	22	**Ordinary business income (loss).** Subtract line 21 from line 8		**22**	

4. **Deductions**

   a. Certain deductions, e.g., charitable contributions, are disallowed in computing taxable income.

      1) These are items that must be separately stated by the partnership.

      2) Each partner may be entitled to his or her distributive share of these items in computing his or her personal tax liability.

5. **Partner's Distributive Share**

   a. Each partner is taxed on his or her share of partnership income, whether or not it is distributed.

   b. A partner's distributive share of any partnership item is allocated by the partnership agreement as long as the allocation has economic effect and is substantial. The partnership agreement includes modifications up to the partnership return due date (without extensions).

      1) An allocation has **economic effect** by satisfying one of three tests defined by the regulations. The applicability of each test is determined in sequential order.

         a) **The Big Three Test.** Economic effect is achieved if the partnership agreement includes the following:

            i) Partners' capital accounts are properly maintained,

            ii) Liquidating distributions are made in accordance with the partners' positive capital account balances, and

            iii) Partners must restore deficit balances in their capital accounts.

      b)   **The Alternate Test.** Economic effect is achieved if the partnership agreement includes items i) and ii) of the Big Three Test on the previous page and contains a qualified income offset provision.

      c)   **Economic Effect Equivalence.** Economic effect is achieved if the resulting allocation achieves the same result as would have been achieved under the Big Three Test without containing the provisions required by the Big Three Test.

   2)   **Substantiality** is present for an allocation if there is a reasonable possibility that the allocation will substantially affect the after-tax economic position of the partners. The allocation is not substantial if it enhances the after-tax economic consequences of one partner and does not diminish the after-tax consequences of another partner.

c.   If the partnership agreement does not allocate a partnership item or lacks substantial economic effect, the item must be allocated to partners according to their interests in the partnership.

d.   **Precontribution gain or loss.** To the extent of gain not recognized on contribution of property to the partnership, gain or loss subsequently recognized on the sale or exchange of an asset must be allocated to the contributing partner.

   1)   Postcontribution gain or loss is allocated among partners as distributive shares, i.e., as any other gain or loss.

EXAMPLE

Tony and Mary form a partnership as equal partners. Tony contributes cash of $100,000, and Mary contributes an asset with a basis of $80,000 and an FMV of $100,000. Two years later, the partnership sells the asset for $110,000. The $30,000 gain ($110,000 selling price – $80,000 basis) is allocated, $25,000 to Mary [$20,000 precontribution gain + (50% partnership interest × $10,000 postcontribution gain)] and $5,000 to Tony (50% partnership interest × $10,000 postcontribution gain).

---

   2)   Accounting for variation between the property's FMV and AB immediately before contribution also applies to related deductions. For example, depreciation must be apportioned and allocated.

e.   **Character.** The character of distributive shares of partnership items is generally determined at the partnership level.

   1)   Any capital loss (FMV < AB) inherent at contribution is capital loss to the extent of any loss realized when the partnership disposes of the property. This applies for 5 years after contribution.

   2)   To the extent of variations between FMV and AB on contribution, partnership gain or loss on inventory and unrealized receivables is ordinary income. This taint on the inventory disappears 5 years after contribution.

f.   If the size of a partner's interest in the partnership varies (e.g., by sale, purchase, exchange, liquidation) during a partnership tax year, the distributive shares of partnership items must be apportioned on a daily basis.

   1)   The partnership may change profit and loss ratios up to the date of the return. However, certain items (such as cash-paid interest) must be allocated based on the number of days of ownership.

   2)   The following items of a cash-basis partnership must be accounted for on an accrual basis but only for apportioning distributive shares: payments for services or the use of property, interest, and taxes.

6.   **Adjustments to Basis**

a.   The basis of a partner's interest in a partnership is adjusted each year for subsequent contributions of capital, partnership taxable income (loss), separately stated items, variations in the partner's share of partnership liabilities, and distributions from the partnership to the partner.

    Initial basis
+   Subsequent contributions to capital
+/– Distributive share of partnership taxable income (loss)
+   Separately stated taxable and nontaxable income
–   Separately stated deductible and nondeductible expenditures
+   Increase in allocable share of partnership liabilities
–   Decrease in allocable share of partnership liabilities
–   Distributions from partnership
=   **Adjusted basis in partnership interest**

EXAMPLE

The taxpayer's ownership and basis in the partnership are 50% and $15,000, respectively, at the beginning of the year. The partnership has ordinary income of $8,000, made charitable contributions of $3,000, and made a $5,000 distribution to the taxpayer. The taxpayer's basis at the end of the year is $12,500 [$15,000 beginning basis + ($8,000 ordinary income × 50% ownership) – ($3,000 charitable contribution × 50% ownership) – $5,000 distribution].

---

    b.   Basis is adjusted for variations in a partner's allocable share of partnership liabilities during the year, e.g., by payments on principal.

        1)   Partner capital accounts are not adjusted for partnership liability variations.

    c.   Basis is not reduced below zero.

    d.   Basis is reduced without regard to losses suspended under passive activity loss rules and at-risk rules.

    e.   No adjustment to basis is made for guaranteed payments received.

7. **Loss Limits**

    a.   A partnership ordinary loss is a negative balance of taxable income.

    b.   **Basis limit.** A partner is allowed to deduct the pro rata share of the partnership's ordinary loss only to the extent of his or her basis in the partnership.

        1)   Excess loss is deductible in a subsequent year in which AB is greater than zero.

    c.   **At-risk rules.** Each partner may deduct only a partnership ordinary loss to the extent (s)he is at risk with respect to the partnership.

        1)   The at-risk limits also apply at the partnership level with respect to each partnership activity.

            a)   The amount of a partnership loss currently deductible (up to an amount for which the partnership bears economic risk of loss with respect to each partnership activity) is allocated to partners as a deductible distributive share.

        2)   A limited partner is at risk in the partnership to the extent of contributions and his or her share of qualified nonrecourse financing, that is, the amount the partner would lose if the partnership suddenly became worthless.

    d.   Passive activity losses are deductible in the current year only to the extent of gains from passive activities (in the aggregate).

        1)   Partnership ordinary loss is generally passive to a partner unless the partner materially participates in the partnership activity.

Past CPA exam questions have tested candidates' knowledge of calculating a partner's share of taxable income and the partner's adjusted basis in the partnership. Also, questions have asked for the calculation of the partnership's income.

8. **Sale of a Partnership Interest**

   a. A sale or exchange of a partnership interest results in capital gain or loss, except that any gain realized attributable to unrealized receivables and inventory is ordinary income (OI).

   b. Gain or loss realized includes the selling partner's share of partnership liabilities.

   c. LTCG results if the partner held the interest more than 1 year.

   d. Gain realized on the sale of a partnership is OI to the extent attributable to the partner's share of Sec. 751, or "hot" assets. These include unrealized receivables (URs) and inventory.

      1) URs are rights to payments to the extent not already included in income under the partnership's accounting method. The rights to payment may be for services or for goods other than capital assets.

         a) URs also include the OI potential (recapture) in Sec. 1245 and Sec. 1250 property and in franchises, trademarks, or trade names.

         b) Note that, to the extent that an accrual-method partnership has basis in an account receivable, the receivable is not unrealized.

      2) "Inventory" in this context includes not only inventory held for sale but also any partnership property characterized as other than Sec. 1231 property or a capital asset in the hands of the partnership, selling partner, or a distributee partner (e.g., copyrights, accounts receivable, unrealized receivables).

         a) The "substantially appreciated" (120%) test no longer applies to sales or exchanges but still applies to distributions. The application to distributions is further explained in item 2.c.1)b)i) in Subunit 13.5.

EXAMPLE

S sells a 25% interest (AB = $100,000) in Partnership to B for $200,000. Partnership's assets are cash ($80,000), land (FMV = $300,000, AB = $160,000), and inventory (FMV = $400,000, AB = $280,000). Of S's realized gain of $100,000, at least $30,000 is ordinary income [($400,000 − $280,000) × 25%].

---

9. **Liability Relief**

   a. A partner's relief from partnership liabilities is treated as a distribution of money.

EXAMPLE

Tami sold her share of a partnership for $29,000. Her basis in the partnership is $24,000, including $10,000 of liabilities. The selling price is considered to be $39,000 ($29,000 cash received plus the $10,000 relief of liabilities). Thus, her gain on the sale of the partnership interest is $15,000 ($39,000 − $24,000).

---

10. **Gift of a Partnership Interest**

    a. Generally, no gain is recognized upon the gift. However, if partnership liabilities allocable to the gifted interest exceed the AB of the partnership interest, the donor must recognize gain. No loss is recognized on the gift.

    b. The donee's basis in the interest is the donor's basis after adjustment for the donor's distributive share of partnership items up to the date of the gift.

    c. For purposes of computing a loss on a subsequent sale of the interest by the donee, the FMV of the interest immediately prior to the gift is used.

    d. Generally, partnership interest gifted to a related minor is attributed to others (e.g., parents).

       1) There are limits on the amount of partnership income that can be allocated to a related minor.

11. **Inheritance**

    a. The tax year of a partnership closes with respect to a partner whose entire interest in the partnership terminates, whether by death, liquidation, or otherwise.

    b. The successor has a FMV basis in the interest.

    c. The partnership tax year does not close with respect to the other partners.

12. **Family Partnerships**

    a. A family partnership is one consisting of a taxpayer and his or her spouse, ancestors, lineal descendants, or trusts for the primary benefit of any of them. Siblings are not treated as members of the taxpayer's family for these purposes.

    b. Services. A services partnership is one in which capital is not a material income-producing factor.

       1) In a family partnership, a family member is treated as a services partner only to the extent (s)he provides services that are substantial or vital to the partnership.

    c. Capital. A family member is treated as a partner in a partnership in which capital is a material income-producing factor, whether the interest is acquired by gift or purchase.

       1) The partnership agreement is disregarded to the extent a partner receives less than reasonable compensation for services.

EXAMPLE

R gives Son a gift of $250,000. Son contributes it in exchange for a 50% interest in a newly formed partnership with R. R&S Partnership continues what was R's sole proprietorship. The reasonable value of R's services the following tax year is $75,000. Of R&S's gross income of $125,000, $75,000 must be allocated to R for his services. Son's distributive share attributable to his capital interest is no more than $25,000 [($125,000 − 75,000) × 50%].

---

       2) This rule applies to all, not just family members.

    d. Spouses filing a joint return may elect out of partnership treatment by choosing to be a qualified joint venture.

       1) The only members of the joint venture must be the spouses, and both must materially participate and make the election.

       2) Each spouse will be treated as a sole proprietor, allowing both to receive Social Security benefits.

13. **Reporting Requirements**

    a. A partnership, as a conduit, is not subject to federal income tax. But it must report information including partnership items of income, loss, deduction, and credit to the IRS.

    b. A partnership is required to file an initial return for the first year in which it receives income or incurs expenditures treated as deductions for federal income tax purposes.

    c. Form 1065 is used for the partnership's information return.

    d. Any partnership item that may vary tax liability of any partner is separately stated on Schedule K.

    e. A Schedule K-1 is prepared for each partner and contains the partner's distributive share of partnership income and separately stated items to be reported on the partner's tax return.

    f. A partnership return is due (postmark date) on or before the 15th day of the 3rd month following the close of the partnership's tax year (March 15 for calendar-year partnerships). Partnership extension periods are, like most others, 6 months (September 15 for a calendar-year partnership).

    g. Signature by any partner is evidence that the partner was authorized to sign the return. Only one partner is required to sign the return.

    h.   Inadequate filing. A penalty is imposed in the amount of the number of persons who were partners at any time during the year, multiplied by $200 for each of up to 12 months (including a portion of one) that the return was late or incomplete.

    i.   Each partner must report his or her share of items consistently with their treatment on the partnership return unless

        1)   The partner identifies inconsistency on a filed statement, or

        2)   The partnership has no more than 10 partners, and no estate or nonresident alien is a partner.

14. **Partnership Tax Administration**

    a.   The IRC provides for designation of a tax matters partner (TMP), e.g., the general partner holding the largest partnership interest.

    b.   When the IRS enters into a settlement agreement with any partner, it must offer consistent settlement terms to any other partner who so requests.

    c.   Each partner is bound to a settlement agreement entered into between the IRS and the TMP unless the partner files notice otherwise.

    d.   Small partnerships. Consistent and binding settlements do not apply to a small partnership, i.e., one that has no more than 10 partners, each being a natural person or an estate.

Operations Attributes Chart

Earnings Implications		Ownership & Basis Adjustments	
Income Characterization	Passed through to partners; character is the same as if a partner received it directly	Death – Basis Adjustments	Basis of partnership interest is generally FMV on the date of death; Sec. 754 election available at partnership level
Allocation of Income	Based on partnership agreement if it has substantial economic reality	Basis Increases from Operations	Increased by profits and additional contributions, and increase in partner's share of debts
Exempt Income (i.e., municipal bond interest)	Passed through to partners; retains character as exempt	Basis Decreases from Operations	Decreased by losses, deductions, distributions, and decreases in partner's share of debts
Capital Losses	Passed through to shareholders with normal limitations applying at partner level	Transferability of Interest/ Ownership	Can sell all or a portion of partnership interest
Charitable Contributions	Generally 50% limitation at partner level	Liquidating and Nonliquidating Distributions	Based on partnership agreement
Deductibility of Losses	Passed through to partners, normal limitations apply, basis, at risk, passive		

Tax Implications	
Pass Through Tax Treatment	Yes
Double Taxation	No
Income Tax Brackets	Income tax brackets of the partner
Business Income Taxability	Business net income taxed as personal income to partners

Stop and review! You have completed the outline for this subunit. Study multiple-choice questions 4 through 6 beginning on page 376.

13.3 PARTNERS DEALING WITH OWN PARTNERSHIP

1. **Overview**

   a. The Code recognizes that a partner can engage in property, services, and loan transactions with the partnership in a capacity other than as a partner, i.e., as an independent, outside third party. The tax result, in general, is as if the transaction took place between two unrelated persons after arm's-length negotiations.

2. **Customary Partner Services**

   a. When a partner performs services for the partnership that are customarily performed by a partner, the partner's return is generally his or her share of profits of the partnership business.

      1) It is gross income, not as compensation, but as a distributive share of partnership income.

      2) The value of the services is not deductible by the partnership.

3. **Guaranteed Payments**

   a. A guaranteed payment (GP) is a payment to a partner for services rendered or capital used that is determined without regard to the income of the partnership.

      1) It is used to distinguish payments that are a function of partnership income and payments connected with partners acting in a nonpartner capacity.

   b. Services. The services must be a customary function of a partner. They are normal activities of a partner in conducting partnership business.

   c. Use of capital. The payment may be stated to be interest on the partner's capital account or to be rent on contributed property.

   d. Fixed amount stated. If the partnership agreement provides for a GP in a fixed amount, e.g., annual salary amount, the GP amount is the stated amount.

   e. Stated minimum amount. The partnership agreement may allocate a share of partnership income to the partner. Any excess over the partner's pro rata share is considered GP.

   GP = Stated minimum amount − Partner's share of partnership income

   f. For purposes of determining the partner's gross income, the GP is treated as if made to a nonpartner.

      1) The partner separately states the GP from any distributive share.

      2) The payment is ordinary income to the partner.

      3) The payment is reported in the tax year in which the partnership makes the GP.

      4) Receipt of a GP does not directly affect the partner's AB in his or her partnership interest.

   g. For purposes of determining deductibility by the partnership, a GP is treated as if made to a nonpartner.

      1) The payment is deductible if it would have been deductible if made to a nonpartner.

      2) Usually, deductible GPs are for a general business expenditure that need not be separately stated.

      3) Investment interest expense is an exception. It should be separately stated even if it is GP and even if it is deductible by a partner.

   NOTE: If the GP exceeds the partnership's ordinary income, the resulting ordinary loss is allocated among the partners (including the partner who receives the GP).

EXAMPLE

Under a partnership agreement, Meena is to receive 30% of the partnership income, but not less than $13,000. The partnership has net income of $30,000. Meena's share, without regard to the minimum guarantee, is $9,000 (30% × $30,000). The guaranteed payment that can be deducted by the partnership is $4,000 ($13,000 – $9,000). Meena's income from the partnership is $13,000, and the remaining $17,000 of partnership income will be reported by the other partners in proportion to their shares under the partnership agreement.

If the partnership net income had been $50,000, there would have been no guaranteed payment since Meena's share, without regard to the guarantee, would have been greater than the guarantee.

---

   h.   For all other purposes, the GP is treated as if made to a partner in his or her capacity as a partner. A partner is not an employee of the partnership. Partnership contributions to a self-employment retirement plan are not deductible by the partnership.

4.   **Nonpartner Capacity**

   a.   Payments to a partner without regard to income of the partnership for property or for services not customarily performed by a partner are generally treated as if the transaction took place between two unrelated persons after arm's-length negotiations.

   b.   Loans. Interest paid to a partner on a (true) loan is all gross income to the partner and a deductible partnership item.

   c.   Services. Payments to the partner for services rendered (of a nature not normally performed by a partner) to or for the partnership are gross income to the partner and generally an ordinary deductible expense of the partnership.

   d.   Property. A partner acting as a nonpartner (independent third party, outsider) can sell (or exchange) property to (or with) the partnership, and vice-versa. Gain or loss on the transaction is recognized, unless an exception applies.

EXAMPLE

Partnership sells land to Partner. Partnership recognizes loss. The loss is a partnership item allocable to partners as distributive shares. Partner takes a cost basis in the property.

---

   e.   Character and loss limit rules.

      1)   Applicability. These character and loss limit rules apply to any transaction between the partnership and either

         a)   A partner who owns more than 50% of the partnership or

         b)   Another partnership, if more than 50% of the capital or profits interest of each is owned by the same persons.

      2)   Character. Any gain recognized is ordinary income if the property is held as other than a capital asset by the acquiring partner or partnership.

EXAMPLE

Dora has held a capital asset for several years. The asset has a basis of $16,000 and an FMV of $24,000. She sells the asset to a partnership in which she is more than a 50% owner. The partnership will hold the property as a depreciable asset. Her gain of $8,000 ($24,000 – $16,000) will be ordinary income since she sold a capital asset to a more than 50% owned partnership that is not a capital asset to the partnership. If the partnership were to hold the asset as a capital asset, her gain would be capital gain.

---

      3)   Loss limit. No deduction is allowed for realized losses.

         a)   The acquiring party has a cost basis.

         b)   A subsequent taxable disposition event results in gain recognition limited to the previously unrecognized gain.

         c)   Expenditures are deductible when, and not before, the amount is includible in gross income by the payee even if the payor is an accrual-method taxpayer.

    f.   Distribution for contribution. When a partner contributes property to a partnership and immediately receives a distribution, the transaction is essentially a sale.

        1)   Gain realized is recognized to the extent the contributed property is deemed purchased by the other partners.

EXAMPLE

P and Q contributed land with FMVs of $250,000 and $500,000, respectively, each in exchange for a 50% interest in PQ Partnership. PQ mortgaged the land for $550,000 and distributed $250,000 of the proceeds to Q. Q recognizes any gain realized on 50% of the land she contributed. Fifty percent of the AB in the land is included in Q's basis in her partnership interest.

Stop and review! You have completed the outline for this subunit. Study multiple-choice questions 7 through 9 beginning on page 377.

13.4 TREATMENT OF PARTNERSHIP LIABILITIES

1.   **Overview**

    a.   A partner's share of partnership liabilities affects the partner's basis in his or her partnership interest and can result in increased gain being recognized by the partner. Any increase in a partner's share of liabilities of the partnership increases the partner's basis. The opposite is true for a decrease in partnership liabilities.

2.   **Recourse Liabilities**

    a.   A liability is a recourse liability if the creditor has a claim against the partnership or any partner for payment if the partnership defaults.

    b.   Partners generally share recourse liabilities based on their ratio for sharing losses.

        1)   However, regulations allocate a recourse liability to the partner(s) who would be liable for it if at the time all partnership debts were due, all partnership assets (including cash) had zero value and a hypothetical liquidation occurred.

        2)   A partner who pays more than his or her proportionate share of a partnership debt that becomes uncollectible is permitted to take a bad debt deduction equal to the amount in excess of that partner's share of the debt.

    c.   A limited partner cannot share in recourse debt in excess of any of his or her obligations to make additional contributions to the partnership and any additional amount(s) (s)he would actually lose if the partnership could not pay its debt.

3.   **Nonrecourse Liabilities**

    a.   The creditor has no claim against the partnership or any partners. At most, the creditor has a claim against a particular secured item of partnership property.

    b.   All partners share in nonrecourse liabilities based on their ratio for sharing profits.

EXAMPLE

Zachary and Paige form a cash-basis general partnership with cash contributions of $40,000 each. Under the partnership agreement, they share all partnership profits and losses equally. To purchase depreciable business equipment, the partnership borrows $98,000. This debt is included in the partners' bases in the partnership because incurring it creates an additional $98,000 of basis in the partnership's depreciable property.

If neither partner has an economic risk of loss in the liability, it is a nonrecourse liability. Each partner's basis would include his or her share of the liability, $49,000.

If Paige is required to pay the creditor if the partnership defaults, she has an economic risk of loss in the liability. Her basis in the partnership would be $138,000 ($40,000 + $98,000), while Zachary's basis would be $40,000.

Stop and review! You have completed the outline for this subunit. Study multiple-choice questions 10 and 11 on page 378.

13.5 DISTRIBUTION OF PARTNERSHIP ASSETS

1. **Overview**

   a. A distribution is a transfer of value from the partnership to a partner in reference to his or her interest in the partnership.

      1) A distribution may be in the form of money, liability relief, or other property.
      2) A draw is a distribution.

   b. Form 1065 Schedule M-2 is the section of the partnership tax return where distributions are required to be recorded.

Schedule M-2	Analysis of Partners' Capital Accounts			
1	Balance at beginning of year . . .		6	Distributions: **a** Cash . . . .
2	Capital contributed: **a** Cash . . .			**b** Property . . . . .
	b Property . .		7	Other decreases (itemize): _____
3	Net income (loss) per books			
4	Other increases (itemize): _____		8	Add lines 6 and 7 . . . .
5	Add lines 1 through 4		9	Balance at end of year. Subtract line 8 from line 5

Form **1065** [Year]

2. **Current Distributions**

   a. A current (or operating) distribution reduces the partner's basis in the partnership interest.

      1) A decrease in a partner's allocable share of partnership liabilities is treated as a distribution of money.

   b. Money distributions. The partnership recognizes no gain.

      1) A partner recognizes gain only to the extent the distribution exceeds the AB in the partnership interest immediately before the distribution.
      2) Gain recognized is capital gain.
      3) Basis in the interest is decreased, but not below zero.
      4) Loss is not recognized.

   c. Property Distributions

      1) Partnership. Generally, no gain or loss is recognized by the partnership when it distributes property, including money. Sections 1245 and 1250 do not trigger recognition on the distribution.

         a) Precontribution gain or loss. If property is distributed to a noncontributing partner within 7 years of contribution, the partnership recognizes gain or loss to the extent of any unrealized gain or loss, respectively, that existed at the contribution date.

            i) Allocate this recognized gain (loss) to the contributing partner.
            ii) The contributing partner's basis in his or her partnership interest is increased.
            iii) Basis in the property is also increased.
            iv) The distributee has a transferred basis.

         b) Disproportionate distributions of unrealized receivables or substantially appreciated inventory (SAI) result in gain recognition.

            i) Inventory is considered substantially appreciated if its FMV exceeds 120% of the partnership's adjusted basis. Gains from such distributions are taxed as ordinary income.

      2) Partner. The distributee partner generally recognizes gain only to the extent that money (including liability relief) exceeds his or her AB in his or her interest.

d. The partner's basis in the distributed property is the partnership's AB in the property immediately before distribution, but it is limited to the distributee's AB in his or her partnership interest minus any money received in the distribution.

e. When the limit in item d. above applies, allocate basis

1) First to unrealized receivables and inventory, up to partnership AB in them, and
2) Second to other (noncash) property.

f. If the available basis is too small, the decrease (partnership basis in assets – basis in partnership interest) is allocated to the assets. The decrease is allocated by the following steps:

1) Assign each asset its partnership basis.
2) Calculate the decrease amount.
3) Allocate the decrease first to any assets that have declined in value.
4) Allocate any remaining decrease to the assets based on relative adjusted basis at this point in the calculation.

EXAMPLE

Karen has a $6,000 basis in the BK partnership immediately before receiving a current distribution (there is no remaining precontribution gain). The distribution consists of $5,000 cash, a computer with a FMV of $1,500 and a $4,000 basis to the partnership, and a desk with a FMV of $500 and a $1,500 basis to the partnership. Karen's basis in the distributed property is determined as follows:

Beginning basis in partnership interest	$6,000	
Less: Money received	(5,000)	
Remaining basis to allocate	$1,000	

		Computer	Desk
Step 1 -- Allocate partnership basis to each asset	Partnership basis in assets	$ 4,000	$ 1,500
Step 2 -- Calculate decrease			
Total partnership basis $ 5,500			
Basis to allocate (1,000)			
Decrease amount $ 4,500			
Step 3 -- Allocate decrease to assets with a decline in FMV	Decline in FMV	(2,500)	(1,000)
	Relative adjusted basis	$ 1,500	$ 500
Step 4 -- Allocate remaining decrease of $1,000 ($4,500 – $2,500 – $1,000) based on relative adjusted basis	Remaining decrease	(750)*	(250)*
	Karen's basis in distributed property	$ 750	$ 250

* $750 = (1,500 ÷ 2,000) × $1,000
$250 = (500 ÷ 2,000) × $1,000

---

g. The partner's holding period in the distributed property includes that of the partnership.

h. The partner's basis in his or her ownership interest in the partnership is reduced by the amount of money and the AB of property received in the distribution.

3. **Disproportionate Distributions**

a. Gain is recognized on a distribution of property that is disproportionate with respect to unrealized receivables (URs) or substantially appreciated inventory (SAI).

b. The distribution will be recharacterized as if the URs or SAI were distributed.

4. **Liquidating Distributions**

a. Distributions liquidating the entire interest of a partner may be due to partnership termination and/or the retirement or death of the partner. Sale to the partnership of a partner's entire interest is treated as a liquidating distribution.

b. Payments to a retired partner that are determined by partnership income are treated as a distributive share of partnership income, regardless of the period over which they are paid. The income is characterized at the partnership level.

c. Amounts received from the partnership in liquidation of a partnership interest are generally treated the same as other (nonliquidating) distributions.

   1) Gain is recognized to the extent money distributed exceeds the liquidating partner's AB in the partnership interest immediately before the distribution.

      a) Decrease of the partner's share of partnership liabilities is treated as a distribution of money.

      b) The gain is capital gain. However, precontribution gain or disproportionate distribution of SAI or URs could result in ordinary income.

   2) The liquidating partner is treated as a partner for tax purposes until all payments in complete liquidation have been made.

d. Loss. A loss is realized when money and the FMV of property distributed are less than the AB of the partnership interest.

   1) No loss is recognized if any property other than money, URs, and inventory is distributed in liquidation of the interest.

   2) Loss recognized is limited to any excess of the AB in the partnership interest over the sum of money and the AB in the URs and inventory.

   3) Loss recognized is characterized as if from sale of a capital asset.

EXAMPLE

Amber has a basis in the partnership of $17,000. In complete liquidation of her interest, she received $11,000 in cash and receivables with a basis of $0. Amber will report a capital loss of $6,000 ($17,000 – $11,000 – $0) from the liquidation. The basis of the receivables will be $0 to her. If she had received a capital asset instead of the receivables, she would not qualify to take a loss, and the capital asset would have a basis to her of $6,000 ($17,000 – $11,000).

---

e. The distributee's basis in (noncash) property received in a distribution in liquidation is any excess of his or her AB in the partnership interest immediately before distribution over any amount of money received.

   1) If the total partnership basis of assets distributed exceeds the partner's basis in the partnership interest, allocate the decrease in the same manner as for current distributions.

   2) For liquidating distributions only, if the basis in the partnership interest exceeds the total partnership basis of distributed assets, allocate the increase by the following steps:

      a) Determine the amount of basis to be allocated.

      Beginning basis
      – Money received
      – Unrealized receivables and inventory
      = **Basis to allocate**

      b) Allocate any appreciation to each asset.

      c) Allocate any remaining basis (basis to allocate – appreciation of distributed assets) to the assets based on FMV prior to the distribution.

f. The distributee's holding period in the distributed property includes that of the partnership.

g.   Gain on the sale of URs distributed by the partnership is ordinary income.

1)   Gain or loss realized on inventory distributed depends on the nature of the property in the distributee's hands.

2)   If the distributee sells or exchanges the inventory 5 years or more after distribution, capital gain treatment may be available.

   Be prepared to answer questions regarding basis and gain (loss) calculations resulting from both current and liquidating distributions of partnership assets.

Stop and review! You have completed the outline for this subunit. Study multiple-choice questions 12 through 15 beginning on page 379.

13.6 TERMINATION OF PARTNERSHIP

1.   **Overview**

a.   A partnership terminates for federal tax purposes only when operations of the partnership cease or 50% or more of the total partnership interests are sold or exchanged within any 12-month period.

1)   The partnership's tax year ends on the date of termination.

b.   Sale or exchange termination is treated as a distribution of assets immediately followed by the contribution of those assets to a new partnership.

c.   The tax year of a partnership closes with respect to a partner whose entire interest in the partnership terminates by death, liquidation, or other means.

1)   A deceased partner's allocable share of partnership items up to the date of death will be taxed to the decedent on his or her final return.

2)   Any items allocated after the date of death will be the responsibility of the successor in interest.

3)   A return must be filed for the short period, which is the period from the beginning of the tax year through the date of termination.

2.   **Merger**

a.   The merging partnership's tax year is used if the partners of the merged firms own more than 50% of the resulting partnership. Otherwise, a new tax year is started.

3.   **Split**

a.   The old partnership's tax year continues; however, if partners owned less than 50% of the original partnership, a new tax year should be started.

EXAMPLE

On January 1 of the current year, the partners' interests in the capital, profits, and losses of Ripple Partnership were

	Percent of Capital, Profits, and Losses
Pebble	20%
Rock	35%
Stone	45%

On February 8, Rock sold his entire interest to an unrelated party. Pebble sold his 20% interest in Ripple to a different unrelated party on December 24. Assuming no other transactions took place in the current year, Ripple Partnership terminated for tax purposes as of December 24 because 50% or more of the total partnership interest in capital and profits had been sold within a 12-month period.

EXAMPLE

Tin-Pan-Alley-Cat Partnership is in the manufacturing and wholesaling business. Tin owns a 40% interest in the capital and profits of the partnership, while each of the other partners owns a 20% interest. All of the partners are calendar-year taxpayers. On November 3 of the current year, a decision is made to separate the manufacturing business from the wholesaling business, and two new partnerships are formed. Tin-Pan Partnership takes over the manufacturing business, and Alley-Cat Partnership takes over the wholesaling business. For tax purposes, Tin-Pan is considered to be a continuation of the Tin-Pan-Alley-Cat Partnership because Tin-Pan owned more than 50% of the original partnership. Alley-Cat Partnership will start a new tax year.

Stop and review! You have completed the outline for this subunit. Study multiple-choice questions 16 and 17 on page 380.

13.7 ELECTING LARGE PARTNERSHIPS

1. **Overview**

    a. Large partnerships meeting certain requirements may elect to use simplified reporting requirements. An electing large partnership combines most items of partnership income, deduction, credit, and loss at the partnership level and passes through net amounts to the partners.

2. **Number of Partners**

    a. An electing large partnership is any partnership with 100 or more nonservice partners during the preceding tax year. Service partnerships and commodity trading partnerships may not make this election.

3. **Sale of Interests**

    a. An electing large partnership will not terminate if 50% or more of its interests are sold or exchanged in a 12-month period.

4. **Separately Stated Items**

    a. Separately stated items include

        1) Net income or loss from passive loss limitation activities
        2) Net income or loss from other activities (e.g., portfolio income)
        3) Net capital gain or loss for portfolio items and passive activity (netting of the gains and losses occurs at the partnership level)
        4) Tax-exempt interest
        5) Net AMT adjustments
        6) General credits
        7) Low-income housing credit
        8) Rehabilitation credit
        9) Foreign income taxes (deduction or credit)

5. **Deductions and Credits Generally Combined at Partnership Level**

    a. An electing large partnership generally does not separately report deductions to partners.

        1) Miscellaneous itemized deductions are generally combined and reduced at the partnership level.

            a) Instead of applying the 2% floor to each deduction, 70% of the total of these deductions is disallowed at the partnership level.

        2) Income and expenses from passive activities are combined to determine net income or loss.

        3) The deduction for charitable contributions is determined at the partnership level and deducted subject to a 10%-of-taxable-income limitation in determining partnership income.

6. **Capital Gains and Losses**

   a. For electing large partnerships, netting of capital gains and losses occurs at the partnership level.

   1) Each partner separately takes into account the partner's distributive shares of net capital gain or loss for each passive activity and for portfolio and active business items.

   2) Net capital gain or loss that is taken into account by a partner is treated as LTCG or LTCL.

   3) Any excess net STCG over net LTCL will be consolidated with the partnership's other taxable income and not separately reported.

Stop and review! You have completed the outline for this subunit. Study multiple-choice questions 18 through 20 on page 381.

QUESTIONS

13.1 Partnership Formation and Tax Year

1. Strom acquired a 25% interest in Ace Partnership by contributing land having an adjusted basis of $16,000 and a fair market value of $50,000. The land was subject to a $24,000 mortgage, which was assumed by Ace. No other liabilities existed at the time of the contribution. What was Strom's basis in Ace?

A. $0
B. $16,000
C. $26,000
D. $32,000

Answer (A) is correct.
   REQUIRED: The partner's basis in a partnership after a contribution of property with a liability in excess of basis.
   DISCUSSION: A partner's basis in a partnership equals the adjusted basis of the property contributed plus the partner's share of all partnership liabilities minus any liability of the partner assumed by the partnership. A liability assumed by the partnership is treated as a distribution to the partner. The basis of this partnership interest is the basis of the contributed land ($16,000) reduced by the liability assumed by the partnership ($24,000) and increased by the partner's share of partnership liabilities ($6,000 = $24,000 × 0.25) and recognized gain on contributed property ($2,000). Thus, the basis will be $0.
   Answer (B) is incorrect. The amount of $16,000 is the basis of the contributed property, which must be reduced by the liability assumed by the partnership and increased by the partner's share of partnership liabilities and recognized gain on contributed property. Answer (C) is incorrect. The amount of $26,000 is the FMV of the land reduced by the liability. The basis of the land, not the FMV, should be used to determine the partner's basis. Additionally, the partner's basis should be increased by his or her share of partnership liabilities and recognized gain on contributed property. Answer (D) is incorrect. The amount of $32,000 results from using the FMV of the land rather than the adjusted basis.

2. The holding period of a partnership interest acquired in exchange for a contributed capital asset begins on the date

A. The partner is admitted to the partnership.

B. The partner transfers the asset to the partnership.

C. The partner's holding period of the capital asset began.

D. The partner is first credited with the proportionate share of partnership capital.

Answer (C) is correct.
   REQUIRED: The partner's holding period for a partnership interest acquired in exchange for a contributed capital asset.
   DISCUSSION: The holding period of the partner's interest includes the holding period of contributed capital and Sec. 1231 assets. The holding period on an interest acquired in exchange for money, ordinary income property, or services begins the day after the exchange.

3. Nolan designed Timber Partnership's new building. Nolan received an interest in the partnership for the services. Nolan's normal billing for these services would be $80,000, and the fair market value of the partnership interest Nolan received is $120,000. What amount of income should Nolan report?

A. $0

B. $40,000

C. $80,000

D. $120,000

Answer (D) is correct.

REQUIRED: The recognized income from services in exchange for interest in a partnership.

DISCUSSION: A partner who receives a partnership interest in exchange for services recognizes compensation income equal to the FMV of the partnership interest. Gross income must be reported when an interest received is subject to neither substantial risk of forfeiture nor restrictions on transfer. The income reported is ordinary.

Answer (A) is incorrect. Income includes compensation for services. This is not a nonrecognition transaction. Answer (B) is incorrect. The value of service performed is also considered income. Answer (C) is incorrect. Income from services exchanged for partnership interest is not valued based on normal billing.

13.2 Partner's Taxable Income

4. On January 2, 2017, Arch and Bean contribute cash equally to form the JK Partnership. Arch and Bean share profits and losses in a ratio of 75% to 25%, respectively. For 2017, the partnership's ordinary income was $40,000. A distribution of $5,000 was made to Arch during 2017. What is Arch's share of taxable income for 2017?

A. $5,000

B. $10,000

C. $20,000

D. $30,000

Answer (D) is correct.

REQUIRED: The partner's share of partnership taxable income.

DISCUSSION: Arch's 75% share of the partnership's $40,000 ordinary income, or $30,000, is Arch's share of taxable income for 2017 even if not distributed. Distributions are received free of tax by the partner, provided (s)he has adequate basis in the partnership, i.e., at least as much basis as the distribution. A partner's basis is increased by his or her share of partnership income and decreased by distributions.

Answer (A) is incorrect. The amount of $5,000 is the distribution to the partner. The partner is taxed on his or her distributive share of partnership taxable income. Answer (B) is incorrect. Arch's profit share is 75%, not 25%. Answer (C) is incorrect. Arch's profit share is 75%, not 50%.

5. Evan, a 25% partner in Vista Partnership, received a $20,000 guaranteed payment in 2017 for deductible services rendered to the partnership. Guaranteed payments were not made to any other partner. Vista's 2017 partnership income consisted of

Net business income before guaranteed payments	$80,000
Net long-term capital gains	10,000

What amount of income should Evan report from Vista Partnership on her 2017 tax return?

A. $37,500

B. $27,500

C. $22,500

D. $20,000

Answer (A) is correct.

REQUIRED: The amount of partner income.

DISCUSSION: A partner will report the ownership portion of the partnership income. Partnership income is the balance of the taxable income of a partnership that is not required to be separately stated. Capital gains and losses are generally segregated from ordinary net income and carried into the income of the individual partners. Any guaranteed payment (GP), while deductible for the partnership, is included in gross income of the receiving partner. Reportable income is calculated as follows:

Business income pre-GP	$80,000
Less: GP	(20,000)
Reportable partnership income	$60,000
25% interest	$15,000
Guaranteed payment	20,000
25% capital gain	2,500
Total	$37,500

Answer (B) is incorrect. The amount of $27,500 results from not deducting the guaranteed payment from net business income and adding only 25% of the guaranteed payment in the income calculation. Answer (C) is incorrect. The amount of $22,500 ignores the partner's share of partnership ordinary income. Answer (D) is incorrect. The amount of $20,000 ignores the business income and net capital gains.

6. At the beginning of 2017, Paul owned a 25% interest in Associates Partnership. During the year, a new partner was admitted, and Paul's interest was reduced to 20%. The partnership liabilities at January 1, 2017, were $150,000 but decreased to $100,000 at December 31, 2017. Paul's and the other partners' capital accounts are in proportion to their respective interests. Disregarding any income, loss, or drawings for 2017, the basis of Paul's partnership interest at December 31, 2017, compared to the basis of his interest at January 1, 2017, was

A. Decreased by $37,500.

B. Increased by $20,000.

C. Decreased by $17,500.

D. Decreased by $5,000.

Answer (C) is correct.

REQUIRED: The change in basis of a partner's interest in the partnership.

DISCUSSION: A decrease in a partner's share of partnership liabilities is treated as a distribution of money to the partner. At the beginning of the year, Paul's 25% share of the $150,000 of partnership liabilities was $37,500. At the end of the year, Paul's 20% share of the $100,000 of partnership liabilities was $20,000. Thus, Paul's share of partnership liabilities decreased by $17,500 ($37,500 – $20,000), and his basis was reduced by the same amount.

Answer (A) is incorrect. The beginning balance of Paul's share of partnership liabilities is $37,500. Answer (B) is incorrect. The ending balance of Paul's share of partnership liabilities is $20,000. Answer (D) is incorrect. A decrease in $5,000 only uses the $100,000 ending amount for partnership liabilities for calculating partner basis.

13.3 Partners Dealing with Own Partnership

7. Sara is a member of a four-person, equal partnership. Sara is unrelated to the other partners. In 2017, Sara sold 100 shares of a listed stock to the partnership for the stock's fair market value of $20,000. Sara's basis for this stock, which was purchased in 2006, was $14,000. Sara's recognized gain on the sale of this stock was

A. $0

B. $1,500

C. $4,500

D. $6,000

Answer (D) is correct.

REQUIRED: The partner's recognized gain on the sale of stock to the partnership.

DISCUSSION: When a partner engages in a transaction with the partnership not in a capacity as a partner, the transaction is considered to occur between the partnership and a nonpartner. Sara recognizes a $6,000 long-term capital gain ($20,000 proceeds less $14,000 AB). If Sara had owned more than 50% of the capital or profit interest of the partnership, a gain could still have been recognized, but a loss on a sale to the partnership would not.

Answer (A) is incorrect. Sara is treated as having sold the stock to an independent third party, and the full amount of realized gain is recognized. Answer (B) is incorrect. The full amount of realized gain is recognized. Answer (C) is incorrect. When a partner engages in a transaction with the partnership not in a capacity as a partner, the transaction is considered to occur between the partnership and a nonpartner.

8. Freeman, a single individual, reported the following income in the current year:

Guaranteed payment from services rendered to a partnership	$50,000
Ordinary income from an S corporation	$20,000

What amount of Freeman's income is subject to self-employment tax?

A. $0

B. $20,000

C. $50,000

D. $70,000

Answer (C) is correct.

REQUIRED: The amount of income subject to self-employment tax.

DISCUSSION: Amounts received as guaranteed payments from services rendered to a partnership are subject to self-employment tax [Reg. Sec. 1.707-1(c)]. The amount is deemed to be similar to a salary to the partner. Ordinary income from an S corporation is simply considered a distribution that passes through to the shareholders and is therefore not subject to the self-employment tax. Therefore, Freeman's income subject to self-employment tax is $50,000.

Answer (A) is incorrect. The guaranteed payment is subject to the tax. Answer (B) is incorrect. The S corporation ordinary income is not subject to the self-employment tax, while the guaranteed payment is. Answer (D) is incorrect. The ordinary income is not subject to the tax.

9. Peterson has a one-third interest in the Spano Partnership. During 2017, Peterson received a $16,000 guaranteed payment, which was deductible by the partnership, for services rendered to Spano. Spano reported a 2017 operating loss of $70,000 before the guaranteed payment. What, if any, are the net effects of the guaranteed payment?

I.   The guaranteed payment increases Peterson's tax basis in Spano by $16,000.

II. The guaranteed payment increases Peterson's ordinary income by $16,000.

    A. I only.

    B. II only.

    C. Both I and II.

    D. Neither I nor II.

Answer (B) is correct.
    REQUIRED: The income from a partnership to be reported by a partner who receives a guaranteed payment.
    DISCUSSION: For purposes of determining the partner's gross income, the guaranteed payment (GP) is treated as made to a nonpartner. The partner separately states the GP from any distributive share. The payment is ordinary income to the partner.
    Answer (A) is incorrect. Receipt of the GP does not directly affect Peterson's tax basis in his partnership interest. Answer (C) is incorrect. The payment is ordinary income to the partner. Answer (D) is incorrect. For purposes of determining the partner's gross income, the guaranteed payment is treated as made to a nonpartner. The partner separately states the GP from any distributive share. The payment is ordinary income to the partner.

13.4 Treatment of Partnership Liabilities

10. A $100,000 increase in partnership liabilities is treated in which of the following ways?

    A. Increases each partner's basis in the partnership by $100,000.

    B. Increases the partners' bases only if the liability is nonrecourse.

    C. Increases each partner's basis in proportion to their ownership.

    D. Does not change any partner's basis in the partnership regardless of whether the liabilities are recourse or nonrecourse.

Answer (C) is correct.
    REQUIRED: The correct treatment of an increase in partnership liabilities.
    DISCUSSION: A partner's share of a partnership liability is treated as if the partner contributed an equivalent amount of money to the partnership. The deemed contribution increases the partner's basis in his or her partnership interest. Normally, general partners share liabilities based on their ratio for sharing economic losses (recourse liability).
    Answer (A) is incorrect. Each partner's share increases based on his or her ratio for sharing economic losses (recourse liability) or partnership profits (nonrecourse liability). Answer (B) is incorrect. A recourse liability also increases a partner's share, but does so based on his or her ratio for sharing losses. Answer (D) is incorrect. The increase in partnership liabilities does affect the partner's basis in his or her partnership interest.

11. On January 4, 2017, Smith and White contributed $4,000 and $6,000 in cash, respectively, and formed the Macro General Partnership. The partnership agreement allocated profits and losses 40% to Smith and 60% to White. In 2017, Macro purchased property from an unrelated seller for $10,000 cash and a $40,000 mortgage note that was the general liability of the partnership. Macro's liability

    A. Increases Smith's partnership basis by $16,000.

    B. Increases Smith's partnership basis by $20,000.

    C. Increases Smith's partnership basis by $24,000.

    D. Has no effect on Smith's partnership basis.

Answer (A) is correct.
    REQUIRED: The effect of an increase in liability on a partner's basis.
    DISCUSSION: A partner's share of a partnership liability is treated as if the partner contributed an equivalent amount of money to the partnership. The deemed contribution increases the partner's basis in the partnership interest. Smith's partnership basis will increase by $16,000 ($40,000 × 40%). The cash payment (exchange) for the property has a net zero effect on partner basis.

13.5 Distribution of Partnership Assets

12. Baker is a partner in BDT with a partnership basis of $60,000. BDT made a liquidating distribution of land with an adjusted basis of $75,000 and a fair market value of $40,000 to Baker. What amount of gain or loss should Baker report?

A. $35,000 loss.

B. $20,000 loss.

C. $0

D. $15,000 gain.

Answer (C) is correct.
REQUIRED: The partner's gain or loss from a liquidating distribution.
DISCUSSION: A partner recognizes gain only to the extent a money distribution exceeds the AB in the partnership interest immediately before the distribution. In the case of capital property distributions, there is no gain or loss; instead, the partner's basis in the property is adjusted for any variance between the partner's partnership basis and the partnership's AB in the property distributed. Therefore, Baker has a $0 gain (loss).
Answer (A) is incorrect. The amount of $35,000 represents a loss by the partnership; however, no gain or loss is recognized by the partnership when it distributes property, including money. Answer (B) is incorrect. A gain can only be recognized when cash is distributed. Losses are never recognized. In addition, the value of distributed property is determined by the partnership's adjusted basis (not the FMV). Answer (D) is incorrect. Gains are only recognized when cash in excess of partnership interest is distributed (not property).

Questions 13 and 14 are based on the following information. The adjusted basis of Jody's partnership interest was $50,000 immediately before Jody received a current distribution of $20,000 cash and property with an adjusted basis to the partnership of $40,000 and a fair market value of $35,000.

13. What amount of taxable gain must Jody report as a result of this distribution?

A. $0

B. $5,000

C. $10,000

D. $20,000

Answer (A) is correct.
REQUIRED: The gain or loss recognized on a distribution with no Sec. 751 assets.
DISCUSSION: Gain is recognized by a partner on a distribution only to the extent that money distributed exceeds the partner's adjusted basis in the partnership interest immediately before the distribution. Gain would be capital. Since Jody's $50,000 adjusted basis in his partnership interest exceeds the $20,000 cash distributed, Jody recognizes no gain.
Answer (B) is incorrect. The amount of $20,000 is less than Jody's AB in the partnership interest immediately before the distribution. Answer (C) is incorrect. The money distributed is less than Jody's AB in the partnership interest immediately before the distribution. Answer (D) is incorrect. No gain is recognized when the money distributed is less than Jody's AB in the partnership interest immediately before the distribution.

14. What is Jody's basis in the distributed property?

A. $0

B. $30,000

C. $35,000

D. $40,000

Answer (B) is correct.
REQUIRED: The partner's basis in the distributed property.
DISCUSSION: The basis of property distributed to a partner (not in liquidation of his or her interest) is the property's AB to the partnership immediately before the distribution. It cannot exceed the AB of the partner's interest in the partnership less any money received in the same distribution.

Basis of partnership interest	$50,000
Less: Cash received	(20,000)
Basis in distributed property	$30,000

Answer (A) is incorrect. The basis in the property is the AB to the partnership immediately before the distribution. Answer (C) is incorrect. The basis is limited to the AB of the partner's interest reduced by any money received in the same distribution, not the fair market value. Answer (D) is incorrect. The basis is limited to the AB of the partner's interest reduced by any money received in the same distribution.

15. Fern received $30,000 in cash and an automobile with an adjusted basis and market value of $20,000 in a proportionate liquidating distribution from EF Partnership. Fern's basis in the partnership interest was $60,000 before the distribution. What is Fern's basis in the automobile received in the liquidation?

A. $0

B. $10,000

C. $20,000

D. $30,000

Answer (D) is correct.

REQUIRED: The distributee's basis in noncash property from liquidating distribution.

DISCUSSION: The distributee's basis in (noncash) property received in a distribution in liquidation is any excess of his or her AB in the partnership interest immediately before distribution over any amount of money received. Therefore, Fern's basis in the automobile is $30,000 ($60,000 basis – $30,000 cash received in distribution).

Answer (A) is incorrect. The cash distributed was only $30,000 and not $60,000 (i.e., equal to Fern's basis in the partnership interest). Answer (B) is incorrect. The amount of $10,000 would be the basis if the distribution included $50,000 in cash. In addition, the basis in the automobile is not equal to the difference between the cash received and the value of the automobile nor the difference between the distribution and the basis in the partnership interest. Answer (C) is incorrect. Carryover basis of capital assets from the partnership is adjusted for any difference in the total distribution and the partner's basis in the partnership interest.

13.6 Termination of Partnership

16. On January 3, 2017, the partners' interests in the capital, profits, and losses of Able Partnership were

	Percent of Capital, Profits, and Losses
Dean	25%
Poe	30%
Ritt	45%

On February 4, 2017, Poe sold her entire interest to an unrelated party. Dean sold his 25% interest in Able to another unrelated party on December 20, 2017. No other transactions took place in 2017. For tax purposes, which of the following statements is true with respect to Able?

A. Able terminated as of February 4, 2017.

B. Able terminated as of December 20, 2017.

C. Able terminated as of December 31, 2017.

D. Able did not terminate.

Answer (B) is correct.

REQUIRED: The result when two partners sell their interests.

DISCUSSION: A partnership terminates for tax purposes only if (1) no part of any business, financial operation, or venture of the partnership continues to be carried on by its partners in a partnership, or (2) within a 12-month period, there is a sale or exchange of 50% or more of the total interest in partnership capital and profits. On December 20, 2017, the partnership ceased to operate as a partnership because over 50% of the partnership interest was sold.

Answer (A) is incorrect. At that time, only 30% of the partnership interest had been sold. Answer (C) is incorrect. The partnership terminates on the date when 50% of the partnership has been sold during any 12-month period, not at the year ending such sales. Answer (D) is incorrect. A partnership terminates when 50% or more of the partnership interests are sold within a 12-month period.

17. Curry's sale of her partnership interest causes a partnership termination. The partnership's business and financial operations are continued by the other members. What, if any, are the effects of the termination?

I. There is a deemed distribution of assets to the remaining partners and the purchaser.

II. There is a hypothetical recontribution of assets to a new partnership.

A. I only.

B. II only.

C. Both I and II.

D. Neither I nor II.

Answer (C) is correct.

REQUIRED: The effects, if any, of the termination.

DISCUSSION: Distributions liquidating the entire interest of a partner occur upon termination. Gain may result, and the partners will have constructively contributed the distributed assets back to the partnership at a stepped-up basis.

Answer (A) is incorrect. There is a second consequence in that a hypothetical recontribution of assets to a new partnership also occurs. Answer (B) is incorrect. A deemed distribution of assets to the remaining partners and the purchaser also occurs. Answer (D) is incorrect. There is at least one effect as a result of the termination.

13.7 Electing Large Partnerships

18. All of the following items are separately reportable items for electing large partnerships **except**

   A. Tax-exempt interest.

   B. Taxable income or loss from passive loss limitation activities.

   C. Section 1231 gains and losses.

   D. Net capital gain or loss.

Answer (C) is correct.
   REQUIRED: The item that is not separately stated for electing large partnerships.
   DISCUSSION: The taxable income of an electing large partnership considers Sec. 1231 gains and losses. Net Sec. 1231 gain is considered long-term capital gain, while net Sec. 1231 loss is considered ordinary and is consolidated with other partnership ordinary income.
   Answer (A) is incorrect. Tax-exempt interest is separately stated for electing large partnerships. Answer (B) is incorrect. Taxable income or loss from passive loss limitation activities is separately stated for electing large partnerships. Answer (D) is incorrect. Net capital gain or loss is separately stated for electing large partnerships.

19. For an electing large partnership, charitable contributions are

   A. Separately reported to the partners.

   B. Allowed as a deduction at the partnership level without limitation.

   C. Allowed as a deduction at the partnership level, subject to a 10%-of-partnership-taxable-income limitation.

   D. Allowed as a deduction at the partnership level, subject to a 50%-of-partnership-taxable-income limitation.

Answer (C) is correct.
   REQUIRED: The treatment of charitable contribution deductions in electing large partnerships.
   DISCUSSION: An electing large partnership does not separately state its charitable contributions to its partners. Instead, the Sec. 170 charitable contribution deduction is allowed at the partnership level in determining partnership taxable income, subject to a 10%-of-taxable-income limitation, similar to the limitation applicable to corporate donors.
   Answer (A) is incorrect. Charitable contributions are not separately stated in an electing large partnership. Answer (B) is incorrect. Charitable contribution deductions are subject to a limitation. Answer (D) is incorrect. The deduction limitation is not 50%.

20. For electing large partnerships, combining capital gains and losses

   A. Occurs completely at the partner level.

   B. Occurs at both the partnership level and at the partner level for all capital gains and losses.

   C. Occurs at the partnership level, except net capital gain or loss for passive activities and other activities are each separately stated.

   D. Occurs at the partnership level, with passive activities and other activities being reported together at the partnership level and all other capital gains and losses being separately stated.

Answer (C) is correct.
   REQUIRED: The treatment of capital gains and losses in electing large partnerships.
   DISCUSSION: For electing large partnerships, netting of capital gains and losses occurs at the partnership level. Each partner separately takes into account the partner's distributive shares of net capital gain or loss for each passive activity and for portfolio and active business items. Net capital gain or loss that is taken into account by a partner is treated as long-term capital gain or long-term capital loss. Any excess net short-term capital gain over net long-term capital loss will be consolidated with the partnership's other taxable income and will not be separately reported.
   Answer (A) is incorrect. The combination occurs at the partnership level. Answer (B) is incorrect. The combination occurs only at the partnership level. Answer (D) is incorrect. Passive activities and other activities are separately stated, and all other capital gains and losses are reported together at the partnership level.

STUDY UNIT FOURTEEN
ESTATES, TRUSTS, AND WEALTH TRANSFER TAXES

(19 pages of outline)

This study unit addresses two different kinds of tax: income taxes and transfer taxes. Estates and trusts are legal entities defined by the assets they hold. These assets produce income. The entities are subject to tax on that income. This is referred to as fiduciary income taxation (Subunit 14.1). The formula for computing this fiduciary tax is the individual income tax formula presented earlier in Study Unit 4, modified for the distribution deduction and other special rules. Furthermore, the beneficiaries of these fiduciary entities, rather than the fiduciary, are personally subject to income tax on certain fiduciary income (Subunit 14.2).

In contrast, the gift and estate taxes (Subunits 14.3 and 14.4) are not income taxes. They are taxes on the transfer of assets from one person to another. Relatively few exclusions and deductions apply, and unified transfer tax rates and an applicable credit amount, or ACA, (formerly referred to as the unified credit) apply against all transfers. The donor or estate, not the recipient, must generally pay the tax. Finally, the generation-skipping transfer tax (Subunit 14.5) limits avoidance of gift and estate taxes.

Some candidates find it helpful to have the entire tax form side-by-side with our Knowledge Transfer Outline when studying. The full versions of the most up-to-date forms are easily accessible at www.gleim.com/taxforms. These forms and the form excerpts used in our outline are periodically updated as the latest versions are released by the IRS.

14.1 INCOME TAXATION

1. **Principal vs. Income**

   a. Tax is imposed on taxable income (TI) of trusts and estates, not on items treated as fiduciary principal.

   b. State law defines **principal** and **income** of a trust or estate for federal income tax purposes.

      1) Many states have adopted the Revised Uniform Principal and Income Act, some with modifications.

         a) The act and state laws provide that trust instrument designations of fiduciary principal and interest components control.

         b) The act and state law also provide default designations.

   c. Generally, principal is property held eventually to be delivered to the remainderman (the person who inherits or is entitled to inherit the property).

      1) Change in form of principal is not taxable income.
      2) Income is return on, or for use of, the principal.
      3) It is held for or distributed to the income beneficiary.

   d. Principal is also referred to as the corpus or res.

Allocation of Fiduciary Receipts and Disbursements

Principal	Income

Receipts

Principal	Income
Consideration for property, e.g.,	Business income
Gain on sale	Insurance proceeds for lost profits
Replacement property	Interest
Nontaxable stock dividends	Rents
Stock splits	Dividends (taxable)
Stock rights	Extraordinary dividends
Liquidating dividends	Taxable stock dividends
Depletion allowance (90%), e.g.,	Royalties (10%)
Royalties	

Disbursements

Principal	Income
Principal payments on debt	Business (ord. & nec.) expenses, e.g.,
Capital expenditures	Interest expense
Major repairs	Production of income expenses, e.g.,
Modifications	Maintenance/repair
Fiduciary fees	Insurance
Tax on principal items, e.g.,	Rent collection fee
Capital gains	Tax on fiduciary income
	Depreciation

---

2. **Tax Rates**

   a. Tax is imposed on taxable income of a trust or estate at the following rates for 2017:

Fiduciary Taxable Income Brackets	Applicable Rate	
$ 0 - $2,550	15%	
> 2,550 - 6,000	25%	(+ $382.50)
> 6,000 - 9,150	28%	(+ $1,245.00)
> 9,150 - 12,500	33%	(+ $2,127.00)
> 12,500	39.6%	(+ $3,232.50)

3. **Simple Trust**

   a. A simple trust is formed under an instrument having the following characteristics:

   1) Requires current distribution of all its income
   2) Requires no distribution of the res (i.e., principal)
   3) Provides for no charitable contributions by the trust

4. **Complex Trust**

   a. A complex trust is any trust other than a simple trust. A complex trust can

   1) Accumulate income,
   2) Provide for charitable contributions, and
   3) Distribute amounts other than income.

5. **Grantor Trust**

   a. A grantor trust is any trust to the extent the grantor is the effective beneficiary.

   1) The income attributable to a trust principal that is treated as owned by the grantor is taxed to the grantor.

2) The trust is disregarded.

    a) A trust is considered a grantor trust when the grantor has greater than 5% reversionary interest.

    b) A grantor is treated as the owner of a trust in which the income may be distributed or accumulated for the grantor's spouse.

    c) The grantor is also taxed on income from a trust in which the income may be applied for the benefit of the grantor. Use of income for the support of a dependent is considered the application of income for the benefit of the grantor. The income that may be applied for the support of a dependent is not taxable to the grantor if it is not actually used.

6. **Application of Rules**

    a. The rules for classifying trusts are applied on a year-to-year basis.

7. **Filing Requirement**

    a. An estate with gross income greater than or equal to $600 is required to file a tax return. A trust is required to file a return if it has either any taxable income or more than $600 of gross income.

        1) The trustee, executor, or administrator must file the return no later than the 15th day of the 4th month after the close of the entity's tax year. The extended due date is 5 1/2 months later.

        2) Form 1041, *U.S. Income Tax Return for Estates and Trusts*, must be used with its own tax rate schedule.

        3) If a domestic estate has a beneficiary who is a nonresident alien, the representative must file a return regardless of income.

        4) Estate gross income includes the gain from the sale of property (not gross proceeds).

8. **Income Tax Formula**

From Form 1041

Income			
1	Interest income	1	
2a	Total ordinary dividends	2a	
b	Qualified dividends allocable to: **(1)** Beneficiaries _____ **(2)** Estate or trust _____		
3	Business income or (loss). Attach Schedule C or C-EZ (Form 1040)	3	
4	Capital gain or (loss). Attach Schedule D (Form 1041)	4	
5	Rents, royalties, partnerships, other estates and trusts, etc. Attach Schedule E (Form 1040) .	5	
6	Farm income or (loss). Attach Schedule F (Form 1040)	6	
7	Ordinary gain or (loss). Attach Form 4797	7	
8	Other income. List type and amount _____	8	
9	**Total income.** Combine lines 1, 2a, and 3 through 8 . . . . ▶	9	

    a. TI of a trust or an estate is computed similarly to that of an individual.

    b. Gross income is computed as for individuals. Capital gain is charged to principal.

    c. Life insurance proceeds are generally includible in the value of the gross estate but are not considered income of the estate.

    d. Income in respect of a decedent is also taxed as income if it is received by the estate.

    e. Capital gains are taxed to the estate; then the gain must be added to the principal of the estate.

f.   AGI does apply to fiduciaries for purposes of computing deduction limits.

1)   The standard deduction is not allowed.

From Form 1041

Deductions	**10** Interest. Check if Form 4952 is attached ▶ ☐	**10**
	11 Taxes	**11**
	12 Fiduciary fees	**12**
	13 Charitable deduction (from Schedule A, line 7)	**13**
	14 Attorney, accountant, and return preparer fees	**14**
	15a Other deductions **not** subject to the 2% floor (attach schedule)	**15a**
	b Net operating loss deduction. See instructions	**15b**
	c Allowable miscellaneous itemized deductions subject to the 2% floor	**15c**
	16 Add lines 10 through 15c . . . . ▶	**16**
	17 Adjusted total income or (loss). Subtract line 16 from line 9 . . . **17**	
	18 Income distribution deduction (from Schedule B, line 15). Attach Schedules K-1 (Form 1041)	**18**
	19 Estate tax deduction including certain generation-skipping taxes (attach computation) . . .	**19**
	20 Exemption	**20**
	21 Add lines 18 through 20 . . . . ▶	**21**

g.   Deductions. They generally follow those allowable to an individual. Trustee fees, or administrator fees, and tax return preparation fees are deductible in full.

1)   Expenses that are directly allocable to tax-exempt income are allocated only to tax-exempt income. A reasonable proportion of expenses indirectly allocable to both tax-exempt income and other income must be allocated to each class of income.

2)   Administration expenses are deductible in full, if not deducted on the estate tax return. The amount of trustee fees deductible is not limited to the excess over 2% of AGI.

3)   Depreciation. In default of a trust instrument designation, the act charges depreciation to income.

   a)   Depreciation is allocated based on the same proportions as income from the estate is allocated.

      i)   EXCEPTION: The estate instrument may contain provisions apportioning the deduction.

   b)   Trusts. The trust may deduct depreciation only to the extent a reserve is required or permitted under the trust instrument or local law, and income is set aside for the reserve and actually remains in the trust.

      i)   Any part of the deduction in excess of the trust income set aside for the reserve is then allocated between the parties according to the instrument.

      ii)   If the instrument is silent, depreciation is allocated in the same proportion as income.

EXAMPLE

In the current year, Beta Trust distributes 40% of its income to Jane. The trust accumulates the remaining 60%. The trust's current-year depreciation is $10,000. The trust instrument is silent concerning the depreciation deduction; therefore, state law, which charges depreciation to principal, governs. Jane receives a $4,000 ($10,000 × 40%) depreciation deduction. The remaining $6,000 ($10,000 × 60%) of depreciation is deducted in calculating the trust's taxable income.

---

4)   Fiduciary NOLs are computed without regard to charitable contributions or distribution deductions. Carryover by the fiduciary is permitted.

   a)   Pass-through for deduction on personal returns of beneficiaries is allowed only in the year the fiduciary terminates.

      b) Pass-through NOLs and capital loss carryovers are used to calculate the beneficiary's AGI and taxable income.

      c) Estates can claim a deduction for a NOL.

         i) The NOL is calculated in a similar manner as an individual's NOL deduction.

         ii) The estate cannot deduct any distributions to beneficiaries or charitable contributions in arriving at the NOL or NOL carryover.

      d) An unused NOL in the final year of the estate may carry over to the beneficiaries succeeding to the property of the estate.

    5) A fiduciary may deduct a capital loss to the extent of capital gains plus $3,000. Carryover is permitted for individuals and estates; however, no carryover is allowed from a decedent's final return to his or her estate or beneficiary.

    6) Miscellaneous itemized deductions are subject to the 2%-of-AGI floor.

    7) Charitable contributions are deductible only if the governing instrument authorizes them. Deduction is not subject to limits based on AGI.

    8) Expenses attributable to tax-exempt income are not deductible.

    9) Personal exemption. A deduction is allowable but not for the year the trust or estate terminates. The amount of the deduction is

      a) $600 for an estate
      b) $300 for a simple trust
      c) $100 for a complex trust

EXAMPLE

Johnnie Rich establishes a trust in Year 1 with Molly Pitcher as the beneficiary. The trust instrument instructs the trustee to make discretionary distributions (i.e., characteristic of a complex trust) of income to Molly from Year 1 through Year 5 and, beginning in Year 6, to pay all of the trust income (i.e., characteristic of a simple trust) to Molly. For Year 1 through Year 5, the trust's exemption is $100. From Year 6 onward, the exemption increases to $300.

---

    h. Credits. Gross regular tax of a fiduciary is offset by most of the same credits available to individuals. Certain "personal" credits are unavailable. A fiduciary, for example, has no dependents.

    i. Losses from a passive activity owned by the estate or trust cannot be used to offset portfolio (interest, dividends, royalties, annuities, etc.) income of the estate or trust in determining taxable income.

  9. **Distribution Deduction**

From Form 1041

Schedule B	Income Distribution Deduction	
1	Adjusted total income. See instructions	1
2	Adjusted tax-exempt interest	2
3	Total net gain from Schedule D (Form 1041), line 19, column (1). See instructions	3
4	Enter amount from Schedule A, line 4 (minus any allocable section 1202 exclusion)	4
5	Capital gains for the tax year included on Schedule A, line 1. See instructions	5
6	Enter any gain from page 1, line 4, as a negative number. If page 1, line 4, is a loss, enter the loss as a positive number	6
7	**Distributable net income.** Combine lines 1 through 6. If zero or less, enter -0-	7
8	If a complex trust, enter accounting income for the tax year as determined under the governing instrument and applicable local law · 8	
9	Income required to be distributed currently	9
10	Other amounts paid, credited, or otherwise required to be distributed	10
11	Total distributions. Add lines 9 and 10. If greater than line 8, see instructions	11
12	Enter the amount of tax-exempt income included on line 11	12
13	Tentative income distribution deduction. Subtract line 12 from line 11	13
14	Tentative income distribution deduction. Subtract line 2 from line 7. If zero or less, enter -0-	14
15	**Income distribution deduction.** Enter the smaller of line 13 or line 14 here and on page 1, line 18	15

a. The deduction for distributions allocates taxable income of a trust or estate (gross of distributions) between the fiduciary and its beneficiaries.

b. Simple trust. The deduction is the lesser of the amount of the distributions (required) or distributable net income (DNI) (computed without including exempt income).

1) Generally, DNI is current net accounting income of the fiduciary reduced by any amounts allocated to principal.

c. Estates and complex trusts. The deduction is the lesser of DNI or distributions.

1) The amount distributed is the lesser of the FMV of the property or the basis of the property in the hands of the beneficiary.

2) The trustee(s) of a complex trust may elect to treat distributions made during the first 65 days of the (trust's) tax year as if they were made on the last day of the preceding tax year.

3) Specific bequests distributed or credited to a beneficiary in no more than three installments are not included as amounts distributed.

4) The fiduciary recognizes no gain on distribution of property, unless an estate executor so elects.

5) A beneficiary's basis in distributed property is transferred, with adjustments for any gain recognized to the fiduciary. Every $1 of value distributed is treated as if (first) from any current DNI.

a) The instrument might allocate the $1 to current income, accumulated income, or principal.

b) Principal (after DNI) is distributed tax-free.

d. Tax-exempt income that is not deductible. The estate cannot take an income distribution deduction for any item of distributable net income not included in the estate's gross income.

EXAMPLE

An estate has distributable net income of $5,000, consisting of $2,500 of dividends and $2,500 of tax-exempt interest. Distributions to the beneficiary total $3,500. Except for the rule in item d. above, the income distribution deduction would be $3,500 ($1,750 of dividends and $1,750 of tax-exempt interest). However, as a result of this rule, the income distribution deduction is limited to $1,750 because no deduction is allowed for the tax-exempt interest distributed.

---

10. **Distributable Net Income**

a. DNI is the maximum deductible at the fiduciary level for distributions and the maximum taxable at the beneficiary level. It is taxable income of the fiduciary (trust or estate), with various adjustments, and calculated as follows:

> Taxable Income (TI) of fiduciary (before the distribution deduction)
> \+ Personal exemption deduction ($600 estate,
> $300 simple trust, $100 complex trust)
> \+ Tax-exempt interest minus any related expenses
> \+ Capital losses allocated to principal
> – Capital gains allocated to principal
> – Taxable stock dividends allocated to principal
> – Extraordinary dividends allocated to principal
> = **Distributable net income**

b. No adjustment to fiduciary TI is made for the following:

1) Dividends, other than those in item a. above.

2) NOL deductions.

3) Depreciation, if a reserve is established and all income is not distributable.

4) Certain expenditures charged to principal, such as trustee fees. They do reduce income taxable to the beneficiary.

11. **Income in Respect of a Decedent (IRD)**

    a.   IRD is all amounts to which a decedent was entitled as gross income but that were not includible in computing taxable income on the final return. The decedent had a right to receive it prior to death; e.g., salary was earned or a sale contract was entered into.

    b.   Not includible on the final income tax return of a cash-method (CM) taxpayer are amounts not received. Not includible on the final income tax return of an accrual-method (AM) taxpayer are amounts not properly accrued. Examples follow:

EXAMPLE

On February 1, Angelo Robertson, a cash-method taxpayer, sold his tractor for $5,000, payable March 1 of the same year. His adjusted basis in the tractor was $3,000. Angelo died on February 15, before receiving payment. The gain to be reported as income in respect of a decedent is the $2,000 difference between the decedent's basis in the property and the sale proceeds. In other words, the income in respect of a decedent is the gain the decedent would have realized had he lived.

---

    c.   IRD is reported by the person receiving the income.

        1)   The cash method applies to income once designated IRD.
        2)   IRD received by a trust or estate is fiduciary income.

    d.   A right to receive IRD has a transferred basis. The basis is not stepped-up to FMV on the date of death, as is generally the case for property acquired from a decedent.

EXAMPLE

Mrs. Hart had earned 2 weeks' salary of $2,000 that had not been paid when she died. As a cash-method taxpayer, her basis in the right to receive the $2,000 was $0. When her estate received the income, it had $2,000 of ordinary income because its basis in the right to receive it was also $0. Note that the $2,000 is not reported on Mrs. Hart's final return.

---

    e.   IRD has the same character it would have had in the hands of the decedent.

    f.   IRD is taxable as income to the recipient and is includible in the gross estate. Double taxation is mitigated by deductions.

        1)   Deductions in respect of a decedent. Expenses accrued before death, but not deductible on the final return because the decedent used the cash method, are deductible when paid if otherwise deductible.

            a)   They are deductible on a fiduciary income tax return.
            b)   They are also deductible on the estate tax return.

        2)   Deduction for estate tax. Estate taxes attributable to IRD included in the gross estate are deductible on the fiduciary income tax return.

            a)   Administrative expenses and debts of a decedent are deductible on the estate tax return (Form 706). Some of them may also be deductible on the estate's income tax return (Form 1041).

                i)   Double deductions are disallowed.
                ii)   The right to deduct the expenses on Form 706 must be waived in order to claim them on Form 1041.

            b)   Deduction is allowed for any excess of the federal estate tax over the amount of the federal estate tax if the IRD had been excluded from the gross estate.

12. **Net Investment Income Tax**

   a. Estates and trusts are required to pay a 3.8% net investment income tax (NIIT) on the lesser of

   1) Undistributed net investment income for the tax year or
   2) Any excess fiduciary taxable income over the amount at which the highest tax bracket for estates and trusts begins for the tax year ($12,500 for 2017).

   b. In general, net investment income for the purpose of this tax includes but is not limited to

   1) Interest, dividends, certain annuities, royalties, and rents (unless derived from an active participation in a trade or business
   2) Income derived in a trade or business that is a passive activity or trading in financial instruments or commodities
   3) Net gains from the disposition of property (to the extent taken into account in computing taxable income) other than property held in an active trade or business

   c. The NIIT does not apply to income excluded for regular income tax purposes such as tax-exempt state or municipal bond interest, Veterans Administration benefits, or excluded gain from the sale of a principal residence.

   d. Undistributed net investment income is net investment income reduced by distributions of net investment income to beneficiaries and deductions for amounts of net investment income paid or permanently set aside for a charitable purpose.

13. **Tax Year**

   a. An estate may adopt any tax year ending within 12 months after death. Most trusts must adopt a calendar tax year. Tax-exempt and wholly charitable trusts may qualify to use a fiscal tax year. A beneficiary includes his or her share of trust income in his or her return for his or her tax year in which the trust's tax year ends, without regard to when distributions are made.

14. **Accounting Method**

   a. Any permissible accounting method may be adopted.

EXAMPLE

Stephen Gabriel owned and operated a pineapple farm. He used the cash method of accounting. He sold and delivered 5,000 bushels of pineapples to a canning factory for $10,000 but did not receive payment before his death. The proceeds from the sale are income in respect of a decedent. When the estate was settled, payment had not been made and the estate transferred the right to the payment to his widow. When Stephen's widow collects the $10,000, she must include that amount in her return. It is not reported on the final return of the decedent or on the return of the estate.

If Stephen used the accrual method of accounting, the amount accrued from the sale of the pineapples would be included on his final return and neither the estate nor the widow would realize income in respect of a decedent when the money is later paid.

---

15. **AMT**

   a. The alternative minimum tax applies to trusts and estates. It is determined in the same manner as for individuals.

16. **Estimated Payments**

From Form 1041

Tax and Payments	22	Taxable income. Subtract line 21 from line 17. If a loss, see instructions	**22**
	23	**Total tax** (from Schedule G, line 7)	**23**
	24	**Payments: a** [Year] estimated tax payments and amount applied from [prior year] return . . .	**24a**
	b	Estimated tax payments allocated to beneficiaries (from Form 1041-T)	**24b**
	c	Subtract line 24b from line 24a	**24c**
	d	Tax paid with Form 7004. See instructions	**24d**
	e	Federal income tax withheld. If any is from Form(s) 1099, check ▶ ☐	**24e**
		Other payments: **f** Form 2439 _____ ; **g** Form 4136 _____ ; Total ▶	**24h**
	25	**Total payments.** Add lines 24c through 24e, and 24h . . . . ▶	**25**
	26	Estimated tax penalty. See instructions	**26**
	27	**Tax due.** If line 25 is smaller than the total of lines 23 and 26, enter amount owed	**27**
	28	**Overpayment.** If line 25 is larger than the total of lines 23 and 26, enter amount overpaid . .	**28**
	29	Amount of line 28 to be: **a Credited to** [next year] **estimated tax** ▶ _____ ; **b Refunded** ▶	**29**

a. Trusts and estates are required to remit payments of estimated tax. The required amount and due dates of installments are determined in the same manner as for individuals. An estate is not required to pay estimated tax for its first 2 tax years. A trustee may elect to treat any portion of an estimated tax payment by the estate as made by the beneficiary. The amount would also be treated as paid or credited to the beneficiary on the last day of the tax year.

Stop and review! You have completed the outline for this subunit. Study multiple-choice questions 1 through 6 beginning on page 401.

14.2 BENEFICIARY'S TAXABLE INCOME

1. **Simple Trust**

    a. A beneficiary of a simple trust is taxed on the lower of the two amounts listed below.

    1) Trust income required to be distributed (even if not distributed)
    2) The beneficiary's proportionate share of the trust's DNI

EXAMPLE

The Triangle Trust reported DNI of $80,000 for the year. If the trustee is required to distribute $60,000 to Neil and $40,000 to Dave each year, then Neil includes $48,000 in GI [$80,000 DNI × ($60,000 Neil's required distribution ÷ $100,000 total required distribution)] and Dave includes $32,000 in GI [$80,000 DNI × ($40,000 Dave's required distribution ÷ $100,000 total required distribution)].

---

2. **Estates and Complex Trusts**

    a. A beneficiary of an estate or complex trust is taxed on amounts of fiduciary income required to be distributed plus additional amounts distributed to the beneficiary. However, the taxable amount is limited to the beneficiary's share of DNI.

3. **Character**

    a. The character of the income in the hands of the beneficiary is the same as in the hands of the trust or estate.

EXAMPLE

A simple trust distributes all of its $10,000 income to its sole beneficiary. Its DNI is also $10,000. Included in the trust income was $1,000 of tax-exempt income. The beneficiary treats $1,000 of the income from the trust as tax-exempt interest and excludes it from his or her personal gross income.

---

4. **Schedule K-1 (Form 1041)**

   a. Schedule K-1 is used to report the beneficiary's share of income deductions and credits from a trust or an estate.

Stop and review! You have completed the outline for this subunit. Study multiple-choice questions 7 through 9 beginning on page 402.

14.3 GIFT TAX

1. **Definition of Gift Tax**

   a. The gift tax is a tax of the transfer imposed on the donor. The table below presents the basic tax formula modified for the gift tax.

GIFT AMOUNT
FMV on date of gift, for
All gifts in the calendar year
– Exclusions
Annual exclusion
$14,000 per donee
Gift splitting between spouses
Paid on behalf of another for
Medical care
Education tuition
– Deductions
Marital
Charitable
= TAXABLE GIFTS FOR CURRENT YEAR
+ Taxable gifts for prior years
= TAXABLE GIFTS TO DATE
× Tax Rate
= TENTATIVE GIFT TAX
– (Prior year's gifts × current tax rates)
– Applicable credit amount
= GIFT TAX LIABILITY

2. **Amount of Gift**

   a. Any excess of FMV of transferred property over the FMV of consideration for it is a gift.

FMV of transferred property: given
– FMV of consideration (property, money, etc.): received
Gift amount

   b. A gift is complete when the giver has given over dominion and control such that (s)he is without legal power to change its disposition.

EXAMPLE

R opens a joint bank account with A, I, and H, with R the only depositor to the account. R, A, I, and H may each withdraw money. A gift is complete only when A, I, or H withdraws money.

---

   c. Gifts completed when the donor is alive (inter vivos gifts) are the only ones subject to gift tax. Transfers made in trusts are included.

   d. Property passing by will or inheritance is not included.

e.   To the extent credit is extended with less than sufficient stated interest, the Code imputes that interest is charged. If the parties are related, the lender is treated as having made a gift of the imputed interest to the borrower each year the loan is outstanding.

   1)   Gift loans are excluded if the aggregate outstanding principal is not more than $10,000.

f.   Basis in a gift is basis in the hands of the donor plus gift tax attributable to appreciation.

EXAMPLE

Thomas made a gift to his daughter of a piece of land with a FMV of $94,000. The land had a basis to Thomas of $60,000. He paid a taxable gift of $80,000 ($94,000 FMV – $14,000 annual exclusion) and a gift tax of $32,000 ($80,000 × 40%). The basis of the land to the daughter is carryover basis of $60,000 plus the gift tax attributable to the appreciation.

$$\$60,000 \quad + \quad \frac{\$34,000 \text{ increase in value}}{\$80,000 \text{ taxable gift}} \quad \times \quad \$32,000 \quad = \quad \$73,600$$

The AICPA has historically tested candidates' knowledge on the various aspects of gift tax, specifically the annual exclusion, gift splitting, medical or tuition costs, and marital deductions.

---

3.   **Annual Exclusion**

   a.   The first $14,000 of gifts of present interest to each donee is excluded from taxable gift amounts. The annual exclusion is indexed to reflect inflation.

   b.   The $14,000 exclusion applies only to gifts of present interests.

   c.   A present interest in property includes an unrestricted right to the immediate possession or enjoyment of property or the income from property (such as a life estate or a term for years). Gifts of future interests in property (such as remainders or reversions) do not qualify for the annual exclusion.

EXAMPLE

Edward sets up a trust with the income going to his daughter for her life and the remainder to his granddaughter. Edward has made a gift of a present interest to his daughter and a future interest to his granddaughter.

---

4.   **Gift Splitting**

   a.   Each spouse may treat each gift made to any third person as made one-half by the donor and one-half by the donor's spouse.

   b.   They must be married at the time of the gift.

   c.   They must make a proper election and signify their consent on the gift tax return.

   d.   Each spouse may exclude $14,000 annually of gifts to each donee allowing for a combined gift of $28,000.

5.   **Medical or Tuition Costs**

   a.   Excluded from taxable gifts are amounts paid on behalf of another individual such as tuition to an educational organization or for medical care.

   b.   The payment must be made directly to the third party, i.e., the medical provider or the educational organization.

   c.   Amounts paid for room, board, and books are not excluded.

6. **Marital Deduction**

    a.   The amount of a gift transfer to a spouse is deducted in computing taxable gifts. Donor and donee must be married at the time of the gift, and the donee must be a U.S. citizen for the unlimited amount. For noncitizen spouses the deduction is limited to $149,000.

    b.   The deduction may not exceed the amount includible as taxable gifts.

    c.   Otherwise, the amount of the deduction is not limited.

EXAMPLE

Sid Smith gave his wife, Mary, a diamond ring valued at $20,000 and cash gifts of $30,000 during 2017. Sid is entitled to a $14,000 exclusion with respect to the gifts to Mary. The marital deduction allows Sid to exclude an additional $36,000 ($20,000 + $30,000 − $14,000).

---

7. **Charitable Deduction**

    a.   The FMV of property donated to a qualified charitable organization is deductible. Like the marital deduction, the amount of the deduction is the amount of the gift reduced by the $14,000 exclusion with respect to the donee.

8. **Spousal Support**

    a.   Transfers that represent support are not gifts.

9. **Political Contributions**

    a.   Political contributions are not subject to gift tax.

10. **Computing the Gift Tax**

    a.   Tentative tax is the sum of taxable gifts to each person for the current year and for each preceding year times the rate. Taxable gifts to a person is the total of gift amounts (FMV) in excess of exclusions and the marital and charitable deductions for a calendar year.

    b.   The unified transfer tax rates are used.

        1)   Current-year applicable rates are applied to both current and preceding years' taxable gifts.

        2)   The rate is 18% for taxable gifts up to $10,000.

        3)   The rates increase in small steps (e.g., 2%, 3%) over numerous brackets.

        4)   The maximum rate is 40% on cumulative gifts in excess of $1 million in 2017.

    c.   The tentative gift tax is reduced by the product of prior years' taxable gifts and the current-year rates.

    d.   Applicable credit amount (ACA). Tentative tax may also be reduced by any ACA. The ACA is a base amount ($2,141,800 in 2017) reduced by amounts allowable as credits for all preceding tax years. This excludes the first $5.49 million of taxable gifts.

> *Gift tax liability for a current year =*
> *Tentative tax − (Prior-year gifts × Current rates) − ACA*

11. **Gift Tax Return**

    a.   A donor is required to file a gift tax return, Form 709, for any gift(s), unless all gifts are excluded under the annual $14,000 exclusion, the exclusion for medical or tuition payments, or the deduction for qualified transfers to the donor's spouse.

        1)   Gift splitting does not excuse the donor from the requirement to file.

    b.   A gift tax return is due on the 15th of April following the calendar year in which a gift was made. But a gift tax return for a year of death is due no later than the estate tax return due date (i.e., the earlier of the regular due date or the estate tax due date).

    c.   A United States donee must report information on gifts from foreign persons if the aggregate of such gifts from all foreign persons exceeds $14,000.

Stop and review! You have completed the outline for this subunit. Study multiple-choice questions 10 through 13 beginning on page 403.

14.4 ESTATE TAX

1. **Components of the Gross Estate**

    a. The estate tax is an excise tax imposed on the transfer of the taxable estate of every decedent who was a U.S. citizen or resident.

    ESTATE TAX Formula

	GROSS ESTATE
–	Deductions
	Expenses, claims, taxes
	Casualty and theft losses
	Charitable bequests
	Marital deduction
=	TAXABLE ESTATE
+	Taxable gifts made after 1976
=	TOTAL TAXABLE TRANSFERS
×	Tax rate
=	TENTATIVE ESTATE TAX
–	Gift taxes paid on post-1976 gifts
–	Applicable credit amount
–	Other credits
=	ESTATE TAX LIABILITY

    b. A decedent's **gross estate (GE)** includes the FMV of all property, real or personal, tangible or intangible, wherever situated, to the extent the decedent owned a beneficial interest at the time of death.

    1) Special tax avoidance rules are established for U.S. citizens or residents who surrender their U.S. citizenship or long-term residency.

    c. Included are items such as cash, personal residence and effects, securities, other investments (e.g., real estate, collector items), other personal assets such as notes and claims (e.g., dividends declared prior to death if the record date had passed), and business interests (e.g., in a sole proprietorship, partnership interest).

    d. Liabilities of the decedent generally do not affect the amount of the GE, unless the estate actually pays them.

    e. The GE includes the value of the surviving spouse's interest in property as dower or curtesy.

    1) Dower and curtesy are common-law rights recognized in some states, usually in modified form.

    a) Dower entitles a surviving wife to a portion of lands her husband owned and possessed during their marriage.

    b) Curtesy entitles a surviving husband to a life estate in all of his wife's land if they had children.

    f. The GE includes the full value of property held as joint tenants with the right of survivorship, except to the extent of any part shown to have originally belonged to the other person and for which adequate and full consideration was not provided by the decedent (i.e., the other tenant provided consideration).

    1) The GE includes 50% of property held as joint tenants by spouses or as tenants by the entirety regardless of the amount of consideration provided by each spouse.

g. The value of property interests over which the decedent had a general power of appointment (POA) are included in the GE. A POA is a power exercisable in favor of the decedent, his or her estate, his or her creditors, or the creditors of his or her estate.

h. Bonds, notes, bills, and certificates of indebtedness of the federal, state, and local governments are included in the GE, even if interest on them is exempt from income tax.

i. Gifts within 3 years of death. The gifts made prior to death are not included in the GE of a decedent.

1) The GE does include gift taxes paid on gifts within 3 years before death.

j. The GE includes insurance proceeds on the decedent's life in certain situations.

1) The insurance proceeds are payable to or for the estate (including if payable to the executor).

2) The decedent had any incident of ownership in the policy at death, e.g.,

a) Right to change beneficiaries
b) Right to terminate the policy

3) The proceeds of insurance policies given to others by the decedent within 3 years of death are included in the estate. This is an exception to the "gifts within 3 years of death rules."

4) The proceeds included in the estate, listed in item c. on the previous page, are allocated proportionately if the premiums are partially paid by the insured and periodically paid by someone else.

EXAMPLE

Twenty years before her death, Joanna bought a $200,000 term insurance policy. One year before her death, she irrevocably transferred the policy and all incidents of ownership to a trust that paid the last year's premiums. Joanna's GE includes $190,000 of proceeds since Joanna paid 95% of the premiums.

---

k. Annuities and survivor benefits including interest. The GE includes the value of any annuity receivable by a beneficiary by reason of surviving the decedent if either of the following statements applies:

1) The annuity was payable to the decedent.
2) The decedent had the right to receive the annuity or payment

a) Either alone or in conjunction with another.
b) For his or her life or for any period not ascertainable without reference to his or her death, or for any period that does not end before his or her death.

l. Medical insurance reimbursements due the decedent at death are treated as property in which the decedent had an interest.

m. Inter vivos transfers. The GE includes assets transferred during life in which the decedent retained, at death, any of the following interests:

1) A life estate, an income interest, possession or enjoyment of assets, or the right to designate who will enjoy the property

2) A 5% or greater reversionary interest if possession was conditioned on surviving the decedent

3) The power to alter, amend, revoke, or terminate the transfer

4) An interest in a qualified terminable interest property (QTIP) trust

2. **Valuing the Gross Estate**

    a.   Value is the FMV of the property unless a special valuation rule is used.

       1)   Real property is usually valued at its highest and best use.

       2)   A transfer of interests in a corporation or partnership to a family member is subject to estate tax-freeze rules.

          a)   Generally, the retained interest is valued at zero.

    b.   The executor may elect to value the estate at either the date of death or the alternate valuation date. An alternate valuation date election is irrevocable.

       1)   The election can be made only if it results in a reduction in both the value of the gross estate and the sum of the federal estate tax and the generation-skipping transfer tax (reduced by allowable credits).

       2)   The alternate valuation date is 6 months after the decedent's death.

          a)   Assets sold or distributed before then are valued on the date of sale or distribution.

          b)   Assets, the value of which is affected by mere lapse of time, are valued as of the date of the decedent's death, but adjustment is made for value change from other than mere lapse of time.

             i)   Examples of such assets are patents, life estates, reversions, and remainders.

             ii)   The value of such assets is based on years.

             iii)   Changes due to time value of money are treated as from more than mere lapse of time.

EXAMPLE

Jenny died on January 1, Year 1. On the date of death, her estate was valued at $15,000,000, of which $10,000,000 was in her stock portfolio. On July 1, Year 1, the value of her portfolio decreased to $7,000,000, and the changes in value of the remaining assets were negligible. In order to minimize the estate's tax liability, the executor of Jenny's estate should elect to use the alternate valuation date of July 1, Year 1.

---

3. **Deductions from the Gross Estate**

    a.   Deductions from the GE in computing the taxable estate (TE) include those with respect to expenses, claims, and taxes.

    NOTE: A deductible amount is allowed against gross income on the decedent's final income tax return only if the right to deduct them from the GE is waived.

    b.   Expenses for selling property of an estate are deductible if the sale is necessary to

       1)   Pay the decedent's debts
       2)   Pay expenses of administration
       3)   Pay taxes
       4)   Preserve the estate
       5)   Effect distribution

    c.   Administration and funeral expenses are deductible.

    d.   Claims against the estate (including debts of the decedent) are deductible.

       1)   Medical expenses paid within 1 year of death may be deducted on either the estate tax return or the final income tax return (not both).

    e.   Unpaid mortgages on property are deductible if the value of the decedent's interest is included in the GE.

    f.   A limited amount of state death taxes is deductible. Federal estate taxes and income tax paid on income earned and received after the decedent's death are not deductible.

    g.   Casualty or theft losses incurred during the settlement of the estate are deductible, if not deducted in the estate's income tax return.

    h.   Charitable contributions. Bequests to qualified charitable organizations are deductible.

        1)   The entire interest of the decedent in the underlying property generally must be donated.

        2)   Trust interests may enable deductible transfer of partial interests in underlying property.

        3)   An inter vivos contribution (vs. a bequest) may result in exclusion from the GE and a current deduction for regular taxable income.

    i.   Marital transfers. Outright transfers to a surviving spouse are deductible from the GE, to the extent that the interest is included in the gross estate.

4.   **Computing the Estate Tax and Credits**

    a.   The estate tax is imposed on the sum of the TE plus gifts subject to the gift tax. However, it is reduced by gift taxes payable on those gifts and by the ACA.

        1)   TE is the GE reduced by deductions.

        2)   Tentative tax is the product of total taxable transfers and the applicable rate.

        3)   Total taxable transfers are the sum of the TE plus taxable gifts after 1976 (valued at FMV on the date of the gifts).

    b.   Applicable rates are the unified transfer tax rates. Current-year applicable rates are applied to both current and preceding years' taxable gifts. The following information is for 2017:

        1)   The rate is 18% for taxable gifts up to $10,000.

        2)   The rates increase in small steps (e.g., 2%, 3%) over numerous brackets.

        3)   The maximum rate is 40% on cumulative gifts in excess of $1,000,000.

    c.   The tentative estate tax is reduced by the credit for gift taxes payable on post-1976 gifts, based on current rates.

    d.   Tentative estate tax reduced by gift taxes paid, the ACA, and other credit is the net estate tax.

    e.   The ACA is a base amount ($2,141,800 in 2017), not reduced by amounts allowable as credits for gift tax for all preceding tax years.

        1)   The ACA offsets the estate tax liability that would be imposed on a taxable estate of up to $5.49 million computed at current rates.

        2)   Any unused amount by a deceased spouse may be used by the surviving spouse in addition to the surviving spouse's own exclusion amount. Under this portability election, the surviving spouse could potentially have an available exclusion amount of $10.98 million.

EXAMPLE

The deceased spouse only used $3.49 million of the allowed exclusion. The surviving spouse is allowed a $7.49 million exclusion ($5.49 million surviving spouse original amount + $2 million unused by the deceased spouse).

---

    f.   Credit is allowable for death taxes paid to foreign governments.

    g.   Credit is allowable on gift tax paid on gifts included in the gross estate.

    h.   Prior transfers. Credit is allowed for taxes paid on transfers by or from a person who died within 10 years before, or 2 years after, the decedent's death.

        1)   Amounts creditable are the lesser of the following:

            a)   Estate tax paid by the (prior) transferor

            b)   Amount by which the assets increase the estate tax

        2)   Adjustment is made to the credit for transfers more than 2 years prior to the decedent's death.

5. **Estate Tax Return**

   a. The executor is required to file Form 706, *United States Estate Tax Return*, if the gross estate exceeds a threshold.

      1) The threshold is $5.49 million in 2017.

      2) Adjusted taxable gifts made by the decedent during his or her lifetime reduce the threshold.

   b. The estate tax return is due 9 months after the date of the decedent's death.

      1) An extension of up to 6 months may be granted.

   c. Time for payment may be extended up to 1 year past the due date. For reasonable cause, the time for payment may be extended up to 10 years.

   d. Estate tax is charged to estate property.

      1) If the tax on part of the estate distributed is paid out of other estate property, equitable contribution from the distributee beneficiary is recoverable.

      2) The executor is ultimately liable for payment of the taxes.

         a) If there is more than one executor, each must verify and sign the return.

   e. An estate that includes a substantial interest in a closely held business may be allowed to delay payment of part of the estate tax, if that interest exceeds 35% of the gross estate.

      1) A closely held business includes the following, if carrying on a trade or business:

         a) A corporation, if it has 45 or fewer shareholders or if 20% or more in value of the voting stock is included in the gross estate

         b) A partnership, if it has 45 or fewer partners or if 20% or more of the capital interests in the partnership is included in the gross estate

6. **Consistent Basis Reporting for Estate Tax and Income Tax**

   a. Those who file a Form 709, *Estate Tax Return*, after July 2015 are required to report the final estate tax value of property distributed from the estate. Form 8971, *Information Regarding Beneficiaries Acquiring Property From a Decedent*, along with a copy of every Schedule A (Form 8971), is used to report values to the IRS. Each beneficiary receiving property is only provided his or her corresponding Schedule A. This filing requirement ties beneficiaries to the value the estate put on the asset when the beneficiary later sells the asset.

EXAMPLE

Peter dies in 2017 and leaves his son Victor a tract of land worth $6 million, which Peter had originally purchased for $1 million. The value of the land listed on Peter's estate tax return is $6 million, the stepped-up basis that Victor will have in the land. Victor cannot use a different appraisal amount to give the land a higher basis.

---

   b. If a decedent has no estate tax filing requirement [perhaps due to the gross estate being valued at less than the basic exclusion amount ($2,141,800 in 2017)] and for whom a return is filed for the sole purpose of making an allocation or election respecting the generation-skipping transfer tax, a Form 8971 is not required.

   c. For estate tax returns filed after June 2016, the due date for the corresponding Form 8971 is 30 days after the due date of the estate tax return.

   d. Form 8971 is subject to both the $260 failure to file penalty and the accuracy-related penalty equal to 20% of the underpayment. The latter applies to the beneficiary overstating the basis upon a subsequent sale. This prevents estates from claiming a low basis to avoid estate tax and a high basis to prevent a gain on the subsequent sale.

Stop and review! You have completed the outline for this subunit. Study multiple-choice questions 14 through 18 beginning on page 405.

14.5 GENERATION-SKIPPING TRANSFER TAX (GSTT)

1. **Overview**

    a. The GSTT is imposed separately and in addition to gift and estate taxes on transfers directly or in trust for the sole benefit of a person at least two generations younger than the transferor. GSTT is generally imposed on each generation-skipping transfer (GST). A GST is a direct skip, a taxable distribution, or a taxable termination.

2. **Direct Skip**

    a. A direct skip is a transfer of an interest in property, subject to estate tax or gift tax, to a skip person. The transferor is liable for the tax.

    b. A **skip person** is either a natural person assigned to a generation that is two or more generations below the transferor or a trust, all interests of which are held by skip persons.

    c. In the case of related persons, a skip person is identified by reference to the family tree.

    1) For example, a grandchild is two generations below the grandparent.

    d. In the case of nonrelated persons, a skip person is identified by reference to age differences.

    1) For example, an individual born between 37 1/2 years and 62 1/2 years after the transferor is two generations below the transferor.

EXAMPLE

Darlene, age 95, left a large estate of property to her neighbor Tom, age 35, in her will. The lawyers managing the estate found that this transfer was subject to estate tax. In addition to the estate tax, Darlene's estate is responsible for the GSTT because Tom is two generations below Darlene and is a skip person.

---

3. **Taxable Distribution**

    a. A taxable distribution is a distribution from a trust to a skip person of income or principal, other than a distribution that is a direct skip or taxable termination. The transferee is liable for the tax.

4. **Taxable Termination**

    a. A taxable termination is a termination of an interest in property held in trust. A taxable termination has not occurred if, immediately after the termination, a nonskip person has an interest in the property or if distributions are not permitted to be made to a skip person at any time following the termination.

    1) Termination may be by lapse of time, release of power, death, or otherwise.
    2) The trustee is liable to pay the tax.

5. **GSTT vs. Estate Tax**

    a. The GSTT approximates the maximum federal estate tax that would have applied to the transfer on the date of the transfer.

6. **Exemption**

    a. Each individual is allowed a $5.49 million exemption in 2017 that (s)he, or his or her executor, may allocate to GST property. The exemption is indexed for inflation. Gift splitting applies to GSTTs; $10.98 million is allocable.

EXAMPLE

Samantha made transfers to her grandson Jeff in the amount of $4,500,000. She made no other generation-skipping transfers during her lifetime. Accordingly, in computing the GSTT, Samantha owed no tax on her transfer to her grandson due to the exemption being greater than the amount of property transferred. Samantha could transfer an additional amount of property, up to the difference between the exemption and the cumulative amount of property transferred.

---

7. **Inter Vivos**

a. Inter vivos gifts are exempt from the GSTT if they are not subject to gift tax due to the $14,000 annual exclusion or the medical/tuition exclusion.

Stop and review! You have completed the outline for this subunit. Study multiple-choice questions 19 and 20 on page 406.

QUESTIONS

14.1 Income Taxation

1. Which of the following is allowed in the calculation of the taxable income of a simple trust?

    A. Exemption.

    B. Standard deduction.

    C. Brokerage commission for purchase of tax-exempt bonds.

    D. Charitable contribution.

Answer (A) is correct.

    REQUIRED: The allowable reduction of income item for simple trust.

    DISCUSSION: Taxable income of a trust is computed similarly to that of an individual; however, there are some significant differences. Expenses for tax-exempt income (e.g., bonds) are not deductible for individuals or trusts. A standard deduction is allowed for individuals but not trusts. In addition, simple trusts are not allowed to make charitable contributions but are allowed a $300 exemption.

    Answer (B) is incorrect. Standard deductions are only available for individuals. Answer (C) is incorrect. Tax-exempt income is excluded from taxable income; therefore, expenses for such income are disallowed deductions. Answer (D) is incorrect. One of the characteristics of simple trusts is that they do not provide charitable contributions.

2. Ross, a calendar-year, cash-basis taxpayer who died in June 2017, was entitled to receive a $10,000 accounting fee that had not been collected before the date of death. The executor of Ross's estate collected the full $10,000 in July 2017. This $10,000 should appear in

    A. Only the decedent's final individual income tax return.

    B. Only the estate's fiduciary income tax return.

    C. Only the estate tax return.

    D. Both the fiduciary income tax return and the estate tax return.

Answer (D) is correct.

    REQUIRED: The correct treatment of income earned before death but not received until after death.

    DISCUSSION: Income that a decedent had a right to receive prior to death but that was not includible on his or her final income tax return is income in respect of a decedent. The $10,000 is properly includible in the estate's income tax return because Ross was a cash-basis taxpayer and would not properly include income not yet received at the time of death in his final return. Since the money was owed to Ross (he had a right to receive it), it is an asset of the estate and must be included on the estate tax return also.

    Answer (A) is incorrect. Ross was a cash-basis taxpayer and would not properly include income not received at the time of death. Answer (B) is incorrect. The $10,000 is an asset of the estate and must also be included on the estate tax return. Answer (C) is incorrect. It must also be included in the fiduciary income tax return.

3. Ordinary and necessary administration expenses paid by the fiduciary of an estate are deductible

    A. Only on the fiduciary income tax return (Form 1041) and never on the federal estate tax return (Form 706).

    B. Only on the federal estate tax return and never on the fiduciary income tax return.

    C. On the fiduciary income tax return only if the estate tax deduction is waived for these expenses.

    D. On both the fiduciary income tax return and the estate tax return by adding a tax computed on the proportionate rates attributable to both returns.

Answer (C) is correct.

    REQUIRED: The deductibility of administration expenses.

    DISCUSSION: Administration expenses (and debts of a decedent) are deductible on the estate tax return, and some may also qualify as deductions for income tax purposes on the estate's income tax return. Double deductions are disallowed. A waiver of the right to deduct them on Form 706 is required in order to claim them on Form 1041.

    Answer (A) is incorrect. Administration expenses are deductible on Form 706. Answer (B) is incorrect. Administration expenses are deductible on Form 1041. Answer (D) is incorrect. Administration expenses are not deductible in full on both Form 706 and Form 1041.

4. Which of the following fiduciary entities are required to use the calendar year as their taxable period for income tax purposes?

	Estates	Trusts (Except Those that Are Tax-Exempt)
A.	Yes	Yes
B.	No	No
C.	Yes	No
D.	No	Yes

Answer (D) is correct.

REQUIRED: The tax year of estates and trusts.

DISCUSSION: An estate may adopt either a calendar tax year or any fiscal year ending not more than 12 months after death. All trusts, other than tax-exempt and wholly charitable trusts, must use a calendar tax year.

5. Raff died in 2016, leaving her entire estate to her only child. Raff's will gave full discretion to the estate's executor with regard to distributions of income. For 2017, the estate's distributable net income was $15,000, of which $9,000 was paid to the beneficiary; no income was tax-exempt. What amount can be claimed on the estate's 2017 income tax return for the distributions deduction?

A. $0

B. $6,000

C. $9,000

D. $15,000

Answer (C) is correct.

REQUIRED: The amount deductible on an estate income tax return for distributions.

DISCUSSION: The deduction for distributions is the lesser of the amount of distributions and distributable net income (DNI). DNI is net accounting income for the tax year reduced by net amounts allocated to principal. A beneficiary is subject to tax on his or her share of DNI. The income is characterized at the fiduciary level.

6. With regard to estimated income tax, estates

A. Must make quarterly estimated tax payments starting no later than the second quarter following the one in which the estate was established.

B. Are exempt from paying estimated tax during the estate's first 2 taxable years.

C. Must make quarterly estimated tax payments only if the estate's income is required to be distributed currently.

D. Are not required to make payments of estimated tax.

Answer (B) is correct.

REQUIRED: The true statement concerning estimated tax payments for estates.

DISCUSSION: Estates are required to make estimated payments of income tax except during the first 2 tax years of existence. No estimated payments are required during the estate's first 2 tax years.

Answer (A) is incorrect. Estates need not make estimated tax payments for the first 2 years of existence. Answer (C) is incorrect. Estimated tax payments are required after the first 2 years regardless of the required distribution of income. Answer (D) is incorrect. Estates are required to make payments of estimated tax after the first 2 years of existence.

14.2 Beneficiary's Taxable Income

7. The Simone Trust reported distributable net income of $120,000 for the current year. The trustee is required to distribute $60,000 to Kent and $90,000 to Lind each year. If the trustee distributes these amounts, what amount is includible in Lind's gross income?

A. $0

B. $60,000

C. $72,000

D. $90,000

Answer (C) is correct.

REQUIRED: The distribution includible in Lind's gross income.

DISCUSSION: Distributable net income (DNI) is the maximum amount of the distribution on which beneficiaries can be taxed. The trust reports DNI of $120,000 and is required to distribute $150,000 ($60,000 to Kent and $90,000 to Lind). Thus, the distribution each beneficiary receives must be prorated to determine his or her share of the distribution includible in gross income. Lind receives 60% of the distribution ($90,000 ÷ $150,000). As a result, she reports $72,000 of the $120,000 DNI.

Answer (A) is incorrect. Beneficiaries of a trust must include distributions to the extent of distributable net income. Answer (B) is incorrect. Only half of the distributable net income equals $60,000. Lind must include an amount equal to her share of total distributions, or 60% ($90,000 Lind's distribution ÷ $150,000 total distribution). Answer (D) is incorrect. The amount of distribution includible in a beneficiary's gross income is limited to the trust's distributable net income. Lind is not the only beneficiary, and her includible distribution must be determined relative to all distributions.

8. Gardner, a U.S. citizen and the sole income beneficiary of a simple trust, is entitled to receive current distributions of the trust income. During the year, the trust reported:

Interest income from corporate bonds	$5,000
Fiduciary fees allocable to income	750
Net long-term capital gain allocable to corpus	2,000

What amount of the trust income is includible in Gardner's gross income?

    A. $7,000

    B. $5,000

    C. $4,250

    D. $0

Answer (C) is correct.
    REQUIRED: The amount of trust income included in Gardner's gross income.
    DISCUSSION: A simple trust is formed under an instrument having the following characteristics:

1. Requires current distribution of all its income
2. Requires no distribution of the principal
3. Provides for no charitable contribution by the trust

Trust income is taxed to the beneficiary of the trust whether distributed or not. Income related to the disposition of corpus is not taxable to the beneficiary because it is not earned income. The fees paid to the fiduciary are deductible from the trust income. Therefore, the trust income equals $5,000 of interest income less $750 of fiduciary fees for a total of $4,250.
    Answer (A) is incorrect. The long-term capital gain allocable to the corpus is not taxable to Gardner and the fiduciary fees are deductible. Answer (B) is incorrect. The $750 of fiduciary fees are deductible in arriving at gross income for Gardner. Answer (D) is incorrect. The income of a simple trust is taxable whether or not it is distributed to Gardner.

9. Bob Jones is sole beneficiary of a trust requiring that all income, but no corpus, be distributed currently. The trust's distributable net income for 2017 was $20,000, of which $4,000 is a long-term capital gain allocated to income and $2,500 is interest on tax-exempt municipal bonds. Jones received a $15,000 distribution on December 20, 2017, and the remaining $5,000 on January 10, 2018. Assuming Jones has no other income for 2017, his adjusted gross income should be

    A. $20,000

    B. $17,500

    C. $15,000

    D. $13,500

Answer (B) is correct.
    REQUIRED: The adjusted gross income of the sole beneficiary of a simple trust.
    DISCUSSION: The beneficiary of a simple trust (one that is required to distribute all income currently) must include in gross income the amount of fiduciary income of the trust (whether distributed or not), limited to the amount of distributable net income. The amount included in a beneficiary's gross income retains the same character as in the hands of the trust.
    Although Jones only received $15,000 in 2017, all of the distributable net income (which is the same as fiduciary income in this case) must be included in his gross income in 2017. Since the income retains the same character in the hands of the beneficiary as in the hands of the trust, Bob is entitled to exclude the $2,500 of interest on municipal bonds. Therefore, Bob's adjusted gross income is $17,500 ($20,000 distributable net income – $2,500 tax-exempt interest).
    Answer (A) is incorrect. Bob is entitled to exclude the $2,500 of interest on municipal bonds. Answer (C) is incorrect. Beneficiary gross income includes income of the trust (whether distributed or not) up to DNI. Answer (D) is incorrect. The LTCG is includible in that it is allocated to income.

14.3 Gift Tax

10. Which of the following payments would require the donor to file a gift tax return?

    A. $30,000 to a university for a spouse's tuition.

    B. $40,000 to a university for a cousin's room and board.

    C. $50,000 to a hospital for a parent's medical expenses.

    D. $80,000 to a physician for a friend's surgery.

Answer (B) is correct.
    REQUIRED: The payment requiring a gift tax return.
    DISCUSSION: Although tuition is an amount excluded as a taxable gift, room and board does not qualify. It must be reported on the gift tax return.
    Answer (A) is incorrect. A payment for tuition to a medical organization may be excluded from gift tax assuming it is paid directly to the third party. Answer (C) is incorrect. Medical expenses are excluded as taxable gifts pending payment directly to the third party providing the medical care. Answer (D) is incorrect. Excluded from taxable gifts are amounts paid on behalf of another individual for medical care. The payment must be directly to the medical provider.

11. Ralph created a joint bank account for himself and his friend's son, Dave. There is a gift to Dave when

A. Ralph creates the account.

B. Ralph dies.

C. Dave draws on the account for his own benefit.

D. Dave is notified by Ralph that the account has been created.

Answer (C) is correct.

REQUIRED: The event that completes the gift.

DISCUSSION: A gift is complete when the donor has so parted with dominion and control as to leave him or her no power to change its disposition. Ralph made an indirect transfer of the money to Dave by opening the bank account. Only once Dave withdraws the money will Ralph lose all dominion and control over the property so that the action will complete the gift.

Answer (A) is incorrect. When Ralph opens the account, he can still withdraw the money so that it is not a completed gift. Answer (B) is incorrect. When Ralph dies, there may be no transfer to Dave, or there may be a devise but not a gift because a gift only occurs during a donor's lifetime. Answer (D) is incorrect. Notice has no effect here since Dave must draw on the account for a completed gift.

12. George and Suzanne have been married for 40 years. Suzanne inherited $3,000,000 from her mother. Assume that the annual gift-tax exclusion is $14,000. What amount of the $3,000,000 can Suzanne give to George without incurring a gift-tax liability?

A. $14,000

B. $28,000

C. $1,500,000

D. $3,000,000

Answer (D) is correct.

REQUIRED: The amount a spouse can transfer to another spouse without incurring gift tax.

DISCUSSION: There is an unlimited marital deduction for taxable gift transfers made between spouses. George and Suzanne qualify because they were married at the time of the transfer and are both U.S. citizens. Therefore, all $3,000,000 is excluded from gift tax.

Answer (A) is incorrect. The annual exclusion is equal to $14,000. There is an unlimited marital deduction for taxable gift transfers made between spouses. George and Suzanne qualify because they were married at the time of the transfer and are both U.S. citizens. Therefore, all $3,000,000 is excluded from gift tax. Answer (B) is incorrect. The annual exclusion allowed for couples under gift splitting is equal to $28,000. There is an unlimited marital deduction for taxable gift transfers made between spouses. George and Suzanne qualify because they were married at the time of the transfer and are both U.S. citizens. Therefore, all $3,000,000 is excluded from gift tax. Answer (C) is incorrect. One-half of the total taxable gift is equal to $1,500,000. There is an unlimited marital deduction for taxable gift transfers made between spouses. George and Suzanne qualify because they were married at the time of the transfer and are both U.S. citizens. Therefore, all $3,000,000 is excluded from gift tax.

13. Don and Linda Grant, U.S. citizens, were married for the entire 2017 calendar year. In 2017, Don gave a $66,000 cash gift to his sister. The Grants made no other gifts in 2017. They each signed a timely election to treat the $66,000 gift as one made by each spouse. Disregarding the unified credit and estate tax consequences, what amount of the 2017 gift is taxable to the Grants for gift tax purposes?

A. $0

B. $38,000

C. $52,000

D. $66,000

Answer (B) is correct.

REQUIRED: The taxable gifts after the gift-splitting election is made.

DISCUSSION: Each spouse may treat each gift made to any third person as made one-half by the donor and one-half by the donor's spouse. Because the Grants made the gift-splitting election, each will be treated as if (s)he made a $33,000 gift to the donee. Since the gift was of a present interest, a $14,000 exclusion is available for each donor. Therefore, after a total of $28,000 in exclusions, the taxable gift will be $19,000 for each donor for a total of $38,000.

Answer (A) is incorrect. A portion of this gift is taxable. Answer (C) is incorrect. The Grants made the gift-splitting election, so each is entitled to the $14,000 exclusion. Answer (D) is incorrect. Each taxpayer is entitled to a $14,000 gift exclusion.

14.4 Estate Tax

14. Under which of the following circumstances is trust property with an independent trustee includible in the grantor's gross estate?

A. The trust is revocable.

B. The trust is established for a minor.

C. The trustee has the power to distribute trust income.

D. The income beneficiary disclaims the property, which then passes to the remainderman, the grantor's friend.

Answer (A) is correct.
REQUIRED: The property includible in a grantor's gross estate.
DISCUSSION: Any beneficial interest held by the decedent at the time of death is included in the gross estate. Retaining a right to revoke the property will cause the property's inclusion in the gross estate.
Answer (B) is incorrect. Once the trust is outside the influence of the grantor, it is no longer a beneficial interest. Thus, no inclusion in the gross estate is necessary. Answer (C) is incorrect. Retaining the power to distribute trust income by the grantor will not cause the property to be included in the gross estate. Answer (D) is incorrect. No beneficial interest remained with the decedent at the time of death. Thus, no inclusion is necessary in the grantor's gross estate.

15. Bell, a cash-basis, calendar-year taxpayer, died on June 1, 2017. In 2017, prior to her death, Bell incurred $2,000 in medical expenses. The executor of the estate paid the medical expenses, which were a claim against the estate, on July 1, 2017. If the executor files the appropriate waiver, the medical expenses are deductible on

A. The estate tax return.

B. Bell's final income tax return.

C. The estate income tax return.

D. The executor's income tax return.

Answer (B) is correct.
REQUIRED: The return on which a decedent's medical expenses are deductible.
DISCUSSION: The executor's waiver precludes a deduction on the estate tax return. Medical expenses incurred but not paid prior to Bell's death are deductible on her final income tax return. Although the expenses were not paid prior to Bell's death, any medical expenses attributed to a decedent should be deducted on the decedent's final income tax return if they were paid within 1 year after the date of death.

16. Alan Curtis, a U.S. citizen, died on March 1, 2016, leaving an adjusted gross estate with a fair market value of $3.4 million at the date of death. Under the terms of Alan's will, $2,375,000 was bequeathed outright to his widow, free of all estate and inheritance taxes. The remainder of Alan's estate was left to his mother. Alan made no taxable gifts during his lifetime. In computing the taxable estate, the executor of Alan's estate should claim a marital deduction of

A. $2,250,000

B. $2,375,000

C. $1,700,000

D. $1,025,000

Answer (B) is correct.
REQUIRED: The amount of the marital deduction.
DISCUSSION: A marital deduction for the value of any interest in property that passes from the decedent to the surviving spouse (which is not a terminable interest) is allowed, but only to the extent that the interest is included in the gross estate. The outright bequest of $2,375,000 is includible and deductible in full.
Answer (A) is incorrect. The full $2,375,000 of the outright transfer by bequest is deductible. Answer (C) is incorrect. The marital deduction is for the amount that passes or passed to the surviving spouse, not an amount that might have passed had intestate succession law applied. Answer (D) is incorrect. The marital deduction is an amount subtracted from the gross estate, not the estate net of the deduction.

17. Daven inherited property from a parent. The property had an adjusted basis to the parent of $1,600,000. It was valued at $2,000,000 at the date of death and valued at $1,800,000 6 months after the date of death. The executor elected the alternative valuation date. What is Daven's basis in the property?

A. $0

B. $1,600,000

C. $1,800,000

D. $2,000,000

Answer (C) is correct.
REQUIRED: The basis in inherited property.
DISCUSSION: The value of the gross estate is the FMV of the property unless a special valuation rule is used. Real property is usually valued at its highest and best use. The executor may elect to use the alternate valuation date instead of the date of death. The election may only be made if it results in a reduction in both the value of the gross estate and the sum of federal estate tax that would be owed. Since the alternate valuation date results in a FMV of $1,800,000, that is the basis that Daven takes in the property inherited.
Answer (A) is incorrect. The basis of the property in the hands of the beneficiary is the FMV on the date of death or the alternate valuation date if elected. Answer (B) is incorrect. The parent's adjusted basis in the property does not determine the basis in the hands of the beneficiary. Answer (D) is incorrect. The election to use the alternate valuation date is irrevocable, and it results in a lower valuation for the estate.

18. Fred and Amy Kehl, both U.S. citizens, are married. All of their real and personal property is owned by them as tenants by the entirety or as joint tenants with right of survivorship. The gross estate of the first spouse to die

- A. Includes 50% of the value of all property owned by the couple, regardless of which spouse furnished the original consideration.
- B. Includes only the property that had been acquired with the funds of the deceased spouse.
- C. Is governed by the federal statutory provisions relating to jointly held property, rather than by the decedent's interest in community property vested by state law if the Kehls reside in a community property state.
- D. Includes one-third of the value of all real estate owned by the Kehls, as the dower right in the case of the wife or curtesy right in the case of the husband.

Answer (A) is correct.

REQUIRED: The survivorship rights includible in the gross estate of a decedent spouse.

DISCUSSION: Generally, the gross estate includes the full value of property held as tenants by the entirety or as joint tenants with the right of survivorship. However, if spouses held the property, the gross estate of the first to die includes only half the value of such property.

Answer (B) is incorrect. The portion of consideration paid for the property by the surviving tenant does not affect the gross estate amount when the property was held by spouses. Answer (C) is incorrect. The amount included in the gross estate when spouses held property jointly is designated by the IRC. Answer (D) is incorrect. The full value of a surviving spouse's dower or curtesy interest is included in the gross estate of a decedent spouse. Furthermore, the question does not address dower or curtesy.

14.5 Generation-Skipping Transfer Tax (GSTT)

19. The generation-skipping transfer tax is imposed

- A. Instead of the gift tax.
- B. Instead of the estate tax.
- C. As a separate tax in addition to the gift and estate taxes.
- D. On transfers of future interest to beneficiaries who are more than one generation above the donor's generation.

Answer (C) is correct.

REQUIRED: The applicability of the GSTT.

DISCUSSION: The generation-skipping transfer tax (GSTT) is imposed, as a separate tax in addition to the gift and estate taxes, on generation-skipping transfers, which are any taxable distributions or terminations with respect to a generation-skipping trust or direct skips.

Answer (A) is incorrect. The GSTT is a separate tax in addition to the gift tax. Answer (B) is incorrect. The GSTT is a separate tax from the estate tax. Answer (D) is incorrect. The GSTT prevents tax avoidance by transferring property directly to a person more than one generation below the donee.

20. Victor and Dawn both retired this year at the age of 65. Victor has decided to give his 16-year-old grandson Peter a cash gift to buy a new car. Dawn is unrelated to Peter, but she has also decided to give him a gift to help him pay for car insurance. Peter is a skip person for generation-skipping tax purposes with respect to the gift from

	Victor	Dawn
A.	No	No
B.	Yes	No
C.	No	Yes
D.	Yes	Yes

Answer (D) is correct.

REQUIRED: The recipient qualifying as a skip person for generation-skipping tax purposes with respect to the gifts from a grandparent and unrelated older donor.

DISCUSSION: Peter is a skip person with respect to the gift from Victor because Peter is two generations below Victor, a related person. Peter is also a skip person with respect to the gift from Dawn. Dawn is unrelated to Peter, but the 49-year age difference between them falls within the 37 1/2-year-to-62 1/2-year range that constitutes two generations.

STUDY UNIT FIFTEEN
NONCORPORATE BUSINESS ENTITIES

(19 pages of outline)

This study unit addresses certain basic business structures. The most basic and common structure is the **sole proprietorship**. It consists of one individual who may be engaged in any kind of business. A **partnership** is an association of two or more persons carrying on a business as co-owners for profit. This study unit covers (1) the form of partnership that may be created without statutory formalities (the **general partnership**), (2) partnerships created only by statute (the **limited partnership**), and (3) the **limited liability company** (a hybrid of the corporation and the partnership).

15.1 SOLE PROPRIETORSHIPS

1. **Formation**

   a. Of all business structures, the sole proprietorship is the easiest and cheapest to create. It is formed at the will of the proprietor. A disadvantage is that it is **not** a separate legal entity because it is not distinct from its owners.

   b. Most filing, registration, and attorneys' fees are avoided.

      1) An advantage is that a sole proprietorship ordinarily can do business in any state without having to file, register, or otherwise qualify to do business in that state.

      2) The Internet allows a sole proprietorship to do business nationally or even internationally.

   c. Formation is subject to few legal requirements, for example, local zoning and licensing laws. States rarely require licensing.

      1) However, a proprietor doing business under a **fictitious name** is usually required to make a d/b/a or "doing business as" filing under state law. This kind of statute also applies to **partnerships**.

2. **Capitalization**

   a. A disadvantage of a sole proprietorship is that it cannot raise equity capital other than the personal resources of the proprietor. For example, it cannot sell shares of the business.

3. **Profits and Losses**

   a. The proprietor has the advantage of receiving all profits.

   b. The proprietor has the disadvantage of **unlimited personal liability** for all losses and debts and his or her personal assets are at risk.

4. **Taxation**

   a. The proprietor and the proprietorship are not distinct entities, so the income or loss of the business passes through to, and is reported by, the proprietor.

   b. The proprietor receives the tax benefits of all business deductions and losses.

   c. Other tax advantages include the need to file only one return and the avoidance of the double taxation of corporate earnings.

5. **Powers of the Proprietor**

    a. The sole proprietorship is the most flexible business structure. The proprietor makes all management decisions without answering to other executives, directors, or owners. Thus, control and accountability are completely centralized.

        1) A disadvantage is that a sole proprietorship may lack the expertise and the checks and balances on decision making found in more complex structures.

6. **Termination**

    a. The duration of the sole proprietorship is at the proprietor's discretion.

    b. The interest of the proprietor may be transferred during his or her life. But the sole proprietorship then is terminated because it is not legally distinct from the owner.

        1) An advantage of a sole proprietorship is that a change in control occurs only with the proprietor's consent.

    c. Lack of continuity of existence is a disadvantage of a sole proprietorship because it automatically terminates upon the proprietor's death.

Stop and review! You have completed the outline for this subunit. Study multiple-choice questions 1 and 2 on page 426.

15.2 GENERAL PARTNERSHIPS

1. **Overview**

Background

In the U.S., partnership law was codified in the Uniform Partnership Act of 1914 (UPA) and updated in the Revised Uniform Partnership Act (RUPA) in 1994. The revised act was amended in 1997 to include provisions for limited liability partnerships (LLPs). These changes conform the law of partnership to modern business practice while retaining many features of the original act.

---

    a. The general partnership is the oldest, simplest, and most common business structure other than the sole proprietorship.

    b. The **Revised Uniform Partnership Act (RUPA)** defines a **partnership** as "an association of two or more persons to carry on as co-owners a business for profit."

        1) A business is any trade, occupation, or profession.

    c. A partnership is considered an entity **distinct** from its partners. The UCC and bankruptcy law treat the partnership as a distinct legal entity. A partnership is an entity separate from its owners (partners) because

        1) The assets of a partnership are treated as those of the business unit.
        2) Title to real property may be acquired in the partnership name.
        3) Each partner is a fiduciary of the partnership.
        4) Each partner is an agent of the partnership.
        5) The partnership may sue and be sued in its own name.

            a) Thus, a legal action against the partnership does not apply to a partner who is not named as a separate defendant.

    d.   However, a partnership is **not** distinct from its partners in certain ways.

        1)   A partnership lacks continuity of existence.

            a)   Its duration is limited by, for example, the will of the partners.

        2)   No person can become a partner without consent of all the partners.

            a)   A transferee of a partnership interest, unlike a transferee of shares in a corporation, does not become an owner.

        3)   Debts of a partnership are ultimately the personal debts of the partners.

        4)   A partnership is not subject to regular federal income tax.

    e.   Partners may by **contract** establish the relationships among themselves and between themselves and the partnership.

        1)   The partnership agreement is determinative in most situations.

            a)   Accordingly, the RUPA consists mostly of guidance that covers matters not addressed by the partnership agreement.

        2)   Nevertheless, the **partnership agreement** cannot do the following:

            a)   Unreasonably restrict access to books and records
            b)   Eliminate the duty of loyalty or the obligation of good faith and fair dealing
            c)   Unreasonably reduce the duty of care
            d)   Vary the power to dissociate
            e)   Waive or vary the right to seek court expulsion of another partner
            f)   Vary the law applying to a limited liability partnership
            g)   Vary the right to dissolution and winding up
            h)   Restrict third-party rights

2. Formation

    a.   An advantage of the general partnership is that it can exist without any formalities. No filings are required, and a partnership may be created without an explicit agreement (oral or written) or even an intent to form a partnership.

        1)   Under the **Statute of Frauds**, a contract (e.g., a partnership agreement), the performance of which cannot be performed within 1 year of its making, must be in writing or proper electronic form to be valid.

            a)   For example, a contract to create a partnership for a specified 2-year period must be in writing.

        2)   Fictitious name statutes have been enacted in most states to protect creditors.

            a)   Registration permits creditors to discover the persons liable for the entity's debts.

    b.   To form a partnership, the co-owners must **intend** to make a profit even if no profit is earned.

        1)   A person who receives a share of the profit is assumed to be a partner. But this assumption is overcome if the amounts received are as payments for debts, principal or interests, rent, wages, etc.

        2)   Not-for-profit entities are not partnerships.

    c.   If the elements of a partnership are present, it is formed even if the parties do not intend to be partners.

EXAMPLE

Jim is doing business as Harvin Shoes, a sole proprietorship. In the past year, Jim has regularly joined with Stewart in the marketing of sport accessories. Jim and Stewart have formed a partnership if they intend to make a profit.

d. A **partnership by estoppel** may be recognized when an actual partnership does not exist to prevent injustice. The duties and liabilities of a partner sometimes may be imposed on a nonpartner (a purported partner).

1) A **purported partner** has represented that (s)he is a partner or has consented to such a representation. Moreover, the purported partner is assumed to be an agent of the partnership.

2) A third party who has reasonably relied on the representation and suffered harm as a result may assert the existence of a partnership. The purported partner then is prevented (estopped) from denying the existence of a partnership.

EXAMPLE

Lawyer A falsely represented to Client that Lawyer A and Lawyer B were partners. Client, in reasonable reliance on this statement, sought legal services from Lawyer B. Because these services were performed without due care, Client suffered harm. Lawyer A (as well as Lawyer B) is liable as a partner despite the absence of an actual partnership.

---

3. **Capitalization**

a. A general partnership is more advantageous than a sole proprietorship because two or more persons (rather than only one person) may contribute cash, property, or services to the business.

1) However, a general partnership cannot raise equity by selling shares.

4. **Profits, Losses, and Distributions**

a. Unless the partnership agreement states otherwise, the RUPA provides that partners share profits and losses equally.

1) If the partnership agreement states otherwise and partners have differing percentages of ownership, losses are shared in the same proportion as profits.

2) A major disadvantage of a general partnership is that each partner has **unlimited personal liability** for all losses and debts of the business.

b. A partner also has the right to distributions. A **distribution** is a transfer of partnership property from the partnership to a partner. A distribution may take various forms:

1) A share of profits

2) Compensation for services

3) Reimbursement for payments made, and indemnification for liabilities incurred, in the ordinary course of business or to preserve the business or its property

4) Reimbursement for advances (loans) in excess of agreed capital contributions

a) The payments made and liabilities incurred are loans that accrue interest.

c. Unless otherwise agreed, the right to compensation for services is generally a right to receive a share of the profits, not to be paid for services.

5. **Partnership Interest**

a. A partner's **transferable interest** only consists of a partner's share of partnership profits and losses and the right to receive distributions.

1) A partner's transfer (assignment) of the partner's interest does **not** by itself result in the (a) loss of rights, duties, and obligations as a partner; (b) dissociation; or (c) dissolution of the partnership.

a) The assignee (or the estate of a deceased partner) is entitled only to the profits the assignor would normally receive. The assignee does **not** automatically become a partner, and cannot act as an agent of the partnership.

b) The assignee (or the estate of a deceased partner) does not have the right to participate in the management of the partnership.

2) The ability to transfer the financial interest but not ownership status is a disadvantage of a partnership.

    a) For example, a partner cannot, during his or her life or through inheritance, transfer ownership to a family member.

3) Partners and their creditors, assignees, and heirs have no interest in any **specific partnership property**. Thus, no creditor can proceed against specific items of partnership property and specific partnership property is not assignable, or subject to attachment by, the partner's individual creditors. Instead, the creditor can only proceed against the partner's interest in the partnership.

    a) Property is partnership property when acquired with partnership assets even if it is in the name of a partner with no indication of the existence of a partnership.

    b) Property acquired without use of partnership assets in the name of a partner, with no indication of the person's capacity as a partner or of the existence of a partnership, is presumed to be **separate property**, even if used for partnership purposes.

        i) The money used in purchasing property is traced to its source to determine ownership.

4) When a partner dies, his or her partnership interest is personal property that may be **inherited** according to a valid will. Heirs of the partnership interest are assignees, not partners.

    a) The estate does not become a partner.

    b) The death of a partner causes dissociation, not dissolution of the partnership.

        i) The remaining partners may choose to continue the partnership.

    c) The estate is responsible for the partner's allocated share of any partnership liabilities.

5) A judgment creditor of a partner may attach the partner's transferable interest only by securing a **charging order** (a lien on the interest) from a court.

The AICPA often tests sharing of profits, losses, and distributions in partnerships. Candidates should understand that sharing is determined by the RUPA's equal distribution default rule only when the partners have not agreed otherwise.

---

6. **Taxation**

    a. An advantage of a partnership is that it is **not** a taxable entity. However, it must file an annual informational return on Form 1065.

    b. The partnership's profit or loss is passed through to the partners, who report their shares of that profit or loss on their personal income tax returns.

7. **Rights of Partners**

    a. The rights, powers, and duties of partners are largely defined by the **law of agency**.

        1) However, partners may agree to limit their rights.

    b.   Each partner has a right to **equal participation in management** of the partnership.

        1)   The general rule for ordinary matters is majority rule.

        2)   A unanimous vote is required to

            a)   Amend a partnership agreement,
            b)   Admit a new partner, and
            c)   Determine other nonroutine matters.

        3)   Different classes of partners may be formed with different management rights.

        4)   A disadvantage of a partnership is that a deadlock may develop when partners have equal management rights.

        5)   Partnership agreements commonly restrict management rights to a few partners or even one partner.

        6)   Without a contrary agreement, a newly admitted partner is entitled to all the rights of a partner.

    c.   A partner's right of **access to partnership information** is the right to inspect and copy the partnership books and records.

        1)   A reasonable demand for other partnership information also must be honored.

    d.   The right to **use or possess partnership property** may be exercised only on behalf of the partnership.

    e.   The right to **choose associates** means that no partner may be forced to accept any person as a partner. Admission as a partner therefore requires the consent of **all** partners. Unanimous consent vests in the new partner all the rights, duties, and powers of a partner.

        1)   When a partner transfers his or her interest, the transferee is entitled only to receive the share of profits and losses and the right to distributions allocated to the interest acquired. The transferee has no management rights.

8.   **Powers of Partners**

    a.   The powers granted to each partner are governed by law and by the specific terms of the partnership agreement.

        1)   Each partner has consented to being both a **principal and an agent** of the partnership.

            a)   Thus, a general partnership and the other general partners are bound by a contract made by a partner acting within the scope of his or her actual or apparent authority.

    b.   A majority of partners may decide ordinary matters and therefore bind the other partners. But an extraordinary matter requires a unanimous vote.

    c.   **Apparent authority** to act as an agent of the partnership results from words or actions of the principal (the partnership) that reasonably induce a third party to rely on the agent's (partner's) authority.

        1)   The scope of apparent authority is limited to conduct in the ordinary course of the partnership business.

        2)   The partnership is bound even if the partner had no actual authority unless the third party knew or had received notice of the lack of actual authority.

        3)   However, if a partner acts without actual or apparent authority, the partnership and the other partners are **not** bound by the act unless the other partners **ratify** the transaction.

        4)   The RUPA provides for filing a **statement of partnership authority** that gives notice of any limitations on the authority of a partner.

9. **Duties of Partners**

    a. Duties imposed upon partners include the **fiduciary** duties of loyalty and care. The duty of **loyalty** is limited to

        1) Not competing with the partnership,
        2) Not dealing with the partnership or winding up the partnership as (or for) a party with an adverse interest, and
        3) Not exploiting a partnership opportunity or secretly using partnership assets for personal gain.

    b. The duty of **care** in the conduct or winding up of the partnership business is not to engage in

        1) Knowing violations of the law,
        2) Intentional wrongdoing,
        3) Gross negligence, or
        4) Reckless behavior.

    c. A partner also has an obligation of **good faith and fair dealing**.

        1) A partner must be honest in fact and meet reasonable (objective) standards of fair dealing.

    d. However, no duty is violated solely because a partner acts in his or her own interest. For example, a partner may lend money to (as a secured or unsecured creditor) or otherwise do business with, the partnership on the same basis as a nonpartner.

10. **Liabilities of Partners**

    a. Partners are **jointly and severally liable** for any partnership obligations. These include the **torts** (e.g., negligence) committed by another partner who acted (1) within the ordinary course and scope of the partnership business or (2) with the authorization of the other partners.

        1) Partners are potentially individually liable for the full amount of a partnership obligation and also liable as a partnership.
        2) A plaintiff may sue one partner, all partners, or the partnership. However, only a partner against whom a judgment has been obtained can be held personally liable.

    b. A partner may obligate the partnership and partners by contract when

        1) Specifically authorized by the partnership agreement,
        2) Apparently carrying on in the ordinary course of the partnership business or business of the kind carried on by the partnership, or
        3) Acting with the actual or implicit consent of the other partners.

            a) When partners agree to limit the authority of a partner to act for the partnership, a third party who has no notice of the limitation is not bound.

    c. **Admission** into an existing partnership results in liability for partnership obligations.

        1) However, a new partner is only liable for obligations incurred prior to admission to the extent of his or her investment.

    d. A **withdrawing** partner remains liable for debts of the partnership incurred before withdrawal unless the creditors contractually agree otherwise.

        1) Termination of the partnership also does not discharge any partner's obligations to third parties.

11. **Termination**

   a. The partners may choose to limit the duration of the partnership to a definite term or the completion of a specific undertaking.

   1) The partnership also may be **at will**. A partnership at will is **not** limited to "a definite term or the completion of a specific undertaking." It continues indefinitely until an act of dissolution.

   b. The RUPA provides for dissociation, dissolution, winding up (also known as liquidation), and termination.

   c. **Dissociation** is the legal effect of a partner's ceasing to be associated in carrying on the business of the partnership. A partner has the power to dissociate at any time, subject to payment of damages if the dissociation is wrongful.

   1) Upon dissociation the partner's management rights (except with regard to winding up) terminate.

   2) After a partner's dissociation, the partnership may continue after purchase of the dissociated partner's interest in accordance with the partnership agreement or the RUPA. If the partnership does not continue to do business, dissolution begins.

   3) Dissociation results from the following:

      a) Notice to the partnership of a partner's express will to withdraw

      b) An event specified in the agreement

      c) Expulsion of a partner under the terms of the partnership agreement

      d) Expulsion by a unanimous vote of the other partners, for example, because (1) it is unlawful to carry on a business with the partner or (2) the partner transferred substantially all of his or her partnership interest (other than for security purposes)

      e) A court order

      f) Incapacity

      g) Death

      h) Bankruptcy or insolvency

      i) Distribution by a trust or estate of its entire transferable interest

   4) The partnership is **not** necessarily dissolved by dissociation of a partner unless it occurs by the partner's notice of an **express will** to leave the partnership.

      a) In a partnership at will, the partners do **not** agree to remain partners until a definite period ends or a specific undertaking is completed. Accordingly, no written agreement exists stating the terms of dissolution. Any partner then can dissolve the at-will partnership by giving notice of an express will to leave.

5) A **statement of dissociation** may be filed by the partnership or a dissociated partner. It is deemed to provide notice of dissociation **90 days** after filing.

    a) Such notice terminates the partner's apparent authority and his or her liability for the partnership's post-dissociation obligations.

    b) A dissociated partner (or the estate of a deceased partner) has apparent authority for **2 years** to bind the partnership to contracts with third parties who (1) reasonably believe the person is a partner, (2) do not have notice of disassociation, and (3) are deemed not to have notice after the filing of a statement of disassociation.

    c) A dissociated partner (or the estate of a deceased partner) remains liable to creditors for obligations incurred prior to dissociation even if the other partners agreed to assume the debts.

    d) A dissociated partner (or the estate of a deceased partner) also may be liable on **post-dissociation** contracts for up to 2 years if third parties reasonably believe that (s)he is still a partner.

6) If the business is **not** wound up, the partnership must **purchase** the dissociated partner's interest from the partner.

    a) The price is determined based on a hypothetical sale of the partnership at the dissociation date.

7) The dissociation provisions support the entity theory by facilitating the continuation of partnerships.

d. **Dissolution and winding up** occur only after certain events. But dissolution may occur without winding up.

1) In a partnership at will, dissolution results from, among other things, notice of a partner's **express will** to withdraw.

    a) Dissolution also may be by **operation of law**, e.g., because of an event that makes the partnership's business illegal. Thus, withdrawal does not dissolve the partnership by operation of law.

    b) Moreover, a **court** may order dissolution, e.g., because the economic purpose of the partnership cannot be achieved.

2) **Actual** authority of a partner to act on behalf of the partnership terminates upon dissolution except as necessary to wind up partnership affairs.

3) **Apparent** authority of a partner may continue to exist throughout the winding up process unless notice of the dissolution has been communicated to the other party to the transaction.

4) A partner's liability for the partnership's obligations continues after dissolution.

5) The fiduciary duties of the partners also remain in effect with the exception of the duty not to compete, which ceases to exist after dissolution.

6) A **statement of dissolution** is not required, but it may be filed by any partner who has not wrongfully dissociated.

    a) It is legally sufficient notice to nonpartners 90 days after the filing regarding dissolution and limitation of partners' authority.

e. A partnership may **continue after dissolution** if certain requirements are met.

1) After dissolution and before winding up, all parties (including any dissociating partner who has not wrongfully dissociated) may waive the right to winding up and termination.

a) In this case, the partnership continues its business as if dissolution had not occurred.

f. **Winding up** is the administrative process of settling partnership affairs, including the use of partnership assets and any required contributions by partners to pay creditors.

1) The RUPA states that the person winding up may do the following:

a) Continue the business as a going concern for a reasonable time
b) Take judicial actions
c) Settle and close the business
d) Dispose of and transfer property
e) Discharge liabilities
f) Distribute assets
g) Settle disputes by mediation or arbitration
h) Perform other necessary acts

2) **Creditors** are paid in full before any distributions are made to partners. However, partners who are creditors share equally with nonpartner creditors under the RUPA.

a) In practice, because partner-creditors also are liable for all partnership debts, partnership creditors are **paid first**.

3) After payment of creditors, any surplus is paid in cash to the partners.

a) A partner has no right to a distribution **in kind (of noncash assets)** and need not accept a distribution in kind.

4) To settle partnership accounts with positive (credit) balances, each partner receives a distribution equal to the amount in his or her account. Thus, no distinction is made between distributions of capital and of profits.

a) Profits and losses from liquidation of assets are increases (credits) and decreases (debits), respectively.

b) Prior credits to an account include contributions made and the partner's share of profits.

c) Prior debits include distributions received and the share of losses.

EXAMPLE

Zoe and Zed are the only partners in a general partnership. Zoe contributes $10,000 in cash, and Zed contributes services only. No partnership agreement states how partnership profits and losses are to be allocated. When the partnership dissolves, Zoe and Zed liquidate its assets. The net receipts are $60,000 in cash. If creditors are owed $45,000, the following is the determination of profit:

Cash	$60,000
Payments to creditors	(45,000)
Available cash	$15,000
Zoe's contribution	(10,000)
Profit	$ 5,000

Zoe and Zed did not agree on the allocation of profit. It therefore is shared equally ($5,000 ÷ 2 = $2,500 to each partner). Zoe receives $12,500 ($10,000 contribution + $2,500), and Zed receives $2,500 ($0 contribution + $2,500).

5) If a partner's account has a negative (debit) balance, the partner is liable to contribute the amount of the balance.

 a) If a partner does not make a required contribution, the other partners must pay the difference in the same proportion in which they share losses.

 b) A partner making an excess contribution may recover the excess from the other partners.

 c) Moreover, the creditors may enforce the obligation of the partners to contribute to the partnership if a partner does not pay his or her share of the losses.

EXAMPLE

In the previous example, assume that the net receipts after liquidation of assets equaled $50,000. The following is the determination of the loss:

Cash	$50,000
Payments to creditors	(45,000)
Available cash	$ 5,000
Zoe's contribution	(10,000)
Loss	$ (5,000)

Zoe and Zed did not agree on the allocation of loss. It therefore is shared equally [$(5,000) ÷ 2 = $(2,500) to each partner]. Zoe receives $7,500 [$10,000 contribution + $(2,500) share of loss], and Zed is liable for $2,500.

6) One effect of these rules is that the priority rules for unsecured partnership creditors and individual partners' unsecured creditors are consistent with the federal Bankruptcy Code. Thus, **unsecured partnership creditors** have priority in **partnership** assets. But, regarding any amounts that cannot be recovered from the partnership assets, they have the same priority in the **partners'** assets as the partners' creditors.

 a) A personal creditor of a personally insolvent partner must obtain a lien on the partner's transferable interest in the partnership.

The AICPA has tested candidates' knowledge of how general partnerships terminate, especially the effects of a partner's death on the partnership and the rights of the deceased partner's heirs.

12. **Limited Liability Partnership (LLP)**

a. An LLP is a general partnership with limited liability. It is a favorable form of organization for professionals who have not incorporated. In many states, this form is restricted to use by professionals.

1) An LLP must file a **statement of qualification** with the secretary of state and maintain professional liability insurance.

2) All partners are general partners who have limited liability for the acts of other parties. In most states, liability is limited for all partnership obligations, including those resulting from contracts. Thus, a **full shield** statute imposes liability only to the extent of the LLP's assets, with certain exceptions.

a) For example, a partner remains liable for obligations s(he) personally guaranteed or incurred and for wrongful acts.

b) Furthermore, a partner who is an immediate **supervisor** is liable for the wrongs committed within the scope of employment by an employee, agent, or another partner.

3) Most CPA and law firms are organized as LLPs because state laws, in general, do not allow professionals limited liability for their actions. However, they do allow professionals the ability to shield their partners from liability.

4) An LLP's statement of qualification is canceled when the partners make a filing with the secretary of state that (a) names the partnership, (b) identifies the statement, and (c) describes the substance of the cancelation.

13. **Joint Ventures**

a. A joint venture is an easily formed business structure common in international commerce. It is an association of persons who as co-owners engage in a specific undertaking for profit.

1) A joint venture is treated as a partnership in most cases.

2) The rights and duties of joint venturers generally are stated in the RUPA.

3) A disadvantage of a joint venture is that it lacks continuity of existence.

a) Moreover, the interests in the entity are not readily transferable.

4) An advantage is that joint venturers have less apparent or implied authority than partners.

Stop and review! You have completed the outline for this subunit. Study multiple-choice questions 3 through 8 beginning on page 426.

15.3 LIMITED PARTNERSHIPS

1. **Limited Partnership**

a. A limited partnership is a partnership formed by two or more persons under a state statute. Most statutes are based on the **Revised Uniform Limited Partnership Act (RULPA)**. A limited partnership has one or more general partners and one or more limited partners.

1) **Person** includes natural person, partnership, limited partnership, trust, estate, association, or corporation.

2) At least one **general partner** must manage the partnership and have full personal liability for debts of the partnership.

a) A general partner may be another partnership or a corporation if its articles of incorporation permit.

b) A person may be both a general partner and a limited partner with the rights and liabilities of each.

3) A **limited partner** is an investor, not a manager or agent. A limited partner's contribution may be cash, services, a note, or other property made in exchange for an interest in the partnership. Limited partnership interests are securities that must be registered with the SEC unless an exemption applies.

    a) A limited partner also may invest in competitor entities or compete in other ways. (S)he does **not** (1) manage the limited partnership or (2) have a fiduciary duty to the limited partnership.

    b) The limited partnership interest is intangible personal property because the limited partner has no right to specific partnership property.

4) A limited partner is not active in management of the partnership.

b. **Formation**

1) A written **certificate of limited partnership** must be filed as a public record with the secretary of state of the state in which it is organized. The certificate gives potential creditors notice of the limited liability of the limited partners. If a certificate is not filed, the organization is treated as a general partnership.

    a) The certificate must contain the following:

        i) Name of the limited partnership
        ii) Name and street address of its agent for service of process
        iii) Name and business address of each general partner
        iv) Latest date upon which the limited partnership is to dissolve
        v) Other matters the general partners include in the certificate

    b) The certificate must be signed by all general partners.

    c) Amendments also must be filed.

2) To do business in any other state, registration as a **foreign limited partnership** with the secretary of state of that state is required.

c. **Operation**

1) The operation of a limited partnership, including its financial structure, capitalization, profit and loss allocation, and distributions, is similar to that of a general partnership.

2) One exception is that, without a contrary agreement, profits and losses are shared on the basis of the value of contributions actually made by each partner.

d. **Partner Rights and Liabilities**

1) Unless the partnership agreement states otherwise, a **general partner** in a limited partnership has

    a) Unlimited liability for partnership liabilities.

    b) Full management powers.

    c) A share in both profits and losses.

    d) The same rights and powers and the same duties as a partner in a general partnership.

    e) No authority to admit additional general or limited partners without the unanimous written consent of all partners. This requirement protects the existing partners' proportionate interests.

        i) But a general partner may assign the interest to creditors or others without dissolving the partnership.

2) A **limited partner** has the right to

    a) Propose and vote on partnership affairs that do not directly control partnership operations, e.g., admission or removal of a general partner.

    b) Withdraw from the partnership upon 6 months' notice or according to the partnership agreement.

        i) The limited partner's right of withdrawal of his or her capital contribution is restricted. It may be withdrawn (a) upon the dissolution of the partnership, (b) at the date specified in the certificate, (c) upon 6 months' notice in writing to all the members, or (d) with the consent of all the members. But all creditors must be paid, or sufficient assets must be available for creditors.

        ii) A limited partner may not withdraw his or her capital contribution if the effect is to impair creditors' rights.

    c) Do business with the partnership, e.g., become a creditor (secured or unsecured) by lending it money.

    d) Inspect and copy the partnership records, including tax returns.

    e) Receive other partnership information (if just and reasonable).

    f) File a derivative action on behalf of the partnership.

    g) Assign the limited partnership interest. But the assignee does not become a substituted limited partner.

        i) If the limited partner is insolvent, a creditor may obtain a charging order from a court that acts as an involuntary assignment.

        ii) The assignee may become a limited partner by unanimous agreement of the partners or if the partnership agreement permits.

    h) Apply for dissolution of the partnership.

    i) Obtain an accounting of partnership affairs.

3) A limited partner is liable for partnership liabilities only to the extent of his or her capital contribution. (S)he has **no** right to participate in control of the business.

    a) **Control** is participation in the day-to-day management decisions of the partnership.

    b) A limited partner may incur personal liability by

        i) Taking part in the control of the entity or

        ii) Knowingly permitting his or her name to be used as part of the partnership name and held out as a participant in management.

    c) Personal liability is incurred only to persons who reasonably believe the limited partner is a general partner.

e.   **Termination**

1)   A limited partnership is **dissolved** and wound up before termination. A limited partnership may be dissolved by any of the following events:

   a)   The time or event specified in the limited partnership agreement occurs.

   b)   All the partners agree, in writing, to dissolve.

   c)   An event of withdrawal of a **general partner** occurs, e.g., death, retirement, bankruptcy, incapacity, or removal. The following are exceptions:

      i)   The written terms of the agreement provide that the business may be carried on by the remaining general partners (if any).

      ii)   If no general partner remains, the limited partners agree in writing within 90 days to continue the business and appoint one or more new general partners.

   d)   The limited partnership is dissolved by court order.

2)   The limited partnership is **not** dissolved by the bankruptcy, incapacity, or death of a limited partner or by the transfer of a limited partner's interest.

   a)   The personal representative of the estate of a deceased limited partner does **not** become a substituted limited partner. However, (s)he has the rights and liabilities of a limited partner for the purpose of settling the estate.

3)   After dissolution, winding up is done by a general partner who has not caused the dissolution. If no general partner exists to conduct the winding up, it may be performed by the **limited partners** or by some person designated by a court.

4)   Remaining assets, if any, are distributed as follows:

   a)   To creditors, including creditors who are partners

   b)   To present partners and former partners for distributions previously due to them and unpaid, except as otherwise provided in the limited partnership agreement

   c)   To the partners as a return of their contributions, except as otherwise provided in the limited partnership agreement

   d)   To the partners according to the terms of the limited partnership agreement in the proportions in which they share distributions (to the extent of any remaining assets)

5)   A **certificate of cancellation** signed by all the general partners must be filed when the entity dissolves and winding up begins.

6)   The final distribution terminates the limited partnership.

Stop and review! You have completed the outline for this subunit. Study multiple-choice questions 9 through 17 beginning on page 428.

15.4 LIMITED LIABILITY COMPANIES (LLCs)

1. **Overview**

   a. An LLC is a noncorporate hybrid business structure that combines the limited liability of the corporation and the limited partnership with the tax advantages of the general partnership and the limited partnership.

   b. Like a corporation, a limited partnership, and an LLP, an LLC is a legal entity separate from its owners-investors (called **members**). Individuals and any corporate and noncorporate business entities may be members.

      1) An LLC may (a) enter into contracts, (b) sue, (c) be sued, (d) own property in its own name, (e) engage in other transactions in property, (f) make donations, (g) be a general or limited partner, and (h) appoint agents.

   c. Like a partnership, the LLC may have owner management, a limited duration, and restricted transfer of interests.

2. **Formation**

   a. An LLC can be formed only under a state statute.

      1) An LLC generally may be formed for any lawful purpose.

      2) An LLC is formed by one or more persons when articles of organization are filed with the appropriate secretary of state (or the equivalent). Thus, formation is more difficult than for a sole proprietorship or a general partnership.

         a) State laws vary as to when the LLC begins its legal existence, e.g., when the articles are (1) filed with the state or (2) officially approved.

   b. The **name** of the LLC must indicate by words or abbreviations that it is an LLC. It should be distinct from the names of other businesses in the state.

   c. The **articles of organization** should state at a minimum (1) the LLC's name, (2) the address of the principal place of business or registered office, and (3) the name and street address of the initial agent for service of process.

      1) The typical statute also requires an indication of whether managers, who may not be members, will manage the LLC.

   d. The members' contract or **operating agreement** ordinarily is **not** legally required. It also may be oral but should be written. One reason is that modification of some statutory provisions may be made only in a written agreement.

      1) Unless the agreement states otherwise, it may be amended only by a unanimous resolution of the members.

      2) The operating agreement may address the following:

         a) Capitalization
         b) Sharing of profits and losses
         c) Amendment of the operating agreement
         d) Management arrangements
         e) Voting rights
         f) Members' rights, including to distributions and access to records
         g) Transfer of members' interests
         h) The circumstances causing dissolution
         i) Admission and withdrawal of members
         j) Death of a member

   e. The LLC must at all times maintain a registered **agent** for service of process and a registered **office** in the state.

      1) These requirements are the same as for limited partnerships and corporations.

   f. The **duration** of LLCs generally is unlimited unless the members agree otherwise.

3. **Capitalization**

    a. Funding of an LLC is from members' **contributions**. Without an agreement to the contrary, it may consist of tangible and intangible property and services, including obligations to contribute cash or property or to perform services.

    b. Partnerships, corporations, and nonresident aliens, unlike the shareholders of an S corporation, may be members of an LLC. (They also may be shareholders of a C corporation, partners in a general partnership, etc.)

        1) Moreover, unlike an S corporation, an LLC (a) has no limit on the number of members, (b) can make disproportionate allocations and distributions, and (c) can distribute appreciated property without incurring a taxable gain.

        2) A member of an LLC can contribute appreciated property in exchange for a membership interest without recognizing a taxable gain.

    c. A disadvantage is that LLC interests may be considered securities subject to federal and state regulation.

4. **Profits, Losses, and Distributions**

    a. Without a contrary agreement, statutes most often provide for profits, losses, and distributions to be shared based on the values of members' **contributions**.

        1) A member is not automatically entitled to compensation, except for winding up.

        2) A right to distributions does not exist until a member gives notice of withdrawal from the entity.

5. **LLC Interest**

    a. A member may transfer (assign) his or her distributional interest without dissolving the LLC. This interest is personal property.

        1) The member has no right in specific property of the LLC.

        2) The transfer may be involuntary, for example, by a charging order obtained by a creditor from a court against the member's interest in the LLC (profits and other distributions).

        3) The transfer also may be through the estate of a deceased member.

        4) A transferee does **not** become a member without consent of all members or a provision in their agreement.

6. **Taxation**

    a. Members may elect to be taxed as partners, and single-member LLCs (called "disregarded entities" for tax purposes) are taxed as sole proprietorships.

    b. Taxation as a corporation may be advantageous if reinvestment in the LLC is desired, and corporate rates are lower than personal rates.

    c. Thus, an LLC has the advantage of being a pass-through entity or a taxable entity at the discretion of the member(s).

        1) But a publicly traded LLC is a taxable entity.

7. **Management**

    a. An LLC is deemed to be member-managed unless the articles provide otherwise.

    b. In a **member-managed LLC**, all members have a right to participate, and most business matters are decided by the majority.

    c. In a **manager-managed LLC**, each manager, who need not be a member, has equal rights, and most business matters are decided by the manager or by a majority of the managers.

8. **Rights and Duties of Members and Managers**

    a. If the articles provide for elected managers, they are agents of the LLC. Any one manager may have the statutory authority to bind the LLC.

        1) In a manager-managed LLC, members are **not** agents.
        2) Most state statutes require unanimous consent to transfer management.

    b. If the articles provide for member-managers, they are agents. Thus, it may be possible, depending on the statute, for any one member to incur indebtedness or otherwise contractually bind the LLC.

    c. The **fiduciary** duties of care and loyalty (and possibly those of good faith and fair dealing) are imposed on those (members or managers) who manage LLCs.

    d. Persons who conduct business as an LLC when requirements of formation have not been met do **not** have limited liability and are jointly and severally liable.

    e. Members have the right to inspect books and records, to be informed about the business, and to file derivative actions.

9. **Voting**

    a. Without a contrary agreement, members usually have voting interests in proportion to their financial interests. Members may vote on

        1) Adoption or amendment of the operating agreement
        2) Election or removal of managers
        3) Admission of members
        4) Selling assets before dissolution
        5) Merger

10. **Liability of Members and Managers**

    a. Members of an LLC who participate in management have limited liability. Thus, creditors of the entity ordinarily have no claim on the personal assets of the members or managers.

    b. However, the members or managers remain liable for their guarantees of LLC debt or for personal misconduct (e.g., negligence or criminal behavior). Moreover, misuse of the LLC form (e.g., to commit fraud or mislead others about who is conducting the business) may cause a court to "pierce the corporate veil."

11. **Termination**

    a. Generally, subject to the LLC's solvency, a member is entitled to a return of his or her capital contribution upon dissolution or other specified event. But a member is liable to the LLC for a deficiency in the agreed contribution. A member also is liable for receipt of a wrongful return of a contribution.

    b. An LLC is dissolved upon

        1) Expiration of a specified time period or occurrence of a specified event.
        2) Consent of a number or percentage of members provided in their agreement.
        3) Judicial determination of the following:

            a) Frustration of purpose
            b) Impracticability of continuing because of a member's conduct
            c) Impracticability of continuing under the articles and operating agreement
            d) Inappropriate behavior of controlling members or managers
            e) The equitability of liquidation

    c. Dissolution requires a public filing.

    d. **Dissociation** occurs when a member no longer is associated with the LLC. In most states, it does **not** result in automatic dissolution.

e.   Liquidation results in payment of proceeds in the following order:

1) Creditors
2) Unpaid distributions to members
3) Members' capital contributions
4) Remaining amounts to members as agreed or in the same ratio as distributions

Characteristics of Noncorporate Business Entities

	Formation	Capitalization	Operation	Liability	Transferability	Taxation	Termination
Sole Proprietorship	No formalities. Formed at will of proprietor.	Only personal resources of proprietor.	All decisions made by proprietor.	Unlimited personal liability for all losses and debts.	Interest may be transferred during proprietor's life. Proprietorship is then dissolved.	Only sole proprietor taxed.	At proprietor's discretion, transfer of interest, and death of proprietor.
General Partnership	No formalities. No filings. Formed based on written or oral agreement.	Resources of general partners.	Each partner has right to equal participation in management. Can restrict management rights to one or more partners.	Partners are jointly and severally liable for any partnership obligation.	Partner may transfer financial interest without loss of rights, duties, and liabilities as partner.	Tax reporting entity only. Partners subject to tax.	Dissociation followed by dissolution and winding up.
Limited Partnership	Formalities. Must file written certificate of limited partnership with state.	Resources of general and limited partners.	General partner has full management rights. Limited partner has no management rights.	General partner has unlimited liability for partnership obligations. Limited partner liable only to extent of capital contribution.	General partner may transfer financial interest without loss of rights, duties, and liabilities as partner. Limited partner may assign interest.	Tax reporting entity only. Partners subject to tax.	Event of withdrawal of a general partner.
Limited Liability Partnership	Formalities. Must file with secretary of state and maintain professional liability insurance.	Resources of partners.	Favorable form of organization for professionals (e.g., lawyers, CPAs, etc.). All partners are general partners with limited liability.	Not personally liable for partnership obligations except to extent of LLP's assets. Partners remain personally liable for their own malpractice.	Partner may transfer financial interest without loss of rights, duties, and liabilities as partner.	Tax reporting entity only. Partners subject to tax.	Dissociation followed by dissolution and winding up.
Limited Liability Company	Formalities. Must file articles of organization with secretary of state.	Contributions of members.	Unless provided otherwise, all members have equal management rights.	Owners who participate in management have limited liability.	A member can transfer his or her distributional interest. This interest is personal property.	May elect flow through taxation or be taxed as an entity.	Dissolution followed by liquidation.

Stop and review! You have completed the outline for this subunit. Study multiple-choice questions 18 through 20 beginning on page 430.

QUESTIONS

15.1 Sole Proprietorships

1. The formation of a sole proprietorship

A. Requires registration with the federal government's Small Business Administration.

B. Requires a formal "doing business as" filing under state law if the proprietor plans to do business under a fictitious name.

C. Requires formal registration in each state the proprietor plans to do business in.

D. Is not as easy and inexpensive to form as an S corporation.

Answer (B) is correct.

REQUIRED: The characteristic of the formation of a sole proprietorship.

DISCUSSION: A proprietor doing business under a fictitious name is usually required to make a d/b/a or "doing business as" filing under state law. Otherwise, the formation of a sole proprietorship is subject to few legal requirements, such as local zoning and licensing. In this respect, the sole proprietorship is the easiest and least expensive to create of all the business organizations.

Answer (A) is incorrect. The Small Business Administration (SBA) is a source of loans for sole proprietorships. No formal registration is required with the SBA. Answer (C) is incorrect. A sole proprietorship may conduct business in any state without having to file, register, or otherwise qualify to do business in that state. Answer (D) is incorrect. Of all business organizations, the sole proprietorship is the easiest and least expensive to create.

2. Bob decides to start a bicycle repair shop. He is the sole owner and raises additional capital by borrowing from a local bank. Which of the following may become at risk if Bob defaults on the repayment of the loan?

	Assets of the Bicycle Repair Shop	Bob's Equity Capital Invested	Bob's Personal Assets
A.	No	No	No
B.	Yes	No	No
C.	Yes	Yes	No
D.	Yes	Yes	Yes

Answer (D) is correct.

REQUIRED: The assets at risk if a sole proprietor defaults on the repayment of the loan.

DISCUSSION: Proprietors have unlimited personal liability for all losses and debts. All of Bob's assets related to the bicycle repair shop and even his personal assets may be at risk. Depending on the extent of the defaulting loan, the bank may claim rights against all of Bob's assets.

Answer (A) is incorrect. The assets of the bicycle repair shop and Bob's equity capital invested and personal assets may be at risk. Answer (B) is incorrect. Bob's equity capital invested and personal assets also may be at risk. Answer (C) is incorrect. Bob's personal assets may be at risk.

15.2 General Partnerships

3. Eller, Fort, and Owens do business as Venture Associates, a general partnership. Trent Corp. brought a breach of contract suit against Venture and Eller individually. Trent won the suit and filed a judgment against both Venture and Eller. Venture then entered bankruptcy. Under the RUPA, Trent will generally be able to collect the judgment in full from

A. Partnership assets but not partner personal assets.

B. The personal assets of Eller, Fort, and Owens.

C. Eller's personal assets only after partnership assets are exhausted.

D. Eller's personal assets.

Answer (D) is correct.

REQUIRED: The assets from which a judgment against a partnership and a specific partner may be collected.

DISCUSSION: The RUPA provides that partners are jointly and severally liable for all obligations of the partnership, including those arising out of a contract. The keys to the question are that (1) Trent sued both the partnership and one partner, (2) that partner can be held individually liable for the entire amount of a partnership obligation (joint and several liability), and (3) only parties who are judgment debtors can be held liable. Because Trent won the lawsuit against Venture and Eller, either Venture or Eller or both are liable for the judgment amount. In this scenario, the partnership is in bankruptcy. A plaintiff with a judgment against a defendant in bankruptcy typically collects very little, if any, of the judgment. The judgment against the partnership will be subordinated to the claims of secured creditors and creditors with priority. As a result, Trent will likely seek to recover the full judgment from Eller's personal assets, given that Eller was a co-defendant in the lawsuit. Furthermore, because Venture is in bankruptcy, the RUPA provides that Trent need not seek a writ of execution against (compel collection of the judgment amount from) Venture before proceeding against Eller's personal assets.

Answer (A) is incorrect. Trent may collect in full from Eller. Answer (B) is incorrect. Fort and Owens must be judgment debtors to be held liable by Trent. Answer (C) is incorrect. Trent need not exhaust the partnership assets. Venture is in bankruptcy.

4. When parties intend to create a partnership that will be recognized under the Revised Uniform Partnership Act, they must agree to

	Conduct a Business for Profit	Share Gross Receipts from a Business
A.	Yes	Yes
B.	Yes	No
C.	No	Yes
D.	No	No

Answer (B) is correct.

REQUIRED: The item(s), if any, that must be agreed to when parties intend to create a partnership under the RUPA.

DISCUSSION: A partnership is an association of two or more persons conducting a business, which they co-own, for profit. Thus, partners must objectively intend that their business make a profit, even if no profit is earned. Each of the parties must be a co-owner. They share profits and losses of the venture and management authority (unless they agree otherwise).

Answer (A) is incorrect. The partnership agreement may specify that gross receipts are not shared. Answer (C) is incorrect. Partners must intend that their business make a profit, but partners do not have to agree to share gross receipts. Answer (D) is incorrect. Partners must intend that their business make a profit.

5. Gillie, Taft, and Dall are partners in an architectural firm. The partnership agreement is silent about the payment of salaries and the division of profits and losses. Gillie works full-time in the firm, and Taft and Dall each work half-time. Taft invested $120,000 in the firm, and Gillie and Dall invested $60,000 each. Dall is responsible for bringing in 50% of the business, and Gillie and Taft 25% each. How should profits of $120,000 for the year be divided?

	Gillie	Taft	Dall
A.	$60,000	$30,000	$30,000
B.	$40,000	$40,000	$40,000
C.	$30,000	$60,000	$30,000
D.	$30,000	$30,000	$60,000

Answer (B) is correct.

REQUIRED: The division of partnership profits when the partnership agreement is silent about salaries and the division of profits and losses.

DISCUSSION: Partners are not entitled to compensation for their actions, skill, and time applied on behalf of the partnership, except when such an arrangement is explicitly provided for in the partnership agreement. The partnership agreement is silent on this point, so salaries are not paid to the partners. Profits and losses may be divided among the partners according to any formula stated in the partnership agreement. Without a contrary agreement, partners share equally in the profits. Thus, each partner will receive $40,000.

6. Cobb, Inc., a partner in TLC Partnership, assigns its partnership interest to Bean, who is not made a partner. After the assignment, Bean may assert the rights to

I. Participation in the management of TLC
II. Cobb's share of TLC's partnership profits

A. I only.

B. II only.

C. I and II.

D. Neither I nor II.

Answer (B) is correct.

REQUIRED: The right(s), if any, of an assignee of a partnership interest.

DISCUSSION: Partnership rights may be assigned without the dissolution of the partnership. The assignee is entitled only to the profits the assignor would normally receive. The assignee does not automatically become a partner and would not have the right to participate in managing the business or to inspect the books and records of the partnership. The assigning partner remains a partner with all the duties and other rights of a partner.

7. Leslie, Kelly, and Blair wanted to form a business. Which of the following business entities does **not** require the filing of organization documents with the state?

A. Limited partnership.

B. Joint venture.

C. Limited liability company.

D. Subchapter S corporation.

Answer (B) is correct.

REQUIRED: The entity created without a statutory filing.

DISCUSSION: A joint venture is an association to accomplish a specific business purpose. It is easily formed and is often organized for a single transaction. No statute requires a filing to create a joint venture.

Answer (A) is incorrect. A limited partnership is required by the RULPA to file a written certificate of limited partnership as a public record with the appropriate secretary of state. Answer (C) is incorrect. A limited liability company must file written articles of organization. Answer (D) is incorrect. A subchapter S corporation must file articles of incorporation with the state.

8. Wind, who has been a partner in the PLW general partnership for 4 years, decides to withdraw from the partnership despite a written partnership agreement that states, "No partner may withdraw for a period of 5 years." Under the Revised Uniform Partnership Act (RUPA), what is the result of Wind's withdrawal?

A. Wind's withdrawal causes a dissolution of the partnership by operation of law.

B. Wind's withdrawal has no bearing on the continued operation of the partnership by the remaining partners.

C. Wind's withdrawal is not effective until Wind obtains a court-ordered decree of dissolution.

D. Wind's withdrawal causes dissociation from the partnership despite being in violation of the partnership agreement.

Answer (D) is correct.

REQUIRED: The result of an early withdrawal from a partnership.

DISCUSSION: Under the RUPA, a partnership is considered an entity substantially separate from its partners. A partner has the power (if not the right) to dissociate at any time. However, if the partner wrongfully dissociates from the partnership, (s)he is liable for any resulting damages to the other partners. After dissociation, the business either continues after purchase of the dissociated partner's interest or dissolution begins.

Answer (A) is incorrect. A partnership is not dissolved by operation of law under RUPA when a partner withdraws. Such a dissolution results from such events as the illegality of the business and certain judicial determinations. Answer (B) is incorrect. Wind will remain liable to creditors for predissociation obligations and any post-dissociation contracts for up to 2 years unless (s)he files a statement of dissociation. Answer (C) is incorrect. A court-ordered decree is not needed for the withdrawal to be effective. The partner may withdraw by notice to the partnership of an express will to withdraw.

15.3 Limited Partnerships

9. Marshall formed a limited partnership for the purpose of engaging in the export-import business. Marshall obtained additional working capital from Franklin and Lee by selling them each a limited partnership interest. Under these circumstances, the limited partnership

A. Will usually be treated as a taxable entity for federal income tax purposes.

B. Will lose its status as a limited partnership if it has more than one general partner.

C. Can limit the liability of all partners.

D. Can exist as such only if it is formed under the authority of a state statute.

Answer (D) is correct.

REQUIRED: The true statement regarding a limited partnership.

DISCUSSION: The limited partnership is not available as a form of business organization under the common law. An organization purporting to be a limited partnership but formed in a state with no statutory authority for such a form of business organization will very likely be treated as a general partnership.

Answer (A) is incorrect. A partnership is not a taxable entity for federal income tax purposes. Partnerships are required to file informational returns only. Answer (B) is incorrect. A limited partnership may have more than one general partner. The minimum is at least one limited and one general partner. Answer (C) is incorrect. At least one general partner must have unlimited personal liability.

10. Stanley is a well-known retired movie personality who purchased a limited partnership interest in Terrific Movie Productions upon its initial syndication. Which of the following is true?

A. If Stanley permits his name to be used in connection with the business and is held out as a participant in the management of the venture, he will be liable as a general partner.

B. The sale of these limited partnership interests is not subject to SEC registration.

C. This limited partnership may be formed with the same informality as a general partnership.

D. The general partners are prohibited from also owning limited partnership interests.

Answer (A) is correct.

REQUIRED: The true statement about a limited partnership.

DISCUSSION: A limited partner who permits his or her name to be used in the name of the partnership or in connection with the business is liable to creditors who give credit without actual knowledge that (s)he is not a general partner. Such a limited partner forfeits limited liability. The use of his or her name may lead unsuspecting creditors to believe that (s)he is a general partner with unlimited liability.

Answer (B) is incorrect. Limited partnership interests are considered to be securities and must be registered with the SEC unless an exemption applies. Answer (C) is incorrect. A limited partnership can be formed only under a statute permitting the formation and existence of limited partnerships. Such statutes require many formalities. Answer (D) is incorrect. A general partner also may be a limited partner.

11. A valid limited partnership

A. Cannot be treated as an "association" for federal income tax purposes.

B. May have an unlimited number of partners.

C. Is exempt from all Securities and Exchange Commission regulations.

D. Must designate in its certificate the name, address, and capital contribution of each general partner and each limited partner.

Answer (B) is correct.

REQUIRED: The true statement regarding a valid limited partnership.

DISCUSSION: A valid limited partnership has no maximum limit on the number of partners (limited or general). The only requirement is that it have at least one limited and one general partner. In contrast, S corporations currently have a limit of 100 shareholders.

Answer (A) is incorrect. A partnership will be treated as an association (and taxed as a corporation) if it has more corporate than partnership attributes. Answer (C) is incorrect. A limited partnership interest is considered a security and generally subject to SEC regulations. Answer (D) is incorrect. Under the RULPA, the name and business address of each general partner (but not information about limited partners) must be included in the certificate.

12. Wichita Properties is a limited partnership created in accordance with the provisions of the Uniform Limited Partnership Act. The partners have voted to dissolve and settle the partnership's accounts. Which of the following will be the last to be paid?

A. General partners for unpaid distributions.

B. Limited partners in respect to capital.

C. Limited and general partners in respect to their undistributed profits.

D. General partners in respect to capital.

Answer (C) is correct.

REQUIRED: The lowest priority of distribution upon liquidation of a limited partnership.

DISCUSSION: Under the RULPA, limited and general partners are treated equally. Unless the partnership agreement provides otherwise, assets are distributed as follows:

1) Creditors (including all partner-creditors)
2) Partners for unpaid distributions (i.e., declared but not paid)
3) Partners for the return of their contributions
4) Partners for remaining assets (i.e., undistributed profits) in the proportions in which they share distributions

13. Which of the following rights would a limited partner **not** be entitled to assert?

A. To have a formal accounting of partnership affairs whenever the circumstances render it just and reasonable.

B. To have the same rights as a general partner to a dissolution and winding up of the partnership.

C. To have reasonable access to the partnership books and to inspect and copy them.

D. To be elected as a general partner by a majority vote of the limited partners in number and amount.

Answer (D) is correct.

REQUIRED: The right that a limited partner is not entitled to assert.

DISCUSSION: A new general partner may be admitted to a limited partnership only with the specific written consent of each and every partner (both limited and general). The limited partners therefore do not have the power to admit new general partners, and unanimous consent is needed unless the partnership agreement provides otherwise.

Answer (A) is incorrect. A limited partner is entitled to an accounting if the circumstances are reasonable. Answer (B) is incorrect. A limited partner has the same rights as a general partner in winding up a partnership. Answer (C) is incorrect. A limited partner has a reasonable right to access books and records.

14. Absent any contrary provisions in the agreement, under which of the following circumstances will a limited partnership be dissolved?

A. A limited partner dies and his or her estate is insolvent.

B. A personal creditor of a general partner obtains a judgment against the general partner's interest in the limited partnership.

C. A general partner retires and all the remaining general partners do not consent to continue.

D. A limited partner assigns his or her partnership interest to an outsider and the purchaser becomes a substituted limited partner.

Answer (C) is correct.

REQUIRED: The circumstance in which a limited partnership is dissolved.

DISCUSSION: Retirement of a general partner generally dissolves a limited partnership or a general partnership. However, dissolution can be avoided if the business is continued by the remaining general partners either with the consent of all partners or pursuant to a stipulation in the partnership agreement.

Answer (A) is incorrect. The death of a limited partner, regardless of the solvency of the estate, does not dissolve the partnership. Answer (B) is incorrect. A judgment against the interest of a general partner is similar to an assignment of that interest, which does not dissolve the partnership. Answer (D) is incorrect. The assignment of a limited partnership interest does not dissolve the partnership. It makes no difference whether the assignee becomes a substituted limited partner.

15. What is a possible disadvantage of forming an LLP as opposed to remaining a general partnership?

    A. Creation and continuation require compliance with statutory provisions.

    B. Partners are subject to a broad personal liability shield.

    C. LLPs are pass-through entities.

    D. Termination of an LLP involves the same process as in a general partnership.

Answer (A) is correct.
    REQUIRED: The possible disadvantage of forming an LLP.
    DISCUSSION: A disadvantage of the LLP is that its creation and continuation require compliance with statutory provisions. Thus, becoming an LLP is more complicated because the partners must amend the partnership agreement and file a statement of qualification with the secretary of state.
    Answer (B) is incorrect. The personal liability shield is an advantage of the formation of an LLP. Answer (C) is incorrect. Avoiding the double taxation of the corporate entity is an advantage of an LLP. Answer (D) is incorrect. The simple dissolution and winding up of a general partnership should be viewed as an advantage of the LLP formation.

16. Under the RUPA, in which of the following situations will a partner in an LLP most likely be personally liable?

    A. The managing partner in the Texas office when individuals in the New York office engaged in fraudulent activities.

    B. The managing partner in the New York office when an employee in the office who was supervised by another partner engaged in fraudulent activities.

    C. The partner who personally incurs an obligation in the conduct of partnership business.

    D. A nonmanaging partner in an office where another partner committed negligence.

Answer (C) is correct.
    REQUIRED: The situation in which a partner in an LLP is liable.
    DISCUSSION: A partner who personally incurs an obligation in the conduct of partnership business is fully liable. The limitation on liability in an LLP applies only to a liability that otherwise would be incurred by a partner solely because of his or her status as a general partner.
    Answer (A) is incorrect. The managing partner in the Texas office has nothing to do with fraudulent activities in the New York office. Answer (B) is incorrect. Unlike the limitation in a limited partnership, the liability shield in an LLP protects the partners who manage the business. Answer (D) is incorrect. Under the RUPA, the liability shield extends to any obligation of the LLP.

17. A limited liability partnership (LLP)

    A. Starts as a corporation.

    B. Is typically adopted by providers of professional services.

    C. Is ordinarily treated as a legal entity to the same extent as a corporation.

    D. Offers a liability shield only for professional malpractice.

Answer (B) is correct.
    REQUIRED: The true statement about an LLP.
    DISCUSSION: An LLP is a general partnership that has been changed to LLP status in accordance with state law. The LLP is a business structure that is often adopted by providers of professional services (e.g., attorneys, CPAs, and physicians) and family enterprises.
    Answer (A) is incorrect. An LLP is typically a general partnership that has been changed to LLP status in accordance with state law. Answer (C) is incorrect. An LLP is ordinarily treated as a legal entity to the same extent as a general partnership. Answer (D) is incorrect. Early statutes provided the limitation on personal liability only for professional malpractice, but most states have now enacted LLP legislation that provides for a broad personal liability shield.

15.4 Limited Liability Companies (LLCs)

18. Which of the following is a legal entity separate from its owners?

    A. Limited partnership.

    B. LLP.

    C. LLC.

    D. All of the answers are correct.

Answer (D) is correct.
    REQUIRED: The entities that are legally separate from their owners.
    DISCUSSION: Limited partnerships, LLPs, and LLCs are legally separate from their owners. Such an entity may enter into contracts, sue, be sued, and own property in its own name.
    Answer (A) is incorrect. A limited partnership is allowed to be legally separate from its owners. Answer (B) is incorrect. An LLP is allowed to be legally separate from its owners. Answer (C) is incorrect. An LLC is allowed to be legally separate from its owners.

19. The owners of a limited liability company are known as which of the following?

    A. Partners.

    B. Members.

    C. Stockholders.

    D. Shareholders.

Answer (B) is correct.

    REQUIRED: The owners of a limited liability company.

    DISCUSSION: An LLC combines the limited liability of the corporation with the tax advantages of the general partnership. Like a corporation, a limited partnership, and an LLP, an LLC is a legal entity separate from its owner-investors (called members) that can be created only under state law.

    Answer (A) is incorrect. Partners are the owners of a partnership. Answer (C) is incorrect. Stockholders (also called shareholders) are the owners of a corporation. Answer (D) is incorrect. Shareholders (also called stockholders) are the owners of a corporation.

20. Which of the following parties generally has the most management rights?

    A. Minority shareholder in a corporation listed on a national stock exchange.

    B. Limited partner in a general partnership.

    C. Member of a limited liability company.

    D. Limited partner in a limited partnership.

Answer (C) is correct.

    REQUIRED: The party that generally has the most management rights.

    DISCUSSION: In a member-managed LLC, all members have a right to participate, and most business matters are decided by the majority. In a manager-managed LLC, each manager has equal rights, but managers are selected or removed by a majority vote of the members. An LLC is deemed to be member-managed unless the articles of organization state otherwise.

    Answer (A) is incorrect. A minority shareholder in a public corporation generally has few or no management rights. Answer (B) is incorrect. A general partnership has no limited partners. Answer (D) is incorrect. In a limited partnership, a limited partner has no authority to participate in management and control of the business.

CANDIDATES L♥VE GLEIM CPA REVIEW

Check out the stories of some of the millions who have succeeded with Gleim.

From first hand experience, practicing the multiple-choice questions with Gleim will give you enough confidence and knowledge to pass each section. Using Gleim will have you well-prepared and conditioned for the exam.

- Thomas Najarian, CPA

The Gleim program was the answer I'd been looking for to finally conquer the exam. I've used other programs before and none of them compared to the step by step process Gleim used, which truly prepared me to conquer all four parts on my first try.

– Eric Murphy, CPA

The testing components simulate the actual exam, so I was completely comfortable with the exam setup when I took the actual exams.

- Tracy Caisse, CPA

Due to passing the exam, I was able to secure an excellent new job as a controller at a large company! Thank you, Gleim, as your products have changed my life!

– Kent Kellenberger, CPA, CIA

I cannot say enough good things about the counselors and the structure of the Gleim system. The structure of the Gleim program keeps you focused and on task.

– Angela Brinley, CPA

I am so glad that I made the decision to take the jump and purchase Gleim. It was so well developed that it didn't feel like I was giving up my entire life just to study.

– Holly Fowler, CPA

The most important piece of advice I can give is follow the order that is laid out in the review material. There is a reason the Gleim Team chose the sequence they did: IT WORKS!

– Benjamin Ziccardy, CPA

In taking all 4 parts, I felt totally confident during the exams because I knew the Gleim products had me prepared!

– Larvizo Wright, CPA, MBA

STUDY UNIT SIXTEEN
CORPORATIONS

(16 pages of outline)

A **corporation** differs from other business organizations because, for all purposes, it is a **separate legal entity** that may exist in perpetuity. Unlike a sole proprietorship or a general partnership, its rights and obligations are separate from those of its owners or managers.

16.1 FORMATION

Background

Corporations are established pursuant to state law. In an effort to provide uniform state laws regarding corporations, the American Bar Association created the **Model Business Corporation Act (MBCA)** as model rules for state laws. The MBCA has been adopted at least in part by every state. The **Revised Model Business Corporation Act of 1984 (RMBCA)** applies to publicly held and closely held corporations. This outline is based on the RMBCA.

1. **Overview**

   a. A corporation is a separate legal entity created under a **state statute** by filing its organizational document (articles of incorporation) with the proper state authority.

      1) The corporation ordinarily is treated as a **legal person** with rights and obligations separate from its owners and managers.

   b. Corporations are governed by **shareholders** (owners) who elect a board of directors and approve fundamental changes in the corporate structure.

      1) **Directors** establish corporate policies and elect or appoint corporate **officers** who carry out the policies in the day-to-day management of the organization.

   c. A **private corporation** may be for-profit or not-for-profit, i.e., for charitable, educational, social, religious, or philanthropic purposes.

      1) A private corporation may be a close corporation or a publicly held corporation.

         a) A **close (closely held) corporation**

            i) Is owned by relatively few shareholders,
            ii) Does not sell its stock to the public,
            iii) Is commonly owned by its officers and directors, and
            iv) Has shareholder-managers.

         b) A **publicly held corporation** sells its shares to the public, generally on a national stock exchange. Its share prices are regularly published.

            i) Shares in the corporation are units of property interests in the net assets of the entity (including an interest in its profits).

   d. A **public corporation** is organized for public purposes related to the administration of government, e.g., an incorporated municipality, and it may be funded by local taxes.

      1) It is formed by specific legislation that defines its purpose and powers.

e.   A **domestic** corporation is one that operates and does business within the state in which it is organized, i.e., where its articles of incorporation are filed. A corporation is only incorporated in one state.

f.   A **foreign** corporation is one that does business in any state other than the one in which it is incorporated. A **certificate of authority** is required to **do business** within the borders of another state.

   1)   An **alien corporation** is a corporation organized in another country. It must obtain a certificate to do business from each host state.

g.   An **S corporation** has elected, under federal law, to be taxed similarly to a partnership. Thus, it usually does not pay corporate income tax but, rather, taxes flow through to its shareholders. (A **C corporation** is taxed at the corporate income tax rate.)

   1)   Study Unit 12 covers S corporations.

h.   **Professional corporations** (professional service associations) give accountants, lawyers, and other professionals the benefits of incorporation. Statutes typically restrict stock ownership to specific professionals licensed within that state.

2.   **Preincorporation Contracts**

a.   A **promoter** arranges for the formation of the corporation. (S)he provides for the financing of the corporation and for compliance with any relevant securities law.

   1)   The promoter also may procure necessary personnel, services, assets, licenses, equipment, leases, etc.

   2)   A promoter has fiduciary duties, including fair dealing, good faith, and full disclosure to subscribers, shareholders, and the corporation.

b.   **Prior to incorporation**, the promoter enters into ordinary and necessary contracts required for initial operation. Liability on preincorporation contracts is:

   1)   Promoters generally are personally liable on their contracts.

   2)   The corporation is not liable because a promoter cannot be an agent of a nonexistent entity. Until its formation, a corporation cannot enter into contracts or employ agents.

   3)   A preincorporation contract made by promoters in the name of a corporation and on its behalf may bind the corporation if permitted by statute.

c.   A corporation may **not ratify** a preincorporation contract because no principal existed at the time of contracting. However, the corporation can **adopt** the preincorporation contract as a legal substitute for ratification. This adoption acts as an assignment of rights and delegation of duties from the promoter to the corporation, but it is not retroactive and does not release the promoter from liability.

   1)   Adoption by the corporation may be implied from accepting the benefits of a contract.

d.   If the promoter, the third party, and the corporation enter into a **novation** substituting the corporation for the promoter, only the corporation is liable and the promoter is released.

e.   The promoter secures potential investors using **preincorporation subscription agreements**. Each subscriber agrees to purchase a certain amount of shares at a specified price, payable at an agreed future time.

   1)   It reflects an intent that the investor become a shareholder at the time of contracting.

   2)   A **preincorporation subscription agreement** is irrevocable for 6 months, unless otherwise provided in the agreement, or all subscribers consent to revocation. Many state statutes require the agreement be written.

3. **Incorporation**

   a. Incorporation may be in any state. **Articles of incorporation** (the corporate charter) must be filed with the secretary of state or another designated official.

   b. **Incorporators** sign the articles. Only one incorporator is required, and it does not have to be a natural person; it may be a corporation or other entity.

   c. **Articles of incorporation** must include the following:

      1) Corporation's name (must differ from the name of any corporation authorized to do business in the state)
      2) Number of authorized shares
      3) Name and street address of the corporation's registered agent
      4) Name and street address of each incorporator

   d. The articles also may contain **optional provisions** (e.g., purpose and powers of the corporation, internal management, or any subject required or allowed to be addressed in the bylaws).

   e. A corporation begins to exist when the articles are filed with the secretary of state or, in some states, from the issuance of a **certificate of incorporation**.

   f. After filing, the incorporators elect the members of the **initial board of directors** if they have not been named in the articles. The incorporators then resign.

   g. The board of directors holds an **organizational meeting** to take all steps needed to complete the organizational structure. The new board

      1) Adopts **bylaws** if they were not adopted by the incorporators.

         a) Bylaws govern the internal structure and operation of the corporation. They may contain any provision for managing the business as long as it does not conflict with the law or the articles.
         b) Initial bylaws are adopted by the incorporators or the board.

      2) Elects officers.
      3) Considers other transactions appropriate for furthering the business.

4. **Types of Corporations**

   a. **De jure corporation.** A corporation formed correctly in full compliance with all mandatory provisions of the incorporation statute.

   b. **De facto corporation.** A corporation formed not in full compliance with all mandatory provisions of the incorporation statute. To be recognized as a de facto corporation, the organization must show a good faith attempt to substantially comply with the incorporation statute and that it has been exercising corporate powers (e.g., holding meetings or transacting business in the corporate name).

   c. **Corporation by estoppel.** When a corporation is neither a de jure nor a de facto corporation, the law recognizes a corporation by estoppel to prevent (1) third parties from denying the existence of a corporation after having dealt with the organization as a corporation or (2) the organization from denying it is a corporation when it held itself out as a corporation and third parties reasonably relied on that representation to their detriment.

EXAMPLE

The XYZ Company, an organization that is neither a de jure nor a de facto corporation, holds itself out to the public as a corporation. XYZ purchases an airplane from Sky Corporation but fails to pay for it. When Sky sues XYZ for payment, XYZ is estopped from asserting as a defense that it is not a valid corporation.

Stop and review! You have completed the outline for this subunit. Study multiple-choice questions 1 through 3 beginning on page 448.

16.2 OPERATION, FINANCING, AND DISTRIBUTIONS

1. **Corporate Powers**

   a. A corporation may exercise the same powers as an individual to do all things necessary or convenient to carry out its business and affairs.

   b. A corporation may do any lawful act to further its business. For example, a corporation can

      1) Sue, be sued, and defend in the corporate name
      2) Acquire real or personal property
      3) Elect directors, appoint officers and agents, hire employees, and set compensation
      4) Engage in transactions involving interests in, or obligations of, another entity
      5) Make contracts, incur liabilities, or give security interests
      6) Be a partner, promoter, manager, or associate of another entity
      7) Lend money, invest funds, and hold collateral
      8) Dispose of all or part of its property by any proper means
      9) Make donations for public welfare, charitable, scientific, or educational purposes
      10) Pay pensions and establish profit-sharing and other benefit or incentive plans
      11) Acquire the corporation's own shares
      12) Be held liable for the actions of its employees

         a) Under the law of agency (**respondeat superior**, or "let the master answer"), a corporate principal may be liable for an agent's **torts** (civil wrongs not resulting from contracts) committed within the scope of employment.
         b) A corporation also may be liable for **crimes** involving (1) violations of statutes imposing strict liability or (2) actions of the board or executives.

   c. Under the doctrine of **ultra vires**, a corporation may not act beyond its implied or express powers. But generally, a corporate action may not be challenged on the ground that the corporation lacked power to act.

   d. **Express powers** are specifically granted by the articles of incorporation.

   e. **Implied powers** are not specifically mentioned in the articles of incorporation but are necessary and appropriate to carry out express powers.

2. **Piercing the Corporate Veil**

   a. Courts disregard the corporate form when it is used merely to (1) commit wrongdoing, (2) shield its shareholders from liability for fraud, or (3) otherwise circumvent the law. Shareholders then are personally liable for corporate acts.

   b. A court might disregard a corporate entity if it finds

      1) The shareholders have not conducted the business on a corporate basis, for example, if

         a) Assets of the corporation and the shareholder(s) are commingled,
         b) The corporation was established for a sham purpose, or
         c) Corporate formalities are ignored.

      2) Two or more entities are related corporations (such as a parent and its subsidiary or corporations that are under common control) and in practice do not maintain a sufficiently independent existence.

      3) A corporation is inadequately capitalized to carry on its intended business.

> ## EXAMPLE
>
> Jennifer organizes a corporation with capital of only $500, intending to buy goods (inventory) worth $1,000,000 on credit. Jennifer expects to pay for the goods from profits generated from sales. If the business is not successful, she expects not to be personally liable because the purchase was made in the corporation's name. Because the corporation is undercapitalized, creditors may be successful in piercing the corporate veil and Jennifer could be held personally liable for the debt.

3. **State Jurisdiction**

   a. A state may only exercise personal jurisdiction ("long-arm jurisdiction") over a foreign corporation that has minimum contacts with the state. **Minimum contacts** consist of activities that are not isolated and that

      1) Are purposefully directed toward the state, e.g., advertising on radio stations heard within the state and intended to generate product demand in the state, or

      2) Place a product in interstate commerce with an expectation or intent that it will ultimately be used in the state.

   b. A minimum contacts analysis is based on the expectation of fairness. A foreign corporation must have sufficient contact with the state to render it fair and reasonable for the foreign corporation to be sued within that state and subject to its laws.

> ## EXAMPLE
>
> A citizen of Florida was injured when a van operated by an employee of California Lawn Care, Inc., struck her in a crosswalk while she was vacationing in California. California Lawn Care's only business is providing landscape services in California. It has no contacts with Florida. California Lawn Care has no reasonable expectation of being, and would be surprised to be, forced to litigate in Florida. Florida may not exercise personal jurisdiction over California Lawn Care, consistent with federal due process requirements, because California Lawn Care does not have minimum contacts with the state of Florida.

4. **Financing**

   a. **Debt** financing increases the corporation's **risk** because it must be repaid at fixed times even if the corporation is not profitable (versus dividends on equity securities, which are discretionary). The following are advantages of debt:

      1) Debt usually provides no voting rights and does not dilute shareholder **control**.
      2) Upon liquidation, debt holders receive no more than their claims.
      3) Interest on debt is **tax deductible**. Dividends on equity securities are not.

   b. **Equity** financing in the form of voting shares (typically called common shares) transfers ownership interests to those who provide financing. But an equity interest does not confer title to any specific property of the corporation. Moreover, shareholders are **not** creditors but, rather, have a share of ownership in the corporation.

      1) During a bankruptcy or liquidation, creditors have **priority** to remaining corporate assets.

5. **Dividends and Other Distributions**

   a. The board has discretion to determine the time and amount of distributions. A distribution ordinarily is a transfer of money or other property (but not the corporation's own shares) to shareholders. A dividend is a distribution.

      1) Payments by an S corporation to shareholders are called distributions.
      2) Payments by a C corporation to shareholders are called dividends.

b.   Generally, two prerequisites are used to determine whether the board is likely to distribute dividends. First, the corporation should not be insolvent after the distribution. Profitability is **not** a legal condition of a distribution. However, a distribution is illegal if the corporation is insolvent or payment would cause insolvency. A dividend also is illegal if not paid from the funds **statutorily** designated to be available for payment. For example, a dividend is not permitted if

    1)   The corporation cannot pay its debts as they become due in the ordinary course of business.

    2)   Total assets are less than the sum of liabilities and liquidation preferences.

c.   Second, the board must authorize the distribution. **Directors** must declare a distribution by resolution. Directors who approve a distribution that violates a statute establishing minimum legal capital requirements have abused their discretion. They are jointly and severally liable to the corporation.

    1)   **Shareholders** generally must repay a distribution only if they knew it was illegal.

6.   **Types of Dividends**

a.   Dividends are returns on capital paid in cash, shares, share rights, or other property (a dividend in kind).

    1)   **Preferred shareholders** are entitled to a fixed amount that must be paid **before common shareholders** are paid.

        a)   If the preferred shares are **cumulative**, any dividends not paid in preceding years (dividends in arrears) are carried forward and must be paid before the common shareholders receive anything.

            i)   Undeclared cumulative dividends are dividends in arrears, not liabilities. They are disclosed in a note to the financial statements.

            ii)   Declared but unpaid dividends are recognized as liabilities.

        b)   **Participating** preferred shareholders receive a residual share of additional dividends after fixed amounts have been paid to common and preferred shareholders.

    2)   **Liquidating dividends** are a return of, not a return on, a shareholder's capital.

b.   **Stock (share) dividends** are payable in the shares of the corporation as a percentage of the shares outstanding. The corporation generally issues new shares for this purpose.

    1)   Stock dividends do not increase the equity of each shareholder because they are distributed in proportion to the shares already owned.

    2)   When a stock dividend is declared, the corporation transfers the legally required amount from earned surplus (retained earnings) to stated capital (common stock). Total equity is not changed. Generally, a stock dividend is in lieu of a cash dividend.

    3)   A stock dividend is **not** a distribution.

c.   **Stock (share) split** is an issuance of shares to reduce the unit value of each share. A stock split does not increase a shareholder's proportionate ownership. It merely increases the number of shares outstanding.

    1)   A stock split is **not** a distribution. It is used to decrease the value of each share for purchasability.

Stop and review! You have completed the outline for this subunit. Study multiple-choice questions 4 through 7 beginning on page 449.

16.3 SHAREHOLDERS' RIGHTS

1. **Shareholders**

   a. A shareholder is an owner but has no direct rights, for example, to manage the corporation.

   b. The shareholders' primary participation is by **meeting annually and electing directors**. Directors are elected by a **plurality** of the votes (the most votes, not a majority) cast by the shares entitled to vote at a meeting at which a quorum is present. A quorum is the minimum number of shareholders necessary to conduct the meeting.

      1) Shareholders must approve **fundamental corporate changes**, including

         a) Mergers and share exchanges other than short-form mergers. (Short-form mergers are described in Subunit 16.5.)

         b) A sale of or a disposition of substantially all assets that leave the corporation with **no significant continuing business activity**.

         c) Dissolutions.

      2) Shareholders may amend or repeal the articles of incorporation and the **bylaws**.

   c. A shareholder has no right to receive dividends unless they have been declared.

   d. Shareholders ordinarily have no right to elect officers.

2. **Voting Rights**

   a. The **articles** may establish the voting rights per share. A **supermajority** may be required for any action subject to a shareholder vote to protect minority shareholders.

      1) Usually, each shareholder is entitled to one vote per share owned for each new director to be elected.

   b. To alter the sometimes harsh effect of straight voting, some states permit **cumulative voting**. Cumulative voting enables minority shareholders to obtain representation on the board in proportion to the number of shares they own.

      1) Under cumulative voting, a shareholder may allocate to any one or more candidates the following number of votes:

Number of Directors to Be Elected	×	Number of Votes to Which Shareholder is Entitled

---

EXAMPLE

Y Corporation is electing five directors to its board. Mary, a shareholder owning 200 of the 1,000 voting shares, can elect at least one director under cumulative voting.

- Five directors to be elected × 200 voting shares = 1,000.
- Mary casts all 1,000 of her votes for the one director of her choice instead of splitting her vote among all five directorships.
- No matter how the other 4,000 votes [5 × (1,000 − 200)] are allocated, the total cast for Mary's candidate must be at least the fifth highest.

3. **Preemptive Rights**

   a. These are important to owners of a closely held corporation. They give a shareholder an option to subscribe to a new issuance of shares in proportion to their current interest in the corporation. Thus, they limit dilution of equity.

   b. Preemptive rights do **not** exist unless they are specifically reserved in the articles.

   c. Preemptive rights do **not** apply to shares issued

      1) As an incentive to officers, directors, or employees;
      2) In satisfaction of conversion or option rights;
      3) For something other than money; or
      4) Within 6 months of incorporation if the shares were authorized in the articles.

4. **Inspection Rights**

   a. Shareholders and their agents have a fundamental **right** to a reasonable inspection of books and records of the corporation. This right cannot be limited by the articles or bylaws.

   b. Inspection must be at the corporation's principal office during regular business hours. The shareholders must give 5 business days' written notice that states the purpose of the demand and the records to be inspected.

   c. Inspection must be in good faith and for a **proper purpose**, involving, for example,

      1) Corporate financial condition,
      2) The propriety of dividends,
      3) Mismanagement of the corporation,
      4) The names and addresses of other shareholders,
      5) Election of directors, or
      6) A shareholder suit.

   d. An **improper purpose** is one that does not relate to the shareholder's interest in the corporation, e.g., to benefit a personal business. Improper purposes include

      1) Harassment of management,
      2) Discovery of trade secrets,
      3) Gaining a competitive advantage for another company, and
      4) Development of a mailing list for sale or similar use.

   e. Courts have permitted a shareholder to obtain a copy of a shareholder list, even when the only purpose was to engage in a takeover battle.

   f. Shareholders have an unconditional right to inspect certain records, such as the articles, bylaws, minutes of shareholder meetings, and the annual report.

5. **Dissenters' (Appraisal) Rights**

   a. Shareholders who disagree with fundamental corporate changes may be paid the **fair value** of their shares in cash.

   b. Before the vote, a shareholder asserting dissenters' (appraisal) rights must make a **written demand** that the corporation purchase his or her stock if the action is approved.

c. Dissenters' rights arise from the following:

1) A disposition of assets that leaves the corporation without a significant continuing business activity.

2) Certain mergers and share exchanges. Shareholder awareness of dissenters' rights is especially important in a **short-form merger** because notice of the merger is not required to be given to shareholders of the parent.

3) Any other action taken by shareholder vote to the extent such a right is provided in the articles, bylaws, or a board resolution.

4) An amendment to the articles that **materially and adversely** affects shareholder rights.

d. Under federal securities law, a dissident shareholder may require the corporation to provide a list of shareholders. The dissident may then mail proxy materials to those shareholders if (s)he pays the cost of the mailing.

6. **Shareholder Suits**

a. **Direct suits** by shareholders are lawsuits filed on their own behalf, either individually or as members of a class.

1) For example, an individual shareholder may sue a corporation to

a) Require payment of properly declared dividends,
b) Recover improper dividends,
c) Obtain a remedy for management's breach of duty, or
d) Compel dissolution.

2) A shareholder also may enforce his or her preemptive, inspection, voting, or other rights.

b. A **shareholder derivative suit** is to recover for wrongs done to the corporation. The action is for the benefit of the corporation, and any recovery belongs to it, not to the shareholder. The corporation is the true plaintiff. An example is a suit to recover damages from management for an **ultra vires** act (actions outside the corporation's authority).

1) In order to bring a shareholder derivative action, a shareholder must first demand that the corporation bring suit unless it is obvious the demand is futile, e.g., when the action is against the directors.

a) A shareholder cannot file a derivative suit until 90 days after the demand (unless notice of rejection has been given or irreparable harm will be done to the corporation).

2) Most states require that the shareholder prove the following:

a) (S)he owned shares at the time of wrongdoing.
b) A written demand was made on the directors.
c) The directors refused to sue.
d) The refusal was in bad faith.

Stop and review! You have completed the outline for this subunit. Study multiple-choice questions 8 through 11 beginning on page 450.

16.4 DIRECTORS AND OFFICERS: AUTHORITY, DUTIES, AND LIABILITY

1. **Composition of the Board**

   a. Each state has a specific requirement with respect to the **number of directors** elected to sit on the board. Many states require a minimum of three. Under the RMBCA, a minimum of one director is required. However, the RMBCA also permits a corporation to dispense with a board by unanimous shareholder agreement.

EXAMPLE

X Corp. has only one shareholder. It is incorporated in a state that requires at least three directors, unless the entity has fewer than three shareholders, in which case the number of directors may equal the number of shareholders. X Corp. is permitted by statute to have one director.

---

   b. A director generally does **not** need to be a shareholder, a resident of the state of incorporation, or meet an age requirement.

   c. The **initial board** is usually appointed by the incorporators or named in the articles, and this board serves until the first meeting of the shareholders.

   d. In most states, shareholders have a right to remove, **with or without cause**, any director or the entire board by a majority vote.

   e. Vacancies resulting from the death, removal, or resignation of directors may be filled by the remaining directors until the next shareholders' meeting.

      1) Directors also may fill positions created by amendment of the bylaws or articles.

2. **Authority of the Board**

   a. Directors formulate overall policy for the corporation, but they are **neither trustees nor agents** of the corporation. A director **cannot** act individually to bind the corporation.

   b. The board establishes and implements corporate policy, including the following:

      1) Selection and removal of officers
      2) Decisions about capital structure, including new issues of shares and their price
      3) Adding, amending, or repealing bylaws (unless shareholders have this power)
      4) Initiation of fundamental changes
      5) Dividends, including whether and when to declare them
      6) Setting of management compensation (including directors)

3. **Directors' Fiduciary Duty**

   a. Directors owe a **fiduciary duty** to the corporation to (1) act in its best interests, (2) be loyal, (3) use due diligence in discharging responsibilities, (4) be informed about information relevant to the corporation, and (5) disclose conflicts of interest. **Controlling or majority shareholders** owe similar duties.

      1) For example, courts often protect the interests of **minority shareholders** by

         a) Ordering the payment of dividends that were withheld in bad faith or

         b) Compelling a seller of a controlling block of shares to distribute ratably among all shareholders any **control premium** paid in excess of the fair value of the stock.

b. A **director's duty of care** is tested objectively.

    1) A director must discharge his or her duties

        a) In good faith,

        b) In a manner (s)he reasonably believes to be in the best interests of the corporation, and

        c) With the care that a person in a similar position would reasonably believe appropriate under similar circumstances.

    2) **Reliance on others.** In exercising reasonable care, a director may rely on information, reports, opinions, and statements prepared or presented by persons (an appropriate officer, employee, or specialist) whom the director **reasonably believes** to be competent in the matters presented.

        a) A director also may rely on the specialized knowledge of lawyers, accountants, investment bankers, and board committees.

c. Directors owe a **duty of loyalty** to the corporation. For example, serving on the board of a competitor may violate this duty.

    1) **Conflicting-interest transactions.** To protect the corporation against self-dealing, a director is required to make **full disclosure** of any financial interest (s)he may have in any transaction to which both the director and the corporation may be a party. A director must not make a secret profit.

        a) A transaction is **not** improper merely on the grounds of a director's conflict of interest. If the transaction (1) is fair to the corporation or (2) has been approved by a majority of informed, disinterested directors or shareholders, it is not voidable and does not result in sanctions even if the director makes a profit.

            i) Under the Sarbanes-Oxley Act, an **issuer** (public company) generally may not make **personal loans** to its directors and officers.

    2) Directors may not usurp any **corporate opportunity**. A director must give the corporation the right of first refusal.

EXAMPLE

Skip, a director of The Fishing Corp., learns in his corporate capacity that a state-of-the-art, deep-sea hydroplane fishing vessel is available for a bargain price. The purchase of this unique hydroplane may be a business opportunity from which the corporation could benefit. If Skip purchases the hydroplane for himself without giving the corporation the right of first refusal, he is usurping a corporate opportunity.

---

4. **Officers**

a. Officers are elected or appointed by the **board**. Generally, officers manage the operations of the corporation. The board may not remove without cause an officer elected or employed by the shareholders.

b. Typically, statutes set a minimum number of officers, not a maximum. A corporation has the officers stated in the bylaws or appointed by the board. Officers need not be shareholders. One officer must be delegated responsibility for

    1) Preparing the minutes of directors' meetings.
    2) Authenticating records of the corporation.

c. The usual officers are a president, vice president, secretary, and treasurer. One person ordinarily may hold more than one office. Moreover, an officer may serve as a director.

    d.   Unlike directors, officers are **agents** of the corporation and manage the corporation.

        1)   Officers have **express authority** conferred by the bylaws or the board.

        2)   Officers have **implied authority** to do things that are reasonably necessary to accomplish their express duties.

        3)   Courts have held that official titles confer limited **inherent authority** on officers.

    e.   Officers, like directors, owe **fiduciary duties** to the corporation.

        1)   Officers are subject to the same duties of care and loyalty as directors.

        2)   According to the RMBCA, corporations may indemnify officers for liability incurred in a suit by shareholders, unless inconsistent with public policy, as provided by the articles, bylaws, board, or contract.

    f.   The SEC requires **issuers** to provide detailed disclosures about **executive compensation** paid to the CEO, CFO, and the next three highest-paid officers.

        1)   It also requires recognition of the **costs of equity awards** over the periods when employees must provide services.

5.   **Liability and the Business Judgment Rule**

    a.   Under the Business Judgment Rule, courts avoid substituting their business judgment for that of **officers or directors**.

        1)   The rule does **not** apply to acts of shareholders.

    b.   The rule protects an officer or a director from **personal liability** for honest errors of judgment if (s)he

        1)   Acted in good faith;

        2)   Was not motivated by fraud, conflict of interest, or illegality; and

        3)   Was not grossly negligent.

    c.   To avoid personal liability, directors and officers must

        1)   Make informed decisions (educate themselves about the issues),

        2)   Be free from conflicts of interest, and

        3)   Have a rational basis to support their position.

    d.   Most states permit corporations to **indemnify** directors and officers for expenses of litigation involving business judgments, subject to some exceptions.

        1)   The RMBCA permits the **articles** to limit the liability of directors to the corporation or shareholders. However, the limitation applies only to **money damages**. The articles may not limit liability for the wrongful acts of a director, such as

            a)   Intentional infliction of harm on the corporation

            b)   Intentional criminal conduct

            c)   Unlawful distributions

            d)   Receipt of financial benefits to which a director is not entitled

        2)   Usually, an officer or director who is liable to the corporation for **negligent** performance is not entitled to indemnification as a matter of public policy.

            a)   However, a **court** may order indemnification of an officer or director (even though found negligent) if the court determines (s)he is fairly and reasonably entitled to it in view of all the relevant circumstances.

Directors' and officers' fiduciary duty and the duties of care and loyalty owed to their corporations have been highly publicized because of the major scandals involving improper practices. You most likely will see questions covering these topics on your exam.

Stop and review! You have completed the outline for this subunit. Study multiple-choice questions 12 through 15 beginning on page 451.

16.5 MERGERS AND TERMINATION

1. **Mergers**

   a. A **merger** combines two or more corporations. One corporation is absorbed by the other and ceases to exist.

      1) The surviving corporation succeeds to the legal rights and duties, liabilities to creditors, and assets of the merged corporation.

      2) In contrast, a corporation can purchase solely the assets of a corporation and then it does not assume the corporation's liabilities.

   b. In a **consolidation**, a new corporation is formed, and the two or more consolidating corporations cease operating as separate entities. Otherwise, the requirements and effects of the combination are similar to those for a merger.

      1) The RMBCA does not mention consolidations because the continuance of one corporation generally is desirable.

   c. The shareholders of a merged corporation may receive shares or other securities issued by the surviving corporation.

      1) Shares of the merged (acquired) corporation are canceled.

   d. A merger requires the approval of (1) each board and (2) shareholders entitled to vote for each corporation. Approval is generally by a majority vote unless state law or the articles require a supermajority. After appropriate notice, shareholder approval must be given at a **special meeting**.

      1) Shareholders of each corporation must be provided a copy of the **plan of merger**.

      2) Shareholders of **each corporation** have appraisal rights.

      3) The sale of substantially all of the corporation's assets outside the regular course of business requires the approval of shareholders.

      4) Under the RMBCA, a corporation (the parent) that owns at least 90% of the shares of another (the subsidiary) may use a **short-form merger**. In a short-form merger,

         a) Approval by the parent's shareholders and the subsidiary's board is **not** required.

         b) The parent's shareholders do **not** have dissenters' rights.

         c) However, the subsidiary's shareholders must be given an appraisal remedy (payment of the fair value of shares + interest) and 10 days' notice.

   e. The purchase or lease of substantially all of the **assets** of another corporation or an acquisition of another corporation's **shares** that allows the acquirer a controlling interest does not imply a merger. Although the acquirer must prepare consolidated financial statements, the acquiree is legally a separate entity.

      1) These transactions are policy decisions that do **not** require shareholder approval.

      2) But if the corporation is selling or leasing substantially all of its assets and is **not** doing so in the regular course of the seller (lessor) corporation's business, its shareholders must approve. Also, the shareholders have dissenters' rights.

         a) A transfer of substantially all assets to a wholly owned subsidiary is an example of a transaction in the regular course of business.

2. **Compulsory Share Exchanges**

    a.   The RMBCA provisions for share exchanges are similar to those for mergers.

        1)   A share exchange occurs when one corporation acquires all of the shares of one or more classes or series of shares of another in exchange for shares, securities, cash, other property, etc.

        2)   A share exchange maintains the separate corporate existence of both entities.

        3)   Only the shareholders of the acquiree must approve, and they have **dissenters' rights**.

3. **Tender Offers**

    a.   An acquirer may bypass board approval of a business combination by extending a tender offer of cash or shares, usually at a higher-than-market price, directly to shareholders to purchase a certain number of the outstanding shares.

    b.   Managements of target corporations have implemented diverse strategies to counter hostile tender offers. The following are examples of antitakeover strategies:

        1)   **Issuing stock.** The target significantly increases its outstanding stock.

        2)   **Self-tender.** The target borrows to tender an offer to repurchase its shares.

        3)   **Legal action.** A target may challenge one or more aspects of a tender offer. A resulting delay increases costs for the raider and enables further defensive action.

4. **Dissolution**

    a.   A corporation that has issued stock and commenced business may be **voluntarily dissolved** by

        1)   Unanimous written consent of all shareholders or

        2)   Majority shareholder vote at a special meeting called for the purpose if the directors have adopted a resolution of dissolution. A majority of the shares entitled to vote must be represented at the special meeting.

    b.   The corporation files **articles of dissolution** with the secretary of state petitioning the state to dissolve the corporation. A dissolution is effective when filed.

    c.   The secretary of state may proceed administratively to dissolve **involuntarily** a corporation that fails to file its annual report, pay its franchise tax, or appoint or maintain a resident agent.

        1)   Written notice is sent to the corporation to correct the default.

    d.   Shareholders may seek a **judicial dissolution** when a deadlock of the board is harmful to the corporation, or the directors' actions are contrary to the best interests of the corporation.

Stop and review! You have completed the outline for this subunit. Study multiple-choice questions 16 through 19 beginning on page 452.

16.6 ADVANTAGES AND DISADVANTAGES OF CORPORATIONS

1. **Advantages**

    a. **Limited liability.** A shareholder owns a property interest in the underlying net assets of the corporation and is entitled to share in its profits. However, a shareholder's exposure to corporate liabilities is limited to his or her investment.

    b. **Separation of ownership from management.** Shareholders have no inherent right to participate in management. They elect a board of directors that sets policy and appoints officers to conduct operations. A shareholder may be an officer or a director.

    c. **Free transferability of interests.** Without contractual or legal restriction, shares may be freely transferred, e.g., by sale, gift, pledge, or inheritance.

        1) A shareholder has no interest in specific property. (S)he owns a proportional, intangible property interest in the entire corporation.

    d. **Perpetual life.** A corporation has perpetual existence unless the articles provide for a shorter life, or it is dissolved by the state. Death, withdrawal, or addition of a shareholder, director, or officer does not end its existence.

    e. **Ease of raising capital.** A corporation raises capital (to start or expand the business) by selling stock or issuing bonds.

    f. **Constitutional rights.** A corporation is considered a **person** for most purposes under the **U.S. Constitution**. Thus, it has the right to equal protection, due process, freedom from unreasonable searches and seizures, and freedom of speech. It also has the right to make nearly unlimited contributions of money for political purposes.

        1) However, commercial speech (e.g., advertising) is given less protection than that provided to the same speech by natural persons.

        2) Moreover, a corporation does **not** have a Fifth Amendment right against **self-incrimination** in criminal cases.

    g. **Transfers of property to a controlled corporation.** A transfer of assets for shares of any corporation is **tax-free** if the transferors are in control of the corporation immediately after the exchange. A person who transfers appreciated property receives the benefit if another transferor transfers property and together they meet the control test. Property includes money.

        1) **Control** is ownership of stock with at least 80% of the

            a) Total combined voting power of all classes of stock entitled to vote and
            b) Total number of shares of all other classes of stock of the corporation.

2. **Disadvantages**

    a. Reduced individual control of a business operated by managers, not owners

    b. Payment of taxes on corporate income and payment by the shareholders of taxes on distributions received from the corporation (unless the entity qualifies for and elects S corporation status)

    c. Substantial costs of meeting the requirements of corporate formation and operation

    d. Becoming subject to state and federal regulation of securities transactions through reporting and registration requirements

    e. Hostile takeover of a publicly traded corporation

    f. Sale or other transfer of unrestricted shares in a close corporation to parties not chosen by all or a majority of current owners

    g. An inability of a minority shareholder in a close corporation to liquidate his or her interest or to influence the conduct of the business

3.   **Summary of Corporate Entities**

	Formation	Capitalization	Operation	Liability	Transferability	Taxation	Termination
S corporation	Formalities. Files articles of incorporation with state. Elects S corporation status.	Members and shareholders (number of shareholders may not exceed 100).	Shareholder-elected board appoints officers to manage daily operations.	Shareholders generally are liable only to the extent of their investment.	Shareholders generally may transfer their interests to qualifying shareholders.	Flow through taxation on a per-day and per-share basis.	If entity ceases to qualify as an S corporation, it becomes a C corporation.
Corporation	Formalities. Files articles of incorporation with state.	May sell common and preferred stock. May issue debt.	Shareholder-elected board appoints officers to manage daily operations.	Shareholders generally are liable only to the extent of their investment.	Shareholders generally are free to transfer their interests.	Income taxed at corporate level. Shareholders pay tax on dividends received.	Perpetual existence. A shareholder's death, bankruptcy, or withdrawal does not terminate corporation.

Stop and review! You have completed the outline for this subunit. Study multiple-choice question 20 on page 454.

QUESTIONS

16.1 Formation

1. Which of the following statements is true with respect to the general structure of a corporation?

A. The corporation is treated as a legal person with rights and obligations jointly shared with its owners and managers.

B. Shareholders establish corporate policies and elect or appoint corporate officers.

C. A corporation is governed by shareholders who elect a board of directors and approve fundamental changes in its structure.

D. The board of directors is responsible for carrying out the corporate policies in the day-to-day management of the organizations.

Answer (C) is correct.
   REQUIRED: The general structure of a corporation.
   DISCUSSION: A corporation is an entity formed under state law that is treated as a legal person with rights and obligations separate from its owners. Shareholders hold the voting power of a corporation. This power gives them the ability to elect a board of directors and to approve fundamental changes in the corporate structure. Thus, the shareholders have the power to govern the corporation.
   Answer (A) is incorrect. A corporation is a legal entity with rights and obligations separate from its owners and managers. Answer (B) is incorrect. Directors establish corporate policies and elect or appoint corporate officers, not shareholders. Answer (D) is incorrect. Corporate officers are responsible for the day-to-day management of the organization.

2. Case Corp. is incorporated in State A. Under the Revised Model Business Corporation Act, which of the following activities engaged in by Case requires that Case obtain a certificate of authority to do business in State B?

A. Maintaining bank accounts in State B.

B. Collecting corporate debts in State B.

C. Hiring employees who are residents of State B.

D. Maintaining an office in State B to conduct intrastate business.

Answer (D) is correct.
   REQUIRED: The interstate business activity that requires a certificate of authority.
   DISCUSSION: A state may exercise authority over a foreign corporation if the corporation has at least minimum contacts with the state. The minimum contacts consist of activities that (1) are not isolated and (2) either are purposefully directed toward the state or place a product in the stream of interstate commerce with an expectation or intent that it will be used in the state. Maintaining an office in State B to conduct intrastate business creates minimum contacts with State B under this test.
   Answer (A) is incorrect. Maintaining bank accounts in State B is an isolated activity that does not meet the minimum contacts test. Answer (B) is incorrect. The collection of debts in State B does not by itself constitute minimum contacts in State B. For example, the debts may not have arisen from activities that involved State B. Answer (C) is incorrect. Hiring employees who reside in State B is not an activity that is purposefully directed toward the state or that places a product in interstate commerce with the expectation or intent that it will be used in the state.

3. Boyle, as a promoter of Delaney Corp., signed a 9-month contract with Austin, a CPA. Prior to the incorporation, Austin rendered accounting services pursuant to the contract. After rendering accounting services for an additional period of 6 months pursuant to the contract, Austin was discharged without cause by the board of directors of Delaney. Absent agreements to the contrary, who will be liable to Austin for breach of contract?

A. Both Boyle and Delaney.

B. Boyle only.

C. Delaney only.

D. Neither Boyle nor Delaney.

Answer (A) is correct.

REQUIRED: The liability of a corporation and a promoter on a preincorporation agreement.

DISCUSSION: A promoter who contracts for a nonexistent corporation is personally liable on such contracts. Delaney is also liable because it impliedly adopted the contract by accepting Austin's performance.

Answer (B) is incorrect. The corporation impliedly adopted the contract by accepting its benefits. Answer (C) is incorrect. A promoter is generally liable on preincorporation contracts. Answer (D) is incorrect. Boyle was not released and a novation did not occur. Delaney adopted the contract by implication.

16.2 Operation, Financing, and Distributions

4. Which of the following acts is most likely to cause a court to pierce the corporate veil?

A. Failure to designate a registered agent in the articles of incorporation (Charter).

B. Retention of excess capital.

C. Failure to conduct a significant portion of business in the chartering state.

D. Using corporate assets for the owner's personal purposes.

Answer (D) is correct.

REQUIRED: The act most likely to cause a court to pierce the corporate veil.

DISCUSSION: Typically, the corporate veil is pierced when a court finds that the corporation is merely the alter ego of a shareholder, for example, when (1) it is undercapitalized, (2) the assets of the corporation and the shareholders are commingled, (3) corporate formalities are ignored, or (4) the corporation is established for a sham purpose.

Answer (A) is incorrect. Failure to designate a registered agent in the articles of incorporation (Charter) while otherwise complying with the formalities of incorporation results in a de facto corporation. Answer (B) is incorrect. Thin capitalization is a basis for piercing the veil. Answer (C) is incorrect. The portion of business conducted in a state does not affect the validity of incorporation.

5. Which of the following statements is correct regarding both debt and common shares of a corporation?

A. Common shares represent an ownership interest in the corporation, but debt holders do not have an ownership interest.

B. Common shareholders and debt holders have an ownership interest in the corporation.

C. Common shares typically have a fixed maturity date, but debt does not.

D. Common shares have a higher priority on liquidation than debt.

Answer (A) is correct.

REQUIRED: The true statement about debt and common shares.

DISCUSSION: Common shares are equity securities. Thus, they are ownership interests. In contrast, debt holders do not have ownership interests. Rather, debt holders have claims on the corporation's assets. In the event of a liquidation, the debt holders' claims must be satisfied before any distribution to common shareholders.

Answer (B) is incorrect. Debt holders do not have an ownership interest in the corporation. Answer (C) is incorrect. Debt securities typically have a fixed maturity date, but common shares do not. Answer (D) is incorrect. In the event of bankruptcy or liquidation, creditors, including bondholders, have first claim on corporate assets.

6. Under modern statutes, the two general prerequisites to the declaration of a dividend are

I. Corporate solvency.

II. A resolution by the directors to declare a dividend.

A. I only.

B. II only.

C. Both I and II.

D. Neither I nor II.

Answer (C) is correct.

REQUIRED: The general prerequisites to the declaration of a dividend.

DISCUSSION: The board has discretion to determine the time and amount of dividends and other distributions. However, two general prerequisites are used to determine whether the board is likely to distribute dividends. Those prerequisites are corporate profitability or solvency and a resolution by the directors to declare a dividend.

7. Which of the following statements is correct regarding the declaration of a stock dividend by a corporation having only one class of par value stock?

    A. A stock dividend has the same legal and practical significance as a stock split.

    B. A stock dividend increases a stockholder's proportionate share of corporate ownership.

    C. A stock dividend causes a decrease in the assets of the corporation.

    D. A stock dividend is a corporation's ratable distribution of additional shares of stock to its stockholders.

Answer (D) is correct.
    REQUIRED: The true statement about the declaration of a stock dividend.
    DISCUSSION: A stock dividend is payable in the stock of the dividend-paying corporation. New stock generally is issued for this purpose. A shareholder's equity in the corporation is not increased because a stock dividend does not increase the recipient's proportional ownership.
    Answer (A) is incorrect. The practical significance of a stock split is to reduce the unit value of each share. Answer (B) is incorrect. A stock dividend is distributed in proportion to shares already owned and has no effect on a shareholder's equity. Answer (C) is incorrect. A stock dividend causes a transfer from retained earnings to stated capital, not from an asset account to stated capital.

16.3 Shareholders' Rights

8. All of the following are legal rights of shareholders in U.S. publicly traded companies **except** the right to

    A. Vote on major mergers and acquisitions.

    B. Receive dividends if declared.

    C. Vote on charter and bylaw changes.

    D. Vote on major management changes.

Answer (D) is correct.
    REQUIRED: The item not a basic legal right of shareholders in publicly traded corporations.
    DISCUSSION: A corporation is owned by shareholders who elect a board of directors to manage the company. The board of directors then hires managers to supervise operations. Shareholders do not vote on major management changes because the powers of the board include selection and removal of officers and the setting of management compensation. Shareholders do have the right to vote on fundamental corporate changes, e.g., mergers and acquisitions, any changes in the corporate charter (the articles of incorporation) and bylaws, and dissolution.
    Answer (A) is incorrect. Shareholders in publicly traded U.S. corporations have the right to vote on fundamental corporate changes. Answer (B) is incorrect. Shareholders have the right to receive declared dividends. Answer (C) is incorrect. Shareholders have the right to vote on charter and bylaw changes.

9. A shareholder's fundamental right to inspect books and records of a corporation will be properly denied if the purpose of the inspection is to

    A. Commence a shareholder's derivative suit.

    B. Obtain shareholder names for a retail mailing list.

    C. Solicit shareholders to vote for a change in the board of directors.

    D. Investigate possible management misconduct.

Answer (B) is correct.
    REQUIRED: The improper purpose of shareholder inspection of corporate books and records.
    DISCUSSION: The fundamental right of a shareholder to inspect the corporation's books and records may be exercised only in good faith for a proper purpose. A proper purpose relates to the shareholder's interest in the corporation, not his or her personal interests, and is not contrary to the corporation's interests. Obtaining a shareholder mailing list is not in itself improper unless it is to further the shareholder's personal interests.

10. A corporate shareholder is entitled to which of the following rights?

    A. Elect officers.

    B. Receive annual dividends.

    C. Approve dissolution.

    D. Prevent corporate borrowing.

Answer (C) is correct.
    REQUIRED: The right of a shareholder.
    DISCUSSION: Shareholders do not have the right to manage the corporation or its business. Shareholder participation in policy and management is through exercising the right to elect directors. Shareholders also have the right to approve charter amendments, disposition of all or substantially all of the corporation's assets, mergers and consolidations, and dissolutions.
    Answer (A) is incorrect. The board elects officers. Answer (B) is incorrect. A shareholder does not have a general right to receive dividends. The board determines dividend policy. Answer (D) is incorrect. Determining capital structure and whether the corporation should borrow are policy and management determinations to be made according to the board's business judgment.

11. Hughes and Brody start a business as a close corporation. Hughes owns 51 of the 100 shares of stock issued by the firm and Brody owns 49. One year later, the corporation decides to sell another 200 shares. Which of the following types of rights would give Hughes and Brody a preference over other purchasers to buy shares to maintain control of the firm?

- A. Shareholder derivative rights.
- B. Preemptive rights.
- C. Cumulative voting rights.
- D. Inspection rights.

Answer (B) is correct.

REQUIRED: The right providing a purchase preference.

DISCUSSION: Preemptive rights are important to owners of a close corporation. They are options to subscribe to a new issuance in proportion to the shareholder's current interest. Thus, they limit dilution of equity.

Answer (A) is incorrect. A shareholder may file a derivative suit to recover for wrongs done to the corporation. The action is for the benefit of the corporation. It is the true plaintiff. Answer (C) is incorrect. Cumulative voting entitles shareholders either to give one candidate as many votes as the number of directors to be elected, multiplied by the number of shares owned, or to distribute that number of votes among as many candidates as (s)he wishes. Answer (D) is incorrect. Shareholders have a fundamental right to inspect the corporation's books and records.

16.4 Directors and Officers: Authority, Duties, and Liability

12. Which of the following corporate actions is subject to shareholder approval?

- A. Election of officers.
- B. Removal of officers.
- C. Declaration of cash dividends.
- D. Removal of directors.

Answer (D) is correct.

REQUIRED: The action that must be approved by the shareholders.

DISCUSSION: A corporation is governed by shareholders (owners) who elect the directors on the corporation's board and who approve fundamental changes in the corporate structure. Directors establish corporate policies and elect or appoint corporate officers who carry out the policies in the day-to-day management of the organization. In most states, the shareholders may by a majority vote remove, with or without cause, any director or the entire board.

Answer (A) is incorrect. The officers are elected by the directors. Answer (B) is incorrect. Officers are removed by the directors. Answer (C) is incorrect. The board of directors has the discretion to determine the nature, time, and amount of dividends and other distributions.

13. Seymore was recently invited to become a director of Buckley Industries, Inc. If Seymore accepts and becomes a director, Seymore, along with the other directors, will **not** be personally liable for

- A. Lack of reasonable care.
- B. Honest errors of judgment.
- C. Declaration of a dividend that the directors know will impair legal capital.
- D. Diversion of corporate opportunities to themselves.

Answer (B) is correct.

REQUIRED: The action for which a director is not personally liable.

DISCUSSION: The directors of a corporation owe a fiduciary duty to the corporation and the shareholders. They also are expected to exercise reasonable business judgment. The law does recognize human fallibility and allows for directors to be safe from liability for honest errors of judgment.

Answer (A) is incorrect. Directors must discharge their duties with the care that a person in a similar position would reasonably believe appropriate under similar circumstances. Answer (C) is incorrect. Directors are prohibited from declaring dividends that would violate a state statute establishing a minimum legal capital. Answer (D) is incorrect. Directors may not usurp any corporate opportunity presented to them in their capacity as directors. The corporation must be given the right of first refusal.

14. Knox, president of Quick Corp., contracted with Tine Office Supplies, Inc., to supply Quick's stationery on customary terms and at a cost less than that charged by any other supplier. Knox later informed Quick's board of directors that Knox was a majority shareholder in Tine. Quick's contract with Tine is

A. Void because of Knox's self-dealing.

B. Void because the disclosure was made after execution of the contract.

C. Valid because of Knox's full disclosure.

D. Valid because the contract is fair to Quick.

Answer (D) is correct.

REQUIRED: The enforceability of a contract entered into by a corporate officer with an interest in the contract.

DISCUSSION: An officer, like a director, owes fiduciary duties of care and loyalty to the corporation and its shareholders. Knox was required to disclose fully the financial interest in the transaction to which the corporation was a party. But a transaction approved by a majority of informed, disinterested directors or shareholders or that is fair to the corporation is valid, regardless of a conflict of interest. Because Tine offers inventory at a cost lower than those charged by other suppliers, the contract is considered fair and valid.

Answer (A) is incorrect. A conflict of interest does not render a transaction voidable if it is fair to the corporation. Answer (B) is incorrect. Nondisclosure does not render a transaction voidable if it is fair to the corporation. Answer (C) is incorrect. Full disclosure merely forms a basis for approval by a majority of informed, disinterested directors or shareholders.

15. Under the Revised Model Business Corporation Act (RMBCA), which of the following statements is true regarding corporate officers of a public corporation?

A. An officer may not simultaneously serve as a director.

B. A corporation may be authorized to indemnify its officers for liability incurred in a suit by shareholders.

C. Shareholders always have the right to elect a corporation's officers.

D. An officer of a corporation is required to own at least one share of the corporation's stock.

Answer (B) is correct.

REQUIRED: The true statement about corporate officers of a public corporation.

DISCUSSION: According to the RMBCA, corporations may indemnify their officers for liability incurred in a suit by shareholders, except when inconsistent with public policy, to the extent provided by the articles of incorporation, bylaws, actions of the board, or contract.

Answer (A) is incorrect. An individual may serve as both a director and an officer. Answer (C) is incorrect. A corporation's officers are appointed by the board of directors, not by shareholders. Answer (D) is incorrect. An officer of a corporation need not be a shareholder.

16.5 Mergers and Termination

16. Generally, a merger of two corporations requires

A. That a special meeting notice and a copy of the merger plan be given to all shareholders of both corporations.

B. Unanimous approval of the merger plan by the shareholders of both corporations.

C. Unanimous approval of the merger plan by the boards of both corporations.

D. That all liabilities owed by the absorbed corporation be paid before the merger.

Answer (A) is correct.

REQUIRED: The prerequisite to a merger.

DISCUSSION: A corporation is merged into another when shareholders of the target corporation receive cash or shares of the surviving corporation in exchange for their target corporation shares. The target shares are canceled, and it ceases to exist. State law generally requires approval by a majority of the board and of shares of each corporation. A special shareholder meeting notice (purpose is stated) and a copy of the merger plan must be provided to shareholders of each corporation to enable informed voting.

Answer (B) is incorrect. Unless a state statute or the charter imposes a supermajority requirement, majority approval is generally required. Answer (C) is incorrect. Unless a state statute or the charter imposes a supermajority requirement, majority approval is generally required. Answer (D) is incorrect. Rights and liabilities of the absorbed company generally become those of the surviving corporation.

17. Acorn Corp. wants to acquire the entire business of Trend Corp. Which of the following methods of business combination will best satisfy Acorn's objectives without requiring the approval of the shareholders of either corporation?

- A. A merger of Trend into Acorn, whereby Trend shareholders receive cash or Acorn shares.

- B. A sale of all the assets of Trend, outside the regular course of business, to Acorn, for cash.

- C. An acquisition of all the shares of Trend through a compulsory share exchange for Acorn shares.

- D. A cash tender offer, whereby Acorn acquires at least 90% of Trend's shares, followed by a short-form merger of Trend into Acorn.

Answer (D) is correct.

REQUIRED: The acquisition method that does not require shareholder approval.

DISCUSSION: A merger, consolidation, or purchase of substantially all of a corporation's assets requires approval of the board of directors of the corporation whose shares or assets are acquired. An acquiring corporation may bypass shareholder approval by using a short-form merger. No shareholder approval is required if a corporation that owns at least 90% of a subsidiary merges with the subsidiary using a short-form merger.

Answer (A) is incorrect. A merger requires the approval of shareholders. Answer (B) is incorrect. A sale of all assets outside the regular course of business requires the approval of shareholders. Answer (C) is incorrect. A compulsory share exchange requires the approval of shareholders.

18. Which of the following actions may be taken by a corporation's board of directors without shareholder approval?

- A. Purchasing substantially all of the assets of another corporation.

- B. Selling substantially all of the corporation's assets not in the regular course of business.

- C. Dissolving the corporation.

- D. Amending the articles of incorporation.

Answer (A) is correct.

REQUIRED: The action by a corporation's board not requiring shareholder approval.

DISCUSSION: The board of directors directly controls a corporation by establishing overall corporate policy and overseeing its implementation. In exercising their powers, directors must maintain high standards of care and loyalty but need not obtain shareholder approval except for fundamental corporate changes. Purchasing substantially all of the assets (or stock) of another corporation is a policy decision properly made by the directors, not a fundamental change. It does not require shareholder approval in the absence of a bylaw or special provision in the articles of incorporation.

Answer (B) is incorrect. Selling substantially all of the corporation's assets not in the regular course of business is a transfer that must be approved by the shareholders. Answer (C) is incorrect. Dissolving the corporation must be approved by the shareholders. Answer (D) is incorrect. Amending the articles of incorporation ordinarily must be approved by the shareholders.

19. Which of the following must take place before a corporation may be voluntarily dissolved?

- A. Passage by the board of directors of a resolution to dissolve.

- B. Approval by the officers of a resolution to dissolve.

- C. Amendment of the certificate of incorporation.

- D. Unanimous vote of the shareholders.

Answer (A) is correct.

REQUIRED: The act usually a precondition to voluntary dissolution.

DISCUSSION: If a corporation has issued stock and commenced business, its voluntary dissolution requires board approval of a dissolution resolution, shareholder vote of approval, and filing of articles of dissolution with the secretary of state. This filing serves to dissolve the corporation on its effective date. Voluntary dissolution without a board resolution is permitted upon unanimous written consent of the shareholders.

Answer (B) is incorrect. A corporation may voluntarily dissolve without approval by its officers. Answer (C) is incorrect. Filing articles of dissolution, not an amendment of the charter, is required. Answer (D) is incorrect. A majority of shares is usually sufficient to approve a board-approved dissolution resolution.

16.6 Advantages and Disadvantages of Corporations

20. Which of the following statements best describes an advantage of the corporate form of doing business?

A. Day-to-day management is strictly the responsibility of the directors.

B. Ownership is contractually restricted and is not transferable.

C. The operation of the business may continue indefinitely.

D. The business is free from state regulation.

Answer (C) is correct.
   REQUIRED: The advantage of the corporate form.
   DISCUSSION: A corporation has perpetual existence unless it is given a shorter life under the articles of incorporation or is dissolved by the state. Death, withdrawal, or addition of a shareholder, director, or officer does not terminate its existence.
   Answer (A) is incorrect. Officers run day-to-day operations. Answer (B) is incorrect. Absent a specific contractual restriction, shares are freely transferable, e.g., by gift, sale, pledge, or inheritance. Answer (D) is incorrect. A corporation can be created only under state law.

Online is better! To best prepare for the CPA exam, access **thousands** of exam-emulating MCQs and TBSs through Gleim CPA Review online courses with SmartAdapt technology. Learn more at www.gleimcpa.com or contact our team at 800.874.5346 to upgrade.

STUDY UNIT SEVENTEEN
CONTRACTS

(24 pages of outline)

This study unit covers the general concepts of contract law, and Study Unit 19 applies specifically to contracts for sales of goods. A contract is formed when its elements (mutual assent, consideration, capacity, and legality) are present. But a writing is not required to form a contract; a contract can be oral. If a valid, enforceable contract is formed, the law provides remedies if an obligation under the contract is breached. The law applies an objective standard (called a reasonable person standard) to determine whether a contract was formed or breached.

17.1 CLASSIFICATION OF CONTRACTS

1. **Express and Implied Contracts**

    a. The terms of an **express contract** are stated, either in writing or orally.

    b. The terms of an **implied contract** are wholly or partially inferred from conduct and circumstances but not from written or spoken words.

    1) A contract is **implied in fact** when the facts indicate a contract was formed.

EXAMPLE

Kelly makes an appointment with a hairdresser. Kelly keeps the appointment and permits the hairdresser to cut her hair. Kelly has promised through her actions to pay for the haircut. A court will infer from Kelly's conduct that an implied contract was formed and a duty to pay was understood and agreed to.

---

2. **Unilateral and Bilateral Contracts**

    a. In a **unilateral contract**, only one party makes a promise. The other party is an actor, not a promisor. If (s)he performs a defined action (an acceptance), the promisor is obligated to keep the promise.

EXAMPLE

Amy tells Bill, "I'll pay you $10 to polish my car." This offer is for a unilateral contract. Amy (the promisor) expects Bill (the actor) to accept by the act of polishing her car, not by making a return promise.

---

    b. In a **bilateral contract**, both parties make promises.

EXAMPLE

Amanda tells Bob that she will provide him lodging in September if he agrees to pay her $200. This is an offer for a bilateral contract. If Bob accepts and promises to pay the $200, a bilateral contract is formed.

3. **Executory and Executed Contracts**

a. An **executory contract** is a contract that is not yet fully performed. If any duty remains to be performed under the contract, then the contract is considered executory.

EXAMPLE

Al says to Brian, "I'll pay you $10,000,000 to play football for me next season." Brian agrees, creating an executory bilateral contract. It is executory because neither party has yet performed.

If Al pays Brian the $10,000,000 and Brian refuses to play, the contract is partially executed.

---

b. An **executed contract** has been fully performed by all parties.

EXAMPLE

If Brian plays football for Al the entire season and Al pays Brian $10,000,000, the contract is fully executed.

---

4. **Other Classifications**

a. A **valid** contract has all the elements of a contract, and the law provides a remedy if breached. A valid contract is legally binding on both parties.

b. An **unenforceable** contract is a valid contract because it has all the elements of a contract; however, the law will not enforce the contract because it does not comply with another legal requirement.

EXAMPLE

Jane enters into an oral contract to sell land to Emily. To be enforceable, a contract for the sale of land must be in writing. Since the real estate contract was not written, it is not enforceable.

---

c. A party may choose to either enforce or nullify a **voidable** contract.

EXAMPLE

Adam was induced to enter into a contract by Ben's intentional deception (i.e., fraud). Adam can choose to either enforce the contract or void the contract since it was fraudulently induced. Adam can also collect damages against Ben for any loss sustained due to fraud.

---

d. A **void** contract is not binding and is considered **"void ab initio,"** which means it was void since its inception. A void contract cannot be ratified and enforced.

EXAMPLE

A contract requiring the commission of a crime is void. It is not recognizable as a contract, and there is no remedy provided by law to enforce it.

Stop and review! You have completed the outline for this subunit. Study multiple-choice questions 1 and 2 beginning on page 478.

17.2 MUTUAL ASSENT (OFFER AND ACCEPTANCE)

1. **Offer**

a. A contract is formed when a party accepts an offer.

   1) An offer is a statement or other communication by which the offeror grants the offeree the power to accept a condition and form a contract.

b. An offer must

   1) Be communicated to an offeree,

   2) Be in a communication authorized by the offeror,

3) **Indicate an objective intent** to enter into a contract as determined in accordance with a reasonable person standard, and

4) Be sufficiently definite and certain.

c. No specific manner of communication of the offer is required. An offer need not take any particular form. For example, **nonverbal** communication may be appropriate.

d. Invitations to negotiate and preliminary negotiations do not constitute an offer. Invitations to negotiate include phrases, such as, "Are you interested in. . ." or "I'll probably take. . ." They differ from the language of an offer, which indicates commitment and intent to contract.

1) Advertisements usually are **not** offers but invitations to submit offers.

a) However, an advertisement can constitute an offer if it uses clear, definite, and explicit language that leaves nothing open for negotiation.

e. Generally, a contract must be reasonably **definite** as to material terms and clearly state the rights and duties of the parties. Essential terms include

1) **Names** of the parties,
2) **Subject matter** involved,
3) **Price and quantity**, and
4) **Time and place** of performance.

f. If a term is missing, it can be implied by the court (with the exception of a quantity term, which must be supplied by the parties). The presumption is that the parties intended to include a reasonable term.

1) A quantity term is sufficiently definite if it is defined by the buyer's reasonable **requirements** or the seller's reasonable **output**.

a) The buyer or seller must act in good faith and not vary substantially from an estimated or normal quantity.

2) If a contract does not specify the time of performance, courts generally decide that performance within a reasonable time was intended.

3) The law has traditionally required definiteness regarding the price term in a contract and generally will not imply the price (e.g., a court will not imply the price of real estate).

g. **An option contract** results in an **irrevocable offer**.

1) The offeree exchanges something of value for the offeror's promise to hold the offer open for a specified period.

h. Under the UCC, a merchant's written, signed **firm offer** to sell goods that are to be held open for a stated or a reasonable period (not greater than 3 months) is irrevocable.

1) The firm offer rule applies to goods and does not apply to sales of services or real estate.

2. **Termination of Offer**

a. **Lapse of time.** An offer may be worded to terminate **after** a specified period or **on** a specified date. Unless otherwise terminated, the offer remains open for the specified time.

1) If no time is stated in the offer, the offer terminates after a reasonable period.

b. **Death or incompetence** of either the offeror or the offeree generally terminates the power of acceptance, whether or not the other party had notice.

1) Incompetence is a lack of legally required qualifications or physical or psychological fitness to bind oneself by contract.

2) Death or incompetence generally does not terminate an existing contract, including an offer in a valid option contract. The offeree has already given consideration.

    c.   **Destruction** or loss of the specific subject matter terminates an offer.

    d.   **Illegality** of a proposed contract or performance terminates the offer.

    e.   **Revocation.** The offeror may revoke an offer at any time prior to acceptance.

        1)   Revocation must be communicated to the offeree prior to the offeree's acceptance.

            a)   Revocation is **effective when received** by the offeree.

        2)   Notice may be communicated by any reasonable means, either directly or indirectly.

            a)   For example, an offeree may receive indirect notice of revocation by learning that the subject matter has been sold to another party.

            b)   The offeree's knowledge that a third party has offered to buy the subject matter of the offer is not a revocation.

        3)   An offer stating it will remain open may be terminated by giving the offeree notice that it has been revoked, unless it is an option contract or a firm offer under the UCC.

    f.   **Rejection** terminates the offer. It implies an intent not to accept the offer. It may be expressed or implied by words or conduct.

        1)   Rejection is **effective when received** by the offeror.

            a)   After rejection is effective, later attempted acceptance becomes a new offer.

        2)   A **counteroffer** is a simultaneous rejection of an offer and the creation of a new offer from the original offeree.

            a)   In contrast, a mere inquiry about the proposed terms of an offer is tentative and does not indicate intent to reject the offer.

EXAMPLE

The statement "Would you consider shipping by air instead of by truck?" is not a counteroffer. It indicates no intent to reject or accept the offer but seeks additional information.

---

   3.   **Acceptance**

    a.   The offeree has an exclusive power of acceptance, but neither the offeror nor the offeree is obligated until acceptance.

        1)   The offeror may expressly limit what constitutes acceptance.

    b.   An acceptance must relate to the terms of the offer and be positive, unequivocal, and unconditional. The acceptance may not vary the offer in any way.

        1)   This principle is the **mirror image rule**.

        2)   If a **conditional acceptance** requires the offeror's agreement to additional or different terms, it is a **counteroffer**, not an acceptance.

    c.   Acceptance **must be communicated** to the offeror by any words or actions that a reasonable person would understand as an acceptance.

        1)   A **unilateral** contract may be accepted by performance instead of a reciprocal promise.

        2)   Possession or control of something may be acceptance.

        3)   **Silence** is acceptance if an intent to accept may be inferred from the facts.

            a)   However, an offeror generally cannot require the offeree to respond to avoid being contractually bound.

d. If an offeror specifies a means of acceptance, it must be used.

1) However, if the offer states nothing about the means of acceptance, the authorized means is any reasonable means (e.g., one that is used by the offeror, customary in similar transactions, or appropriate in the specific circumstances).

2) Generally, acceptance by an unauthorized means is effective upon receipt by the offeror, assuming the offer has not expired or been revoked.

e. If the offer specifies a **time for acceptance**, the acceptance must be communicated within that time.

f. The offeror may waive compliance with particular terms of an offer regarding acceptance. For example, a deficient or late acceptance may be a new offer that the original offeror chooses to accept.

The AICPA has consistently tested candidates on the mailbox rule, including when an offeror attempts revocation after an acceptance has been dispatched.

4. **Mailbox Rule**

a. The offer may state that acceptance is effective on receipt. If it does not, then the law applies the mailbox rule to determine when the offer is accepted.

b. Under the mailbox rule, acceptance is effective at the **moment of dispatch** if (1) the offeree has used an **authorized** means of acceptance to communicate to the offeror and (2) the offer is still open. Acceptance is effective even if the offeror attempts revocation while it is in transit.

EXAMPLE

An offer is sent by mail. It does not specify a particular medium for acceptance. A letter of acceptance is deposited in the mail. If it was properly addressed and had proper postage affixed, the acceptance is considered legally effective even if it never reaches the offeror.

---

1) An acceptance **following prior dispatch of a rejection** is effective only if received by the offeror before receipt of the rejection.

2) The mailbox rule does not apply to an option contract.

3) Making acceptance effective only upon receipt negates the mailbox rule.

EXAMPLE

The offeror mailed a revocation on July 15. It arrived on July 17, after the offeree had mailed an acceptance on July 16. The revocation is invalid because the acceptance was in transit before the offeree had notice of the revocation and a contract was formed. This outcome is avoided if the offeror explicitly states that the "acceptance must be received to be effective." The first item received by the offeror controls whether a contract is formed.

Stop and review! You have completed the outline for this subunit. Study multiple-choice questions 3 and 4 on page 479.

17.3 CONSIDERATION

1. **Definition**

a. Consideration is something of value given in a bargained-for exchange. It is the **promise, act, or forbearance** to do or not do something that parties agree to as part of their agreement.

EXAMPLE

Amanda tells Bob that she will provide him lodging in September if he agrees to pay her $200. Amanda's consideration is the promise of an obligatory future action. Bob's consideration is the act of paying $200. Both parties have provided consideration that was not legally required of them before the contract was created.

---

    b.   The elements of consideration are

        1)   Legal sufficiency and
        2)   A bargained-for exchange (mutuality of consideration).

2.   **Legal Sufficiency**

    a.   Consideration is legally sufficient to render a promise enforceable if the promisee (1) incurs a legal detriment or (2) the promisor receives a legal benefit.

        1)   To incur a legal detriment, the promisee must

            a)   Do something (s)he is not legally obligated to do or
            b)   Forebear to do something (s)he has a legal right to do.

        2)   Almost any legal detriment is legally sufficient. Parity of value is **not** required.

            a)   But extreme inadequacy or inequality of consideration may be evidence of fraud, mistake, or a gift.

        3)   In a **bilateral contract**, one promise is consideration for the other.
        4)   Consideration may be legally sufficient without a simultaneous exchange and despite the form of the consideration.

3.   **Bargained-for Exchange**

    a.   A bargained-for exchange occurs when one party makes a promise or performance in exchange for a return promise or performance by the other party. The promise or performance given by the promisor must induce the promisee to incur a legal detriment or provide a legal benefit to the promisor.

4.   **Items Not Sufficient Consideration**

    a.   **Nominal** consideration. Something almost without value (e.g., a symbolic payment of $1) generally is not sufficient.

    b.   **Past consideration** cannot be bargained for. Such acts have already happened, and the acting party cannot effectively promise to incur any legal detriment.

EXAMPLE

Father said to Daughter, "If you graduate, I promise to pay you $10,000 at the end of next month." If Daughter had already graduated at the time of the promise, Father is not obligated. Daughter incurred no legal detriment to support his promise.

---

    c.   **Pre-existing legal duty.** Consideration does not exist if

        1)   An existing duty was imposed by law, or
        2)   A person is already under contract to render a specified performance.

EXAMPLE

A contractor tells a homeowner that, unless she pays him an extra $500, he will leave her roof half repaired. Because the contractor has a pre-existing duty to repair the entire roof, he has not incurred any new consideration.

---

    d.   **Part payment of an undisputed (liquidated) debt** is not consideration for a promise by the creditor to accept the part payment in full satisfaction of the debt.

        1)   A promise to pay part of a **disputed (unliquidated)** debt is consideration for the creditor's forgiveness of the remainder. But the dispute must be in good faith.
        2)   Early payment of an undisputed debt is legally sufficient consideration for the creditor's acceptance of a lesser amount.

5. **Substitutes for Consideration**

   a. **Promissory estoppel** applies when

      1) A promise is given that the promisor should reasonably expect to induce action or forbearance by the promisee,

      2) The promise induces the action or forbearance, and

      3) Injustice can be avoided only by enforcing the promise.

EXAMPLE

John pledged $5 million to University. In reliance on the pledge, University began construction of a new building. If John retracts the pledge, a court will most likely enforce the promise. University has acted upon John's promise and likely incurred a significant debt to its detriment.

---

   b. A **quasi-contract** (contract implied in law) occurs when the parties make no promises and reach no agreement; however, one of the parties is substantially benefited at the expense of the other party, and no adequate legal remedy is available. The court finds that a quasi-contract applies so that an **equitable** remedy may be given.

      1) To avoid **unjust enrichment** of the receiving party, the party who provided the benefit is entitled to the **reasonable** value (not the contract price) of the services rendered or property delivered. The court provides an equitable remedy because a contractual remedy is **not** available.

         a) The terms **unjust enrichment** and **restitution** are modern equivalents of the traditional phrases quasi-contract, **quantum meruit**, and implied-in-law contract.

EXAMPLE

A doctor found an unconscious person on the sidewalk and provided medical treatment. To avoid unjust enrichment, the patient must pay the doctor a reasonable fee even though the aid was unsolicited and no contract existed.

Stop and review! You have completed the outline for this subunit. Study multiple-choice question 5 on page 480.

17.4 CAPACITY

1. **Overview**

   a. Parties to a contract must have the legal capacity to contract. Minors, persons lacking mental capacity, and intoxicated persons do not have legal capacity.

   b. The UCC adopts the common law in determining legal capacity to contract.

2. **Minors**

   a. Because a minor does not have legal capacity to enter contracts, a minor may **disaffirm** his or her contract. Thus, the contract is **voidable** by the minor.

      1) However, the minor is liable until disaffirmance. Moreover, regardless of disaffirmance, a minor is always liable based on a **quasi-contract** for the reasonable value, **not** the contract price, of **necessaries** (e.g., food, shelter, and clothing).

      2) According to the majority rule, disaffirmance is allowed even if the minor misrepresented his or her age.

      3) A party contracting with a minor is bound to the contract.

      4) An emancipated minor is free of parental control but still lacks capacity.

      5) However, some contracts cannot be voided, e.g., those for student loans and medical care.

b.   Power to disaffirm continues until a **reasonable** time after the minor reaches the age of majority.

1)   Any unequivocal act that indicates an intent to disaffirm is sufficient. A written disaffirmance is not required.

a)   Performance is not a condition of disaffirmance.

2)   When the contract has been partially or wholly performed, the minor must, if possible, return any consideration received from the other party.

3)   A minor may disaffirm even if (s)he cannot return the consideration or the consideration is damaged.

c.   A contract entered into by a minor may be **ratified** by the minor orally or in writing **after** (s)he has reached the age of majority.

1)   Ratification may be either expressed or implied.

2)   Ratification dates back to the beginning of the contract and is for all of its terms.

3)   A contract is ratified if the minor retains the consideration for an unreasonable time after (s)he reaches majority.

a)   New consideration is **not** needed.

b)   Ratification may result from accepting benefits incidental to ownership, such as rents, dividends, or interest.

c)   Selling or donating the property is ratification by the minor.

4)   Failure to disaffirm for a reasonable period after reaching majority is a ratification.

3.   **Persons Lacking Mental Capacity**

a.   A person lacking mental capacity is unable to understand the nature and consequences of his or her acts and therefore does not have legal capacity to enter contracts.

1)   If a person was **judicially** determined to be insane or otherwise incompetent **before** contract formation, the contract is **void** and cannot be ratified.

2)   Judicial determination of incompetence **after** the formation of a contract renders the contract merely **voidable**.

4.   **Intoxicated Persons**

a.   If mental capacity is lacking due to intoxication, the contract is **voidable** at the option of the intoxicated person.

1)   But the other party must have had reason to know that the intoxicated person (a) did not understand the nature and consequences of his or her actions or (b) was unable to act reasonably.

2)   However, extreme intoxication may prevent contract formation.

Stop and review! You have completed the outline for this subunit. Study multiple-choice question 6 on page 480.

17.5 LEGALITY

1.   **Overview**

a.   Contracts are unenforceable if they violate the U.S. Constitution, a civil or criminal statute or other law, or public policy.

1)   A promise to commit, or induce the commission of, a tort or crime is void on grounds of public policy.

2)   Agreements not to press criminal charges are **not** enforceable. They interfere with the state's duty to protect society by prosecuting criminals.

2. **Effects of Illegality**

    a. Courts ordinarily do not assist either party to an illegal contract. There is no judicial means to enforce it.

3. **Statutory Violations**

    a. A contract that cannot be performed without violating a statute is void.

    b. Commission of an illegal act during performance of a contract does not make the contract illegal. If the formation of the contract violated no law and the contract could be performed without violating any law, the contract is enforceable.

    c. A party who agrees to supply goods or services while unaware that such goods or services will be used for an unlawful purpose can enforce the contract.

        1) However, a person who intends to accomplish an unlawful purpose may not enforce a contract made for that purpose.

4. **Licensing Statutes**

    a. A **regulatory** statute is enacted for the protection of the public against unqualified or incompetent persons.

        1) If a licensing statute is regulatory, a person cannot recover for services unless (s)he holds the required license, regardless of whether the statute so states.

        2) A **revenue** collection statute is enacted merely to collect revenue, such as requiring a vendor's license. Recovery on the contract is possible, but a fine may be payable.

5. **Contracts in Restraint of Trade**

    a. A contract in restraint of trade restricts competition or otherwise interferes with the normal flow of goods or services. Thus, courts are reluctant to enforce them and they are narrowly construed.

    b. A typical restraint on trade is a **covenant not to compete**. It is an agreement not to engage in a particular trade, profession, or business. This restraint may be valid if

        1) The purpose is to protect a property interest of the promisee and

        2) The restraint is no more extensive in scope and duration than is reasonably necessary to protect that property or legitimate business interest.

    c. An **employment contract** may include a covenant not to compete during or after the period of employment.

        1) It may prohibit the employee from

            a) Setting up a business in competition with the former employer,

            b) Entering the employment of a competitor, or

            c) Revealing the former employer's trade secrets (a nondisclosure agreement).

        2) Restrictions on future employment tend to be more strictly scrutinized than covenants not to compete in agreements to sell a business. A restraint that is unreasonable, e.g., because of its effect on the ability to find other employment, may be voided or revised by the court to an acceptable form.

6. **Contracts of Adhesion**

    a. A contract of adhesion is between parties with a great disparity of bargaining power. The weaker party must accept the terms imposed by the stronger party or forgo the transaction entirely (examples are rental agreements and insurance contracts).

        1) Most such contracts are upheld in the interest of efficiency.

7. **Unconscionability**

    a. If one party to a contract has excessive economic power over another, the courts may find that a contract is unenforceable. Unconscionability relates to unscrupulous or unreasonable activity and fundamental fairness. If a contract or term is unconscionable when the contract is made, a court may

        1) Refuse to enforce the contract,
        2) Enforce the remainder of the contract without the unconscionable term, or
        3) Limit the application of the term to avoid an unconscionable result.

    b. Unconscionability may be **procedural** (an unfair negotiating process or procedural irregularity) or **substantive** (excessively unfair terms).

8. **Exculpatory Clauses**

    a. Exculpatory clauses excuse one party from liability for harm caused by his or her acts.

        1) Generally, courts do not enforce a term that excuses a party's criminal conduct, intentional torts, or gross negligence.

    b. If the parties have approximately equal bargaining power, the courts are more likely to uphold an exculpatory clause.

        1) If one party has a decidedly weaker position, the contract may be held invalid as contrary to public policy.

Stop and review! You have completed the outline for this subunit. Study multiple-choice question 7 on page 480.

17.6 LACK OF GENUINE ASSENT

1. **Fraud**

    a. A contract induced by an intentional misrepresentation or the omission of a material fact is considered procured by fraud and is therefore voidable.

    b. The following are the **elements of fraud**:

        1) An actual or implied false representation (or concealment) of a material fact,
        2) Intent to misrepresent (scienter),

            a) The intent element is satisfied if the defendant (1) knew the representation was false or (2) **recklessly disregarded** its truth of falsity.

        3) Intent to induce reliance,
        4) Justifiable actual reliance by the innocent party based on the misrepresentation, and
        5) Damage (loss) suffered by the innocent party.

    c. A statement of opinion is not usually the basis of a fraud claim. A fact is objective and verifiable, but an opinion is generally subject to debate. Generally, sellers are allowed a certain amount of "puffery" in selling their products.

        1) Statements of probabilities and predictions of future business results do not usually constitute fraudulent statements unless they are known to be false when made.

    d. The misrepresentation must be **material**. It must relate to an important inducement into entering into the contract. Thus, it is a basis of the bargain.

    e. **Constructive fraud** arises from gross negligence.

        1) Gross negligence occurs when a misrepresentation is made with a willful and reckless disregard for its truth or falsity rather than with actual intent to deceive (scienter).

    f.   **Fraud in the inducement** occurs when the defrauded party is aware of entering into a contract and intends to do so, but the contract is procured by fraud.

        1)   (S)he is intentionally deceived about a material fact to the contract (e.g., the nature of the goods or services).

        2)   Thus, the contract is **voidable**.

    g.   **Fraud in the execution** occurs when the signature of a party is obtained by a fraudulent misrepresentation that directly relates to the signing of a contract.

        1)   The purported contract is **void**.

    h.   A **duty to disclose facts** exists when

        1)   The parties have a fiduciary relationship creating a duty to disclose.
        2)   One party knows a material fact, and the other could not reasonably discover it.
        3)   An important fact is misstated. It must be corrected as soon as possible.
        4)   Failure to do so constitutes actual fraud in these circumstances.

    i.   The remedy in cases of fraudulent representation is either a claim for damages or rescission of the entire contract.

        1)   For a tort claim based on fraud, the injury sustained must have been caused by the misrepresentation.

2. **Negligent Misrepresentation**

    a.   Negligent misrepresentation is a false representation of a material fact intended to be reasonably relied upon. It is made by a party that has **no knowledge** of its falsity but has acted **without due care**.

    b.   The remedy to the injured party for negligent misrepresentation is a claim for damages. Only actual losses are recoverable.

3. **Innocent Misrepresentation**

    a.   Innocent misrepresentation is a false representation of a material fact that is intended to be relied upon and that is reasonably relied on.

        1)   The party that makes the misrepresentation has **no knowledge** of its falsity, believes the statement to be true, and has acted **with due care**.

        2)   The remedy for innocent misrepresentation generally is rescission and occasionally damages (reliance damages only).

4. **Mistake**

    a.   A mistake is an unintended act, omission, or error in the formation of a contract.

    b.   Mistakes of **fact** have legal significance. Mistakes in judgment of value or quality, whether mutual or unilateral, do not.

    c.   A **mutual mistake** occurs when both parties to a contract are mistaken about the same material fact. A mutual mistake of material fact is

        1)   A basis for rescission or
        2)   A sufficient defense for failure to perform the contract.

EXAMPLE

Katie has a truck she uses for business. Curt offers to buy Katie's truck. She agrees to sell. Curt accepts her price and pays Katie. However, without the knowledge of either party, the truck was actually destroyed by fire a few hours before their contract was formed. Given that neither party was aware that the truck had been destroyed, a mutual mistake has occurred, and rescission is available to either party.

    d.   A **unilateral mistake** occurs when only one party to a contract acts on the basis of a mistaken belief or assumption. The party is generally not relieved of the contractual obligation. However, the remedy of **rescission** by the mistaken party is available in limited circumstances when the mistake is material and

        1)   The other party knew or should have known of the mistake;

        2)   Enforcement would result in extreme hardship constituting injustice;

        3)   The error was due to a mathematical mistake or omission of items in computing the cost of the contract; or

        4)   The mistake was due to fraud, duress, or undue influence.

5.   **Duress**

    a.   One form of duress occurs when one party, by means of an **improper threat** that instills fear in a second party, effectively denies the second party's exercise of free will.

        1)   The improper threat must have **sufficient coercive effect** so that it actually induces the particular person to agree to the contract.

            a)   A threat based on a legal right and not constituting a tort or a crime may be improper if made in bad faith and with an ulterior motive.

        2)   The contract entered into is **voidable** by the innocent party.

    b.   **Economic duress** may arise when one party exerts extreme economic pressure that leaves the threatened party with no reasonable alternative but to comply.

        1)   Economic duress may be created by threats of economic harm if the buyer does not accept the seller's terms.

            a)   Merely taking advantage of another's financial difficulty is not duress.

            b)   Inadequacy of consideration is not an element of duress.

    c.   A threat of criminal prosecution is improper. Although a person has a legal right to report a crime to the police, (s)he may not do so for private gain.

        1)   A threat of a civil suit is not improper unless it is made in bad faith, that is, when such an action has no legal basis.

    d.   **Physical compulsion** with threats of personal violence renders the contract **void**.

6.   **Undue Influence**

    a.   Undue influence occurs when a dominant party (e.g., a trusted lawyer, physician, or guardian) wrongly exploits a confidential relationship to persuade a second party to enter into an unfavorable contract.

        1)   A contract is **voidable** as a result of undue influence.

Stop and review! You have completed the outline for this subunit. Study multiple-choice questions 8 and 9 on page 481.

17.7 STATUTE OF FRAUDS

1.   The original Statute of Frauds was passed by the British Parliament in 1677. U.S. jurisdictions have adopted and amended it to require certain contracts be in writing. The signed writing requirement only applies to those contracts that are covered by the statute as set forth below and on the next page.

2.   **Contracts Covered by the Statute**

    a.   An oral contract is usually enforceable. However, the statute of frauds requires certain contracts to be in writing and signed by the defendant. The statute of frauds relates to enforcement, not formation, of contracts.

1) **Agreements that cannot be performed within 1 year of the making of the contract.** If performance, however difficult or improbable, is possible within 1 year, the agreement is **not** covered by the statute of frauds.

    a) The day the contract is made is excluded, and the 1-year period expires at the close of the contract's express termination date.

EXAMPLE

John orally contracts to perform maintenance services on Mary's truck for as long as she owns it. The contract may be performed within 1 year if Mary decides to sell the truck within that time. Thus, the agreement is not required to be in writing. If John had contracted to maintain Mary's truck for the next 4 years, the contract would be unenforceable without a writing.

---

2) **Agreements for the sale of an interest in land.** An interest may be a long-term lease (more than 1 year), mortgage, full ownership, or any other interest in land.

3) **Agreements for the sale of goods for $500 or more.** An agreement for the sale of goods for $500 or more is not enforceable without a writing sufficient to indicate that a contract for sale has been made between the parties.

4) **Agreements to answer for the debt of another.** A suretyship agreement must be in writing if the promise is secondary.

    a) **Main purpose rule.** A promise is **secondary** if its main purpose is to benefit the debtor.

EXAMPLE

Parent cosigns an educational loan for Child as a favor based on familial affection. Parent receives no economic benefit from the guarantee. Accordingly, the promise is secondary and must be in writing.

---

    b) A promise is **primary** if its main purpose is to benefit the promisor (the surety, i.e., the party who agrees to pay if the debtor defaults).

EXAMPLE

Company A agrees to buy inventory from Company B. B offers a favorable price if A will guarantee payment of a debt that B owes to supplier. This promise is primary because its main purpose is to obtain an economic advantage for A, not to benefit B. Primary promises are enforceable even if not in writing.

---

    c) The statute of frauds does not apply to an oral promise made to the **debtor**.

5) **Agreements made in contemplation of marriage.** A promise to marry must be made in writing with consideration other than mutual promises to marry.

3. **The Required Writing**

    a. A written memorandum complies with the statute if it contains the following:

        1) A reasonably certain description of the parties and the subject matter,

        2) The essential terms and conditions of the contract,

        3) A description of the consideration (no minimum or adequate amount is required), and

        4) The signatures of the parties against whom the writing is to be enforced.

    b. The agreement may consist of several writings if

        1) One is signed and

        2) The facts clearly indicate that they all relate to the same transaction.

4.   **Alternatives to the Writing Requirement**

a.   The statute does **not** apply when both parties to an oral contract have fully performed.

1)   An oral agreement to **rescind** a completely unperformed (executory) written contract is generally valid.

b.   Lack of written evidence ordinarily does not prevent enforcement if one party has fully performed.

1)   An oral acceptance of a written offer signed by the offeror is binding only on the offeror if the statute of frauds applies to the contract.

c.   **Part performance.** An oral contract for the sale of land may be enforced when the contract has been partially performed.

1)   The purchaser must have (a) taken action that is clearly based on the oral agreement and (b) reasonably relied on it to his or her substantial detriment.

a)   Mere payment of a deposit is not part performance.

2)   In most states, the party seeking to enforce the oral contract for land must have done at least **two** of the following:

a)   Paid part or all of the price,
b)   Taken possession, or
c)   Made valuable improvements.

3)   If part performance is established, a court may grant specific performance and force the transfer of the land.

Stop and review! You have completed the outline for this subunit. Study multiple-choice questions 10 and 11 on page 481.

17.8 PAROL EVIDENCE RULE

The AICPA often tests whether the parol evidence rule applies to terms in a contract.

1.   **Definition**

a.   Parol evidence is a rule courts apply to determine whether a party may introduce into evidence prior written agreements or contemporaneous oral agreements (one made at the same time as the final agreement) to modify, explain, or supplement the contract before the court. The rule states that where the parties intended the contract to be the **full and final expression** of their bargain, then other written agreements or oral agreements that were made prior or simultaneous with the contract are **inadmissible** for the purpose of changing the terms of the contract before the court.

b.   The parol evidence rule prohibits admission of oral evidence when a writing is intended to be the final and complete expression (integration) of the agreement of the parties. The terms of such a contract **cannot be contradicted or varied** by extrinsic evidence of

1)   Any prior understanding (oral or written) or
2)   An oral understanding reached at the same time as the final writing.

c.   A writing apparently complete on its face is assumed to be completely integrated at the time of its making.

1)   Most contracts contain a merger or integration clause that states the writing constitutes the entire and final agreement between the parties.

2) To determine the meaning of the contract, the parties must rely upon the wording within the four corners of the document and cannot enter other evidence as to its meaning.

2. **Exceptions**

a. Parol evidence is admissible to prove or explain the following:

1) Circumstances that make the written contract void, voidable, or unenforceable. The following are examples:

a) Illegality or lack of capacity to make a contract
b) Fraud, mistake, duress, or undue influence
c) Failure of a condition precedent

2) The meaning of ambiguous terms in the contract, such as

a) Custom and usage not inconsistent with the agreement or
b) Typographical or obvious drafting errors that clearly do not represent the intention of the parties.

3) A subsequent modification or rescission.

Stop and review! You have completed the outline for this subunit. Study multiple-choice question 12 on page 482.

17.9 PERFORMANCE, DISCHARGE, AND BREACH

1. **Discharge by Performance**

a. **Strict performance.** A party discharges his or her contractual obligations by performing according to the terms of the contract.

1) **Part performance** is generally insufficient to discharge contractual duties.

b. **Substantial performance** is a lesser standard of performance. It applies when duties are difficult to perform without some deviation from perfection.

1) Substantial performance may be achieved even with an immaterial breach of contract.

EXAMPLE

A contractor has just completed a mansion. Upon inspection, the homeowner finds that cheap water fixtures were used even though she explicitly required an expensive brand. Accordingly, she refuses to pay for or accept the home, attempting to void the contract. Because the breach is immaterial in relation to the total contract, the homeowner must pay for and accept the house. The contractor must pay damages for the repair or replacement of the fixtures.

---

2) A party who in **good faith** completes performance in substantial compliance with the contract has discharged his or her duties. The party can enforce the contract and collect the contract price even if damages are owed.

3) The doctrine is **not** applied if the party has intentionally committed this immaterial breach.

c. **Good faith** is expected of the parties in performing contractual promises.

1) A party has a duty to act in good faith to fulfill a condition to the extent to which (s)he is able, for example, to obtain financing.

2) Each party has a duty not to prevent another party from performing.

2. **Discharge by Agreement**

a. **Mutual rescission** occurs when the parties to a contract agree to cancel it.

b. Parties to a contract may make a new contract (an **accord**) in which the prior and the new contracts are to be discharged by performance (**satisfaction**) of the new contract.

EXAMPLE

A general contractor and a homeowner contract for the construction of a deck on the back of the house. The contract specifies that the deck is to be constructed of pine, and the homeowner will pay $5,000. As construction is nearing completion, the homeowner discovers that pine has not been used in the deck and addresses this issue with the contractor. Both parties agree that the price of the deck construction will be lowered to $4,000 given the contractor's mistake. After the construction is completed, and the homeowner pays the contractor $4,000, neither party can sue successfully because of the inferior wood or decreased payment. The accord and satisfaction bars this legal action.

---

    c.   In a **composition with creditors**, the participating creditors agree to extend time for payment, take lesser sums in satisfaction of the debts owed, or accept some other plan of financial adjustment.

        1)   The consideration for the promise of one creditor to accept less than the amount due is the similar promise of each of the other creditors.

        2)   These agreements are not as common and have generally been replaced by federal bankruptcy laws.

    d.   **Modification** of an existing contract's term(s) traditionally requires new consideration.

        1)   However, the Restatement (Second) of Contracts does not require consideration if

            a)   The contract is executory and

            b)   The modification is fair given facts the parties did not anticipate when the contract was formed.

        2)   Under the UCC, modifications involving a sale of **goods** do not require consideration if made in good faith.

    e.   A **substituted contract** is an agreement among all parties that cancels an existing contract. The new contract is supported by new consideration, which may include a promise made by a new party.

        1)   A **novation** is a special form of substituted contract that replaces a party to the prior contract with another who was not originally a party. It completely releases the replaced party.

            a)   The promise of the new party to perform in accordance with the novation is consideration for release of the replaced party.

            b)   For example, a real estate mortgagor (the landowner-borrower) generally may sell or otherwise transfer the property. However, the mortgagor may not delegate performance and avoid liability under the mortgage unless specifically released by the lender-mortgagee. Without the lender-mortgagee's agreement to substitute the delegatee for the mortgagor (a novation), the mortgagor remains liable.

                i)   A transfer of real property **subject to the mortgage** is not a novation. The buyer pays the seller his or her equity but is not personally liable on the existing mortgage loan.

                ii)   **Assumption** of a mortgage by the buyer also is not a novation. The buyer pays the mortgagor the value of the property minus the debt secured by the mortgage and **promises** to pay the balance of the debt.

                iii)   The mortgagor is a **surety**. If the buyer defaults, the mortgagor is liable.

    f.   **Release.** One party releases another of performance obligations without restoration to all parties' original positions. Releases are commonly used to settle differences if liability is contingent or disputed.

3. **Discharge by Operation of Law**

   a. **Illegality.** The nonperformance of a contractual duty may be excused if, after formation, the contract becomes objectively impossible to perform (e.g., the law changes, making the contract illegal).

   b. **Impossibility** is an exception to the general rule of strict performance.

      1) Circumstances must have changed so completely since the contract was formed that the parties could **not** reasonably have foreseen and expressly provided for the change.

         a) For example, an essential party to the performance of a contract dies or is incapacitated, an essential item or commodity is destroyed, or an intervening change of law makes performance illegal.

         b) However, the death, incapacity, or bankruptcy of a party who is to receive the performance does not discharge the duty.

      2) The impossibility must be **objective** in the sense that no one could perform the duty or duties specified in the contract.

         a) A promise to supply a commodity is not impossible to perform when a substitute supply is available.

      3) If performance is partially impossible, discharge is partial.

   c. **Commercial impracticability** results from an **unforeseen** and unjust hardship. It is a less rigid doctrine than the impossibility exception.

      1) Impracticability results from occurrence of an event if its occurrence was unexpected and a basic assumption of the contract.

         a) Common events creating commercial impracticability include shortages caused by war, crop failures, or labor strikes.

      2) It permits discharge when a party's performance is no longer feasible for reasons that are not his or her fault. But discharge does not result from a mere significant cost increase.

      3) An issue is whether the promisor assumed the risk of such an event.

   d. **Frustration of purpose** is a doctrine that permits discharge of parties even though performance is still possible. Frustration occurs when a contract becomes valueless, that is, when the purpose for which it was entered is no longer available because it has been destroyed by an intervening event that was not reasonably foreseeable.

4. **Conditions**

   a. A condition is an act, an event, or a set of facts that creates, limits, or extinguishes an absolute contractual duty to perform.

      1) Failure of a condition does not subject either party to liability because it is an event that must occur for the contract to continue.

   b. Conditions may be classified based on their timing.

      1) A condition **precedent** is an event that must occur before performance is due.

      2) A **concurrent** condition must occur or be performed simultaneously.

      3) A condition **subsequent** is an event that terminates one party's duty and another party's right to damages for breach of the duty. For example, if a company closes its business, a supplier is relieved from its contractual duty to deliver widgets.

  c. Conditions also may be classified as express or implied.

    1) An **express** condition is explicitly stated, usually preceded by such terms as "on condition that" or "subject to."

    2) An **implied** condition is not expressly stated in the contract but inferred.

      a) **Implied-in-fact** conditions are understood by both parties to be part of the agreement.

      b) **Implied-in-law** conditions are imposed by law to promote fairness.

Conditions
Timing
• Precedent
• Concurrent
• Subsequent
Express
Implied
• In-fact
• In-law

5. **Breach of Contract**

  a. A breach of contract is the failure of a party to perform a duty required under a contract.

  b. A **material breach** is an unjustified failure to perform obligations arising from a contract, such that one party is deprived of what (s)he bargained for.

    1) A material breach discharges the nonbreaching party from any obligation to perform under the contract and entitles that party to sue for breach of contract.

  c. A **nonmaterial breach** is the failure to perform a minor or less important obligation of a contract that does not deprive the nonbreaching party of the benefit of the bargain. Therefore, the nonmaterial breach does not discharge the nonbreaching party from its obligation. Instead, the nonbreaching party may only sue for actual damages.

    1) A breach generally is considered nonmaterial if it is unintended and the injured party receives substantially all of the benefits reasonably anticipated.

  d. An **anticipatory breach** occurs when one party **repudiates** the contract.

    1) An **anticipatory repudiation** is an express or implied indication that (s)he has no intention to perform the contract prior to the time set for performance.

    2) After anticipatory repudiation, the nonbreaching party may suspend his or her own performance and

      a) Await a change of mind by the breaching party,

      b) Act to find a substitute performance, or

      c) Immediately sue for damages.

  e. A **statute of limitations** is a law that designates a time period after which litigation may not be commenced. Expiration of the time period bars a judicial remedy. The period of limitations varies from state to state and by the type of action (e.g., a civil breach of contract claim generally is 4 or 5 years). But the duration of litigation once commenced is not limited.

    1) The statutory period begins to run for a breach of contract claim from the later of the date of the breach or the date when a party should reasonably have discovered the breach.

    2) The statute of limitations applies to all contracts. The ability of a party to sue for nonperformance no longer exists after the statute of limitations runs out.

Stop and review! You have completed the outline for this subunit. Study multiple-choice questions 13 and 14 on page 482.

17.10 REMEDIES

1. **Damages**

    a. The most common remedy for breach of contract is a judgment awarding an amount of money to compensate for damages.

    1) **Compensatory** (actual or general) damages are damages incurred from the wrongful conduct of the breaching party. Compensatory damages are intended to place the injured party in as good a position as if the breaching party had performed under the contract. The following are measures of compensatory damages:

        a) **Expectation** damages compensate the nonbreaching party for the monetary loss suffered or the expectancy interest or benefit of the bargain.

        b) **Incidental** damages result directly from the breach.

        c) **Consequential** damages are not incidental damages. They are additional damages resulting from special circumstances that the defendant had reason to foresee. For example, the plaintiff might have given notice of a possible loss of profits in the event of breach.

    2) **Reliance** damages are intended to put the injured party in as good a position as if the contract had **not** been formed.

    3) **Punitive** damages punish a breaching party and set a public policy example for others.

        a) A court awards punitive damages only when the breach is malicious, willful, or physically injurious to the nonbreaching party.

    4) **Liquidated** (undisputed) damages clauses are favored by public policy. They are agreed upon money damages in advance of an actual breach. Such a clause is enforceable if

        a) The clause is not intended as a penalty,
        b) It reasonably forecasts the probable loss due to the breach, and
        c) The loss is difficult to calculate.

    b. **Mitigation.** An injured party is required to take reasonable steps to mitigate damages (s)he may sustain as a result of the breach. The nonbreaching party must

    1) Not accumulate losses after notice of breach,
    2) Not incur further costs, and
    3) Make reasonable efforts to limit losses by obtaining a substitute.

2. **Other Remedies**

    a. **Specific performance** is a nonmonetary judgment entered by the court requiring the breaching party to perform the duties specified in the contract.

    1) This is an extraordinary remedy that is rarely granted and only under the following conditions:

        a) No other legal remedy is adequate.

            i)   Monetary damages are not available or are not adequate.
            ii) The subject matter of the contract is unique. For example, each parcel of land or each patent is deemed to be unique, so damages rarely are adequate.

        b) Irreparable injury will result if specific performance is not granted.

    2) A judge will not order specific performance for a personal service contract.

b.   **Rescission** cancels a contract and returns the parties to the positions they would have been in if the contract had not been made. It results from mutual consent, conduct of the parties, or a court order in the following situations:

   1)   Nonperformance or a material breach by the other party
   2)   Negligent or innocent misrepresentation
   3)   A mutual or unilateral mistake in contract formation

c.   **Reformation.** When the parties' written agreement imperfectly expresses the parties' intent, it can be rewritten.

d.   **Replevin** is an action to recover personal property taken unlawfully.

e.   An **injunction** is a court's order to do or not do some act.

f.   **Restitution** is available when a party's performance conferred a recoverable benefit on the other party.

   1)   A valid contract need not have existed.
   2)   Restitution is an equitable remedy to prevent unjust enrichment, correct an erroneous payment, or recover advances.
   3)   Study Unit 19, Subunit 5, provides further discussion.

Stop and review! You have completed the outline for this subunit. Study multiple-choice questions 15 and 16 on page 483.

17.11 CONTRACT BENEFICIARIES

1.   **Third-Party Beneficiaries**

a.   In a third-party beneficiary contract, at least one performance is intended for the direct benefit of a person not a party to the contract (not in **privity** of contract). This person is an **intended beneficiary**.

b.   Intended third-party beneficiaries have rights under the contract.

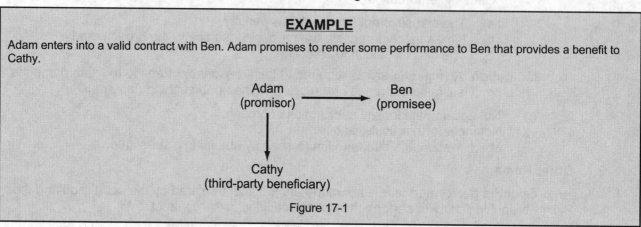

EXAMPLE

Adam enters into a valid contract with Ben. Adam promises to render some performance to Ben that provides a benefit to Cathy.

Adam
(promisor) → Ben
(promisee)

Cathy
(third-party beneficiary)

Figure 17-1

   1)   If a promisee's main purpose in entering the contract with promisor is to discharge a debt (s)he owes to a third party, the third party is an intended **creditor beneficiary**.

      a)   If the contract in the example above is breached, the creditor (Cathy) may sue the promisor (Adam) as a third-party beneficiary. But the creditor also may sue the original debtor (Ben).

   2)   If a promisee's main purpose is to confer a benefit on a third party as a gift, the third party is a **donee beneficiary**.

      a)   A typical donee beneficiary is the beneficiary of life insurance.

c. An intended third-party beneficiary's rights are derivative and therefore they are the same rights as the promisee's.

   1) The promisor may assert any defense against the beneficiary that the promisor could have asserted against the promisee.

d. An **incidental beneficiary** is a nonparty who might benefit if the contract is performed but whom the parties did not intend to benefit directly.

   1) Because an incidental beneficiary is not an intended beneficiary, (s)he has no legal right to sue for performance of the contract.

EXAMPLE

Adam enters into a valid contract to sell goods to Ben. Cathy will benefit unintentionally from performance of the contract because Ben purchases the goods from his wholesaler, Cathy. Because Cathy is an unintentional beneficiary, she has no legal rights to enforce.

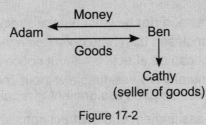

Figure 17-2

Stop and review! You have completed the outline for this subunit. Study multiple-choice questions 17 and 18 beginning on page 483.

17.12 ASSIGNMENT AND DELEGATION

1. **Assignment of Rights**

   a. A party to a contract ordinarily **may transfer his or her rights** under the contract to a third person without discharging the other party's duty to perform.

      1) The recipient of the payment or benefit is the **obligee** and the **obligor** is contractually committed to provide the payment or benefit to the obligee.

      2) The right of the obligee is the obligor's performance (e.g., a payment).

EXAMPLE

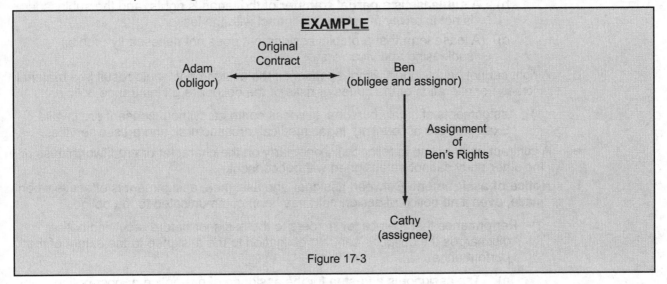

Figure 17-3

b. An assignment is a manifestation of the assignor's **intent** to transfer the right to the obligor's performance (due to the obligee) to a third party, the assignee.

1) The party making the assignment is an **assignor**. The person to whom the assignment is made is an **assignee**.

2) The assignor's right to the obligor's performance is extinguished in whole or in part if the assignment is **unconditional**.

a) The assignee then acquires the right transferred to the exclusion of the assignor.

3) The assignment may be gratuitous (without consideration).

4) After an assignment, the assignee is in **privity of estate** with the original obligor.

a) For example, if the original obligor is a lessor, the assignee (1) acquires the assignor-lessee's rights but (2) is liable to pay rent to the obligor-lessor.

5) An assignment need **not** be written unless required by statute.

6) The obligor can assert the same defenses against the assignor and assignee.

7) An assignment can be effective without notice to the obligor.

c. **Contract rights** generally are assignable without consent of the obligor and without a written document. But a signed assignment is required if the statute of frauds applies.

1) An attempted assignment of a contract right is not effective if the contract expressly states that it is not assignable. Nevertheless, the following are assignable despite an agreement not to assign:

a) A right to receive money

b) Negotiable instruments

c) An option contract

d) The right to receive damages for breach of contract or for payment of an account owed in a contract for the sale of goods

2) A tenant may have the **right to assign or sublease** the premises without the consent of the landlord. The right may be restricted by the lease agreement.

a) An **assignment** transfers the lessee's interest for the **entire unexpired term** of the original lease.

b) A **sublease** is a **partial transfer** of the tenant's rights, and the sublessee is not in privity of estate or contract with the lessor.

c) A lease term that prohibits assignment does not necessarily prohibit subleasing and vice versa.

d. A right cannot be assigned without consent if the assignment would result in a material increase or alteration of the duties or risks of the obligor (e.g., insurance policies).

1) Assignments of highly personal services contracts without consent are invalid. Examples are accounting, legal, medical, architectural, and artistic services.

e. A contract entered into in reliance by one party on the character or creditworthiness of the other party cannot be assigned without consent.

f. **Notice of assignment.** Between assignor and assignee, assignment is effective when made, even if no notice of assignment has been communicated to the obligor.

1) Performance that the obligor renders to the assignor before receiving notice discharges the obligor's contract obligation to the assignee to the extent of the performance.

a) The assignor is a trustee for the assignee of pre-notice or post-notice amounts received from the obligor after the assignment. The assignor must account to the assignee for these amounts.

2) If the assignee does **not** give proper notice, (s)he cannot sue the obligor and force a repeat performance but instead must sue the assignor.

   a) After notice of the assignment is given, the assignee has the additional option of suing the obligor for payments made to the assignor.

EXAMPLE

Jayhawk Corp. has $70,000 of outstanding accounts receivable. On March 10, Jayhawk assigned a $30,000 account receivable due from Tiger, one of Jayhawk's customers, to Clemons Bank for value. On March 30, Tiger paid Jayhawk the $30,000. On April 5, Clemons notified Tiger of the March 10 assignment from Jayhawk to Clemons. Clemons is entitled to collect $30,000 from Jayhawk only.

---

g. **Revocability of Assignments**

   1) An assignment given for consideration is irrevocable.

   2) A gratuitous assignment is usually revocable by the assignor. The following are means of revocation:

      a) Notice of revocation communicated by the assignor to the assignee or obligor

      b) Assignor's receipt of performance directly from the obligor

      c) Assignor's subsequent assignment of the same right to another assignee

      d) Bankruptcy of the assignor

      e) Death or insanity of the assignor

   3) However, an effective **delivery** of the gratuitous assignment to the assignee by the assignor prevents revocation. An example is a physical delivery of a signed, written assignment of the right.

   4) Revocation also is ineffective if the assignee has (a) collected from the obligor and (b) made a further assignment for consideration.

h. **Assignor's Warranties**

   1) Unless the assignment is with recourse, the assignor does not warrant that the obligor will perform.

   2) However, if assignment is for consideration, the assignor impliedly warrants

      a) (S)he will do nothing to impair the value of the assignment and has no knowledge of any fact that would;

      b) The right assigned exists and is not subject to any limitations or defense against the assignor, except any that are stated or apparent; and

      c) Any writing shown to the assignee as evidence of the right is genuine.

i. If an assignee releases the obligor, the assignor also is released.

j. **Assignee's rights.** The assignee acquires all the assignor's rights. The assignee stands in the shoes of the assignor.

2. **Delegation of Performance**

   a. A contract involves rights and duties.

      1) Delegation means that a person under a duty to perform authorizes another person to render the performance.

EXAMPLE

Adam and Ben have a contract under which Adam delegates his duties to Cathy. Adam is the delegator (obligor), Cathy is the delegatee, and Ben is the obligee.

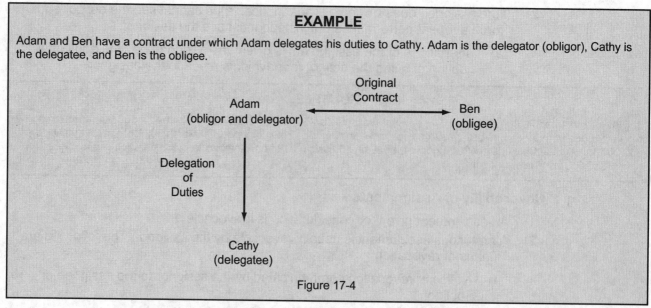

Figure 17-4

b.   A delegator may delegate performance if the delegatee's performance will be substantially similar to the delegator's (e.g., paying money, manufacturing ordinary goods, building according to a set of plans and specifications, or delivering standard merchandise).

1)   But highly personal services contracts generally are **not** delegable. The obligee has a strong interest in having the delegator perform. For example, a CPA firm cannot delegate performance of an audit.

c.   General language, such as "I hereby assign the contract," is a delegation of performance as well as an assignment of rights.

3.   **Liability after Delegation**

a.   Delegation of performance does not relieve the obligor liability even if notice is given to the obligee (unless the contract provides otherwise).

1)   The obligee may sue the delegatee, the obligor, or both after a breach.

Stop and review! You have completed the outline for this subunit. Study multiple-choice questions 19 and 20 on page 484.

QUESTIONS

17.1 Classification of Contracts

1. When a client accepts the services of an accountant without an agreement concerning payment, the result is

A.   An implied-in-fact contract.

B.   An implied-in-law contract.

C.   An express contract.

D.   No contract.

Answer (A) is correct.
   REQUIRED: The type of contract formed when a client accepts an accountant's services.
   DISCUSSION: Enforceable contracts may be formed without an express agreement of terms if the facts of the situation indicate (imply) an objective intent of both parties to contract. Objective intent means the apparent intent of an ordinary, reasonable person and not the actual (subjective) intent. When a client accepts the services of an accountant, an agreement to pay for them is implied. Because the facts indicate a contract was formed, it is an implied-in-fact contract.
   Answer (B) is incorrect. The equitable remedy of restitution or quasi-contract (contract implied in law) prevents unjust enrichment of one party when the facts do not indicate both parties intended to form a contract. Answer (C) is incorrect. An express contract is one in which the terms (such as payment) are specifically agreed upon. Answer (D) is incorrect. A contract implied in fact was formed.

2. Which of the following represents the basic distinction between a bilateral contract and a unilateral contract?

    A. Specific performance is available if the contract is unilateral but not if it is bilateral.

    B. Only one promise is involved if the contract is unilateral, but two are involved if it is bilateral.

    C. The statute of frauds applies to a bilateral contract but not to a unilateral contract.

    D. Rights under a bilateral contract are assignable, whereas rights under a unilateral contract are not assignable.

Answer (B) is correct.
    REQUIRED: The basic distinction between a unilateral and a bilateral contract.
    DISCUSSION: In a bilateral contract, the promise of one party to perform is consideration for the promise of the other. In a unilateral contract, one party makes a promise in exchange for the other party's act, instead of in exchange for a promise from the other party (as in a bilateral contract). Thus, a unilateral contract involves only one promise, but a bilateral contract involves two promises.
    Answer (A) is incorrect. The availability of specific performance is not affected by the distinction between unilateral and bilateral contracts. They may apply to either a unilateral or bilateral contract. Answer (C) is incorrect. The applicability of the statute of frauds is not affected by the distinction between unilateral and bilateral contracts. They may apply to either a unilateral or bilateral contract. Answer (D) is incorrect. The assignability of rights is not affected by the distinction between unilateral and bilateral contracts. They may apply to either a unilateral or bilateral contract.

17.2 Mutual Assent (Offer and Acceptance)

3. On September 10, Harrin, Inc., a new car dealer, placed a newspaper advertisement stating that Harrin would sell 10 cars at its showroom for a special discount only on September 12, 13, and 14. On September 12, King called Harrin and expressed an interest in buying one of the advertised cars. King was told that five of the cars had been sold and that King should come to the showroom as soon as possible. On September 13, Harrin made a televised announcement that the sale would end at 10:00 p.m. that night. King went to Harrin's showroom on September 14 and demanded the right to buy a car at the special discount. Harrin had sold the 10 cars and refused King's demand. King sued Harrin for breach of contract. Harrin's best defense to King's suit would be that Harrin's

    A. Offer was unenforceable.

    B. Advertisement was not an offer.

    C. Television announcement revoked the offer.

    D. Offer had not been accepted.

Answer (B) is correct.
    REQUIRED: The legal effect of a newspaper advertisement quoting sales prices.
    DISCUSSION: Newspaper advertisements that merely cite prices on items in stock are invitations to negotiate, not offers. In rare instances, an advertisement may be so definite and indicate such clear intent that it constitutes an offer and not a solicitation of offers, e.g., a promise to give one mink stole for $1 to the first person requesting it on April 5.
    Answer (A) is incorrect. If an offer had existed, and King's telephone call was an acceptance, the resulting agreement would have been enforceable. Answer (C) is incorrect. No offer existed that could have been revoked. Answer (D) is incorrect. If the newspaper advertisement constituted an offer, King might argue that the offer was accepted on September 12.

4. Ann Mayer wrote Tom Jackson and offered to sell Jackson a building for $200,000. The offer stated it would expire 30 days from July 1. Mayer changed her mind and does not wish to be bound by the offer. If a legal dispute arises between the parties regarding whether there has been a valid acceptance of the offer, which of the following is true?

    A. The offer cannot be legally withdrawn for the stated period of time.

    B. The offer will not expire prior to the 30 days even if Mayer sells the property to a third person and notifies Jackson.

    C. If Jackson phoned Mayer on August 1 and unequivocally accepted the offer, a contract would be formed, provided Jackson had no notice of withdrawal of the offer.

    D. If Jackson categorically rejects the offer on July 10, Jackson cannot validly accept within the remaining stated period of time.

Answer (D) is correct.
    REQUIRED: The true statement about termination of an offer.
    DISCUSSION: Rejection of an offer terminates it. An offeree cannot accept an offer after rejection is effective. An attempted acceptance after rejection is a new offer.
    Answer (A) is incorrect. The offer may be legally withdrawn at any time prior to acceptance, even though it states it will be held open for a specified period. An offer for sale of a building is not a firm offer under the UCC because it is not for a sale of goods. Answer (B) is incorrect. Notice to the offeree of sale of the property to a third person has the effect of terminating the offer. Answer (C) is incorrect. Acceptance on August 1 would be ineffective. The time provided for acceptance expires on July 31.

17.3 Consideration

5. For there to be consideration for a contract, there must be

A. A bargained-for detriment to the promisor(ee) or a benefit to the promisee(or).

B. A manifestation of mutual assent.

C. Genuineness of assent.

D. Substantially equal economic benefits to both parties.

Answer (A) is correct.

REQUIRED: The element that is necessary for consideration.

DISCUSSION: The consideration provided by one party (the promisee) to support the enforceability of the other party's (the promisor's) promise may be a bargained-for legal detriment to the promisee or a legal benefit to the promisor. Consideration is always in the form of a promise, act, or forbearance.

Answer (B) is incorrect. A manifestation of assent is an element of a contract distinct from consideration. Answer (C) is incorrect. Genuineness of assent is a contractual element distinct from consideration. Answer (D) is incorrect. Courts rarely question adequacy or equality of consideration.

17.4 Capacity

6. Green was adjudicated incompetent by a court having proper jurisdiction. Which of the following statements is true regarding contracts subsequently entered into by Green?

A. All contracts are voidable.

B. All contracts are valid.

C. All contracts are void.

D. All contracts are enforceable.

Answer (C) is correct.

REQUIRED: The consequence of an adjudication of mental incompetence.

DISCUSSION: An incompetent person is one whose mental capacity is such that (s)he is unable to understand the nature and consequences of his or her acts. If a person is adjudicated insane or otherwise incompetent before a contract is entered into, the contract is void and cannot be ratified (even after the person is later adjudged competent).

17.5 Legality

7. West, an Indiana real estate broker, misrepresented to Zimmer that West was licensed in Kansas under the Kansas statute that regulates real estate brokers and requires all brokers to be licensed. Zimmer signed a contract agreeing to pay West a 5% commission for selling Zimmer's home in Kansas. West did not sign the contract. West sold Zimmer's home. If West sued Zimmer for nonpayment of commission, Zimmer would be

A. Liable to West only for the value of services rendered.

B. Liable to West for the full commission.

C. Not liable to West for any amount because West did not sign the contract.

D. Not liable to West for any amount because West violated the Kansas licensing requirements.

Answer (D) is correct.

REQUIRED: The recovery for services rendered in violation of a regulatory statute.

DISCUSSION: A person who performs services without obtaining a statutorily required license may recover only if the statute is solely a revenue measure. If the legislative intent was to protect the public from incompetent work by unqualified persons, the statute is regulatory and the contract is unenforceable, even if the defendant was benefited and the work performed was satisfactory.

Answer (A) is incorrect. A court will not give any remedy to a party who violates a regulatory statute. West will not recover in quasi-contract although Zimmer was unjustly enriched. Answer (B) is incorrect. A violator of a regulatory statute is not permitted any recovery. Answer (C) is incorrect. The contract is not subject to the statute of frauds. (It is not a contract to sell real property.) If it were, failure of West to sign would not relieve Zimmer of liability.

17.6 Lack of Genuine Assent

8. The intent, or scienter, element necessary to establish a cause of action for fraud will be met if the plaintiff can show that the

A. Defendant made a misrepresentation with a reckless disregard for the truth.

B. Defendant made a false representation of fact.

C. Plaintiff actually relied on the defendant's misrepresentation.

D. Plaintiff justifiably relied on the defendant's misrepresentation.

Answer (A) is correct.

REQUIRED: The proof of intent to defraud.

DISCUSSION: The essence of fraud is that one party intentionally deceives to take advantage of another. The scienter, or intent, element of a fraud action is satisfied if the defendant knew of the falsity of a representation, or (s)he made it with reckless disregard for whether it was true. The defendant must have intended that the other party rely on the representation.

9. A building subcontractor submitted a bid for construction of a portion of a high-rise office building. The bid contained material computational errors. The general contractor accepted the bid with knowledge of the errors. Which of the following statements best represents the subcontractor's liability?

A. Not liable because the contractor knew of the errors.

B. Not liable because the errors were a result of gross negligence.

C. Liable because the errors were unilateral.

D. Liable because the errors were material.

Answer (A) is correct.

REQUIRED: The effect of a material unilateral mistake.

DISCUSSION: Generally, a unilateral mistake in fact does not invalidate a contract except in limited circumstances. In this case, the subcontractor is not liable. The mistake was an obvious mathematical error, and the general contractor was aware of the mistake and was not acting in good faith. The contract is voidable at the subcontractor's option.

Answer (B) is incorrect. The subcontractor would be liable under the contract if the error were the result of gross negligence. Answer (C) is incorrect. The other contracting party knew of the mistake and was acting unfairly. Answer (D) is incorrect. Only if the unilateral mistake was material to formation would it be voidable by the mistaken party in limited circumstances.

17.7 Statute of Frauds

10. Which of the following statements is true with regard to the statute of frauds?

A. All contracts involving consideration of $500 or more must be in writing.

B. The written contract must be signed by all parties.

C. The statute of frauds applies to contracts that can be fully performed within 1 year from the date they are made.

D. The contract terms may be stated in more than one document.

Answer (D) is correct.

REQUIRED: The true statement about the statute of frauds.

DISCUSSION: If a contract is within the statute of frauds, it is not enforceable at law unless requirements of the statute are satisfied. There must be a sufficient written memorandum of the contract. It may be stated in more than one document if evidence shows they are all related. One of them must be signed by the party against whom enforcement is sought.

Answer (A) is incorrect. Under the UCC, contracts for the sale of goods for $500 or more must be in writing. All contracts for $500 or more are not within the general statute of frauds. Answer (B) is incorrect. A party who signs a sufficient writing may be bound to performance, even if the other parties do not sign. Answer (C) is incorrect. The statute of frauds applies to a contract that cannot be performed within a year of its making.

11. Kram sent Fargo, a real estate broker, a signed offer to sell a specified parcel of land to Fargo for $250,000. Kram, an engineer, had inherited the land. On the same day that Kram's letter was received, Fargo telephoned Kram and accepted the offer. Which of the following statements is correct under the statute of frauds?

A. No contract could be formed because Fargo's acceptance was oral.

B. No contract could be formed because Kram's letter was signed only by Kram.

C. A contract was formed and would be enforceable against both Kram and Fargo.

D. A contract was formed but would be enforceable only against Kram.

Answer (D) is correct.

REQUIRED: The true statement under the statute of frauds about oral acceptance of a written offer to sell real property.

DISCUSSION: An agreement to sell an interest in real property is within the statute of frauds. An agreement that meets the criteria for the formation of an oral contract (offer and acceptance, consideration, mutual assent, capacity of the parties, and legality) but is within the statute of frauds is enforceable only against a party who signs a written memorandum of the offer. Fargo's oral acceptance bound Kram but not Fargo.

Answer (A) is incorrect. A contract was formed, but it is enforceable only against the party who signed the writing. The statute of frauds addresses the enforceability of a contract, not its formation. Answer (B) is incorrect. The statute of frauds only requires the signature of the defendant. No writing needs to be signed by Fargo. Answer (C) is incorrect. Under the statute of frauds, a contract is generally not enforceable against a party who did not sign a writing.

17.8 Parol Evidence Rule

12. Two individuals signed a written contract that was intended to be their entire agreement. The parol evidence rule will prevent the admission of evidence that is offered to

A. Prove the existence of a contemporaneous oral agreement that modifies the contract.

B. Prove the existence of a subsequent oral agreement that modifies the contract.

C. Explain the meaning of an ambiguity in the written contract.

D. Establish that fraud had been committed in formation of the contract.

Answer (A) is correct.
REQUIRED: The applicability of the parol evidence rule.
DISCUSSION: The parol evidence rule excludes any prior agreement or an oral agreement made at the time of the final writing that would tend to vary or contradict the terms of a written agreement intended to be complete. If the parties meant their written agreement to be entire, only terms incorporated directly or by reference are part of the contract as it existed at the time it was set forth in writing and signed.
Answer (B) is incorrect. Evidence of a later agreement does not modify the contract as it existed at the time it was made. Answer (C) is incorrect. Evidence to clarify an ambiguity is admissible. Answer (D) is incorrect. Evidence to prove fraud is admissible.

17.9 Performance, Discharge, and Breach

13. Dell owed Stark $9,000. As the result of an unrelated transaction, Stark owed Ball that same amount. The three parties signed an agreement that Dell would pay Ball instead of Stark, and Stark would be discharged from all liability. The agreement among the parties is

A. A novation.

B. An executed accord and satisfaction.

C. Voidable at Ball's option.

D. Unenforceable for lack of consideration.

Answer (A) is correct.
REQUIRED: The true statement about an agreement to discharge a debtor from liability.
DISCUSSION: A novation is a new contract that replaces and releases a party to the prior contract with another who was not originally a party. Replacing in the Stark-Ball contract the former promisor (Stark) with a new promisor (Dell) is a novation.
Answer (B) is incorrect. By an accord, a promisee agrees to accept a substituted performance by the promisor. Performance of the accord (execution of the contract) is the satisfaction. Answer (C) is incorrect. No basis for voidability is apparent. Answer (D) is incorrect. The promise by Dell to pay Stark's debt is consideration for Ball's discharge of Stark.

14. On May 25, Year 1, Smith contracted with Jackson to repair Smith's cabin cruiser. The work was to begin on May 31, Year 1. On May 26, Year 1, the boat, while docked at Smith's pier, was destroyed by arson. Which of the following statements is true with regard to the contract?

A. Smith would not be liable to Jackson because of mutual mistake.

B. Smith would be liable to Jackson for the profit Jackson would have made under the contract.

C. Jackson would not be liable to Smith because performance by the parties would be impossible.

D. Jackson would be liable to repair another boat owned by Smith.

Answer (C) is correct.
REQUIRED: The parties' liability when the subject matter of a contract is destroyed.
DISCUSSION: Nonperformance is excused when circumstances change so completely that performance is objectively impossible because no one could perform the duty. Impossibility discharges contractual obligations by operation of law. It occurs when the subject matter of, or an item or commodity essential to, the contract is destroyed. The impossibility must arise after and could not have been reasonably contemplated at contract formation.
Answer (A) is incorrect. Mutual mistake is present at, not after, contract formation. It would apply if, without the knowledge of the parties, the boat were destroyed before formation. Answer (B) is incorrect. To the extent the doctrine of impossibility applies, performance by both parties is excused, and the contract is canceled. Answer (D) is incorrect. Under the doctrine of impossibility, duties are discharged, not substituted. But performance of a promise to supply a commodity is not impossible when an alternative supply is available.

17.10 Remedies

15. In June, Mullin, a general contractor, contracted with a town to renovate the town square. The town council wanted the project done quickly, and the parties placed a clause in the contract that for each day the project extended beyond 90 working days, Mullin would forfeit $100 of the contract price. In August, Mullin took a 3-week vacation. The project was completed in October, 120 working days after it was begun. What type of damages may the town recover from Mullin?

A. Punitive damages because taking a vacation in the middle of the project was irresponsible.

B. Compensatory damages because of the delay in completing the project.

C. Liquidated damages because of the clause in the contract.

D. No damages because Mullin completed performance.

Answer (C) is correct.
    REQUIRED: The damages, if any, that may be collected given a contract clause providing for penalties for late performance.
    DISCUSSION: By a liquidated damages clause, the parties to a contract agree in advance to the damages to be paid in the event of a breach. A liquidated damages clause is enforceable if all of the following apply: (1) It is not intended as a penalty, (2) it reasonably forecasts the probable loss due to the breach, and (3) the loss is difficult to calculate.
    Answer (A) is incorrect. Punitive damages are intended to punish a wrongdoer and to set an example for others. It is extremely rare for a court to award punitive damages in a contract suit. It might if a breach is malicious, willful, or physically injurious to the nonbreaching party, e.g., willful and malicious refusal to pay valid medical claims of an insured. Answer (B) is incorrect. Compensatory damages (also called actual damages or general damages) are damages incurred from the wrongful conduct of the breaching party. The usual measure of compensatory damages is the amount of money necessary to compensate the nonbreaching party for the breach. Answer (D) is incorrect. Mullin breached the clause in the contract requiring completion within 90 days.

16. For which of the following contracts will a court generally grant the remedy of specific performance?

A. A contract for the sale of a patent.

B. A contract of employment.

C. A contract for the sale of fungible goods.

D. A contract for the sale of stock that is traded on a national stock exchange.

Answer (A) is correct.
    REQUIRED: The contract for which a court will generally grant specific performance.
    DISCUSSION: Specific performance is granted when no other remedy is adequate, and irreparable injury will result if it is not granted. Thus, monetary damages are not available or are not adequate, and the subject matter of the contract is unique, e.g., a rare painting or land. A patent meets the requirements for specific performance because it is unique. In addition, monetary damages are not adequate because no reliable method exists for determining how much money the purchaser would have earned from the use of the patent.
    Answer (B) is incorrect. Specific performance of a service contract is never granted. Answer (C) is incorrect. Fungible goods are not unique. Answer (D) is incorrect. Monetary damages are adequate for stock traded on a national exchange.

17.11 Contract Beneficiaries

17. Ferco, Inc., claims to be a creditor beneficiary of a contract between Bell and Allied Industries, Inc. Allied is indebted to Ferco. The contract between Bell and Allied provides that Bell is to purchase certain goods from Allied and pay the purchase price directly to Ferco until Allied's obligation is satisfied. Without justification, Bell failed to pay Ferco and Ferco sued Bell. Ferco will

A. Not prevail, because Ferco lacked privity of contract with either Bell or Allied.

B. Not prevail, because Ferco did not give any consideration to Bell.

C. Prevail, because Ferco was an intended beneficiary of the contract.

D. Prevail, provided Ferco was aware of the contract between Bell and Allied at the time the contract was entered into.

Answer (C) is correct.
    REQUIRED: The rights of a creditor who is a payee of a contract between the payor and the debtor.
    DISCUSSION: A creditor beneficiary has standing to enforce a contract to which (s)he is a third party. Because the intent of the promisee (Allied) in entering into the contract with Bell was specifically to have return performance (payment) to discharge the debt to a third party (Ferco), the third party is a creditor beneficiary.
    Answer (A) is incorrect. Ferco was an intended beneficiary of the contract between Bell and Allied. Also, Ferco is in privity of contract with Allied. Answer (B) is incorrect. An intended beneficiary may enforce a contract enforceable between the parties. An essential element of the contract was consideration, but not from Ferco. Answer (D) is incorrect. Creditor awareness is not sufficient. The parties to the contract must have intended direct benefit to the third party.

18. Rice contracted with Locke to build an oil refinery for Locke. The contract provided that Rice was to use United pipe fittings. Rice did not do so. United learned of the contract and, anticipating the order, manufactured additional fittings. United sued Locke and Rice. United is

A. Entitled to recover only from Rice because Rice breached the contract.

B. Entitled to recover from either Locke or Rice because it detrimentally relied on the contract.

C. Not entitled to recover because it is a donee beneficiary.

D. Not entitled to recover because it is an incidental beneficiary.

Answer (D) is correct.
    REQUIRED: The status of a manufacturer regarding a construction contract stipulating the use of its product.
    DISCUSSION: A person who is neither a primary contracting party nor an intended third-party beneficiary has no right to sue on a contract. United is a mere incidental beneficiary, a person who may have been indirectly affected by the agreement but was not intended to be directly benefited.
    Answer (A) is incorrect. United was not an intended beneficiary. Answer (B) is incorrect. United's reliance is irrelevant. It is merely an incidental beneficiary. Answer (C) is incorrect. A person is a donee beneficiary if the promisor's performance was intended as a gift to that person.

17.12 Assignment and Delegation

19. Moss entered into a contract to purchase certain real property from Shinn. Which of the following statements is **false**?

A. If Shinn fails to perform the contract, Moss can obtain specific performance.

B. The contract is nonassignable as a matter of law.

C. The statute of frauds applies to the contract.

D. Any amendment to the contract must be agreed to by both Moss and Shinn.

Answer (B) is correct.
    REQUIRED: The legal effect and assignability of a valid real estate contract.
    DISCUSSION: Contracts are generally assignable. Assignment is ineffective if a risk or duty of a party to the contract is materially increased, or an exception otherwise applies.
    Answer (A) is incorrect. Each parcel of real property is considered unique. Thus, monetary damages are deemed an inadequate remedy for the buyer. (S)he may seek specific performance. Answer (C) is incorrect. A contract for the purchase and sale of real property is within the statute of frauds. Answer (D) is incorrect. To be enforceable, a contract modification must be agreed to by both parties. But consideration may not be required.

20. One of the criteria for a valid assignment of a sales contract to a third party is that the assignment must

A. Be supported by adequate consideration from the assignee.

B. Be in writing and signed by the assignor.

C. Not materially increase the other party's risk or duty.

D. Not be revocable by the assignor.

Answer (C) is correct.
    REQUIRED: The requirement for a valid assignment of a sales contract.
    DISCUSSION: Unless agreed otherwise, most contract rights can be assigned. However, a contract right cannot be assigned if it would materially increase the risk or duty of the other party. If an assignment would materially increase the risk or duty sustained by the other party, the assignment is invalid.
    Answer (A) is incorrect. Adequate consideration is not a required element of a valid assignment. Gratuitous assignments are permissible. Answer (B) is incorrect. Generally, no writing is required for an assignment of contract rights to be valid. However, the statute of frauds requires a writing in certain situations. Answer (D) is incorrect. A gratuitous assignment is generally revocable by the assignor.

STUDY UNIT EIGHTEEN
AGENCY AND REGULATION

(18 pages of outline)

The law of agency is a common law concept that allows one person to employ another to do his or her work. The American Law Institute's Restatement (Second) of the Law of Agency summarizes the common law. In 2006, the ALI published a new version, the Restatement of the Law Third, Agency, which was adopted by most states. The law of agency relates to the rights and duties of the principal, the agent, and third parties. The emphasis on the CPA exam will be (1) the formation and termination of an agency, (2) the duties of the agent to the principal and third parties, (3) the duties of the principal to the agent and third parties, (4) the agent's actual and apparent authority, and (5) the significance of whether the agency is disclosed.

The remainder of this subunit relates to employer compliance with the federal laws and regulations governing employment taxes and the Affordable Care Act.

18.1 AGENCY FORMATION

1. **Overview**

   a. Agency describes an express or implied consensual relationship whereby two parties mutually agree that one party (the "agent") will act on behalf of the other party (the "principal") in dealing with third parties.

      1) The **agent** has authority to act on behalf of the principal and is subject to the principal's **control**.

      2) The **principal** must intend for the agent to act on the principal's behalf.

      3) Courts apply an objective standard, the "reasonable person standard," in determining whether parties have consented to an agency relationship.

EXAMPLE

Bud overheard Harold say, "I wish I had a boat." Bud went to Boatworld and told the salesperson that, acting as Harold's agent, he wanted to buy a boat. An agency was not formed since Harold never intended for Bud to act on his behalf.

---

   b. An agent must agree to act on the principal's behalf as a **fiduciary**.

   c. An agency must have a **legal purpose**.

      1) Agencies formed for an illegal purpose are terminated by operation of law

   d. A **principal** must have legal **capacity** to perform an act assigned to the agent. Legal **incapacity** applies to individuals the law considers incapable of incurring any binding contractual obligations.

      1) A contract entered into with a third party by an agent on behalf of an incompetent principal is voidable by the principal.

      2) An incompetent agent, such as a minor, can bind a competent principal because the agent's act is deemed to be the act of the principal.

   e. Personal acts, such as executing a will, may not be delegated.

f. An agency relationship itself is not a contract. **The doctrine of consideration belongs exclusively to contracts.**

1) Agents who act without receiving consideration are **gratuitous agents**. The rights and powers of gratuitous agents are the same as the rights and powers of agents who do receive consideration.

2) If an agency relationship is formed through a contractual transaction, then the principal must provide consideration.

2. **Formation**

a. The general rule is that conduct, by itself, is **sufficient** to form an agency relationship. An agency relationship can be formed by actions even if the parties do not verbally or in writing express their consent.

1) However, an agency must be in writing to comply with the statute of frauds if performance under the contract cannot be fulfilled within 1 year of contract formation.

2) Some states require the agency to be in writing if the contract involves a sale of land.

3) Some states apply the **equal-dignities rule**, which requires that the agency relationship be in writing if the agent is entering contractual transactions with third parties that must be in writing to be enforceable under the statute of frauds.

b. An agency may be **implied in law** without intent to form the relationship.

1) A person may be held liable as a principal for the act of another person regardless of whether the principal intended to grant any authority. For example, a court may determine that an agent acted properly outside of a delegated authority in an emergency when the principal was unavailable.

c. **Agency by Estoppel**

1) This condition may arise if

a) A person presents himself or herself as an agent,

b) The alleged principal knows (or should know) of the representation and fails to make an effective denial, and

c) A third party detrimentally relies on the existence of this presumed agency.

2) The principal is prevented from asserting the nonexistence of an agency after a third party has taken some action in reasonable reliance on its existence.

d. A **power of attorney** is a formal written appointment of an agent signed by the principal. But it need not be for a definite period.

1) A **general power of attorney** authorizes the agent to do anything that may be necessary to transact the principal's legal affairs.

2) A **special power of attorney** grants authority for only specific transactions.

3) General and special powers of attorney ordinarily terminate upon incapacity of the principal. But any power of attorney may be exercised in good faith and with no knowledge of the principal's incapacity.

4) A **durable power of attorney** is effective during a period of incapacity of the principal.

a) This power of attorney must be expressly conferred in writing before the principal becomes incapacitated.

5) All powers of attorney ordinarily terminate upon the **death** of the principal. But any power of attorney may be exercised in good faith and with no knowledge of the principal's death.

e. An agency may be formed by **ratification** of another's acts.

3. **Types of Agents**

    a.   **General agents** are authorized to perform all acts relevant to the purpose for which they are engaged.

    b.   **Universal agents** are authorized to conduct all of the principal's business that the principal may legally delegate.

    c.   **Special agents** are engaged for a particular transaction and are authorized to perform specific activities subject to specific instructions.

    d.   A **del credere agent** acts not only as a salesperson or broker for the principal, but also as a guarantor of credit extended to the buyer. The del credere agent guarantees a third party's obligation to the principal.

        1)   Because the primary purpose of the agent's guarantee is for the agent's benefit (to close the deal), it is not subject to the statute of frauds and, unlike other suretyship promises, it need not be in writing.

    e.   Under the Third Restatement, a **power given as security** confers the ability to affect the legal relations of its creator. The power itself does **not** establish an agency or confer actual authority. However, it is created in the form of a manifestation of actual authority held for the benefit of the holder or a third party.

        1)   For example, Debtor (the creator) and Creditor (the holder) agree in writing that, if Debtor defaults, Creditor will have Debtor's authority to transfer ownership of specified property to Creditor.

        2)   The broad definition of a power given as security includes the traditional **agency coupled with an interest**. In this form of agency, the agent has a specific, current, beneficial interest in the subject matter of the agency.

            a)   The principal does **not** have the right or power of termination.

            b)   The agent's interest in the subject matter is **not** exercised for the benefit of the principal. An example is an agent-creditor's power to sell collateral if the debt is not paid.

EXAMPLE

A stockbroker working on commission does not have an agency coupled with an interest. Receipt of a commission depends on whether the shareholder receives a benefit from the sale of the stock. The interest need not be an ownership or security interest in the stock itself.

Stop and review! You have completed the outline for this subunit. Study multiple-choice questions 1 through 4 beginning on page 502.

18.2 AGENT'S AUTHORITY AND DUTIES

    The CPA exam has tested candidates' knowledge of an agent's actual and apparent authority. Candidates need to remember that the principal is liable on contracts made by an agent who has actual, apparent, or emergency authority.

1. **Authority**

    a.   An agent has the authority to act on behalf of the principal under the principal's direction and control.

        1)   The most important legal consequence of the agency relationship is the agent's power to bind the principal to third parties.

        2)   In order to hold a principal liable for the acts of an agent, the agent must have **actual or apparent authority** to act on the principal's behalf.

b.   **Actual Authority**

1)   Actual authority is conveyed to the agent by the principal's words or conduct. The agent receives the right and power to bind the principal to third parties.

   a)   **Express actual authority** results when the agent has been expressly told either by written or spoken words that (s)he may act on behalf of the principal.

   b)   **Implied actual authority** is incidental authority the agent has inferred from words or conduct by the principal.

      i)   It may be inferred from custom and usage of the business or by virtue of the agent's position relative to the purposes of the agency.

      ii)   Express authority to achieve a result necessarily implies the authority to use reasonable means to accomplish the expressly authorized action.

      iii)   Secret limitations on an agent's actual authority create **apparent authority**.

c.   **Apparent Authority**

1)   Apparent authority is determined by looking at the principal's words, conduct, and other facts and circumstances a reasonable person would justifiably use to conclude the agent has actual authority.

   a)   It gives the agent the power, but not necessarily the right, to bind the principal to third parties.

   b)   A third party's rights against the principal are **not** affected by secret limits placed on the agent's actual authority by the principal.

   c)   The agent is liable to the principal for exceeding actual authority but **not** to the third party.

2)   Apparent authority is **not** based on the words or actions of the agent, and it cannot exist if the principal is **undisclosed** (the third party is unaware of any agency). It is based on justifiable reliance on the conduct of the principal.

   a)   The agent has no apparent authority if the third party knows the agent lacks actual authority.

3)   Apparent authority may continue after termination of the agency until the third party receives notice.

4)   Under the Second Restatement, apparent authority ends when the agency is automatically terminated by operation of law.

5)   Under the Third Restatement, apparent authority ends if it is unreasonable for third parties who deal with the agent to believe that (s)he has actual authority.

d.   A court may grant **emergency authority** when prompt action is needed.

1)   An agent's delegated authority may be extended if the public interest is served.

Authority of an Agent
• Actual
1) Express
2) Implied
• Apparent
• Emergency

2. **Subagents**

    a.   Generally, an agent is chosen because of his or her personal qualities. Thus, an agent does **not** have the power to **delegate** authority or to appoint a subagent unless the principal intends to grant it. But delegation that is not expressly authorized may be appropriate in an emergency.

    b.   Evidence that the principal intends that the agent be permitted to delegate authority may include

        1)   An express authorization,
        2)   The character of the business,
        3)   Usage or trade, or
        4)   Prior conduct of the principal and agent.

    c.   If the agent makes an unauthorized appointment of a subagent, the subagent is **not** able to bind the principal.

    d.   If the agent is authorized to appoint a subagent, the subagent

        1)   Is an agent of both the principal and the agent,
        2)   Binds the principal as if (s)he were the agent, and
        3)   Owes a fiduciary duty to the principal and the agent.

3. **Agent's Duties to the Principal**

    a.   **Types of Duties**

        1)   Parties to an agency relationship often form contractual relationships regarding the terms of the principal-agent agreement.

        2)   The agency relationship itself, however, is independent of any contractual relationships the parties may have formed. The agency relationship is subject to the five duties and obligations set forth under agency law.

            a)   Loyalty
            b)   Care
            c)   Notification
            d)   Obedience
            e)   Accounting

    b.   **Duty of Loyalty**

        1)   The agency is a **fiduciary** relationship that imposes a **duty of loyalty** on the agent to act solely in the principal's interest with utmost loyalty and in good faith.

        2)   The agent's duty of loyalty encompasses specific duties of selflessness that serve to protect the principal's economic interest.

        3)   The agent is obligated to refrain from

            a)   Competing with the principal;
            b)   Purchasing goods from the agent for the principal without the principal's knowledge or permission;
            c)   Accepting secret profits or transactions entered into on behalf of the principal;
            d)   Representing the principal, if doing so creates a conflict of interest between parties;
            e)   Misappropriating the principal's property; and
            f)   Disclosing the principal's confidential information for the agent's own benefit or for the benefit of third parties.

c.   **Duty of Care**

1)   The agent must use the care and skill of a reasonable person in like circumstances and with his or her special skills or knowledge in performing agency duties.

2)   The agent must act prudently and cautiously to avoid injury to the interests of the principal.

d.   **Duty of Notification (Duty of Disclosure)**

1)   When an agent possesses information relating to the business that the principal may need or desire to know, the agent has **a duty to notify** the principal of all material facts.

2)   The agent must make reasonable efforts to provide information to the principal that

a)   Is relevant to the subject matter of the agency, and

b)   The agent knows or should know will be imputed to the principal.

i)   An example is an agent's knowledge of dangerous conditions. The principal may be held liable to an injured third party to the same extent as if (s)he had actual knowledge of the dangerous condition.

3)   A person receives notice by actual knowledge of a fact, having reason to know of its existence, or receiving formal notice.

a)   Thus, notice to an agent authorized to receive it is notice to the principal.

b)   Moreover, knowledge possessed by an agent is assumed to be known by the principal if it is important to an authorized transaction.

EXAMPLE

Allan is Peter's agent for the sale of art. Allan falsely and intentionally overstates the value of a painting to a buyer. Peter is assumed to have knowledge of the fraud.

---

e.   **Duty of Obedience**

1)   The agent must follow lawful, explicit instructions of the principal within the bounds of authority conferred.

2)   If the instructions are not clear, the agent must act in good faith and in a reasonable manner considering the circumstances.

3)   If an emergency arises and the agent cannot reach the principal, the agent may deviate from instructions to the extent that is appropriate.

f.   **Duty of Accounting**

   1)   The agent must

      a)   Account for money or property received or expended on behalf of the principal and

      b)   **Not** commingle his or her money or property with that of the principal.

Agent's Duties to the Principal
• Contractual Duties
• Duty of Loyalty 1) Loyalty and good faith 2) Duty not to compete 3) Duty not to engage in self-dealing 4) No secret profits 5) Avoidance of conflicts of interest 6) No misappropriation 7) Protection of confidential information
• Duty of Care
• Duty of Notification (Duty of Disclosure)
• Duty of Obedience
• Duty of Accounting

4.   **Agent's Breach of Duty and Liability to Principal**

   a.   The agent is liable to the principal for losses resulting from the agent's breach of a duty.

   b.   Transactions between the principal and the agent may be voidable by the principal.

   c.   A constructive trust in favor of the principal is imposed on profits obtained by the agent as a result of breaching the fiduciary duty.

      1)   The agent, in effect, holds the profits in trust for the benefit of the principal.
      2)   The principal recovers the profits by suing the agent.

   d.   If the principal is sued for the agent's negligence or the agent ignores the principal's instructions, the principal has a right to indemnification from the agent.

5.   **Agent's Contractual Liability to Third Parties**

   a.   The agent may assume liability on any contract by

      1)   Making the contract in his or her name,
      2)   Being a party to the contract with the principal, or
      3)   Guaranteeing the principal's performance.

   b.   The agent is liable if the principal is undisclosed or partially disclosed.

6.   **Agent's Tort Liability to Third Parties**

   a.   A person is liable for his or her torts (e.g., negligence) even when acting as an agent of another.

Stop and review! You have completed the outline for this subunit. Study multiple-choice questions 5 through 8 beginning on page 503.

18.3 PRINCIPAL'S DUTIES AND LIABILITIES

1. **Duties to the Agent -- Financial**

    a.   If a contract exists between the agent and the principal, the principal has a duty to comply with the contractual terms. For example, if the duty to compensate is not expressly excluded, the principal should **compensate** the agent for services. This duty includes keeping accurate **records** of payments made to the agent.

       1)   If compensation is **not** stated expressly, the reasonable value of the agent's services is implied.

       2)   But if the agent agrees to act gratuitously, (s)he is **not** owed a duty of compensation.

    b.   Whether the agency is gratuitous or contractual, the principal has a duty to **reimburse** the agent for authorized payments made or expenses incurred by the agent on behalf of the principal.

    c.   Regardless of whether the agency is gratuitous or contractual, the principal has a duty to **indemnify** the agent. The indemnity is for losses suffered or expenses incurred while the agent acted

       1)   As instructed in a legal transaction or

       2)   In a transaction that the agent did not know to be wrongful.

    d.   The principal does **not** owe a fiduciary duty to the agent.

2. **Duties to the Agent -- Occupational**

    a.   The principal has a duty **not to impair** the agent's performance.

    b.   The principal owes a **general duty of care** to the agent because a principal-agent relationship exists.

    c.   The principal has a duty to **disclose known risks** involved in the task for which the agent is engaged and of which the agent is unaware.

    d.   The principal has a duty to provide an agent who is an employee with reasonably **safe working conditions**.

    e.   The principal does **not** owe a fiduciary duty to the agent.

Principal's Duties to the Agent

• Financial
    1) Compensation
    2) Reimbursement
    3) Indemnification

• Occupational
    1) Nonimpairment of agent's performance
    2) General duty of care
    3) Disclosure of known risks
    4) Provision of reasonably safe working conditions

---

3. **Agent's Remedies against Principal**

    a.   The agent's remedies for a principal's breach of a duty include

       1)   Withholding performance or terminating the agency relationship,

       2)   Counterclaiming if the principal sues,

       3)   Demanding an accounting, and

       4)   Filing a civil action seeking tort and contract remedies.

          a)   But certain contract remedies, e.g., specific performance, may not be available if the agency is not based on a contract.

4. **Contractual Liability to Third Parties**

    a.   If the agent has actual or apparent authority, the principal generally will be held liable on contracts that the agent entered into with a third party.

    b.   Whether the principal is disclosed, partially disclosed, or undisclosed determines the principal's and agent's contractual liability.

        1)   **Disclosed principal.** If the third party knows the agent is acting for a principal and the identity of the principal, an agent who acts within actual or apparent authority ordinarily is not liable to the third party.

        2)   **Partially disclosed principal.** The third party knows the agent is acting for a principal but does not know the identity of the principal.

            a)   The liability of the agent and a partially disclosed principal is **joint and several liability**. The third party may sue either or both the principal and agent and collect any amount from either until the judgment is satisfied.

        3)   **Undisclosed principal.** The third party is unaware of any agency and believes that (s)he is dealing directly with a principal, not an agent.

            a)   The third party has no legal right to disclosure.

            b)   **Actual** authority is unaffected. By definition, however, **apparent** authority does **not** exist.

            c)   To enforce the contract, the third party may sue the agent of an undisclosed principal.

                i)   The third party intended to deal only with the agent, and the agent is a party to the contract.

            d)   The undisclosed principal generally may sue or be sued on the contract except when it would be unfair or unjust to the other party. But the undisclosed principal may not be able to enforce a contract that

                i)   Requires that credit be extended by the third party,

                ii)   Involves unique personal services of the agent,

                iii)   Involves nondelegable duties, or

                iv)   Is a negotiable instrument signed by the agent with no indication of his or her status.

EXAMPLE

If the agent issues a check to a third party on behalf of an undisclosed principal, the third party cannot enforce the check against the principal. The principal has not endorsed it.

---

            e)   Under traditional rules, if the undisclosed principal is discovered, the third party must elect whether to hold the principal or the agent liable for performance. But the third party has no right to void an otherwise valid contract.

            f)   If the agent does **not** have actual authority, the undisclosed principal generally is not liable to the third party.

            g)   Whether the principal is disclosed does not affect the duties of the principal and agent to each other.

Contractual Liabilities					
Principal	Agent's Authority	Principal's Liability to Third Party	Principal's Duty to Reimburse Agent	Principal's Right to Indemnity from Agent	Agent Liable to Third Party
Disclosed	Actual	Yes	Yes	No	No
	Apparent	Yes	No*	Yes*	No
	No Authority	No	No	No	Yes
Partially Disclosed	Actual	Yes	Yes	No	Yes
	Apparent	Yes	No*	Yes*	Yes
	No Authority	No	No	No	Yes
Undisclosed	Actual	Yes	Yes	No	Yes
	Apparent	N/A	N/A	N/A	N/A
	No Authority	No	No	No	Yes

* The agent has exceeded actual authority, and the principal has not ratified the actions of the agent. If the principal ratifies the actions of the agent, the principal has a duty to reimburse the agent but not the right to indemnity.

5. **Ratification**

   a. Ratification is a voluntary election to treat as authorized an unauthorized act or contract purportedly done or entered into on the principal's behalf.

      1) Notice to a third party is not needed for ratification.
      2) Ratification is unnecessary if the agent's act is authorized.

   b. The principal must be aware of **all material facts** when assenting to the agent's act. The agent need not have performed his or her fiduciary duty or duty of due care.

   c. Ratification may be either express or implied. It may be inferred from the principal's words or conduct that reasonably indicates intent to ratify.

EXAMPLE

Tony contracted to purchase 500 pounds of fish from Greg on behalf of Teresa's restaurant. Teresa did not know Tony or Greg and was unaware of the transaction. When the fish arrived, Teresa accepted the shipment. Her ratification of the transaction may be inferred.

---

   d. Ratification is all-or-nothing. The principal may not ratify part of a transaction.

   e. Ratification is irrevocable.

   f. Ratification relates back to the time of the act. The act is treated as if it had been authorized at the time it was performed.

   g. An agent has no liability to the third party after ratification.

      1) The rights, duties, and remedies of the parties are the same as if the agent had actual authority.
      2) If a principal does not ratify, the agent also is liable to the third party for breach of the **implied warranty of authority**.

   h. Under the Second Restatement, an undisclosed principal cannot ratify.

      1) Under the Third Restatement, a person may ratify (e.g., by accepting the benefits of the contract) if the unauthorized act was done or purported to be done on that person's behalf. However, the person who performed the unauthorized act need **not** have disclosed that (s)he was acting on behalf of a principal.
      2) The third party has no right to ratification.

    i.   An **undisclosed principal** may not be able to ratify certain contracts involving (1) personal services, (2) credit extended by the third party, or (3) nondelegable duties.

        1)   If the agent's unauthorized act is purportedly for an identified principal, only that person may ratify it.

            a)   Thus, the agent cannot substitute another principal if the identified principal does not ratify it.

    j.   Certain conditions terminate the power of ratification. Examples include

        1)   The third party's withdrawal, death, or loss of capacity;
        2)   Changes in circumstances; or
        3)   Failure to ratify within a reasonable time.

    k.   The principal must have the capacity to contract at the time of the unauthorized act and at the time of ratification.

6.   **Tort Liability**

    a.   A principal may be liable in tort because of a personal act or the agent's wrongful act that results in harm to a third party.

        1)   The principal's liability is greater when the agent is an employee rather than an independent contractor.

    b.   **Direct liability** results from the principal's negligent or reckless action or failure to act in conducting business through agents. Examples include

        1)   Negligently selecting an agent,
        2)   Failing to give proper orders or make proper regulations,
        3)   Failing to employ the proper person or machinery given risk of harm,
        4)   Failing to supervise the agent, or
        5)   Allowing wrongful conduct.

    c.   **Vicarious liability** results from the actions of the agent for which the principal, whether or not disclosed, is liable. Thus, both the principal and the agent are liable.

        1)   This type of liability is based upon the doctrine of **respondeat superior** (Latin for "let the master reply"). Vicarious liability holds employers liable for the tortious conduct of their employees.

        2)   An employer may be held vicariously liable for the employee's conduct when the employee

            a)   Commits a tort, whether negligently or intentionally;
            b)   Was not authorized by the principal to perform the act; or
            c)   Performs the act **within the scope of employment**.

                i)   An act is within the scope of employment when it is work assigned by the employer or a course of conduct subject to the employer's control.

                ii)   An act is **not** within the scope of employment when it is within an independent course of conduct not intended by the employee to serve a purpose of the employer.

        3)   A principal may be vicariously liable for an agent's material **misrepresentation** regardless of whether the agent is an **employee** or an **independent contractor**.

            a)   This misrepresentation must be within the scope of actual or apparent authority. It may be (1) fraudulent, (2) negligent, (3) innocent but with all the elements of fraud except wrongful intent (scienter), or (4) defamatory.

EXAMPLE

Mary Lou hired John, a real estate broker, as an independent contractor to market her 15-year-old home. John told Michelle that the home was only 5 years old. Michelle bought the home. Both Mary Lou and John are liable for any harm suffered by Michelle as a result of the misrepresentation. Moreover, Mary Lou is entitled to be indemnified by John if she must pay damages to Michelle for John's misrepresentation.

---

    d.   Any agreement between a principal and agent limiting the principal's liability has no effect on the liability of the principal to third parties.

7.   **Criminal Liability**

    a.   A principal is liable for his or her own criminal conduct.

    b.   A principal is generally **not** liable for a crime committed by the agent but may be held criminally liable for a crime of the agent if

        1)   The principal approves or directs the crime,

        2)   The principal participates or assists in the crime, or

        3)   Violation of a regulatory statute constituted the crime.

8.   **Employee vs. Independent Contractor**

    a.   An agent is either an employee or an independent contractor.

        1)   A principal employer controls or has the right to control the manner and means of an employee's work.

        2)   An employer does not control or have the right to control the manner and means of an independent contractor's work.

        NOTE: The Third Restatement does not use the term "independent contractor."

    b.   Whether an agent is an employee depends on

        1)   The parties' agreement about the degree of control by the principal;

        2)   The extent of supervision by the principal;

        3)   Whether the agent provides services exclusively for the principal;

        4)   The relationship of the nature of the business and the work of the agent;

        5)   The skills and specialization required for the task;

        6)   How the agent is paid, whether at the end of all work or periodically per unit of time;

        7)   Which party provides the agent's place of work, tools, and supplies; and

        8)   The duration of the relationship.

    c.   **Independent Contractors**

        1)   The principal generally is not liable for the torts of the independent contractor.

        2)   However, tort liability may result from a principal's own negligence, e.g., in the selection of the contractor.

        3)   The principal also may be subject to **strict liability**.

            a)   This liability of a principal is generally not vicarious.

            b)   Some duties cannot be delegated as a matter of law or public policy, for example, an employer's duty to provide employees with a safe workplace.

            c)   Persons engaging in ultrahazardous activity have strict liability. Contracting out ultrahazardous activities is not a shield against liability.

        4)   The principal is liable for representations made on behalf of the principal by the independent contractor that are actually or apparently authorized or ratified by the principal.

Stop and review! You have completed the outline for this subunit. Study multiple-choice questions 9 through 12 on page 505.

18.4 AGENCY TERMINATION

1. **Termination by the Parties**

   a. An agency is based on the mutual consent of the parties. Thus, it may be terminated at will by either party or both even if the termination breaches a contract between principal and agent.

   b. A principal may revoke a grant of authority at any time.

      1) **Revocation** may be implicit or explicit.

   c. An agent may renounce the grant of authority by giving notice to the principal.

   d. If termination breaches a contract, the nonbreaching party has remedies provided by contract law.

   e. An agency for a specific period terminates when the period ends.

2. **Termination by Operation of Law**

   a. Under the Second Restatement, termination by operation of law terminates actual or apparent authority in the following cases:

      1) **Death** or **incapacity** of either the principal or the agent.

      2) The **illegality** of duties to be performed by an agent.

EXAMPLE

An agency has been formed in which the agent is expected to sell the principal's real estate. If the agent fails to obtain a real estate license, the agency is void. An unlicensed agent cannot legally sell real estate for the principal.

---

        a) A change of law that makes an authorized act illegal also terminates the agency.

      3) The principal's filing of a petition in **bankruptcy**.

      4) **Destruction** of the subject matter of the agency that makes fulfilling the purpose of the agency impossible.

      5) A **change in circumstances** (a change in business conditions or the value of a property) so significant that a reasonable person would infer that actual authority is terminated.

        a) The agency might be revived upon a return to the initial circumstances.

        b) If the agent knows that the principal is aware of the change and the principal does not give new directions, the agency may not terminate.

        c) If the agent has reasonable doubts as to how or whether the principal wants the agent to act, the agent may act reasonably. That is, the agency is not terminated.

   b. The Third Restatement provides a broad rule. It states that an agent has actual authority when, at the time of performing an act that results in legal consequences for the principal, the agent reasonably believes that the principal wants the agent to perform the act. This belief should be based on the principal's manifestations to the agent.

      1) Accordingly, when changes have occurred so that the act on behalf of the principal is unreasonable, the agent has no actual authority.

      2) **Actual** authority is deemed to continue until the agent receives **notice**. Thus, the Third Restatement produces a different result in cases in which the Second Restatement automatically terminates actual authority, e.g., death, incapacity, or bankruptcy of the principal.

      3) The Third Restatement also provides that termination of actual authority does **not** end apparent authority.

Termination of an Agency

• By the Parties
  1) Mutual consent
  2) Principal's revocation of authority
  3) Agent's renunciation of authority
  4) Lapse of the period of the agency

• By Operation of Law
  1) Bankruptcy
  2) Death or incapacity
  3) Illegality of agent's duties
  4) Destruction of subject matter
  5) Agent's breach of a fiduciary duty
  6) Change in circumstances

3. **Agency Coupled with an Interest**

   a.   An agency coupled with an interest may be terminated

   1)   According to the terms of the agreement,
   2)   By surrender of the authority by the agent, or
   3)   Upon destruction of the subject matter of the agency.

   b.   An agency coupled with an interest generally is **not** terminated by

   1)   Revocation by the principal,
   2)   Death of the principal, or
   3)   Loss of legal capacity of the principal.

4. **Termination of Apparent Authority**

   a.   Apparent authority of the agent continues to exist until the third party receives notice of the termination if the termination is by an act of the parties.

   1)   **Actual** notice (an effective notification) to the third party is required if the third party has already dealt with the agent.
   2)   **Constructive** notice generally suffices for other third parties.

   a)   The requirement is satisfied by a message posted in a trade journal or in a paper of general circulation where the agent operated.

   b.   According to the Third Restatement, terminations by operation of law may **not** end apparent authority.

   1)   Apparent authority ends only when it is **unreasonable** for a third party to believe the agent has actual authority. For example, the death, incapacity, or bankruptcy of the principal does not automatically end apparent authority.

   a)   It is unreasonable for a third party to believe the agent has actual authority when

   i)   **Notice** is received that the principal has revoked actual authority

   •   A third party has **notice** if (s)he (1) knows the fact, (2) has reason to know it, (3) has received an effective notification, or (4) should know it to perform a duty owed to another.

   ii)   Other circumstances have changed so that reasonable belief is no longer warranted
   iii)   The agent has renounced actual authority

   c.   If the authorization of the agent was in writing, the revocation of authorization also must be written.

Stop and review! You have completed the outline for this subunit. Study multiple-choice questions 13 through 16 beginning on page 506.

18.5 EMPLOYMENT TAX

1. **Federal Insurance Contributions Act (FICA)**

   a. FICA provides programs for disabled employees and families of retired, disabled, and deceased workers, including, in some cases, divorced spouses. Employers and employees contribute under this program.

   b. Employers must contribute (pay tax) based on the employee's pay.

      1) An employer subject to FICA taxes must file quarterly returns and deposit appropriate amounts on a monthly or semiweekly basis with an authorized depository institution.

         a) For example, a monthly depositor must deposit each month's taxes on or before the 15th day of the following month.

      2) Failure to deposit appropriate amounts results in penalties.

      3) Penalties also are imposed on persons who file returns and other documents without supplying taxpayer identification numbers.

   c. The employer must generally pay **6.20%** of the first **$127,200** of wages paid for 2017 plus **1.45%** of all wages for the Medicare portion. The employer generally must withhold the same amounts from the employee's wages. An employer that underwithholds and underpays is liable for the unpaid amount. But an employer that pays an employee's share has a right of reimbursement.

      1) Employers are responsible for withholding an additional 0.9% of an individual's wages paid in excess of $200,000 as Additional Medicare Tax ($250,000 married filing jointly or surviving spouse; $125,000 married filing separately).

      2) No employer match exists for Additional Medicare Tax.

   d. A **net investment income tax (NIIT)** of 3.8% is imposed. The tax applies to the lesser of (1) NII or (2) the excess of modified AGI over the applicable threshold amount. These amounts are used to calculate the Additional Medicare Tax.

   e. **Wages** are all forms of consideration paid for employment, including cash and the cash value of compensation in any medium other than cash. They include

      1) Wages and salaries,
      2) Commissions (including contingent fees),
      3) Bonuses,
      4) Productivity awards,
      5) Tips,
      6) Vacation and sick pay,
      7) Severance allowances, and
      8) Fringe benefits.

         a) Wages exclude (1) payments for moving expenses to the extent that it is reasonable to believe a corresponding deduction is allowable and (2) medical care reimbursements under a self-insured plan.

         b) Investment income is not subject to FICA tax except for the NIIT.

   f. **Group term life insurance** payments for retirees are treated as wages to the extent they constitute gross income and are for periods during which retirees no longer have employee status.

   g. The employer must **withhold FICA tax** from an employee's wages. The employee's contribution (tax) must be withheld upon each payment of wages, up to the maximum bases and at the same rates.

   h. Contributions made by the employee are **not tax deductible** by the employee. Those made by the employer are deductible by the employer.

   i. **Self-employed persons** are required to report their own taxable income and pay FICA taxes. FICA is calculated based on net income.

2.   **Federal Unemployment Tax Act (FUTA)**

    a.   FUTA provides for a system of temporary financial assistance for unemployed workers.

    b.   FUTA tax is imposed on employers who

        1)   Employ one or more covered individuals for some portion of a day in each of the 20 weeks in the current or preceding calendar year, or

        2)   Pay actually or constructively $1,500 or more in wages in any calendar quarter of the current or preceding calendar year.

    c.   The FUTA tax is **6.0%** of the **first $7,000** of wages paid annually to each employee.

        1)   The employee does not pay any part of the FUTA tax.

        2)   The employer pays the FUTA tax to the IRS.

            a)   FUTA tax is a deductible business expense of the employer.

    d.   A credit against FUTA tax liability is provided to an employer who pays state unemployment tax.

        1)   The credit cannot exceed 5.4% of the first $7,000 of wages.

        2)   The amount paid to a state usually depends on the employer's past experience regarding the frequency and amount of unemployment claims.

    e.   **Benefits** are determined on a state-to-state basis. Thus, the state fixes the amount and duration of compensation. To collect unemployment compensation, the worker ordinarily must

        1)   Have been employed and laid off without fault;

        2)   Have filed a claim for the benefits; and

        3)   Be able, available, and willing to work but not be able to find employment.

    f.   A state may refuse benefits to employees who

        1)   Have voluntarily quit work without good cause,

        2)   Have been discharged for good cause (misconduct), or

        3)   Refuse to actively seek or accept suitable work.

Stop and review! You have completed the outline for this subunit. Study multiple-choice questions 17 and 18 on page 507.

18.6 AFFORDABLE CARE ACT

1.   **Means of Increasing Health Insurance Coverage**

    a.   The Patient Protection and Affordable Care Act of 2010 (ACA) is intended to increase health insurance coverage by the following means:

        1)   Expanding Medicaid

            a)   However, the U.S. Supreme Court ruled that states cannot be compelled to participate in the Medicaid expansion.

        2)   Requiring employers with at least 50 **full-time or full-time equivalent employees** (FTEs) to offer **affordable essential** health insurance coverage or pay a penalty

        3)   Providing insurance premium subsidies for certain low- and middle-income individuals

        4)   Requiring individuals without health insurance (e.g., employer coverage or Medicare) to purchase health insurance or pay a penalty

        5)   Creating insurance exchanges (markets in which individuals can buy health insurance)

            a)   If a state does not set up an exchange, a federal exchange is established.

        6)   Outlawing lifetime limits on or arbitrary cancelations of health insurance coverage

7) Allowing a parent's policy to cover his or her nondependent children until age 26

8) Requiring employers to disclose to employees

    a) The employer's coverage (or absence of coverage),

    b) Information about the use of exchanges,

    c) A **summary of benefits and coverage** (not a summary plan description) that facilitates comparison of health insurance plans, and

    d) The cost of coverage on W-2 forms (mandatory for employers that filed at least 250 W-2 forms the previous year).

2. **Grandfathered Plans**

    a. If an employer plan was in effect when the ACA was enacted on March 23, 2010, many of its elements may continue if, for example, the employer does not (1) reduce benefits, (2) change insurers, or (3) materially increase co-payments or deductibles.

3. **Employer Mandate**

    a. An employer with at least 50 FTEs must **pay** a penalty if it does not provide affordable essential coverage.

        1) If any employee receives a tax credit to buy coverage, the annual penalty for choosing not to provide coverage is determined as follows:

$$\$2,260 \times (Total\ FTEs - First\ 30\ FTEs)$$

        2) An employer that offers coverage to FTEs still may be penalized. If the coverage (a) is unaffordable or (b) does not provide the minimum essential care or have the minimum actuarial value, the annual penalty is the lesser of the following:

            a) $\$2,260 \times (Total\ FTEs - First\ 30\ FTEs)$

            b) $\$3,390 \times (FTEs\ who\ received\ a\ tax\ credit)$

        3) An IRS rule makes tax credits under the ACA available through a federal exchange in a state that has declined to establish a state exchange.

    b. An employer offering coverage to full-time employees must include all employees who are regularly scheduled to work an average of 30 or more hours per week.

        1) The plan's waiting period for coverage cannot exceed 90 days.

        2) The employer also must determine the number of FTEs for (a) current employees who work variable hours and (b) new employees whose hours are variable or have not yet been specified.

4. **Affordability**

    a. Affordability is based on the following factors:

        1) The lowest applicable wage paid by the employer
        2) The employer's lowest-cost eligible plan
        3) Employee-only coverage (excluding family or any other tier of coverage)
        4) The employee's premium contribution

    b. The cost of the employee's premium contribution should not exceed 9.69% of his or her household income. The affordability requirement, however, is also met if the monthly premium contribution is not greater than 9.69% of any of the following:

        1) The annual federal poverty level for a single person, divided by 12
        2) The employee's monthly income based on rate of pay and monthly hours worked
        3) The annual income reported in Form W-2, Box 1, divided by 12

5.   **Essential Care**

    a.   The insurance must cover the following medical services:

        1)   Ambulatory patient services
        2)   Emergency services
        3)   Hospitalization
        4)   Maternity and newborn care
        5)   Mental health and substance use disorder services, including behavioral health treatment
        6)   Prescription drugs
        7)   Rehabilitative and habilitative services and devices
        8)   Laboratory services
        9)   Preventive and wellness services and chronic disease management
        10)   Pediatric services, including oral and vision care

6.   **Actuarial Value**

    a.   Actuarial value is the expected percentage of covered expenses that the plan will pay. The following are the tiers of plans and expected reimbursement levels:

Tier	Reimbursement
Bronze	60% ± 2%
Silver	70% ± 2%
Gold	80% ± 2%
Platinum	90% ± 2%

    b.   The **minimum** actuarial value allowed for an eligible employer plan is 60%. Thus, an employee should **not** pay more than 40% in deductibles, co-payments, and co-insurance (excluding the premium contribution).

        1)   Employer contributions to health-savings accounts (HSAs) or health-reimbursement arrangements (HRAs) may increase the minimum actuarial value.

Stop and review! You have completed the outline for this subunit. Study multiple-choice questions 19 through 22 beginning on page 507.

QUESTIONS

18.1 Agency Formation

1. Jim entered into an oral agency agreement with Sally in which he authorized Sally to sell his interest in a parcel of real estate, Blueacre. Within 7 days, Sally sold Blueacre to Dan, signing the real estate contract on behalf of Jim. Dan failed to record the real estate contract within a reasonable time. Which of the following most likely is true?

A.   Dan may enforce the real estate contract against Jim because it satisfied the statute of frauds.

B.   Dan may enforce the real estate contract against Jim because Sally signed the contract as Jim's agent.

C.   The real estate contract is unenforceable against Jim because Sally's authority to sell Blueacre was oral.

D.   The real estate contract is unenforceable against Jim because Dan failed to record the contract within a reasonable time.

Answer (C) is correct.
    REQUIRED: The true statement about an oral agency to sell realty.
    DISCUSSION: Oral agreement usually suffices to form an agency, but a contract involving a sale of land is required to be in writing in some states. Furthermore, the equal dignity rule applies in many states. In these states, the agency must be in writing if the authority granted to the agent is to enter into a contract required to be in writing. For example, an agreement to transfer an interest in land is subject to the statute of frauds and therefore must be in writing. The contract is therefore most likely to be voidable at Jim's option. It was required by the statute of frauds to be written, and Sally's agency was oral. In most other situations, the agent's authority may be oral.
    Answer (A) is incorrect. The contract most likely operates only as an offer because the agency was oral. Answer (B) is incorrect. The contract most likely operates only as an offer because the agency was oral. Answer (D) is incorrect. If Jim and Dan had entered into a binding agreement, it would be effective without recording. Compliance with the recording statute is necessary to protect against parties not privy to the contract.

2. Forming an agency relationship requires that

A. The agreement between the principal and agent be supported by consideration.

B. The principal and agent not be minors.

C. Both the principal and agent consent to the agency.

D. The agent's authority be limited to the express grant of authority in the agency agreement.

Answer (C) is correct.
REQUIRED: The requirement to form an agency relationship.
DISCUSSION: Agency is an express or implied consensual relationship. Both the principal and agent must manifest consent to the grant of authority. The purpose and subject matter of the agency must be legal. The principal must have legal capacity to perform the act authorized.
Answer (A) is incorrect. Consideration is not required to form an agency. Answer (B) is incorrect. An agent need not have legal capacity to enter into a contract to be able to bind a principal on the contract. Answer (D) is incorrect. An agent's authority can extend to more than acts specifically expressed in the agreement. For example, a universal agent is authorized to conduct all business that the principal may legally delegate.

3. Noll gives Carr a written power of attorney. Which of the following statements is true regarding this power of attorney?

A. It must be signed by both Noll and Carr.

B. It must be for a definite period of time.

C. It may continue in existence after Noll's death.

D. It may limit Carr's authority to specific transactions.

Answer (D) is correct.
REQUIRED: The true statement about a power of attorney.
DISCUSSION: A power of attorney is a written authorization for the agent to act on behalf of the principal. It can be general, or it can grant the agent restricted authority, such as for specific transactions.
Answer (A) is incorrect. A power of attorney is a delegation of authority and need only be signed by the principal. Answer (B) is incorrect. To be effective, a written power of attorney need not be for a definite period of time. Answer (C) is incorrect. In the absence of a special statute, the death of a principal terminates an agency relationship.

4. Which of the following actions requires an agent for a corporation to have a written agency agreement?

A. Purchasing office supplies for the principal's business.

B. Purchasing an interest in undeveloped land for the principal.

C. Hiring an independent general contractor to renovate the principal's office building.

D. Retaining an attorney to collect a business debt owed to the principal.

Answer (B) is correct.
REQUIRED: The action requiring a written agency agreement.
DISCUSSION: Oral agreement usually suffices to form an agency, but a contract involving a sale of land is required to be in writing in some states. Furthermore, the equal dignity rule applies in many states. In these states, the agency must be in writing if the authority granted to the agent is to enter into a contract required to be in writing. For example, an agreement to transfer an interest in land is subject to the statute of frauds and therefore must be in writing.
Answer (A) is incorrect. Purchasing office supplies does not require any formality and is not subject to the requirement of a writing unless the price of the goods is $500 or more. Answer (C) is incorrect. An independent contractor may be an agent, but the object of the agency, providing the service of office renovation, is not subject to the formality of a writing. Answer (D) is incorrect. A written agreement is not required. The object of the agency, collecting a debt, does not require a writing.

18.2 Agent's Authority and Duties

5. Ace engages Butler to manage Ace's retail business. Butler has **no** implied authority to

A. Purchase inventory for Ace's business.

B. Sell Ace's business fixtures.

C. Pay Ace's business debts.

D. Hire or discharge Ace's business employees.

Answer (B) is correct.
REQUIRED: The agent's implied authority.
DISCUSSION: An agent's actual authority is conveyed by communication to the agent from the principal. It is not feasible to state expressly each act an agent is authorized to perform. Thus, an agent may have express and implied actual authority. Implied actual authority is for acts reasonably necessary to execute express authority. Selling the business fixtures is not necessary to manage a retail business.
Answer (A) is incorrect. Buying inventory is an act necessary to execute the express authorization to manage the store. Answer (C) is incorrect. Paying business debts is an act necessary to execute the express authorization to manage the store. Answer (D) is incorrect. Hiring or discharging employees is an act necessary to execute the express authorization to manage the store.

6. Bo Borg is the vice president of purchasing for Crater Corp. He has authority to enter into purchase contracts on behalf of Crater, provided that the price under a contract does not exceed $2 million. Dent, who is the president of Crater, is required to approve any contract that exceeds $2 million. Borg entered into a $2.5 million purchase contract with Shady Corp. without Dent's approval. Shady was unaware that Borg exceeded his authority. Neither party substantially changed its position in reliance on the contract. What is the most likely result of this transaction?

    A.   Crater will be bound because of Borg's apparent authority.

    B.   Crater will not be bound because Borg exceeded his authority.

    C.   Crater will only be bound up to $2 million, the amount of Borg's authority.

    D.   Crater may avoid the contract because Shady has not relied on the contract to its detriment.

Answer (A) is correct.
    REQUIRED: The most likely result when an agent exceeds his or her authority.
    DISCUSSION: Apparent authority exists when a third party has reason to believe that an agent has the authority to enter into contracts of the nature involved based upon a principal's representations. Secret limitations placed on the agent's normal authority create apparent authority. In this case, it was reasonable for Shady to believe that Borg had the authority to enter into the contract, given Borg's position in the company as vice president of purchasing. That Dent secretly limited Borg's authority has no effect, and Crater Corp. can be held liable under the contract.
    Answer (B) is incorrect. An agent with apparent authority has the power to bind a principal even if the agent exceeds his express authority. Answer (C) is incorrect. A principal is liable to the extent of an agent's apparent authority, not an agent's express authority. Answer (D) is incorrect. Reliance is irrelevant when the parties are bound to the contract.

7. Which act, if committed by an agent, will cause a principal to be liable to a third party?

    A.   A negligent act committed by an independent contractor in performance of the contract that results in injury to a third party.

    B.   An intentional tort committed by an employee outside the scope of employment that results in injury to a third party.

    C.   An employee's failure to notify the employer of a dangerous condition that results in injury to a third party.

    D.   A negligent act committed by an employee outside the scope of employment that results in injury to a third party.

Answer (C) is correct.
    REQUIRED: The act of an agent causing a principal to be liable to a third party.
    DISCUSSION: An agent, such as an employee, has a duty to give notice to the principal of all information relevant to the agency. Thus, an agent's knowledge of a relevant, dangerous condition is assumed to be known by the principal. The principal is then liable to an injured third party to the same extent as if the principal had actual knowledge of the condition.
    Answer (A) is incorrect. A nonnegligent principal generally is not liable for the negligence of an independent contractor. Answer (B) is incorrect. The principal is not liable for intentional torts outside the scope of employment. Answer (D) is incorrect. The principal is not liable for negligent acts outside the scope of employment.

8. North, Inc., hired Sutter as a purchasing agent. North gave Sutter written authorization to purchase, without limit, electronic appliances. Later, Sutter was told not to purchase more than 300 of each appliance. Sutter contracted with Orr Corp. to purchase 500 tape recorders. Orr had been shown Sutter's written authorization. Which of the following statements is true?

    A.   Sutter will be liable to Orr because Sutter's actual authority was exceeded.

    B.   Sutter will not be liable to reimburse North if North is liable to Orr.

    C.   North will be liable to Orr because of Sutter's actual and apparent authority.

    D.   North will not be liable to Orr because Sutter's actual authority was exceeded.

Answer (C) is correct.
    REQUIRED: The true statement about liability for a contract beyond the agent's actual authority.
    DISCUSSION: A principal is liable on contracts made by an agent who has actual or apparent authority. Sutter had apparent authority to make the contract because of the principal's communication (letter) shown to the third party. Moreover, the third party's rights against the principal are not affected by the secret limits placed on actual authority. Sutter had actual authority to buy up to 300 units and apparent authority to buy the rest.
    Answer (A) is incorrect. The agent is not liable to the third party. The agent had apparent authority to buy all 500 tape recorders. Answer (B) is incorrect. The agent is liable to the principal for acting beyond actual authority. Answer (D) is incorrect. The principal is liable for acts of the agent within actual or apparent authority.

18.3 Principal's Duties and Liabilities

9. Which of the following statements, if any, represent a principal's duty to an agent who works on a commission basis?

I. The principal is required to maintain pertinent records and pay the agent according to the terms of their agreement.

II. The principal is required to reimburse the agent for all authorized expenses incurred unless the agreement calls for the agent to pay expenses out of the commission.

A. I only.

B. II only.

C. Both I and II.

D. Neither I nor II.

Answer (C) is correct.

REQUIRED: The duties, if any, owed by a principal to an agent who works on commission.

DISCUSSION: Two implied fundamental duties of a principal to an agent are to compensate the agent for his or her services and to indemnify or reimburse the agent for authorized expenses incurred on behalf of the principal. Any renunciation of these duties requires an express agreement.

10. Neal, an employee of Jordan, was delivering merchandise to a customer. On the way, Neal's negligence caused a traffic accident that resulted in damages to a third party's automobile. Who is liable to the third party?

	Neal	Jordan
A.	No	No
B.	Yes	Yes
C.	Yes	No
D.	No	Yes

Answer (B) is correct.

REQUIRED: The liability of the employer and employee for the employee's negligence.

DISCUSSION: A principal is strictly liable for a tort committed by an agent within the scope of the agent's employment (vicarious liability). This liability is without regard to the fault of the principal. Vicarious liability does not apply when the agent is an independent contractor. A person is liable for his or her own negligent acts even if acting as an agent of another.

Answer (A) is incorrect. Agent status is not a shield to liability for one's own negligence, and an employer is vicariously liable for his or her employees' acts. Answer (C) is incorrect. An employer is vicariously liable for employees' acts. This rule reflects the doctrine of respondeat superior. Answer (D) is incorrect. Agent status is not a shield to liability for a person's own negligence.

11. Generally, a disclosed principal will be liable to third parties for its agent's unauthorized misrepresentations if the agent is an

	Employee	Independent Contractor
A.	Yes	Yes
B.	Yes	No
C.	No	Yes
D.	No	No

Answer (A) is correct.

REQUIRED: The type(s) of agents, if any, for whose unauthorized misrepresentations the principal is liable.

DISCUSSION: The principal is liable for torts involving misrepresentations regardless of whether the agent is an employee or an independent contractor. The agent's misrepresentation must be (1) fraudulent, (2) negligent, or (3) innocent but material and with all of the elements of fraud except intent. A tort involving misrepresentation is an an example of vicarious liability. An example of tortious misrepresentation by an agent-independent contractor is the sale by a homeowner through a real estate broker who made a material misrepresentation to make the sale. But the principal generally is not liable for the tortious acts of an independent contractor that involve physical acts.

12. An agent will usually be liable under a contract made with a third party when the agent is acting on behalf of a

	Disclosed Principal	Undisclosed Principal
A.	Yes	Yes
B.	Yes	No
C.	No	Yes
D.	No	No

Answer (C) is correct.

REQUIRED: The liability of an agent to a third party when the principal is disclosed and undisclosed.

DISCUSSION: When a principal is undisclosed, the third party believes (s)he is dealing directly with the agent. Thus, under general contract law, an agent is liable to the third party because the third party intended to deal only with the agent. An agent who discloses the principal and acts within actual or apparent authority ordinarily binds only the principal.

18.4 Agency Termination

13. Under the Restatement of the Law Third, Agency, which of the following does **not** terminate an agency relationship?

- A. War between the principal and agent's countries.
- B. An agent's act of filing a bankruptcy petition.
- C. Changing circumstances that make it unreasonable to believe the agent has actual authority.
- D. Agent fails to obtain a required license.

Answer (B) is correct.
REQUIRED: The circumstance that does not terminate an agency relationship under the Third Restatement.
DISCUSSION: A principal's act of filing a voluntary petition in bankruptcy, not an agent's, terminates an existing agency.
Answer (A) is incorrect. War between the principal's and agent's countries terminates the agency because the relationship cannot be enforced. Answer (C) is incorrect. Under the Third Restatement, an agent's actual authority ends when (s)he does not have a reasonable belief that the principal wants the agent to perform an act with legal consequences for the principal. Apparent authority ends when it is not reasonable to believe the agent has actual authority. For example, a serious change in the value of property or in business conditions may terminate the agency. However, the agency might be revived upon recovery or a return to the initial circumstances. Answer (D) is incorrect. The illegality of duties to be performed by the agent ends actual and apparent authority. Third parties have reason to know of the illegality.

14. Bolt Corp. dismissed Ace as its general sales agent and notified all of Ace's known customers by letter. Young Corp., a retail outlet located outside of Ace's previously assigned sales territory, had never dealt with Ace. Young knew of Ace as a result of various business contacts. After his dismissal, Ace sold Young goods to be delivered by Bolt and received from Young a cash deposit for 20% of the purchase price. It was not unusual for an agent in Ace's previous position to receive cash deposits. In an action by Young against Bolt on the sales contract, Young will

- A. Lose because Ace lacked any implied authority to make the contract.
- B. Lose because Ace lacked any express authority to make the contract.
- C. Win because Bolt's notice was inadequate to terminate Ace's apparent authority.
- D. Win because a principal is an insurer of an agent's acts.

Answer (C) is correct.
REQUIRED: The outcome of a suit by a third party against a principal whose agent had no actual authority.
DISCUSSION: When a principal discharges an agent, (s)he must give (1) actual notice of the discharge to those the agent had previously dealt with and (2) constructive notice to others who might have known of the agency. Ace continued to have apparent authority because of Bolt's failure to give constructive notice by publication in a newspaper of general circulation in the place where the agency activities occurred. Publication in trade journals of the termination would have provided such notice and effectively terminated Ace's apparent authority.
Answer (A) is incorrect. Young will win. Ace had apparent, although not actual (express or implied), authority. Answer (B) is incorrect. Ace's lack of express authority did not preclude the existence of apparent authority. Answer (D) is incorrect. A principal is not an insurer of an agent's acts. A principal is only liable when an agent acts with actual or apparent authority.

15. According to the Restatement (Second) of the Law of Agency, the apparent authority of a general agent for a disclosed principal will terminate without notice to third parties when the

- A. Principal dismisses the agent.
- B. Principal or agent dies.
- C. Purpose of the agency relationship has been fulfilled.
- D. Time period set forth in the agency agreement has expired.

Answer (B) is correct.
REQUIRED: The occurrence automatically terminating a general agent's apparent authority.
DISCUSSION: According to the Restatement (Second) of the Law of Agency, an agency and the agent's power to bind the principal terminate instantly upon the death of the principal because the principal must exist at the time the agent acts. NOTE: According to the Restatement of the Law, Third, Agency, the principal's death does not automatically terminate actual or apparent authority. Continuation of actual and apparent authority protects from liability the agent and the parties who do business with the agent, respectively.
Answer (A) is incorrect. When an agent is dismissed, existing customers must be given actual notice. Other persons must be given constructive notice to terminate apparent authority. Answer (C) is incorrect. Fulfillment of the purpose of the agency does not terminate apparent authority. Answer (D) is incorrect. The expiration of the agency does not terminate apparent authority.

16. Pell is the principal and Astor is the agent in an agency coupled with an interest. In the absence of a contractual provision relating to the duration of the agency, who has the right to terminate the agency before the interest has expired?

	Pell	Astor
A.	Yes	Yes
B.	No	Yes
C.	No	No
D.	Yes	No

Answer (B) is correct.
REQUIRED: The person with the right to terminate an agency coupled with an interest.
DISCUSSION: In an agency coupled with an interest, the agent has a specific, current, beneficial interest in property that is the subject matter of the agency. A principal does not have the right or power to terminate an agency coupled with an interest. In any agency, the agent may terminate at any time without liability if no specific period for the agency has been established.

18.5 Employment Tax

17. Under the Federal Insurance Contributions Act (FICA), which of the following acts will cause an employer to be liable for penalties?

	Failure to Supply Taxpayer Identification Numbers	Failure to Make Timely FICA Deposits
A.	Yes	Yes
B.	Yes	No
C.	No	Yes
D.	No	No

Answer (A) is correct.
REQUIRED: The acts for which an employer is liable.
DISCUSSION: An employer subject to FICA taxes must file quarterly returns and deposit appropriate amounts on a monthly or semiweekly basis with an authorized depository institution. For example, a monthly depositor must deposit each month's taxes on or before the 15th day of the following month. Failure to deposit appropriate amounts results in penalties. Penalties are also imposed on persons who file returns and other documents without supplying taxpayer identification numbers.

18. Other than the net investment income (NII) tax, which of the following types of income is subject to taxation under the provisions of the Federal Insurance Contributions Act (FICA)?

A. Interest earned on municipal bonds.

B. Capital gains of $3,000.

C. Car received as a productivity award.

D. Dividends of $2,500.

Answer (C) is correct.
REQUIRED: The type of income to which Social Security tax applies.
DISCUSSION: The Social Security tax imposed by the FICA applies to virtually all compensation received for employment, including money or other forms of wages, bonuses, commissions, vacation pay, severance allowances, and tips. A car received as a productivity award is a form of compensation for employment. It is not excepted from application of FICA tax. Income derived from an investment, as opposed to compensation for employment, is not subject to FICA tax. But the NII tax applies to the lesser of (1) NII or (2) the excess of modified AGI over an applicable threshold amount.
Answers (A), (B), and (D) are incorrect. Income derived from an investment, as opposed to compensation for employment, is not subject to FICA tax.

18.6 Affordable Care Act

19. The Patient Protection and Affordable Care Act of 2010 (ACA) is intended to increase health insurance coverage by all of the following means **except**

A. Allowing nondependent children up to age 21 to be covered by a parent's policy.

B. Expanding Medicaid.

C. Creating insurance exchanges and markets in which individuals can buy health insurance.

D. Providing insurance premium subsidies for individuals with low- or middle-incomes.

Answer (A) is correct.
REQUIRED: The means of increasing health insurance coverage under the ACA.
DISCUSSION: Among the primary ways by which the ACA increases health insurance coverage are (1) expanding Medicaid, (2) providing insurance premium subsidies for certain low- and middle-income individuals, (3) creating insurance exchanges, (4) allowing nondependent children up to age 26 to be covered by a parent's policy, and (5) mandating that certain employers provide coverage.
Answer (B) is incorrect. Expanding Medicaid is a means of increasing health insurance coverage. Answer (C) is incorrect. Creating insurance exchanges and markets in which individuals can buy health insurance is a means of increasing health insurance coverage. Answer (D) is incorrect. Providing insurance premium subsidies for individuals with low- or middle-incomes is a means of increasing health insurance coverage.

20. The Affordable Care Act (ACA) requires an employer with at least 50 full-time or full-time equivalent employees (FTEs) to offer them affordable essential health insurance coverage or pay a penalty. In which situation is the penalty **not** imposed?

   A. An employer offers coverage to FTEs but the coverage is not affordable.

   B. Any employee receives a tax credit to buy coverage and the employer does not provide affordable essential coverage.

   C. An employer offers coverage to FTEs but the coverage does not provide the minimum essential care.

   D. None of the answers are correct.

Answer (D) is correct.
   REQUIRED: The circumstance in which the employer mandate of the ACA does not apply.
   DISCUSSION: According to the ACA, an employer with at least 50 full-time employees or full-time equivalent employees (FTEs) must offer them affordable essential health insurance coverage or pay a penalty. If any employee receives a tax credit to buy coverage, the annual penalty for choosing not to provide coverage is imposed. An employer offering coverage to FTEs also may be penalized if the coverage (1) is unaffordable or (2) does not meet minimum coverage or actuarial value standards.
   Answer (A) is incorrect. The penalty is imposed when an employer offers coverage to FTEs but the coverage is not affordable. Answer (B) is incorrect. The penalty is imposed when any employee receives a tax credit to buy coverage but the employer does not provide affordable essential coverage. Answer (C) is incorrect. The penalty is imposed when an employer offers coverage to FTEs, but the coverage does not provide the minimum essential care.

21. The Affordable Care Act (ACA) sets a 60% minimum actuarial value for an eligible employer plan. All of the following statements are true **except** that

   A. Actuarial value indicates what percentage of covered expense the health plan will pay.

   B. Employer contributions to health-savings accounts may decrease the minimum actuarial value.

   C. An employee would not pay more than 40% of the covered expenses excluding the premium contribution.

   D. The lowest tier of plan allowed by the ACA is bronze.

Answer (B) is correct.
   REQUIRED: The true statement about the minimum actuarial value for an eligible employer plan.
   DISCUSSION: According to the ACA, actuarial value is the expected percentage of covered expenses that the plan will pay. The minimum actuarial value allowed for an eligible employer plan is 60%. The minimum actuarial value is set by the ACA and will not be reduced by employer contributions.
   Answer (A) is incorrect. The actuarial value is the expected percentage of covered expenses that the plan will pay. Answer (C) is incorrect. The minimum actuarial value allowed for an eligible employer plan is 60%. Thus, an employee should not pay more than 40% in deductibles, co-payments, and co-insurance (excluding the premium contribution). Answer (D) is incorrect. The four tiers of health plans, from highest to lowest, are platinum, gold, silver, and bronze.

22. Meen Co. has 40 full-time employees and 20 full-time equivalent employees. Meen does not offer its employees affordable essential health insurance coverage. Furthermore, its employees received tax credits to buy coverage for this fiscal year. According to the Affordable Care Act (ACA), what amount must Meen pay as an annual penalty?

   A. $0

   B. $45,200

   C. $67,800

   D. $135,600

Answer (C) is correct.
   REQUIRED: The penalty paid by an employer under mandate of the ACA.
   DISCUSSION: If any employee receives a tax credit to buy coverage, the annual penalty paid by an employer with at least 50 full-time or full-time equivalent employees (FTEs) is determined as follows:

   Annual penalty = $2,260 × (total FTEs – first 30 FTEs)

The employer has 60 FTEs and must pay a penalty for not providing coverage. Accordingly, the amount paid is $67,800 [$2,260 × (60 – 30)].
   Answer (A) is incorrect. A penalty must be paid. Answer (B) is incorrect. To calculate the penalty, $2,260 should be multiplied by total FTEs in excess of 30, not the number of full-time equivalent employees in excess of full-time employees. Answer (D) is incorrect. To calculate the penalty, $2,260 should not be multiplied by total FTEs.

STUDY UNIT NINETEEN
SALES AND SECURED TRANSACTIONS

(27 pages of outline)

UCC **Article 2**, *Sales*, governs **all contracts for the sale of goods**. The general law of contracts (covered in Study Unit 17) also applies to sales of goods except to the extent Article 2 states different rules.

UCC **Article 9**, *Secured Transactions*, governs debtor-creditor transactions. Article 9 applies to security interests created under Articles 2, 2A, 4, and 5 as well as (1) security interests in personal property and fixtures created by contract; (2) agricultural liens; (3) consignments; and (4) sales of accounts, promissory notes, and certain other items. A secured transaction is a loan or purchase secured by collateral to protect the seller or creditor from the buyer's or debtor's default.

19.1 CONTRACT FORMATION

1. **Overview**

   a. A sale is a contract in which title to goods passes from the seller to the buyer for a price.

      1) **Goods** are a form of personal property. The UCC defines goods as all things movable and tangible at the time they are identified as goods to be sold. The following items are not defined as goods for UCC purposes:

         a) The money in which the price is to be paid

         b) Investment securities

         c) Things in action (property rights in intangibles that can only be enforced by legal action, not possession)

   b. Special standards apply to certain aspects of sales of goods if they involve merchants. **Merchant** is defined as one who

      1) Regularly deals in goods of the kind involved in the sales contract or

      2) Represents (or employs, one who represents) himself or herself, by occupation, as having specific knowledge or skill regarding the goods.

EXAMPLE

Marilyn owns Jewelry Co. where Green, an expert in faux jewelry, is employed as operations manager. Jewelry Co. distributes direct mail order sales to the general public and wholesales the same products to trinket retail stores throughout the country. For purposes of the UCC, Marilyn is a merchant in faux jewelry.

---

   c. The UCC imposes an obligation of **good faith** in the performance of every contract or duty under the UCC.

      1) Good faith is honesty in fact and the observance of reasonable commercial standards of fair dealing.

EXAMPLE

In a contract for the sale of goods, Seller and Buyer agree that Seller will set the price term. Seller must establish the price in good faith. In most instances, good faith requires that the price be set at fair value.

---

   d. **Course of dealing** is the prior conduct involving transactions between the parties that may be regarded as establishing a common basis of their understanding.

   e. **Usage of trade** is a practice or method regularly observed in a place, vocation, or trade. It justifies an expectation that it will be followed with respect to the specific transaction.

   f. **Course of performance** is conduct involving (1) repeated occasions for performance by a party and (2) acceptance by the other party despite knowledge of the performance and an opportunity to object.

2. **Merchant's Firm Offer**

   a. When a **merchant** seller makes an offer that includes assurances to hold the offer open, the offer cannot be revoked for the stated period or, if no period is stated, then for a reasonable time (but in no event may the duration exceed 3 months).

   b. The offer must be in **writing and signed** by the merchant offeror.

      1) If the offeree supplies the form, the firm offer term must be signed separately.

      2) The offeree need **not** be a merchant.

   c. Consideration is **not** necessary. (See Study Unit 17, Subunit 3, for consideration.)

   d. An example of a firm offer is a rain check. It is a writing issued by a merchant when the supply of a sale item is insufficient.

      1) It offers the goods at the advertised price, but no period of effectiveness need be stated.

3. **Acceptance**

   a. Unless the offer indicates otherwise, an offer invites acceptance in any manner and by any medium reasonable under the circumstances.

      1) If the offeror indicates that a particular medium of acceptance must be used, only the indicated medium is authorized.

EXAMPLE

Big Corp. writes Small Corp. offering to sell $1 million worth of computers (goods). The offer states that Big will keep the offer open for 20 days from the date of the letter. Before the 20th day arrives, Small sends Big an acceptance by registered letter. Because this medium of acceptance is commercially reasonable under the circumstances, the acceptance is probably valid. Acceptance is effective upon delivery to the post office.

---

   b. The beginning of performance by the offeree may be an appropriate acceptance. But the offeree must notify the offeror within a reasonable time.

EXAMPLE

Rob (offeror) sends a fax to Lisa (offeree) requesting that Lisa begin manufacturing and shipping goods immediately. Lisa begins the requested performance but does not inform Rob. Thus, Rob may acquire goods from another source without liability to Lisa even if Lisa has begun performance.

---

   c. If the offer does not require a particular manner or medium for acceptance, acceptance may be by either (1) a prompt promise to ship or (2) prompt shipment of the goods to the buyer.

      1) If the seller ships **nonconforming goods**, the shipment is both an acceptance and a breach.

EXAMPLE

Steven orders 1,000 orange sweatshirts from Victor. Victor ships 1,000 garnet sweatshirts without informing Steven that the goods are offered only as an accommodation. Victor's shipment is both an acceptance of the offer and a breach of the resulting contract. Steven may reject the shipment and sue for damages.

---

2) If the seller seasonably notifies the buyer that a nonconforming shipment is offered only as an **accommodation**, no breach occurs.

    a) No contract has been formed, and the shipment is a counteroffer.

EXAMPLE

In the example above, assume that, before the goods arrive, Victor notifies Steven that the garnet sweatshirts were sent as an accommodation. The shipment is a counteroffer. If Steven accepts delivery, a contract for the purchase and sale of garnet sweatshirts is formed.

---

4. **Open Terms**

  a. Under general contract law, the terms of a contract must be **definite and complete**.

    1) The UCC has modified this strict approach. Thus, a contract for the sale of goods may be made in any manner sufficient to show agreement.

  b. Leaving open one or more terms does not prevent formation of a contract under the UCC. But (1) the parties must have intended to enter into a contract and (2) a reasonably certain basis must exist for granting a remedy.

  c. If the **quantity term** is left open, the general rule is that a court may have no basis to grant a remedy. Thus, a contract may not have been formed.

    1) A contract is not too indefinite because it measures the quantity by the seller's **output** or the buyer's **requirements** that occur in good faith.

      a) The amount should not be unreasonably different from (1) a stated estimate or (2) given no estimate, any normal prior amount.

  d. If the parties have not agreed on **price**, a court determines a reasonable price at the time of delivery.

    1) If the buyer or seller is to determine price, it should be fixed in good faith.
    2) The price determined is generally the market price.

  e. When parties do not specify **payment or credit terms**, payment is due at the time and place at which the buyer is to receive the goods.

    1) Tender of payment suffices if made by any means current in the ordinary course of business, e.g., by check. But the seller may demand **cash** if a reasonable extension of time is given.

  f. When **delivery** terms are not specified, the buyer normally takes delivery at the **seller's** place of business (or home if no place of business exists).

    1) Otherwise, delivery is at the place where both parties know the goods are located at the time of sale.

  g. If the time for shipment or delivery is not clearly specified, it is a reasonable time.

5. **Additional or Different Terms**

  a. Article 2 does not apply the **mirror image rule** covered in Study Unit 17, Subunit 2. If the offeree's overall response indicates a definite acceptance, a contract is formed.

    1) But acceptance may be conditioned on agreement to the terms.

      a) The result is a counteroffer (and rejection). No contract exists unless the original offeror agrees to the counteroffer.

    2) If the seller or the buyer is a **nonmerchant**, additional or different terms in an acceptance are mere proposals, not part of the contract.

EXAMPLE

Tammy offers to sell a boat and trailer to Nan for $2,000. Nan replies, "I accept and want you to put new tires on the boat trailer." She has indicated a definite expression of acceptance, forming a contract. Her acceptance suggests an added term modifying the offer. Because Tammy is not a merchant, the additional term is merely a proposal. Tammy is not legally obligated to comply.

---

    3) Between **merchants**, the additional or different terms automatically become part of the contract unless

        a) The terms materially alter the original contract,
        b) The offer expressly limits acceptance to the terms of the offer, or
        c) The offeror objects in a reasonable time.

    4) If the offer was definitely accepted but the additional or different terms are not included in the contract, they are mere proposals for changes in the contract.

6. **Modifications**

    a. Under the UCC, an agreement modifying a contract does **not** need to be supported by additional **consideration** to be binding regardless of whether the parties are merchants or nonmerchants.

    b. An oral modification may be enforceable unless

        1) A written agreement signed by the parties excludes oral modification or rescission or
        2) The modified contract is within the **statute of frauds**.

    c. A **waiver** (a voluntary, intentional choice not to enforce a term of a contract) may be withdrawn after reasonable notice. However, this retraction is not allowed if it would be unjust because of a material change in position by the other party in reliance on the waiver.

7. **Parol Evidence**

    a. A writing intended by the parties to be the final expression of their agreement cannot be contradicted by

        1) Evidence of any prior agreement or
        2) An oral agreement made at the same time as the final writing.

    b. The final expression of the agreement may be explained or supplemented by

        1) Course of dealing (prior conduct between the parties),
        2) Usage of trade (a regular practice or method),
        3) Course of performance (past performance accepted without objection), or
        4) Consistent additional terms (unless a court finds the writing to be complete).

8. **Statute of Frauds**

    a. Generally, contracts for the **sale of goods for $500 or more** are not enforceable without a writing. The writing must (1) suffice to indicate that a contract was formed and (2) be signed by the party against whom it is being enforced.

        1) The **quantity** of goods must be specified.
        2) The writing need not contain all essential terms, e.g., payment, delivery, and express warranties.
        3) One merchant may send a written confirmation to another merchant that is binding on the sender. If the confirmation is sent within a reasonable time after an oral understanding, it satisfies the statute.

            a) The statute is **not** satisfied if the recipient objects within 10 days.

4) A writing is unnecessary in the following situations:

    a) If the goods are to be specially made or extensively modified and cannot be sold to others in the ordinary course of business.

        i) The seller must make either a substantial beginning in their manufacture or commitment for their purchase before a notice of repudiation is received from the buyer.

    b) To the extent goods are actually received and accepted or payment has been made.

    c) If a party admits in pleadings or in court that a contract exists.

9. **Auctions**

    a. An auction is a public sale where various buyers offer bids for the goods, which are sold to the highest bidder. An auction is **with reserve** unless it is explicitly without reserve. An auction with reserve means that the seller has set a minimum acceptable price, which may or may not be disclosed to the bidders. In an auction with reserve, an auctioneer may withdraw the goods at any time until (s)he announces completion of the sale. An auction **without reserve** may be withdrawn only if no bid is made within a reasonable time.

        1) A bid is an offer and may be revoked at any time before acceptance by the auctioneer. However, no prior bid is revived by the revocation and must be rebid.

        2) If a bid is made during the auctioneer's acceptance (while the hammer is falling), the auctioneer may reopen the bidding or declare the goods sold.

Stop and review! You have completed the outline for this subunit. Study multiple-choice question 1 on page 536.

19.2 PERFORMANCE

1. **Seller's Performance**

    a. The **seller** must transfer and deliver the goods.

    b. Under the **perfect tender rule**, if the goods and the seller's tender of delivery fail in any way to conform to the contract, the buyer may reject the goods or the tender.

        1) A **tender** is an unconditional offer to perform with a current ability to do so. If it is unjustifiably refused, the tendering party has remedies for breach of contract.

        2) The perfect tender rule is subject to the seller's rights, e.g., the right to **cure** (correct the nonconformity).

            a) After rightful (1) rejection or (2) revocation of acceptance, the seller may seasonably notify the buyer of an intent to cure. If the seller then delivers conforming goods within the time allowed by the contract, no breach occurs.

        3) The seller's duty is to put and hold conforming goods at the buyer's disposition for a time sufficient for the buyer to take possession.

            a) The seller must give reasonable notice to enable the buyer to take delivery.

    c. If the delivery term is **FOB** (free on board) a particular point, the tender of delivery must be made at the FOB point.

        1) "Delivery to be FOB the place of shipment" indicates a shipment contract.

        2) "Delivery to be FOB the place of destination" indicates a destination contract.

        3) In carrier cases, unless otherwise explicitly stated, a shipment contract is assumed.

d.   In a **shipment contract**, the seller must

1)   Place the goods in the care of the designated (or a reasonable) carrier and make a reasonable contract for their transportation to the buyer,

2)   Obtain and tender in due form any documents necessary to enable the buyer to take possession, and

3)   Promptly notify the buyer.

e.   In a **destination contract**, the seller must transport the goods at its own risk and expense to the destination and duly tender them. The seller must

1)   Put and hold conforming goods at the buyer's disposal at a reasonable hour and for a reasonable time and

2)   Provide reasonable notice to the buyer.

2.   **Buyer's Performance**

a.   After a proper tender of conforming goods, the buyer must (1) accept them and (2) pay the price. These obligations are usually subject to a right to inspect.

1)   Without an agreement to the contrary, the buyer must

a)   Provide facilities reasonably suited for receipt of the goods and
b)   Pay at the time and place of **receipt**.

b.   The buyer has a **right to inspect the goods** at any reasonable time and place and in any reasonable manner before payment or acceptance, unless agreed otherwise.

1)   If the buyer fails to inspect the goods within a reasonable time after receipt, (s)he loses his or her right to inspect.

2)   Generally, if the contract provides for (a) payment against documents of title (a **documentary sale** is customary in **shipment** contracts) or (b) delivery **COD** (collect on delivery), the buyer has no right of inspection (or possession) before payment. In these circumstances, payment is not acceptance.

a)   In a documentary sale, the documents ordinarily arrive and are tendered while the goods are in transit.

EXAMPLE

Buyer Co. in New Mexico and Seller Co. in Florida contract for the sale of goods to be shipped to New Mexico. The contract provides for payment against an order bill of lading. Thus, Buyer must pay when the bank or other seller's agent in New Mexico notifies Seller that the bill of lading is ready, and Buyer does not have a right of inspection prior to payment. Under these facts, the buyer is required to pay first and inspect later.

---

3)   The buyer may **reject** nonconforming goods when tender is not perfect. The buyer may (a) keep them and sue for damages or (b) reject them and either cancel the contract or sue for damages.

a)   The buyer's right to reject (or revoke acceptance) is subject to the seller's right to cure the nonconformity.

4)   A buyer who accepts goods and later discovers nonconformity that substantially impairs their value to the buyer may **revoke acceptance** within a reasonable time.

a)   Acceptance must have been reasonably induced by the difficulty of discovery or the seller's assurance.

c.   **Acceptance** precludes the buyer from exercising the right of rejection, but acceptance may be revocable.

d.   In noncarrier cases, the price is due at tender.

3. **Failure of Presupposed Conditions**

   a. A seller's duty to perform is excused by failure of presupposed conditions. Breach does **not** occur if

      1) Performance as agreed has been made **impracticable** by the occurrence of a contingency, the nonoccurence of which was a **basic assumption** of the contract, or

      2) The seller complies in good faith with governmental regulations.

   b. An unexpected circumstance must arise subsequent to formation of the contract.

   c. Hardship or increase in costs alone is not an excuse. Objectively, current circumstances must be such that no one could reasonably perform the contract.

EXAMPLE

An unforeseen international embargo cuts off Seller's supply. If an alternative supply is available at a cost that will merely render performance unprofitable, impracticability will not excuse nonperformance.

---

4. **Substitute Performance**

   a. The agreed-upon manner of delivery may become commercially impracticable due to failure of loading or unloading facilities or the unavailability of an acceptable carrier. If neither party is at fault, a substitute manner of performance must be tendered and accepted if it is commercially reasonable.

Stop and review! You have completed the outline for this subunit. Study multiple-choice questions 2 through 4 beginning on page 536.

19.3 TITLE AND RISK OF LOSS

1. **Overview**

   a. The parties may agree on who has the risk of loss. Otherwise, the UCC assigns it by means of practical rules.

   b. Risk of loss is **not** determined by **title** to the goods.

   c. Without a breach of contract, and if no carrier or bailee is involved, risk of loss passes to the buyer when:

      1) The buyer takes **receipt** of the goods from a **merchant**,

---

EXAMPLE

Merchant seller sells goods to Buyer, who must take delivery at Merchant's place of business. Risk of loss does not pass to Buyer until (s)he actually picks up the goods.

---

   2) A **nonmerchant** seller places the goods at the buyer's disposal (a **tender of delivery**), and/or

---

EXAMPLE

Seller, a nonmerchant, sells goods to Buyer, and the parties agree that the goods will be picked up by Buyer at 3:00 p.m. on Wednesday at a specified place. Seller has goods ready for Buyer at that time and place, but Buyer does not arrive. The goods are destroyed at 4:30 p.m. that day. Risk of loss passed to Buyer because Seller tendered delivery at 3:00 p.m. when (s)he had the goods ready for pick-up by Buyer.

---

   3) A seller may be entitled to recover the full contract price for conforming goods that are lost or damaged after risk of loss has passed to the buyer.

    d.   If the buyer has a **right to reject** the goods because they do not conform to the contract, the risk of loss remains on the seller even in a shipment contract.

        1)   Risk of loss does not pass to the buyer until

            a)   The nonconformity is cured (i.e., corrected) or

            b)   The buyer accepts the goods despite the nonconformity.

EXAMPLE

Buyer orders gold kazoos from Seller in Orlando, FOB Orlando. Seller ships silver kazoos, giving Buyer a right to reject. The kazoos are destroyed in transit. The risk of loss was on Seller. If gold kazoos had been shipped, the risk of loss would have been on Buyer.

---

    e.   If the buyer **rightfully revokes acceptance**, the risk of an uninsured loss is treated as having rested on the seller from the origination of the contract.

EXAMPLE

Boat Co. accepted delivery of a shipment of life vests from Seller. Boat discovered a hidden defect in the vests and rightfully revoked acceptance. Boat then notified Seller and waited for instructions. But before any action could be taken, the vests were destroyed through no fault of Boat. Boat's insurance covers only 30% ($30,000) of the fair value of the vests ($100,000). Seller bears the remaining loss of $70,000.

---

2.   **Use of Carrier**

    a.   If a carrier is involved, the shipping terms control. Whether a party is a merchant is irrelevant.

        1)   In a **destination** contract, title and risk of loss pass to the buyer when the goods have reached the destination and are tendered to (not accepted by) the buyer.

EXAMPLE

Seller in Tampa sells 10,000 tons of beans to Buyer in Denver FOB Denver. Risk of loss during shipment is on Seller. If the goods are damaged during shipment, the loss falls on Seller.

---

        2)   If the contract does not require delivery at a specified destination, it is a shipment contract. In a **shipment** contract, title and risk of loss pass to the buyer when the seller delivers the goods to the carrier.

EXAMPLE

Seller in Tampa sells 10,000 tons of beans to Buyer in Denver FOB Tampa. The contract authorizes shipment by carrier but does not require Seller to tender them in Denver. Risk of loss passes to Buyer when the goods are placed in possession of the carrier. If the goods are damaged in shipping, the loss falls on Buyer.

---

            a)   The shipping term **CIF** (cost, insurance, freight) or **C&F** indicates a shipment contract.

        3)   The buyer can rightfully reject goods because of damages incurred during shipment in a destination contract but not a shipment contract.

3.   **Sale on Approval**

    a.   In a sale on approval, the risk of loss and title do not pass until the buyer accepts.

        1)   The buyer takes the goods to use and may return them even if they conform to the contract. A sale on approval is a conditional sale whereby the buyer is allowed to use the item for a given amount of time and then decide to return it or buy it.

        2)   If the buyer decides not to take the goods, the seller has the risk of loss for the return.

4. **Sale or Return**

    a. A sale or return contract is treated as an ordinary sale. Thus, title passes when the seller completes physical delivery.

        1) The buyer takes the goods to resell them but may return those unsold.

        2) If the goods are returned, the buyer bears the expense and risk of loss while they are in transit.

5. **Identification**

    a. Title to goods **cannot** pass until the goods exist and the seller identifies goods as those referred to under the contract. Identification is designation of specific goods referred to under the contract.

        1) The buyer has a special property interest and insurable interest in identified goods.

    b. If the parties do not agree upon the time and manner of identification of existing goods to the contract, the time of identification is determined as follows:

        1) Identification of already existing goods occurs when the contract is made.

        2) When the contract is for **future goods**, identification occurs when the goods are designated by the seller for the buyer.

            a) By definition, future goods are not yet existing or identified.

EXAMPLE

Jean and Ellen contract for the sale of widgets when Jean has a barn filled with identical widgets. Until identification, the contract is one for the sale of future goods. Identification does not occur until either Jean or Ellen designates a quantity of the fungible widgets to which the contract refers. Until identification occurs, title cannot pass to Ellen.

---

6. **Passage of Title**

    a. Unless the parties explicitly agree, the following rules apply:

        1) Title passes to the buyer at the time and place at which the seller completes performance of physical delivery even if the goods are nonconforming. Passage of title does not depend on payment.

        2) Under a destination contract, title passes when delivery is tendered.

        3) Under a shipment contract, title passes when the goods are delivered to the carrier.

    b. Reservation of a security interest has no effect on passage of title.

    c. Title passes back to the **seller** by operation law as a result of the buyer's

        1) Rejection or other refusal to receive or retain the goods, whether or not justified and before return to the seller, or

        2) Justified revocation of acceptance.

7. **Sales by Nonowners**

    a. A purchaser receives the title that the seller has power to transfer.

    b. If the seller is a **thief**, the seller's title is void. Thus, the buyer acquires no title. The actual owner can reclaim the goods from the buyer.

    c. A seller has voidable title if the goods were obtained by **fraud**. A **voidable** title becomes valid when the goods are sold to a good-faith purchaser for value.

EXAMPLE

Jim sells a boat to Ted, who pays for the boat by check. Ted's check is dishonored because of insufficient funds. Jim has the right to rescind the contract and recover the boat from Ted. If Ted has already resold the boat to Scott, and Scott is a good-faith purchaser for value, Jim cannot recover the boat from Scott because title has passed to Scott. Jim still has a right of action against Ted for the purchase price, but Scott retains title to the boat.

---

    d.   Any **entrusting** of goods to a merchant who deals in goods of that kind gives the merchant power to transfer all rights of the entruster to a buyer in the ordinary course of business.

EXAMPLE

Candace leaves her watch with a jeweler for repair. The jeweler sells (deals in) both new and used watches. The jeweler sells the watch to Eileen, a customer, who does not know that the jeweler has no right to sell the watch. Eileen receives good title against Candace's claim of ownership. But the good-faith purchaser (Eileen) has only those rights held by the person entrusting the goods. Thus, if a thief of the watch had entrusted it to the jeweler, Eileen would have good title against the entruster (thief). However, she would not have good title against Candace, who neither entrusted the watch to the thief nor authorized the thief to entrust the watch to the jeweler.

---

  8. **Insurable Interest**

    a.   A buyer has a special property interest and an insurable interest in identified goods even without title or risk of loss.

    b.   A seller has an insurable interest if (s)he has title or a security interest. (Security interests are covered in Subunit 19.7.)

Stop and review! You have completed the outline for this subunit. Study multiple-choice questions 5 through 7 on page 537.

19.4 WARRANTIES

  1. **Types of Warranties**

    a.   A warranty is an assurance by one party (regardless of whether a warranty was actually intended) of the existence of a fact upon which the other party may rely.

    b.   **Express warranties** are a seller's oral or written statements of fact or promises that are made (whether or not a merchant) to the buyer that become part of the basis of the bargain. Express warranties include any (1) description of the goods (e.g., in promotional materials), (2) sample, or (3) model.

        1)   To become part of the agreement, the communication must be made when the buyer could have relied upon it when (s)he entered into the contract.

        2)   A statement relating to the value of the goods or a statement of the seller's opinion is not an express warranty.

EXAMPLE

Sporty is browsing at the Copter Co. She is a new pilot and is considering purchasing a particular helicopter but is concerned about its safety. Bud, the owner, tells Sporty, "Don't worry. All of our aircraft are nearly indestructible and cannot crash under any circumstances." Sporty purchases the helicopter. Subsequently, the aircraft crashes. Sporty sues Bud for breach of express warranty. Bud claims that it was not a warranty because he did not use language such as "guarantee" or "warranty" and was merely puffing. Bud will probably lose. As long as a seller makes the affirmation of fact or promise relating to the goods that becomes part of the basis of the bargain, the seller is expressly warranting the goods. It is not relevant that Bud did not intend to guarantee the goods.

---

    c.   An **implied warranty of merchantability** arises by operation of law and need not be written. This warranty is implied in every sale by a **merchant** who deals in goods of the kind sold. The buyer need **not** be a merchant.

        1)   The issue is whether the goods are fit for the ordinary purposes for which such goods are used.

    d.   An **implied warranty of fitness for a particular purpose** also arises by operation of law and need not be written. This warranty is implied whenever any seller knows

        1)   The particular purpose for which the goods are to be used and
        2)   That the buyer is relying on the seller to select suitable goods.

EXAMPLE

KBW is interested in climbing a mountain. KBW goes to a sporting goods store and purchases rope, hooks, pins, and maps. She tells the sales associate, "I need climbing shoes as well," and the sales associate recommends the Bumps. KBW purchases them. In fact, the Bumps are great for basketball but are useless and dangerous for mountain climbing. The Bumps shred on KBW's first outing under normal use. KBW sues for breach of warranty of fitness for a particular purpose. The store defends on the grounds that KBW never specifically said the shoes were for mountaineering. KBW will win because the store had reason to know that (1) the goods were to be used for a particular purpose (mountain climbing) and (2) the buyer would rely on the seller's skill and judgment in selecting suitable goods.

---

    e.   Any seller, whether or not a merchant, makes the **warranty of title**, which states that

        1)   The title is good,
        2)   Its transfer is rightful, and
        3)   The goods are free of liens and other encumbrances (unless specifically agreed to by the buyer).

    f.   Unless otherwise agreed, a **merchant** seller warrants that the goods are free of rightful third-party claims based on **infringement** (unauthorized use, e.g., of a patented device).

        1)   But a buyer who gives manufacture or design specifications to the seller must protect the seller from infringement claims.

EXAMPLE

Bo purchases a piano from Ben for cash. Two months later, Abe repossesses the piano from Bo. Abe proves that (1) he has a security interest in the piano and (2) Ben is in default. Bo demands his money back from Ben. Bo can recover because the seller of goods warrants that they are delivered free from any security interest or other lien of which the buyer has no knowledge.

---

  2. **Disclaimer of Warranties**

    a.   For all practical purposes, it is impossible for a seller to disclaim an **express** warranty.

        1)   Words or conduct that (a) create an express warranty and (b) negate or limit the warranty are construed whenever reasonable as consistent with each other. But negation or limitation of the warranty is ineffective to the extent such construction is unreasonable.

    b.   **Implied** warranties are disclaimed by (1) the use of certain language, for example, **"as is"** or **"with all faults;"** (2) the buyer's examination; or (3) the course of dealing, course of performance, or usage of trade.

        1)   Without such circumstances,
            a)   An oral or written disclaimer of the implied warranty of merchantability must use the word **merchantability**, which must be conspicuous if made in a writing.
            b)   The disclaimer of the implied warranty of fitness must be written and conspicuous.

    c.   The warranty of title may be disclaimed orally or in writing but only by (1) specific language or (2) the buyer's knowledge of circumstances relating to title.

        1)   A general disclaimer of warranty is ineffective.

d. A court may refuse to enforce a disclaimer on the grounds that it is unconscionable. For example, a disclaimer of liability for **personal injury** is not permitted.

1) Regarding personal injury, the UCC provides three statutory options to determine which third-party beneficiaries of a warranty are covered. The most widely adopted option extends to any individual in the family or household of the buyer or a house guest. It must be reasonable to expect the person to use, consume, or be affected by the goods.

a) However, in most states, the courts have extended warranty protection to other noncontracting parties who suffer personal injury because of defective goods.

Stop and review! You have completed the outline for this subunit. Study multiple-choice questions 8 and 9 on page 538.

19.5 REMEDIES

1. **Overview**

a. The purpose of a remedy is not to penalize the breaching party or to enrich the nonbreaching party. Remedies available under the UCC are intended to place the injured party in approximately the same position (s)he would have been had no breach of contract occurred.

2. **Remedies of the Buyer or Seller**

a. A party has a right to demand written assurances if there exists a reasonable basis for believing that the other party will **not** tender performance. Until receipt of adequate assurance, the party may suspend further performance if commercially reasonable.

1) If adequate assurance is not provided within a reasonable period (not over 30 days), the party may treat the contract as repudiated.

EXAMPLE

Seller hears a false rumor that Buyer is in financial difficulty. Seller reasonably believes the rumor. Seller may demand assurances and withhold any unpaid-for goods. Buyer sends an audited financial statement showing good financial condition. The statement is adequate assurance, and Seller must resume performance.

---

b. A party has **rights after anticipatory repudiation** of a performance not yet due.

1) If the loss will substantially impair the value of the contract, the injured party may

a) Await performance for a commercially reasonable time;
b) At any time resort to any remedy for breach, including immediate suit; or
c) Suspend performance.

2) The repudiating party's words, actions, or conduct must be clear.

3) A repudiating party may, at any time before his or her next performance is due, **retract** repudiation unless the non-repudiating party has

a) Canceled,
b) Materially changed his or her position in reliance on the repudiation, or
c) Otherwise indicated that (s)he considers the repudiation final.

EXAMPLE

During March Year 1, BigCo contracts to sell 1,000 earth-moving machines to Roadbuilders Corp., delivery to be April 1, Year 2. Early in Year 2, BigCo's employees' union calls a strike. On February 15, Year 2, BigCo notifies Roadbuilders in writing, unequivocally, that it repudiates the contract for April 1 delivery. Roadbuilders simply waits and does not change its position. On March 15, BigCo notifies Roadbuilders that it retracts its repudiation. The retraction is effective.

---

    c.   The parties may **modify the contract** to limit the available remedies or provide an exclusive remedy.

        1)   Substantial freedom of contract is permitted. However, any remedy must not be unconscionable or fail to accomplish its essential purpose.

    d.   The parties may agree to **liquidated damages**. The amount must be a reasonable forecast of damages for breach. Such a provision must be a reasonable reflection of (1) anticipated losses, (2) the difficulties of proof of loss, and (3) the inconvenience of obtaining another remedy.

        1)   The provision usually sets a ceiling on the defaulting party's liability.

        2)   If the provision is not a good-faith estimate of probable damages, it will be treated as a penalty and declared void.

        3)   If a seller has properly withheld delivery of goods, the buyer may receive a refund of amounts paid minus any liquidated damages. If damages are unliquidated (not specified in the contract), the seller may retain 20% of the value of the total contract price or $500, whichever is less.

        4)   The buyer's right of restitution is subject to offset to the extent the seller establishes either

            a)   A right to damages other than liquidated damages or
            b)   Benefits received by the buyer directly or indirectly under the contract.

    e.   Under the **statute of limitations**, a contracting party may sue another party for breach only if suit is filed within 4 years after the breach occurred. The parties may reduce (but not extend) the period, but not to less than 1 year.

        1)   A plaintiff must notify the defendant within a reasonable time of the breach or be barred from any remedy.

        2)   A **breach of warranty** occurs and establishes a cause of action when the seller tenders **delivery** of the goods.

            a)   But if (1) a warranty explicitly extends to future performance and (2) discovery must await the performance, the statute begins to run when the breach is or should have been discovered. For example, if a heating system is installed in the summer, discovery of a defect is likely to be delayed until winter.

    f.   The innocent party may **rescind the contract** because of **fraud** in its formation.

        1)   A party who rescinds must return the consideration received from the other party.

        2)   But rescission does not bar a claim for damages or any other remedy.

        3)   The elements of fraud must be present.

3.   **Seller's Breach of Contract**

    a.   The following actions constitute a breach by the seller:

        1)   Repudiating (renouncing) all or part of the contract,
        2)   Making a nonconforming tender of delivery, and
        3)   Failing to deliver conforming goods.

    b.   The **buyer's rights** after a seller's **nonconforming tender** are to either (1) accept, (2) reject the whole, (3) accept any commercial unit(s) and reject the rest, or (4) resort to any of the following remedies:

        1)   A buyer who (a) rightfully rejects nonconforming goods or (b) justifiably revokes acceptance has a **right to cover**.

            a)   To cover means to purchase substitute goods in the marketplace.
            b)   Cover is not mandatory. The buyer may choose between cover and damages.

      c)   The buyer must act reasonably and in good faith. (S)he may recover any excess of the cover price over the contract price, minus any savings on expenses, and damages.

      d)   If reasonable efforts to cover have failed or are likely to fail, the buyer may have a right to obtain possession of goods wrongly withheld. However, the goods must have been identified to the contract.

2)   The buyer's basic remedy when (s)he rejects the goods or justifiably revokes acceptance, or the seller fails to deliver, is to **sue for monetary damages**.

      a)   Damages ordinarily are the excess of market price over contract price.

      b)   The buyer may choose to measure damages by the difference between the contract price and the amount actually paid.

      c)   The buyer is entitled to **incidental** damages. They are expenses reasonably related to the breach.

      d)   The buyer may be entitled to **consequential** damages (e.g., lost profits). Recovery of these damages is permitted if the seller knew or had reason to know, at the time of contracting, of the buyer's general or particular needs.

EXAMPLE

Digit agrees to sell Macro a software package for use during the upcoming tax season. Digit knows that (1) Macro intends to earn $150,000 by using this software package and (2) the software is not readily available elsewhere. Digit telephones Macro in February and informs Macro that she plans to keep the software for use during the entire tax season. Macro is unable to find replacement software. Macro may be entitled to consequential damages because Digit knew of special circumstances that made Macro unable to mitigate the circumstances in the event of breach. Digit may be liable to Macro for her lost profits.

---

      e)   The UCC normally does **not** allow recovery of **punitive** damages.

3)   A buyer may **recover** goods from an **insolvent seller** if

      a)   The goods have been identified to the contract,

      b)   The seller became insolvent within 10 days of receipt of the first payment, and

      c)   Tender of any unpaid portion of the price is made and kept open.

4)   If the goods are unique and in other proper circumstances, a court may order **specific performance**.

      a)   The commercial feasibility of replacement determines whether the remedy is available to a buyer (but not a seller).

5)   A buyer has a right of **replevin** (recovery of possession) of goods identified to the contract that have been wrongfully withheld if the buyer cannot reasonably obtain cover.

  c.   A merchant buyer who rightfully rejects **perishables** may have a duty to resell.

EXAMPLE

Cotton Co. contracts to buy all cotton planted, produced, and ginned by Farmers Co-op during the annual season at $.30/lb. The market price of cotton rises to $.80/lb. Farmers Co-op attempts to avoid performance of the contract when most of the U.S. cotton crop for the season has already been sold. Cotton Co. seeks and obtains from a court an order of good faith specific performance.

---

4. **Buyer's Breach of Contract**

   a. The buyer's basic duty is to accept and pay for goods in accordance with the contract. The **seller's remedies** when a buyer breaches include the following:

      1) A seller may **withhold delivery of goods** when the buyer

         a) Is insolvent (unless the buyer pays cash, including payment for prior deliveries)
         b) Fails to make a payment due on or before delivery
         c) Wrongfully rejects, or revokes acceptance of, the goods
         d) Repudiates the contract

      2) A seller may **identify conforming goods to the contract** when a buyer breaches or repudiates a contract while the seller is still in possession.

         a) When the goods are unfinished at the time of breach, the seller must exercise reasonable commercial judgment to mitigate the loss and obtain maximum value for the unfinished goods. The seller may

            i) Stop work and resell the goods for scrap or salvage value or
            ii) Complete manufacture and wholly identify the goods to the contract.

      3) A seller may **recover goods in transit** (in the possession of a carrier or other bailee) when (s)he discovers the buyer to be insolvent.

      4) A seller may **recover goods from an insolvent buyer** when the buyer has received goods on credit and is insolvent. Demand must be made within 10 days after the buyer's receipt of the goods.

         a) No time limit applies if a misrepresentation of solvency was made in writing to the seller within 3 months prior to the delivery of the goods.
         b) The seller's right to reclaim is subject to the rights of a good-faith purchaser or other buyer in the ordinary course of business.

      5) A seller may **resell the goods** when (s)he (a) possesses or controls the goods at the time of breach or (b) duly reacquires the goods in transit.

         a) The resale must be in good faith and commercially reasonable.
         b) The seller can recover any deficiency between the market price and the contract price, plus incidental damages from breach, less any savings.

            i) If this measure of damages is inadequate, the seller may recover the profit it would have made from full performance by the buyer, plus incidental damages. But due allowance must be made for costs reasonably incurred and payments or proceeds of resale.

         c) Perishable goods must be sold as rapidly as possible to mitigate damages.
         d) A good-faith purchaser takes free of any rights of the original buyer.
         e) The UCC provides expressly that an aggrieved buyer, not a seller, may recover consequential damages. However, it does not prohibit recovery by a seller.

            i) Resale is not a prerequisite to their recovery.

      6) A seller may **recover the price plus incidental damages** but only under specific circumstances.

         a) The buyer accepted the goods and has not revoked acceptance,
         b) Risk of loss passed to the buyer before conforming goods were lost or damaged, or

c)   The buyer breached after the goods were identified to the contract and the seller is unable to resell the goods.

    i)   If a seller is unable to resell, the goods must be held for the buyer.

    ii)   The net proceeds from the sale must be credited to the buyer.

7)   A seller may seek damages for **wrongful repudiation** or **nonacceptance**. The seller may also resell the goods.

8)   A seller may **cancel the sales contract** if the buyer

    a)   Wrongfully rejects, or revokes acceptance of, conforming goods duly delivered;

    b)   Fails to make proper payment; or

    c)   Repudiates the contract in whole or in part.

9)   A contract clause may allow a party to **accelerate** payment or performance or require collateral at will or when the party deems itself insecure. This power may be used only if the party, in good faith, believes the possibility of payment or performance is impaired.

Stop and review! You have completed the outline for this subunit. Study multiple-choice questions 10 through 12 beginning on page 538.

19.6 SECURITY INTERESTS AND ATTACHMENT

1.   **Security Agreements**

    a.   A security agreement provides a seller (or lender) an interest in a specific asset that is pledged as collateral. The pledged collateral can be seized and sold if the buyer (or borrower) defaults.

        1)   A **secured party** is the lender or seller who holds a security interest in the pledged asset.

        2)   A lien is a form of a security interest in a collateral asset that provides the lender with a legal claim to the asset until the debt has been paid back. If the borrower defaults, the secure party is entitled to the proceeds from the sale of the asset.

    b.   A security agreement may include the following optional items:

        1)   An **after-acquired property** clause creates an interest in most types of personal property to be acquired in the future. Such a clause is important to a lender that finances inventory.

            a)   The clause provides for a **floating** lien that will attach (float) to specified property that the debtor may acquire in the future.

            b)   The security interest attaches in favor of the lender once the debtor has obtained an interest in the property.

EXAMPLE

A typical after-acquired property clause might apply to "all inventory now owned or hereafter acquired by the debtor."

---

            c)   A security interest attaches to **consumer goods** under the clause only if the debtor acquires rights in the goods within 10 days after the secured party gives value.

        2)   A **future advances** clause permits the secured party to advance additional funds to the borrower using the same collateral, for example, under a continuing line of credit.

EXAMPLE

Bank lends David $50,000 to purchase equipment. David gives Bank a security interest in the equipment. A future advances clause provides that the liability for any funds lent by Bank to David in the future will be secured by the original equipment.

---

        3)   A **waiver-of-defenses** is a clause in a contract where the debtor waives (prohibited from raising) all his defenses to the enforcement of the security interest in the collateral. A waiver of defenses clause in a security agreement is not always binding. There are certain public policy arguments against enforcing such clauses against consumers. However, they have been upheld between merchants.

            a)   For a waiver of defense clause to be effective against an assignee of a security interest, the debtor is bound by the waiver only if the assignee has taken (1) for value, (2) in good faith, and (3) without notice of a claim or defense.

            b)   A **holder in due course** status under the UCC protects a purchaser of debt against claims or defenses the parties to the original transaction had against each other.

2. **Security Interest**

    a.   UCC Article 9 covers any transaction (regardless of form or name) intended to create a security interest in personal property or fixtures. A security interest secures payment or performance of an obligation.

        1)   But mere identification of the goods to the contract or passage of title does **not** give the buyer a security interest. A security interest is a separate right that must be agreed to by the parties.

            a)   An exception is a reservation of title by a **lessor** or **consignor**, which is intended to act as a security interest in the property.

        2)   **Personal property** consists of all things movable and ownable.

            a)   **Goods** are tangible personal property that is movable when the security interest attaches. The following are goods:

               i)   **Consumer goods** are used for personal, family, or household purposes.

               ii)   **Inventory** includes goods held for sale or lease or to be provided under a contract for service.

EXAMPLE

Wholesaler buys milk from farmers and sells it to restaurants. The milk is Wholesaler's inventory.

---

               iii)   **Farm products** are crops, livestock, supplies, and unprocessed products of crops or livestock.

EXAMPLE

Milk in the possession of a dairy farmer is a farm product.

Sap that has been boiled into maple syrup is a farm product because boiling is so closely related to harvesting the sap. But once the syrup is bottled for resale, it becomes inventory.

---

               iv)   **Equipment** consists of goods that are not consumer goods, inventory, or farm products. For example, a refrigerator purchased for use in a laboratory is equipment.

               v)   **Fixtures** are goods that become part of real property (buildings or land) under state law. An example is a central heating system or built-in cabinets.

3.   **Purchase Money Security Interest (PMSI)**

a.   A PMSI results when

1)   A person obtains credit,
2)   The credit is used to acquire property, and
3)   That property is collateral for the debt.

EXAMPLE

Debtor purchases an office copier. One week later, Debtor borrows $10,000 from Bank and gives Bank a security interest in all its office equipment. Bank's security interest in the copier is **not** a PMSI.

EXAMPLE

Debtor borrows $10,000 from Bank to purchase office equipment. Debtor gives Bank a security interest in the equipment to be purchased. The next day, Debtor purchases a desk. Bank's security interest in the desk is a PMSI.

EXAMPLE

Debtor purchased a computer on credit from Seller. Debtor also purchased in the same transaction additional software to install in the computer. Thus, Seller (the party that financed the purchase) has a PMSI in the computer and the software.

---

4.   **Attachment**

a.   A security interest in collateral is not effective against the debtor or third parties until it attaches. Attachment must occur to be enforceable against the debtor, barring an explicit agreement stating otherwise. The debtor must agree to the security interest.

b.   The security interest attaches and becomes **enforceable** against the debtor when the following 3 events have occurred:

1)   The debtor has **authenticated** (signed manually or electronically) a security agreement (contract) that describes the collateral. The description suffices if it reasonably identifies the collateral. For example, with certain exceptions, identification may be by a type of collateral defined in the UCC, such as inventory.

a)   But other evidence of authentication may suffice if it is in accordance with the security agreement:

i)   The secured party's **possession** of the collateral and/or
ii)   The secured party's **control** of collateral in the form of deposit accounts (e.g., savings and checking) or investment property (e.g., securities)

b)   If the collateral cannot be possessed or controlled (e.g., in the case of accounts such as receivables), a signed writing (or one in electronic form) is necessary for attachment.

2)   The secured party has given **value**.

a)   Contract consideration suffices and need not be new. An example is an agreement to take a security interest instead of enforcing a previously existing debt is considered value.

3)   The debtor (a) has **rights** in the collateral or (b) can transfer such rights (but not necessarily title).

c.   Attachment of a security interest in collateral gives the secured party rights to proceeds.

Stop and review! You have completed the outline for this subunit. Study multiple-choice questions 13 and 14 on page 539.

19.7 PERFECTION OF SECURITY INTERESTS

1. **Overview**

   a. A secured party perfects its security interest to prioritize its claim over any other third party's interest in the collateral. Third parties include buyers from the debtor, creditors of the debtor, or a trustee in bankruptcy.

      1) Perfection gives priority over most unperfected interests and subsequent perfected secured interests.
      2) Perfection is **not** required to enforce the secured party's rights against the debtor.

   b. Perfection of a security interest occurs only after

      1) It has attached and
      2) Other requirements have been satisfied that relate to the particular collateral.

   c. Depending on the collateral, security interests are perfected in various ways:

      1) By filing a financing statement
      2) By possession or control of the collateral
      3) Automatically (but in certain cases for a brief period only)

2. **Perfection by Filing a Financing Statement**

   a. Filing a financial statement gives notice of the filer's security interest. It is not required for attachment. But it is required to perfect a security interest without a specific exception. The debtor's location controls the place of filing.

      1) Security interests in most forms of collateral may be perfected by filing a financing statement with the appropriate public official, e.g., the Secretary of State.

   b. The UCC requires the financing statement to contain

      1) The name of the debtor (but not a trade name only),
      2) The name of the secured party, and
      3) An indication (description) of the covered collateral.

         a) For example, a **fixture filing** must (1) indicate that it covers fixtures, (2) be filed in the **real property** records, and (3) describe the real property.

EXAMPLES

Ralph Ortega is a sole proprietor of Small Business. Ortega borrowed money from Bank and gave a security interest in the equipment of Small Business. Bank should file the financing statement under Ortega.

XYZ Partnership owns Dave's Plumbing. XYZ borrowed money from Bank and conveyed a security interest in its fleet of trucks. Bank should file the financing statement under XYZ Partnership, not Dave's Plumbing.

---

   c. A financing statement may be filed before a security agreement is reached or a security interest attaches. But filing is not a condition of attachment.

   d. A filed financing statement is effective for 5 years. A **continuation statement** extending perfection for 5 years may be filed during the last 6 months of this period.

   e. If a debtor moves out of the jurisdiction where the security interest is perfected, it remains perfected until the earliest of (1) lapse of the original period of perfection, (2) 4 months after the debtor changed location, or (3) 1 year after transfer of the collateral to a debtor in another jurisdiction.

3. **Perfection by Possession**

   a.   An example is a pawnbroker's loan of money and receipt of personal property as collateral. A security interest may be perfected by possession of the following:

      1)   Goods

      2)   Negotiable documents of title (e.g., warehouse receipts and bills of lading)

          a)   A security interest in a negotiable document of title perfects a security interest in the goods it represents while the goods are held by the issuer of the document.

      3)   Tangible chattel paper

      4)   Instruments

          a)   Possession is optimal for negotiable instruments. A security interest not perfected by possession is defeated by a holder in due course.

              i)   Also, perfection by possession is not limited to the 20-day automatic perfection period.

      5)   Money

          a)   Possession is the only way to perfect a security interest in money other than identifiable cash proceeds.

   b.   If attachment occurs when the secured party takes possession of the collateral according to the security agreement, perfection and attachment are **simultaneous**.

EXAMPLE

John arranged to borrow $10,000 from Julie for 30 days and to provide Julie a security interest in his boat on June 1. On June 2, John surrendered possession of the boat to Julie, and Julie gave John $10,000. Attachment occurred on June 2 because (1) John had rights in the collateral, (2) Julie had given value, and (3) Julie was in possession of the collateral. Perfection occurred simultaneously with attachment because Julie had possession of the boat when attachment occurred.

---

      1)   Generally, the security interest becomes unperfected when possession ceases unless the secured party files a financing statement while in possession.

4. **Perfection by Control**

   a.   Control perfects a security interest only in investment property, electronic chattel paper, and deposit accounts. Perfection ends when the secured party no longer has control.

      1)   For example, a secured party has control over (a) a savings account if the secured party is the bank in which the account is maintained or (b) a certificated security delivered to the secured party.

5. **Automatic Perfection**

   a.   In some cases, perfection is automatic upon attachment. The primary example is **PMSI in consumer goods**.

EXAMPLES

Finance Co. lent Lori $1,000 to purchase a couch for use in her home and took a security interest in the couch. Lori used the $1,000 to purchase a couch. The security interest is a PMSI and is perfected without filing a financing statement or taking possession of the couch.

Finance Co. lent Factory, Inc., $1,000 to purchase a forklift and took a security interest in the forklift. Factory purchased a forklift with the $1,000. The PMSI is not automatically perfected because the forklift is equipment, not consumer goods.

---

    b.   The factoring of **accounts** is an outright sale that the UCC treats as a secured transaction. Perfection of a security interest in accounts ordinarily is only created by filing because nothing exists to possess. A purchaser, therefore, must file to perfect an ownership interest.

        1)   But if an insignificant amount of the assignor's accounts is transferred, perfection is by attachment only.

    c.   With respect to security interests in **instruments, certificated securities, or negotiable documents**,

        1)   Perfection is automatic for the 20-day period after attachment to the extent that new value is given to obtain the security interest under an authenticated security agreement.

        2)   The security interest becomes unperfected at the end of 20 days unless the secured party perfects by other means.

6.   **Proceeds**

    a.   Proceeds include all items received upon disposition of collateral. Proceeds consist of any collateral that has changed in form.

EXAMPLE

A sheep rancher obtains credit and grants the creditor a security interest in the wool (goods in the form of a farm product). If the rancher exchanges the wool for a truck or cash, the truck or cash constitutes proceeds.

---

    b.   A security interest generally continues in collateral after its sale or other disposition. Moreover, a security interest attaches to **identifiable** proceeds.

        1)   The proceeds are perfected if the security interest in the collateral was perfected.

        2)   A perfected security interest in proceeds becomes unperfected on the 21st day after attachment. But perfection continues if the proceeds are identifiable amounts of cash or in certain other cases.

    c.   Proceeds are paid in the following order:

        1)   Reasonable expenses incurred by the sale

        2)   Certain buyers of goods

            a)   Buyer in the ordinary course of business

            b)   Buyer of consumer goods from a consumer under certain circumstances

        3)   Balance of debt owed to primary secured creditor

        4)   The debt owed any creditor with a subordinate security interest in the collateral

    d.   Once all interests have been paid, the debtor receives any surplus.

Stop and review! You have completed the outline for this subunit. Study multiple-choice questions 15 and 16 on page 540.

19.8 PRIORITIES

1.   **Overview**

    a.   The protection provided by a security interest varies with its priority.

        1)   One general rule is that a perfected security interest has priority over an unperfected security interest in the same collateral.

        2)   A second general rule is that if unperfected security interests conflict, the first to attach or become effective has priority.

        3)   A third general rule is that if continuously perfected security interests conflict, priority depends upon the order of filing or perfection with respect to the collateral.

2.   **Priority of Unperfected Interests**

    a.   An unperfected security interest is subordinate to, among others, the following:

        1)   A perfected security interest in the same collateral.

EXAMPLE

On June 1, Bank lent Debtor $20,000 and took a security interest in Debtor's equipment. Bank did not file a financing statement or take possession of the equipment. On July 15, Finance Co. lent Debtor $30,000 and took a security interest in the same equipment. Finance Co. properly filed a financing statement. On August 1, Debtor filed for bankruptcy. Finance Co.'s security interest is perfected and has priority over Bank's unperfected security interest and over claims of Debtor's other unsecured creditors (to the extent of the value of the equipment).

---

        2)   The rights of a **lien creditor**. Lien creditors include (a) a creditor who acquires a lien by judicial process, (b) an assignee for the benefit of creditors, or (c) a trustee in bankruptcy.

            a)   The rights of lien creditors are subordinate to a prior perfected security interest.

EXAMPLE

Bank has an unperfected security interest in Debtor's equipment as of June 1. Debtor files a petition in bankruptcy on August 1. The bankruptcy trustee has priority over Bank's security interest as of August 1. Knowledge of the unperfected claim by the trustee is not relevant to priority.

---

        3)   A buyer of tangible chattel paper, documents, goods, instruments, or certificated securities who gives value, takes delivery, and has no knowledge of the security interest.

    b.   An unperfected security interest has priority over claims of the debtor's general creditors.

EXAMPLE

Bank lends Debtor $15,000 and takes a security interest in Debtor's fleet of trucks. Bank fails to perfect the security interest by filing or taking possession of the collateral. Second Bank lends Debtor $20,000 but does not take a security interest in collateral. In a priority contest between Bank and Second Bank, Bank prevails.

---

3.   **Priority of Perfected Interests**

    a.   Priority usually dates from the time of filing or perfection, whichever is first.

EXAMPLE

Bank agreed to lend Debtor up to $50,000 as needed during the next year. On January 2, Year 1, Debtor executed a financing statement covering all owned or after-acquired equipment. The statement included a future advances clause. Bank filed the financing statement on January 3. Finance, Inc., lent Debtor $10,000 on March 1. Debtor executed a financing statement covering all owned or after-acquired equipment. Finance perfected its security interest by filing the financing statement on March 9. On July 1, Bank lent Debtor $30,000. On July 31, Debtor declared bankruptcy. Bank's security interest has priority over Finance's security interest because Bank filed before Finance filed or perfected. If Bank's financing statement had been filed on July 1, rather than on January 3, Finance's security interest would have priority over Bank's security interest. Finance's priority would date from March 9 and Bank's from July 1. Further, Bank's security interest would cover all $80,000 since it contained a future advances clause.

---

    b.   Without filing or perfection in a subsequent period, priority no longer dates from the time of filing or perfection. Thus, the filing or perfection must be continuous.

EXAMPLE

In the example under 3.a. above, assuming no bankruptcy, Bank's filed financing statement lapses on January 3, Year 6. On January 4, Year 6, assuming no filing of a continuation statement, Finance has a perfected security interest and Bank has an unperfected security interest.

---

c. If the security agreement contains a future advances clause, the perfected security interest ordinarily has the same priority for future advances as for the first advance.

4. **Buyers of Goods**

a. Generally, a perfected security interest in goods is effective against subsequent purchasers. However, certain third parties may acquire the collateral (goods) free of the security interest, even though the interest has been perfected.

1) A buyer in the **ordinary course of business** (other than a buyer of farm products from a farmer) is not subject to any security interest given by the seller to another. The buyer's knowledge of the security interest is only relevant if the buyer knows that the purchase violates that interest.

EXAMPLE

Family Grocery purchased frozen yogurt from Wholesaler. Wholesaler had given a security interest in its inventory to Freezers, Inc. Freezers had properly perfected the security interest. The president of Wholesaler disclosed the security interest to Family's president before selling the yogurt. If Wholesaler defaults on its obligation to Freezers, Freezers cannot exercise its rights as a secured party against Family.

---

2) A buyer of **consumer goods from a consumer** is not subject to a security interest if the purchase is (a) made without knowledge of the security interest, (b) for value, (c) for consumer purposes, and (d) **prior to the secured party's filing**.

EXAMPLE

Sam bought a dining table (a consumer good) from Tables, Inc., on credit. Tables took a PMSI in the dining table that was automatically perfected. Several months later, Sam paid 50% of the purchase price to Tables. Sam then sold the table to Don. Don, unaware of Tables' security interest, paid $200 for the table and placed it in his dining room. Tables' security interest is unenforceable against Don. However, if Tables had filed a financing statement before Don purchased the table, Tables' security interest would be enforceable against Don.

---

5. **PMSIs**

a. A perfected PMSI in **goods (other than inventory)** has priority over a conflicting security interest in the goods if the PMSI is perfected when, or within 20 days after, the debtor takes possession. This priority is recognized even if the conflicting interest was perfected first. Moreover, it ordinarily extends to a perfected security interest in the identifiable proceeds of goods.

1) Even in bankruptcy, a secured creditor with a perfected PMSI may seek its remedy against the specific collateral.

EXAMPLE

On January 2, Bank lent Debtor $50,000 and took a security interest in Debtor's currently owned and after-acquired equipment. On June 2, Equip Corp. sold Debtor equipment on credit and took a PMSI in the equipment. On June 19, Equip perfected the PMSI. Equip has priority over Bank.

---

b. A perfected PMSI in **inventory** has priority over a conflicting security interest if

1) The PMSI is perfected when the debtor takes possession,
2) An authenticated notice is sent to the other secured party,
3) The notice is received within 5 years before the debtor takes possession, and
4) The notice describes the collateral and states that the sender has or expects to have a PMSI in the debtor's inventory.

EXAMPLE

Bank is secured by Debtor's inventory. The security agreement contains an after-acquired property clause. Bank's security interest was perfected by filing. Subsequently, Expansion, Inc., began supplying Debtor with a new line of inventory. Expansion sold the inventory to Debtor on credit and retained a PMSI. Expansion filed a financing statement covering the collateral on June 1. Debtor took possession of the new products on June 23. On July 1, Expansion disclosed the PMSI in a letter to Bank. Expansion will not have priority over Bank with respect to the security interest in the new inventory in Debtor's possession. Notice was given to Bank after Debtor took possession. If Expansion had notified Bank of the PMSI prior to June 23, however, Expansion's claim to the new inventory would have had priority over Bank's.

---

        5)   The notice requirement applies only if (a) the PMSI is perfected and (b) the other secured party filed prior to perfection of the PMSI.

        6)   A perfected PMSI in inventory extends to identifiable cash **proceeds** received no later than the time of delivery to a buyer.

EXAMPLE

Bank has a perfected PMSI in Debtor's car inventory. Sam buys a car from Debtor and pays with a check. Bank's perfected PMSI floats to the check as identifiable cash proceeds.

---

        7)   When perfected PMSIs in goods conflict, the PMSI securing all or part of the price of the collateral has priority over a PMSI securing an obligation incurred to obtain rights in the collateral.

    c.   A secured party with a security interest in **fixtures** has priority over any earlier recorded **real estate** interest if the security interest is a PMSI that has been perfected by a fixture filing before or within 20 days after the goods became fixtures.

        1)   A nonpurchase money security interest perfected by a fixture filing has priority over a later recorded real estate interest.

        2)   A construction mortgage has priority over a security interest in fixtures if (a) the **construction mortgage** is recorded before the goods become fixtures and (b) the goods become fixtures before construction is completed.

6.   **Liens Arising by Operation of Law**

    a.   The holder of the lien typically has provided services or materials with respect to the goods in the ordinary course of business and has possession of the goods.

        1)   With possession, the lien has priority over a perfected security interest unless a state statute provides otherwise.

        2)   Without possession, the lien is subordinate to a perfected security interest.

        3)   A lienholder's knowledge of a security interest does not affect priority.

EXAMPLE

Debtor borrows $5,000 from Bank to purchase a car and conveys a security interest in the car to Bank. Bank perfects the security interest. A week later Debtor takes the car to Best Body Shop for a new paint job. Best Body Shop knew of Bank's security interest. When Best Body finishes the job, Debtor cannot pay. Best retains possession of the car. Debtor defaults on payment to the bank. Bank sues Best, demanding delivery of the car. Best alleges its lien, based upon common law, has priority over Bank's perfected security interest. Best's lien is not granted by statute. The court holds that Best's lien has priority. Best's awareness of Bank's interest is irrelevant.

Stop and review! You have completed the outline for this subunit. Study multiple-choice questions 17 and 18 on page 541.

19.9 RIGHTS AND DUTIES OF DEBTORS, CREDITORS, AND THIRD PARTIES

1. **Possession or Control of Collateral**

    a. The secured party in possession of collateral is a **bailee** who is **strictly liable** for unauthorized use or misdelivery. The obligations and rights of the secured party in possession are to

    1) Use reasonable care at all times to preserve the collateral, for example, in the case of instruments or chattel paper, by preserving rights against prior parties. Failure to use reasonable care is negligence, and the bailee may be liable for damages.

    2) Keep the collateral identifiable, although interchangeable collateral, such as grain, may be commingled.

    3) Bear the cost of reasonable expenses incurred for preservation, use, or custody of the collateral, e.g., insurance and taxes.

        a) This cost is chargeable to the debtor.

        b) The debtor has the risk of accidental loss or damage to the extent effective insurance coverage is deficient.

    b. A secured party with possession or control may either

    1) Keep proceeds from the collateral as security (excluding money or funds) or
    2) Create a security interest in the collateral.

    c. A secured party must file a termination statement of record within 1 month if (1) the collateral consists of consumer goods, (2) no obligation is secured by the collateral, and (3) no commitment to give value exists.

    1) The filing must be within 20 days after receipt of an authenticated demand from the debtor, if earlier.

    2) If the property is not consumer goods, a termination statement must be filed or sent to the debtor within 20 days after the debtor makes an authenticated demand given that no obligation is secured and no commitment to give value exists.

2. **Duty to Respond to Requests**

    a. A secured party generally must comply with a debtor's request for an accounting (e.g., the unpaid amount of the debt), a statement of account, or a list of collateral within 14 days.

3. **Default**

    a. Default occurs when the debtor fails to fulfill obligations under the security agreement. Typical events constituting default are (1) lack of current payments, (2) removal of or failure to insure the collateral, and (3) bankruptcy or insolvency of the debtor.

    b. The secured party has three options if the debtor defaults: (1) Sue the debtor for the amount due (reduce the claim to a judgment for the deficiency), (2) peaceably take possession and dispose of the collateral, or (3) accept (retain) the collateral.

4. **Repossession**

    a. Upon the debtor's default, the secured party may resort to self-help repossession or repossession by judicial action.

    1) Self-help repossession is without judicial action. It must be peaceable.
    2) Repossession by judicial action requires a court order or judgment against the debtor.

b. After repossession, the secured party may **dispose** of the collateral by **public or private** sale. The debtor cannot prevent sale.

1) Reasonable authenticated **notice** of the disposition must be given to the debtor. Notice of public disposition must include the time and place. Notice of a private disposition must include only the time after which disposition may occur.

   a) Other appropriate parties must be notified. For example, failure to notify another secured party may result in liability.

   b) Notice is reasonable if the debtor has adequate time to protect its interests.

   c) The debtor may waive notice.

   d) Notice to other secured parties is unnecessary if the collateral is consumer goods. The reason is that a PMSI in consumer goods is perfected by attachment alone.

EXAMPLE

Leo, with a loan from Local Bank, purchases a van and a boat. He signs, with respect to each purchase, a promissory note for half the loan amount and a security agreement. Leo thereby conveys to Bank a security interest in both the van and the boat, each securing payment when due of half the remaining amount on the loan. Leo defaults on payments to Bank. Bank takes lawful possession of both van and boat. Bank sends proper written notice to Leo that the van will be sold at auction 4 weeks after date of notice. The boat and van are sold at auction. Bank sues Leo for a deficiency in the net proceeds. With regard to the half of the amount secured by the van, the court awards a judgment for the deficiency. Because no reasonable notice was given regarding the sale of the boat, Bank is not entitled to a deficiency judgment for the part of the loan it secured.

---

2) Notice to the debtor is **not** required if the collateral is normally sold on a recognized market, perishable, or likely to decline quickly in value.

3) All aspects of the disposition must be commercially reasonable, including the time, place, manner, method, and terms.

4) A secured party's disposition of collateral

   a) Transfers to a **transferee for value** all of the debtor's rights,

   b) Discharges the security interest under which the disposition was made, and

   c) Discharges subordinate security interests or liens (unless a statute provides otherwise).

   d) A transferee who acts in good faith is not subject to such interests even if the secured party does not comply with applicable requirements.

5) The secured party may buy the collateral at any public disposition. If the collateral is customarily sold in a recognized market or is the subject of widely distributed price quotations, the secured party may buy it at private disposition.

6) The proceeds of collection or enforcement are applied in the following order:

   a) Payment of reasonable expenses of collection or enforcement
   b) Satisfaction of the debt owed to the secured party
   c) Satisfaction of the debts owed to subordinate secured parties
   d) Payment of any surplus to the debtor

7) If the disposition is commercially reasonable but the proceeds are insufficient, the obligor is liable for any deficiency.

8) The underlying transaction may be a sale of accounts, chattel paper, promissory notes, and certain other items. In these cases, the debtor has no right to a surplus or an obligation for a deficiency.

5. **Acceptance of the Collateral**

    a. Acceptance of the collateral (strict foreclosure) may be an alternative to disposition.

    b. The secured party keeps the collateral in satisfaction of the debt.

    c. The secured party must send an authenticated notice to other claimants.

    d. The debtor must consent to the acceptance.

    e. Acceptance of collateral in partial satisfaction of the obligation is **not** permitted if the collateral is consumer goods.

    f. Disposition is required if the amount paid is at least (1) 60% of the cash price in the case of a PMSI in consumer goods or (2) 60% of the principal amount of the secured obligation in the case of a non-PMSI in consumer goods.

        1) The secured party must dispose of collateral within 90 days of taking possession. But the debtor and all secondary obligors may agree to a longer period in an authenticated agreement.

    g. Acceptance of collateral is not permitted if the debtor or any other party that is required to receive notice objects within 20 days of having received such notice. Then the secured party must dispose of the collateral.

6. **The Debtor's Remedies**

    a. The debtor may **redeem** his or her interest in the collateral at any time before

        1) The debt is satisfied by acceptance of the collateral,
        2) The collateral has been collected,
        3) The collateral is disposed of, or
        4) A contract for the disposition of the collateral is entered into.

    b. The secured party's failure to comply with Article 9 provides the debtor with a right to damages for any resulting losses from the disposition of collateral.

Stop and review! You have completed the outline for this subunit. Study multiple-choice questions 19 and 20 on page 542.

QUESTIONS

19.1 Contract Formation

1. Smith contracted in writing to sell Peters a used personal computer for $600. The contract did not specifically address the time for payment, place of delivery, or Peters's right to inspect the computer. Which of the following statements is true?

A. Smith is obligated to deliver the computer to Peters's home.

B. Peters is entitled to inspect the computer before paying for it.

C. Peters may not pay for the computer using a personal check unless Smith agrees.

D. Smith is not entitled to payment until 30 days after Peters receives the computer.

Answer (B) is correct.

REQUIRED: The true statement about a contract with terms left open.

DISCUSSION: A contract for the sale of goods is enforceable if missing terms can be supplied. The buyer has a right to inspect the goods before payment unless contract terms waive the right, e.g., when delivery is COD or payment is against documents of title (a documentary sale).

Answer (A) is incorrect. Unless otherwise agreed, tender is generally due at the seller's place of business. Answer (C) is incorrect. Tender of payment by check suffices unless the seller demands legal tender (currency) and gives the buyer a reasonable amount of time to obtain it. Answer (D) is incorrect. Unless otherwise agreed, the price is due upon tender of delivery.

19.2 Performance

2. Rowe Corp. purchased goods from Stair Co. that were shipped COD. Under the Sales Article of the UCC, which of the following rights does Rowe have?

A. The right to inspect the goods before paying.

B. The right to possession of the goods before paying.

C. The right to reject nonconforming goods.

D. The right to delay payment for a reasonable period of time.

Answer (C) is correct.

REQUIRED: The right of a buyer of goods shipped COD.

DISCUSSION: The seller has an obligation to deliver goods that conform to the contract. The perfect tender rule allows the buyer an absolute right to reject nonconforming goods. When goods are shipped COD, payment is not considered to be an acceptance.

Answer (A) is incorrect. When goods are shipped COD, the buyer does not have the right to inspect the goods before payment. Answer (B) is incorrect. When goods are shipped COD, the buyer does not have the right to take possession before payment. Answer (D) is incorrect. When goods are shipped COD, the buyer does not have the right to tender payment at a later time.

3. With regard to a contract governed by Article 2 of the UCC, which one of the following statements is true?

A. Merchants and nonmerchants are treated alike.

B. The contract may involve the sale of any type of personal property.

C. The obligations of the parties to the contract must be performed in good faith.

D. The contract must involve the sale of goods for a price of $500 or more.

Answer (C) is correct.

REQUIRED: The true statement about contracts governed by UCC Article 2.

DISCUSSION: Good faith means honesty in fact. The UCC imposes an obligation of good faith in the performance or enforcement of every contract or duty within its scope.

Answer (A) is incorrect. Article 2 applies to both merchants and nonmerchants, but special rules are provided for certain aspects of transactions between or with merchants. Answer (B) is incorrect. Article 2 applies to sales of goods. Goods do not include such items of personal property as accounts, documents of title, instruments, money, investment securities, copyrights, and patents. Answer (D) is incorrect. No dollar amount is required to bring a sale of goods within Article 2.

4. Buyer and Seller contracted for Buyer to purchase all of Seller's output for 1 year. The stated price was subject to decreases of up to 5% if the market price decreased. The market price fell by 2%, and Seller doubled its usual output. Accordingly, Buyer refuses to purchase Seller's output. In a suit by Seller against Buyer, Buyer's best defense is that

A. The quantity was not definite.

B. Seller supplied an unreasonable amount.

C. Mutual assent was not present.

D. The contract was impossible to perform.

Answer (B) is correct.
REQUIRED: The best argument for avoiding performance on a requirements contract.
DISCUSSION: Requirements and output contracts are permitted if the parties act in good faith and demand or tender reasonable quantities. Without stated estimates, Seller's normal or otherwise comparable prior output is the measure of a reasonable amount. No estimates were made. Thus, if Seller's output is twice the reasonable amount, Buyer may avoid performance.
Answer (A) is incorrect. The contract is not indefinite if the parties act in good faith and demand or tender reasonable quantities. Answer (C) is incorrect. An agreement that one party will buy the other's output for a specified period within a given price range indicates an intention to enter into a contract with terms that are reasonably definite and certain. Answer (D) is incorrect. The facts do not indicate that Buyer is unable to purchase the increased output.

19.3 Title and Risk of Loss

5. Under the Sales Article of the UCC, which of the following factors is most important in determining who bears the risk of loss in a sale of goods contract?

A. The method of shipping the goods.

B. The contract's shipping terms.

C. Title to the goods.

D. The manner in which the goods were lost.

Answer (B) is correct.
REQUIRED: The most important factor in determining who has the risk of loss.
DISCUSSION: The agreement as to risk of loss may be express. It also may be implicit from trade usage, course of dealing, or course of performance. If the parties do not have an agreement about risk of loss but a carrier is involved, the shipping terms control. In a destination contract, risk of loss passes to the buyer when the goods have reached the destination and are tendered to the buyer. In a shipment contract, risk of loss passes to the buyer when the seller delivers the goods to the carrier.
Answer (A) is incorrect. The type of carrier is irrelevant. Answer (C) is incorrect. The UCC never assigns risk of loss based on the location of the title. Answer (D) is incorrect. The manner in which the goods were lost by the carrier is irrelevant.

6. On Monday, Wolfe paid Aston Co., a furniture retailer, $500 for a table. On Thursday, Aston notified Wolfe that the table was ready to be picked up. On Saturday, while Aston was still in possession of the table, it was destroyed in a fire. Who bears the loss of the table?

A. Wolfe, because Wolfe had title to the table at the time of loss.

B. Aston, unless Wolfe is a merchant.

C. Wolfe, unless Aston breached the contract.

D. Aston, because Wolfe had not yet taken possession of the table.

Answer (D) is correct.
REQUIRED: The true statement about risk of loss given that the seller was a merchant.
DISCUSSION: If (1) the parties have no agreement as to risk of loss, (2) no carrier is involved, and (3) the goods are not in the possession of a bailee, the risk of loss passes to the buyer on his or her receipt of the goods if the seller is a merchant. Otherwise, the risk passes to the buyer on tender of delivery. Because Aston is a merchant (a person engaged in selling goods of the kind), risk did not pass to Wolfe on tender of delivery.
Answer (A) is incorrect. The UCC never assigns risk of loss to goods on the basis of title. Answer (B) is incorrect. The seller's, not the buyer's, status is relevant. Answer (C) is incorrect. Risk of loss would not have passed prior to receipt by Wolfe.

7. Under the Sales Article of the UCC, unless a contract provides otherwise, before title to goods can pass from a seller to a buyer, the goods must be

A. Tendered to the buyer.

B. Identified to the contract.

C. Accepted by the buyer.

D. Paid for.

Answer (B) is correct.
REQUIRED: The prerequisite for passage of title to goods.
DISCUSSION: In every contract for the sale of goods, a seller has a duty to pass title to the buyer in exchange for the price. An express or explicit understanding between the buyer and the seller will determine when title passes. Before title can pass, two conditions must be satisfied: (1) The goods must be in existence, and (2) they must be identified to the contract. Identification is the method for designating the specific goods as the subject matter of the sales contract. It is the time at which the buyer obtains an insurable interest. A contract to sell goods not existing and identified is subject to Article 2 as a contract to sell future goods.

19.4 Warranties

8. Under the Sales Article of the UCC, most goods sold by merchants are covered by certain warranties. An example of an express warranty is a warranty of

  A. Usage of trade.

  B. Fitness for a particular purpose.

  C. Merchantability.

  D. Conformity of goods to the sample.

Answer (D) is correct.
  REQUIRED: The example of an express warranty by a merchant in a sale of goods.
  DISCUSSION: Any statement of fact or promise made by a seller to the buyer that (1) relates to the goods and (2) becomes part of the basis of the bargain is an express warranty that the goods conform to the statement or promise. Express warranties also may be created by description, model, or sample. A sample that is part of the basis of the bargain is an express warranty that the goods conform to the sample.

9. Larch Corp. manufactured and sold Oak a stove. The sale documents included a disclaimer of warranty for personal injury. The stove was defective. It exploded, causing serious injuries to Oak's spouse. Larch was notified 1 week after the explosion. Under the UCC Sales Article, which of the following statements concerning Larch's liability for personal injury to Oak's spouse is true?

  A. Larch cannot be liable because of a lack of privity with Oak's spouse.

  B. Larch will not be liable because of a failure to give proper notice.

  C. Larch will be liable because the disclaimer was not a disclaimer of all liability.

  D. Larch will be liable because liability for personal injury cannot be disclaimed.

Answer (D) is correct.
  REQUIRED: The true statement about liability for personal injury under the UCC Sales Article.
  DISCUSSION: The warranty provisions were not intended to enlarge or restrict legal remedies for personal injuries. Strict liability for an unreasonably dangerous product may be viewed as the implied warranty of merchantability stripped of the contract defenses of notice of defect, privity, and disclaimer. Thus, strict liability for personal injury caused by a defective product cannot be disclaimed.
  Answer (A) is incorrect. The most restrictive option under the UCC allows a member of the purchaser's family to sue for physical injury. Answer (B) is incorrect. Oak gave reasonable notice by informing Larch of the injury within 1 week of its occurrence. Answer (C) is incorrect. Even if a disclaimer of the warranty of merchantability met all technical requirements, disclaimer of liability for personal injury is presumed to be unconscionable. Furthermore, strict liability for personal injury caused by a defective product cannot be disclaimed.

19.5 Remedies

10. Unless the parties have otherwise agreed, an action for the breach of a contract within the UCC Sales Article must be commenced within

  A. Four years after the cause of action has accrued.

  B. Six years after the cause of action has accrued.

  C. Four years after the effective date of the contract.

  D. Six years after the effective date of the contract.

Answer (A) is correct.
  REQUIRED: The time within which an action for the breach of a contract within the UCC Sales Article must be commenced.
  DISCUSSION: A 4-year statute of limitations applies to cases involving sales of goods. The parties, however, may reduce (but not extend) the period for suit, but not to less than 1 year. The limitations period generally begins to run when the cause of action has accrued.
  Answer (B) is incorrect. The applicable period is 4 years. Answer (C) is incorrect. The limitations period begins when cause of action has accrued (generally when the breach occurs). Answer (D) is incorrect. An action for the breach of a contract must be commenced within 4 years after the cause of action has accrued.

11. Bush Hardware ordered 300 Ram hammers from Ajax Hardware. Ajax accepted the order in writing. On the final date allowed for delivery, Ajax discovered it did not have enough Ram hammers to fill the order. Instead, Ajax sent 300 Strong hammers. Ajax stated on the invoice that the shipment was sent only as an accommodation. Which of the following statements is true?

  A. Ajax's note of accommodation cancels the contract between Bush and Ajax.

  B. Bush's order can be accepted only by Ajax's shipment of the goods ordered.

  C. Ajax's shipment of Strong hammers is a breach of contract.

  D. Ajax's shipment of Strong hammers is a counteroffer, and no contract exists between Bush and Ajax.

Answer (C) is correct.
  REQUIRED: The true statement about the shipment of goods solely as an accommodation.
  DISCUSSION: Shipment of a brand different from that stipulated in the contract was a breach of the contract. Bush may (1) accept the goods despite their nonconformity, (2) rightfully reject them, or (3) resort to any of the buyer's other remedies under the UCC. Accommodation shipments and the ability to cure, are not applicable. Notice of acceptance was sent, and a cure must be made within the time for performance in most cases.
  Answer (A) is incorrect. The breaching party cannot cancel the contract. Only a mutual rescission or the promised performance discharges the seller's obligation unless the nonconforming goods are accepted. Answer (B) is incorrect. Bush's order is an offer to enter into either a bilateral or unilateral contract. It can be accepted either by a prompt promise to ship or by a prompt shipment, respectively. Answer (D) is incorrect. The shipment is not a counteroffer. The acceptance had already created a contract.

12. Under the Sales Article of the UCC, the remedies available to a seller when a buyer breaches a contract for the sale of goods may include

	The Right to Resell Goods Identified to the Contract	The Right to Stop a Carrier from Delivering the Goods
A.	Yes	Yes
B.	Yes	No
C.	No	Yes
D.	No	No

Answer (A) is correct.
    REQUIRED: The remedies available to a seller when a buyer breaches a contract for the sale of goods.
    DISCUSSION: A buyer may breach or repudiate a sales contract while the seller is still in possession of the goods. The seller then can identify to the contract the conforming goods that are still in his or her possession or control. The seller can do so even if the goods were not identified at the time of the breach. The seller can resell the goods, holding the buyer liable for any loss. The seller also may recover goods in transit. The seller may stop delivery of goods in the possession of a carrier or other bailee if a buyer breaches or repudiates a sales contract. The right to stop delivery can be exercised only for a truckload, planeload, carload, or larger freight shipment unless the buyer is insolvent.

19.6 Security Interests and Attachment

13. Shemwell Co. purchased a printing press from Jones Equipment, Inc. Shemwell signed a promissory note for the purchase price and signed a security agreement stating, "The buyer waives as against any assignee of the security interest any claim or defense that the buyer may have against the seller." Jones assigned the promissory note and security agreement to 1st Bank. The waiver-of-defenses clause is **not** enforceable against Shemwell if

A. Jones had issued a written warranty on the press.

B. 1st Bank did not give value for the assignment from Jones.

C. Jones knew the printing press could malfunction.

D. After the assignment, 1st Bank learned the printing press had malfunctioned.

Answer (B) is correct.
    REQUIRED: The true statement about enforceability of a waiver-of-defenses clause.
    DISCUSSION: A waiver-of-defenses clause in a security agreement is not always binding. For personal defenses effective against an assignee of a security interest, the debtor is bound by the waiver only if the assignee has taken (1) for value, (2) in good faith, and (3) without notice of a claim or defense. However, the clause is not binding with respect to real defenses, i.e., effective against a holder in due course of a negotiable instrument.
    Answer (A) is incorrect. A written warranty has no bearing on the enforceability of the waiver. Answer (C) is incorrect. Whether Jones knew the printing press could malfunction has no bearing on the enforceability of the waiver. Answer (D) is incorrect. Knowledge of possible defenses is immaterial if it is learned after the assignee has given value in good faith.

14. Under the UCC Secured Transactions Article, which of the following after-acquired property may be covered by a debtor's security agreement with a secured lender?

	Inventory	Equipment
A.	Yes	Yes
B.	Yes	No
C.	No	Yes
D.	No	No

Answer (A) is correct.
    REQUIRED: The scope of an after-acquired property clause.
    DISCUSSION: A security agreement may provide for a security interest in after-acquired property. The security interest does not attach to consumer goods, unless the debtor acquires rights in them within 10 days after the secured party gives value. An after-acquired property clause can apply to both inventory and equipment.

19.7 Perfection of Security Interests

15. Perfection of a security interest permits the secured party to protect its rights by

    A. Avoiding the need to file a financing statement.

    B. Preventing another creditor from obtaining a security interest in the same collateral.

    C. Establishing priority over the claims of most subsequent secured creditors.

    D. Denying the debtor the right to possess the collateral.

Answer (C) is correct.

    REQUIRED: The true statement about perfection of a security interest.

    DISCUSSION: Unless perfection is by attachment, to establish priority over a previous unperfected creditor or a subsequent secured creditor, a secured party must give notice by perfecting its security interest. The methods of perfection include (1) filing a financing statement, (2) taking possession of the collateral, or (3) obtaining control of the collateral. The steps taken will depend upon the nature of the collateral.

    Answer (A) is incorrect. Filing a financing statement is required to perfect an interest in certain types of collateral, such as the debtor's inventory not in the possession of the secured party. Answer (B) is incorrect. Perfection of a security interest does not bar other creditors from obtaining a security interest in the same collateral. Answer (D) is incorrect. Possession is one means of perfecting a security interest, but the parties ordinarily expect the debtor to maintain possession.

16. Burn Manufacturing borrowed $500,000 from Howard Finance Co., secured by Burn's current and future inventory, accounts receivable, and its proceeds. Burn's representative authenticated a sufficient security agreement that described the collateral. The security agreement was filed in the appropriate state office. Burn subsequently defaulted on the repayment of the loan, and Howard attempted to enforce its security interest. Burn contended that Howard's security interest was unenforceable. In addition, Green, who subsequently gave credit to Burn without knowledge of Howard's security interest and filed a financing statement but did not have a purchase money security interest (PMSI) in inventory, is also attempting to defeat Howard's alleged security interest. The security interest in question is valid with respect to

    A. Both Burn and Green.

    B. Neither Burn nor Green.

    C. Burn but not Green.

    D. Green but not Burn.

Answer (A) is correct.

    REQUIRED: The true statement about the validity of a security interest in inventory, both current and after-acquired, and accounts receivable.

    DISCUSSION: Before attachment of the security interest, the creditor gave value, the debtor had rights in the collateral, and the debtor authenticated a sufficient security agreement. Thus, attachment has occurred, and the security interest is enforceable between the debtor (Burn) and the secured party (Howard). Because Howard's security interest was perfected by filing a financing statement, Green is assumed to have notice of Howard's security interest. Howard's claim has priority over Green's because Howard filed and perfected before Green. However, if Green had perfected a PMSI in inventory and met the notice requirements, Green would have priority.

19.8 Priorities

17. On June 15, Harper purchased equipment for $100,000 from Imperial Corp. for use in its manufacturing process. Harper paid for the equipment with funds borrowed from Eastern Bank. Harper gave Eastern an authenticated security agreement covering Harper's existing and after-acquired equipment. On June 21, Harper was petitioned involuntarily into bankruptcy under Chapter 7 of the Federal Bankruptcy Code. A bankruptcy trustee was appointed. On June 23, Eastern duly filed a sufficient financing statement. Which of the parties will have a superior security interest in the equipment?

A. The trustee in bankruptcy, because the filing of the financing statement after the commencement of the bankruptcy case would be deemed a preferential transfer.

B. The trustee in bankruptcy, because the trustee became a lien creditor before Eastern perfected its security interest.

C. Eastern, because it had a perfected purchase money security interest without having to file a financing statement.

D. Eastern, because it perfected its security interest within the permissible time limits.

Answer (D) is correct.

REQUIRED: The party with a superior security interest in equipment after bankruptcy.

DISCUSSION: The equipment is purchase money collateral that secures the purchase money obligation arising from the lender's giving value to permit the debtor to obtain rights in the collateral. Thus, Eastern Bank has a PMSI. A PMSI in goods other than inventory or livestock has priority over a perfected conflicting security interest in the same collateral if it is perfected at the time the debtor receives possession of the collateral or within 20 days thereafter. Even in bankruptcy proceedings, a secured creditor with a perfected security interest may pursue its remedy against the particular property. Thus, Eastern Bank's perfected PMSI in the equipment is superior (it is not inventory). However, the trustee in bankruptcy has the status of a hypothetical lien creditor and can defeat a nonperfected security interest in the equipment.

Answer (A) is incorrect. Filing is not a transfer. It perfects the PMSI. Answer (B) is incorrect. Eastern could perfect its PMSI and retain its priority in the equipment by filing for up to 20 days after the debtor received possession. Answer (C) is incorrect. Filing was required for perfection, even though it could be done up to 20 days after the debtor received possession of the collateral.

18. Under the UCC Secured Transactions Article, what is the order of priority for the following security interests in store equipment?

I. Security interest perfected by filing on April 15.

II. Security interest attached on April 1.

III. Purchase money security interest attached April 11 and perfected by filing on April 20.

A. I, III, II.

B. II, I, III.

C. III, I, II.

D. III, II, I.

Answer (C) is correct.

REQUIRED: The order of priority for the security interests in equipment.

DISCUSSION: The basic rule is that conflicting security interests in the same collateral will rank in priority according to the time of filing or perfection. If a purchase money security interest (PMSI) in goods (e.g., equipment) other than inventory or livestock is perfected when the debtor receives possession of the collateral, or within 20 days afterward, the PMSI has priority over a conflicting security interest even if it was perfected first. The reasonable assumption is that the debtor took possession between April 11 (when the security interest attached) and April 20 (when perfection occurred). Furthermore, a perfected security interest generally has priority over a security interest that has attached but is not perfected.

19.9 Rights and Duties of Debtors, Creditors, and Third Parties

19. Under the UCC Secured Transactions Article, if a debtor is in default under a payment obligation secured by goods, the secured party has the right to

	Reduce the Claim to a Judgment	Sell the Goods and Apply the Proceeds toward the Obligations Secured	Peacefully Repossess the Goods without Judicial Process
A.	Yes	Yes	No
B.	Yes	No	Yes
C.	No	Yes	Yes
D.	Yes	Yes	Yes

Answer (D) is correct.

REQUIRED: The rights of a secured party when a debtor defaults on a payment obligation.

DISCUSSION: After default by a debtor, a secured party essentially may choose among three remedies. The secured party may (1) sue the debtor for the amount owed (reduce the claim to judgment); (2) peaceably take possession of (foreclose on) the collateral, with or without judicial process, and dispose of it in a commercially reasonable manner that includes applying the proceeds to the costs of disposition and to the obligations secured; and (3) accept (retain) the collateral in full or partial satisfaction of the obligations secured if certain conditions, for example, consent of the debtor, are met. These remedies are cumulative and allow the creditor, if unsuccessful by one method, to pursue another remedy. They also may be exercised simultaneously.

20. Under the UCC Secured Transactions Article, which of the following statements is most likely true concerning the disposition of collateral by a secured creditor after a debtor's default?

A. A good-faith transferee for value and without knowledge of any defects in the sale takes free of any subordinate liens or security interests.

B. The debtor may not redeem the collateral after the default.

C. Secured creditors with subordinate claims retain the right to redeem the collateral after the collateral is sold to a third party.

D. The collateral may only be disposed of at a public sale.

Answer (A) is correct.

REQUIRED: The statement most likely to be true about disposition of collateral.

DISCUSSION: When a secured party disposes of collateral after default, (1) the transferee for value receives all of the debtor's rights in the collateral, (2) the security interest under which the disposition occurs is discharged, and (3) subordinate security interests or liens are discharged unless a specific statute provides for a lien that is not dischargeable in this manner. As long as the transferee acts in good faith, (s)he will receive the property free of the foregoing interests even if the secured party does not comply with the requirements for the sale under Article 9 or any judicial proceeding.

Answer (B) is incorrect. The debtor always may redeem his or her interest in the collateral after default and before the secured party (1) collects the collateral (e.g., from account debtors); (2) disposes of, or enters into a contract for disposition of, the collateral; or (3) accepts collateral in full or partial satisfaction of the obligations secured. Answer (C) is incorrect. A good-faith transferee for value takes the property free of any subordinate security interests or liens unless a specific statute provides for a lien that is not dischargeable in this manner. Answer (D) is incorrect. Disposition sales may be either public or private.

STUDY UNIT TWENTY
DEBTOR-CREDITOR RELATIONSHIPS

(29 pages of outline)

This study unit covers issues related to debtor-creditor relationships. The first two subunits review the rights and duties of debtors and creditors under general contract law. Solutions to the conflict between debtor relief and creditor protection may be formal (bankruptcy) or informal. The next three subunits review federal bankruptcy law, including bankruptcy proceedings under Chapters 7, 11, and 13 of the Bankruptcy Code. The sixth subunit outlines the rights and duties of sureties.

20.1 LIENS AND ENFORCEMENT METHODS

1. **Overview**

   a. A **lien** is a legal claim on property, either real or personal, as security for payment or performance of a debt or obligation.

   b. The relative priority of liens usually is in the **order of their acquisition**.

      1) Certain liens attach only when possession is obtained and exist only as long as it is retained (e.g., artisan's liens).

      2) Concurrent liens attach simultaneously and have equal rank in distribution.

      3) A government has the power to establish the priorities of liens. It may give a statutory lien (e.g., a tax lien) priority over other liens or exempt certain property from collection by creditors.

   c. This subunit describes the most common procedures for enforcing liens.

2. **Statutory Liens**

   a. A statutory lien attaches when a party adds value to another party's property by agreement. The authority for statutory liens is based on state law.

      1) Many such liens are based on the right of one person to retain possession of the property of another until the owner pays for the goods or services. However, certain statutory liens are nonpossessory.

      2) Statutory liens include (a) artisan's liens, (b) mechanic's liens, (c) bailee's liens, and (d) tax liens.

   b. An **artisan's lien** is held by a repairer or improver of **personal** property, such as an automobile or computer, who retains **possession** of the property until paid.

      1) The work or improvement must be performed subject to an express or implied agreement for cash payment.

c. **Mechanic's liens** (including **materialman's liens**) are liens against the **real** property benefited. Thus, they are not possessory.

1) The liens secure unpaid debts from **contracts** for materials or services to improve specific real property. For example, a mechanic's lien may be held by the builder of a house or by someone who has merely remodeled a room in a house.

2) The holder of a mechanic's lien normally files a document (a notice of lien) that identifies the property within 60 to 120 days after work is complete.

3) Attachment of the lien to the property dates back to when the first work is done or materials are supplied, and priority is determined by when liens attach. Thus, a real estate mortgage that was properly recorded (attached) before the work was done has priority.

d. A **bailee's lien** is granted to a common carrier (e.g., trucker, airline, or railroad) or warehouser to whom the debtor has entrusted goods. This possessory lien secures payment of shipment or storage charges.

1) The goods must be covered by a document of title.

e. A **tax lien** secures payment of taxes owed to a governmental entity. For example, it may be imposed on specific land on which the landowner has not paid the real property taxes. Moreover, a federal tax lien may be placed on all property of a delinquent tax payer. Only federal statutes, not state statutes, may exempt debtor assets from federal tax liens. For example, federal law exempts Social Security benefits from garnishment.

EXAMPLE

State **homestead exemption acts** may shield a debtor's equity in his or her home from most liens. However, mortgage liens and tax liens are not exempted.

---

1) Artisan's and mechanic's liens have priority over all other security interests in property unless a statute expressly provides otherwise.

2) Statutes typically give tax liens priority over otherwise superior liens.

3. **Enforcement of a Statutory Lien**

a. A statutory lien is enforceable only as to items to which liens may legally attach.

1) Statutes may allow the lienholder to foreclose the lien judicially and sell the property if the owner does not pay the debt.

a) The lienholder must give notice to the owner prior to foreclosure and sale.

b) Sale proceeds are used to pay the costs of foreclosure and sale and to satisfy the debt. Any remaining proceeds are paid to the former owner.

2) The statutory remedy is generally exclusive.

4. **Judicial Liens**

a. A judicial lien is acquired by judgment, seizure (levy), or another judicial process.

1) A court, after a civil proceeding, may issue a monetary judgment for one of the parties, e.g., the plaintiff. The party who is owed a money judgment is a judgment creditor.

2) If the other party (the judgment debtor) fails to pay, the judgment creditor may petition the court to issue a **writ of execution**. This order authorizes the sheriff to seize and sell specific nonexempt property of the judgment debtor to satisfy the judgment.

3) **Attachment**, a prejudgment remedy, is the seizure of a defendant's nonexempt property prior to the court's final judgment. The court allows seizure of property and placement of it in the custody of the court so that the judgment creditor cannot sell the property during the pendency of the litigation. Attachment is intended to secure satisfaction of a pending judgment.

a) **Replevin** is a prejudgment remedy intended to secure property already subject to a lien or a right of repossession.

EXAMPLE

A lender seeks repossession of an automobile after the debtor's default. The lender obtains a writ of replevin by filing an affidavit and posting a bond. The sheriff then seizes (replevies) the property and turns it over to the lender pending resolution of legal proceedings.

---

b) **Garnishment** is a prejudgment or postjudgment collection remedy. It is directed against a third party (the garnishee) who holds property, or is a debtor, of the defendant. For example, wages or bank accounts of the defendant may be garnished.

NOTE: Filing a petition in bankruptcy stays garnishment.

5. **Termination of Liens**

a. A lien is discharged by payment or tender of payment.

1) **Tender** is an offer to pay combined with a present ability to pay. It also discharges liability for further interest or damages. It does **not** discharge the debt.

2) A debtor may owe separate debts to one creditor. If the debtor makes a **partial** payment, the creditor may apply the payment to whichever debt (s)he chooses. But the debtor may instruct otherwise.

b. A lien is effective only as long as the property exists.

c. A lien dependent on possession terminates if the lienholder voluntarily and unconditionally surrenders possession or control of the property.

1) If the surrender is subject to an agreement that the property will be returned, the lien does not terminate. However, if a third party obtains rights to the property before it is returned, the lien terminates.

d. A lien may be terminated by waiver (i.e., a voluntary surrender of a right).

6. **Foreclosure on a Real Estate Mortgage by Judicial Sale**

a. The right to foreclose results from the debtor's default. Foreclosure is an action by the **mortgagee-lender** (or assignee) to (1) take the property from the **mortgagor-debtor**, (2) sell it to pay the debt, and (3) end the mortgagor's rights in the property.

b. To foreclose, the mortgagee must initiate a **judicial proceeding** to secure an order of sale. The sheriff or other officer of the court then conducts a sale by auction as specified by state statute.

c. The sale is confirmed by court order following a hearing.

d.   The debt then is satisfied with **proceeds** of the sale.

1)   A **purchase money mortgage** (PMM) is entitled to preference over other claims or liens. It is granted by a purchaser to secure payment of the purchase price. The money or credit is provided to purchase the property.

a)   The mortgage must be granted at the same time that the deed is delivered.

2)   An owner of property subject to a mortgage can grant a **second mortgage** (and others) on the same property to secure a debt.

a)   After foreclosure, the first mortgage has priority. It is satisfied in full from sale proceeds before any payment to another mortgagee.

3)   If the proceeds are less than the sum of the debt costs and interest, the mortgagor is liable for the deficiency unless released by the mortgagee.

a)   A state may restrict a deficiency to the excess of the debt over the **fair value**.

b)   In a state with an **antideficiency** statute, a purchase money mortgagor is not liable for a deficiency.

4)   **Surplus** proceeds belong to the mortgagor.

e.   The mortgagee may buy the property at the sale.

f.   The mortgagor has an **equitable right of redemption**. Prior to foreclosure, the mortgagor may regain rights by paying the mortgage debt plus interest and costs.

1)   The equity of redemption cannot be relinquished by agreement. Any such attempt is against public policy and considered void.

2)   Redemption might be accomplished by refinancing.

g.   The mortgagor may also have a **statutory right of redemption**. The mortgagor may repurchase the property by paying the auction sale price after the foreclosure sale during the statutorily specified period (not exceeding 1 year).

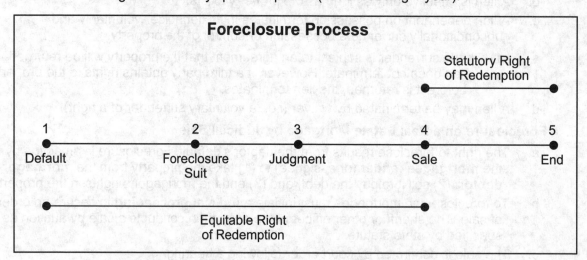

Figure 20-1

h.   The **purchaser** at a judicial sale takes the property free of any claim.

i.   **Foreclosure by sale** is an alternative permitted in most states. The mortgagee may sell the property at public auction without resorting to the legal system.

1)   The mortgage agreement must permit this procedure, and the sale must comply with strict statutory requirements.

Stop and review! You have completed the outline for this subunit. Study multiple-choice questions 1 and 2 on page 572.

20.2 STATE COLLECTIVE REMEDIES AS AN ALTERNATIVE TO FEDERAL BANKRUPTCY

1. **Composition**

   a. A **composition** with creditors is a nonstatutory alternative to bankruptcy. It is a contract in which the debtor agrees to pay the creditors part of the amounts owed in full satisfaction of their claims. The **mutual** promises among the creditors provide consideration.

      1) The agreement does not affect the rights of a nonconsenting creditor.
      2) The original debts are not discharged until the debtor has performed the new obligations.
      3) In an **extension** agreement, the debtor agrees to pay the full amount of all debts over a longer period.

   b. **Liquidation** of a **disputed** claim is an agreement by a debtor and creditor about the payoff amount of a disputed debt.

   c. No receiver is appointed. The court appoints a **receiver** to preserve property that is the subject of litigation.

2. **Assignment**

   a. Another alternative to bankruptcy is a **general assignment** for the benefit of creditors under a state statute. With a general assignment, the debtor of title **voluntarily** transfers assets to a third party (i.e., an assignee or trustee).

   b. The trustee (1) receives the debtor's property, (2) converts it to cash, and (3) distributes the cash to creditors in exchange for their promises to release the debtor.

   c. An assignment differs from a composition because the consent of creditors is **not** required.

   d. The assignee has **legal title** to the debtor's property.

      1) The debtor must act in good faith.
      2) Retention of any benefit from the property most likely is a fraudulent conveyance.
      3) If otherwise valid, the assignment is effective unless the creditors file an involuntary bankruptcy petition.
      4) The debtor cannot revoke the assignment, and creditors cannot use judicial process to seize the property.
      5) The assignment discharges debts only if they are paid in full by the trustee. It does not affect nonassenting creditors' claims.

   e. Another possibility is to transfer the debtor's business to a **creditor's committee** that has full management authority.

3. **Fraudulent Transfers**

   a. Transfers of property made with the intent to delay, hinder, or defraud creditors are voidable by the transferor's creditors pursuant to state law. Such transfers include the following:

      1) The debtor's retention of possession or a beneficial interest
      2) A transfer of substantially all assets
      3) A transfer in secret
      4) A transfer to a family member or insider
      5) A transfer for inadequate consideration
      6) A transfer in anticipation of legal action or financial problems
      7) Removal or concealment of assets

   b. As described in Subunit 20.4, a trustee in a bankruptcy also has the power to void fraudulent transfers.

Stop and review! You have completed the outline for this subunit. Study multiple-choice questions 3 and 4 beginning on page 572.

20.3 BANKRUPTCY ADMINISTRATION

1. The **U.S. Constitution** (Article I) gives Congress the exclusive power to establish "uniform Laws on the subject of Bankruptcies throughout the United States." The federal statute is the Bankruptcy Reform Act of 1978.

    a. Notable amendments have been made by the Bankruptcy Reform Act of 1994 and the Bankruptcy Abuse Prevention and Consumer Protection Act of 2005.

2. **The Bankruptcy Code**

    a. Bankruptcy is a formal way of resolving the conflict between creditor rights and debtor relief. The objectives are to ensure that (1) debtor assets are fairly distributed to creditors and (2) the debtor is given a fresh start.

    b. This outline covers the specific proceedings under the following chapters of the Code, with an emphasis on Chapters 7, 11, and 13:

        1) Chapter 7: Liquidation
        2) Chapter 9: Adjustment of Debts of a Municipality
        3) Chapter 11: Reorganization
        4) Chapter 12: Adjustment of Debts of a Family Farmer or Fisherman with Regular Annual Income
        5) Chapter 13: Adjustment of Debts of an Individual with Regular Income
        6) Chapter 15: Ancillary and Other Cross-Border Cases

    c. The following summarizes the eligibility for filing under Chapters 7, 11, and 13:

TYPES OF BANKRUPTCY	ELIGIBLE	INELIGIBLE
Chapter 7 Liquidation (voluntary or involuntary)	Individuals, including couples (subject to disqualification by the means test) Partnerships Corporations	Municipalities (eligible under Ch. 9) Railroads Insurers Banks Credit unions S&Ls
Chapter 11 Reorganization (voluntary or involuntary)	Railroads Most persons that may be debtors under Chapter 7	Shareholders Commodities and stockbrokers Insurers Banks Credit unions S&Ls
Chapter 13 Adjustment of debts of an individual (voluntary only)	Individuals	Nonindividuals Individuals without regular income

3. **Administration of Proceedings**

    a.   Each federal judicial district has its own bankruptcy court. A judge hears the case after the moving party files a petition that identifies the applicable chapter.

        1)   The result is an estate consisting of the debtor's property (a) at the time of filing or (b) that becomes subject to the proceeding. It is a separate legal entity.

        2)   Insolvency or any prior filing is **not** a requirement for filing a petition.

    b.   The filing of **any** petition operates as an **automatic stay** of most civil actions, including those by secured parties, against the debtor or his or her property until the court acts. The filed petition, however, does not terminate security interests or liens. The following are activities **not** stayed:

        1)   Alimony and child support collection
        2)   Criminal proceedings
        3)   Issuance of a notice of tax deficiency

    c.   The bankruptcy judge conducts the **core proceedings**. They resolve issues most directly related to reorganization or discharge, such as

        1)   Allowing creditor claims,
        2)   Determining the relative priority of creditor claims,
        3)   Confirming a plan of reorganization, and
        4)   Granting a discharge.

    d.   **Noncore proceedings** are resolved in state or other federal courts but may affect rights of the creditors or debtor. They involve property rights, personal injury claims, divorce, etc.

4. **Termination of the Stay**

    a.   A secured creditor may ask the court to recognize the priority of the existing security interest and allow foreclosure.

    b.   The stay may be terminated because of serial filings suggestive of bad faith or abuse. If a Chapter 7, 11, or 13 case is filed within a year after dismissal of another case, the stay generally terminates after 30 days. However, the stay continues in effect if the new filing is shown to be in good faith.

        1)   After a third filing within 1 year, the stay will not go into effect unless good faith is shown.

5. **Voluntary Proceedings**

    a.   Most petitions are voluntary. Any person eligible to be a **debtor** under a chapter may file under it. The debtor need **not** be insolvent, and no minimum debt or number of creditors is required.

        1)   A voluntary petition results in an **automatic order for relief**. In the order, the court assumes exclusive authority over the case. The mandatory creditors' meeting is held within a reasonable time after the order.

        2)   Amendments to the bankruptcy code in 2005 made filing more extensive. Among the additional requirements are (a) a statement of affairs, (b) a schedule of income and expenses, (c) lists of creditors and property, and (d) itemized monthly net income.

6.   **Involuntary Proceedings**

   a.   An involuntary petition may be filed against an eligible debtor exclusively under **Chapter 7** or **Chapter 11**. The number or timing of involuntary petitions is not limited.

   1)   An involuntary petition cannot be filed against the following:

   a)   Farmers
   b)   Banks
   c)   Insurers
   d)   Nonprofit corporations
   e)   Railroads
   f)   Persons who owe less than $15,775

   2)   If the debtor has **12 or more** different creditors, any **3 or more** who together hold unsecured claims of at least $15,775 may file an involuntary petition.

   3)   If the debtor has **fewer than 12** creditors, any **1 or more** who alone or together have unsecured claims of at least $15,775 may file an involuntary petition.

   a)   Any creditors who are the debtor's employees or are insiders, e.g., officers or directors of a corporation, relatives, or a partner, are **not** counted.

   4)   Filing an involuntary petition results in an **automatic stay** but does **not** result in an automatic order for relief. If the debtor does **not** oppose the petition, however, the court will enter an order for relief.

   5)   If the debtor opposes the petition, the court must hold a hearing, and the petitioner must post a bond to compensate a debtor if the case is dismissed.

   a)   The court orders relief on behalf of the creditors if it finds that either of two **statutory grounds** for involuntary bankruptcy exists:

   i)   The debtor is not paying undisputed debts as they become due.
   ii)   Within 120 days before the filing of the petition, a custodian, assignee, or general receiver took possession of all or most of the debtor's property to enforce a lien against the property.

   b)   If the case is dismissed, the creditors may have to pay the debtor's costs, attorney's fees, and damages caused when the trustee took possession of the debtor's property.

   i)   A petitioner who acted in bad faith may have to pay punitive damages for harm caused to the debtor's reputation.

7.   **Debtor Rights and Duties**

   a.   The debtor may continue to use, acquire, and dispose of his or her property until the court orders otherwise. The debtor also may incur new debts and operate a business.

   1)   If necessary, the court may order the appointment of a **temporary** trustee to preserve the debtor's assets.

   b.   A debtor must comply with various requirements, which include

   1)   Attending and submitting to all court-scheduled examinations,
   2)   Testifying if called as a witness in a hearing,
   3)   Informing the trustee in writing of the location of all real property in which the debtor has an interest, and
   4)   Receiving credit counseling.

8. **Trustees**

   a. Within a reasonable time after the order for relief, which may be delayed in an involuntary case, the U.S. Trustee (an administrator for a federal district court) appoints an **interim trustee**. The interim trustee (1) represents the debtor's estate, (2) investigates the financial affairs of the debtor, and (3) holds the first meeting of creditors.

      1) A trustee is required in Chapter 7, 12, and 13 cases. A trustee is **not** required in a Chapter 9, 11, or 15 case, but the court may order the appointment of an interim trustee who then may be elected by the creditors as the permanent trustee.

      2) Under Chapter 7, the **permanent** trustee may be elected by qualified creditors at their required meeting. But the interim trustee may continue to serve.

      3) Under all other chapters, the trustee, if any, is appointed.

      4) **Creditor committees** may be required or permitted. The committee is responsible for facilitating communication among the debtor, the trustee, and the creditors.

   b. The following are among the powers of the trustee:

      1) Collecting and accounting for property

         a) But a court may allow the debtor to file a bond and reacquire property from the trustee.

      2) Performing investigations

      3) Setting aside fraudulent conveyances and certain other property transfers

      4) Assuming and performing an unperformed contract or unexpired lease, rejecting it, or assigning it to a third party

         a) But rejection is assumed unless the trustee acts within 60 days after the order for relief.

      5) Operating the debtor's business

      6) Selling, using, or leasing estate property

      7) Investing estate money

      8) Hiring professionals

         a) A qualified trustee may perform professional services for reasonable compensation with court approval.

         b) Service as a trustee impairs a CPA's independence regarding the debtor.

      9) Filing reports

      10) Objecting to creditor claims

      11) Objecting to a discharge in a proper case

      12) Distributing assets and closing the estate

Be prepared to answer bankruptcy questions. The AICPA tests this topic often. Exam questions have tested the details of bankruptcy law, such as the number of creditors and dollar amounts involved in filing an involuntary bankruptcy petition against a debtor.

Stop and review! You have completed the outline for this subunit. Study multiple-choice questions 5 through 8 beginning on page 573.

20.4 BANKRUPTCY LIQUIDATIONS

1. **Chapter 7**

    a. The liquidation approach converts a debtor's nonexempt assets to cash distributed in conformity with the Code. An honest debtor then is discharged from most of the remaining debts and given a fresh start.

    b. Eligible parties are most debtors, including individuals, partnerships, and corporations. Among others, the following entities are not eligible to file under Chapter 7:

        1) Municipalities
        2) Railroads
        3) Insurers
        4) Banks, savings and loan associations, and credit unions

2. **Abuse by an Individual Debtor**

    a. The availability of bankruptcy protection is limited by means testing to avoid abuse. Abuse by an individual debtor with primarily consumer debts (for example, credit card debt) results in dismissal or conversion to a Chapter 13 case. Abuse is found when (1) the debtor does not pass the **means test** (if it results in a presumption of abuse), or (2) **general grounds** exist for the finding (bad faith or all circumstances indicate abuse).

    b. If the **debtor's income** exceeds the state median income, any interested party may seek dismissal for abuse. Otherwise, only the judge and certain administrators may move to dismiss (and then only on general grounds of abuse).

        1) The debtor's income for this purpose equals current monthly income (CMI) times 12.

    c. The **means test** determines the debtor's ability to repay general unsecured claims.

        1) **Current monthly income (CMI)** is a 6-month average of all income received by the debtor (and spouse if the case is joint). Social Security and certain other items are excluded.

        2) Presumed deductions from CMI are permitted for support and payment of higher priority debt, for example, (a) living expenses for which allowances are specified by the IRS, (b) actual expenses recognized by the IRS, and (c) secured debt coming due within 5 years.

        3) The debtor's **CMI after deductions** creates a **presumption of abuse** if it is at least

            a) $214.17 ($12,850 ÷ 60 months) regardless of the amount of general unsecured debt.

            b) $128.33 ($7,700 ÷ 60 months) if it suffices to pay at least 25% of general unsecured debt over 5 years.

                i) If CMI after deductions is less than $128.33, no presumption of abuse arises.

EXAMPLE

If CMI after deductions is $150, abuse is presumed if general unsecured debt is no more than $36,000.

($150 CMI after deductions × 60 months) ÷ 25% = $36,000

---

        4) The presumption of abuse may be overcome by proof of special circumstances.

3. **Debtor's Estate**

    a. The estate consists of all the debtor's nonexempt interests in property at the beginning of the case.

        1) The estate **excludes** the following:

            a) Earnings of the debtor for services after the beginning of a Chapter 7 case (but not a Chapter 11 or 13 case)

            b) Contributions to employee retirement plans

            c) Contributions made more than 365 days prior to filing to educational retirement accounts and state tuition programs

            d) Most property acquired after the filing of the petition, including (1) gifts, (2) Social Security payments, (3) welfare benefits, (4) disability payments, (5) alimony and support awards, and (6) most pension proceeds.

        2) The estate **includes** the following:

            a) All **nonexempt** property currently held (wherever located)

            b) Interests in property to which the debtor becomes entitled within 180 days after filing, such as

                i) Life insurance payments

                 ii) Divorce settlements

                iii) Amounts (e.g., inheritances) received upon the death of another person, whether or not through a will

                iv) Proceeds, products, offspring, rents, or profits received from property in the estate (e.g., interest on bonds, rent from a building, or property insurance proceeds)

                v) Property acquired by the estate after the commencement of the case

                vi) Property recovered by the trustee under the avoidance powers

4. **Exempt Assets**

    a. Exempt assets are basic necessities for a fresh start (e.g., rights to receive Social Security, disability benefits, alimony, and child support). Only individual debtors, not corporations, are eligible for exemptions.

    b. **States** are permitted to require their citizens to accept the exemptions of property defined by state law. If a state has not rejected the federal exemptions, the debtor has a choice.

        1) The state homestead exemption may be decreased by the value of an addition to the homestead during the 10 years before filing. This rule applies if the added value resulted from a disposition by the debtor of nonexempt property that operated as a fraud on creditors.

    c.   **Federal exemptions** and other amounts are indexed to inflation and adjusted every 3 years.

       1)   Up to $23,675 in equity in the debtor's residence and burial plot

       2)   An interest in a motor vehicle up to a value of $3,775

       3)   An interest up to a value of $600 in any item of household goods and furnishings, clothing, appliances, books, animals, crops, or musical instruments, with a total limited to $12,265

       4)   An interest in jewelry up to a value of $1,600

       5)   Any other property worth up to $1,250, plus any unused part of the $23,675 exemption in item 1) above, up to an amount of $11,850

       6)   An interest in tools of the debtor's trade up to a total value of $2,375

       7)   Any unmatured life insurance contract owned by the debtor

       8)   Certain interests in accrued dividends or interest under life insurance contracts owned by the debtor not exceeding $12,265

       9)   Professionally prescribed health aids

      10)   The right to receive Social Security, certain welfare benefits, veterans' benefits, disability benefits, alimony and support, and certain pension benefits

      11)   The right to receive certain personal injury and other awards up to $23,675

      12)   Unemployment compensation

      13)   The ability to void certain judicial liens, e.g., on exempt property

      14)   Regardless of which exemptions (federal or state) apply, amounts in tax exempt retirement accounts (but the amount in IRAs is capped at $1,283,025)

5.   **Trustee Powers**

    a.   To collect the property that belongs in the estate, the trustee can (1) exercise the rights and (2) assert any defenses of the **debtor**. The trustee also can exercise the rights that would be held by an actual creditor who has obtained a **judicial lien** on the property of the debtor through legal proceedings.

       1)   However, no such actual creditor needs to exist. Thus, the trustee is a hypothetical (ideal) lien creditor, one with the greatest power allowed under state law.

          a)   For example, the trustee has priority over a secured creditor whose security interest is unperfected.

       2)   The trustee does **not** have the right to void **statutory liens** against the debtor's property that were effective before filing.

          a)   But certain statutory liens on real property (e.g., mechanic's liens) are voidable. These are liens that are not effective until the petition is filed or the time when the debtor becomes insolvent.

       3)   The trustee also may void liens that are not enforceable against a **good-faith purchaser for value (GFP)** on the date of the filing. A GFP is a purchaser who (a) acted honestly, (b) gave value, and (c) had no notice of an adverse claim.

       4)   Accordingly, the trustee can void any transfer of property or debt incurred by the debtor that could be defeated by an (a) judicial lien creditor, (b) judgment creditor, or (c) GFP.

          a)   Thus, the trustee can exercise the same rights as

             i)   The debtor,

             ii)   Any actual creditors, and

             iii)   The hypothetical creditors or purchasers described above.

b. The trustee can **void preferential transfers**. The transfer may be (1) a voluntary property transfer, (2) a voluntary creation of a lien (a mortgage or a security interest whether or not perfected), or (3) the involuntary creation of a lien (e.g., a creditor's judgment lien).

   1) A voidable preferential transfer is made

     a) To or for the benefit of a creditor,

     b) For or on account of an antecedent (pre-existing) debt,

     c) During the debtor's insolvency,

     d) Within 90 days prior to filing the petition, and

     e) For the purpose of entitling the creditor to receive a larger portion of its claim than otherwise would be received under a distribution in bankruptcy.

   2) Property purchased by an innocent third party from a preferential transferee cannot be recovered. However, the preferential transferor may be liable for its value.

   3) Other transfers **not** voidable as preferences include the following:

     a) Payments of accounts payable in the ordinary course of the debtor's and transferee's business or financial affairs

     b) If the debtor is an individual, payment of up to $600 on a consumer debt within 90 days preceding the filing of the petition

     c) If an individual's debts are primarily nonconsumer debts, any transfer worth less than $6,425

     d) Transfers that involve a contemporaneous exchange for new value, such as materials or goods acquired in exchange for cash or a security interest

---

EXAMPLE

A purchase money security interest (PMSI) (one that enables the debtor to acquire the property) is not a voidable preference because new value is received. However, the PMSI must be perfected within 20 days after the debtor takes possession of the property.

---

     e) Bona fide transfers for domestic support obligations

EXAMPLE

On August 1, Hall filed a voluntary petition under Chapter 7 of the Federal Bankruptcy Code. Hall's assets are sufficient to pay general creditors 40% of their claims. The following transactions occurred before the filing:

- On May 15, Hall gave a mortgage on Hall's home to National Bank to secure payment of a loan National had given Hall 2 years earlier. When the loan was made, Hall's sibling was a National employee.
- On June 1, Hall purchased a boat from Olsen for $10,000 cash.
- On July 1, Hall paid off an outstanding credit card balance of $500. The original debt was $2,500.

The National mortgage was preferential because the mortgage was given to secure an antecedent debt. The payment to Olsen was not preferential because the payment was a contemporaneous exchange for new value. The credit card payment made by Hall on July 1 was not preferential because the payment was for a consumer debt of less than $600.

---

   4) The trustee has the power to void **preferential liens**, including judgment liens and other liens obtained by any judicial proceeding. These liens arise in the circumstances described for preferential transfers.

   5) The trustee may void preferential transfers and grants of security interests to **insiders** if made within 1 year before the filing of the petition.

     a) The debtor must have been insolvent at the time of the transfer or grant.

     b) Insiders are related parties, including the following:

       i) Relatives

       ii) Partners and partnerships

       iii) Corporate directors and officers

       iv) Controlling shareholders

       v) A corporation controlled by the debtor

   c.   The trustee can **void fraudulent transfers**.

      1)   A property transfer is voidable if it was made within 2 years prior to filing with actual **intent** to hinder, delay, or defraud creditors.

      2)   A trustee may also void a transfer or obligation for which the debtor received less than reasonably equivalent consideration if the debtor

         a)   Was insolvent or was made insolvent by the transfer,
         b)   Was operating a business with an unreasonably small capital, or
         c)   Expected to incur debts that (s)he could not repay.

EXAMPLE

Burton's business was faltering, and the creditors were demanding immediate payment. Burton's brother had recently set up a new corporation for real estate investments. With the intent to save some of her assets, Burton transferred them to the new corporation with an understanding that Burton would receive stock after resolution of her financial problems. Five months later, Burton filed for bankruptcy. Without regard to whether the new corporation had knowledge of Burton's fraud or insolvency, the trustee can recover the assets because Burton transferred them with intent to defraud creditors within 2 years of bankruptcy.

---

6. **Claims**

   a.   The distribution process commences with creditors' filing of proofs of claim.

      1)   A proof of claim must be filed within **90 days** after the first meeting of creditors.
      2)   Only unsecured creditors are required to file.
      3)   Upon filing, the claim is deemed valid and allowable.

         a)   However, if an interested party such as a creditor or the trustee objects, the bankruptcy court must decide whether to allow the claim.

         b)   If a debtor has a defense to an alleged debt (e.g., fraud or failure of consideration), the claim will not be allowed.

         c)   Claims are denied if they

            i)   Are for unearned interest,
            ii)   Can be offset by a claim against the creditor, or
            iii)   Exceed the reasonable value of services performed by an insider or attorney.

7. **Rights of Creditors**

   a.   The creditors involved in the distribution of the debtor's estate are (1) secured creditors, (2) priority creditors (unsecured), and (3) general creditors (other unsecured creditors).

   b.   **Secured creditors' rights**

      1)   The trustee cannot defeat a secured creditor's rights.
      2)   They are paid in full if the collateral is sufficient.
      3)   To the extent of any deficiency, the secured creditor is a general creditor.
      4)   A perfected property tax lien on the debtor's property is satisfied before support obligations.
      5)   Between secured creditors with interests in the same collateral, the first perfected interest has priority.

    c. **Priority creditors** are unsecured creditors that are paid after the secured creditors. They have priority over the claims of general creditors.

        1) Members of a higher class of priority creditors are paid in full before members of a lower class receive anything. If the assets are insufficient to pay all claims in a given class, the claimants in the class share pro rata.

        2) The classes of priority claims listed in order of payment are as follows:

            a) Domestic support obligations to a spouse, former spouse, or child have priority over those assigned or owed directly to a government.

            b) Claims for administrative expenses and expenses incurred in preserving and collecting the estate.

            c) Claims of tradespeople (gap creditors) who extend unsecured credit in the ordinary course of business after the filing of an involuntary petition but before the earlier of the appointment of a trustee or the entry of the order for relief.

            d) Wages (compensation) up to $12,850 owed to employees earned within 180 days prior to the earlier of (1) filing or (2) cessation of the debtor's business.

            e) Certain contributions owed to the debtor's employee benefit plans resulting from employee services performed within 180 days prior to the earlier of (1) filing or (2) cessation of the debtor's business.

            f) Claims of grain or fish producers up to $6,325 each for grain or fish deposited with the debtor but not paid for or returned.

            g) Claims of consumers for the return of up to $2,850 each in deposits.

            h) Certain income and other taxes owed to governmental entities.

            i) Death and injury claims arising from operation of a motor vehicle or vessel by a legally intoxicated person.

    d. If any money remains after payments to secured creditors and priority creditors, the general creditors are paid.

        1) General creditors are unsecured creditors that are not priority creditors.

        2) Higher-ranking claims are paid in full before lower-ranking claims receive anything. The rankings under this final set of priorities are as follows:

            a) Permitted unsecured claims for which creditors filed proofs of claim in time or had acceptable excuses for filing late

            b) Permitted unsecured claims for which proofs of claim were filed late and without acceptable excuse

            c) Interest on claims already paid for the period between the filing of the petition and the date of payment of the claims

EXAMPLE

A corporation filed for bankruptcy under Chapter 7. The total cash in the bankruptcy estate after the sale of all assets and payment of administration expenses is $100,000. The following is a listing of creditors:

- Bank is owed $75,000 on a mortgage loan secured by real property that was sold by the trustee for $71,000.
- The IRS has a $12,000 recorded judgment for unpaid taxes.
- Creditor X has an unsecured, nonpriority claim of $3,000 that was timely filed.
- Creditor Z has an unsecured claim of $1,200 that was not timely filed.
- Creditor Q has a claim of $15,000. Of this amount, $2,000 is secured by equipment sold by the trustee for $2,000. The claim was timely filed.

How is the available cash distributed?

Secured creditors are paid in full to the extent of their security before other claimants are paid anything. Priority creditors also are paid in full before general creditors. Bank has a secured claim for $75,000. Because sale of the security recovered only $71,000, Bank is a general creditor for $4,000 ($75,000 – $71,000). Creditor Q is a general creditor for its unsecured claim of $13,000 ($15,000 – $2,000 recovery from sale of equipment collateral). The IRS is a priority creditor for its $12,000 claim.

Accordingly, the cash available to pay the general creditors is $15,000 ($100,000 – $71,000 – $2,000 – $12,000). Creditor Z receives $0 because its claim was not timely filed. The general creditors entitled to payment are Bank ($4,000), Creditor X ($3,000 claim timely filed), and Creditor Q ($13,000). They share pro rata in the available cash.

Cash available to pay creditors	$100,000
Payment to Bank as secured creditor	(71,000)
Payment to Creditor Q as secured creditor	(2,000)
Payment to IRS as priority creditor	(12,000)
Cash available to pay general creditors	$ 15,000
Bank	
[$4,000 ÷ ($4,000 + $3,000 + $13,000)] × $15,000 =	(3,000)
Creditor X	
[$3,000 ÷ ($4,000 + $3,000 + $13,000)] × $15,000 =	(2,250)
Creditor Q	
[$13,000 ÷ ($4,000 + $3,000 + $13,000)] × $15,000 =	(9,750)
	$ 0

8. **Discharge**

    a. Individual debtors under Chapter 7 may receive a discharge from most debts that are unpaid after distribution of the debtor's estate, including the unsatisfied part of a secured debt.

    1) A discharge frees the debtor from further liability on certain debts.
    2) The court generally grants a discharge in a Chapter 7 proceeding.
    3) Corporations and partnerships cannot receive a Chapter 7 discharge.
    4) Most debtors are eligible for a discharge only once every 8 years.

b. The following acts, failures to act, or circumstances of the debtor are grounds for **denial of a general discharge**:

1) Fraudulently transferring or concealing (a) property within 1 year preceding the filing of the bankruptcy petition or (b) the property of the estate after filing

2) Unjustifiably concealing or destroying business records or failing to keep adequate business records

3) Making a false oath, a fraudulent account, or a false claim in connection with the case

4) Failing to explain satisfactorily any loss or deficiency of assets

5) Refusing to testify or to obey lawful orders of the court

6) Filing a written waiver of discharge approved by the court

7) Giving or receiving a bribe in connection with the case

8) Committing within 1 year before filing any of these acts in a case involving an insider

9) Being subject to a proceeding that may limit the homestead exemption

10) Failing to complete a personal financial management course

---

EXAMPLE

On June 9, Amy Aker transferred property she owned to her son. The property was collateral for Aker's obligation to Simon. Aker transferred the property with the intent to defraud Simon. On July 7, Aker filed a voluntary bankruptcy petition. Because Aker transferred the property with the intent to defraud Simon within 1 year of filing the petition for relief, she will be denied a general discharge.

---

c. A Chapter 7 discharge does not cover certain debts. These debts remain binding on the debtor but do not prevent a general discharge. **Nondischargeable debts** include

1) Most taxes, including federal income tax coming due within 3 years prior to bankruptcy

2) Debts incurred on the basis of materially false financial statements if (a) they were issued with the intent to deceive and (b) the creditor reasonably relied on them

3) Unscheduled debts not included in required filings in time to permit a creditor without notice of the case to timely file a proof of claim

4) Debts resulting from fraud (including securities fraud), misrepresentation, embezzlement, larceny, or breach of fiduciary duty but not negligence

5) Debts resulting from alimony, maintenance, or child support awards

6) Debts resulting from willful and malicious (but not unintentional) injury to another person or conversion of that person's property

7) Debts resulting from certain educational loans made, funded, or guaranteed by a governmental unit

8) Governmental fines and penalties, except those relating to dischargeable taxes

9) Debts resulting from liability for operating a motor vehicle while legally intoxicated

10) Credit card debts greater than $675 owed to a single creditor by an individual debtor for luxury goods or services incurred on or within 90 days prior to filing

11) Credit card debts for cash advances aggregating more than $950 under an open-end credit plan obtained by an individual debtor within 70 days prior to filing

12) Nondischarged debts from a prior bankruptcy

13) Certain debts incurred as a result of committing securities fraud

9. **Dismissal**

    a. If a Chapter 7 case is dismissed, the debtor is not discharged.

        1) Dismissal may result from, among other things, the debtor's

            a) Unreasonable delay

            b) Failure to pay fees

            c) Failure to provide (1) creditor's lists, (2) financial statements, (3) tax returns, (4) evidence of payment by an employer, and (5) the certificate from a credit counselor

            d) Lack of good faith

            e) Failure to complete a course in personal financial management

        2) If the debtor is an individual whose debts are mostly consumer debts, the court may dismiss if a discharge would result in a substantial abuse of Chapter 7.

10. **Reaffirmation of Debt**

    a. A debtor must receive extensive disclosures and sign a statement disclosing his or her income, expenses, and amounts available to pay the debt. The debtor then may enter into a reaffirmation agreement to perform an obligation to be discharged.

        1) To be legally enforceable, such an agreement must

            a) Be entered into prior to the discharge (in bankruptcy),

            b) Be in writing and filed with the court, and

            c) Conspicuously state the debtor's right to rescind until the later of the discharge or 60 days after the agreement is filed with the court.

        2) If the debtor does **not** have an attorney, the court must conduct a hearing to approve the agreement. If the debtor has an attorney, the attorney must file an affidavit stating that (a) the debtor has been advised of the legal effect of reaffirmation, (b) the debtor voluntarily and knowingly entered into the agreement, and (c) it creates no undue hardship.

11. **Revocation of a Discharge**

    a. A discharge previously granted may be revoked within 1 year if the trustee or a creditor proves that (1) the discharge was obtained fraudulently, (2) the debtor knowingly and fraudulently retained property of the estate, or (3) the debtor failed to obey a court order.

Stop and review! You have completed the outline for this subunit. Study multiple-choice questions 9 through 13 beginning on page 574.

20.5 REORGANIZATIONS AND ADJUSTMENTS

1. **Chapter 11 Plans**

    a. Partnerships, corporations, railroads, and debtors qualified for relief under Chapter 7 (except stock or commodity brokers) are eligible for a **reorganization**, not a liquidation. This procedure allows for (1) a debtor (including an individual or a business) to restructure its finances, (2) the business to continue, and (3) the creditors to be paid.

    b. A case is commenced by filing a petition requesting an order for relief.

        1) Petitions may be **voluntary or involuntary**.
        2) A petition results in a suspension of creditors' actions.
        3) An involuntary petition must meet the Chapter 7 tests.
        4) Insolvency is not a condition precedent to a voluntary petition.

c. An individual or company seeking protection under Chapter 11 generally is permitted to operate its own business as a **debtor-in-possession**. A trustee is **not** required.

   1) A debtor-in-possession has the same rights and duties as a trustee.
   2) The court may order the appointment of a trustee if such action is in the best interests of the parties. The creditors may elect the trustee.
   3) A court may appoint an examiner to investigate fraud, misconduct, or mismanagement if all of the following apply:

      a) Appointment is requested by an interested party.
      b) It is in the interests of creditors or equity security holders.
      c) The debtor's fixed, undisputed, unsecured debts exceed $5 million.

d. A **committee of unsecured creditors** is appointed as soon as feasible after an order for relief has been granted. The committee generally consists of persons holding the seven largest unsecured claims. Its functions include the following:

   1) Consulting with the debtor-in-possession or the trustee
   2) Requesting appointment of a trustee
   3) Independently investigating the debtor's affairs
   4) Participating in formulating the plan of reorganization
   5) Employing professionals to perform services

e. A **plan of reorganization** must be prepared and filed.

   1) The debtor has the exclusive right to file a plan during the 120 days after the order for relief and may file a plan at any time. If the creditors or shareholders do not approve the plan within 180 days, **any party** may file. Moreover, any party may file if a trustee has been appointed.

f. A reorganization plan must (1) divide creditors' claims and shareholders' interests into classes, (2) state the treatment of each class and whether it is impaired, and (3) provide for payment. Members of each class must be treated equally unless they agree otherwise.

   1) A class is **impaired** unless the plan leaves its legal, equitable, and contractual rights unaltered.

g. The **court's confirmation** of the plan binds the debtor, creditors, equity security holders, and others. Confirmation may occur after acceptance or by cramdown.

   1) **Acceptance** by a **class** of claims requires the holders of more than 50% of the claims representing at least two-thirds of the dollar totals to approve the plan. A class of equity interests accepts the plan if the holders of at least two-thirds of the voting interests in dollar amount approve.

      a) To avoid a cramdown, the plan must be accepted by each class unless it is not adversely affected by the plan.
      b) The court may not confirm a plan not in the creditors' best interests.
      c) A spouse or child whose claims will not be paid in cash may block the plan.

   2) The bankruptcy court may confirm (approve and put into effect) the plan only if

      a) It is proposed in good faith,
      b) It provides for full payment of administrative expenses,
      c) Each class has accepted the plan or its interests are not impaired, and
      d) Each member of an impaired class has (1) accepted the plan or (2) will receive at least the amount (s)he would have received under Chapter 7.

       3)   Confirmation over the objection of one or more classes is a **cramdown**. Even if a class rejects the plan, the court may confirm if the other requirements are met and

           a)   At least one impaired class (but not an insider) accepts the plan.

           b)   The court finds that the plan is fair to the interests of the impaired class, e.g., secured creditors retain their security interests and payments equal the present value of the collateral.

           c)   The court finds that the plan does not discriminate unfairly against any creditors.

  h.   **Consumer cases** under Chapter 11 are relatively similar to those under Chapter 13. Thus, (1) property of the estate includes after-acquired property, (2) discharge occurs only after plan completion, (3) plan funding is from future earnings, and (4) a 5-year minimum contribution of disposable income is required.

  i.   After confirmation, the plan is implemented, and assets are distributed accordingly.

  j.   After the debtor has made all payments required under the plan, a debtor that is not an individual is discharged from most debts. Exceptions include debts that are provided for in the plan of reorganization approved by the creditors, the order of confirmation, and certain nondischargeable debts (e.g., those resulting from fraud or tax evasion).

       1)   An individual's nondischargeable debts under Chapter 7 cannot be discharged under Chapter 11.

CHAPTER 11 REORGANIZATION

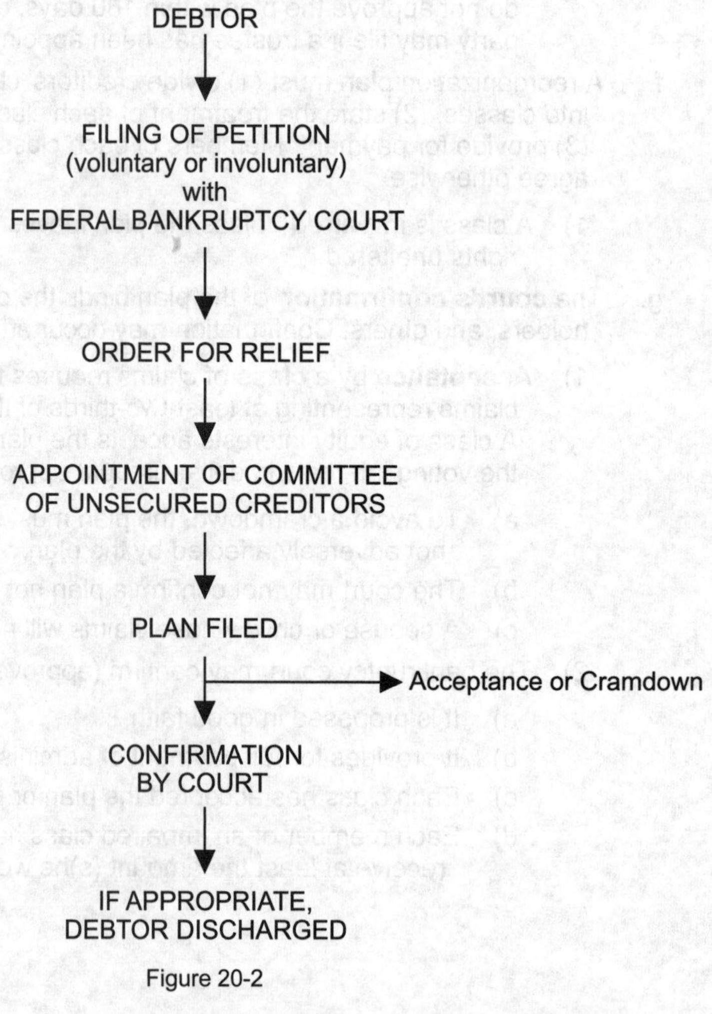

DEBTOR

↓

FILING OF PETITION
(voluntary or involuntary)
with
FEDERAL BANKRUPTCY COURT

↓

ORDER FOR RELIEF

↓

APPOINTMENT OF COMMITTEE
OF UNSECURED CREDITORS

↓

PLAN FILED

↓   → Acceptance or Cramdown

CONFIRMATION
BY COURT

↓

IF APPROPRIATE,
DEBTOR DISCHARGED

Figure 20-2

2. **Chapter 13 Plans**

   a.   Chapter 13 provides for **adjustment of debts of an individual**. Its focus is on payment from future income. Thus, it may be preferable to liquidation because the debtor often is able to retain more assets.

      1)   The debtor must have regular income and owe unsecured debts of less than $394,725 and secured debts of less than $1,184,200.

      2)   Sole proprietorships also are eligible if the debt limitations are met.

   b.   A proceeding may be initiated only by the debtor's filing a **voluntary petition**.

   c.   A **trustee** is appointed.

   d.   The plan requires the approval of the bankruptcy judge only. It may modify the rights of secured or unsecured creditors. To be confirmed, the plan must meet the following requirements:

      1)   The debtor submits all earnings (or any part necessary to the plan) to the trustee.

      2)   The plan provides for deferred payment of priority claims (unless a holder agrees otherwise).

      3)   Each claim in a class must be treated the same.

      4)   If the debtor's net monthly income is at least equal to the state median income, the maximum payment period is 5 years. Otherwise, it is 3 years.

      5)   The plan is proposed in good faith and complies with the Code.

      6)   The debtor can comply with the plan.

      7)   Required amounts have been paid.

      8)   The present value of property to be distributed on each unsecured claim equals at least the Chapter 7 amount.

      9)   With regard to each secured claim,

         a)   The holder has accepted the plan;

         b)   The holder retains the lien on the collateral, the value of the distributed property is not less than the claim, and the plan provides for adequate payments to protect the holder from any loss in the collateral's fair value; or

         c)   The debtor surrenders possession of the collateral to the holder.

   e.   The debtor generally proposes either a composition or an extension plan.
A **composition** plan allows the debtor to pay less than 100% of claims on a pro rata basis for each class of claims. Also, a debtor is entitled to relief from creditors while the plan is being executed.

      1)   An **extension** plan extends the payment period but does not reduce the debt.

   f.   The court must hold a confirmation hearing.

   g.   For the protection of creditors, the court may dismiss the proceeding or convert it into a Chapter 7 proceeding after a request by an interested party, including the debtor.

   h.   After a debtor completes all or substantially all payments under the plan, the court grants a discharge of most debts. With few exceptions, the nondischargeable debts are the same as under Chapter 7.

   i.   The Chapter 13 discharge upon completion of the plan bars another discharge in a Chapter 13 case for a 2-year period.

      1)   If the prior discharge was in a Chapter 7 or 11 case, a 4-year period applies.

   j.   A hardship discharge is available if (1) the debtor's failure is due to circumstances for which (s)he is not justly accountable, (2) creditors have received what they would have been paid under Chapter 7, and (3) modification of the plan is not feasible.

GENERAL MODEL FOR CHAPTER 13 PLANS

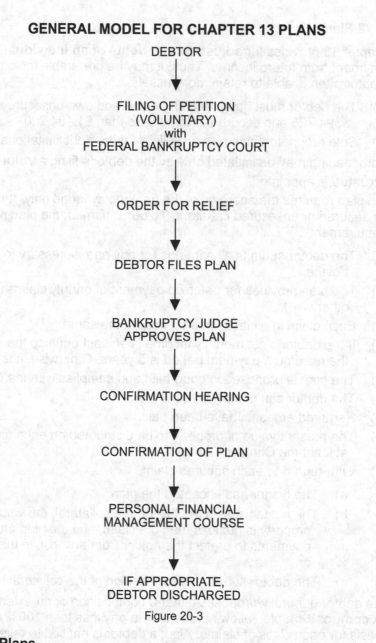

DEBTOR

FILING OF PETITION
(VOLUNTARY)
with
FEDERAL BANKRUPTCY COURT

ORDER FOR RELIEF

DEBTOR FILES PLAN

BANKRUPTCY JUDGE
APPROVES PLAN

CONFIRMATION HEARING

CONFIRMATION OF PLAN

PERSONAL FINANCIAL
MANAGEMENT COURSE

IF APPROPRIATE,
DEBTOR DISCHARGED

Figure 20-3

3. **Chapter 12 Plans**

    a. Chapter 12 applies to **family farmers** or **family fishermen**. A debtor proposes a plan to make payments to creditors over 3 to 5 years.

        1) The plan must provide for payments over 3 years unless the court approves a longer period for cause. Plans extended for cause must (a) propose to pay 100% of domestic support claims (child support and alimony) if any exist and (b) include all of the debtor's disposable income. A plan cannot provide for payments over more than 5 years.

    b. Chapter 12 eliminates many barriers to reorganization under Chapter 11 or 13. For example, Chapter 12 is more efficient and less expensive than Chapter 11, which is better suited to large corporate reorganizations. Also, Chapter 13 may not be advantageous because it is designed for wage earners who have smaller debts.

        1) Only a family farmer (fisherman) with **regular annual income** may file a petition. The purpose is to ensure that the debtor's annual income is sufficiently stable and regular to permit the debtor to make payments. But Chapter 12 allows for situations in which income is seasonal.

        2) Relief is voluntary, and only the debtor may file a petition.

    c.   Family farmers (fishermen) may be

        1)   An individual or individual and spouse or

        2)   A corporation or partnership.

    d.   An individual (and spouse) must meet the following criteria at the filing date:

        1)   The individual (and spouse) must be engaged in a farming operation or a commercial fishing operation.

        2)   The total debts (secured and unsecured) of the operation must not exceed $4,153,150 (if farming) or $1,924,550 (if fishing).

        3)   For a family farmer, at least 50% (80% for a fisherman) of the total fixed debts (exclusive of debt for a home) must be related to the operation.

        4)   More than 50% of the gross income of the individual (and spouse) for the preceding tax year (or, for family farmers only, each of the 2nd and 3rd prior tax years) must have come from the operation.

    e.   For a **corporation or partnership** to be an eligible debtor, it must meet the following criteria at the date of the filing:

        1)   More than 50% of the outstanding stock or equity must be owned by one family (or one family and relatives).

        2)   The family (and relatives) must conduct the operation.

        3)   More than 80% of the value of the assets must be related to the operation.

        4)   The total indebtedness must not exceed $4,153,150 (if farming) or $1,924,550 (if fishing).

        5)   At least 50% (farming) or 80% (fishing) of the total fixed debts (exclusive of debt for a home occupied by a shareholder) must be related to the operation.

        6)   Corporate stock cannot be publicly traded.

    f.   A case begins by **filing a petition** with the bankruptcy court in the area where (1) the individual lives or (2) the corporation or partnership has its principal place of business or principal assets.

        1)   Unless the court orders otherwise, the debtor also must file

            a)   Schedules of assets and liabilities,

            b)   A schedule of current income and expenditures,

            c)   A schedule of executory contracts and unexpired leases, and

            d)   A statement of financial affairs.

        2)   Spouses may file a joint petition or individual petitions.

        3)   The debtor must compile the following information:

            a)   A list of all creditors and the amounts and nature of their claims;

            b)   The source, amount, and frequency of the debtor's income;

            c)   A list of all of the debtor's property; and

            d)   A detailed list of the debtor's monthly farming (fishing) and living expenses.

        4)   Married individuals must gather this information for each spouse.

    g.   When a petition is filed, an impartial **trustee** is appointed to administer the case. As under Chapter 13, the trustee evaluates the case and serves as a disbursing agent, collecting payments from the debtor and making distributions to creditors.

    h.   Filing the petition **automatically stays** most collection actions against the debtor or the debtor's property. The stay is by operation of law and requires no judicial action. As long as the stay is in effect, creditors generally cannot initiate or continue collection efforts (including phone calls). The bankruptcy clerk notifies all creditors whose names and addresses are provided by the debtor.

        1)   A special automatic stay provision protects co-debtors. Unless the bankruptcy court authorizes otherwise, a creditor may not seek to collect a **consumer debt** from any individual who is liable to the debtor.

i.   After the petition is filed, the trustee holds a **meeting of creditors**. During the meeting, the debtor answers questions under oath. The debtor must attend the meeting and answer questions about financial matters and the repayment plan. If spouses have filed jointly, both must attend.

j.   After the meeting of creditors, the debtor, the trustee, and interested creditors attend a **hearing on confirmation** of the debtor's repayment plan.

1)   Payments to **secured creditors** can sometimes continue longer than 3 to 5 years. For example, if the debtor's underlying debt obligation was scheduled to be paid over more than 5 years (e.g., an equipment loan or a mortgage), the debtor may be able to pay the loan over the original repayment schedule as long as any arrearage is made up during the period of the plan.

4.   **Chapter 9 Plans**

a.   Chapter 9 provides a financially-distressed **municipality** with protection from its creditors while it negotiates a plan for adjusting its debts.

b.   Reorganization is accomplished by (1) extending debt maturities, (2) reducing principal or interest, or (3) refinancing by obtaining a new loan.

c.   Chapter 9 differs significantly from other Chapters. It does **not** provide for liquidation of assets and distribution of the proceeds to creditors. Such action violates the Constitution and the reservation to the states of sovereignty over their internal affairs. Due to this severe limitation, the bankruptcy court is not as active in managing a municipal case as it is in corporate reorganizations under Chapter 11. Its functions are limited to (1) approving the petition (if the debtor is eligible), (2) confirming a plan of debt adjustment, and (3) ensuring implementation of the plan.

1)   However, the municipality may consent to the court's jurisdiction in many of the traditional areas of court oversight in bankruptcy. Thus, it obtains the protection of court orders and eliminates the need for multiple forums to decide issues.

5.   **Chapter 15 Plans**

a.   Chapter 15 applies to insolvency cases involving debtors, assets, claimants, and other parties of interest from **more than one country**.

b.   The objectives of the statute are to

1)   Promote cooperation between U.S. courts and parties of interest and the courts and other competent authorities of foreign countries involved in cross-border insolvency cases;

2)   Establish greater legal certainty for trade and investment;

3)   Provide for the fair and efficient administration of cross-border insolvencies that protects the interests of all creditors and other interested entities, including the debtor;

4)   Protect and maximize the value of the debtor's assets; and

5)   Facilitate the rescue of financially troubled businesses, thereby protecting investment and preserving employment.

c.   A Chapter 15 case is ancillary to a primary proceeding brought in another country, typically the debtor's home country. An alternative for the debtor or a creditor is to commence a full Chapter 7 or Chapter 11 case in the U.S. if the assets there are sufficiently complex. In addition, a U.S. court may authorize a trustee or other entity to act in a foreign country on behalf of a U.S. bankruptcy estate.

Stop and review! You have completed the outline for this subunit. Study multiple-choice questions 14 through 16 beginning on page 575.

20.6 SURETIES

 The AICPA has tested candidates' knowledge of the rights, duties, and liabilities of the various parties under a suretyship contract.

1. **Definitions**

   a. Suretyship involves at least three parties: the debtor, the creditor, and the surety.

   b. The person who actually receives the money or the credit is the debtor, principal, principal debtor, or obligor.

   c. The creditor (obligee) is the person who has permitted the debtor to receive goods, services, money, or other value without having fully paid the price.

   d. A **surety** is a legal person (an individual, a corporation, etc.) contractually liable to a creditor for another's debt or default.

   e. **Cosureties** are two or more persons obligated to pay the same debt if the debtor defaults.

   f. Essentially the same rules apply whether or not a surety is compensated.

2. **Overview**

   a. The surety's promise is security for the payment of a debt or the performance of a duty if the debtor or obligor fails to make payment or otherwise perform. But the surety arrangement is **not** a security interest held by the creditor.

      1) If a debtor owes more than one debt to a creditor, (s)he may give instructions about the application of a payment. The creditor must comply.

      2) Without instructions, the creditor may apply the payment as (s)he chooses.

   b. Under the ALI's Restatement of Law Third, a surety is primarily liable for the debtor's obligation. Upon default, the creditor may proceed first against the surety, for example, without resorting to collateral.

      1) Under the Restatement, a **guarantor** is synonymous with a surety. But a person described as a **guarantor of collection** is not liable until the creditor has sued the debtor and is unable to collect the judgment.

3. **Formation of Suretyship Contract**

   a. Suretyship arises by express contract at the request of either the debtor or the creditor.

      1) The elements of a contract, including legal capacity and sufficient consideration, must be present.

         a) Separate consideration is required unless the surety's promise is made **at the same time** that the creditor provides consideration to the debtor.

EXAMPLE

Mom is engaged as surety on a note signed by Son. The surety contract is between Mom and Lender (not Son). The legally sufficient consideration received by Mom is the legal benefit of Lender's promise to continue dealing with Son. This consideration also supports Son's promise to repay Lender.

2) The **statute of frauds** requires that a contract to answer for the debt of another be written and signed by the surety.

    a) A writing is needed to enforce a **secondary** promise, which is a promise to pay a debt of another if the principal debtor fails to pay.

    b) The statute of frauds does not apply when the promise is **original** (primary).

EXAMPLE

If a buyer directs the seller to ship goods to a third person and agrees to pay $300 for them, the promise is original, and the promisor does not undertake to answer for the debt of another.

---

    c) If the **main purpose** of a promise to answer for the debt of another is to secure some new economic benefit, the promise may be enforced even if it is oral.

EXAMPLE

X is an essential supplier to Z. If Z guarantees X's debts to protect its supply of a vital component, the suretyship promise is not covered by the statute of frauds.

---

  b. An important use of a suretyship arrangement is a sale of mortgaged real estate to a buyer who **assumes** the mortgage. Between the new buyer and the seller, the new buyer becomes the primary debtor and the seller (the original debtor who took out the mortgage) becomes a surety.

    1) If the buyer defaults, the seller is liable. The creditor (the person who holds the mortgage on the real estate) then may sue either or both parties (the new buyer or seller).

  c. Another use of a suretyship arrangement is an **official bond**. A statute may require a public official to provide a performance bond. The bonding company is the surety liable for losses caused by the official's misconduct.

4. **Creditor's Duty to Disclose**

  a. A creditor must communicate to the surety, prior to formation of the contract, information about significant risk to the surety.

    1) The duty exists only if the creditor has reason to believe that the surety does not know the facts, and the creditor has reasonable opportunity to communicate them.

    2) The creditor should disclose what (s)he knows about the debtor if the surety inquires.

  b. A surety may **not** void the surety contract on the basis of misconduct of the debtor that induced the surety to enter into the surety agreement. The surety contract is between the surety and the **creditor**, not the debtor.

  c. The creditor may notify the surety when the debtor defaults but is not required to.

5. **Rights of a Surety**

    a. If required to perform, the surety has rights of reimbursement, subrogation, and exoneration against the principal debtor. The surety has no right to compel the creditor to proceed legally against the debtor or the collateral.

    b. **Reimbursement** is the right to sue the debtor for amounts the surety paid the creditor.

        1) The surety may enforce a security interest the creditor acquired in collateral.

        2) The surety is not entitled to reimbursement of amounts paid after receiving notice of a valid defense of the debtor to the payment.

        3) If the debtor has received a discharge in bankruptcy as to the creditor's claim, the surety's claim for reimbursement is barred.

        4) **Indemnification** is not a right of a surety. It results from an agreement by one party to protect an obligor (debtor), not an obligee (creditor), from loss.

    c. The right of **subrogation** entitles the surety to enforce the debt against the debtor. After payment to the creditor, the surety has the following rights of the creditor:

        1) Rights in collateral provided by the debtor
        2) Rights against other parties indebted on the same obligation
        3) Rights against cosureties
        4) Priority in bankruptcy

    d. **Exoneration** is the right of a surety to request that a court compel a capable but reluctant debtor to pay the debt before the creditor collects from the surety.

6. **Co-surety's Right of Contribution**

    a. A co-surety who pays more than the share (s)he agreed to pay is entitled to contribution from the other cosureties.

        1) Each co-surety is liable for the agreed-to proportionate part of a loss.

        2) A co-surety's contributive share is computed based on the following formula:

$$\frac{\text{Maximum liability of the co-surety}}{\text{Sum of maximum liabilities of all co-sureties}} \times \text{Default amount}$$

        3) Contribution cannot be obtained from a co-surety whose obligation was discharged in bankruptcy.

EXAMPLE

PD borrowed $100,000 from C. CS1 agreed to act as surety for up to $100,000. CS2 agreed to act as surety for up to $50,000. PD defaulted when the principal owed was $90,000. C recovered the full $90,000 from CS1. The co-sureties' contributive shares are computed as follows:

CS1: $100,000 ÷ ($100,000 + $50,000) = (2 ÷ 3) × $90,000 = $60,000
CS2: $50,000 ÷ ($100,000 + $50,000) = (1 ÷ 3) × $90,000 = $30,000

CS1 has a right to a $30,000 contribution from CS2.

---

        4) Co-sureties, like sureties, have rights of subrogation and exoneration.

        5) A co-surety's relative interest in collateral is in the proportion used to determine his or her contributive share.

        6) Without a contrary agreement, co-sureties have joint and several liability. Each is liable for the entire loss caused by the debtor's default up to the stated amount of each co-surety's maximum liability.

7. **Discharge of a Surety**

   a.   The discharge of a surety's liability is governed by the contract.

   b.   A surety is **discharged by performance** of his or her obligations (i.e., those of the principal debtor). Who tenders the performance is irrelevant.

      1)   Partial payment discharges a surety to the extent of the payment.

      2)   If a note, bond, or draft is accepted as payment, the surety is discharged.

      3)   A creditor's refusal to accept tender by the principal debtor or a surety discharges the surety.

      4)   Death of a surety does not necessarily terminate liability, particularly if terms of the surety agreement bind the surety's heirs and representatives.

      5)   Death or insolvency of the the debtor does **not** discharge the surety.

   c.   An agreement between the creditor and the debtor **extending time of payment** discharges a surety only to the extent of any loss to the surety.

      1)   This agreement also extends the time for performance by the debtor of duties (exoneration and reimbursement) owed to the surety unless the agreement reserves the surety's right of recourse.

   d.   The creditor's **release of the debtor** may discharge the surety unless the creditor:

      1)   Reserves his or her rights against the surety, and

      2)   The instrument states that (a) the creditor retains rights against the surety, and (b) the surety retains rights against the debtor.

   e.   **Modification** of the debtor-creditor contract, without consent of the surety, also may discharge the surety.

      1)   Discharge is complete only if (a) the modification constitutes a substituted contract or (b) the risks of loss imposed on the surety differ fundamentally from those resulting from the original contract.

      2)   Otherwise, the surety guarantees the modified contract except to the extent of actual loss caused to the surety by the modification.

   f.   The creditor's **impairment of collateral** discharges the surety to the extent of the value of the lost collateral. Examples are returning collateral to the debtor or failing to maintain a perfected security interest in it.

   g.   **Rescission** or **revocation** of the principal contract releases the surety from any further liability but not from liability already incurred.

   h.   **Release by the creditor of a surety** releases the co-sureties to the extent they cannot obtain contribution from the released surety. If a surety is released, the total liability of the co-sureties equals the total liabilities of all sureties prior to the release reduced by the portion for which the released surety would have been responsible.

      1)   The co-sureties are **not** released if (a) they consent to the underlying release or (b) the creditor expressly **reserves** rights against them. The reservation of rights puts the released surety on notice that the release is effective only between the creditor and the released surety. Thus, the right of contribution held by the other sureties against the released surety is not impaired, and their obligations are not reduced.

EXAMPLE

If, in the previous example, C released CS1 without consent of CS2 and without reserving rights against CS2, CS2 can no longer obtain the contribution of $60,000 from CS1, and CS2 is released to that extent. Thus, CS2's liability to C is limited to $30,000.

8. **Defenses of a Surety**

    a. A surety has three kinds of defenses.

        1) Personal defenses of the surety include the following:

            a) A valid contract of suretyship never existed.

            b) A valid contract existed, but the surety exercised a right to void it, e.g., for failure to comply with the statute of frauds or because of his or her incapacity.

            c) The creditor obtained the surety's promise by means of fraud or duress.

            d) The surety performed the contract by performing the debtor's promise.

            e) The surety tendered performance of the suretyship contract.

            f) An intended co-surety did not sign the suretyship contract.

        2) The surety may assert certain **debtor's defenses** against the creditor.

            a) But the following **personal** defenses of a debtor are **not** available to the surety:

                i) The debtor's incapacity due to infancy or mental incompetence

                ii) Discharge of the debtor's obligation in bankruptcy

                iii) A debtor's claim against the creditor for set-off

---

EXAMPLE

A debtor may have a claim against its creditor. The debtor could offset what it is owed against what it owes. The surety on the obligation owed to the creditor by the debtor cannot be offset because the set off was personal to the debtor.

---

            b) It is **not** a defense that an insolvent debtor induced the creditor and surety to enter into a contract.

            c) Defenses available to the debtor and surety include the following:

                i) Forgery of the debtor's signature on an instrument

                ii) Fraudulent or material alteration of the contractual document or other fraud by the creditor, including the creditor's failure to disclose known fraud by the debtor

                iii) Lack of a valid creditor-debtor contract (except in the case of the debtor's incapacity)

                iv) Illegality or impracticability of performing the creditor-debtor contract

                v) Performance by the debtor

                vi) The creditor's refusal to accept tender of performance by debtor or surety

        3) **Special surety defenses** include the following:

            a) The creditor's release of the debtor unless the creditor reserves his or her rights against the surety

            b) Modification of the debtor-creditor contract without consent by the surety

            c) The creditor's impairment of collateral

Stop and review! You have completed the outline for this subunit. Study multiple-choice questions 17 through 20 beginning on page 576.

QUESTIONS

20.1 Liens and Enforcement Methods

1. Which of the following liens generally require(s) the lienholder to give notice of legal action before selling the debtor's property to satisfy the debt?

	Mechanic's Lien	Artisan's Lien
A.	Yes	Yes
B.	Yes	No
C.	No	Yes
D.	No	No

Answer (A) is correct.

REQUIRED: The lien(s), if any, requiring notice before sale of the debtor's property.

DISCUSSION: A mechanic's lien is a statutory lien against realty that secures an unpaid debt arising from a contract for labor, materials, or services to improve the property. An artisan's lien arises in favor of a repairer or improver of personal property who retains possession of the property until paid. Failure to pay the debt permits the lienholder to foreclose on the property and sell it. Statutes require notice to the owner prior to foreclosure and sale.

2. If a mortgagor defaults in the payment of a purchase money mortgage, and the mortgagee forecloses, the mortgagor may do any of the following **except**

A. Obtain any excess monies resulting from a judicial sale after payment of the mortgagee.

B. Remain in possession of the property after a foreclosure sale if the equity in the property exceeds the balance due on the mortgage.

C. Refinance the mortgage with another lender and repay the original mortgage.

D. Assert the equitable right of redemption by paying the mortgage.

Answer (B) is correct.

REQUIRED: The right not held by a defaulting mortgagor.

DISCUSSION: Most states recognize the mortgage as a security interest. The mortgagor-debtor signs a promissory note for the sum borrowed from the mortgagee-creditor. (S)he also signs a mortgage document representing the right of the mortgagee to seek judicial foreclosure of the mortgage and sale of the property upon default. The purchaser will receive a right to possession after the sale (or, in some states, after the redemption period elapses).

Answer (A) is incorrect. The mortgagor has an equity in the process equal to any amount left after payment of the debt, interest, and costs. Answer (C) is incorrect. Redemption might be accomplished by refinancing. Answer (D) is incorrect. A defaulting mortgagor has an equitable right to redeem the property before the foreclosure proceedings are complete by payment of the debt, interest, and costs. In many states, the mortgagor also has a statutory right of redemption after foreclosure.

20.2 State Collective Remedies as an Alternative to Federal Bankruptcy

3. A client has joined other creditors of the Martin Construction Company in a composition agreement seeking to avoid the necessity of a bankruptcy proceeding against Martin. Which statement describes the composition agreement?

A. It provides a temporary delay, not to exceed 6 months, insofar as the debtor's obligation to repay the debts included in the composition.

B. It does not discharge any of the debts included until performance by the debtor has taken place.

C. It provides for the appointment of a receiver to take over and operate the debtor's business.

D. It must be approved by all creditors.

Answer (B) is correct.

REQUIRED: The description of a composition among creditors.

DISCUSSION: A composition with creditors is a common-law contractual undertaking between the debtor and the creditors. The participating creditors agree to (1) extend time for payments, (2) take lesser sums in satisfaction of the debts owed, or (3) accept some other plan of financial adjustment. Under general contract law, the original debts will not be discharged until the debtor has performed the new obligations.

Answer (A) is incorrect. Although a composition may involve an extension of time, it is not limited to 6 months. Furthermore, the more common composition is to take lesser sums in satisfaction. Answer (C) is incorrect. Only a court appoints a receiver. A composition is a contractual agreement not involving judicial intervention. Answer (D) is incorrect. A composition need not be approved by all creditors but is binding only upon those participating.

4. A debtor may attempt to conceal or transfer property to prevent a creditor from satisfying a judgment. Which of the following actions will be considered an indication of fraudulent conveyance?

	Debtor Remaining in Possession after Conveyance	Secret Conveyance	Debtor Retains an Equitable Benefit in the Property Conveyed
A.	Yes	Yes	Yes
B.	No	Yes	Yes
C.	Yes	Yes	No
D.	Yes	No	Yes

Answer (A) is correct.

REQUIRED: The indications of fraudulent conveyance.

DISCUSSION: Transfers of property made to delay, hinder, or defraud creditors are voidable by the transferor's creditors. They include (1) the debtor's retention of possession or a beneficial interest, (2) a transfer of substantially all assets, (3) a transfer in secret, (4) a transfer to a family member or insider, (5) a transfer for inadequate consideration, (6) a transfer in anticipation of legal action or financial problems, (7) removal or concealment of assets, and (8) insolvency at the time of or shortly after the transfer.

Answer (B) is incorrect. Retention of possession is an indication of a fraudulent conveyance. Answer (C) is incorrect. Secrecy is an indication of a fraudulent conveyance. Answer (D) is incorrect. Retention of a beneficial interest is an indication of a fraudulent conveyance.

20.3 Bankruptcy Administration

5. Green owes the following amounts to unsecured creditors: Rice, $5,700; Zwick, $5,200; Young, $15,800; and Zinc, $4,900. Green has not paid any creditor since January 1, Year 1. On March 15, Year 1, Green's sole asset, a cabin cruiser, was seized by Xeno Marine Co., the holder of a perfected security interest in the boat. On July 1, Year 1, Rice, Zwick, and Zinc involuntarily petitioned Green into bankruptcy under Chapter 7 of the Federal Bankruptcy Code. If Green opposes the involuntary petition, the petition will be

A. Upheld because the three filing creditors are owed more than $15,775.

B. Upheld because one creditor is owed more than $15,775.

C. Dismissed because there are fewer than 12 creditors.

D. Dismissed because the boat was seized more than 90 days before the filing.

Answer (A) is correct.

REQUIRED: The status of an involuntary petition under Chapter 7.

DISCUSSION: If the debtor has fewer than 12 creditors, any 1 or more creditors who alone or together have unsecured claims of $15,775 or more can file an involuntary petition under Chapter 7 or Chapter 11. If the debtor has 12 or more creditors, any 3 or more who together hold unsecured claims of at least $15,775 can file an involuntary petition. The three filers are owed $15,800 ($5,700 + $5,200 + $4,900).

Answer (B) is incorrect. Young did not join in filing the petition. Answer (C) is incorrect. A debtor with fewer than 12 creditors may be involuntarily petitioned into bankruptcy by one or more creditors who alone or together are owed more than $15,775. Answer (D) is incorrect. A challenged involuntary petition is not dismissed if the debtor is generally not paying his or her bills as they become due or, within 120 days before filing, a custodian or receiver took possession of all or most of the debtor's property to enforce a lien against the property.

6. To file for bankruptcy under Chapter 7 of the Federal Bankruptcy Code, an individual must

A. Have debts of any amount.

B. Be insolvent.

C. Be indebted to more than three creditors.

D. Have debts in excess of $15,775.

Answer (A) is correct.

REQUIRED: The requirement to file for protection under Chapter 7 of the Bankruptcy Code.

DISCUSSION: Under Chapter 7, generally, a debtor's nonexempt assets are converted into cash, the cash is distributed among creditors, and the debtor is discharged from most remaining obligations. Any person eligible to be a debtor under Chapter 7 may file a petition.

Answer (B) is incorrect. Insolvency is not required to file a voluntary petition. It is only necessary that the person be under Chapter 7. Answer (C) is incorrect. Number-of-creditors thresholds apply only to involuntary petitions filed by creditors. Answer (D) is incorrect. Amount-of-debt thresholds apply only to involuntary petitions.

7. A party involuntarily petitioned into bankruptcy under Chapter 7 of the Federal Bankruptcy Code who succeeds in having the petition dismissed could recover

	Court Costs and Attorney's Fees	Compensatory Damages	Punitive Damages
A.	Yes	Yes	Yes
B.	Yes	Yes	No
C.	No	Yes	Yes
D.	Yes	No	No

Answer (A) is correct.
   REQUIRED: The recovery allowed a debtor whose involuntary bankruptcy was dismissed.
   DISCUSSION: A debtor who successfully contests an involuntary bankruptcy petition could recover his or her costs, including reasonable attorney's fees. The court may require the petitioner to pay damages if (s)he is found to have acted in bad faith. A petitioner whose conduct is malicious or otherwise egregious also may be required to pay punitive damages.

8. Which of the following statements is true with respect to a voluntary bankruptcy proceeding under the liquidation provisions of the Bankruptcy Code?

A. The debtor must be insolvent.

B. The liabilities of the debtor must total $15,775 or more.

C. It may be properly commenced and maintained by any person who is insolvent.

D. The filing of the bankruptcy petition constitutes an order for relief.

Answer (D) is correct.
   REQUIRED: The true statement about a voluntary bankruptcy proceeding.
   DISCUSSION: The voluntary bankruptcy petition is a formal request by the debtor to the court for an order for relief. Under the liquidation provisions, an order for relief is automatically given to the debtor upon the filing of the petition.
   Answer (A) is incorrect. Insolvency is not required. A statement that the debtor has debts is all that is needed. Answer (B) is incorrect. In a voluntary bankruptcy proceeding, there is no minimum amount of debtor liabilities. Answer (C) is incorrect. The courts have discretion not to grant relief that would constitute a substantial abuse of the bankruptcy laws. Also, certain entities, e.g., banks, are not eligible for voluntary bankruptcy.

20.4 Bankruptcy Liquidations

9. Which asset is included in a debtor's bankruptcy estate in a liquidation proceeding?

A. Proceeds from a life insurance policy received 90 days after the petition was filed.

B. An inheritance received 270 days after the petition was filed.

C. Property from a divorce settlement received 365 days after the petition was filed.

D. Wages earned by the debtor after the petition was filed.

Answer (A) is correct.
   REQUIRED: The asset included in a debtor's bankruptcy estate.
   DISCUSSION: Most assets in which the debtor has a legal or equitable interest at the date Chapter 7 proceedings began are included in the estate. Other property may be added to the estate. For example, it includes property acquired by the debtor within 180 days after filing the petition if the property was acquired (1) by inheritance, (2) as proceeds of a life insurance policy, or (3) from a property settlement in a divorce case.

10. A person who voluntarily filed for bankruptcy and received a discharge under Chapter 7 of the Federal Bankruptcy Code

A. May obtain another voluntary discharge in bankruptcy under Chapter 7 after 5 years have elapsed from the date of the prior filing.

B. Will receive a discharge of all debts owed.

C. Is precluded from owning or operating a similar business for 2 years.

D. Must surrender for distribution to the creditors any amount received as an inheritance within 180 days after filing the petition.

Answer (D) is correct.
   REQUIRED: The true statement about a discharge under Chapter 7.
   DISCUSSION: The bankruptcy estate available for distribution to creditors includes all the debtor's nonexempt legal and equitable interests in property on the date of filing. It includes proceeds and profits from that estate. Certain property acquired after filing is also included: inheritances, property settlements (divorce), and life insurance proceeds to which the debtor becomes entitled within 180 days after filing.
   Answer (A) is incorrect. Discharge is barred if there was a Chapter 7 discharge within the 8 years preceding filing the petition. Answer (B) is incorrect. Certain debts are nondischargeable. Answer (C) is incorrect. A debtor who receives a Chapter 7 discharge may own or operate a similar business without a time restriction.

11. Which of the following transfers by a debtor, within 90 days of filing for bankruptcy, could be set aside as a preferential payment?

- A. Making a gift to charity.
- B. Paying a business utility bill.
- C. Borrowing money from a bank secured by giving a mortgage on business property.
- D. Prepaying an installment loan on inventory.

Answer (D) is correct.

REQUIRED: The transfer that is preferential.

DISCUSSION: A preferential transfer is made for the benefit of a creditor within 90 days prior to filing the petition and on account of an antecedent (pre-existing) debt. The transfer must have (1) been made when the debtor was insolvent and (2) resulted in the creditor's receipt of a larger portion of its claim than it otherwise would have received as a distribution in bankruptcy. A prepayment is on account of an existing debt and is therefore a voidable preference.

Answer (A) is incorrect. A gift to a charity is not on account of an antecedent (pre-existing) debt. Answer (B) is incorrect. Payment of accounts payable in the ordinary course of the debtor's business is not a voidable preference. Answer (C) is incorrect. A contemporaneous exchange between the debtor and another, even a creditor, for new value may not be set aside. The transfer of a security interest enables the debtor to acquire the new property.

12. Which of the following claims will be paid first in the distribution of a bankruptcy estate under the liquidation provisions of Chapter 7 of the Bankruptcy Code if the petition was filed July 15, Year 1?

- A. A secured debt properly perfected on March 20, Year 1.
- B. Inventory purchased and delivered August 1, Year 1.
- C. Employee wages due April 30, Year 1.
- D. A federal tax lien filed June 30, Year 1.

Answer (A) is correct.

REQUIRED: The claim paid first.

DISCUSSION: The Bankruptcy Code classifies creditors into several categories according to the priority of their claims against the debtor. It states that secured creditors' claims will be satisfied in full to the extent of the value of the security before unsecured creditors' claims will be considered. To the extent the security is insufficient, the secured creditor becomes an unsecured creditor. The tax lien, even if a security interest, would have lower priority than the secured debt perfected earlier.

Answer (B) is incorrect. A secured claim has priority over the inventory purchase before unsecured claims are satisfied. Answer (C) is incorrect. The secured claim has priority over employee wages. Answer (D) is incorrect. Even if the federal tax lien is a secured claim, the first perfected of two security interests has priority.

13. By signing a reaffirmation agreement on April 15, Year 1, a debtor agreed to pay certain debts that would be discharged in bankruptcy. On June 20, Year 1, the debtor's attorney filed the reaffirmation agreement and an affidavit with the court indicating that the debtor understood the consequences of the reaffirmation agreement. The debtor obtained a discharge on August 25, Year 1. The reaffirmation agreement would be enforceable only if it was

- A. Made after discharge.
- B. Approved by the bankruptcy court.
- C. Not for a household purpose debt.
- D. Not rescinded before discharge.

Answer (D) is correct.

REQUIRED: The enforceable reaffirmation of debt.

DISCUSSION: To be enforceable, a reaffirmation agreement must conspicuously state the debtor's right of rescission. The debtor has the right to rescind the reaffirmation until the later of the discharge or 60 days after the agreement is filed with the court.

Answer (A) is incorrect. To be legally enforceable, the reaffirmation agreement must be entered into prior to the general discharge in bankruptcy. Answer (B) is incorrect. Court approval is required if the debtor has no attorney. In the alternative, the reaffirmation agreement may be accompanied by an affidavit filed by the debtor's attorney that the debtor voluntarily and knowingly entered into the agreement and it caused no undue hardship. Answer (C) is incorrect. Almost any debt, including one incurred for household purposes, may be reaffirmed.

20.5 Reorganizations and Adjustments

14. Under Chapter 11 of the Federal Bankruptcy Code, which of the following would **not** be eligible for reorganization?

- A. Retail sole proprietorship.
- B. Advertising partnership.
- C. CPA professional corporation.
- D. Savings and loan association.

Answer (D) is correct.

REQUIRED: The entity ineligible for Chapter 11 reorganization.

DISCUSSION: Reorganization under Chapter 11 of the Bankruptcy Code is available only for eligible debtors. These include partnerships and corporations, railroads, and any person that may be a debtor under Chapter 7 (but not stock or commodity brokers). Ineligible debtors under Chapter 7 include municipalities, insurance companies, banks, credit unions, and savings and loan associations.

15. Under Chapter 11 of the Federal Bankruptcy Code, which of the following actions is necessary before the court may confirm a reorganization plan?

A. Provision for full payment of administration expenses.

B. Acceptance of the plan by all classes of claimants.

C. Preparation of a contingent plan of liquidation.

D. Appointment of a trustee.

Answer (A) is correct.

REQUIRED: The prerequisite to court confirmation of a reorganization plan.

DISCUSSION: The debtor generally has the exclusive right to file a reorganization plan during the 120 days after the order of relief. To be effective, the plan must be confirmed by the bankruptcy court. The plan must provide for full payment of administration expenses.

Answer (B) is incorrect. A plan that is fair and equitable may be confirmed without approval of all classes of creditors (a cramdown plan). Answer (C) is incorrect. Chapter 11 enables restructuring instead of liquidation. A contingent plan of liquidation is not required. Answer (D) is incorrect. The court has discretion to appoint a trustee given evidence of dishonesty or mismanagement or if such action is in the best interests of the parties. But the debtor normally remains in possession of his or her assets and continues to operate the business.

16. Under the reorganization provisions of Chapter 11 of the Federal Bankruptcy Code, after a reorganization plan is confirmed and a final decree closing the proceedings entered, which of the following events usually occurs?

A. A reorganized corporate debtor will be liquidated.

B. A reorganized corporate debtor will be discharged from all debts except as otherwise provided in the plan and applicable law.

C. A trustee will continue to operate the debtor's business.

D. A reorganized individual debtor will not be allowed to continue in the same business.

Answer (B) is correct.

REQUIRED: The status of a debtor after completing a Chapter 11 reorganization.

DISCUSSION: At the conclusion of Chapter 11 proceedings, a corporate debtor is discharged from most debts of the business. Exceptions include debts that are provided for in the plan of reorganization approved by the creditors and certain nondischargeable debts.

Answer (A) is incorrect. A Chapter 11 reorganization allows the debtor's finances to be restructured, not liquidated. Answer (C) is incorrect. A trustee is usually not appointed to run the debtor's business. The court may, however, order the appointment of a trustee for cause or if such action is in the best interests of the parties. Answer (D) is incorrect. A reorganized individual debtor may continue in the same business without any restrictions.

20.6 Sureties

17. A party contracts to guarantee the collection of the debts of another. As a result of the guaranty, which of the following statements is true?

A. The creditor may proceed against the guarantor without attempting to collect from the debtor.

B. The guaranty must be in writing.

C. The guarantor may use any defenses available to the debtor.

D. The creditor must be notified of the debtor's default by the guarantor.

Answer (B) is correct.

REQUIRED: The true statement about a guaranty of collection.

DISCUSSION: A person who guarantees payment without qualification must pay upon default. A guarantor of collection guarantees the debt on condition that the creditor first use ordinary legal means to collect. Surety and guaranty arrangements that are secondary promises are within the statute of frauds and must be in writing.

Answer (A) is incorrect. A guarantor of collection is not liable until the creditor exercises due diligence in enforcing its remedies against the debtor. Answer (C) is incorrect. A guarantor may not use defenses that are personal to the debtor, e.g., infancy. Answer (D) is incorrect. The creditor ordinarily notifies the guarantor of the debtor's default.

18. Which of the following defenses would a surety be able to assert successfully to limit the surety's liability to a creditor?

    A. A discharge in bankruptcy of the principal debtor.

    B. A personal defense the principal debtor has against the creditor.

    C. The incapacity of the surety.

    D. The incapacity of the principal debtor.

Answer (C) is correct.
    REQUIRED: The defense a surety could assert to limit his or her liability to a creditor.
    DISCUSSION: The surety may assert a defense personal to the surety to limit his or her liability to a creditor. The surety may use the defense of incapacity of the surety to avoid liability to the principal debtor's creditor.
    Answer (A) is incorrect. A surety may not assert a principal debtor's discharge in bankruptcy as a defense. Bankruptcy is a common reason for a debtor to use a surety. Answer (B) is incorrect. A surety may assert only a limited number of contractual defenses of the principal debtor. A surety may not ordinarily assert a defense personal to the principal debtor. Answer (D) is incorrect. A surety may not assert the incapacity of the principal debtor as a defense. A debtor's incapacity is a common reason to use a surety.

19. If a debtor defaults and the debtor's surety satisfies the obligation, the surety acquires the right of

    A. Subrogation.

    B. Primary lien.

    C. Indemnification.

    D. Satisfaction.

Answer (A) is correct.
    REQUIRED: The surety's right after (s)he satisfies the principal debtor's obligation.
    DISCUSSION: Subrogation is the right of a surety, after paying the obligation of a debtor who has defaulted, to succeed to the legal rights of the creditor against the principal debtor, co-sureties, or any collateral.
    Answer (B) is incorrect. The surety stands in the shoes of the creditor, who may or may not have had a senior security interest or a priority in bankruptcy. Answer (C) is incorrect. A right of indemnification arises from a contract by which one party agrees to hold another party harmless. Indemnity (e.g., insurance) protects a debtor from loss. A suretyship contract protects a creditor. Answer (D) is incorrect. Satisfaction is the creditor's acceptance of a performance stipulated in an accord, which is an agreement to accept some performance by the debtor that is different from, and usually less than, what was originally agreed.

20. Which of the following events will release a noncompensated surety from liability to the creditor?

    A. The principal debtor was involuntarily petitioned into bankruptcy.

    B. The creditor failed to notify the surety of a partial surrender of the principal debtor's collateral.

    C. The creditor was adjudicated incompetent after the debt arose.

    D. The principal debtor exerted duress to obtain the surety agreement.

Answer (B) is correct.
    REQUIRED: The event releasing a noncompensated surety from liability to the creditor.
    DISCUSSION: The creditor's impairment of collateral, for example, by returning it to the principal debtor or failing to maintain a perfected security interest in it, discharges the surety to the extent of the value of the lost collateral. The reason for permitting this defense is to protect a surety who assumed the obligation solely because the creditor held the security for the debt.
    Answer (A) is incorrect. The manner in which the principal debtor entered into bankruptcy proceedings is irrelevant. It is one of the reasons a creditor enters into a surety contract. Answer (C) is incorrect. The mental capacity of the creditor after the debt arose is irrelevant. Answer (D) is incorrect. The principal debtor is not a party to the surety agreement. Accordingly, the duress defense is not valid.

APPENDIX A
AICPA UNIFORM CPA EXAMINATION
BLUEPRINTS WITH GLEIM CROSS-REFERENCES

The AICPA has indicated that the Blueprints have several purposes, including to

- *Document the minimum level of knowledge and skills necessary for initial licensure.*
- *Assist candidates in preparing for the Exam by outlining the knowledge and skills that may be tested.*
- *Apprise educators about the knowledge and skills candidates will need to function as newly licensed CPAs.*
- *Guide the development of Exam questions.*

For your convenience, we have reproduced the AICPA's Regulation Blueprint. We also have provided cross-references to the study units and subunits in this book that correspond to the Blueprint's coverage.

REGULATION (REG)

Area I – Ethics, Professional Responsibilities and Federal Tax Procedures (10-20%)

A. ETHICS AND RESPONSIBILITIES IN TAX PRACTICE

1. Regulations governing practice before the Internal Revenue Service - SU 1
2. Internal Revenue Code and Regulations related to tax return preparers - SU 1

B. LICENSING AND DISCIPLINARY SYSTEMS - SU 1

C. FEDERAL TAX PROCEDURES

1. Audits, appeals and judicial process - SU 3
2. Substantiation and disclosure of tax positions - SU 1, SU 3
3. Taxpayer penalties - SU 3
4. Authoritative hierarchy - SU 3

D. LEGAL DUTIES AND RESPONSIBILITIES

1. Common law duties and liabilities to clients and third parties - SU 2
2. Privileged communications, confidentiality and privacy acts - SUs 1-2

Area II – Business Law (10-20%)

A. AGENCY

1. Authority of agents and principals - SU 18
2. Duties and liabilities of agents and principals - SU 18

B. CONTRACTS

1. Formation - SU 17, SU 19
2. Performance - SU 17, SU 19
3. Discharge, breach and remedies - SU 17, SU 19

C. DEBTOR-CREDITOR RELATIONSHIPS

1. Rights, duties, and liabilities of debtors, creditors and guarantors - SU 20
2. Bankruptcy and insolvency - SU 20
3. Secured transactions - SU 19

D. GOVERNMENT REGULATION OF BUSINESS

1. Federal securities regulation - SU 2
2. Other federal laws and regulations (e.g., employment tax, Affordable Care Act and worker classification) - SU 18

E. BUSINESS STRUCTURE

1. Selection and formation of business entity and related operation and termination - SUs 15-16
2. Rights, duties, legal obligations and authority of owners and management - SUs 15-16

Area III – Federal Taxation of Property Transactions (12-22%)

A. ACQUISITION AND DISPOSITION OF ASSETS

1. Basis and holding period of assets - SU 8
2. Taxable and nontaxable dispositions - SU 8
3. Amount and character of gains and losses, and netting process (including installment sales) - SU 8
4. Related party transactions (including imputed interest) - SU 8

B. COST RECOVERY (DEPRECIATION, DEPLETION AND AMORTIZATION) - SU 8

C. ESTATE AND GIFT TAXATION

1. Transfers subject to gift tax - SU 14
2. Gift tax annual exclusion and gift tax deductions - SU 14
3. Determination of taxable estate - SU 14

Area IV – Federal Taxation of Individuals (including tax preparation and planning strategies) (15-25%)

A. GROSS INCOME (INCLUSIONS AND EXCLUSIONS) (INCLUDES TAXATION OF RETIREMENT PLAN BENEFITS) - SUs 3-5

B. REPORTING OF ITEMS FROM PASS-THROUGH ENTITIES - SU 4, SUs 12-14

C. ADJUSTMENTS AND DEDUCTIONS TO ARRIVE AT ADJUSTED GROSS INCOME AND TAXABLE INCOME - SUs 5-6

D. PASSIVE ACTIVITY LOSSES (EXCLUDING FOREIGN TAX CREDIT IMPLICATIONS) - SU 7

E. LOSS LIMITATIONS - SU 7

F. FILING STATUS AND EXEMPTIONS - SU 3

G. COMPUTATION OF TAX AND CREDITS - SU 7

H. ALTERNATIVE MINIMUM TAX - SU 7

Area V – Federal Taxation of Entities (including tax preparation and planning strategies) (28-38%)

A. TAX TREATMENT OF FORMATION AND LIQUIDATION OF BUSINESS ENTITIES - SU 9, SU 11

B. DIFFERENCES BETWEEN BOOK AND TAX INCOME(LOSS) - SU 9

C. C CORPORATIONS

1. Computations of taxable income (including alternative minimum taxable income), tax liability and allowable credits - SU 4, SUs 9-10
2. Net operating losses and capital loss limitations - SU 9
3. Entity/owner transactions, including contributions, loans and distributions - SU 11
4. Consolidated tax returns - SU 10
5. Multijurisdictional tax issues (including consideration of local, state and international tax issues) - SU 11

D. S CORPORATIONS

1. Eligibility and election - SU 12
2. Determination of ordinary business income (loss) and separately stated items - SU 12
3. Basis of shareholder's interest - SU 12
4. Entity/owner transactions (including contributions, loans and distributions) - SU 12
5. Built-in gains tax - SU 12

E. PARTNERSHIPS

1. Determination of ordinary business income (loss) and separately stated items - SU 13
2. Basis of partner's interest and basis of assets contributed to the partnership - SU 13
3. Partnership and partner elections - SU 13
4. Transactions between a partner and the partnership (including services performed by a partner and loans) - SU 13
5. Impact of partnership liabilities on a partner's interest in a partnership - SU 13
6. Distribution of partnership assets - SU 13
7. Ownership changes - SU 13

F. LIMITED LIABILITY COMPANIES - SU 15

G. TRUSTS AND ESTATES

1. Types of trusts - SU 14
2. Income and deductions - SU 14
3. Determination of beneficiary's share of taxable income - SU 14

H. TAX EXEMPT ORGANIZATIONS

1. Types of organizations - SU 12
2. Obtaining and maintaining tax exempt status - SU 12
3. Unrelated business income - SU 12

APPENDIX B
OPTIMIZING YOUR SCORE ON
THE TASK-BASED SIMULATIONS (TBSs)

Each section of the CPA exam contains multiple testlets of Task-Based Simulations. The number of TBS testlets and the number of TBSs in each testlet are the same for each exam section except BEC.

TBSs per Exam Section

	Testlet 3	Testlet 4	Testlet 5	Total
AUD	2	3	3	8
BEC	2	2	N/A*	4
FAR	2	3	3	8
REG	2	3	3	8

*Testlet 5 of BEC is Written Communications.

Task-Based Simulations are constructive response questions with information presented either with the question or in separate information tabs. Question responses may be in the form of entering amounts or formulas into a spreadsheet, choosing the correct answer from a list in a pop-up box, completing accounting or tax forms, or reviewing and completing or correcting a draft of a document. In the AUD, FAR, and REG exam sections, you will also have to complete a Research task, which requires you to research the relevant authoritative literature and cite the appropriate guidance as indicated. You will not have to complete a Research task in BEC.

It is not productive to practice TBSs on paper. Instead, you should use your online Gleim CPA Review Course to complete truly interactive TBSs that emulate exactly how TBSs are tested on the CPA exam. As a CPA candidate, you must become an expert on how to approach TBSs, how to budget your time in the TBS testlets, and the different types of TBSs. This appendix covers all of those topics for you and includes examples of typical TBSs. Use this appendix only as an introduction to TBSs, and then practice hundreds of exam-emulating TBSs in your Gleim CPA Review Course.

Task-Based Simulations -- Toolbar Icons and Operations**

The following information and toolbar icons are located at the top of the testlet screen of each TBS. All screen shots are taken from the AICPA Sample Test (www.aicpa.org). The CPA exam, the Sample Test, and all screenshots are Copyright 2017 by the AICPA with All Rights Reserved. The AICPA requires all candidates to review the Sample Tests and Tutorials before sitting for the CPA exam.

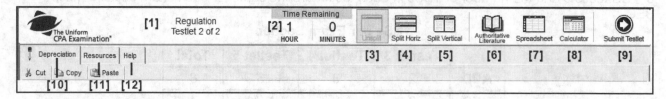

1. **Exam Section and Testlet Number:** The testlet number will always be 3, 4, or 5 of 5 for the simulations.

2. **Time Remaining:** This information box displays how much time you have remaining in the entire exam. Consistently check the amount of time remaining to stay on schedule.

3. **Unsplit:** This icon, when selected, will unsplit the screen between two tabs.

4. **Split Horiz:** This icon, when selected, will split the screen horizontally between two tabs, enabling you to see, for example, both the simulation question and the help tab at the same time.

5. **Split Vertical:** This icon, when selected, will split the screen vertically between two tabs, enabling you to see, for example, both the simulation question and the help tab at the same time.

6. **Authoritative Literature:** The Authoritative Literature for AUD, FAR, and REG is available in every TBS testlet. You can use either the Table of Contents or the Search function to locate the correct guidance.

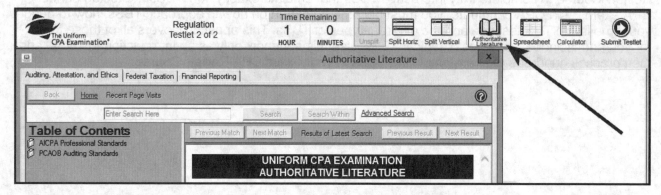

**IMPORTANT NOTE: The AICPA has announced the launch of new, more user-friendly software for the CPA exam sometime in 2018. At time of print, the finalized interface and actual launch date had not been released. Gleim will keep candidates up-to-date on all news and will provide the most realistic emulations within our course and in an update PDF for book users as soon as they are available. Be sure to check the Gleim CPA Blog at www.gleim.com/cpablog for breaking news on this development.

7. **Spreadsheet:** The spreadsheet operates like most others and is provided as a tool for complex calculations. You may enter and execute formulas as well as enter text and numbers.

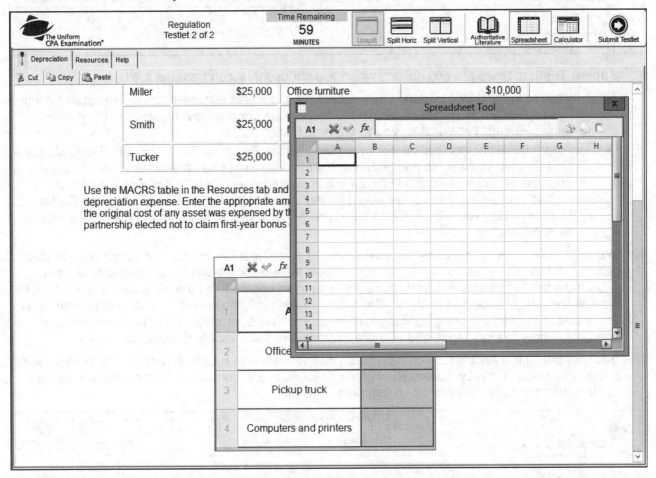

8. **Calculator:** The calculator provided is a basic tool for simple computations. It is similar to calculators used in common software programs.

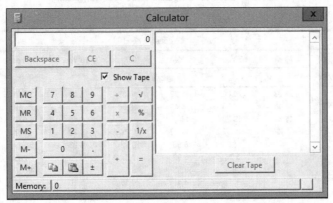

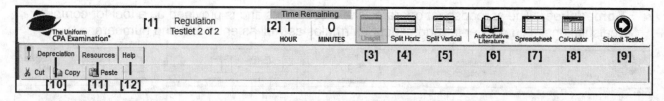

9. **Submit Testlet:** There are two options when you choose this icon from the toolbar.

   - In any of the first four testlets, you will be asked to select either Return to Testlet or Submit Testlet. Return to Testlet allows you to review and change your answers in the current testlet. Submit Testlet takes you to the next testlet.

   - In the final testlet, you will be asked to select either Return to Testlet or Quit Exam. Choose Quit Exam if you wish to complete the exam. You will not be able to return to any testlet, and you will not receive credit for any unanswered questions. To prevent accidentally ending your exam, you will be asked to verify your selection, or you can choose Go Back. Upon verifying you wish to End Exam, you will be required to leave the test center with no re-admittance.

10. **Work Tabs:** A work tab requires you to respond to given information. Each task will have at least one work tab (distinguished by a pencil icon), and each work tab will have specific directions you must read to complete the tab correctly. You must complete all the work tabs in each task to maximize your chance for full credit. The format of the work tab varies. You may encounter work tabs that require you to complete forms, fill in spreadsheets, or select an option from multiple choices. The TBSs on pages 593-609 are examples of each variety of work tab.

11. **Information Tabs:** An information tab gives you information to help with responding to work tabs. These tabs are generally labeled Resources or Exhibits and contain various resources and tools to use with the current work tab. An example is below.

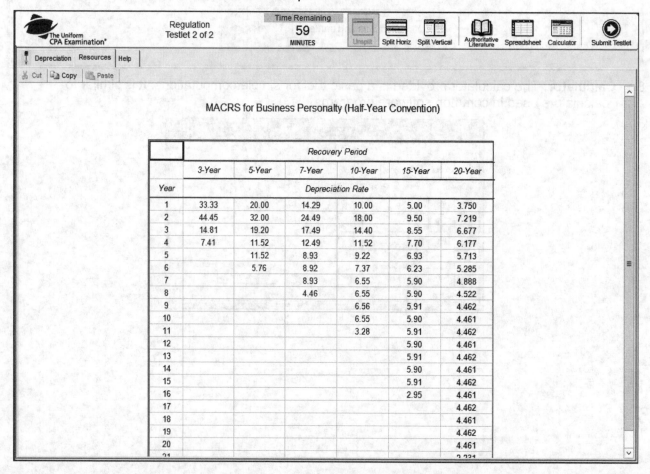

12. **Help:** This tab, when selected, provides a quick review of certain functions and tool buttons specific to the type of task you are working in. It will also provide directions and general information but will not include information related specifically to the test content.

The **navigation toolbar** below appears at the bottom of every TBS screen.

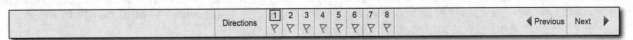

Clicking on a number takes you to that TBS; hovering over the number shows the name of the TBS. Clicking on the flag under a number marks the TBS. You can use the flag as a reminder to go back and check that TBS again if you have time.

Answering Task-Based Simulations

Do not be intimidated by TBSs. Just learn the material and practice answering the different question types. Knowing **how** to work through the simulations is nearly as important as knowing what they test.

You can maximize your score on the TBS testlets of each exam section by following these suggested steps for completing Task-Based Simulations.

A. **Budget your time so you can finish before time expires.**

   1. Allot small segments of the total testing time to each specific task. We recommend you budget 18 minutes for each TBS.

   2. Track your progress to ensure that you will have enough time to complete all the tasks.

   3. Use our Time Allocation Table to determine the time at which you need to start and finish each TBS testlet.

B. **Devote the first few minutes to reading the directions and scanning each TBS.**

   1. Spend no more than 3 minutes reading the directions and previewing the TBSs you received by clicking through the navigation bar at the bottom of the screen.

   2. You will not need to spend any time on the directions for your second and third TBS testlets, so you can dedicate the full time (minus a minute for scanning to preview) to responding.

   3. You will be familiar with the layout of the TBSs if you have been practicing with Gleim TBSs under exam conditions.

C. **Answer all the tasks within the time limit for each testlet.**

   1. Read all information tabs (e.g., financial statements, memos, etc.) associated with the tab you are working on before you attempt to answer the simulation.

      a. We have included detailed directions on using exhibits as source documents in the next section on Document Review Simulations. Much of those instructions can also be used when answering regular TBSs that contain exhibits.

   2. Do not skip any of the questions within a tab. Make an educated guess if you are unsure of the answer and set a reminder for yourself by clicking the flag icon under the number of the TBS in the navigation toolbar at the bottom of the screen. There is no penalty for incorrect answers, so do not move on without at least selecting your best guess.

D. **Spend any remaining time wisely to maximize your points.**

   1. Ask yourself where you will earn the most points.

   2. Move from task to task systematically, reviewing and completing each one. Focus specifically on any TBS you flagged.

   3. Move on to the next TBS within the testlet or to the next testlet at the end of 18 minutes.

DOCUMENT REVIEW SIMULATIONS

Within the Task-Based Simulation testlets included in each CPA exam section, you may find a Document Review Simulation (DRS), which will be named Document Review. You are required to review various exhibits to determine the best phrasing of a particular document. The document will contain highlighted words, phrases, sentences, or paragraphs that may or may not be correct. You then must select answer choices that indicate which (if any) changes you believe should be made in the highlighted words, phrases, sentences, or paragraphs.

The DRSs always include the actual document you must review and correct, a help tab, and one or more information tabs. Information tabs vary from one DRS to the next because they contain the exhibits to be used as sources for your conclusions. For example, these exhibits may be financial statements, emails, letters, invoices, memoranda, or minutes from meetings. You must read each DRS tab so that you are always aware of the resources available.

Answering Document Review Simulations

A. **Familiarize yourself with every part of the DRS.**

    Review each information tab so you know what information is available. If your subject-matter preparation has been thorough, you should be able to identify quickly the most relevant information in each part of the DRS.

B. **Address every underlined portion of text in the DRS.**

    You must make an answer selection for every modifiable section of a DRS because each counts as a separate question. You will know an answer has been selected when you see that the white outline in the blue icon has changed to a white checkmark.

C. **Read the underlined section and answer choices carefully and completely.**

    Each underlined portion of text may have five to seven answer choices that may include the options to revise the text, retain the original text, or delete the text. Verify that each word or amount is correct in your choice before making your final selection.

D. **Clearly understand the information in the exhibits.**

    Quickly survey the various items; then analyze the most relevant facts specifically and refer to them to reduce the possible answer choices. Keep in mind that the relevant information may be presented or worded differently than the document you are revising.

E. **Double-check that you have officially responded to each underlined portion of text.**

    If you have time, go through the entire DRS once more to confirm that every underlined section has a white checkmark next to it.

MANAGING TIME ON THE TBSs

Managing your time well during the CPA exam is critical to success, so you must develop and practice your time management plan before your test date. The only help you will receive during your actual CPA exam is a countdown of the hours and minutes remaining. When there are less than 2 minutes left in an exam section, the exam clock will begin to include the seconds, but you should be doing your final review by that point.

Each of the testlets on the exam is independent, and there are no time limits on individual testlets. Therefore, you must budget your time effectively to complete all five testlets in the allotted 4 hours.

The key to success is to become proficient in answering all types of questions in an average amount of time. When you follow our system, you'll have 2-17 minutes of total extra time (depending on the section) that you will be able to allocate as needed.

Each exam will begin with three introductory screens that you must complete in 10 minutes. (Time spent in the introductory screens does not count against the 240 minutes you get for the exam itself.) Then you will have two MCQ testlets. Each testlet contains half the total number of MCQs for that section (36/testlet for AUD, 31/testlet for BEC, 33/testlet for FAR, and 38/testlet for REG.). Based on the total time of the exam and the amount of time needed for the other testlets, you should average 1.25 minutes per MCQ.

The final three testlets in AUD, FAR, and REG will have eight TBSs each: two in Testlet #3, three in Testlet #4, and three in Testlet #5. BEC will have four TBSs in two testlets, then a final testlet of three Written Communications (WCs). We suggest you allocate approximately 18 minutes to answering each TBS. On BEC, budget 25 minutes for each of the three WCs (20 minutes to answer, 5 minutes to review and perfect your response). **

To make the most of your testing time during the CPA exam, you will need to develop a time management system and commit to spending a designated amount of time on each question. To assist you, please refer to the Gleim Time Management System.

The table below shows how many minutes you should expect to spend on each testlet for each section. Remember, you cannot begin a new testlet until you have submitted a current testlet, and once you have submitted a testlet, you can no longer go back to it.

Time Allocation per Testlet (in minutes)

Testlet	Format	AUD	BEC**	FAR	REG
1	MCQ	45	38*	41*	47*
2	MCQ	45	38*	41*	47*
3	TBS	36	36	36	36
15-Minute Break					
4	TBS	54	36	54	54
5	TBS/WC	54	75	54	54
Total		234	223	226	238
Extra Time		6	17	14	2
Total Time Allowed		240	240	240	240

*Rounded down

**BEC candidates may prefer to allocate more time to the TBSs and reduce the 17 minutes of extra review time after the WCs. In this case, we suggest 20 minutes per TBS, for a total time of 40 minutes in Testlet 3 and 40 minutes in Testlet 4, leaving 9 minutes of final review after the WCs.

The exam screen will show hours:minutes remaining. Focus on how much time you have, NOT the time on your watch. Using the times on the previous page, you would start each testlet with the following hours:minutes displayed on-screen:

Completion Times and Time Remaining

	AUD	BEC**	FAR	REG
Start	4 hours 0 minutes	4 hours 0 minutes	4 hours 0 minutes	4 hours 0 minutes
After Testlet 1	3 hours 15 minutes	3 hours 22 minutes	3 hours 19 minutes	3 hours 13 minutes
After Testlet 2	2 hours 30 minutes	2 hours 44 minutes	2 hours 38 minutes	2 hours 26 minutes
After Testlet 3	1 hour 54 minutes	2 hours 8 minutes	2 hours 2 minutes	1 hour 50 minutes
15-Minute Break				
After Testlet 4	1 hour 0 minutes	1 hour 32 minutes	1 hour 8 minutes	0 hours 56 minutes
After Testlet 5	0 hours 6 minutes	0 hours 17 minutes	0 hours 14 minutes	0 hours 2 minutes

Next, develop a shorthand for hours:minutes. This makes it easier to write down the times on the noteboard you will receive at the exam center.

	AUD	BEC**	FAR	REG
Start	4:00	4:00	4:00	4:00
After Testlet 1	3:15	3:22	3:19	3:13
After Testlet 2	2:30	2:44	2:38	2:26
After Testlet 3	1:54	2:08	2:02	1:50
15-Minute Break				
After Testlet 4	1:00	1:32	1:08	0:56
After Testlet 5	0:06	0:17	0:14	0:02

**BEC candidates may prefer to allocate more time to the TBSs and reduce the 17 minutes of extra review time after the WCs. In this case, we suggest 20 minutes per TBS, for a total time of 40 minutes in Testlet 3 and 40 minutes in Testlet 4, leaving 9 minutes of final review after the WCs.

The following pages of this appendix contain the AICPA TBS directions and the following eight example TBSs:

> Research
> Form 1120 Reported Amounts: Tax Form 1
> Schedules M-1 and M-2: Tax Form 2
> Net Operating Loss: Numeric Entry 1
> Liquidation: Numeric Entry 2
> Gains and Losses: Numeric Entry and Drop-Down
> Bases for Liability: Drop-Down
> Document Review Simulation (DRS)

We have included a variety of TBS types, including Research, Drop-Down, Numeric Entry, and DRS, along with suggestions on how to approach each type. The answer key and our unique answer explanations for each TBS appear at the end of the appendix.

Again, do not substitute answering TBSs in your Gleim CPA Review Course with answering the TBSs presented here. Refer to these TBSs only for guidance on how to answer this difficult element of the exam. It is vital that you practice answering TBSs in the digital environment of our online course so that you are comfortable with such an environment during your CPA exam.

DIRECTIONS

Below and on the next page are reproductions of the Directions screen that appears at the beginning of each TBS testlet. Take the time now to read these directions line by line so that you do not have to spend time reading this screen when you take your exam. This preparation, along with completing numerous TBSs under exam conditions in the Gleim CPA Review Course, will help you refine your TBS-answering techniques.

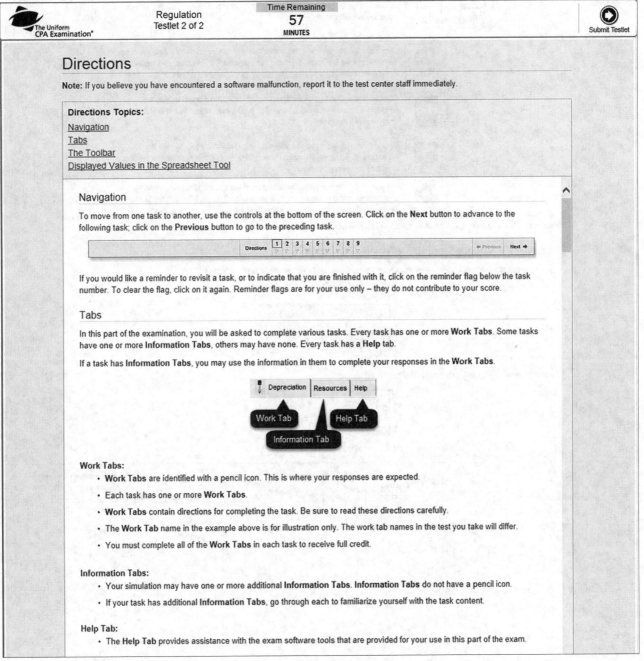

-- Continued on next page --

-- Continued

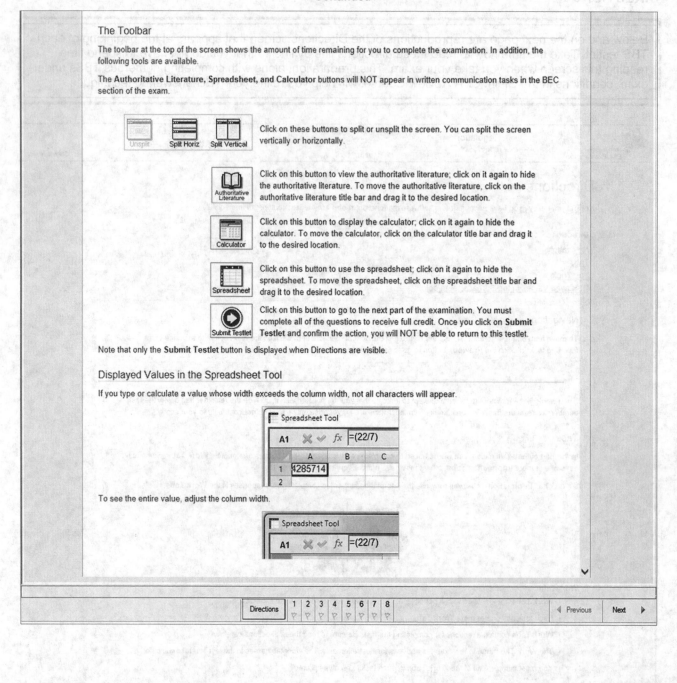

The Toolbar

The toolbar at the top of the screen shows the amount of time remaining for you to complete the examination. In addition, the following tools are available.

The **Authoritative Literature, Spreadsheet, and Calculator** buttons will NOT appear in written communication tasks in the BEC section of the exam.

Click on these buttons to split or unsplit the screen. You can split the screen vertically or horizontally.

Click on this button to view the authoritative literature; click on it again to hide the authoritative literature. To move the authoritative literature, click on the authoritative literature title bar and drag it to the desired location.

Click on this button to display the calculator; click on it again to hide the calculator. To move the calculator, click on the calculator title bar and drag it to the desired location.

Click on this button to use the spreadsheet; click on it again to hide the spreadsheet. To move the spreadsheet, click on the spreadsheet title bar and drag it to the desired location.

Click on this button to go to the next part of the examination. You must complete all of the questions to receive full credit. Once you click on **Submit Testlet** and confirm the action, you will NOT be able to return to this testlet.

Note that only the **Submit Testlet** button is displayed when Directions are visible.

Displayed Values in the Spreadsheet Tool

If you type or calculate a value whose width exceeds the column width, not all characters will appear.

To see the entire value, adjust the column width.

RESEARCH

This type of TBS requires that you research within the Authoritative Literature, which is accessible from the top right corner of the TBS toolbar (shown below), to find the best supporting guidance for the presented scenario. Although there is only one question to answer in the Research TBS, it counts as much as a TBS with multiple questions, so you must treat it with the same gravity as any other TBS. Our suggested steps on how to answer this task type follow:

1. Read through the given scenario to identify the question being asked and, within that, the key terms to search for in the literature. In this example, the question is asking for the penalties assessed to a return preparer for failing to sign a return, so the key terms are preparer, penalty, and sign.

2. Type the key term(s) into the search box and click "Search."

3. Review the first 10 results. Use your knowledge of the topic to decide whether the search results fit the question you are researching. Often, the first search will not yield the correct answer, and it is necessary to narrow your scope.

4. Restrict your search to only the most relevant section of the literature by using the "Search Within" function. To do so, choose the subtitle of the literature from the Table of Contents that is most likely to contain the related section. Click on that subtitle, type your term into the search box, and click "Search Within." This will populate the results with only matches from that specific subtitle. For example, this Research question refers to penalties assessed to a return preparer. Therefore, Subtitle F, Procedure and Administration, is the subtitle to search within.

5. From these streamlined results, select the exact paragraph (350-40-25-2 for this example) that corresponds to the given scenario and enter your response using the on-screen formatting prompts.

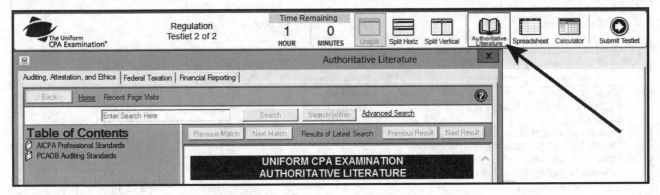

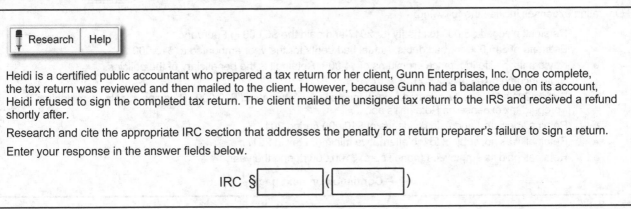

Heidi is a certified public accountant who prepared a tax return for her client, Gunn Enterprises, Inc. Once complete, the tax return was reviewed and then mailed to the client. However, because Gunn had a balance due on its account, Heidi refused to sign the completed tax return. The client mailed the unsigned tax return to the IRS and received a refund shortly after.

Research and cite the appropriate IRC section that addresses the penalty for a return preparer's failure to sign a return.

Enter your response in the answer fields below.

IRC § [   ] ([   ])

FORM 1120 Reported Amounts: TAX FORM 1

> The following two TBSs are Tax Forms. This type of task requires that you complete a tax form based on a set of given facts, such as a company's condensed income statement. Some cells will require that you enter amounts, and other cells will then automatically calculate based on your entries.

Form 1120 Reported Amounts   Help

Following is the Retainall Corp.'s condensed income statement before federal income tax for the year ended December 31, 2017:

Sales		$1,000,000
Cost of sales		(550,000)
Gross profit		$ 450,000
Operating expenses		(250,000)
Operating income		$ 200,000
Other income (loss):		
Interest	$ 8,000	
Dividends	33,180	
Net long-term capital loss	(6,400)	34,780
Income before federal		
income tax		$ 234,780

Additional Information

Interest arose from the following sources:

U.S. Treasury notes	$4,000
Municipal arbitrage bonds	1,000
Other municipal bonds	3,000
Total interest	**$8,000**

Dividends arose from the following sources:

Taxable Domestic Corporation	Date Stock Acquired	Percent Owned by Retainall	
Blanko Corp.	09/01/13	10	$10,000
Fathers Corp. (sold 1/10/17)	12/01/16	5	10,000
Silver Corp.	07/01/11	30	8,750
Real estate investment trust	06/01/16	1	3,750
Mutual fund corp. (capital gains dividends)	04/01/15	0.1	400
Money market fund (interest-paying securities only)	03/01/14	0.1	280
Total dividends			**$33,180**

Operating expenses include the following:

- Retainall pledged $5,000 to charity for 2017 and paid the $5,000 in February.
- Estimate of $15,000 for bad debts. Actual bad debts for the year amounted to $10,000.
- Key employee life insurance premiums of $4,000. Retainall is the beneficiary of the policies.
- State income taxes of $12,000.
- During 2017, Retainall estimated federal income tax payments of $30,000. These payments were debited to prepaid tax expense on Retainall's books.
- Retainall declared and paid dividends of $10,000 during 2017.
- Retainall was not subject to the alternative minimum tax in 2017.
- Retainall paid its employees (nonofficers) $100,000 during the year.

-- Continued on next page --

| ✏ Form 1120 Reported Amounts | Help | -- **Continued** |

Using the information for Retainall Corp. on the previous page, enter the appropriate amount in each of the shaded cells below.

Form 1120
Department of the Treasury
Internal Revenue Service

U.S. Corporation Income Tax Return
For calendar year [Year] or tax year beginning _____ , [Year], ending _____ , 20 _____
▶ Information about Form 1120 and its separate instructions is at *www.irs.gov/form1120.*

OMB No. 1545-0123
[Year]

A Check if:
1a Consolidated return (attach Form 851) . ☐
  b Life/nonlife consolidated return . . ☐
2 Personal holding co. (attach Sch. PH) . ☐
3 Personal service corp. (see instructions) . ☐
4 Schedule M-3 attached ☐

TYPE OR PRINT

Name
Retainall Corporation
Number, street, and room or suite no. If a P.O. box, see instructions.
12345 Ace Avenue
City or town, state, or province, country, and ZIP or foreign postal code
Newtown, PA 35000

B Employer identification number
98 7654321
C Date incorporated
1-1-01
D Total assets (see instructions)
$10,000,000

E Check if: (1) ☐ Initial return   (2) ☐ Final return   (3) ☐ Name change   (4) ☐ Address change

Income	1a	Gross receipts or sales	1a	
	b	Returns and allowances	1b	
	c	Balance. Subtract line 1b from line 1a . . .	1c	
	2	Cost of goods sold (attach Form 1125-A)	2	
	3	Gross profit. Subtract line 2 from line 1c	3	
	4	Dividends (Schedule C, line 19)	4	
	5	Interest	5	
	6	Gross rents	6	
	7	Gross royalties	7	
	8	Capital gain net income (attach Schedule D (Form 1120)) . . .	8	
	9	Net gain or (loss) from Form 4797, Part II, line 17 (attach Form 4797) .	9	
	10	Other income (see instructions—attach statement)	10	
	11	**Total income.** Add lines 3 through 10 . . . . . . ▶	11	
Deductions (See instructions for limitations on deductions.)	12	Compensation of officers (see instructions—attach Form 1125-E) . . . ▶	12	
	13	Salaries and wages (less employment credits)	13	
	14	Repairs and maintenance	14	
	15	Bad debts	15	
	16	Rents	16	
	17	Taxes and licenses	17	
	18	Interest	18	
	19	Charitable contributions	19	
	20	Depreciation from Form 4562 not claimed on Form 1125-A or elsewhere on return (attach Form 4562) .	20	
	21	Depletion	21	
	22	Advertising	22	
	23	Pension, profit-sharing, etc., plans	23	
	24	Employee benefit programs	24	
	25	Domestic production activities deduction (attach Form 8903) . . .	25	
	26	Other deductions (attach statement)	26	
	27	**Total deductions.** Add lines 12 through 26 . . . . . ▶	27	
	28	Taxable income before net operating loss deduction and special deductions. Subtract line 27 from line 11.	28	
	29a	Net operating loss deduction (see instructions)	29a	
	b	Special deductions (Schedule C, line 20)	29b	
	c	Add lines 29a and 29b	29c	
Tax, Refundable Credits, and Payments	30	**Taxable income.** Subtract line 29c from line 28. See instructions . .	30	
	31	Total tax (Schedule J, Part I, line 11)	31	
	32	Total payments and refundable credits (Schedule J, Part II, line 21) . .	32	
	33	Estimated tax penalty. See instructions. Check if Form 2220 is attached . . ▶ ☐	33	
	34	**Amount owed.** If line 32 is smaller than the total of lines 31 and 33, enter amount owed . .	34	
	35	**Overpayment.** If line 32 is larger than the total of lines 31 and 33, enter amount overpaid . .	35	
	36	Enter amount from line 35 you want: **Credited to [next year] estimated tax ▶**	Refunded ▶ 36	

For Paperwork Reduction Act Notice, see separate instructions.   Cat. No. 11450Q   Form **1120** [Year]

SCHEDULES M-1 AND M-2: TAX FORM 2

| ⬧ Schedules M-1 and M-2 | Help |

Based on the facts below, complete Schedules M-1 and M-2.

Fort, Linda, and Yolanda formed the FLY partnership on January 1, 2012, and properly adopted a calendar tax year. The partnership elected to use the cash receipts and disbursements method of accounting. Among FLY's items of income, expense, loss, and credit for its 2016 tax year were a guaranteed payment to Linda for services rendered, expenses attributable to investment income, and a long-term capital loss. FLY had no other capital gains or losses during the tax year. Linda, a domestic partner, has a $7,000 basis in the FLY partnership immediately before receiving a current distribution. The distribution consists of $6,000 cash, a computer with a FMV of $2,500 and a $5,000 basis to the partnership, and a desk with a FMV of $1,500 and a $2,500 basis to the partnership.

In addition, FLY has the following items in its current-year financial statements:

1) FLY received $15,000 in prepaid rent from a tenant leasing one of FLY's offices.
2) FLY also earned $16,000 of tax-exempt interest during the year. FLY incurred $6,000 in interest expense on a loan used to purchase the tax-exempt bonds.
3) One of FLY's key partners died during the year, and FLY received $30,000 in life insurance proceeds, which was included in book income.
4) FLY spent $8,000 on meals and entertainment to attract new clients. Business was discussed at each meeting.
5) FLY purchased a new machine during the year to assist in operations. FLY elected to immediately expense $39,000 of the machine under code section 179. FLY uses the same depreciation method for book and tax purposes for the machine.
6) During the year, Yolanda contributed an additional $10,000 cash to the partnership. No property was contributed.
7) Yolanda also received $20,000 in a guaranteed payment during the year.
8) Net income recorded on the books for financial accounting purposes for the year was $100,000. The partners' combined capital accounts at the beginning of the year totaled $50,000.

Schedule M-1	Reconciliation of Income (Loss) per Books With Income (Loss) per Return		
	Note. Schedule M-3 may be required instead of Schedule M-1 (see instructions).		

1	Net income (loss) per books	[1]		6	Income recorded on books this year not included on Schedule K, lines 1 through 11 (itemize):		
2	Income included on Schedule K, lines 1, 2, 3c, 5, 6a, 7, 8, 9a, 10, and 11, not recorded on books this year (itemize):	[2]		a	Tax-exempt interest $		
							[6]
3	Guaranteed payments (other than health insurance)	[3]		7	Deductions included on Schedule K, lines 1 through 13d, and 16l, not charged against book income this year (itemize):		
4	Expenses recorded on books this year not included on Schedule K, lines 1 through 13d, and 16l (itemize):			a	Depreciation $		
a	Depreciation $						[7]
b	Travel and entertainment $			8	Add lines 6 and 7		[8]
		[4]		9	Income (loss) (Analysis of Net Income (Loss), line 1). Subtract line 8 from line 5 .		[9]
5	Add lines 1 through 4	[5]					

Schedule M-2	Analysis of Partners' Capital Accounts		

1	Balance at beginning of year . . .	[10]		6	Distributions: **a** Cash		[15]
2	Capital contributed: **a** Cash . . .	[11]			**b** Property		[16]
	b Property . .	[12]		7	Other decreases (itemize):		
3	Net income (loss) per books	[13]					
4	Other increases (itemize):						
				8	Add lines 6 and 7		[17]
5	Add lines 1 through 4	[14]		9	Balance at end of year. Subtract line 8 from line 5		[18]

Form **1065** (201X)

| | Directions | 1 ▽ | 2 ▽ | **3** ▽ | 4 ▽ | 5 ▽ | 6 ▽ | 7 ▽ | 8 ▽ | ◀ Previous | Next ▶ |

NET OPERATING LOSS: NUMERIC ENTRY 1

The following two TBSs are all Numeric Entries. This type of TBS requires that you calculate and then respond with some kind of number, e.g., an amount of currency, a ratio, etc. The spreadsheet functions much like an Excel document would. Negative numbers should be entered using a leading minus sign and will be automatically formatted with parentheses. Some Numeric Entry TBSs may also have Drop-Down type responses required. The Drop-Down TBSs are in essence multiple-choice questions.

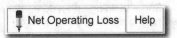

For each of the following situations, enter the correct amounts in the shaded cells below. Enter all values as positive whole numbers. If no entry is necessary, or the answer is zero, enter a zero (0).

Situation	Answer
1. For the tax year ended December 31, Year 4, Kustan Co. had gross income of $300,000 and operating expenses of $500,000. Included in the operating expenses is a contribution of $7,000 made to qualifying charities. What is Kustan's net operating loss for Year 4?	
2. During Year 3, Tennis Corporation had gross income of $70,000 and operating expenses of $95,000. Tennis Co. also received dividend income of $60,000 from a domestic corporation in which Tennis is a 25% shareholder. What is Tennis Co.'s net operating loss for Year 3?	
3. For each of the following years, Gobby Corporation had net income (loss) per books as follows: • Year 1 -- $20,000 • Year 2 -- $15,000 • Year 3 -- $(65,000) What amount of NOL may be carried forward to Year 4?	
4. For Year 3, Association Corporation had taxable income of $60,000 before using any of its net operating loss from Year 2. Association's books and records reflect the following income (losses): • Year 1 -- $15,000 • Year 2 -- $(40,000) If Association does not elect to forgo the carryback period, what amount of taxable income must Association report on its Year 3 tax return?	

Directions | 1 2 3 [4] 5 6 7 8 | ◀ Previous   Next ▶

LIQUIDATION: NUMERIC ENTRY 2

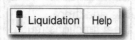

Son, Inc., and Clef, Inc., are both taxable domestic C corporations. On January 1, 2017, Son owned 800 of the outstanding shares of the only class of stock of Clef. Dawn owned the other 200 shares of Clef but owned none of the outstanding shares of Son. Son's basis in its Clef stock was $200,000, and Dawn's basis in her stock in Clef was $50,000. Clef had $10,000 of accumulated earnings and profits on January 1, 2017. On October 13, 2016, Clef contributed numerous copyrights to a tax-exempt organization. By July 4, 2017, Clef had paid all its liabilities to third parties. Clef was subsequently liquidated on August 31, 2017. In the complete liquidation, Clef distributed to Son a building and a computer, and to Dawn a concert grand piano, an electronic keyboard, and $82,000 in cash. Clef had no other assets other than an amount reserved for taxes.

Immediately before the distribution, the fair market values and Clef's adjusted bases are as follows:

Asset	FMV	Clef's Adjusted Basis
Building	$550,000	$250,000
Computer	25,000	30,000
Piano	15,000	10,000
Keyboard	3,000	4,000

The building was subject to a $175,000 mortgage. All of the noncash assets Clef distributed were purchased on August 31, 2013, 2 months after the corporation was formed. Clef had claimed allowable depreciation on the building using the straight-line method.

Enter either the correct amount or holding period (in number of months) for each item below.

Item	Answer
1. Loss recognized by Clef, Inc., on the distribution of the computer	
2. Gain recognized by Clef, Inc., on the distribution of the concert piano	
3. Son, Inc.'s basis in the building	
4. Son, Inc.'s basis in the computer	
5. Dawn's gain or loss recognized on the distribution of the piano, keyboard, and cash	
6. Dawn's holding period for the piano on December 31, 2017	
7. Dawn's holding period for the keyboard on December 31, 2017	

GAINS AND LOSSES: NUMERIC ENTRY AND DROP-DOWN

This TBS is an example of both Numeric Entry and Drop-Down type questions being asked in the same TBS.

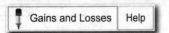 Gains and Losses | Help

For each of the following transactions, (1) enter the amount of the gain or loss, and (2) select from the list provided the character of the gain or loss. Each choice may be used once, more than once, or not at all. Enter all amounts as positive numbers.

Transaction	Amount	Character		Character Choices
1. Sale of 1,000 shares of XYZ common stock purchased on 10/15/16 for $20,000 and sold on 2/15/17 for $23,000.				A) Ordinary Income
				B) Ordinary Loss
2. Sale of 2,000 shares of ABC common stock purchased on 3/23/17 for $125,000 and sold on 12/31/17 for $139,000.				C) Short-Term Capital Gain
				D) Long-Term Capital Gain
3. Sale of van purchased on 1/25/16 for $10,000 and sold on 6/03/17 for $9,000.				E) Short-Term Capital Loss
				F) Long-Term Capital Loss
4. Sale of land purchased on 06/30/03 for $110,000 and sold on 7/04/17 for $169,000.				
5. $45,000 of insurance recovery received from a 5-year-old building that was destroyed in a fire. The building was used in a business, had a FMV of $65,000, and an adjusted basis of $50,000.				

Directions | 1 2 3 4 5 6 7 8 | ◀ Previous Next ▶

BASES FOR LIABILITY: DROP-DOWN

> This TBS is an example of a Drop-Down, which is in essence a series of multiple-choice questions. This type of task requires that you select a response from a list of choices. Some Drop-Down TBSs may also have Numeric Entry type responses required.

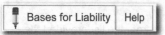 Bases for Liability | Help

The CPA firm of Martinson, Brinks, & Sutherland, a partnership, was the auditor for Masco Corporation, a medium-sized wholesaler. Masco leased warehouse facilities and sought financing for leasehold improvements to these facilities. Masco assured its bank that the leasehold improvements would result in a more efficient and profitable operation. Based on these assurances, the bank granted Masco a line of credit.

The loan agreement required annual audited financial statements. Masco submitted its audited financial statements to the bank. They showed an operating profit of $75,000, leasehold improvements of $250,000, and net worth of $350,000. In reliance on the statements, the bank lent Masco $200,000. The audit report that accompanied the financial statements disclaimed an opinion because the cost of the leasehold improvements could not be determined from the company's records. The part of the audit report applicable to leasehold improvements reads as follows:

> Additions to fixed assets for the year were found to include principally warehouse improvements. Most of this work was done by company employees, and the costs of materials and overhead were paid by Masco. Unfortunately, complete, detailed cost records were not kept of these leasehold improvements, and no exact determination could be made of the actual cost of the improvements. The total amount capitalized is set forth in note 4.

Late in the following year, Masco went out of business, at which time it was learned that the claimed leasehold improvements were totally fictitious. The labor expenses charged as leasehold improvements proved to be operating expenses. No item of building material cost had been recorded. No independent investigation of the existence of the leasehold improvements was made by the auditors.

If the $250,000 had not been capitalized, the income statement would have reflected a substantial loss from operations, and the net worth would have been correspondingly decreased.

The bank has sustained a loss on its loan to Masco of $200,000 and now seeks to recover damages from the CPA firm.

Items 1 through 8 are questions regarding CPA liability. Select the correct answer from the list provided. Each choice may be used once, more than once, or not at all.

Item	Answer
1. What basis for liability does not apply to an accountant?	
2. What basis for liability applies to Martinson, Brinks, & Sutherland?	
3. What is the class of persons to which the bank belongs for the purpose of determining the accountant's liability for negligence?	
4. What element of fraud is not included in negligent misrepresentation?	
5. Intent is an element of fraud. What may be substituted for intent?	
6. What type of causation is an element of negligence?	
7. One characteristic of a primary beneficiary is that the accountant is retained principally for its benefit. What is another characteristic, if any, of a primary beneficiary?	
8. What is the class of persons to which a defendant is liable for fraud?	

Choices

A)	Negligence	I)	Primary beneficiaries
B)	Gross negligence	J)	Privity of contract
C)	Fraud	K)	Proximate cause
D)	Relationship to a specific transaction	L)	Identification of the third party
E)	Strict liability in tort	M)	Duty to discover fraud
F)	Foreseen third parties	N)	Supervening cause
G)	Reasonably foreseeable users	O)	Scienter
H)	Implied cause	P)	None of the answer choices

DOCUMENT REVIEW SIMULATION (DRS)

This type of TBS requires that you analyze certain words or phrases in a document to decide whether to (1) keep the current text, (2) replace the current text with different text, or (3) delete the text. You must review various exhibits (e.g., financial statements, emails, invoices, etc.; see the second row of tabs in the image below) presented with the original document in order to find the information necessary for each response.

| Document Review | Exhibits | Help |

| 📄 OSHA Form 301 | 📄 Notice of Action/Change | 📄 Warning Letter | 📄 Wildcat Complaint | 📄 Installation Agreement | 📄 OSHA Form 300a |

| 📄 Distributor Agreement | 📄 Martha Jones Complaint |

During the audit of Jayhawk Corporation, your audit manager has instructed you to meet with Bob Smith, Jayhawk's director of internal auditing, to obtain information on the two pending civil claims against the company and on the sole workers' compensation claim. After meeting with Bob Smith and reviewing the relevant support, you drafted the below memorandum for your audit manager's review. Using the information from the exhibits presented on the following pages, select the option from the list provided that corrects the underlined portion of each of your answers. If the underlined text is already correct in the context of the document, select *[Original Text]* from the list. If removal of the underlined text is the best revision to the document, select *[Delete Text]* from the list if available.

To: Manager
From: You
Re: Information provided by Bob Smith, Jayhawk Corp.'s director of internal auditing

Bob Smith is concerned that Jayhawk Corp. needs to disclose a potential liability in a slip-and-fall lawsuit. <u>Jayhawk is potentially liable because California Distributor, LLC, is Jayhawk's agent as of the date of the alleged slip-and-fall incident.</u>

- [A] *[Original Text]* Jayhawk is potentially liable because California Distributor, LLC, is Jayhawk's agent as of the date of the alleged slip-and-fall incident.
- [B] Jayhawk may be liable, but California Distributor, LLC, will indemnify Jayhawk for any losses.
- [C] Jayhawk is not liable because California Distributor, LLC, is an independent contractor.
- [D] Jayhawk is not liable because California Distributor, LLC, is not an agent as of the date of the alleged slip-and-fall incident.
- [E] Jayhawk is not liable because the agency was for an illegal purpose.

Jayhawk Corp. and Wildcat, Inc., entered into a contract on December 7, 20X0, by which Jayhawk agreed to sell a Jayhawk Widget to Wildcat. The agreement also provided for installation of a Jayhawk Widget at Wildcat's premises. This equipment was essential to the functioning of Wildcat's production facility. Jayhawk then hired Ace Installer, LLC, to perform the installation, which was completed on December 10, 20X0. When the defective Jayhawk Widget malfunctioned, Ace Installer made repairs and agreed to pay damages to Wildcat. Ace Installer made this agreement because of its obligation to indemnify Jayhawk. But Ace Installer failed to pay, and Wildcat sued Jayhawk for $750,000 of lost revenue. <u>Jayhawk is not liable to Wildcat because of Ace Installer's indemnification agreement.</u>

- [A] *[Original Text]* Jayhawk is not liable to Wildcat because of Ace Installer's indemnification agreement.
- [B] Jayhawk is not liable to Wildcat because Ace Installer is an independent contractor.
- [C] Jayhawk is liable to Wildcat because it materially breached its contract with Wildcat.
- [D] Jayhawk is liable only for the price paid by Wildcat for the Jayhawk Widget and its installation.

Jayhawk South is the southeastern distributor of widgets manufactured by Jayhawk Corp. of Fort Scott, Kansas. On January 11, 20X0, one of its employees sustained a work-related injury resulting in a workers' compensation claim. Jayhawk South also reports to the Occupational Safety and Health Administration (OSHA). <u>Jayhawk South must recognize a liability for potential fines from OSHA due to employee safety issues.</u>

- [A] *[Original Text]* Jayhawk South must recognize a liability for potential fines from OSHA due to employee safety issues.
- [B] [Delete Text]
- [C] Jayhawk South must recognize in its financial statements the workers' compensation settlement.
- [D] Jayhawk South must recognize a contingent liability for damages exceeding the workers' compensation settlement.
- [E] Jayhawk South's insurer need not pay the claim if the employee was contributorily negligent.

DRS: EXHIBITS

OSHA's Form 301
Injury and Illness Incident Report

U.S. Department of Labor
Occupational Safety and Health Administration

Form approved OMB no. 1218-0176

This *Injury and Illness Incident Report* is one of the first forms you must fill out when a recordable work-related injury or illness has occurred. Together with the *Log of Work-Related Injuries and Illnesses* and the accompanying *Summary*, these forms help the employer and OSHA develop a picture of the extent and severity of work-related incidents.

Within 7 calendar days after you receive information that a recordable work-related injury or illness has occurred, you must fill out this form or an equivalent. Some state workers' compensation, insurance, or other reports may be acceptable substitutes. To be considered an equivalent form, any substitute must contain all the information asked for on this form.

According to Public Law 91-596 and 29 CFR 1904, OSHA's recordkeeping rule, you must keep this form on file for 5 years following the year to which it pertains.

If you need additional copies of this form, you may photocopy and use as many as you need.

Attention: This form contains information relating to employee health and must be used in a manner that protects the confidentiality of employees to the extent possible while the information is being used for occupational safety and health purposes.

Information about the employee

1) Full name __Robert Dean__

2) Street __200 Longfellow Dr.__
   City __Gainesville__ State __FL__ ZIP __32608__

3) Date of birth __10__ / __30__ / __1960__

4) Date hired __5__ / __24__ / __2008__

5) ☒ Male
   ☐ Female

Information about the physician or other health care professional

6) Name of physician or other health care professional __Dr. Williams__

7) If treatment was given away from the worksite, where was it given?
   Facility __Stoneridge Medical Center__
   Street __Stoneridge Drive__
   City __Gainesville__ State __FL__ ZIP __32606__

8) Was employee treated in an emergency room?
   ☒ Yes
   ☐ No

9) Was employee hospitalized overnight as an in-patient?
   ☐ Yes
   ☒ No

Information about the case

10) Case number from the Log __02__ *(Transfer the case number from the Log after you record the case.)*

11) Date of injury or illness __1__ / __11__ / __XO__

12) Time employee began work __8:00__ ☒ AM ☐ PM

13) Time of event __8:30__ ☒ AM ☐ PM ☐ Check if time cannot be determined

14) **What was the employee doing just before the incident occurred?** Describe the activity, as well as the tools, equipment, or material the employee was using. Be specific. *Examples:* "climbing a ladder while carrying roofing materials"; "spraying chlorine from hand sprayer"; "daily computer key-entry."
   Employee was working on building a fence around Jayhawk South's building. A bee flew out of the building materials and stung employee on upper left thigh.

15) **What happened?** Tell us how the injury occurred. *Examples:* "When ladder slipped on wet floor, worker fell 20 feet"; "Worker was sprayed with chlorine when gasket broke during replacement"; "Worker developed soreness in wrist over time."
   Lifted building materials and bee flew out from under them.

16) **What was the injury or illness?** Tell us the part of the body that was affected and how it was affected; be more specific than "hurt," "pain," or "sore." *Example:* "strained back"; "chemical burn, hand"; "carpal tunnel syndrome."
   Upper left thigh was stung. It became red, swollen, and achy because of an allergic reaction.

17) **What object or substance directly harmed the employee?** *Examples:* "concrete floor"; "chlorine"; "radial arm saw." *If this question does not apply to the incident, leave it blank.*
   Bee

18) **If the employee died, when did death occur?** Date of death __N/A__ / __ / __

Completed by __Peggy Prince__
Title __Operations Officer__
Phone __555__ - __555__ - __5555__ Date __5__ / __15__ / __XO__

NOTICE OF ACTION/CHANGE

DIVISION OF WORKERS' COMPENSATION
Attention: Information Management
200 East Gaines Street
Tallahassee, FL 32399-4226
For assistance call 1-800-342-1741 or contact your local EAO Office

COMPLETE ALL APPLICABLE SECTIONS BEFORE FILING WITH THE DIVISION

SENT TO DIVISION DATE	DIVISION RECEIVED DATE
2/29/20X0	

PLEASE PRINT OR TYPE ■

SOCIAL SECURITY NUMBER	EMPLOYEE NAME (First, Middle, Last)	DATE OF ACCIDENT (Month-Day-Year)
222-44-6666	Robert Dean	1/11/20X0

INDICATE ONLY ACTION OR CHANGE - PLEASE REFER TO KEY FOR DWC-4 TYPES/CODES ON REVERSE SIDE

ALL INDEMNITY SUSPENDED: EFFECTIVE DATE ____-____-____   REASON CODE: _____

INDEMNITY REINSTATED AFTER SUSPENSION: EFFECTIVE DATE ____-____-____   DISABILITY TYPE: _____

RELEASED TO RETURN TO WORK DATE: ____-____-____   RESTRICTIONS?: ☐ YES ☐ NO

ACTUAL RETURN TO WORK DATE: ____-____-____   RESTRICTIONS?: ☐ YES ☐ NO

DATE FINAL SETTLEMENT ORDER MAILED: ____-____-____

OVERALL MMI DATE: ____-____-____   PI RATING: _____ % BAW   DATE OF DEATH ____-____-____

PERMANENT IMPAIRMENT BENEFITS (D/A'S PRIOR TO 01/01/94):   DATE PAID: ____-____-____

IMPAIRMENT INCOME BENEFITS (D/A'S ON OR AFTER 01/01/94):   START DATE: 1 . 11 . X0   WEEKLY RATE: $ 391.83

TOTAL NUMBER OF WEEKS OF ENTITLEMENT: 1

PERMANENT TOTAL: DATE ACCEPTED/ADJUDICATED ____-____-____

WEEKLY PT SUPPLEMENTAL RATE $ _____

WEEKLY PT SUPP EFFECTIVE DATE ____-____-____

AVERAGE WEEKLY WAGE AND/OR COMPENSATION RATE AMENDMENTS:	
PREVIOUS AWW:	$ 527.12
PREVIOUS COMP RATE:	$ 351.43
AMENDED AWW:	$ 587.74
AMENDED COMP RATE:	$ 391.83
RETROACTIVE TO D/A:	☑ YES ☐ NO
IF NO, GIVE EFFECTIVE DATE:	____-____-____

BENEFIT ADJUSTMENTS

BENEFIT ADJUSTMENT CODE _____   BENEFIT ADJUSTMENT CODE _____

DISABILITY TYPE ADJUSTED _____   DISABILITY TYPE ADJUSTED _____

WEEKLY ADJ AMOUNT $ _____   WEEKLY ADJ AMOUNT $ _____

EFFECTIVE DATE _____   EFFECTIVE DATE _____

ADJUSTMENT END DATE _____   ADJUSTMENT END DATE _____

CORRECTIONS OF:

☐ SOCIAL SECURITY NUMBER/CORRECT #: _____

☐ DATE OF ACCIDENT/CORRECT DATE: ____-____-____

☐ EMPLOYEE'S NAME/CORRECT NAME: _____

☐ CLAIMS-HANDLING ENTITY: _____

CLASS CODE

NAICS CODE

REMARKS: A change has been made to the Average Weekly Wage and/or Compensation Rate.

CC:

Hopper Tax Consultants
5562 Wellington Lane
Briston, FL 34418

INSURER CODE #	DATE PREPARED: (Month-Day-Year)
2233	04 . 30 . 20X0

SERVICE CO/TPA CODE #   CLAIMS-HANDLING ENTITY FILE #
3399

INSURER NAME
Plymouth Insurance Company

CLAIMS-HANDLING ENTITY NAME, ADDRESS & TELEPHONE

4292 Main Street
Barstow, FL 36614

Form DFS-F2-DWC-4 (03/2009) Rule 69L-3.025, F.A.C.

Department of Health and Human Services

Public Health Service
Food and Drug Administration
College Park, MD 20740

SEP 28 20X0

WARNING LETTER

CERTIFIED MAIL
RETURN RECEIPT REQUESTED

Jayhawk Corporation
Fort Scott, Kansas

Re: CFS-AA-03-0X

Dear Sir or Madam:

This is to advise you that the Food and Drug Administration (FDA) obtained a sample packet of your Special Health Remedies product and promotional literature at the American Society of Pharmacognosy (ASP) conference in Portland, Maine, during the week of June 14, 20X0. FDA has reviewed the labeling for Special Health Remedies on your website, as well as the label of the sample packet we collected. This review found serious violations of the Federal Food, Drug, and Cosmetic Act (the Act). You can find the Act and its implementing regulations on FDA's website at http://www.fda.gov.

New Drug

Furthermore, the therapeutic claims in your labeling indicate that the product is intended for the diagnosis, cure, mitigation, treatment, or prevention of disease in man. Similar claims and testimonials also appear on your website.

These claims are evidence that your product is intended for use as a drug within the meaning of section 201(g)(1)(B) of the Act [21 U.S.C. § 321(g)(1)(B)]. Your product is also a new drug under section 201(p) of the Act [21 U.S.C. § 321(p)] because this product is not generally recognized as safe and effective for its intended uses. New drugs may not be legally marketed in the U.S. without prior approval from FDA as described in section 505(a) of the Act [21 U.S.C. § 355(a)].

The above violations are not meant to be an all-inclusive list of deficiencies in your product and its labeling. It is your responsibility to ensure that products marketed by your firm comply with the Act and its implementing regulations.

The Act authorizes the seizure of illegal products and injunctions against manufacturers and distributors of those products. You should take prompt action to correct these deviations and prevent their future recurrence. Failure to do so may result in enforcement action without further notice. Federal agencies are advised of the issuance of all Warning Letters about drug products so that they may take this information into account when considering the award of contracts.

Please notify this office, in writing, within fifteen (15) working days of the receipt of this letter, as to the specific steps you have taken to correct the violations noted above and to assure that similar violations do not occur. Include any documentation necessary to show that correction has been achieved. If corrective actions cannot be completed within fifteen working days, state the reason for the delay and the time within which the corrections will be completed.

Your response should be directed to Compliance Officer, Food and Drug Administration, Center for Food Safety and Applied Nutrition, Office of Compliance, Division of Enforcement, 5100 Paint Branch Parkway (HFS-608), College Park, Maryland 20740.

Sincerely,

Office of Compliance
Center for Food Safety and Applied Nutrition

IN THE SIXTH JUDICIAL DISTRICT
DISTRICT COURT OF BOURBON COUNTY, KANSAS

WILDCAT, INC.,	)	
	)	
Plaintiff,	)	
	)	
v.	)	Case No. 23 BR 195 RT
	)	
JAYHAWK CORP.,	)	
	)	
Defendant.	)	
	)	

<u>COMPLAINT</u>

COMES NOW Plaintiff, Wildcat, Inc., by and through its undersigned attorney, and sues the Defendant, Jayhawk Corp., and alleges:

1. This is an action for damages that do not exceed $750,000.

2. On 12/7/20X0, Plaintiff purchased a Jayhawk Widget and the installation of a Jayhawk Widget at Wildcat, Inc.'s premises.

3. On 12/10/20X0, Jayhawk notified Wildcat, Inc., that the Jayhawk Widget was installed, operational, and ready for use.

4. On 12/27/20X0, the Jayhawk Widget malfunctioned, causing Wildcat, Inc.'s production facility to cease all operations.

5. On 12/27/20X0, subsequent to the malfunction, Plaintiff notified Defendant of the failure of the Jayhawk Widget.

6. On 1/14/20X1, Ace Installer repaired the Jayhawk Widget and certified it to be operational and ready for use.

7. Between 12/27/20X0 and 1/14/20X1, Plaintiff's loss of revenue was $750,000. Plaintiff then negotiated a settlement with Ace Installer, which agreed to pay Plaintiff $750,000. But Generic Bank did not pay Plaintiff the sum it was legally and contractually required to receive due to insufficient funds in Ace Installer's account.

Wherefore Plaintiff demands judgment against Defendant for damages, interest, court costs, and attorney's fees.

Harkon Davis
_____
Harkon Davis, #92367
Attorney For Plaintiff
101 S.W. Litigation Drive
Fort Scott, KS 66701

AGREEMENT FOR THE INSTALLATION
OF ONE (1) JAYHAWK CORPORATION WIDGET

This Agreement is made this [___7th___] day of [_____December 20X0_____] by and between **JAYHAWK CORPORATION** ("JAYHAWK"), a company incorporated in Fort Scott, Kansas, company registration no. 63947XX62G and ACE INSTALLER, LLC ("the Contractor").

WHEREBY IT IS AGREED BETWEEN THE CONTRACTOR AND JAYHAWK as follows:

1   QUANTITY AND PRICE OF WORK

1.1   The Contractor shall, subject to the terms and conditions of this agreement, install one (1) Jayhawk Widget and all the components and accessories as specified in Annex A attached hereto (collectively "the Equipment") for the aggregate price of five hundred thousand U.S. dollars ($500,000.00) ("the price"). The installation will be at the premises of WILDCAT, INC., in Fort Scott, Kansas. Annex A hereto shall be read together with and form an integral part of this agreement.

1.2   The Contractor shall be responsible for the furnishing of all designs, labor, and tools for the installation of the Equipment.

2   WARRANTY AND MAINTENANCE

2.1   The Contractor **HEREBY WARRANTS** that the Equipment shall be free from installation defect for a period of not less than twelve (12) calendar months from the date of commencement of warranty as specified in the Certificate of Acceptance issued by JAYHAWK. The Contractor also **HEREBY WARRANTS** that the Equipment has no design flaws or defects for a period of not less than five (5) years from such date of commencement of warranty.

2.2   Any fault due to material, workmanship, or structural faults or design flaws or defects that may be observed during the relevant warranty period specified in Clause 2.1 shall be made good by the Contractor at its own expense, which shall include the cost of labor and replacement of parts.

3   INSURANCE AND INDEMNITY

3.1   The Contractor shall also insure against any damage, loss, death, or injury that may occur to any person or property whatsoever in carrying out or omitting to carry out its duties under this agreement and shall **INDEMNIFY** and **keep JAYHAWK and its related and associate companies INDEMNIFIED** in respect of all claims, costs, and other expenses arising out of such damage, loss, death, or injury.

3.2   The Contractor **INDEMNIFIES JAYHAWK and its related or associated companies** in full from and against all actions, proceedings, liability, loss, damage, costs, and expenses whatsoever (including without limitation legal costs and expenses on a full indemnity basis, and any fines, penalties, levies, and charges) that may be brought against any of them or that any of them may suffer or incur.

IN WITNESS WHEREOF, the parties hereto have hereunto set their hands on the day and the year first above written.

SIGNED BY: ____*Caleb Green*_____

                         (Name)

for and on behalf of:

JAYHAWK CORPORATION

SIGNED BY: ____*Jean Taylor*_____

                         (Name)

for and on behalf of:

ACE INSTALLER, LLC

OSHA's Form 300A (Rev. 01/2004)

Summary of Work-Related Injuries and Illnesses

Year 20 X0

U.S. Department of Labor
Occupational Safety and Health Administration

Form approved OMB no. 1218-0176

All establishments covered by Part 1904 must complete this Summary page, even if no work-related injuries or illnesses occurred during the year. Remember to review the Log to verify that the entries are complete and accurate before completing this summary.

Using the Log, count the individual entries you made for each category. Then write the totals below, making sure you've added the entries from every page of the Log. If you had no cases, write "0."

Employees, former employees, and their representatives have the right to review the OSHA Form 300 in its entirety. They also have limited access to the OSHA Form 301 or its equivalent. See 29 CFR Part 1904.35, in OSHA's recordkeeping rule, for further details on the access provisions for these forms.

Establishment Information

Your establishment name Jayhawk South

Street 1 Bill Self Dr.

City Gainesville State FL ZIP 32601

Industry description (e.g., *Manufacture of motor truck trailers*)
Widget distribution

Standard Industrial Classification (SIC), if known (e.g., 3715)
__ __ __ __

OR

North American Industrial Classification (NAICS), if known (e.g., 336212)
5 1 1 1 1 9

Employment information (If you don't have these figures, see the Worksheet on the back of this page to estimate.)

Annual average number of employees 25

Total hours worked by all employees last year 48,300

Sign here

Knowingly falsifying this document may result in a fine.

I certify that I have examined this document and that to the best of my knowledge the entries are true, accurate, and complete.

Tricia Testament   HR Manager
Company executive   Title

555 555 - 5555   1 30 X0
Phone   Date

Number of Cases

Total number of deaths

0
(G)

Total number of cases with days away from work

1
(H)

Total number of cases with job transfer or restriction

0
(I)

Total number of other recordable cases

0
(J)

Number of Days

Total number of days away from work

5
(K)

Total number of days of job transfer or restriction

0
(L)

Injury and Illness Types

Total number of . . .
(M)

(1) Injuries 1

(2) Skin disorders ___

(3) Respiratory conditions ___

(4) Poisonings ___

(5) Hearing loss ___

(6) All other illnesses ___

Post this Summary page from February 1 to April 30 of the year following the year covered by the form.

Public reporting burden for this collection of information is estimated to average 38 minutes per response, including time to review the instructions, search and gather the data needed, and complete and review the collection of information. Persons are not required to respond to the collection of information unless it displays a currently valid OMB control number. If you have any comments about these estimates or any other aspects of this data collection, contact: US Department of Labor, OSHA Office of Statistical Analysis, Room N-3644, 200 Constitution Avenue, NW, Washington, DC 20210. Do not send the completed forms to this office.

DISTRIBUTOR AGREEMENT

THIS AGREEMENT is made this 6th day of July, 20X0, by and between Jayhawk Corporation, with its principal place of business located in Fort Scott, Kansas (the "Company"), and California Distributor, LLC, located in Berkeley, California (the "Distributor").

NOW, THEREFORE, in consideration of the promises hereinafter made by the parties hereto, it is agreed as follows:

ARTICLE I
APPOINTMENT OF DISTRIBUTORSHIP

1. <u>Distribution Right</u>. The Company hereby appoints and grants Distributor the exclusive and non-assignable right to sell **ONLY** the special health remedies of the Company ("Remedy") listed in the then current "Price List" (Exhibit "A" attached hereto). The distribution right shall be limited to customers who have places of business in, and will initially use the Company's products in, the geographic area in California.

2. <u>Prices</u>. All prices stated are FOB the Company's offices in Fort Scott, Kansas. Prices do not include transportation costs which shall be borne by Distributor.

3. <u>Terms</u>. Terms are net cash upon delivery, except where satisfactory credit is established in which case terms are net thirty (30) days from date of delivery.

ARTICLE II
DELIVERY

1. <u>Purchase Orders</u>. Distributor shall order Remedy by written notice to Company. Each order shall specify the number of units to be shipped, the type of units to be shipped, and the desired method of shipment and the installation site.

2. <u>Shipment</u>. All shipments of Remedy shall be made FOB Company's plant.

ARTICLE III
DURATION OF AGREEMENT

1. <u>Term</u>. The term of this Agreement shall be for five (5) years from the date hereof, unless sooner terminated. Termination shall not relieve either party of obligations incurred prior thereto.

2. <u>Termination</u>. This Agreement may be terminated only:

(a) By either party for substantial breach of any material provision of this Agreement by the other.
(b) Upon termination of this Agreement all further rights and obligations of the parties shall cease.

ARTICLE IV
GENERAL PROVISIONS

1. <u>Relationship of Parties</u>. The agency relationship between the parties established by this Agreement shall be solely that of Company and Distributor and all rights and powers not expressly granted to the Distributor are expressly reserved to the Company.

2. <u>Assignment</u>. This Agreement constitutes a personal contract and Distributor shall not transfer or assign same or any part thereof without the advance written consent of Company.

3. <u>Entire Agreement</u>. The entire Agreement between the Company and the Distributor covering the Remedy is set forth herein and any amendment or modification shall be in writing.

IN WITNESS WHEREOF, the parties have caused this Agreement to be executed by their duly authorized officers as of the date and year indicated above.

COMPANY   DISTRIBUTOR

By: _____*Herm Cooper*_____   By: _____*Lucienne Tanaquil*_____
(Authorized Officer)   (Authorized Officer)

Belinda Holiday, State Bar #923697
10 N.W. Main Street
Berkeley, CA 94704

Attorney for: Plaintiff Martha Jones

SUPERIOR COURT OF CALIFORNIA

ALAMEDA COUNTY

MARTHA JONES,	) Case No.: A03-19576
Plaintiff,	)
vs.	)
CALIFORNIA DISTRIBUTOR, LLC, and JAYHAWK CORP.,	)
Defendants.	)

<u>COMPLAINT</u>

COMES NOW Plaintiff, Martha Jones, by and through her undersigned attorney, and sues the Defendants, California Distributor, LLC, and Jayhawk Corp., and alleges:

1. This is an action for damages that do not exceed $1,250,000.00.

2. On 9/1/20X0, Plaintiff visited California Distributor on its premises in Berkeley, California.

3. California Distributor is Jayhawk Corp.'s agent in California.

4. Defendants were grossly negligent by allowing a pool of water to form on their recently polished marble flooring.

5. As Plaintiff walked into California Distributor's office, she did not notice the water, slipped, and fell onto her back.

6. An ambulance took Plaintiff to Mercy Hospital where she was diagnosed with a broken back.

7. Plaintiff is no longer able to walk normally and is unable to be employed.

8. Plaintiff is suing for pain, suffering, and permanent disability.

9. Plaintiff requests a trial by jury.

Wherefore Plaintiff demands judgment against the Defendants, jointly and severally, for damages, interest, court costs, and attorney's fees.

Belinda Holiday

Belinda Holiday
Attorney For Plaintiff

ANSWERS 1 OF 5

1. Research (1 Gradable Item)

Answer: IRC § 6695(b)

§ 6695. Other assessable penalties with respect to the preparation of tax returns for other persons

(b) Failure to sign return

Any person who is a tax return preparer with respect to any return or claim for refund, who is is required by regulations prescribed by the Secretary to sign such return or claim, and who fails to comply with such regulations with respect to such return or claim shall pay a penalty of $50 for such failure, unless it is shown that such failure is due to reasonable cause and not due to willful neglect. The maximum penalty imposed under this subsection on any person with respect to documents filed during any calendar year shall not exceed $25,000.

2. Form 1120 Reported Amounts (12 Gradable Items)

Form **1120**	U.S. Corporation Income Tax Return		OMB No. 1545-0123
Department of the Treasury Internal Revenue Service	For calendar year [Year] or tax year beginning _____, [Year], ending _____, 20 ____ ▶ Information about Form 1120 and its separate instructions is at *www.irs.gov/form1120.*		**[Year]**

A Check if:
1a Consolidated return (attach Form 851) ☐
 b Life/nonlife consolidated return ☐
2 Personal holding co. (attach Sch. PH) ☐
3 Personal service corp. (see instructions) ☐
4 Schedule M-3 attached ☐

TYPE OR PRINT

Name **Retainall Corporation**
Number, street, and room or suite no. If a P.O. box, see instructions. **12345 Ace Avenue**
City or town, state, or province, country and ZIP or foreign postal code **Newtown, PA 35000**

B Employer identification number 98 7654321
C Date incorporated 1-1-01
D Total assets (see instructions) $ 10,000,000

E Check if: (1) ☐ Initial return   (2) ☐ Final return   (3) ☐ Name change   (4) ☐ Address change

Income

1a	Gross receipts or sales	1a	1,000,000	[1]
b	Returns and allowances	1b	0	
c	Balance. Subtract line 1b from line 1a	1c	1,000,000	[2]
2	Cost of goods sold (attach Form 1125-A)	2	550,000	[3]
3	Gross profit. Subtract line 2 from line 1c	3	450,000	[4]
4	Dividends (Schedule C, line 19)	4	33,180	[5]
5	Interest	5	5,000	[6]
6	Gross rents	6		
7	Gross royalties	7		
8	Capital gain net income (attach Schedule D (Form 1120))	8		
9	Net gain or (loss) from Form 4797, Part II, line 17 (attach Form 4797)	9		
10	Other income (see instructions—attach statement)	10		
11	**Total income.** Add lines 3 through 10 ▶	11	488,180	[7]

Deductions (See instructions for limitations on deductions.)

12	Compensation of officers (see instructions—attach Form 1125-E) ▶	12		
13	Salaries and wages (less employment credits)	13	100,000	[8]
14	Repairs and maintenance	14		
15	Bad debts	15	10,000	[9]
16	Rents	16		
17	Taxes and licenses	17	12,000	[10]
18	Interest	18		
19	Charitable contributions	19	5,000	[11]
20	Depreciation from Form 4562 not claimed on Form 1125-A or elsewhere on return (attach Form 4562)	20		
21	Depletion	21		
22	Advertising	22		
23	Pension, profit-sharing, etc., plans	23		
24	Employee benefit programs	24		
25	Domestic production activities deduction (attach Form 8903)	25		
26	Other deductions (attach statement)	26		
27	**Total deductions.** Add lines 12 through 26 ▶	27	127,000	[12]
28	Taxable income before net operating loss deduction and special deductions. Subtract line 27 from line 11	28		
29a	Net operating loss deduction (see instructions)	29a		
b	Special deductions (Schedule C, line 20)	29b		
c	Add lines 29a and 29b	29c		

ANSWERS 2 OF 5

[1] $1,000,000. The facts indicate that Retainall had sales of $1,000,000 for 2017.
[2] $1,000,000. Since there were no returns and allowances, the total gross receipts are still $1,000,000.
[3] $550,000. The situation indicates that Retainall has $550,000 of COGS related to its sale of inventory.
[4] $450,000. Gross profits equal sales revenue less COGS ($1,000,000 – $550,000).
[5] $33,180. The dividends received from Retainall's portfolio are fully included in gross income, and a dividends-received deduction is provided later.
[6] $5,000. The $4,000 of interest from U.S. Treasury notes is included in gross income as well as the $1,000 interest from the arbitrage bonds. The $3,000 of municipal bond interest is not taxable and is excluded from gross income.
[7] $488,180. The total income for Retainall is gross profit plus dividends and interest ($450,000 + $33,180 + $5,000).
[8] $100,000. The situation indicates that Retainall pays its nonofficer employees $100,000 in wages for 2017.
[9] $10,000. Bad debts can only be deducted when they are written off. Because Retainall only wrote off $10,000 of bad debts, only $10,000 is deductible.
[10] $12,000. State income taxes are a deductible expense of a corporation that is ordinary and necessary.
[11] $5,000. Charitable contributions that are pledged by a corporation are deductible if they are paid within 2 1/2 months after the close of the corporation's tax year. In addition, the $5,000 is not in excess of 10% limitation.
[12] $127,000. The total deductions for line 12 through line 26 equals $127,000 ($100,000 + $10,000 + $12,000 + $5,000). The dividends received deduction appears on line 29b so this amount is not considered for "total deductions."

3. Schedules M-1 and M-2 (18 Gradable Items)

Schedule M-1 — **Reconciliation of Income (Loss) per Books With Income (Loss) per Return**

Note. Schedule M-3 may be required instead of Schedule M-1 (see instructions).

1	Net income (loss) per books	100,000	[1]	6	Income recorded on books this year not included on Schedule K, lines 1 through 11 (itemize):	
2	Income included on Schedule K, lines 1, 2, 3c, 5, 6a, 7, 8, 9a, 10, and 11, not recorded on books this year (itemize): prepaid rent	15,000	[2]	a	Tax-exempt interest $ 16,000 insurance proceeds $30,000	$46,000 [6]
3	Guaranteed payments (other than health insurance)	20,000	[3]	7	Deductions included on Schedule K, lines 1 through 13d, and 16l, not charged against book income this year (itemize):	
4	Expenses recorded on books this year not included on Schedule K, lines 1 through 13d, and 16l (itemize):			a	Depreciation $ Sec. 179 expense $39,000	
a	Depreciation $					39,000 [7]
b	Travel and entertainment $ 4,000 interest expense $6,000	10,000	[4]	8	Add lines 6 and 7	85,000 [8]
5	Add lines 1 through 4	145,000	[5]	9	Income (loss) (Analysis of Net Income (Loss), line 1). Subtract line 8 from line 5 .	60,000 [9]

Schedule M-2 — **Analysis of Partners' Capital Accounts**

1	Balance at beginning of year . . .	$50,000	[10]	6	Distributions: a Cash	6,000 [15]
2	Capital contributed: a Cash . . .	10,000	[11]		b Property	7,500 [16]
	b Property . .	0	[12]	7	Other decreases (itemize):	
3	Net income (loss) per books	100,000	[13]			
4	Other increases (itemize):					
				8	Add lines 6 and 7	13,500 [17]
5	Add lines 1 through 4	160,000	[14]	9	Balance at end of year. Subtract line 8 from line 5	146,500 [18]

Form **1065** (201X)

[1] $100,000. Net income per books is provided in the situation.

[2] $15,000. Prepaid rent was considered income for tax purposes but not for financial accounting. Therefore, prepaid rent must be added back to reconcile book to tax income.

[3] $20,000. The $20,000 guaranteed payment to Yolanda was provided in the situation.

[4] $10,000. The entire $8,000 of meals and entertainment expenses was deductible for financial accounting purposes. However, for tax purposes, only 50% of meals and entertainment expenses are deductible. Therefore, you must add back 50% of the $8,000 that is not deductible for tax purposes. In addition, the $6,000 in interest expense to purchase tax-exempt bonds is not deductible for tax purposes but is deductible for book purposes. It also must be added back to reconcile book to tax income.

[5] $145,000. The total of lines 1 through 4 equals $145,000 ($100,000 + $15,000 + $20,000 + $10,000).

[6] $46,000. The $16,000 of tax-exempt interest was included in arriving at book income; however, it is not deductible for tax purposes. Therefore, it will have to be deducted to reconcile book to tax income. The $30,000 of life insurance proceeds was included in income for book purposes but is not income for tax purposes. Therefore, it also must be subtracted to reconcile book to tax income.

ANSWERS 3 OF 5

[7] $39,000. The Sec. 179 expense of $39,000 taken this year is deductible for tax purposes but not for book purposes. Therefore, it will have to be subtracted to reconcile book to tax income.

[8] $85,000. The total of lines 6 and 7 is $85,000 ($46,000 + $39,000).

[9] $60,000. Line 5 less line 8 equals $60,000 ($145,000 – $85,000).

[10] $50,000. The partners' total capital account balances are provided in the situation.

[11] $10,000. Yolanda contributed $10,000 cash to the partnership.

[12] $0. The situation states that no property was contributed to the partnership.

[13] $100,000. The net income per books is given as $100,000.

[14] $160,000. The total of lines 1, 2, and 3 is $160,000 ($50,000 + $10,000 + $0 + $100,000).

[15] $6,000. Linda received a $6,000 cash distribution from the partnership during the year.

[16] $7,500. The adjusted basis of the property distributed to Linda was $2,500 for the desk and $5,000 for the computer.

[17] $13,500. The total of lines 6 and 7 is $13,500 ($6,000 + $7,500).

[18] $146,500. Line 5 less line 8 equals $146,500 ($160,000 – $13,500).

4. Net Operating Loss (4 Gradable Items)

1. $193,000. A deduction for charitable expenses is not allowed in computing a current NOL; thus, this amount should be subtracted from operating expenses. Therefore, Kustan's NOL for Year 4 is $193,000 [$300,000 – ($500,000 – $7,000)].

2. $13,000. When calculating an NOL, the dividends-received deduction (DRD) is computed without regard to the 80% of taxable income limitation (i.e., $35,000 × 80% = $28,000 deduction limit). Thus, Tennis will have a DRD of $48,000 ($60,000 × 80%). Therefore, Tennis will have an NOL of $13,000 ($70,000 gross income + $60,000 dividend income – $95,000 operating expenses – $48,000 DRD).

3. $30,000. An NOL may be carried back to each of the 2 preceding taxable years and forward to the 20 succeeding taxable years. The NOL must be carried to the earliest possible year unless an election is made to give up the 2-year carryback. Since Gobby did not make this election, the $65,000 loss in Year 3 must be carried back to Year 1 and Year 2. Gobby will therefore be able to carry over a $30,000 NOL ($65,000 NOL in Year 3 – $20,000 Year 1 income – $15,000 Year 2 income) to Year 4.

4. $35,000. An NOL can be carried back 2 years and forward 20 years. The NOL must be carried back to the earliest year to which such a loss may be carried. The Year 2 NOL of $40,000 must first be carried back to offset the $15,000 of income from Year 1. This leaves a $25,000 NOL carryover, which is carried forward to reduce Year 3's $60,000 taxable income to $35,000.

5. Liquidation (7 Gradable Items)

1. $0. A corporation recognizes no loss in a complete liquidation on a distribution of appreciated property to a parent corporation (one that owns 80% or more of the voting power and the total value of the stock of the liquidating subsidiary).

2. $5,000. When an 80%-or-more-owned subsidiary is liquidated, the rules generally applicable to complete liquidations apply to distributions to shareholders other than the parent corporation. Thus, the liquidating corporation recognizes the $5,000 gain realized on the piano as if it were sold to Dawn at its FMV.

3. $250,000. A parent corporation's basis in property received in a distribution in complete liquidation of its 80%-or-more-owned subsidiary is the subsidiary corporation's basis in the property immediately before the distribution.

4. $30,000. A parent corporation's basis in property received in a distribution in complete liquidation of its 80%-or-more-owned subsidiary is the subsidiary corporation's basis in the property immediately before the distribution.

5. $50,000. When an 80%-or-more-owned subsidiary is completely liquidated, the rules generally applicable to complete liquidations apply to distributions to shareholders other than the parent corporation. Thus, Dawn treats the amounts distributed (the cash and the FMV of the other property) as realized in exchange for her stock. She realizes and recognizes a gain of $50,000 [$82,000 (cash) + $15,000 (piano) + $3,000 (keyboard) – $50,000 basis in her stock].

6.   4 months. Dawn's basis in the piano was not determined by reference to Clef's basis in it. Thus, her holding period began the day after she acquired the piano (September 1).

7.   4 months. Dawn's basis in the keyboard was not determined by reference to Clef's basis in it. Thus, her holding period began the day after she acquired the keyboard (September 1).

ANSWERS 4 OF 5

6. Gains and Losses (10 Gradable Items)

1. <u>$3,000 and Short-Term Capital Gain.</u> Taxpayer realized $23,000 on the sale when he had a $20,000 cost basis in the stock. Thus, he realized and recognized a gain of $3,000. The stock was a capital asset. Gain from the sale or exchange of a capital asset held for less than 1 year is short-term capital gain.

2. <u>$14,000 and Short-Term Capital Gain.</u> Taxpayer realized $139,000 on the sale when he had a $125,000 cost basis in the stock. Thus, he realized and recognized a gain of $14,000. The stock was a capital asset. Gain from the sale or exchange of a capital asset held for less than 1 year is short-term capital gain.

3. <u>$1,000 and Long-Term Capital Loss.</u> Taxpayer realized $9,000 on the sale when he had a $10,000 cost basis in the van. Thus, he realized a loss of $1,000. The van was personal-use property, not depreciable. Thus, it was a capital asset. Loss from the sale or exchange of a capital asset held for more than 1 year is long-term capital loss.

4. <u>$59,000 and Long-Term Capital Gain.</u> The amount realized was $169,000. Vacant land is not depreciable, so its basis was the $110,000 cost. Thus, there is a $59,000 gain ($169,000 – $110,000). The vacant land is personal-use property held as a capital asset. Since the property was held for over 12 months and sold after May 5, 2003, it is included in the 15% basket.

5. <u>$5,000 and Ordinary Loss.</u> Sec. 1033 nonrecognition does not apply to losses. The amount of the casualty loss is the adjusted basis, net of amounts recovered, e.g., insurance proceeds. Thus, taxpayer recognizes a loss of $5,000 ($50,000 adjusted basis – $45,000 recovery). Sec. 1231 property is depreciable or real property used in a trade or business and held for more than 1 year, and nonpersonal capital assets held for more than 1 year and involuntarily converted. If there is a net loss for the year from involuntary conversion of property, including by fire, used in the trade or business or capital assets held long-term for investment or in connection with a trade or business, the loss is treated as an ordinary loss. If so, even if the involuntarily converted properties are otherwise Sec. 1231 property, the gains and losses are not included further in Sec. 1231 computations.

7. Bases for Liability (8 Gradable Items)

1. <u>Strict liability in tort.</u> Liability without fault is not a basis for recovery from an accountant.

2. <u>Negligence.</u> The auditors failed to exercise reasonable care and diligence. Omitting an investigation of the leasehold improvements was negligent. The accountant breached a legal duty, and the breach actually and proximately caused the defendant's damages. The auditors were not grossly negligent because the facts do not indicate that they failed to use even slight care.

3. <u>Foreseen third parties.</u> The majority rule is that the accountant is liable to foreseen (but not necessarily individually identified) third parties (foreseen users and users within a foreseen class of users). Foreseen third parties are those to whom the accountant intends to supply the information or knows the client intends to supply the information. They also include persons who use the information in a way the accountant knows it will be used. Financial statements are commonly distributed to lenders.

4. <u>Scienter.</u> Negligent misrepresentation includes all elements of fraud except scienter. Scienter is actual or implied knowledge of fraud.

5. <u>Gross negligence.</u> Gross negligence is failure to use even slight care. The element of intent required to prove fraud is satisfied by gross negligence.

6. <u>Proximate cause.</u> The plaintiff must prove that (1) the defendant breached a legal duty to the plaintiff and (2) the breach actually and proximately caused the plaintiff's damages. The concept of proximate cause limits liability to damages that are reasonably foreseeable.

7. <u>Identification of the third party.</u> A third party is considered to be a primary beneficiary if (1) the accountant is retained principally to benefit the third party, (2) the third party is identified, and (3) the benefit pertains to a specific transaction.

8. <u>Reasonably foreseeable users.</u> Liability for fraud extends to all reasonably foreseeable users of the accountant's work product.

ANSWERS 5 OF 5

Document Review (3 Gradable Items)

1. A. *[Original Text]* <u>Jayhawk is potentially liable because California Distributor, LLC, is Jayhawk's agent as of the date of the alleged slip-and-fall incident.</u> A principal generally is not liable for a tort (e.g., negligence committed by an independent contractor).

   B. <u>Jayhawk may be liable, but California Distributor, LLC, will indemnify Jayhawk for any losses.</u> The agreement between Jayhawk and California Distributor does not address indemnification. Moreover, the duty to reimburse or indemnify generally extends from the principal to the agent.

   C. **Correct:** <u>Jayhawk is not liable because California Distributor, LLC, is an independent contractor.</u> An agent ordinarily is either an employee or an independent contractor. A principal-employer has an actual right of control over the physical efforts of an employee. But an independent contractor is responsible only for a result. Based on the facts given, the principal has no physical control over the agent's sales efforts or the maintenance of its premises. Accordingly, the agent is an independent contractor. A principal generally is not responsible for the torts (e.g., negligence) of an independent contractor unless the principal has itself committed a tort (e.g., negligent hiring of the independent contractor).

   NOTE: Jayhawk may argue that no agency existed because an agency for an illegal purpose is terminated by operation of law. However, although the FDA has determined that the product is an illegal drug, the plaintiff will argue that an agency by estoppel was created. This condition results when (1) a person presents himself or herself as an agent, (2) the alleged principal knows (or should know) of the representation and fails to make an effective denial, and (3) a third party detrimentally relies on the existence of this presumed agency. Consequently, Jayhawk's best argument is that California Distributor is an independent contractor.

   D. <u>Jayhawk is not liable because California Distributor, LLC, is not an agent as of the date of the alleged slip-and-fall incident.</u> The accident occurred on September 1, 20X0. But the term of the agency was for 5 years from July 6, 20X0.

   E. <u>Jayhawk is not liable because the agency was for an illegal purpose.</u> Plaintiff can argue persuasively that an agency by estoppel was created.

2. A. *[Original Text]* <u>Jayhawk is not liable to Wildcat because of Ace Installer's indemnification agreement.</u> Jayhawk has a direct contractual obligation to Wildcat that is unaffected by Jayhawk's contract with Ace Installer.

   B. <u>Jayhawk is not liable to Wildcat because Ace Installer is an independent contractor.</u> Jayhawk's liability is based on its sale of a defective product, not by a defective installation.

   C. **Correct:** <u>Jayhawk is liable to Wildcat because it materially breached its contract with Wildcat.</u> An implied warranty of merchantability arises in every sale by a merchant who deals in goods of the kind sold. The issue is whether the goods are fit for the ordinary purposes for which such goods are used. Accordingly, the buyer may recover damages because the goods were not as warranted. The measure of damages appropriately includes consequential damages for lost revenue. These damages are awarded if they are foreseeable to a reasonable person at the time of contracting.

   D. <u>Jayhawk is liable only for the price paid by Wildcat for the Jayhawk Widget and its installation.</u> It was reasonably foreseeable that the failure of the Jayhawk Widget, equipment essential to the production facility's operations, would result in lost revenue.

3. A. *[Original Text]* <u>Jayhawk South must recognize a liability for potential fines from OSHA due to employee safety issues.</u> The entity's minimal amount of work-related injuries and illnesses does not justify imposition of fines. Employers are required to provide a workplace free of recognized hazards, not a risk-free workplace.

   B. **Correct:** *[Delete Text]* The entity's minimal amount of work-related injuries and illnesses does not justify imposition of fines. Employers are required to provide a workplace free of recognized hazards, not a risk-free workplace.

   C. <u>Jayhawk South must recognize in its financial statements the workers' compensation settlement.</u> The employer's insurer pays the claim. Thus, the employer recognizes only insurance expense.

   D. <u>Jayhawk South must recognize a contingent liability for damages exceeding the workers' compensation settlement.</u> Recovery under the state workers' compensation statute is the employee's exclusive remedy against the employer.

   E. <u>Jayhawk South's insurer need not pay the claim if the employee was contributorily negligent.</u> Neither contributory negligence nor comparative negligence of the worker is a defense of the employer. Assumption of the risk also is not a permissible defense.

INDEX